Routledge Handbook of Digital Media and Communication

What are we to make of our digital social lives and the forces that shape it? Should we feel fortunate to experience such networked connectivity? Are we privileged to have access to unimaginable amounts of information? Is it easier to work in a digital global economy? Or is our privacy and freedom under threat from digital surveillance? Our security and welfare being put at risk? Our politics undermined by hidden algorithms and misinformation? Written by a distinguished group of leading scholars from around the world, the *Routledge Handbook of Digital Media and Communication* provides a comprehensive, unique, and multidisciplinary exploration of this rapidly growing and vibrant field of study. The *Handbook* adopts a three-part structural framework for understanding the sociocultural impact of digital media: the *artifacts* or physical devices and systems that people use to communicate; the communicative *practices* in which they engage to use those devices, express themselves, and share meaning; and the organizational and institutional *arrangements*, structures, or formations that develop around those practices and artifacts. Comprising a series of essay-chapters on a wide range of topics, this volume crystallizes current knowledge, provides historical context, and critically articulates the challenges and implications of the emerging dominance of the *network* and *normalization* of digitally mediated relations. Issues explored include the power of algorithms, digital currency, gaming culture, surveillance, social networking, and connective mobilization. More than a reference work, this *Handbook* delivers a comprehensive, authoritative overview of the state of new media scholarship and its most important future directions that will shape and animate current debates.

Leah A. Lievrouw is Professor of Information Studies at the University of California, Los Angeles. Her research focuses on the relationship between digital/new media technologies and social change. She is the author of *Alternative and Activist New Media* (Polity, 2011; second ed. in preparation) and editor of *Challenging Communication Research* (Peter Lang, for the International Communication Association, 2014). With Sonia Livingstone, she edited two editions of the *Handbook of New Media* (Sage, 2002, 2006). Her current works in progress include *Foundations of Communication Theory: Communication and Technology* (Wiley–Blackwell). Currently, she is also North American editor for the international journal *Information, Communication & Society*.

Brian D. Loader is an honorary fellow in the Department of Sociology at the University of York, UK. His academic interests are focused around the social relations of power in a digitally mediated world, including social media and citizenship participation. More specifically, his research interests are primarily concerned with young citizens, civic engagement, and social media; social movements and digital democracy; and community informatics and the digital divide. He has written widely on these subjects for the past 25 years. He is the founding Editor in Chief of the international journal *Information, Communication & Society*.

Routledge International Handbooks

ROUTLEDGE HANDBOOK OF ART, SCIENCE, AND TECHNOLOGY STUDIES
Edited by Hannah Star Rogers, Megan K. Halpern, Kathryn de Ridder-Vignone, and Dehlia Hannah

ROUTLEDGE HANDBOOK OF BOUNDED RATIONALITY
Edited by Riccardo Viale

ROUTLEDGE INTERNATIONAL HANDBOOK OF CHARISMA
Edited by José Pedro Zúquete

ROUTLEDGE INTERNATIONAL HANDBOOK OF WORKING-CLASS STUDIES
Edited by Michele Fazio, Christie Launius, and Tim Strangleman

ROUTLEDGE HANDBOOK OF DIGITAL MEDIA AND COMMUNICATION
Edited by Leah A. Lievrouw and Brian D. Loader

ROUTLEDGE INTERNATIONAL HANDBOOK OF RELIGION IN GLOBAL SOCIETY
Edited by Jayeel Cornelio, François Gauthier, Tuomas Martikainen, and Linda Woodhead

THE ROUTLEDGE HANDBOOK ON THE INTERNATIONAL DIMENSION OF BREXIT
Edited by Juan Santos Vara and Ramses A. Wessel; Assistant Editor, and Polly R. Polak

ROUTLEDGE HANDBOOK OF CRITICAL FINANCE STUDIES
Edited by Christian Borch and Robert Wosnitzer

For more information about this series, please visit: www.routledge.com/Routledge-International-Handbooks/book-series/RIHAND

Routledge Handbook of Digital Media and Communication

Edited by Leah A. Lievrouw and Brian D. Loader

LONDON AND NEW YORK

First published 2021
by Routledge
2 Park Square, Milton Park, Abingdon, Oxon OX14 4RN

and by Routledge
52 Vanderbilt Avenue, New York, NY 10017

Routledge is an imprint of the Taylor & Francis Group, an informa business

British Library Cataloguing-in-Publication Data
A catalogue record for this book is available from the British Library

Library of Congress Cataloging-in-Publication Data
A catalog record for this book has been requested

ISBN: 978-1-138-67209-3 (hbk)
ISBN: 978-1-315-61655-1 (ebk)

Typeset in Bembo
by Apex CoVantage, LLC

For Daniel, as ever, as always

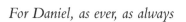

". . . being together solves most of it, in fact, solves all of it"

− Charles Bukowski

. . . and

For Kim, joyous companion, constructive critic, and constant foundation. Also, for Christopher, Will, and Emma for sharing their effervescent fun and creativity.

Contents

Illustrations

Images

Figures

Notes on the contributors

The editors

Leah A. Lievrouw is Professor of Information Studies at the University of California, Los Angeles. Her research focuses on the relationship between digital/new media technologies and social change. She is the author of *Alternative and Activist New Media* (Polity, 2011; second ed. in preparation) and editor of *Challenging Communication Research* (Peter Lang, for the International Communication Association, 2014). With Sonia Livingstone, she edited two editions of the *Handbook of New Media* (Sage, 2002, 2006). Her current works in progress include *Foundations of Communication Theory: Communication and Technology* (Wiley-Blackwell). Currently, she is also North American editor for the international journal *Information, Communication & Society*.

Brian D. Loader is an honorary fellow in the Department of Sociology at the University of York, UK. His academic interests are focused around the social relations of power in a digitally mediated world, including social media and citizenship participation. More specifically, his research interests are primarily concerned with young citizens, civic engagement, and social media; social movements and digital democracy; and community informatics and the digital divide. He has written widely on these subjects for the past 25 years. He is the founding Editor in Chief of the international journal *Information, Communication & Society*.

The contributors

Stuart Allan is Professor and Head of the School of Journalism, Media and Culture at Cardiff University, UK. He is the author of *Citizen Witnessing: Revisioning Journalism in Times of Crisis* (Polity, 2013), editor of *Photojournalism and Citizen Journalism: Co-operation, Collaboration and Connectivity* (Routledge, 2017), and coeditor of *Journalism, Gender and Power* (Routledge, 2019). He is currently co-writing *The Visual Citizen* with Chris Peters for Oxford University Press.

Mark Andrejevic is Professor in the School of Media, Film, and Journalism at Monash University. He is the author of *Reality TV: The Work of Being Watched*; *iSpy: Surveillance and Power in the Interactive Era*; and *Infoglut: How Too Much Information Is Changing the Way We Think and Know*. He writes about surveillance, digital media, and popular culture and is currently working on a book titled *Automated Media*.

Peng Hwa Ang is Professor at the Wee Kim Wee School of Communication and Information, Nanyang Technological University, Singapore. He was a past president of the International Communcations Association. His research interests lie in media law and policy, and he has consulted on the subject for the governments of Singapore, Thailand, and Bhutan.

Veronica Barassi is Professor of Media and Communication Studies in the School of Humanities and Social Sciences at the University of St. Gallen. She is the author of *Activism on the Web: Everyday Struggles against Digital Capitalism* (Routledge, 2015) and *Child | Data | Citizen: How Tech Companies Are Profiling Us from Before Birth* (MIT Press, 2020). Her research focuses on digital citizenship, activism, big data, and the digital transformation of new forms of society and of governmental, scientific, entrepreneurial, and individual action. In addition to her work on social media technologies, she is currently analyzing the datafication of citizens, including children. Her current and future research projects examine the misconceptions and inaccuracies of algorithms in human−computer relations ("machines care about you"), for example using voice-controlled artificial intelligence. She was previously Associate Professor of Media, Communications, and Cultural Studies at Goldsmiths College, University of London. Recently, she has also been a visiting scholar in the Department of Information Studies at the University of California Los Angeles and a visiting professor in visual and media anthropology at the University of Münster.

David Beer is Professor of Sociology at the University of York. He is the author of *The Data Gaze, Metric Power, Punk Sociology, Popular Culture and New Media: The Politics of Circulation*, and editor of *New Media: The Key Concepts* (with Nicholas Gane). He is also the editor of *The Social Power of Algorithms*.

Geoffrey C. Bowker is Donald Bren Chair at the School of Information and Computer Sciences, University of California at Irvine, where he directs the Evoke Laboratory, which explores new forms of knowledge expression. Recent positions include Professor of and Senior Scholar in Cyberscholarship at the University of Pittsburgh School and Executive Director, Center for Science, Technology and Society, Santa Clara. Together with Leigh Star he wrote *Sorting Things Out: Classification and Its Consequences*; his most recent books are *Memory Practices in the Sciences* and (with Stefan Timmermans, Adele Clarke and Ellen Balka) the edited collection *Boundary Objects and Beyond: Working with Leigh Star*. He is currently working on big data policy and on scientific cyber infrastructure, as well as completing a book on social readings of data and databases. He is a founding member of the Council for Big Data, Ethics, and Society.

Finn Brunton is an Assistant Professor in the Department of Media, Culture, and Communication at New York University. He is the author of *Spam: A Shadow History of the Internet* (MIT 2013) and *Digital Cash: The Unknown History of the Anarchists, Utopians, and Technologists Who Created Cryptocurrency* (Princeton 2019) and the coauthor of *Obfuscation: A User's Guide for Privacy and Protest* (MIT 2015) and *Communicate* (University of Minnesota 2018).

Taina Bucher is an Associate Professor in the Department of Media and Communication, University of Oslo. Her research focuses on social media and the power of algorithms in everyday life, at the intersection of software studies, Science and Technology Studies (STS), and media theory. She is the author of *IF . . . THEN: Algorithmic Power and Politics* (Oxford University Press, 2018), and her work on software and sociality has appeared in journals such as *New Media & Society; Information, Communication & Society; Television & New Media; Computational Culture*; and *Culture Machine*.

Mary Chayko is a sociologist, social media researcher, and Professor at Rutgers University's School of Communication and Information (SC&I). Her research is on the impact of digital technology and social media on relationships, community, society, and self. She is the author of *Superconnected: The Internet, Digital Media, and Techno-Social Life* (Sage Publications), now in its second edition; *Portable Communities: The Social Dynamics of Online and Mobile Connectedness* and *Connecting: How We Form Social Bonds and Communities in the Internet Age*, both with SUNY Press; and many published articles. Connect with Dr. Chayko on her website http://marychayko.com, her book blog http://superconnectedblog.com, on LinkedIn, and on Twitter @MaryChayko.

Julie E. Cohen is the Mark Claster Mamolen Professor of Law and Technology at the Georgetown University Law Center. She teaches and writes about surveillance, privacy and data protection, intellectual property, information platforms, and the ways that networked information and communication technologies are reshaping legal institutions. She is the author of *Between Truth and Power: The Legal Constructions of Informational Capitalism* (Oxford University Press, 2019), *Configuring the Networked Self: Law, Code, and the Play of Everyday Practice* (Yale University Press, 2012), and numerous articles and book chapters, and she is a coauthor of *Copyright in a Global Information Economy* (Wolters Kluwer, 5th ed. 2020). Professor Cohen is a faculty codirector of the Institute for Technology Law and Policy at Georgetown Law, a faculty codirector of the Center on Privacy and Technology at Georgetown Law, and a member of the Advisory Board of the Electronic Privacy Information Center.

Nick Couldry is Professor of Media, Communications, and Social Theory in the Department of Media and Communications at the London School of Economics. As a sociologist of media and culture, he approaches media and communications from the perspective of the symbolic power that has been historically concentrated in media institutions. He is interested in how media and communications institutions and infrastructures contribute to various types of order (social, political, cultural, economic, and ethical). His work has drawn on, and contributed to, social, spatial, democratic, and cultural theory; anthropology; and media and communications ethics. His analysis of media as "practice" has been widely influential. He is the author or editor of 15 books and many journal articles and book chapters.

Paul Dourish is Chancellor's Professor of Informatics and Associate Dean for Research in the Donald Bren School of Information and Computer Sciences at the University of California, Irvine, with courtesy appointments in computer science and in anthropology. His research lies at the intersection of computer science and social science, with a particular interest in ubiquitous and mobile computing and the cultural practices surrounding digital media.

Natalie Fenton is Professor of Media and Communications in the Department of Media, Communications, and Cultural Studies at Goldsmiths, University of London, where she is codirector of the Centre for the Study of Global Media and Democracy. She has published widely on issues relating to news, journalism, civil society, radical politics, and new media and is particularly interested in issues of media reform and democracy. She was on the Board of Directors of the campaign group Hacked Off for seven years and is Chair of the Media Reform Coalition. Her latest books are *Digital, Political, Radical* (Polity, 2016); *The Media Manifesto*, coauthored with Des Freedman, Justin Schlosberg, and Lina Dencik (Polity, 2020); and *Media, Democracy and Social Change: Re-imagining Political Communications*, coauthored with Aeron Davis, Des Freedman, and Gholam Khiabany (Sage, 2020).

Terry Flew is Professor of Communication and Creative Industries at the Queensland University of Technology, Brisbane, Australia. He is the author of *Understanding Global Media* (Palgrave Macmillan, 2018); *Politics, Media and Democracy in Australia* (Routledge, 2017); *Media Economics* (Palgrave, 2015); and *Global Creative Industries* (Polity, 2013). He was President of the International Communications Association (ICA) from 2019 to 2020, and organized the

69th ICA Annual Conference in Washington, DC, in 2019. He is a fellow of the Australian Academy of the Humanities (FAHA) and a fellow of the ICA.

Shiv Ganesh is Professor in the Department of Communication Studies at the University of Texas at Austin. He studies communication and collective organizing in the context of globalization and digital technologies. His work spans critical-institutional and poststructural approaches to communication, and is currently comprised of two strands: studies of technological transformations in collective action and studies of dialogue, conflict, and social change. Current research projects include a study of advocacy and voice among indigenous people displaced by the creation of environmental reserves in India, as well as a large-scale survey of digital interaction and engagement dynamics among global networks of activists. Ganesh is on the editorial board of *Information, Communication & Society*, as well as several other journals.

Radhika Gajjala (PhD, University of Pittsburgh, 1998) is Professor of Media and Communication (jointly appointed faculty in American Culture Studies) at Bowling Green State University. She has published books such as *Online Philanthropy in the Global North and South: Connecting, Microfinancing, and Gaming for Change* (2017), *Cyberculture and the Subaltern* (Lexington Press, 2012) and *Cyberselves: Feminist Ethnographies of South Asian Women* (Altamira, 2004). She has coedited collections on *Cyberfeminism 2.0* (2012), *Global Media Culture and Identity* (2011), *South Asian Technospaces* (2008), and *Webbing Cyberfeminist Practice* (2008). During the year 2015–2016 she was Fulbright Professor in Digital Culture at the University of Bergen, Bergen, Norway. She is currently finishing a manuscript on *Digital Diasporas: Gendered Labour, Affect and Technomediation of South Asia*.

Antero Garcia is an Assistant Professor in the Graduate School of Education at Stanford University, where he studies how technology and gaming shape both youth and adult learning, literacy practices, and civic identities. Prior to completing his PhD, Antero was an English teacher at a public high school in South Central Los Angeles. Based on his research focused on equitable teaching and learning opportunities for urban youth through the use of participatory media and gameplay, Antero codesigned the Critical Design and Gaming School – a public high school in South Central Los Angeles. His most recent books are *Good Reception: Teens, Teachers, and Mobile Media in a Los Angeles High School*, *Doing Youth Participatory Action Research: Transforming Inquiry with Researchers, Educators, and Students*, and *Pose, Wobble, Flow: A Culturally Proactive Approach to Literacy Instruction*. Antero received his PhD in the Urban Schooling division of the Graduate School of Education and Information Studies at the University of California, Los Angeles.

Keith N. Hampton is a Professor in the Department of Media and Information in the College of Communication Arts and Sciences at Michigan State University. He received his PhD and MA in sociology from the University of Toronto, and a BA (Honors) in sociology from the University of Calgary. His research interests focus on the relationship between new information and communication technologies, social networks, democratic engagement, and the urban environment.

Larissa Hjorth is a digital ethnographer, artist, distinguished Professor and director of the Design & Creative Practice ECP platform at RMIT University. The Platform focuses on interdisciplinary collaboration and creative solution to real-world problems. Hjorth is committed to cross-cultural, intergenerational, and interdisciplinary approaches to the social dimensions of mobile technology. She has published 6 single-authored books and

6 coauthored books along with over 30 journal articles and over 50 book chapters. Research projects include *Locating the Mobile*: http://locatingthemobile.net/and *Games of Being Mobile*: http://gamesofbeingmobile.com/.

Lee Humphreys is an Associate Professor in communication at Cornell University. She studies the social uses and perceived effects of communication technology, specifically focusing on mobile and social media. She is the author of *The Qualified Self: Social Media and the Accounting of Everyday Life* (MIT Press, 2018). Her research has appeared in *Information, Communication & Society, Journal of Communication, New Media & Society*, and the *Journal of Computer-Mediated Communication*, among others. She received her PhD from the University of Pennsylvania's Annenberg School in 2007.

Nancy Jennings is Associate Professor and the Director of the Children's Education and Entertainment Research Lab (CHEER) in the Department of Communication at the University of Cincinnati. Dr Jennings studies the impact of media on the lives of children and their families and public policies and practices involved with children's media. Her research focuses on children's cognitive and social development and their use of media. She has authored one book, *Tween Girls and Their Mediated Friend (2014)*, and coedited another book, *20 Questions about Youth and the Media (2018)*, with Sharon Mazzarella. She has published on a variety of topics, including virtual environments, children's advertising, families and media, and media violence in peer-reviewed journals and book chapters.

Curtis McCord is a PhD student at the Faculty of Information Studies, University of Toronto. His research explores government online consultation processes to examine how they elicit and construct information, and how they might begin to constitute democratic institutions.

Brittany Paris is an Assistant Professor of library and information science in the School of Communication and Information at Rutgers, the State University of New Jersey. She is a critical informatics scholar using methods from discourse analysis and qualitative social science to study how groups build, use, and understand information systems according to their values, and how these systems influence evidentiary standards and political action. Her publications include work on Internet infrastructure projects, audiovisual footage generated through artificial intelligence, digital labor, and civic data analyzed through the lenses of critical, feminist, and de-colonial theory. She holds an MA in media studies from the New School in New York City and a PhD in information studies from the University of California, Los Angeles. Prior to joining the Rutgers faculty she was a researcher at Data & Society in New York.

Elena Pavan is Senior Assistant Professor at the Department of Sociology and Social Research of the University of Trento. She holds a degree in communication sciences (University of Padova, Italy, 2004) and a PhD in sociology (University of Trento, 2009). Her most recent research interests pertain to the relationships between collective action/political participation and digital media use. She adopts an interdisciplinary approach combining technical and social knowledge as well as traditional qualitative and quantitative research methods with digital methods and big data approaches.

Chris Peters is Professor with Special Responsibilities in Audience Research at Roskilde University, Denmark, and principal investigator of "Beyond the Here and Now of News," a project funded by the Independent Research Fund Denmark. His research focuses on media sociology, journalism, and audience studies, investigating the sociocultural transformations associated with news and information in everyday life. Peters is the editor of six books and special issues, including *Rethinking Journalism* and *Rethinking Journalism Again* (Routledge, 2013 & 2016, both with Marcel Broersma), "The Places and Spaces of News Audiences" (*Journalism Studies*, 2015), and "Conceptualizing Change in Journalism Studies" (*Journalism*, 2019, with Matt Carlson). He is currently co-writing *The Visual Citizen* with Stuart Allan for Oxford University Press.

Donatella della Porta is Professor of Political Science, Dean of the Department of Political and Social Sciences, and Director of the Ph.D. program in Political Science and Sociology at the Scuola Normale Superiore in Florence, where she also leads the Center on Social Movement Studies (Cosmos). Among the main topics of her research are social movements, political violence, terrorism, corruption, the police, and protest policing. She has directed a major ERC project Mobilizing for Democracy, on civil society participation in democratization processes in Europe, the Middle East, Asia, and Latin America. In 2011, she was the recipient of the Mattei Dogan Prize for distinguished achievements in the field of political sociology. She is Honorary Doctor of the universities of Lausanne, Bucharest, and Goteborg. She is the author or editor of 90 books, 135 journal articles, and 135 contributions in edited volumes.

Jack Linchuan Qiu is Professor in the Department of Communications and New Media, National University of Singapore. Recipient of the 2019 C. Edwin Baker Award for the Advancement of Scholarship on Media, Markets and Democracy from the International Communication Association (ICA), Qiu has published more than 100 research articles and chapters and 10 books in both English and Chinese, including *Goodbye iSlave: A Manifesto for Digital Abolition* (U of Illinois Press, 2016), *World Factory in the Information Age* (Guangxi Normal U Press, 2013), and *Working-Class Network Society* (MIT Press, 2009). He also works with grassroots NGOs and provides consultancy services for international organizations, while serving as the President of the Chinese Communication Association (CCA).

Matt Ratto is an associate professor in the Faculty of Information at the University of Toronto, Director of the Bachelor of Information degree program, and the Bell University Labs Chair in Human–Computer Interaction. His work explores the intersections between digital technologies and the human life world, with a particular focus on new developments that trouble the divide between online and offline modes of production. His work crosses both the boundaries between the digital and physical world and the divide between humanities and engineering disciplines. He coined the term "critical making" in 2007 to describe work that combines humanities insights and engineering practices, and has published extensively on this concept. A current project involves the development of a cost-effective software and hardware tool chain for the scanning, design, and 3D printing of lower-limb prostheses for use in the developing world. This work is being carried out in partnership with Hope and Healing International and rehabilitation hospitals in Canada, Uganda, and Tanzania.

Gabby Resch is a postdoctoral researcher in the Synaesthetic Media Lab at Ryerson University. He studies tangible, embodied, and multisensory methods for data interaction. His current research projects focus on tangible interfaces for augmenting spatial skills, collaborative interaction tools for infrastructure planning, and methods for fostering critical visualization literacy.

Irina Shklovski is Professor of Communication and Computing at the University of Copenhagen. Working across the disciplines of human–computer interaction, communication and science and technology studies, she seeks to answer how to design to exploit technology's usefulness without exploiting its users. Irina's recent projects address responsible technology design, online information disclosure, the use of self-tracking technologies, data leakage on mobile devices and the sense of powerlessness people experience in the face of massive personal data collection. She is concerned with how everyday technologies are becoming increasingly "creepy" and how people come to normalize and ignore those feelings of discomfort. Most recently, she coordinated a Horizon 2020 project VIRT-EU funded by the European Commission, examining how *Internet of Things* (IoT) developers enact ethics in practice and co-designing interventions into the IoT development process to support ethical reflection on data and privacy in the EU context (www.virteuproject.eu/servicepackage).

Aubrey Slaughter is a doctoral student in informatics at the University of California, Irvine. His research examines the intersection of activism, occultism, and infrastructure.

Stephen C. Slota is a postdoctoral researcher at the University of California, Irvine. His areas of research interest include infrastructure studies, information and data ethics, and the role of knowledge production in policy processes.

Holly Steel is a media sociologist specializing in the field of digital media and conflict, with a focus on the role of social media in the ongoing Syria conflict. Her work centers on questions of media representation and power in the digital age. She holds a PhD from the University of York, UK, and is currently a lecturer in media and communication at the University of Leeds, UK.

Cynthia Stohl is a Distinguished Professor in the Department of Communication and a past director of the Center for Information Technology and Society at the University of California Santa Barbara. Professor Stohl's work connects several areas in organizational and group studies. She is concerned with the relationships among internal and external communication processes as they are manifest in global collaborations. Her most recent work addresses a diversity of network and collective action organizations in the global context focusing specifically on the role of new communication technologies in contemporary organizing. She is a member of the Editorial Board of *Information, Communication & Society* as well as several other journals.

Dawn Walker is a PhD student in the Faculty of Information at the University of Toronto. Her research focuses on participation in civic technology and design practices. Her previous research includes co-design to investigate how community mapping increases participation in urban agriculture. She completed her Master of Information at the University of Toronto in 2016, and also holds an Honors Bachelor of Arts with distinction in philosophy and history.

Kaitlyn Wauthier is a doctoral candidate in the American Culture Studies program at Bowling Green State University, where she has taught courses in women's studies, ethnic studies, and American culture studies. Her research interests include questions of access and mobility as they relate to critical disability studies, tourism, and immigration. Her dissertation is titled "'I Wish to Be, I Wish to Give, I Wish to Go, I Wish to Meet': Make-A-Wish and the Construction of Disability, 1980-Present."

Barry Wellman (PhD Sociology, Harvard University) directs the NetLab Network, based in Toronto. He's a Fellow of the Royal Society of Canada and the author of more than 300 articles, often with collaborators. With Lee Rainie, he coauthored *Networked: The New Social Operating System* (2012: MIT Press).

Acknowledgments

Like editors of other collections addressing a rapidly changing topic, as coeditors of the *Routledge Handbook of Digital Media and Communication* we have faced the lightning-in-a-bottle challenge of crystallizing the field's immediacy, significance, and impact out of an editorial project that has taken years to plan and produce.

Originally conceived by one of us (Lievrouw) and long-time collaborator Sonia Livingstone as a completely new follow-up to the coedited *Handbook of New Media* (Lievrouw & Livingstone, 2002, 2006), discussions began with the original publishers nearly a decade ago, in 2012. Those plans were put on hold in late 2013, however, when Sonia had to withdraw from the project due to her other expanding research obligations and commitments. So she is one of the first people we want to acknowledge and thank, certainly for her creativity and comradeship on the earlier volumes, but especially for her contributions to the artifacts-practices-arrangements theorizing of infrastructure that has been carried forward here as our basic intellectual armature, and to the early stage development of this book.

Leah thought a new edition would still be worth pursuing, perhaps with another coeditor, so she began to ask colleagues for advice. One of those she consulted was Brian D. Loader at the University of York, the founding Editor in Chief of the highly ranked journal *Information, Communication & Society*. After rounds of correspondence, we agreed that in fact *he* would be the ideal coeditor for the new volume given his extensive publishing experience and wide acquaintance with the various fields related to new media, digital technologies, and society. We framed the scope and themes of the new volume over lunch in Seattle during the annual conference of the International Communication Association in July 2014. In the following months we developed a new list of chapter topics we hoped to include and a "dream team" roster of prospective contributors we wanted to write for us. Since then our amiable professional collaboration has developed into a real friendship, and we look forward to other collaborations in the years to come.

After extensive negotiations among different publishers, in 2015 we were pleased to sign with Routledge in London, where our original commissioning editor Gerhard Boomgaarden was an enthusiastic champion, committed to finding the widest possible global audience for the book. We have been grateful for his unstinting support from the outset, and although he recently moved on to handle new projects at another publishing house, in a real sense the *Handbook* is as much his accomplishment as it is ours and our contributors'. We hope he is pleased with the results. Rebecca Brennan, who took over Gerhard's *Handbook* duties at Routledge, has continued his style of steady encouragement, and we appreciate her dedication and help through the final editorial stages. Special thanks must also go to Mihaela Diana Ciobotea, who has unstintingly been available to assist with queries and provide guidance.

Throughout the project we have been fortunate to work with a truly superb group of contributing authors with an exceptional range of disciplinary, intellectual, cultural, and national perspectives. In the process we (i.e., Leah) have learned that in the current academic "economy," recruiting chapter writers for an edited volume like this one can be a bit more challenging than it was 20 years ago, particularly with respect to outstanding early and mid-career scholars whose institutions might prefer them to be publishing in journals or to "write their book." Yet these colleagues often have the most perceptive, creative viewpoints in complex fields like this one and are prepared to explore new technological and theoretical developments across disciplinary boundaries and in different intellectual registers – exactly what we needed for the *Handbook*. At the same time, more established and recognized scholars are often heavily committed and may require deadline flexibility. Consequently, to get the range of expertise we needed, our recruitment process had to proceed in several waves and took longer than expected. Thus, we are especially thankful not only for the high caliber of our contributors but also for their great patience throughout the editorial process.

Finally, a personal note or two. An important part of any long-term editorial project is the experience and life-courses of the editors, which naturally shape their personal priorities as well as their intellectual horizons. The period of collaboration on the *Handbook* has also been full of major life events for one of us (Lievrouw), including serious health problems for both aging parents (one of whom died in late 2018) and, more recently and unexpectedly, the life-threatening illness of her spouse (who as of this writing has been treated successfully, we are relieved and happy to say). Brian carried the weight of editorial responsibilities throughout these episodes and pressed ahead, despite Leah's periods of distraction and neglected correspondence that were surely frustrating for both him and the authors. From Leah: Brian, you have been the ideal coeditor, steady, persistent, and (not least) organized. Our book would not exist without you. Dear authors, I am lucky and indebted for your flexibility, kindness, and supportive notes and condolences, which have risen so far above any usual standards of simple academic courtesy. Thank you all.

Introduction

Leah A. Lievrouw and Brian D. Loader

No longer new, digital media and communication technologies – and their associated infrastructures, practices, and cultural forms – have become woven into the very social fabric of contemporary human life. The editors of this *Handbook of Digital Media and Communication*, together with many of the contributors, have witnessed, documented, and attempted to interpret the significant changes arising from this process of normalization throughout the formative years of the digital age. Despite the cautiously optimistic accounts of the potential of the Internet to foster stronger democratic governance (Loader, 1997; Hague & Loader, 1999), enable connective forms of mobilization (Van de Donk et al., 2004; Lievrouw, 2011), stimulate social capital (community, social, or crisis informatics) (Loader, 1998a; Keeble & Loader, 2001), restructure education and learning (Dutton & Loader, 2002), support remote health care (Loader et al., 2009), or facilitate networked flexible organization (Loader, 1998b), the actual development of digital media and communication has been far more problematic. Indeed, recent commentary has been more pessimistic about the disruptive impact of digital media and communication upon our everyday lives (Zuboff, 2019). The promise of personal emancipation and free access to unlimited digital resources has, some argue, led us to sleepwalk into a world of unremitting surveillance, gross disparities in wealth, precarious employment opportunities, a deepening crisis in democracy, and an opaque global network of financial channels and transnational corporations with unaccountable monopoly power.

A critical appraisal of the current state of play of the digital world is thus timely, indeed overdue, and required if we are to examine these assertions and concerns clearly. It is essential to avoid narrow, technologically deterministic explanations, as well as socially or culturally deterministic ones trading solely in constructions, representations, discourses, or other abstractions. Instead, we must examine the complex co-construction of digital media technologies and economic, social, political, and cultural forces and interests. There is no preordained technological pathway that digital media must follow or are following. But this is not to deny that digital media and communication have developed within and, in turn, facilitated new forms of digital capitalism (e.g., *platform capitalism* [Srnicek, 2016]; *surveillance capitalism* [Zuboff, 2019]) with their own logics of accumulation and control. A measure of these changes is the inadequacy of many familiar concepts – such as commons, public sphere, social capital, class, and others – to capture contemporary power relations or to explain transitions from "mass society" to networked sociality – or even from mass to personalized consumption. Even the strategies of resistance to these transitions draw upon traditional appeals to unionization, democratic accountability, mass mobilization, state regulation, and the like, all part of the legacy of earlier capitalist and political forms.

How then to examine the current digitalscape? We believe that by adopting the basic structure developed by Lievrouw and Livingstone (2002, 2006), organized around three co-determining elements of new media infrastructure (artifacts, practices, and arrangements), in this *Handbook* we are well placed to critically explore the changes that have occurred in the nearly two decades since their work first appeared, in terms of both the research domain and the presence and significance of digital and algorithmic media in contemporary society. Internet-based and data-driven systems, applications, platforms, and affordances now play a pivotal role in every domain of social life. And, whether under the rubric of new media research, computer-mediated communication, social media or Internet studies, media sociology, or media anthropology, research and scholarship in the area have moved from the fringe to the theoretical and empirical center of many disciplines, dominating conferences and spawning a whole generation of new journals and publishers' lists. Within communication research and scholarship itself, digital technologies and their consequences have become central topics in every area of the discipline – indeed, they have helped blur some of the most enduring boundaries dividing many of the field's traditional specializations. Meanwhile, the ubiquity, adaptability, responsiveness, and networked structure of online communication, the advantages of which – participation, convenience, engagement, connectedness, community – were often celebrated in earlier studies, have also introduced troubling new risks, including pervasive surveillance, monopolization, vigilantism, cyberwar, worker displacement, intolerance, disinformation, and social separatism.

This new collection reflects this landscape. We decided to recruit new voices and contributors who would not just sum up developments in their respective areas of study but could reflect more deeply and critically on the changed state of communication and contemporary life under conditions of ubiquitous digital mediation. The present *Handbook* brings together a group of writers who represent as much as possible the current gender, ethnic, and national composition, and the intellectual range, of research on digital media and communication. About half of our contributing authors are women. Most contributors work in the United Kingdom, Europe, or North America, but others work in Australia, Singapore, and Hong Kong. The roster includes anthropologists, attorneys, cultural critics, designers, education specialists, engineers, historians, journalists, and philosophers, as well as communication/media scholars.

We invited these colleagues to address key topics related to one of the three aspects of infrastructure, for corresponding sections of the book, but with the understanding that each aspect – artifacts, practices, arrangements – is necessarily and inextricably articulated with the other two. And, as Leigh Star and Geof Bowker theorized in the Lievrouw and Livingstone volumes (in chapters which strongly influenced the three-dimensional framing of infrastructure carried over into this work and became seminal early works in the field now known as "infrastructure studies"), technology infrastructure has several defining features that make it a distinctive object of study. Infrastructures are *embedded*; *transparent* (support tasks invisibly); have *reach or scope* beyond a single context; *learned* as part of membership in a social or cultural group; are *linked to existing practices* and routines; embody *standards*; are built on an *existing, installed base*; and, perhaps most critically, ordinarily become "visible" or apparent to users only *when they break down*: when "the server is down, the bridge washes out, there is a power blackout" (Star & Bowker, 2002, 152).

As of this writing, as the world undergoes breakdowns in social, institutional, and technological systems across every domain of human affairs in the wake of a biological and public health crisis of unprecedented scale and scope, such a framework for understanding communicative action, technology, and social forms has never been so apt or so urgently needed.

We also asked our authors to consider two cross-cutting themes that we felt had come to characterize the quality and processes of mediated communication over the prior two decades. The first is a broad shift from *the mass* and toward *the network* as the defining structure and dominant logic of communication technologies, systems, relations, and practices; the second is the growing *enclosure* of those technologies, relations, and practices by private ownership and state security interests. These two features of digital media and communication have joined to create socio-technical conditions for communication today that would have been unrecognizable even to early new media scholars of the 1970s and 1980s, to say nothing of the communication researchers before them specializing in classical media effects research, political economy of media, interpersonal and group process, political communication, global/comparative communication research, or organizational communication, for example.

While not every chapter responds directly to all aspects of our brief, on the whole the collection reveals an extraordinarily faceted, nuanced picture of communication, and communication studies, today. For example, the opening part, "Artifacts," richly portrays the infrastructural qualities of digital media tools and systems. We are particularly pleased to have Stephen C. Slota, Aubrey Slaughter, and Geoffrey C. Bowker's piece on "occult" infrastructures of communication as the first chapter in the book, expanding and elaborating on the infrastructure studies perspective. In the same part, Paul Dourish provides perhaps the most incisive discussion published to date on the nature and meaning of *ubiquity* for designers and users of digital systems. Chapters on big data and algorithms (Taina Bucher), mobile devices and communicative gestures (Lee Humphreys and Larissa Hjorth), digital embodiment and financial infrastructures (Kaitlyn Wauthier and Radhika Gajjala), interfaces and affordances (Matt Ratto, Curtis McCord, Dawn Walker, and Gabby Resch), hacking (Finn Brunton), and digital records and memory (David Beer) demonstrate how computation and data generation/capture have transfigured both the material features and the human experience of engagement with media technologies and systems.

The second part, "Practices," shifts focus from devices, tools, and systems to the communicative practices of the people who use them. Digital media and communication today have fostered what some writers have called *datafication* – capturing and rendering all aspects of communicative action, expression, and meaning into quantified data that are often traded in markets and used to make countless decisions about, and to intercede in, people's experiences (e.g., Kennedy, 2018; Mayer-Schönberger & Cukier, 2013). Systems that allow people to make and share meaning are also configured by private-sector firms and state security actors to capture and enclose human communication and information. As our contributors show, this dynamic is played out in routine monitoring and surveillance (Mark Andrejevic), in the construction and practice of personal identity (Mary Chayko), in family routines and relationships (Nancy Jennings), in political participation (Brian Loader and Veronica Barassi), in our closest relationships and sociality (Irina Shklovski), in education and new literacies (Antero Garcia), in the increasing precarity of "information work" (Leah Lievrouw and Brittany Paris), and in what Walter Lippmann famously called the "picture of reality" portrayed in the news (Stuart Allan and Chris Peters, Holly Steel). Many of the chapters here suggest that the erosion and contestation of boundaries between public and private, true and false, and ourselves and others are increasingly taken for granted, with mediated communication as likely to create a destabilizing, chronic sense of disruption and displacement as it is to promote deliberation, cohesion, or solidarities.

In the third part, contributors explore the broader social, organizational, and institutional arrangements that shape and regulate the tools and the practices of digital communication and information, and which themselves are continuously reformed by those tools and practices. It begins with Nick Couldry's overview of *mediatization*, the growing centrality of media in what he calls the "institutionalization of the social" and the establishment of social order, at every level of sociality from micro-scale interaction to the jockeying among nation-states. Again, in their essays several contributors present evidence of the instability, uncertainty, and delegitimation associated with digital media, from Terry Flew's reflections on globalization, Peng Hwa Ang's survey of governance and regulation and Jack Linchuan Qiu's revisitation of political economy, to Natalie Fenton's assessment of the prospects for the public sphere, Julie Cohen's trenchant reconsideration of the notion of property, and Elena Pavan and Donatella della Porta's examination of the role of digital media in social movements. In contrast, Keith Hampton and Barry Wellman argue that digital technologies may, in fact, help reinforce people's senses of community and belonging; communities continue to form and thrive, both online and offline. Shiv Ganesh and Cynthia Stohl show that while much past research has focused on of the "fluidity" or formlessness of organization afforded by "digital ubiquity," in fact contemporary organizing is a more subtle process comprising "opposing tendencies and human activities, of both form and formlessness."

Taken together, the contributions present a complex, interwoven technical, social/cultural, and institutional fabric of society, which nonetheless seems to be showing signs of wear, or perhaps even breakdown in places, in response to systemic environmental and institutional crises. As digital media and communication technologies have become routine, even banal, features of interaction, commerce, and culture, the rosy confidence in what economists call the *positive externalities*, or network effects, of digital communication and information systems – convenience, immediacy, connectedness – is increasingly accompanied by a growing recognition of their *negative* externalities – monopoly and suppressed competition, incumbency and rent-seeking, ethical and leadership failures, and technological lock-in and "more like this" instead of genuine, pathbreaking innovation. The promise and possibility of new media and digitally mediated communication are increasingly tempered with sober assessments of risk, path-dependency, conflict, and exploitation.

This scenario may seem pessimistic, but perhaps one way to view the current state of digital media and communication studies is that it has matured, or reached a plateau or moment of consolidation, in which the visionary enthusiasms and forecasts of earlier decades have grown into a more developed or skeptical perspective. Digital media platforms and systems have diffused across the globe into cultural, political, and economic contexts and among diverse populations that often challenge the assumptions and expectations that were built into the early networks. The systems themselves, and their ownership and operations, have stabilized and become routinized, much as utilities and earlier media systems have done before, so they are more likely to resist root-and-branch change. They are as likely to reinforce and sustain patterns of knowledge and power as they are to "disrupt" them.

So, if we look ahead to imagine what a future *Handbook*-type compendium might look like in another decade – in whatever forms or genres it might take – we might expect to find that, consistent with the infrastructural perspective advanced here, the devices, practices, and institutional arrangements will have become even more integrated into common activities, places, experiences, and culture. That is, they will be unremarkable, embedded, woven into cultural practices, standardized, and *invisible* or transparent in Star and Bowker's sense – just as satellite transmissions and undersea cables, or content streaming and social media platforms, are to us today. These socio-technical qualities will pose new kinds of challenges for communication researchers and scholars, but they also herald possibilities for a fuller, deeper understanding of the role communication plays at the center of human experience and endeavor.

References

Dutton, W., and Loader, B. D. (2002). *Digital Academe: The New Media and Institutions of Higher Education and Learning*. London: Routledge.

Hague, B., and Loader, B. D. (1999). *Digital Democracy: Discourse and Decision-Making in the Information Age*. London: Routledge.

Keeble, L., and Loader, B. D. (2001). *Community Informatics: Shaping Computer-Mediated Social Networks*. Edited by L. Keeble. London: Routledge.

Kennedy, H. (2018). Living with Data: Aligning Data Studies and Data Activism Through a Focus on Everyday Experiences of Datafication. *Krisis: Journal for Contemporary Philosophy*, 1, 17–30. https://eprints.whiterose.ac.uk/129959.

Lievrouw, L. A. (2011). *Alternative and Activist New Media*. Cambridge: Polity Press.

Lievrouw, L. A., and Livingstone, S. (2002). *The Handbook of New Media*. London: Sage.

Lievrouw, L. A., and Livingstone, S. (2006). *The Handbook of New Media* (updated student ed.). London: Sage.

Loader, B. D. (1997). *The Governance of Cyberspace: Politics, Technology and Global Restructuring*. London: Routledge.

Loader, B. D. (1998a). *The Cyberspace Divide: Equality, Agency and Policy in the Information Society*. London: Routledge.

Loader, B. D. (1998b). Welfare Direct: The Emergence of a Self-Service Welfare State? In J. Carter (ed.), *Postmodernity and the Fragmentation of Welfare*. London: Routledge, pp. 220–233.

Loader, B. D., Hardey, M., and Keeble, L. (2009). *Digital Welfare for the Third Age: Health and Social Care Informatics for Older People*. London: Routledge.

Mayer-Schönberger, V., and Cukier, K. (2013). *Big Data: A Revolution That Will Transform How We Live, Work, and Think*. New York: Houghton Mifflin Harcourt.

Srnicek, N. (2016). *Platform Capitalism*. Cambridge: Polity Press.

Star, S. L., and Bowker, G. (2002). How to Infrastructure. In L. A. Lievrouw and S. Livingstone (eds.), *The Handbook of New Media*. Thousand Oaks, CA: Sage, pp. 151–162.

Van de Donk, W., Loader, B. D., Nixon, P., and Rucht, D. (2004). *Cyberprotest: New Media, Citizens and Social Movements*. London: Routledge.

Zuboff, S. (2019). *The Age of Surveillance Capitalism*. New York: Public Affairs.

Part I
Artifacts

1

The hearth of darkness
Living within occult infrastructures

Stephen C. Slota, Aubrey Slaughter, and Geoffrey C. Bowker

Infrastructure is the story of what happens when the "real story" is taking place. Behind the spectacles of permanent technocultural revolution, effervescent personal expression, and the vertiginous proliferation of new modes of expression lies the operation of physical, computing, organizational forms of action (*dispositifs*). Often, the most visible products of our culture reflect and represent substantive changes in infrastructure and infrastructural capacity – behind the scenes of film production are attendant infrastructures of chemical reactions and assorted associated refinements for film development, broadly available and reliable electricity, all the industry and science that went into the production of electric lighting (not to mention the substantial complexity of audio recording) (Sterne, 2006). These are prior to the broader cultural infrastructure that supports and responds to particular forms of expression. Silent films, for example, presume a significant visual as well as written skill set for the audience (cf. Deleuze, 1986). The early history of US national broadcast television – especially the content controls enforced by the Federal Communications Commission (FCC) – speaks to the notion of resource availability and societal responsibility (Aufderheide, 1991). Similarly, the apportionment and use of radio spectra depend to some extent on both the technology that is used to broadcast and broader societal assumptions as to the best use of that quite limited spectra (Aufderheide, 1999).

In recent times we are experiencing an unusual proliferation of infrastructural goods. Where previously infrastructure that spanned broad distance required significant investment and management of physical space and material, extant communications infrastructure provides a ground in which new infrastructure might be more easily built and integrated. The infrastructure of the Internet, for example, was largely built upon the existing infrastructure of telephone communication, which itself was partly built on the telegraph, which followed and was built alongside roadways and canal infrastructure (cf. Castells and Blackwell, 1998; Edwards et al., 2007; Edwards, 2010). New infrastructures emerged out of the generic, formal http: protocol, defined largely by their role relative to particular activities – often called "platforms" (Gillespie, 2010). Infrastructure, as defined by Star and Ruhleder (1996), is embedded and transparent; it exists (metaphorically) within or underneath other social, technological, and built worlds and does not need to be reconsidered at the moment of each task it enables. Infrastructure is learned as a part of membership and linked with the conventions of practice therein and embodies some set of standards. It is built over the top of an installed base, becoming visible upon breakdown, and is of a scale or scope that exceeds a single "site" – however that might be conceived (Star & Ruhleder, 1996). This definition of infrastructure allows us to consider the complex plurality of social, organizational, and physical infrastructures that together inform and support our day-to-day activities – something that expansively is referred to as knowledge infrastructures (Borgman et al., 2013). It is important to remember, here, that infrastructure occupies not just a material place but also a social, political and organizational one – hence the emphasis on knowledge infrastructures – and can in fact be almost totally immaterial (Karasti et al., 2016; Borgman et al., 2013). It is difficult to argue, for example, that the TCP/IP routing and addressing protocols are not infrastructural to Internet communication, but it is equally difficult to understand those objects according to their material properties alone (DeNardis, 2012). One of the major methodologies for social scientists interested in infrastructure studies is the notion of "infrastructural inversion" (Bowker et al., 2009), where the supportive technologies, standards, and material are intentionally and specifically foregrounded in order to explore their effect on work, expression, or policy.

The core reason for making this move is the postulate that infrastructure matters. Infrastructure is not a neutral background enabling an infinite set of activities; infrastructure holds values, permits certain kinds of human and nonhuman relations while blocking others, and shapes the very ways in which we think about the world. This is evident in Veyne's (2005) proposition that it is impossible to trace the development of the concept of democracy over time because "democracy" changes fundamentally with new infrastructural developments. Meeting in an agora or town square to determine matters of concern is fundamentally different from holding discussions through print media or following a 24-hour news cycle on electronic media (Boczkowski, 2005). Or as Richard John (2009) has pointed out, we could not have the American state without the cheap circulation of newspapers nationally through the infrastructure of the post office, permitting the engagement of a national debate among residents of the otherwise remote states. Infrastructural inversion has been applied to work in health care (Jensen, 2008), water management in Thailand and the role of rice production (Morita, 2017), sociotechnical analyses of Wi-Fi (Mackenzie, 2005), as a generative resource in the digital humanities (Kaltenbrunner, 2015), and in studies of policy and development (Pelizza, 2016; Suarez-Villa, 1997; Zick, 2013; Korn & Voida, 2015; Hetherington & Campbell, 2014). It, however, seems most comfortably applied to the area of science studies for its revelations on knowledge production practices (Mayernik et al., 2013; Georgiadou et al., 2009; Lee et al., 2006). Throughout this writing, we "invert" the notion of infrastructure itself to consider it as a relational quantity – something that exists *as infrastructure* only in relation to particular activities, modes of work, expression, and performance.

We examine how systems and technologies infrastructural to new media such as social media platforms, recommender systems, and entertainment apps serve to inform certain kinds of performance of the self, and we examine broadly the concept of infrastructure as it relates to digital media and communication. Infrastructural systems are deeply embedded in a wide ecology of social interactions, political realities, and assumptions among its users with respect to affordances (Gibson, 1979). As we explore the impact and consideration of the place of knowledge infrastructure in our daily interactions with media, we are talking about effects and assumptions infrastructural to our current interactions and are describing a *relational, changing* system impacted by a wide array of social, political, and technological factors. In the following sections, we discuss the specific example of the End User License Agreement (EULA), exploring how our basic interactions, legal rights, and assumptions of value are coded into an occluded, often-unread, potentially unenforceable document. Infrastructural to our interactions with service providers, the law, and by extension to the communities enabled and propagated within our services, the place of the EULA is nevertheless in flux – what is reality one day might be history a few days later. The deployment and relationality of infrastructure are subject to relatively rapid changes – as soon as it must be reconsidered at the moment of work there is a substantive difference from the initial infrastructural relationship.

Infrastructure encodes values, influences behavior

Critical reflection on the design of information systems and other artifacts shows that humans embody their values and morality, often unconsciously, in the things that they create (Winner, 1980; Latour, 1992; Nissenbaum, 1998). These values may be intentionally designed into the physical state of the artifact or system (Flanagan et al., 2008; Friedman et al., 2002) or be observed as resulting from a myriad of social factors (Pinch & Bijker, 1984). These values can produce bias (Friedman & Nissenbaum, 1996) or otherwise be seen to have and carry politics of their own (Introna & Nissenbaum, 2000). Successful infrastructures serve those with a variety of values but may prioritize certain values in their design (Knobel & Bowker, 2011). For example, mobile technology that automatically reports your location through GPS to your friends and family values connectedness and intimacy above privacy. Although these value propositions are evident in the objects themselves, often they are the result of unconscious assumptions on the part of the designer, making it quite difficult to avoid their potential negative impacts on the quality of life (Introna & Nissenbaum, 2000).

Engagement with media in different platforms has significant and unconscious effects on user behavior (Valkenburg & Peter, 2013; Greenfield, 2014; Johnson et al., 1997). Similarly, with the use of hidden A/B testing, where users are unknowingly presented with one of two different versions of a site or service in order to test the effect of that design choice on use, the potential for emotional and social manipulation by those managing platforms (Kramer et al., 2014) is increasingly problematic – the medium itself is designed to disguise or otherwise impede awareness of the variety of ways in which behavior is being manipulated, information and inference about an individual are collected and put to use (Schüll, 2014), and certain interactions are trivialized while others are highlighted (Metcalf & Crawford, 2016). In design literature, such work is often characterized as a "nudging technology," which is defined by Thaler and Sunstein as "any aspect of the choice architecture that alters people's behavior in a predictable way without forbidding any options or significantly changing their economic incentives" (2009, 6). A nudge, in the sense of Thaler and Sunstein, is not a mandate – it is the careful curation of choices presented to users of a system through their notifications, menu layout, and other design aspects of the overall information architecture of that system (cf. Obama, 2015). Nudging is designed to act aggregately over a population, rather than deterministically over a single user (Spiegler, 2015; Marteau et al., 2011).

Nudging technologies play upon the human machine and seek to create certain conformities of behavior according to unconscious responses. This is performance of the human as machine in a way that can only be done in a specific media regime – requiring both the tranching of behaviors sufficient to predict responses and the willingness to engage with a system, device, or environment on "its own terms." That is to say, the system performs a mode of engagement and interaction that works simultaneously to encourage particular performances of the individual as machine, the individual as a collective uniqueness, the individual as self-representation, and the individual in the production of narratives of the self as presented through media conforming to that system.

This is transhumanism in the mode of De Chardin (1964), or Kurzweil (2000), and Butler in *Erewohn* (1974) – exceeding the performance of the self through technologies of representation, sharing, and re-presentation of that self: "Firstly, the power of invention, so rapidly intensified at the present time by the rationalised recoil of all the forces of research that it is already possible to speak of a forward leap of evolution" (De Chardin, 1964, 305). Increasingly, we self-curate, creating an archive of the self-reflective not just of a self-product but also of the system in which we are performing ourselves. This is integrally a new mode of being human – one where the global and local are brought to the same level through communication technology; where marginalized populations are able to constitute themselves in ways that would not have otherwise been possible (Cormack & Hourigan, 2007); and where the formation, dissolution, and reconstitution of communities are far more rapid than before (Alonso & Oiarzabal, 2010).

What we need to understand people's politics is to see what they don't consider to be political, what is a "natural" form of governance, whether that is democracy, capitalism, or nature-red-in-tooth-and-claw (Schmitter & Karl, 1991). Even before we were "nudged" by technology and intentional design, social cues, interactions, and reactions served a similar role in unconsciously modifying our behavior. We do not consider our unconscious responses to be a part of infrastructural systems; we prefer to believe that we interact with systems agentially (Luhmann, 2000). But people's reactions and their unconscious, reflexive, immanent responses are perhaps much more relevant to the builder of infrastructural systems than anything else (Tosa, 2010). These are perhaps the most vital elements of infrastructure because they cannot be easily changed by either users or designers, but still invisibly inflect all forms of human-infrastructural relations. In many ways, the unconscious, reactive human is itself an infrastructure of relevance to system designers, particularly in the field of human–computer interaction (Zafar et al., 2017; Van House, 2011; Karashima & Ishibashi, 2007). Now, we characterize the influence of the 'machine' on the human in terms of the characteristic ability of infrastructure to 'fade into the background' of our daily lives in terms of the *occult*. This is not (just) the occult in the sense of the magical, the unexplained, or the ineffable but also in the sense of that which is hidden, unseen, or blocked from view. In various ways, we find infrastructural relations both fading from view in daily practice and as actively occluded.

The invisible actor: infrastructure as occult, occulting, and occulted

The complexity of 'nudging' in technology design is partly in the *occulting* of its action through the manipulation of autonomic or unconsidered responses to design choices. Much as infrastructure itself fades from awareness, so too do its influences – even those that may be harmful, in the case of Schüll's study of how gambling is designed to provoke addiction-like responses (Schüll, 2014). There is a sense in which design that does not nudge its users toward certain behaviors could be equated to just bad design (design that fails to engage, fails to encourage repeat use, fails to create healthier or safer behaviors, etc.) (Goldhaber, 1997; Ciampaglia et al., 2015). However, a user might be *nudged* to spend more on microtransactions than they can afford, compromise their privacy and safety through oversharing, or otherwise be led toward harmful behavior through nudging technologies – the potential broader social connections enabled through that platform being modified and controlled through our unconscious reactions becomes a substantial issue in its own right (Sunstein, 2015). This is a particularly noticeable effect of an information-oriented infrastructure – the very way in which information and choices are presented to us has a significant impact on how we interact with that system, how we perceive that interaction, and the behaviors and choices we make within it. Operated on our unconscious reactions as humans, the *nudging* of behavior through choice architectures is both a metaphor for how infrastructure impacts our lives and a prime example of how the *occulting* of that infrastructure leads away from momentary consideration of those behaviors.

Bowker and Star discussed how we see infrastructure – they argued that by and large we do not; infrastructures are perspectivally invisible (2000). We tend to abstract infrastructural systems through representations or discourses, which, Knobel (2010) argues, could always be otherwise; infrastructures are perspectivally representational. A defining aspect of human-infrastructural relations is that infrastructures are, in their relation to their users, differentially perspectivally occult.

New infrastructures are built upon their elders, a *matryoshka* of obsolescence and path dependence (Edwards et al., 2007). Infrastructures, then, do not arise de novo; similarly, human-infrastructural relations are built upon precedent. While a user introduced to a novel infrastructure learns how to use the system as part of assimilating into a community of practice (Star & Ruhleder, 1996), these community practices have lineages of their own, and how one relates to a given infrastructure is formed and informed by how one has related to past instances of infrastructure.

Of course, how one has related to past instances of infrastructure is formed and informed by how your parents related to infrastructures, and their communities of practice, and their parent's practices, all the way down the line. This sort of infinite regress, in terms of theory, generically cannot go very far – "Prehistorians must resign themselves to doing without the evidence that would have been most significant" (Leroi-Gourhan, 1993, 107), and even the most nimble of researchers are left groping in the dark, imaginatively constructing explanatory frameworks to account for what little concrete evidence remains. It is rare to talk with one's parents or elders about their own relationship with infrastructure – one infers it on slight evidence. Assembling some sort of constructive abstraction is a natural response toward systems that we must grapple with but are unable to understand, and we argue that such a stance also characterizes how humans approach and relate to the infrastructural systems that undergird their daily lives.

The first infrastructures were the first assemblages that humans recognized as systemic. They were certainly not man-made: the weather, the cycle of seasons, and the natural rhythms of growth and decay that predominated and defined the field of primal systems (Durham Peters, 2012). Humans made use of these systems as they needed in order to survive. Crucially, users of these systems did not understand how they worked. While users of primal infrastructures necessarily had some mytho-poetic representation as to how these systems functioned, the mechanics of the weather were esoteric to these early humans as they are for most of us. Little has changed, "how much of society is already homeostatically regulated by machines that are ultimately under human control, but practically speaking, are almost never meddled with?" (Mckenna, 1999, 26, 29). Centrally, we have retained a commonality with our primal ancestors, in that we do not understand most of the systems that we use in our daily lives. Digital communication media are in general occult.

We cannot directly observe how our primal ancestors related to the mysterious networks of forces that allowed for their continued existence. The archaeological record is of some use, certainly, but time has rendered these already occult relations ever more obscure. For example, Serres speaks of the early origins of both mathematics and law arising from a religious group of measurers and surveyors, known as the *harpedonaptai* drawing on Herodotus' history of Egypt. He describes the *harpedonaptai* as surveyors/priests who were responsible for marking the boundaries of tillable land following the annual flooding of the Nile River, which would destroy the prior markers of those boundaries. He claims this practice both as the practical origin of geometry and as the functional beginning of the law.

But, once again, since the flood erased the limits and markers of tillable fields, properties disappeared at the same time. Returning to the now chaotic terrain, the harpedonaptai redistribute them and thus give new birth to law, which had been erased. Law reappears at the same time as geometry; or rather, both are born along with the notion of limit, edge, and definition, with analytic thought. The definition of precise form implies properties: for geometry, those of the square or the parallelogram; for law, it implies the proprietor. Analytic thought takes root in the same word and the same operation, from which grow two branches, science and law.

(Serres, 1995, 52)

While it is unclear whether Herodotus ever visited Egypt, or if his descriptions (as analyzed and interpreted by Serres) were derived from experience or hearsay, we do derive a picture of early infrastructure brought about through ritual, through bounding and measuring, and through resolving disagreement over land rights to appeals to an early scientific authority. The *harpedonaptai* worked by attaching a cord to a stake, and using that cord as both boundary and instrument when surveying. This cord is significant to Serres; he suggests that the *harpedonaptai's* "mysterious title can be broken down into two words, a noun expressing the bond and a verb denoting his act of attaching it" (ibid.) That cord is both boundary and attachment – in surveying, dividing, and describing the land the surveyors attach themselves to the object of study just as surely as they stake out its boundary and are themselves characterized and described by the technologies of that practice. The act of stretching the cord is meaningless without a field upon which to work, and the geometries practiced by the *harpedonaptai* are sensible primarily in terms of that field.

It is in this context that we wish to point to the *occulting* of infrastructure. Rather than being invisible, infrastructure is "visible upon breakdown" and "embedded in practice" (Star & Ruhleder, 1996). Not something entirely unseen, but, like a celestial body, it is occulted. Where the occulting of distant stars gives us information not only on the makeup of the star itself but also on that which moves across its path to our perspective (Simon et al., 1995), infrastructure is occulted by the work that is done upon it, and in that occulting is something revelatory about both that work and the infrastructure itself. That work which does not need to consider systems, organizations, and material at the moment of action reveals, through its assumptions of availability, an infrastructural relationship. And as in astronomy, the nature of how infrastructure is occulted in practice is revelatory of its nature. Labeling infrastructure as 'occult' extends Bowker's concept of infrastructural inversion; if you can see an infrastructure working, something has gone awry – if you need to deeply reconsider the infrastructure when acting, it is no longer infrastructural to your work, but rather the site of it. Infrastructures can only be captured when dead, never alive; a freeze-frame cross section of a functioning infrastructural assemblage is a virtual impossibility, much in the same way it is difficult to extract a functioning nervous system for clinical examination. Dissection is far easier than vivisection, as any surgeon will readily attest; "Death is a great revealer of infrastructures" (Peters, 2015, 383). Thus, we consider the nature of the infrastructure as *occult* and as *occulted*, and discuss how that which is *occulted into* the infrastructure behaves and acts upon us.

Occult media: tracing infrastructural effects in the performance of the self

Connected self-expression is always already infrastructural – it is tied to a performance, not just of the self but of the self by means of the platform (Gillespie, 2010). In the ever-varying spaces of digital communication platforms, of mediated discourse, and of broad, many-to-many connectedness, there is a cyclical reciprocity to the performance of self. Even as a certain image of the self, the family, and other immediate social units can be performed through media selection, through text, and through the production of ephemeral moments of sharing (Bayer et al., 2016; Androutsopoulos, 2014), the system algorithmically and automatically produces a representation of that self that is performed back to the user through their mediated feedback mechanisms (likes, shares, notes) as well as through an image of the individual as consumer in recommender systems. The user is interpellated (Haraway, 2003). Through social media platforms, we can see presentations of the self as falling more closely into categories of performance (where feedback is expected relatively synchronously) and exhibition (which bears a bit more expectation of asynchronous interaction) (Hogan, 2010). Increasingly, platforms for engagement cast the act of presenting the self as both artist and curator, and the production of shareable moments is often performed in light of that self-presentation.

Self-expression through social media presumes a many-to-many relationship between content creation and consumption rather than the broadcast one-to-many relationship of television, movies, radio, and printed books enabled through a particular communications and technology infrastructure. Just as, in the tradition of McLuhan, the development of an infrastructure of printing and distribution of text had significant effects on expression (McLuhan et al., 2011; McLuhan & Fiore, 1967; Eisenstein, 1957) – the assumptions present in self-expression over Internet-connected media significantly enable certain behaviors while limiting others, create means of understanding the self that previously had gone unseen, and develop new modes of interaction not limited by geography or group membership (Livingstone, 2008). One cannot imagine the epistelatory novel without the infrastructure of the post office – nor the proliferation of spam without email.

We consider infrastructure as present in and relevant to studies of digital media and communication along two axes. The first is in its representation and narrative, and the second is as a technological substrate that enables certain activities, communities, networks, and representations. In the narrative mode of infrastructure we see infrastructural goods presented as political pathways toward idealized futures (Larkin, 2013) and as a character in narratives of technology development and social formation.

What would it mean, analytically speaking, to consider the Internet as infrastructurally occult, and how does doing so serve the field of infrastructural studies? First, this perspective privileges the relationality of infrastructure, reinforcing the argument that infrastructures are defined through their relations to the human. This is not to say that infrastructural systems are intrinsically occult, or ultimately ineffable, but rather that we act toward these systems as if they were. We view infrastructure from the perspective of the human; the system, regrettably, is silent. Second, examining infrastructure through an occult lens emphasizes the abstract and representational nature of our infrastructural imaginaries, the notional constructions that inform our understandings of and interactions with infrastructural systems. This anthropocentric approach is unconcerned with how infrastructures actually function; the lower mysteries are always an object of faith. Rather, an occult perspective on infrastructure is more concerned with how infrastructures are *imagined* to operate, the routinized rituals of a modern-day mythos. According to Larkin, infrastructure presupposes some future and presents a pathway toward that future. Politically, infrastructure speaks closely to how we understand our own capacity, capability, and room for growth (Larkin, 2013). Representations of infrastructure growth are tied to notions of expanding that capacity and not only reflect a pathway toward an idealized future but also present an image of what it is that enables important work. Investment, time, and resources spent building the first American cross-country railroad, for example, was presaged on the imagined future of a large, connected country capable of rapid transportation from the Atlantic coast to the Pacific (Cronon, 2009).

The question is not 'How can we build a better infrastructure?' but rather 'How are our imaginaries of infrastructure informed?' More than any technical constraints or cultural norms, it is these imaginaries that shape how we relate to infrastructural systems. A superior infrastructure is a poor replacement for a deprecated system when it is used in the same fashion, just as the computer is a poor typewriter and the electric turbine a poor steam dynamo (David, 1990). Establishing an understanding of how infrastructural imaginaries are formed is useful for scholars looking to apply an infrastructural lens to systems seen as outside the ambit of the field. It can be difficult to examine the infrastructural imaginaries that undergird one's every day. However, our perceptions, interpretations, and performances of infrastructural and infrastructural goods enact a specific ordering of the world, present us with certain choices that would not exist outside that infrastructure, and operate upon us in significant ways, often through the work of a system 'black-boxed' into the platform, underneath the structure of our interaction. Increasingly, it is important to consider not only the world of media that is presented to us but also the operation of media upon us and provide some accounting of how to interpret an increasingly curated life – one that presents us with a performance of ourselves as mediated through a technology platform and provides a ground for interaction with that performance. Next, we explore a particularly 'infrastructural' media genre that serves to structure a given consumer's interactions with a platform as well as enforcing an order of society, notions of value, and accounts of what constitutes a human. The EULA is a significant mode of writing that generically goes unseen and unread by its intended audience yet is consistently addressed, updated, and worked upon; it will be the focus of the next section.

Performance and the EULA – showing you to you and us through you

Increasingly, we understand ourselves and perform our identities, goals, and reality through the recording, visualization, and interpretation of data. New technologies, sensors, and other systems have created an infrastructure from which we might interpret our health and the functioning of our bodies (Berson, 2015), as well as presenting "stories" about the world as represented and contained in trace and other data (Madhavan et al., 2012; Knaflic, 2015; Boy et al., 2015).

Recommender systems – platforms and technologies that reason algorithmically about our prior behavior in order to predict what we might want to purchase, listen to, or befriend next – illuminate some of the dynamics of this self-performance (Seaver, 2012). I perform myself in different ways over Pandora in accord with the structured means by which I might interact with the recommender system, for example, choosing between whether to 'thumbs-down' a song or just to skip it, depending on my goals in interacting with that system – whether I want similar songs, a diverse channel, or a mood will all produce certain performances of that goal to the system, even when the mechanics of that system are not fully disclosed. This is advertisement and recommendation through play, supported and enabled through instantiations of technology and through the affordances (Gibson, 1979) present within that technology. Without large libraries and multifaceted, self-created in addition to imposed, systems of categorization, the recommender is incapable of supporting exploratory and investigative play (Seaver, 2012). Technological systems are becoming deeply intentional.

In addition to this notion of the self being performed to you by the platform, we also draw attention to the implicit, unintentional, or invisible production of media about a person through the creation of digital traces. Even while performing other activities, the basic substrate of connected, online expression creates a narrative of activities that are recorded and expressed outside of the immediate control, or even awareness, of the user. This is evident in the reuse of user data of 87 million users of Facebook by the Cambridge Analytica corporation, used to influence political elections from 2014 to 2017, which resulted in significant international outcry and the broad questioning of the privacy, sale, and potential reach of data collected about social media behaviors often without the users being made fully aware (Metcalf, 2018). The extent to which our self-performance can be reasoned upon and influential of the world as aggregate can be interpreted as surprising, invasive, or just plain wrong for a variety of reasons, but it remains that the actual reach of data collection and capacity for inference about uncollected information is well hidden in the infrastructure of communication (Metcalf, 2018).

EULAs are a contract between a customer and a seller that detail each side's rights, responsibilities, and duties in regard to the product in question. These "non-negotiable, often inaccessible contracts" bind the users of nearly all digital or virtual products, dictating what a customer can and cannot do with their purchase (Jankowich, 2006, 9). EULAs are endemic to software licensing, where it "is the most common format for disclosing information about software behavior," and in games, where generally "the EULA is the sole form of governance" (Good et al., 2006, 284; De Zwart, 2010, 607). These agreements are ubiquitous and come in many forms, but all share common issues that make their implementation problematic.

Image 1.1 was described by its artist, Dimo Yarvinsky, as an attempt to

> [take] the content of the "terms of service" [ToS] of the leading online services that we use on a daily basis (including Facebook, Snapchat, Instagram, Tinder etc.). I've printed them on a standard A4 wide scroll with a standard legal contract font size and type. After printing these so-called terms, I hanged the scrolls in the gallery at the academy, added the number of words and the time it takes to read each scroll on the floor. My main goal was to emphasize how small, helpless and harmful are we against this giant corporates.
>
> *(quote from the Visualizing Knowledge exhibition)*

This artwork serves to describe both how extensive and, ultimately, how inaccessible the EULA or ToS might be to a user approaching a service for the first time. The most common complaint about the contractual fine print of the EULA is that, empirically speaking, no one reads them before agreeing to their terms (Bakows et al., 2009). There are a number of reasons why customers don't read EULAs; the length (Fairer Finance Survey in Nejad et al., 2016), complexity (Reidenberg et al., 2015), and obligatory nature of the documents (De Paoli & Kerr, 2009) lead many consumers to believe that EULAs "all say the same thing and that they are irrelevant" (Plaut & Bartlett, 2012, 305). While EULAs are almost universally one-sided and pro-seller (Mann & Siebneicher, 2008), these same attributes often lead courts to declare the contracts unconscionable in the legal sense, or extremely unjust and therefore invalid (Gilbert, 2009). As consumers are often unaware of the terms of agreement, and sellers uncertain about their enforceability, it has been argued that EULAs do not serve either party well (Kunze, 2008). Even unread, however, they serve as the 'first word' in a legal dispute between the user and the platform provider; infrastructure the nature of the platform and how it operates; and instantiate what is valuable to users, to the platform provider, and often to society at large.

There have been a number of attempts to mitigate these issues, ranging from technical interventions that offer to read (Nejad et al., 2016) and rate (TOS:DR Team, 2019) EULAs, through algorithmic or crowd-sourced initiatives, to calls for the legal regulation of EULAs, through private (Braman & Roberts, 2003), governmental (Terasaki, 2013), or nonprofit institutions (Gomulkiewicz, 2003). Other scholars have aimed at the reclamation of EULAs as a tool to fight data collection and corporate overreach, which these documents discreetly enable

Image 1.1 Yarvinsky "Terms of Service"

(Cherry, 2014). Despite their flaws, and scholarly attention to them, it would appear as though EULAs will remain a relevant concern for the foreseeable future (Gomulkiewicz & Williamson, 1996).

While the immediate, contractual ramifications of EULAs are spelled out within the document, keen observers have also picked up on a variety of consequential and concurrent effects that stretch beyond the legal writ of the text. Not only do consumers agree to EULAs without reading them, they'll do the same with documents that simply resemble EULAs (Böhme & Köpsell, 2010). This 'blind consent' has much to do with the onerous nature of reading EULAs

(Grimes et al., 2008), but has just as much to do with our (often wildly incorrect) beliefs about EULAs (Plaut & Bartlett, 2012). It has been argued that it is these beliefs, rather than an unread click-through agreement, that form and inform our behaviors in regard to virtual goods and services (Kennedy et al., 2016).

Infrastructural inflection: orienting the cattle

EULAs are generally not about the end users. Much confusion comes down to there being 'End User' in the title; what else could such a contract possibly be about other than between a corporation and a person? Though EULAs are ostensibly binding agreements between two parties, it can be difficult to ascertain whether or not they are binding, whether they are agreements, or even whether there are two parties involved. Some courts (*ProCD, Inc. v. Zeidenberg* (1996), *Microsoft v. Harmony Computers* (1994), *Novell v. Network Trade Center* (1997)) have upheld the validity of particular EULAs, while others have not (*Step-Saver Data Systems, Inc. v. Wyse Technology* (1991), *Vault Corp. v. Quaid Software Ltd* (1988)), leaving the binding capacities of any given EULA a matter of litigation, not fact. Their status as agreements is equally nebulous, as EULAs are essentially unread by the vast majority of end users (Vila et al., 2003). It is difficult to feel bound by terms to which you agreed but remained ignorant. It is especially difficult when the terms of ignorance can change without notice (Luger et al., 2013). EULAs constitute agreements in the same manner that unconditional surrender can be considered an agreement; that is to say, technically it lies between two parties where practically it is simply an imposition. Often the EULA is used to spell out the responsibilities, rights, and liabilities of both parties. At other times it is used as an oblique way to bring suit against competing businesses by claiming that these competitors enticed users to break the EULA (Static Control Components, Inc. v. Lexmark International, Inc.). Other EULA documents attempt to secure blanket immunity from end-user litigation through questionably conscionable clauses (Fiesler et al., 2016), while still others do little more than give carte blanche for user data to be harvested for sale or research (Chee et al., 2012). In these cases, the EULA is not *for* the end user; while the EULA impacts the end user's activities, it can be argued that this impact is incidental, a side effect of the real work of quashing competition or commodifying user data.

For (distant) context, let us take cows: they are a good subject for analysis; humans have learned a good deal about them over the period of their becoming one of our companion species (Haraway, 2003). One of the interesting things we've learned about cows over the years is that, given their druthers, cows will tend to orient themselves along a North/South (N/S) axis (Begall et al., 2008). How and why this happens is still a matter of scholarly debate, and recent research disputes the methodology used in these studies (Weijers et al., 2018). That said, there is substantial support for claiming that cows do indeed orient themselves along the N/S axis — that is, unless the herd is grazing underneath a high-voltage powerline. Generally speaking, there is not much in the way of a relationship between cows and high-voltage powerlines. Cows are not especially relevant to electrical infrastructures; they neither buy nor sell electricity, and are only tangentially energy producers in the sense that their manure produces methane. Likewise, electrical infrastructures are not a pressing concern for cattle; power pylons make poor fodder and worse mates. Yet despite this seeming lack of a connection, our electrical infrastructure incidentally impacts the arrangement of nearby cows, leading them to align with the magnetic field given off by the power lines, rather than the N/S geomagnetic field of the earth (Burda et al., 2009). If, for example, the cattle in question are resting under a powerline producing an East/West (E/W) magnetic field, the herd would orient itself along the E/W axis rather than the N/S axis.

This constitutes a case of incidental infrastructural impact, in which an actor is not in a direct relation to a given infrastructure but their actions are still impacted by its presence. Outside of an abattoir, it may seem irrelevant how cows need orienting, and inside an abattoir there is little need to orient cattle gently (cf. Temple Grandin (1997) on the comfort of animals in transport and care). *That* cows are affected by magnetic fields is trivial; *how* cows are affected and the mechanisms through which this effect occurs are of vital interest.

The case of the compass cows is fairly cut and dry: high-voltage powerlines produce magnetic fields, and cows somehow sense these and use them as orientation. The EULA case is much more complex; we know that the legal assemblage produces EULAs, and it appears as though consumer behavior is both directly and incidentally impacted by these nebulous documents. One of the reasons that the cow case is simpler to parse is because we can see that the cows' orientation is impacted, and we can measure the electromagnetic force producing said impact. What we do not know, and what biologists are still struggling to ascertain, is the mechanism through which cows receive and process this data. Similarly, infrastructural studies have many times demonstrated the effects of infrastructure upon humans (Anand, 2017), and produced metrics to explain these effects (Ottinger, 2010), but the mechanisms through which infrastructural imaginaries are produced, made mobile, and implemented are an understudied area. That EULAs, and other infrastructurally adjacent or contingent assemblages, have an impact upon human action is trivial; it is *how* this impact is produced and perceived that is essential to further study of infrastructural assemblages.

Cambridge Analytica and the Facebook terms of service

In late 2017 to early 2018 it was revealed in newspapers and popular press that the Cambridge Analytica political consulting firm was making broad use of Facebook user data in crafting political strategy toward influencing elections in several countries over a period of several years (Rosenberg et al., 2018; Hern, 2018). This use of Facebook's user data represented a significant breach of data control as that data was not intended to be shared outside of the academic analysis for which it had previously been collected and brought questions of privacy, security, and the potential reach of the effects of large-scale analysis of data collected about user behaviors to popular light (Metcalf, 2018). In response to the Cambridge Analytica data breach, and the apparent broad effects of using that data to target political intervention (Cadwalladr, 2017), Facebook rewrote and reissued their Terms of Service and License Agreement into apparently more readable, clear, and explanatory form. This was done in response to claims that Facebook did little to protect its users from misuse of their data and that there existed broad, potentially harmful, social, and individual effects that might emerge from the use of that data.

In the Facebook terms of service and license agreement, and EULAs writ large, we see an (infra)structuring of our engagement with those services, with companies, and with each other. The EULA encodes some certain definition of value – we see in it what is both valuable to the corporation drafting the EULA and a conception of what is valuable to the user: "Our partners pay us to show their content to you, and we design our services so that the sponsored content you see is as relevant and useful to you as everything else that you see on our Products" (Facebook, 2018, Terms of Service). The EULA and similar documents (Terms of Service, Data Policies, etc.) also describe *social value* that may well occlude the financial operation and organization of that corporation. "Stronger ties make for better communities, and we believe that our services are most useful when people are connected to people, groups and organisations that they care about" (Facebook, 2018, Terms of Service). Facebook "Connect[s] you . . . Empower[s] you . . . Help[s] you . . . protect[s] and support[s] our community . . . provide[s] safe and functional service" (Facebook, 2018, Terms of Service). Important in these terms of service is the notion that this document works to structure your interaction with Facebook, according to their terms. The terms are the infrastructure of expectation, of power of action, and of legal right that subtends the ability of users to take part in the platform.

In a similar way, Facebook's Data Policy (a subset of their overall Terms of Service, along with about a dozen other specific areas of structured interaction) works to structure and provide a social infrastructure for the user's interactions with the service, discursively responds to criticisms and establishes conceptions of value, and defines the stakeholders and interested groups. In these terms, for example, only the user and corporation (and implicitly, advertisers and researchers) are interested parties. There is little said about the protections for those in your life who you might share information about, little control over long-term multiparty reuse of that data, and no ability to control information you submit should it be shared or repeated by someone else (a fundamental feature of the platform). The Facebook Data Policy is not about limiting harm but about providing a structure through which value might be drawn from data about users and their activities. Sharing of data, despite broad criticism of how it might be used, is not limited by potential use, nor is it especially limited in terms of how many might have access to it:

> Here are the types of third parties we share information with: Partners who use our analytics services . . . Advertisers . . . Measurement partners . . . Vendors and service providers . . . Researchers and academics . . . Law enforcement or legal requests.
>
> *(Facebook, 2018, Data Policy)*

This is a broad group, especially keeping in mind that the Cambridge Analytica breach came about when an academic researcher conjured a new use for the data to which he was supplied. Addressing potential harms through data reuse, data proxies, or privacy implications is not a part of the Terms of Service, or the Data Policy, though these agreements structure the sharing of information that might lead to those harms.

The EULA is itself simultaneously performance and structure – it is performative in a vital, legal way, while also working to establish terms of value and describe ideal interactions with the system. In limiting its scope to simple one-to-one interactions it avoids the implications and broad societal effects of having such quantities of data available for analysis. Machine learning classically often leads to counterintuitive results that are also factually wrong and misleading. For example, a machine-learning tool designed to predict recidivism and reduce sentencing might instead work to reinforce societal racial bias through biased data, lack of attention to issues of social condition, or simple design issues (Angwin et al., 2016; Skeem & Lowenkamp, 2016; Harcourt, 2008). Disproportionate police action among urban poor communities, for example, might produce a biased prediction of recidivism on the basis of detainment by policy prior to the age of 18 – something very common for minor offenses in poor, urban areas but not so in wealthier rural and suburban ones. Such algorithms and risk prediction tools are highly complex and frequently proprietary (Gillespie, 2014), introducing issues of accountability and the assessment of bias specific to these tools and complicated by their use in policy and sentencing. The terms of agreement in the Facebook EULA do not serve to protect their users from algorithmic harm, nor do they work to sensitize their users to such issues such that the user might better protect themselves. Rather, the terms, data policy, and other agreements are structured in such a way as to avoid a discussion of aggregate harms, to limit the scope of responsibility to one person interacting singly with the system, and their immediate individual rights. In short, it does little to "empower you . . . Help you . . . protect and support our community . . . provide safe and functional service" (Facebook, 2018, Terms of Service), except within the limits of scope and aggregation present within the EULA itself.

To a certain extent, this discussion of EULAs is also a discussion of the social role of data science as it operates across the existing infrastructures of communication. Data science and machine learning are substantially about the ability to predict social trends, consumer activity, the stock market, crime, and health. Traditionally, scientific reasoning has drawn a bright line between correlation, causation, and prediction by assigning distinct epistemic statuses to each. Yet the methods of data science blur the epistemic distinctions between causation and correlation – with some arguing that causality is no longer needed for explanation (Anderson, 2008; Latour, 2002; Latour et.al. 2012; Candea, 2015). Whereas ethics is often focused on discrete harms caused to individual human lives, 'big data' operates on distributed, aggregated, and partial knowledge, thus producing a profile that is mismatched to the conceptual frameworks, research methods, and regulatory apparatuses developed over the last century to help guide scientific knowledge production. Harms may occur at the aggregate rather than the individual level – this is clearly visible in the recent data breaches involving Facebook and Cambridge Analytica. Even if the data is recovered and deleted, models of behavior produced from that data would persist, as would the strategies, media, and generalizations drawn from that data (Metcalf, 2018).

Reflections on the design of infrastructure – isolation through connection

Our relationship with data is changing, both as individuals and as a society. Self-tracking and quantification provide a data-oriented mode of understanding our own behaviors, bodies, and lives (Berson, 2015). As a society, we are rendering ourselves increasingly computable, with greater portions of our lives tracked, quantified, and analyzed as part of our daily activities (Cheung et al., 2017). Similarly, we are changing the nature of our society – creating new kinds of 'social facts' built around the ubiquity and presence of tracking, data collection, and the presentation of results of that collection to us (Boullier, 2015). We are witnessing fundamentally new modes of social organization such as the widespread use of predictive analytics in a variety of fields, which can work to create new ways in which our behaviors and practices might be governed (Foucault, 2012; Mackenzie, 2013; Lövbrand et al., 2009; Williamson, 2016; Schüll, 2014). Even disregarding these external or societal orientations toward data and analytics, there is reason to believe that our own relationships, attitudes, and priorities around data collected about us are changing. For example, both the scope of the available technology and our social understanding of the nature of a right to privacy are fundamentally different from the situation 50, or even 20, years ago (Solove, 2015; Martin, 2014; Nissenbaum, 2009).

"[O]ne of the best ways to determine someone's politics is to see what they don't consider to be political" (Holkins, 2018). One could argue that the same is true of infrastructure. The best possible infrastructural imaginary would be one that is never imagined, an infrastructure that is not only not thought of as infrastructural but not thought of, is not a thing to think of, and does not occupy an ontological space in which it could be considered a thing to think of, in which the infrastructure could be imagined. Think of water to a fish, or air to us. Air can be thought of as an infrastructure. But we imagine that you might have had a momentary resistance to the idea. We certainly did. Air, infrastructural? Medial, yes; the aether has long been thought of as a medium for other entities, but structural? What offers less support than air? But, of course, air is a critical infrastructure, as a quick inversion will tell you. But air qua air has no imaginary, or at the very least no popular imaginary (imaginaries of initiates are hardly ever popular). Wind, now wind has imaginaries. Winds are personified, anthropomorphisized; winds blow. But air does not blow; air is an undifferentiated milieu. Air is not seen to move; air is not *seen*.

While air is a decent example of a perfect infrastructure, it is not quite ideal. We do relate to the air as infrastructure, although, of course we can only do so through its rupture by way of pollution. One of the more enticing candidates for an 'ideal' infrastructure is, in keeping with our theme of the occult, darkness. We do not have an infrastructural imaginary for the provision of darkness, despite the fact that the provision of darkness subtends a vast array of activities. We have vast, sprawling imaginaries for the provision of light, from early mytho-poetic explanations of the sun to contemporary representations of the electrical grid. We see darkness as a lack of light, an absence, a consequence rather than a result (cf. O'Brien, 1999). In a metaphorical but similar sense, we talk about designing for transparency, for visibility; opacity and darkness may also be designed for, but in order for it to be produced purposely it's production must be imagined.

What makes darkness an 'ideal' infrastructure, as opposed to merely 'perfect'? A perfect infrastructure lacks the capacity to fail. Of course, a lack of a capacity to fail also means a lack of a capacity to interact. Any infrastructure that is completely foolproof is made so in the only way possible − by keeping the fools (i.e., everyone) out. The infrastructure that is the N−O mix of gases of our air could fail, and no longer provide the necessaries for respiration, and would then only provide an infrastructure in the sense that atmospheric pressure could be considered infrastructural. But the infrastructure of darkness lacks the capacity to fail because we do not interact with darkness, even when it subtends our other activities. Rather, our actions and relations are *inflected* by the provision of darkness, their trajectory altered without any sort of direct engagement. If we take this to a logical extreme, eventually we will cease to directly interact with systems at all and instead will only be inflected by the constant, perfect, invisibly infrastructural assemblage that remains.

Trivial mass communication encourages 'sound bites' and the isolation of facts from the contexts of their creation. Called by Latour and Woolgar (1986) the "deletion of modalities," the representations of science and research we see in the world often do not contain information sufficient to evaluate the reliability of their results. Sharing of information in short form, through limited length, limited attention, or emotionally nudging "clickbait" style description, distances readers from the scientific process, limits readers' ability to properly assess its results, and encourages an engagement with scientific progress closer to a matter of faith than active consideration. Here we see a different impingement of infrastructure: the processes of peer review, scientific certification and education, and ongoing academic social control have occulted the process of scientific inquiry. The results presented emerge from a trusted infrastructure and as such do not need further visibility in order to be acted upon. Like in the Star and Ruhleder (1996) depiction of infrastructure, this knowledge infrastructure (Borgman et al., 2013) serves to confirm trustworthiness and epistemologically stands in for ongoing inquiry and investigation. However, the effects of this infrastructure become more negative upon its breakdown − particularly when the results of science become politicized according to social agendas distinct from those that produced the science to begin with. This is perhaps the end result of the deletion of modalities (Latour & Woolgar, 1986) − immutable mobiles so thoroughly distant from the contexts of their creation that they are indistinguishable from outright falsehood.

Managed and curated information flows produce what might be thought of as 'walled gardens' of information. While there is reason to believe that these walled gardens do not necessarily cause an individual to be completely isolated from opposing viewpoints (Bortoli et al., 2009; Landale and Meinrath, 2017), they do provide for that possibility to the extent that a person wishes to isolate themselves. While it may not often happen in practice, it is certainly possible should a person be motivated to do so. Is this necessarily a bad thing? In general we would want to think that a diversity of viewpoints is better, but the short-term, low-evidence presentation of ideas also produces a leveling effect. Opposing viewpoints might be overrepresented due to a more aggressive media strategy or more engaged small group, where majority opinions do not generally provoke similar passion in argument. The medium, here, allows 1,000 very active people to appear the same as 1,000,000 relatively disinterested individuals.

Here we have a system that allows for media without news – increasingly evident in a mass convergence of 'mainstream' media as more and more news sources repurpose centrally produced news items (AP Feeds, in particular) that are not subjected to local standards of journalism or integrity (Boczkowski, 2005). Convergence of voice may even result in critique and loss of authority – once it appears there are 'two sides' those sides become level. Broad consensus appears identical to passionate disagreement, and selective effects reduce exposure to evidence that may change opinions.

Conclusion

Infrastructure is more present and pervasive than it is generally considered – even in terms of infrastructural studies. A variety of infrastructural relationships exist in natural cycles; the operation of our bodies; and in objects of policy, agreement, and technology, as well as in the more traditionally accounted material forms.

It is important to consider and account for the ways these infrastructural relationships work to structure our interactions with ourselves, each other, technology, and groups. This importance is especially highlighted when the infrastructure itself is occluded from our attention. There exists design and technology that operate upon us without our being aware in a variety of ways in order to produce particular, predictable behaviors. While these might not work well in terms of making a given individual do something, when considered in the aggregate it produces a substantial effect.

There exist infrastructures of policy, agreement, and value that work to structure our interactions with each other in nonobvious ways. The EULA is the most telling example of this, but we often remain unaware of the preponderance of law, contract, and agreement that operates behind the scenes of even temporary interactions (Metcalf, 2018). This is significant work that is often not considered within the media space. STS in the broad sense and infrastructure studies in particular provide the tools and perspective to assess, understand, and reconsider these infrastructural relationships, primarily through the notion of infrastructural inversion, but in a broader sense by considering the networks of people, policy, technology, and other actors attendant to most engagements with large systems.

Simultaneous moves toward generalization and specificity both reduce individual identity while making increasingly smaller and more focused groups amenable to nudging design (Latour et al., 2012). This works to influence the way we perceive and structure our interactions with an information space that exceeds casual assessment due to size, fragmentation, and isolation. We perform ourselves to performances and have the performances of ourselves performed back to us. This is a curation of the self through media structured by and through the platforms and infrastructures with which we engage (Hogan, 2010).

Considering and drawing attention to infrastructural relationships are worthwhile and important activities despite the fact that nearly anything can at some time be infrastructural to almost any activity. Pointing out infrastructural relationships, and working to invert the infrastructure in terms of specified activities, serves to highlight the occult in our lives and draw attention to those things that are meaningful, impactful, and invisible. It is arguable that much of scholarship – particularly in the media space – inverts infrastructural relationships in practice in order to better understand their mechanics and dynamics toward its goals (often defined politically or socially more so that attendant to an isolated progress of that scholarship).

The infrastructure of media, and its ability to support the performance of user data, has fairly broad-ranging consequence – consequence that seems baffling, random, or arbitrary without accounting for those infrastructural effects. Understanding the landscape of digital media, its evidentiary and authoritative claims, and the means by which individuals perform themselves through their communicative practices necessarily engages with the technologies, policies, and systems through which those practices are performed.

The real story here is a confluence of the person and the technology – a transhuman landscape of communication where the medium of expression exerts significant influence on the expression of personhood and the act of self-understanding and self-expression. Increasingly, our selves are performed to us based on our digital traces and data produced about us from outside of our control and even experience (Mitchell, 2004).

You can imagine, here, a person 'without a body' – a person existing only as data traces and collections of communicative practices. Occasionally, this bodiless person will interact with an embodied self, but it is more common that decisions made about the embodied self are on the basis of the bodiless self that exists as trace data, market segments, and analyzed communication. There is here no ideal self; the world as one experiences it is formed from the 'bodiless self' of data even as the performance of the self is linked to and influenced by the platform of that performance.

References

Alonso, A., and Oiarzabal, P. J. (2010). *Diasporas in the New Media Age: Identity, Politics, and Community*. Reno: University of Nevada Press.

Androutsopoulos, J. (2014). Moments of Sharing: Entextualization and Linguistic Repertoires in Social Networking. *Journal of Pragmatics*, 73, 4–18.

Anand, N. (2017). *Hydraulic City – Water and the Infrastructures of Citizenship in Mumbai*. Durham: Duke University Press.

Angwin, J., Larson, J., Mattu, S., and Kirchner, L. (2019). *Machine Bias: There's Software Used Across the Country to Predict Future Criminals and It's Biased Against Blacks, 2016*. www.propublica.org/article/machine-bias-risk-assessments-in-criminal-sentencing.

Aufderheide, P. (1991). Public Television and the Public Sphere. *Critical Studies in Media Communication*, 8(2), 168–183.

Aufderheide, P. (1999). *Communications Policy and the Public Interest: The Telecommunications Act of 1996*. New York: Guilford Press.

Bakows, Y., Marotta-Wurgler, F., and Trossen, D. R. (2009). *Does Anyone Read the Fine Print: A Test of the Informed Minority Hypothesis Using Clickstream Data*. New York University School of Law Working Paper.

Bayer, J. B., Ellison, N. B., Schoenebeck, S. Y., and Falk, E. B. (2016). Sharing the Small Moments: Ephemeral Social Interaction on Snapchat. *Information, Communication & Society*, 19(7), 956–977.

Begall, S., Červený, J., Neef, J., Vojtěch, O., and Burda, H. (2008). Magnetic Alignment in Grazing and Resting Cattle and Deer. *Proceedings of the National Academy of Sciences*, 105(36), 13451–13455.

Berson, J. (2015). *Computable Bodies: Instrumented Life and the Human Somatic Niche*. London: Bloomsbury Publishing.

Boczkowski, P. J. (2005). *Digitizing the News: Innovation in Online Newspapers*. Cambridge, MA: MIT Press.

Böhme, R., and Köpsell, S. (2010). *Trained to Accept? A Field Experiment on Consent Dialogs*. Proceedings of the SIGCHI Conference on Human Factors in Computing Systems, pp. 2403–2406, April.

Borgman, C. L., Edwards, P. N., Jackson, S. J., Chalmers, M. K., Bowker, G. C., Ribes, D., Burton, M., and Calvert, S. (2013). *Knowledge Infrastructures: Intellectual Frameworks and Research Challenges.* Ann Arbor: Deep Blue.

Bortoli, S., Palpanas, T., and Bouquet, P. (2009). *Pulling Down the Walled Garden: Towards a Paradigm for Decentralized Social Network Management.* Iadis Multi Conference on Computer Science and Information Systems, Web Based Communities.

Boullier, D. (2015). The Social Sciences and the Traces of Big Data: Society, Opinion, or Vibrations? *Revue française de science politique (English Edition)*, 65(5–6), 71–93.

Bowker, G. C., Baker, K., Millerand, F., and Ribes, D. (2009). Toward Information Infrastructure Studies: Ways of Knowing in a Networked Environment. In *International Handbook of Internet Research.* Dordrecht: Springer, pp. 97–117.

Bowker, G. C., and Star, S. L. (2000). *Sorting Things Out: Classification and Its Consequences.* Cambridge, MA: MIT Press.

Boy, J., Detienne, F., and Fekete, J. D. (2015). *Storytelling in Information Visualizations: Does It Engage Users to Explore Data?* Proceedings of the 33rd Annual ACM Conference on Human Factors in Computing Systems, pp. 1449–1458, April.

Braman, S., and Roberts, S. (2003). Advantage ISP: Terms of Service as Media Law. *New Media & Society*, 5(3), 422–448.

Burda, H., Begall, S., Červený, J., Neef, J., and Němec, P. (2009). Extremely low-frequency Electromagnetic Fields Disrupt Magnetic Alignment of Ruminants. *Proceedings of the National Academy of Sciences*, 106(14), 5708–5713.

Butler, S. (1974). *Erewhon.* London: Penguin.

Cadwalladr, C. (2017). The Great British Brexit Robbery: How Our Democracy Was Hijacked. *The Guardian*, p. 7.

Candea, M. (ed.). (2015). *The Social after Gabriel Tarde: Debates and Assessments.* London: Routledge.

Castells, M., and Blackwell, C. (1998). The Information Age: Economy, Society and Culture: Volume 1. The Rise of the Network Society. *Environment and Planning B: Planning and Design*, 25, 631–636.

Chee, F. M., Taylor, N. T., and de Castell, S. (2012). Re-Mediating Research Ethics: End-User License Agreements in Online Games. *Bulletin of Science, Technology & Society*, 32(6), 497–506.

Cherry, M. A. (2014). A Eulogy for the EULA. *Duquesne Law Review*, 52, 335.

Cheung, C., Bietz, M. J., Patrick, K., and Bloss, C. S. (2017). Conceptualizations of Privacy Among Early Adopters of Emerging Health Technologies. *Annals of Behavioral Medicine*, 51, S2586–S2586, Springer, March.

Ciampaglia, G. L., Flammini, A., and Menczer, F. (2015). The Production of Information in the Attention Economy. *Scientific Reports*, 5, 9452.

Cormack, M. J., and Hourigan, N. (eds.). (2007). *Minority Language Media: Concepts, Critiques and Case Studies* (vol. 138). Clevedon: Multilingual Matters.

Cronon, W. (2009). *Nature's Metropolis: Chicago and the Great West.* New York: W.W. Norton & Company.

David, P. A. (1990). The Dynamo and the Computer: An Historical Perspective on the Modern Productivity Paradox. *The American Economic Review*, 80(2), 355–361.

De Chardin, P. T. (1964). *The Future of Man.* London: Collins.

Deleuze, G. (1986). *Cinema 1: The Movement-Image.* Translated by H. Tomlinson and B. Habberjam. Minneapolis: University of Minnesota.

DeNardis, L. (2012). Hidden Levers of Internet Control: An Infrastructure-Based Theory of Internet Governance. *Information, Communication & Society*, 15(5), 720–738.

De Paoli, S., and Kerr, A. (2009). *The Cheating Assemblage in MMORPGs: Toward a Sociotechnical Description of Cheating.* Breaking New Ground: Innovation in Games, Play, Practice and Theory. Proceedings of DiGRA 2009, pp. 1–12.

De Zwart, M. (2010). Contractual Communities: Effective Governance of Virtual Worlds. *University of New South Wales Law Journal*, 33, 605.

Edwards, P. N. (2010). *A Vast Machine: Computer Models, Climate Data, and the Politics of Global Warming.* Cambridge, MA: MIT Press.

Edwards, P. N., Jackson, S. J., Bowker, G. C., and Knobel, C. P. (2007). *Understanding Infrastructure: Dynamics, Tensions, and Design*. Ann Arbor: Deep Blue.

Eisenstein, S. (1957). *Film Form [and]: The Film Sense; Two Complete and Unabridged Works*. New York: Meridian Books.

Facebook, 2018. Terms of Service. Facebook [online]. https://www.facebook.com/terms.php (Accessed February 2, 2018).

Fiesler, C., Lampe, C., and Bruckman, A. S. (2016). *Reality and Perception of Copyright Terms of Service for Online Content Creation*. Proceedings of the 19th ACM Conference on Computer-Supported Cooperative Work & Social Computing, pp. 1450–1461.

Flanagan, M., Howe, D. C., and Nissenbaum, H. (2008). Embodying Values in Technology: Theory and Practice. *Information Technology and Moral Philosophy*, 322.

Foucault, M. (2012). *Discipline and Punish: The Birth of the Prison*. New York: Vintage.

Friedman, B., Howe, D. C., and Felten, E. (2002). *Informed Consent in the Mozilla Browser: Implementing Value-Sensitive Design*. Proceedings of the 35th Annual Hawaii International Conference on System Sciences, IEEE, p. 10, January.

Friedman, B., and Nissenbaum, H. (1996). Bias in Computer Systems. *ACM Transactions on Information Systems (TOIS)*, 14(3), 330–347.

Georgiadou, Y., Harvey, F., and Miscione, G. (2009). *A Bigger Picture: Information Systems and Spatial Data Infrastructure Research Perspectives*. Global Spatial Data Infrastructure 11 World Conference: SDI Convergence: Building SDI Bridges to Address Global Challenges, Rotterdam, The Netherlands, June 15–19.

Gibson, J. J. (1979). *The Theory of Affordances: The Ecological Approach to Visual Perception*. Boston, MA: Houghton Mifflin.

Gilbert, B. J. (2009). Getting to Conscionable: Negotiating Virtual Worlds' End User License Agreements Without Getting Externally Regulated. *International Journal of Law and Information Technology*, 4, 238.

Gillespie, T. (2010). The Politics of 'Platforms'. *New Media & Society*, 12(3), 347–364.

Gillespie, T. (2014). The Relevance of Algorithms. *Media Technologies: Essays on Communication, Materiality, and Society*, 167.

Goldhaber, M. H. (1997). The Attention Economy and the Net. *First Monday*, 2(4).

Gomulkiewicz, R. W. (2003). Getting Serious About User-Friendly Mass Market Licensing for Software. *George Mason Law Review*, 12, 687.

Gomulkiewicz, R. W., and Williamson, M. L. (1996). A Brief Defense of Mass Market Software License Agreements. *Rutgers Computer & Technology Law Journal*, 22, 335.

Good, N., Grossklags, J., Thaw, D., Perzanowski, A., Mulligan, D. K., and Konstan, J. (2006). User Choices and Regret: Understanding Users' Decision Process About Consensually Acquired Spyware. *I/S: A Journal of Law and Policy for the Information Society*, 2(2), 283–344.

Grandin, T. (1997). Assessment of Stress During Handling and Transport. *Journal of Animal Science*, 75(1), 249–257.

Greenfield, P. M. (2014). *Mind and Media: The Effects of Television, Video Games, and Computers*. London: Psychology Press.

Grimes, J. M., Jaeger, P. T., and Fleischmann, K. R. (2008). Obfuscatocracy: A Stakeholder Analysis of Governing Documents for Virtual Worlds. *First Monday*, 13(9).

Haraway, D. J. (2003). *The Companion Species Manifesto: Dogs, People, and Significant Otherness* (vol. 1). Chicago: Prickly Paradigm Press, pp. 3–17.

Harcourt, B. E. (2008). *Against Prediction: Profiling, Policing, and Punishing in an Actuarial Age*. Chicago: University of Chicago Press.

Hern, A. (2018). Cambridge Analytica: How Did It Turn Clicks Into Votes. *The Guardian*, May 6, 2018. https://www.theguardian.com/news/2018/may/06/cambridge-analytica-how-turn-clicks-into-votes-christopher-wylie (Accessed March 18, 2020).

Hetherington, K., and Campbell, J. M. (2014). Nature, Infrastructure, and the State: Rethinking Development in Latin America. *Journal of Latin American and Caribbean Anthropology*, 19(2), 191–194.

Hogan, B. (2010). The Presentation of Self in the Age of Social Media: Distinguishing Performances and Exhibitions Online. *Bulletin of Science, Technology & Society*, 30(6), 377–386.

Holkins, J. (2018). Penny Arcade – News – Everything Old Is New Again. *Penny Arcade* [online]. www.penny-arcade.com/news/post/2018/03/09/everything-old-is-new-again1?utm_source= feedburner&utm_medium=feed&utm_campaign=Feed%3A+pa-mainsite+%28Penny+Arcade%29 (Accessed March 18, 2020).

Introna, L. D., and Nissenbaum, H. (2000). Shaping the Web: Why the Politics of Search Engines Matters. *The Information Society*, 16(3), 169–185.

Jankowich, A. (2006). EULAw: The Complex Web of Corporate Rule-Making in Virtual Worlds. *Tulane Journal of Technology and Intellectual Property*, 8, 1.

Jensen, C. B. (2008). Power, Technology and Social Studies of Health Care: An Infrastructural Inversion. *Health Care Analysis*, 16(4), 355–374.

John, R. R. (2009). *Spreading the News: The American Postal System from Franklin to Morse*. Cambridge, MA: Harvard University Press.

Johnson, J. D., Adams, M. S., Hall, W., and Ashburn, L. (1997). Race, media, and violence: Differential Racial Effects of Exposure to Violent News Stories. *Basic and Applied Social Psychology*, 19(1), 81–90.

Kaltenbrunner, W. (2015). Infrastructural Inversion as a Generative Resource in Digital Scholarship. *Science as Culture*, 24(1), 1–23.

Karashima, M., and Ishibashi, Y. (2007). *Unconscious Transmission Services of Human Feelings*. Symposium on Human Interface and the Management of Information, Springer, Berlin, Heidelberg, pp. 68–76, July.

Karasti, H., Millerand, F., Hine, C. M., and Bowker, G. C. (2016). Knowledge Infrastructures: Part I. *Science & Technology Studies*, 29(1).

Kennedy, J., Meese, J., and van der Nagel, E. (2016). Regulation and Social Practice Online. *Continuum*, 30(2), 146–157.

Knaflic, C. N. (2015). *Storytelling with Data: A Data Visualization Guide for Business Professionals*. Hoboken: John Wiley & Sons.

Knobel, C. P. (2010). *Ontic Occlusion and Exposure in Sociotechnical Systems* (Doctoral dissertation).

Knobel, C. P., and Bowker, G. C. (2011). Values in Design. *Communications of the ACM*, 54(7), 26–28.

Korn, M., and Voida, A. (2015). *Creating Friction: Infrastructuring Civic Engagement in Everyday Life*. Proceedings of the Fifth Decennial Aarhus Conference on Critical Alternatives. Aarhus University Press, pp. 145–156, August.

Kramer, A. D., Guillory, J. E., and Hancock, J. T. (2014). Experimental Evidence of Massive-Scale Emotional Contagion Through Social Networks. *Proceedings of the National Academy of Sciences*, 111(24), 8788–8790.

Kunze, J. T. (2008). Regulating Virtual Worlds Optimally: The Model End User License Agreement. *Northwestern Journal of Technology and Intellectual Property*, 7, 102.

Kurzweil, R. (2000). *The Age of Spiritual Machines: When Computers Exceed Human Intelligence*. New York: Penguin.

Landale, J., and Meinrath, S. (2017). The Future of Digital Enfranchisement. In *Media Activism in the Digital Age*. London: Routledge, pp. 10–27.

Larkin, B. (2013). The Politics and Poetics of Infrastructure. *Annual Review of Anthropology*, 42, 327–343.

Latour, B. (1992). Where Are the Missing Masses? The Sociology of a Few Mundane Artifacts. In W. Bijker and J. Law (eds.), *Shaping Technology/Building Society: Studies in Sociotechnical Change*. Cambridge, MA: MIT Press, pp. 225, 258.

Latour, B. (2002). Gabriel Tarde and the End of the Social. In P. Joyce (ed.), *The Social in Question: New Bearings in History and the Social Sciences*. London and New York: Routledge.

Latour, B., Jensen, P., Venturini, T., Grauwin, S., and Boullier, D. (2012). 'The Whole Is Always Smaller Than Its Parts' – a Digital Test of Gabriel Tardes' Monads. *The British Journal of Sociology*, 63(4), 590–615.

Latour, B., and Woolgar, S. (1986). *Laboratory Life: The Construction of Scientific Facts*. Princeton, NJ: Princeton University Press.

Lee, C. P., Dourish, P., and Mark, G. (2006). *The Human Infrastructure of Cyberinfrastructure*. Proceedings of the 2006 20th Anniversary Conference on Computer Supported Cooperative Work, pp. 483–492, November.

Leroi-Gourhan, A. (1993). *Gesture and Speech*. Cambridge, MA: MIT Press.

Livingstone, S. (2008). Taking Risky Opportunities in Youthful Content Creation: Teenagers' Use of Social Networking Sites for Intimacy, Privacy and Self-Expression. *New Media & Society*, 10(3), 393–411.

Lövbrand, E., Stripple, J., and Wiman, B. (2009). Earth System Governmentality: Reflections on Science in the Anthropocene. *Global Environmental Change*, 19(1), 7–13.

Luger, E., Moran, S., and Rodden, T. (2013). *Consent for All: Revealing the Hidden Complexity of Terms and Conditions.* Proceedings of the SIGCHI Conference on Human Factors in Computing Systems, pp. 2687–2696, April.

Luhmann, N. (2000). *The Reality of the Mass Media.* Stanford, CA: Stanford University Press, p. 1.

Mackenzie, A. (2005). Untangling the Unwired: Wi-Fi and the Cultural Inversion of Infrastructure. *Space and Culture*, 8(3), 269–285.

Mackenzie, A. (2013). Programming Subjects in the Regime of Anticipation: Software Studies and Subjectivity. *Subjectivity*, 6(4), 391–405.

Madhavan, J., Balakrishnan, S., Hurley, K., Gonzalez, H., Gupta, N., Halevy, A., Jacqmin-Adams, K., Lam, H., Langen, A., Lee, H., and McChesney, R. (2012). Big Data Storytelling Through Interactive Maps. *IEEE Data Engineering Bulletin*, 35, 46–54.

Mann, R. J., and Siebneicher, T. (2008). Just One Click: The Reality of Internet Retail Contracting. *Columbia Law Review*, 108, 984.

Marteau, T. M., Ogilvie, D., Roland, M., Suhrcke, M., and Kelly, M. P. (2011). Judging Nudging: Can Nudging Improve Population Health? *British Medical Journal*, 342, d228.

Martin, J. P. (2014). Brief History of Privacy and Selected Electronic Surveillance Laws. *Cloud Computing and Electronic Discovery*, 37–54.

Mayernik, M. S., Wallis, J. C., and Borgman, C. L. (2013). Unearthing the infrastructure: Humans and Sensors in Field-Based Scientific Research. *Computer Supported Cooperative Work (CSCW)*, 22(1), 65–101.

McLuhan, M., and Fiore, Q. (1967). The Medium Is the Message. *New York*, 123, 126–128.

McLuhan, M., Gordon, W. T., Lamberti, E., and Scheffel-Dunand, D. (2011). *The Gutenberg Galaxy: The Making of Typographic Man.* Toronto: University of Toronto Press.

McKenna, T. (1999). *Psychedelics in the Age of Intelligent Systems* [online]. www.youtube.com/watch?v=J5yOaTgWu6Y (Accessed June 18, 2019).

Metcalf, J. (2018). Facebook May Stop the Data Leaks, but It's Too Late: Cambridge Analytica's Models Live on. *MIT Technology Review*, April 9. [online]. www.technologyreview.com/s/610801/facebook-may-stop-the-data-leaks-but-its-too-late-cambridge-analyticas-models-live-on/(Accessed October 5, 2018).

Metcalf, J., and Crawford, K. (2016). Where Are Human Subjects in Big Data Research? The Emerging Ethics Divide. *Big Data & Society*, 3(1). http://bds.sagepub.com/content/3/1/2053951716650211.

Microsoft v. Harmony Computers & Electronics. (1994). 846 F. Supp. 208.

Mitchell, W. J. (2004). *Me++: The Cyborg Self and the Networked City.* Cambridge, MA: MIT Press.

Morita, A. (2017). Multispecies Infrastructure: Infrastructural Inversion and Involutionary Entanglements in the Chao Phraya Delta, Thailand. *Ethnos*, 82(4), 738–757.

Nejad, N. M., Scerri, S., Auer, S., and Sibarani, E. M. (2016). *Eulaide: Interpretation of End-User License Agreements Using Ontology-Based Information Extraction.* Proceedings of the 12th International Conference on Semantic Systems, pp. 73–80, September.

Nissenbaum, H. (1998). Values in the Design of Computer Systems. *Computers and Society*, 28(1), 38–39.

Nissenbaum, H. (2009). *Privacy in Context: Technology, Policy, and the Integrity of Social Life.* Stanford: Stanford University Press.

Novell, Inc. v. Network Trade Center, Inc. (1997). 25 F. Supp. 2d 1218.

Obama, B. (2015). *Executive Order – Using Behavioral Science Insights to Better Serve the American People.* New York: Office of the Press Secretary.

O'Brien, F. (1999). *The Third Policeman: A Novel.* Normal, IL: Dalkey Archive Press.

Ottinger, G. (2010). Buckets of Resistance: Standards and the Effectiveness of Citizen Science. *Science, Technology, & Human Values*, 35(2), 244–270.

Pelizza, A. (2016). Developing the Vectorial Glance: Infrastructural Inversion for the New Agenda on Government Information Systems. *Science, Technology, & Human Values*, 41(2), 298–321.

Peters, J. D. (2012). *Speaking into the Air: A History of the Idea of Communication*. Chicago: University of Chicago Press.

Peters, J. D. (2015). *The Marvelous Clouds: Toward a Philosophy of Elemental Media*. Chicago: University of Chicago Press.

Pinch, T. J., and Bijker, W. E. (1984). The Social Construction of Facts and Artefacts: Or How the Sociology of Science and the Sociology of Technology Might Benefit Each Other. *Social Studies of Science*, 14(3), 399–441.

Plaut, V. C., and Bartlett III, R. P. (2012). Blind Consent? A Social Psychological Investigation of Non-Readership of Click-Through Agreements. *Law and Human Behavior*, 36(4), 293.

ProCD, Inc. v. Zeidenberg. (1996). 908 F. Supp. 640.

Reidenberg, J. R., Breaux, T., Cranor, L. F., French, B., Grannis, A., Graves, J. T., Liu, F., McDonald, A., Norton, T. B., and Ramanath, R. (2015). Disagreeable Privacy Policies: Mismatches Between Meaning and Users' Understanding. *Berkeley Technology Law Journal*, 30, 39.

Rosenberg, M. et al. (2018). How Trump Consultants Exploited the Facebook Data of Millions. *The New York Times*, March 17, 2018. https://www.nytimes.com/2018/03/17/us/politics/cambridge-analytica-trump-campaign.html (Accessed April 26, 2018).

Schmitter, P. C., and Karl, T. L. (1991). What Democracy Is . . . and Is Not. *Journal of Democracy*, 2(3), 75–88.

Schüll, N.D. (2014). Addiction by design: Machine gambling in Las Vegas. Princeton University Press.

Seaver, N. (2012). Algorithmic Recommendations and Synaptic Functions. *Limn*, 1(2).

Serres, M. (1995). *The Natural Contract*. Ann Arbor, MI: University of Michigan Press.

Simon, M., Ghez, A. M., Leinert, C., Cassar, L., Chen, W. P., Howell, R. R., Jameson, R. F., Matthews, K., Neugebauer, G., and Richichi, A. (1995). A Lunar Occultation and Direct Imaging Survey of Multiplicity in the Ophiuchus and Taurus Star-Forming Regions. *The Astrophysical Journal*, 443, 625–637.

Skeem, J. L., and Lowenkamp, C. T. (2016). Risk, Race, and Recidivism: Predictive Bias and Disparate Impact. *Criminology*, 54(4), 680–712.

Solove, D. J. (2015). The Meaning and Value of Privacy. *Social Dimensions of Privacy: Interdisciplinary Perspectives*, 71.

Spiegler, R. (2015). On the Equilibrium Effects of Nudging. *The Journal of Legal Studies*, 44(2), 389–416.

Star, S. L., and Ruhleder, K. (1996). Steps Toward an Ecology of Infrastructure: Design and Access for Large Information Spaces. *Information Systems Research*, 7(1), 111–134.

Step-Saver Data Systems, Inc. v. Wyse Technology. (1991). 939 F.2d 91.

Sterne, J. (2006). The Death and Life of Digital Audio. *Interdisciplinary Science Reviews*, 31(4), 338–348.

Suarez-Villa, L. (1997). Innovative Capacity, Infrastructure and Regional Inversion: Is there a Long-Term Dynamic? In *Innovative Behaviour in Space and Time*. Berlin, Heidelberg: Springer, pp. 291–305.

Sunstein, C. R. (2015). The Ethics of Nudging. *Yale Journal on Regulation*, 32, 413.

Terasaki, M. (2013). Do End User License Agreements Bind Normal People. *Western State University Law Review*, 41, 467.

Thaler, Richard H., and Cass R. Sunstein. (2009). *Nudge: Improving Decisions About Health, Wealth, and Happiness*. New York, NY: Penguin.

ToS;DR Team. (2019). Terms of Service; Didn't Read. *Tosdr.org* [online]. https://tosdr.org/ (Accessed June 10, 2018).

Tosa, N. (2010). Cultural Computing – Creative Power Integrating Culture, Unconsciousness and Software. In *Entertainment Computing Symposium*. Berlin, Heidelberg: Springer, pp. 223–232, September.

Valkenburg, P. M., and Peter, J. (2013). The Differential Susceptibility to Media Effects Model. *Journal of Communication*, 63(2), 221–243.

Van House, N. A. (2011). Feminist HCI Meets Facebook: Performativity and Social Networking Sites. *Interacting with Computers*, 23(5), 422–429.

Vault Corp. v. Quaid Software Ltd. (1988). 847 F.2d 255.

Veyne, P. (2005). Did the Greeks Know Democracy? *Economy and Society*, 34(2), 322–345.

Vila, T., Greenstadt, R., and Molnar, D. (2003). *Why We Can't Be Bothered to Read Privacy Policies Models of Privacy Economics as a Lemons Market*. Proceedings of the 5th International Conference on Electronic Commerce, pp. 403–407, September.

Weijers, D., Hemerik, L., and Heitkönig, I. M. (2018). An Experimental Approach in Revisiting the Magnetic Orientation of Cattle. *PloS One*, 13(4).

Williamson, B. (2016). Digital Education Governance: Data Visualization, Predictive Analytics, and 'Real-Time' Policy Instruments. *Journal of Education Policy*, 31(2), 123–141.

Winner, L. (1980). Do Artifacts Have Politics? *Daedalus*, 121–136.

Zafar, H., Randolph, A. B., and Martin, N. (2017). Toward a More Secure HRIS: The Role of HCI and Unconscious Behavior. *AIS Transactions on Human-Computer Interaction*, 9(1), 59–74.

Zick, P. (2013). CSR Infrastructure for Communication and the Nike Controversy. *Journal Of Management and Sustainability*, 3, 63–73.

2

Mobile media artifacts

Genealogies, haptic visualities, and speculative gestures

Lee Humphreys and Larissa Hjorth

Much has been written about the practices and political economy of mobile media. From the ethnographic analysis of cultural practice (Horst & Miller, 2006) to the industry political economy (Donner, 2008), studies on mobile media have grown over the past decade into its own scholarly field globally. And yet in this burgeoning field, the role of mobile media as artifacts that are part of broader symbolic and material conditions encompassing materiality and infrastructures has received less attention. In this chapter, we draw on various interdisciplinary studies of mobile media from game studies, mobile communication, and digital media to consider how we can contextualize the various ways in mobile media as artifacts plays out – in the past, present, and speculative futures. Through these three rubrics we seek to explore ways in which mobile media as artifacts have shaped, and been shaped by, their material and infrastructural characteristics.

As one of the most quotidian media today, mobile media's ubiquity makes it a compelling and yet difficult field to study. Increasingly, it is the sole device for Internet and social media use, making it an assemblage of competing practices, platforms, and infrastructures. Over the past decade and half, mobile media have been studied in a variety of qualitative and quantitative ways to understand the emerging practices and political economies. As an artifact it can be understood in a variety of ways – the material dimensions and 'thingyness' of the device, how it is part of practices, and how it is part of broader infrastructures (i.e., technological networks and corporate platforms). Mobile media embody the politics of personalization – they have embodied personalization practices of the user and the algorithmic personalization of platforms. So much so that they epitomize Jose van Dijck's (2014) discussion of the tension around datafication – personal data is being given over to corporate platforms.

Core to this tension is a broader debate around the relationship between the user and media – do media shape us, or do we shape media? In this chapter we draw on medium theory, social constructionism, and affordance approaches to explore mobile media artifacts in terms of three rubrics of the past, present, and speculative futures.

To understand mobile media as artifacts means to put them into a longer historical genealogy of mobile media. From this, we can better situate contemporary mobile media, which, we argue, embody haptic visuality. And with any evolving sociotechnical system (MacKenzie & Wajcman, 1999), the future imaginaries play an important role in the mobilities and materialities of media.

We argue that gestural systems of control can help illuminate how mobile media artifacts are increasingly understood through anticipatory work of speculative futures.

Genealogies of mobile media: past

From media archeology, we see traces of the mobile media through many different kinds of media that emerge historically. Defined by Erkki Huhtamo (1997) as the cultural study of recurring media discourses, media archeology has grown to encompass what Jussi Parikka (2012) identifies as material media cultures in relation to historical perspectives.

The genealogy of mobile media can be seen through "cultures of mobility" (Parikka & Suominen, 2006), in which a series of phenomenon emerges around 19th-century industrialization – the rise of transport and mobile technologies (i.e., wristwatch) interconnected increasingly with forms of individualization, constructions of intimacy, and the family in the private sphere (Plummer, 2003). These competing forms of mobility – technological, geographic, temporal, spatial, socioeconomic and social – develop with paradoxes and tensions. In order to understand these cultures of mobility and associated tensions, we discuss the materiality and affordances that define mobile media as artifacts. We then finish this genealogical section discussing more recent cultures of mobility.

Materiality

While the significance of materiality and the multisensorial nature of media has been identified by anthropologists (Appadurai, 1988; Miller, 2005; Pink, 2009), materiality in new media studies was lacking until approaches such as media archaeology grounded the discussions (Coole & Frost, 2010). For Parikka, "the task of new materialism is to address how to think materialisms in a multiplicity in such a methodological way that enables a grounded analysis of contemporary culture" (2012, 99). For Paterson et al., the sensory turn in the digital humanities has sought to weave together "historical, theoretical and empirical studies" (2012, 4).

Historically, we see the materiality of mobile media emerging in Innis' (1951) medium theory. While Innis doesn't use the term *mobile*, his argument regarding different media's biases are particularly relevant to our understanding of mobile media today. Space biases of communication media, according to Innis, mean that they are relatively "light and easily transportable" (Innis, 1951, 33). This is contrasted with time bias media, which are heavy, durable, and not transportable. Innis argues that as the primary medium of communication shifted from stone tablets to papyrus, we saw greater diffusion of ideas across geographical space due to a relative shift from a time-biased to space-biased dominant medium of communication. The relative mobility of papyrus from stone meant that ideas and information were moveable and thus able to spread. The space biases of papyrus enabled the spread of ideas and the codification of laws over geographical terrain. According to Innis's medium theory, the values embedded in the materiality of the dominant medium of communication shape a civilization.

The space biases of media are not unique to papyrus or mobile media today. Before we used the word *mobile* to describe media, the term *pocket* was a common way to characterize the space bias or portability of media. Whether it be pocket books (von Schneidemesser, 1980), pocket diaries (McCarthy, 2000), pocket watches (Agar, 2003), or pocket telegraphs (Parikka & Suominen, 2006), the term *pocket* conveys that an artifact is not just transportable but also miniaturized to be small enough to fit into a pocket. It also conveys that an artifact is personal, that is, something to be kept near people's bodies. In the United States in the 1700s and 1800s, pocket books and diaries were small books where people could write down notes throughout their day (McCarthy, 2000; von Schneidemesser, 1980). Like the term *mobile*, the term *pocket* articulates a set of material characteristics of media that shape how they can be used. Even to this day the pocket notion can be found in discussions of mobile media use by Japanese children as "mom in the pocket" (Matsuda, 2009, 67).

But terms like *mobile* and *pocket* can belie an artifact's infrastructural embeddedness. While an individual artifact like a phone or watch may be quite portable, some mobile and pocket media rely on and are linked to broader infrastructural systems. Agar (2003) argues that the pocket watch is an important predecessor to the mobile phone because it felt very mobile in its every-day practice, but was highly reliant on centralized systems of time keeping. The mobility of the artifact, much like that of contemporary mobile media, overshadows nonmobile infrastructures on which it relies. The materiality of pocket or mobile artifacts does not necessarily convey the variety of material forms and structures that enable mobile media.

Affordances

The notion of affordance has often been ascribed to the work of psychologist James Gibson (1979). Gibson used the term to characterize the various material dimensions and its "possi-bilities for action." It was then reappropriated by Donald Norman in 1988 (Norman, 2002) in the field of human computer interaction (HCI) to describe the design of an object and how it should be used. The term was then further nuanced to HCI scholar William Gaver (1991), who divided it into three sections – perceptible, hidden, and false.

The material characteristics of mobile media are seldom understood just as inherent physical characteristics but as complex attributes that become relevant in perceived situational contexts (Graves, 2007). Therefore, we suggest situating mobility as an affordance of mobile media that allows these artifacts to not only be moved but, moreover, be seen as mutually constitutive of the situational context, the actors, and technological artifacts (Humphreys et al., 2018).

While Carolyn Marvin (1988) does not use the framework of affordances, her analysis of roles of the electronic lightbulb, telegraph, and telephone in the 19th century can be under-stood through an affordance lens. While not mobile in artifactual form, as sociotechnical sys-tems they enabled the exchange and mobility of mediated communication. Indeed, many of the tensions such exchange of communication brings about can map onto mobile media today. For example, these electronic technologies that were brought into the home blurred distinctions between private and public and raised important privacy issues, such as young women engaging in unchaperoned interactions with strangers over the telephone or being able to see into sitting rooms after sunset due to electric light use in the home. The domestic yet networked nature of these technologies also raised important questions about technological ubiquity in society and fears of overreliance and excess. Further, these systems highlighted the emergent role of the technological 'expert.' In the 19th century, as Marvin shows, the electrician held the esteemed technological literacy and with it power in society. Today, app developers and coders hold this expertise and control the modes of communication on which we become reliant. These long-standing tensions emerge as a result of the shared affordances in late 19th-century electronically mediated communication and in contemporary mobile media today.

Amateur photography also emerges in the late 19th century and affords, what might be called, user-generated production of mediated visual content (Humphreys, 2018; Palmer, 2014). The Kodak camera was the key mobile artifact bringing photography to the mass market (Jenkins, 1975). Needing natural light to properly expose the film, the Kodak camera also pushed amateur photography outdoors and into the hands of novices (Becker, 1993; Gye, 2007; West, 2000). The mobility of these cameras was embodied not only in their handheld nature but also in the content of their photographic subjects. Often depicting leisure activities, play, or travel, Kodak advertisements of the early 20th century typically showed people using the camera in moments of mobility or movement (West, 2000). Photography scholars such as Daniel Palmer (2014) have highlighted these tensions of mobility by linking the aspirational ideologies of Kodak advertisements with Nokia, whereby photographing something renders it worthy of remembering.

While the history of photography has always been about touching, intimacy, and mobility, cameraphones magnify this entanglement. Pink and Hjorth (2014) have described this phenomenon in terms of digital wayfaring, whereby mobility and immobility are played out through cameraphone sharing and non-sharing. Wayfaring here is an embodied way of knowing through movement (i.e., proprioception) that is entangled with the digital.

Wayfaring acknowledges the core paradox to the camera's mobility – immobility. To capture a photo both photographer and subject need to remain still to avoid blurring. Given the prominence of the camera in mobile media today, early amateur photography can again help to reveal the complex ways that mobile media afford mobility and immobility. Parikka and Suominen (2006) similarly argue that reading on trains was also a simultaneous act of movement and stillness. Just as the pocket book or the Kodak camera embodies a mobility, the same technology simultaneously also demands immobilities. Thus, a kind of mechanical wayfaring can be seen as analogous to Pink and Hjorth's (2014) digital wayfaring.

Mobile gaming can also trace its roots back to the late 19th century. In particular, Parikka and Suominen (2006) focus on the situational context of modernization at this time, processes including industrialization, transportation, and urbanization, that enabled and relied on notions of mobility and movement. These processes with regard to mobile gaming practices entangle questions of leisure, spectatorship, and the personal position which are central affordances of contemporary mobile gaming (Hjorth & Richardson, 2014). From playing cards to portable chess and the stereoscope, these games were part of the Victorian mediascape, which emphasized mechanization, consumption, and mobility.

These historical antecedents of mobile media are found not just in shared material characteristics but in shared affordances. Rather than just examining the artifactual similarities, affordances can reveal similar practices and tensions across sociotechnical systems and historical time periods. Mobile gaming, mediated communication, and information exchange, as well as amateur photography, are essential practices for understanding mobile media today.

Recent genealogies

More recent predecessors of mobile media are also helpful to understand mobile media genealogy – in particular, the prominence of portable music and gaming devices. Sony's Walkman is an example of the popular portable music players in the 1980s (du Gay et al.,1997; Hosokawa, 1984). Highly influential as both a cultural product and practice, Sony's Walkman also represented the global media marketplace within the everyday experience of people's lives. As Lasen (2018) argues, mobile listening can also be understood as a form of public engagement with urban spaces, which has a long history of portable media, including the transistor radio, boom boxes (Schloss & Boyer, 2014), personal stereos (Bull, 2000), and the boom car (Bull, 2007; Labelle, 2010).

The mobility of music listening exacerbated an important concern that resonates with mobile media today – the privatization of media consumption and subsequent "tuning out" of others in public space. While the car brought about an auto-mobility which led to greater privatization and suburbanization (Packer, 2008), the personal listening device was seen as further trend toward atomization of society. It was of concern that these devices with their earphones or earbuds took people out of their inhabited worlds and created bubbles in which they alone lived (Bull, 2007). We have seen this atomization at work in the concept of absent presence, which, Ken Gergen (2002) argues, occurs when people are physically present in one place but emotionally and cognitive absent, drawn into the world on their mobile phones.

Portable listening devices can be viewed as part of a broader set of paradoxes encapsulated by Raymond William's (1975) notion of mobile privatization. When Williams coined the term to discuss TV, he was highlighting the deep contradictions around domestic media whereby the media traversed the public but made users feel more 'at home.' Mobile privatization has been heightened within the rise of mobile media which has seen a further tethering to notions of the home while also setting the user 'free' to roam (Morley, 2003). For cultural studies scholar David Morley (2003), the 'home' involves contradictory dynamics whereby domestication of technology (i.e., Silverstone's (1994) domestication or "taming" of wild new technology) sees a dislocation of domesticity.

Domestication approaches acknowledge the blurring distinctions between work and leisure with mobile media (Ling & Haddon, 2003). One way of understanding this entanglement between work and leisure in terms of contemporary mobile media is through the notion of 'playfulness' (Sicart, 2015). Kerr identifies play as a "key concept for understanding the interaction of users with new media" (2006, 69), in which all media interfaces could be said to be part of the "collective playful media landscape" (Frissen et al., 2015, 29). Much of the affordances of media devices and apps draw on the playful and sometimes the gamified – although many game scholars have allergies to this concept due to the way it commodifies media into 'game-like' affordances (Deterding et al., 2011). Wilmott et al. (2017) argue that geographic positioning systems (GPS) enabled smart-watches and smart-bands invite us to redefine our quotidian environments as laborious playgrounds where leisure activities are redefined in terms of work and quantifiable data. The blurring of work and leisure practices has been highlighted by many cultural scholars such as Melissa Gregg (2013) and Judy Wajcman (1991). It is encapsulated by Julian Kücklich's (2005) term *playbour* to define the various player labor practices (social, creative, and cultural capital) emerging, such as computer modification (modding), which companies then capitalize upon. Therefore, mobile media can be mutually characterized by what Larissa Hjorth (2017) calls "ambient play and soft labor."

From papyrus to the Walkman, mobile media have a long artifactual history. The datafication of contemporary mobile media may be unique (Humphreys, 2018), but shared material characteristics and affordances reveal much longer genealogies for contemporary mobile media.

Haptic visuality: present

As we have explored, understanding wearables and the rise of haptic mobile media within this historical context – the pocket watch and novel – can provide insight into how the personal and private, work and leisure, are intimately entwined. In this section we focus upon the notion of haptic visuality as a way to not only capture the multisensorial nature of materiality but also define some key characteristics of contemporary "mobile media" – a term coined by cinema scholar Laura Marks (2002) to talk about the affective and embodied ways in which cinema can tap into multisensorial memories and corporeal experiences. Our usage here draws on Marks's emphasis on materialist and multisensory approaches to the screen.

The rise of haptic screens as now an everyday part of smartphone practices has led to scholars such as David Parisi (2009) defining a subarea of media studies – haptic media studies. Haptic screens have a long history in games studies whereby the "touch" of the screen was normalized (Parisi, 2009; Paterson, 2009). As Parisi (2008) notes through the example of the Nintendo DS, the advertisements had to teach people to learn to touch the screen after decades of etiquette *not* touching the screen (Nintendo's slogan "touching is good"). These behaviors are taught, untaught, and retrained.

Paterson (2007) explores both the historical and the contemporary theorizations and dimensions of touch. In Paterson's terms, haptic media engage the manifold facets of touch – involving kinesthetic, proprioceptive, somatic, mimetic, metaphoric, and affective modes of perception. Over the past decade such analyses of the haptic interface have enabled fertile connections between media theory and the disciplinary fields of sensory studies and new materialism.

Parisi (2008) argues that what constitutes touching is culturally and historically specific. Parisi observes aptly, "touch is defined by a fundamental instability" that understands that "touch is itself multimodal – composed of and constituted by a range of imperceptibly interwoven component sensations" (2008, 229). Parisi and colleagues (2017) argue for the importance of haptic media studies in understanding the historical, material, and multisensorial dimensions of contemporary mobile media.

The work in animal computer interaction (ACI) has been pivotal in questioning the human-centric nature in which we define media practice. In particular, the work of Anne Galloway (2017) and Hanna Wirman (2014) highlights the ways in which we can learn from animals (more-than-humans) in terms of the haptic possibilities of screens. Far from just using hands or digits, animals will use their whole body – tongues, bums, and tails. These types of practices take the haptic visuality affordances of mobile screens to new dimensions.

Haptic visuality can also be understood through embodiment (Farman, 2012). As Brendan Keogh (2015) observes in his phenomenology of videogame play, we need an attunement to the multisensorial dimensions of play through, in, and around screenplay. Keogh argues, "through an entanglement of eyes-at-screens, ears-at-speakers, and muscles-against interfaces players perceive videogames as worlds consisting of objects and actors with texture, significance, and weight" (2015, 1). Game consoles such as Nintendo Wii have been important in understanding and addressing the multisensorial experience of mobile media, not just through haptics but through visualized bodies in space (Giddings & Kennedy, 2010).

Haptic visuality of location

Our use of haptic visualities of mobile media highlights the need for understanding the multisensorial ways in which mobile media contribute to multiple cartographies – physical, geographic, social, and cultural. Locative media are an intrinsic part of this overlay and are often a default for many mobile media apps (Frith, 2015). For example, the shift from maps to map apps signifies an important infrastructural distinction. Maps have always relied on infrastructures such as transportation to present and represent space. However, the networked capabilities of map apps turn the visual representations of space into datafied form. While the user merely sees a dot on the map representing where they are, the app collects longitudinal and latitudinal coordinates of the phone itself. Map apps not only allow us to see our bodies in space but feed such data back into a networked infrastructural system concerning patterns of movement of populations and markets. In turn, these coordinates then shape the visual representations of the maps themselves (Frith, 2015). For example, different venues may be featured on different maps for different users. The prominence and visuality of map apps belie their datafied infrastructural presence.

Gestural systems and speculative futures

As we turn to thinking about the futures of mobile media artifacts, we move from haptic visuality to gestural systems. Drawing on Baudrillard (2005), Bart Simon (2009) distinguishes between a gestural system of control and a gestural system of effort. Gestural systems of effort are systems where cause and effect are direct and knowable, whereas gestural systems of control are indirectly tied whereby the means of cause and effect are unknowable. For example, a hammer and nail would be a gestural system of effort while a button that turns something on would be a gestural system of control. Simon argues that the introduction of the Nintendo Wii signaled an important shift in video games from gestural systems of control (e.g., joystick based) toward gestural systems of effort. However, Simon notes, there are still gestural excess and in-excess within the system which must be learned through experience over time.

Gestural systems of control and effort are a helpful framework for mobile media artifacts because they are about cause and effect (Baudrillard, 2005) – thus introducing an important temporal element to these systems. Whereas touch is fundamentally presentist in practice, gestural systems can be understood as anticipatory in nature. We anticipate the effects through these systems. As mobile media increasingly move from haptics to gestures, we see greater anticipatory and speculative work of mobile media.

Speculative futures

Fundamentally, speculative futures of mobile media artifacts can be understood in their connection to communication as an inherent act of surveillance. In 1949, Harold Lasswell (Lasswell, 1949) argued that the surveillance of the environment was one of the most fundamental functions of communication. Surveillance here is defined as anticipatory monitoring. As Steve Wicker (2011) argues, mobile networks are by necessity networks of surveillance, as they must anticipate potential mobile network use. Mobile phones can receive calls because they periodically send registration messages so that telecommunication service providers can route the call through proximate cellphone towers. Even if people are not actively using their mobile phones, as long as the phone is turned on it regularly communicates with a cellular network. Locations of the phone and by proxy its owner are collected by telecommunication service providers such as AT&T or Vodafone as part of the mobile network infrastructure.

Lee Humphreys (2011) argues there are multiple kinds of surveillance practices at work through mobile media. First is what she calls "voluntary panopticon" (Whitaker, 1999), whereby people willingly give up their personal information to corporate entities in exchange for some kind of benefit. Within mobile media, people often use "free" social media apps, which collect detailed information about them because they enjoy being able to communicate with their friends and family. In this case, the corporate entity engages in a kind of speculative surveillance of users and their communication for future commodification.

The second kind of surveillance of mobile media is lateral surveillance (Andrejevic, 2007), where users of mobile social media engage in a kind of monitoring of other users. Much like participatory or social surveillance (Albrechtslund, 2008; Marwick, 2012), users often engage in mobile media assuming a kind of mutual monitoring of each other (Humphreys, 2011). Jansson uses the term *interveillance* to describe the growing ways in which people mutually share and disclose various forms of private information. Interveillance is dialectical, whereby it "reinforces" and "integrates" "overarching ambiguities of mediatization" in which "freedom and autonomy" are "paralleled by limitations and dependencies vis-à-vis media" (2015, 81). Mutual disclosure and monitoring are woven into the everyday practice of mobile media.

A third kind of surveillance on mobile media, according to Humphreys (2011), is self-surveillance. Here users of mobile media come to understand their mediated communicative exchanges as superseding their lived experience. People engage in the anticipatory monitoring of their own behavior to better understand themselves. Much like the self-tracking movement

(Neff & Nafus, 2016), self-surveillance relies on an assumption that in the future one will desire to look back at one's experiences or behaviors to better understand oneself.

A fourth surveillance of mobile media is of citizens by state actors (Lyon, 2001; Morozov, 2011; Park, 2013). Within the United States, law enforcement agencies regularly rely on cell-site evidence, that is, inferential work to determine the approximate location of a phone based on which cell towers were activated during the time period in question (Wicker, 2011). This kind of evidence, however, raises important legal issues. The Supreme Court case Carpenter v. US (SCOTUS, 2018) questioned the publicness of cell-site data. Within US law, a phone number dialed is considered more public than the conversation that is held over the phone. Similarly, an address on an envelope is more public than the contents of the letter inside the envelope. Thus, law enforcement has different requirements with regard to access and usage of various communication within legal cases (e.g., it is harder to legally attain the content of a phone call than the phone number called). Carpenter v. US considered whether cell-site information is really as public as a phone number or an address, because most citizens do not realize their phones are transmitting such information. Ultimately, the US Supreme Court decided that cell-site data requires a warrant to access and is more private than a phone number or address. This example demonstrates the ways the legal infrastructures overlap with technical infrastructures to shape how mobile media's speculative futures become enacted in everyday life.

The infrastructural, commercial, state, social, and intrapersonal surveillances of mobile media rely on speculative futures and anticipatory monitoring to coordinate interaction, exchange communication, and simply operate mobile media. Mobile media research points to the ways that mobile media surveillances are multiple with various potential implications, some more negative and some more positive. Mobile media artifacts are part of complex gestural systems of control that embody various kinds of anticipatory monitoring. In some cases, mobile media systems rely on in-excessive gestural work whereby little to no effort on the part of the user can generate significant effects within the broader systems.

Conclusion

This chapter has outlined three primary frames through which to understand the artifactual nature of mobile media. By articulating a long genealogy of mobile media, we demonstrated how materiality and affordances both shape and are shaped by a complex understanding of 'mobile.' Historical terms like 'pocket' convey many of the attributes of mobile media today but lack the contemporary fluidity and flows associated with networked global capitalism (Castells, 2000). Nevertheless, historicizing mobile media can help to identify key affordances and social tensions that are shared among many historical artifacts and mobile media as well as key differences. In particular, the ways mobile media are intricately linked to capitalistic incentives through the datafication and commodification of use mark an important change in the genealogy of mobile media (Couldry & Hepp, 2017; Humphreys, 2018).

With a historical sensibility, we then argued that the rise of the smartphone environment can be best understood through haptic visuality. Touch has become the primary mode through which our experiences with mobile media artifacts are embodied. But touch is inherently multisensory and therefore quite complex for digital and social media scholars to study. Emerging from screen and game studies, the haptic visuality of mobile media artifacts represents an important shift within new media studies toward embodied interaction (Dourish, 2001; Farman, 2012).

Lastly, as we shifted from a present to future-oriented frame for mobile media artifacts, we moved from touch to gesture, which not only conveys greater mobility but also introduces anticipatory elements to our understanding of media. Situating mobile media within gestural systems of control we make explicit the way these systems indirectly articulate cause and effect. We argue mobile media artifacts are inherently systems of surveillances that infrastructurally and socially rely on anticipatory monitoring. The multiplicity of surveillances enabled through mobile media artifacts reveals the complex ways mobile media's speculative futures manifest and matter in everyday life.

References

Agar, J. (2003). *Constant Touch: A Global History of the Mobile Phone*. Cambridge: Icon Books.

Albrechtslund, A. (2008). Online Social Networking as Participatory Surveillance. *First Monday*, 13(3), article 6.

Andrejevic, M. (2007). *iSpy: Surveillance and Power in the Interactive Era*. Lawrence, KS: University Press of Kansas.

Appadurai, A. (ed.). (1988). *The Social Life of Things: Commodities in Cultural Perspective*. Cambridge: Cambridge University Press.

Baudrillard, J. (2005). *The System of Objects*. Translated by J. Benedict. London: Verso.

Becker, K. (1993). The Aesthetics of Amateur Photography. *Adomus*, 15, 19–25.

Bull, M. (2000). *Sounding out the City. Personal Stereos and the Management of Everyday Life*. Oxford: Berg Publishers.

Bull, M. (2007). *Sound Moves. iPod Culture and Urban Experience*. London: Routledge.

Castells, M. (2000). *The Rise of the Network Society* (2nd ed.). Malden, MA: Blackwell Publishers.

Coole, D. and Frost, S. (eds.). (2010). *New Materialisms: Ontology, Agency, and Politics*. Durham: Duke University Press.

Couldry, N., and Hepp, A. (2017). *The Mediated Construction of Reality*. Cambridge: Polity Press.

Deterding, S., Dixon, D., Khlaed, R. and Nacke, L. (2011). *From Game Design Elements to Gamefulness: Defining 'Gamification'*. Proceedings of the 15th International Academic Mindtrek Conference, pp. 9–15.

Donner, J. (2008). Research Approaches to Mobile Use in the Developing World: A Review of the Literature. *The Information Society*, 24(3), 140–159.

Dourish, P. (2001). *Where the Action Is: The Foundations of Embodied Interaction*. Cambridge, MA: MIT Press.

du Gay, P., Hall, S., Janes, L., MacKay, H., and Negus, K. (1997). *Doing Cultural Studies: The Story of the Sony Walkman*. Milton Keynes: The Open University.

Farman, J. (2012). *Mobile Interface Theory: Embodied Space and Locative Media*. New York: Routledge.

Frissen, V., Lammes, S., de Lange, M., de Mul, J., and Raessens, J. (2015). *Playful Identities: The Ludification of Digital Media Cultures*. Amsterdam: Amsterdam University Press.

Frith, J. (2015). *Smartphones as Locative Media*. Malden, MA: Polity Press.

Galloway, A. (2017). More-Than-Human Lab: Creative Ethnography After Human Exceptionalism. In L. Hjorth, H. Horst, A. Galloway, and G. Bell (eds.), *The Routledge Companion to Digital Ethnography*. New York: Routledge, pp. 470–477.

Gaver, W. W. (1991). *Technology Affordances*. Proceedings of the SIGCHI Conference on Human Factors in Computing Systems: Reaching Through Technology. New Orleans, pp. 79–84.

Gergen, K. (2002). The Challenge of the Absent Presence. In J. E. Katz and M. Aakhus (eds.), *Perpetual Contact: Mobile Communication, Private Talk, Public Performance*. Oxford: Oxford University Press, pp. 227–241.

Gibson, J. (1979). *The Ecological Approach to Visual Perception*. Boston, MA: Houghton Mifflin.

Giddings, S., and Kennedy, H. W. (2010). 'Incremental Speed Increases Excitement': Bodies, Space, Movement, and Televisual Change. *Television & New Media*, 11(3), 163–179.

Graves, L. (2007). The Affordances of Blogging: A Case Study in Culture and Technological Effects. *Journal of Communication Inquiry*, 31(4), 331–346. doi:10.1177/0196859907305446.

Gregg, M. (2013). *Work's Intimacy*. Cambridge: Polity Press.

Gye, L. (2007). Picture This: The Impact of Mobile Camera Phones on Personal Photographic Practices. *Continuum*, 21(2), 279–288.

Hjorth, L. (2017). Ambient and Soft Play: Play, Labour and the Digital in Everyday Life. *European Journal of Cultural Studies*. doi:10.1177/1367549417705606.

Hjorth, L., and Richardson, I. (2014). *Gaming in Social, Locative and Mobile Media*. London: Palgrave Macmillan.

Horst, H., and Miller, D. (2006). *The Cell Phone: An Anthropology of Communication*. New York: Berg Publishers.

Hosokawa, S. (1984). The Walkman Effect. *Popular Music*, 4, 65–180.

Huhtamo, E. (1997). From Kaleidoscomaniac to Cybernerd: Notes Toward an Archaeology of the Media. *Leonardo*, 30(3), 221–224.

Humphreys, L. (2011). Who's Watching Whom? A Study of Interactive Technology and Surveillance. *Journal of Communication*, 61, 575–595.

Humphreys, L. (2018). *The Qualified Self: Social Media and the Accounting of Everyday Life*. Cambridge, MA: MIT Press.

Humphreys, L, Karnowski, V., and Von Pape, T. (2018). Smartphones as Metamedia: A Framework for Identifying the Niches Structuring Smartphone Use. *International Journal of Communication*, 12, 17. https://ijoc.org/index.php/ijoc/article/view/7922.

Innis, H. (1951). *The Bias of Communication*. Toronto: University of Toronto Press.

Jansson, A. (2015). Interveillance: A New Culture of Recognition and Mediatization. *Media and Communication*, 3(3), 81–90.

Jenkins, R. V. (1975). Technology and the Market: George Eastman and the Origins of Mass Amateur Photography. *Technology and Culture*, 16(1), 1–19.

Kerr, A. (2006). *The Business and Culture of Digital Games*. London: Sage.

Keogh, B. (2015). *A Play of Bodies: A Phenomenology of Videogame Experience* (PhD thesis), RMIT, Melbourne, Australia.

Kücklich, J. (2005). Precarious Playbour: Modders and the Digital Games Industry. *Fibreculture*. http://five.fibreculturejournal.org/fcj-025-precarious-playbour-modders-and-the-digital-games-industry/.

LaBelle, B. (2010). *Acoustic Territories: Sound Culture and Everyday Life*. New York: Continuum.

Lasen, A. (2018). Disruptive Ambient Music: Mobile Phone Music Listening as Portable Urbanism. *European Journal of Cultural Studies*, 21(1), 96–110. doi:10.1177/1367549417705607.

Laswell, H. (1949). Structure and Function of Communication in Society. In L. Bryson (ed.), *The Communication of Ideas*. New York: Harper.

Ling, R., and Haddon, L. (2003). Mobile Telephony, Mobility, and the Coordination of Everyday Life. In J. E. Katz (ed.), *Machines That Become Us: The Social Context of Personal Communication Technology*. New Brunswick, NJ: Transaction Publishers, pp. 245–265.

Lyon, D. (2001). *Surveillance Society: Monitoring in Everyday Life*. Buckingham: Open University Press.

MacKenzie, D., and Wajcman, J. (1999). *The Social Shaping of Technology* (2nd ed.). Buckingham: Open University Press.

Marks, L. U. (2002). *Touch: Sensuous Theory and Multisensory Media*. Minneapolis: University of Minnesota Press.

Marvin, C. (1988). *When Old Technologies Were New: Thinking About Electric Communication in the Late Nineteenth Century*. New York: Oxford University Press.

Marwick, A. E. (2012). The Public Domain: Social Surveillance in Everyday Life. *Surveillance and Society*, 9(4), 378–393.

Matsuda, M. (2009). Mobile Media & the Family. In G. Goggin and L. Hjorth (eds.), *Mobile Technologies: From Telecommunications to Media*. London: Routledge, pp. 62–71.

McCarthy, M. (2000). A Pocketful of Days: Pocket Diaries and Daily Record Keeping Among Nineteenth-Century New England Women. *The New England Quarterly*, 73(2), 274–296.

Miller, D. (ed.). (2005). *Materiality*. Durham, NC: Duke University Press.

Morley, D. (2003). What's Home Got to Do with It? *European Journal of Cultural Studies*, 6(4), 435–458.

Morozov, E. (2011). *The Net Delusion: How Not to Liberate the World*. New York: Public Affairs.

Neff, G., and Nafus, D. (2016). *The Self-Tracking*. Cambridge, MA: MIT Press.

Norman, D. A. (2002). *The Design of Everyday Things*. New York: Basic Books.

Packer, J. (2008). *Mobility Without Mayhem*. Durham, NC: Duke University Press.

Palmer, D. (2014). Mobile Media Photography. In G. Goggin and L. Hjorth (eds.), *Routledge Companion to Mobile Media*. New York: Routledge, pp. 245–255.

Parikka, J. (2012). New Materialism as Media Theory: Medianatures and Dirty Matter. *Communication and Critical/Cultural Studies*, 9(1), 95–100.

Parikka, J., and Suominen, J. (2006). Victorian Snakes? Towards a Cultural History of Mobile Games and the Experience of Movement. *Game Studies*, 6(1).

Parisi, D. (2008). Fingerbombing, or 'Touching Is Good': The Cultural Construction of Technologized Touch. *Senses & Society*, 3(3), 307–327.

Parisi, D. (2009). Game Interfaces as Bodily Techniques. In R. Ferdig (ed.), *Handbook of Effective Research on Electronic Games*. New York: IGI Global, pp. 111–126.

Parisi, D., Paterson, M., and Archer, J. E. (2017). Haptic Media Studies. *New Media & Society*, 19(10), 1513–1522.

Park, Y. J. (2013). Offline Status, Online Status: Reproduction of Social Categories in Personal Information Skill and Knowledge. *Social Science Computer Review*, 31(6), 680–702.

Paterson, M. (2007). *Senses of Touch: Haptics, Affects and Technologies*. London: Berg Publishers.

Paterson, M. (2009). Haptic Geographies: Ethnography, Haptic Knowledges and Sensuous Dispositions. *Progress in Human Geography*, 33(6), 766–88.

Paterson, M., Dodge, M., and MacKian, S. (2012). Introduction: Placing Touch Within Social Theory and Empirical Study. In M. Paterson and M. Dodge (eds.), *Touching Space, Placing Touch*. Farnham, MA: Ashgate, pp. 1–28.

Pink, S. (2009). *Doing Sensory Ethnography*. London: Sage.

Pink, S., and Hjorth, L. (2014). New Visualities and the Digital Wayfarer: Reconceptualizing Camera Phone Photography. *Mobile Media & Communication*, 2(1), 40–57.

Plummer, K. (2003). *Intimate Citizenship: Private Decisions and Public Dialogues*. Seattle, WA: University of Washington Press.

Schloss, J., and Boyer, B. (2014). Urban Echoes: The Boombox and Sonic Mobility in the 1980s. In S. Gopinath and J. Stanyek (eds.), *The Oxford Handbook of Mobile Music Studies* (vol. 1). Oxford: Oxford University Press, pp. 399–412.

SCOTUS Blog. (2018). *Carpenter v. United States, Docket 16-402*. www.scotusblog.com/case-files/cases/carpenter-v-united-states-2/.

Sicart, M. (2015). *Playfulness: A BIT of Play Matters*. Cambridge, MA: MIT Press.

Silverstone, R. (1994). *Television and Everyday Life*. London: Routledge.

Simon, B. (2009). Wii Are Out of Control: Bodies, Game Screens and the Production of Gestural Excess. *Social Science Research Network*. SSRN. http://dx.doi.org/1354010.1352139/ssrn.1354043.

van Dijck, J. (2014). Datafication, Dataism and Dataveillance: Big Data Between Scientific Paradigm and Ideology. *Surveillance and Society*, 12(2), 197–208.

von Schneidemesser, L. (1980). Purse and Its Synonyms. *American Speech*, 55(1), 74–76.

Wajcman, J. (1991). *Feminism Confronts Technology*. University Park, PA: Penn State Press.

West, N. M. (2000). *Kodak and the Lens of Nostalgia*. Charlottesville, VA: University of Virginia.

Whitaker, R. (1999). *The End of Privacy: How Total Surveillance Is Becoming a Reality*. New York: The New Press.

Wicker, S. B. (2011). Cellular Telephony and the Question of Privacy. *Communications of the ACM*, 54(7), 88–98.

Williams, R. (1975). *Television: Technology and Cultural Form*. New York: Schocken Books.

Wilmott, C., Fraser, E., and Lammes, S. (2017). 'I am He. I am He. Siri Rules': Work and Play with the Apple Watch. *European Journal of Cultural Studies*. https://doi.org/10.1177/1367549417705605.

Wirman, H. (2014). Games for/with Strangers-Captive Orangutan (pongo pygmaeus) Touch Screen Play. *Antennae*, 30, 105–115.

3

Digital embodiment and financial infrastructures

Kaitlyn Wauthier and Radhika Gajjala

This chapter examines the digital (subaltern)[1] body and how it is produced through financial infrastructures. Our everyday engagement with and immersion in the digital body puts into question the experience of embodiment "coherent, whole and unified" through "a sense 'corporeal wholeness'" (Grosz, 1994, 32). The digital body, as in the case of body image – albeit differently, through immersion and relational affective intensities – is also experienced as "a collection of 'felt intensities' that are derived from bodily sensations" (Blackman, 2008, 77). Yet in the case of the production of digital subaltern presence through microfinance platforms (such as kiva.org) and in online philanthropy projects, there is an attempt to reproduce an authentic and essentialized image of the subaltern through registers of 'Otherness' that most westernized viewers are familiar and comfortable with. Acts of giving motivated through affective intensities resulting from encounters and interactions with such an assemblage of digital subalternity contribute to our sense of self as a global citizen. Our global digital body thus travels through carefully curated sites of 'identity tourism' (Nakamura, 1995) materialized as real by financial infrastructures. It is the link with financial banking structures that makes us view these digital subaltern bodies as real and the success stories posted in these online microfinance sites as evidence.

In order to highlight the differences in how digital bodies emerge and how digital subalternity is produced and to reveal hierarchies within which digital embodiment shifts corporeality and subjectivity, we interweave personal journeys of 'becoming digital' and 'becoming transnational' with a look at how a certain image of the offline subaltern is staged as the original representation in digital space while being brought into the digital infrastructures through digital financialization. Thus, in the first section we narrate chosen digital entry stories, and in the second section we describe the staging and visualization of the digital subaltern body that in turn serve to connect subaltern bodies to digital financial debt infrastructures. As Federici notes:

> Microfinance enables international capital to directly control and exploit the world proletariat, bypassing the mediation of the national states and thus ensuring that any profit made accrues directly to the banks and is not appropriated by local governments. It also enables it to bypass the world of male relatives as mediators in the exploitation of women's labor and

to tap the energies of a population of women who in the wake of "structural adjustment" have been able to create new forms of subsistence outside or at the margins of the money economy, which microcredit attempts to bring under the control of monetary relations and the banks. Last but not least, like other debt-generating policies, microfinance is a means of experimentation with different social relations where the tasks of surveillance and policing are "internalized" by the community, the group, and the family and where exploitation appears to be self-managed, failure is experienced as an individual problem and disgrace is more burning.

(2014, 239)

The goal, therefore, is to think through shifting ontologies of subjectivity and corporeality (Blackman, 2012) by examining how digital financialization platforms influence states of mobility and immobility through the monetizing of labor/leisure, affect, and visuality. This chapter seeks to understand how these structures redefine the 'body' beyond assumptions and through expectations of becoming ideal "empowered, autonomous, agential subjects of history" (Jarrett, 2016, 65).

Through these interweaving and overlapping self/digital/corporeal narratives of access and literacy and labor and leisure, we raise ontological issues around the body and its existence as simultaneously digital and material/corporeal/enfleshed. We consider how the body extends into, as well as emerges from, our geo-social and political ecologies of being. This approach implicitly resurfaces various interdisciplinary explorations that bring together the sciences, social sciences, and the humanities in conversation. As has been noted by various scholars, while 'biology' and metaphysics have been interconnected and contemplated for centuries, in the current moment of encounter with the digital and with awareness of anthropogenic climate change issues, "there has been a resurgence of interest in this connection in the last couple of decades (e.g., Hull, 1989; Millstein, 2009; Clarke, 2011; Dupré, 2012; Pradeu, 2012; Godfrey-Smith, 2013; Ferner, 2016; Wiggins, 2016). Rediscovering this connection brings both opportunities and challenges" (Ferner & Pradeu, 2017, 1). Further, as Lisa Blackman notes, "Speed, movement, mobility, immateriality, fluidity, multiplicity and flows are all concepts that are profoundly reorganizing how the ontology of both subjectivity and corporeality are examined" (2012, ix).

By examining ontological and epistemological issues around the 'existence' of a body in digital space, we note how spatio-temporal shifts, physical geographical border crossings, and digital infrastructures produce particular intersections and relationships between subjectivity and corporeality. In the production of economic citizens – a central focus in our contemporary global digital capitalist ethos – through mechanisms of invoking consumer subjectivities, forms of free, digital, and subaltern labor are called upon to physically move into formation around computer-networked socioeconomic systems. A case in point is the digital-corporeal and affective-economic assemblages through which online microfinance functions. Further, the human-ness of the software engineer and architect are kept invisible as the technological interface/algorithm is attributed with agency as an artificial intelligence–based subjectivity as corporeality gets refigured through visual and textual stagings.

We therefore frame this chapter against the binary and continuum of digital/offline and consider the techno-social ensemble that includes various technological gadgets – the sociocultural as well as political-economic contexts of engaging these gadgets – and the biological body as part of a relational-digital-corporeal habitus.

In the case of the individual with access to digital technologies in whatever limited or extended capacity – whether 'digital native,' 'digital immigrant,' or 'digital subaltern' – the virtual is indeed real. The virtual/digital is a part of everyday life reality. This way of understanding the digital as an extension of the real self then leads to ontological shifts in how the body is experienced and defined. It centers the everydayness of how we produce ourselves and bodies as we weave through the many digital and offline modes of communication and affective exchange by raising questions of what it means to be offline and online simultaneously – and how this reconfigures our everyday spatio-temporalities.

Digital everyday interactions provide a range of opportunities to examine the relationship of the digital body to the physical body. In fact, these interactions between the physical self and representations of the body with gadgets that produce digitality of interaction, exchange, and embodiment allow us to extend the notions of 'body' and to work against and beyond the binary of the digital versus physical/material. Discussions of the body in relation to informationalization, digitality, and mediation cover a range of understandings based in various configurations of the relationship of the digital to the physical, tactile, affective, and material body supported by analog infrastructures and architectures. Such discussions reveal shifting definitions of 'the body' as we look at particular instances of how we 'become' digital in the contemporary sociocultural, political, and economic ethos of market-centered globalization as digitality both opens up the definition of body through "direct involvement of immaterial activity and goods, such as affect and care, into the economic calculations of capital" (Jarrett, 2017, 14)[2] and recodes it and tightens surveillance of it through algorithmic infrastructures.

The work in small teams to produce code that is replicable across platforms creates parts that are moveable and reusable in many kinds of platforms interchangeably. Coders are thus producing parts of a machine, but these are immaterial – written – rather than made from physical tactile circuits, nuts, and bolts. Further, the human coder must function mechanically and with a certain speed without organizational/structural support to incorporate diverse users and contexts across time and space. Code has to be 'scalable' and reproducible, which is also why it needs to have a dynamism and flexibility built into it. The problem is that coders most often are not given structural/organizational incentives to code for a very diverse user base. Instead, speed of output and a narrow vision of scalability are privileged.

Algorithms are produced by human beings, and we lose sight of this as we talk of "code as law" in ways that scholars such as Lessig (2006, 1) do. As a software engineer interviewed as part of one of the coauthors' larger research project notes in a discussion on how algorithms produce structural bias:

> Algorithms are instructing a computer how to think. That's literally all programing is. Since everything a programmer does is algorithms. Then they're intervening constantly. Their personal feelings and biases are baked into every facet of their work [and] more complex code can embody more complex biases. It's a boring day job for most normal programmers. So you made the text on that button a bit small. You can read it because you're 20. But an older person might struggle to read it. And that's a bias right there. Baked into the simple work of a button.
>
> *("Q," personal communication with R. Gajjala, January 2018)*

The interviewee continues to note that workplace incentives and employee empowerment are important factors that would contribute to the diversification of algorithmic infrastructures. The model that merely adds diverse bodies and stirs may not work to automatically cure the problem. In fact, "Q" noted that in discussions of diversity in hiring within software organizations we forget that there is geographical diversity in labor – a large quantity of routine coding work is sent offshore to Global South locations as we know.

Cheney-Lippold (2011) has also noted how algorithmic coding is far more dynamic and flexible than 'code as law' (Lessig, 2006). Similar to what the software engineer notes in the interview referred to previously, Cheney-Lippold writes:

> Code is part of a dynamic relationship to the real world, one that can 'automatically and continuously' affect life chances offered to users based on a pre-configured but also reflexive programmed logic. But rather than look at code as just an automated and adaptive gatekeeper of critical information, we can explore its function much more constitutionally. An analysis that centers on code allows us to look at a list of lines of a computer language and see how it uses certain representations of the world (variables and data) to produce new value.
>
> *(2011, 166–167)*

An analysis that centers code must also center the human coder and the conditions of work that contribute to their production of social value through code. Thus, in the production of the digital body, concepts of subjectivity, voice, performativity, affect, digital labor, value, and algorithmic identity work together and are brought into being through discourse and through audio-visual performativity as different body parts engage tactile and architectural structures around us through everyday practice.

The corporeal/subjective/digital body emerges through an interplay of digital infrastructures and offline access to offline bodies – the immaterial and the affective – as we come into being through affects engaged around us and through memories and extrasensory perception. The digital body is produced in relational space: it is performative, but it is also connected to capital through digital financial tools and embedded within a surveillance structure. Digital connectivity and sociality are threaded through the corporeal offline body, once again impacting the ontology of subjectivity and corporeality.

Becoming digital

In this section, we narrate our individual digital entry stories to think through how our material and digital embodiment interweave with each other.

Digital diasporas and connectivity: Radhika's story

Long ago when I was in graduate school I learned that "everything is text" (Derrida, 1996) – I also learned about the "death of the author" (Foucault, 1977). Inevitably, these discussions would end with some of us trying to touch the material artifacts around us or trying to articulate some "authorial" intention and uniqueness in thought. We were physical, embodied *individuals* with authorial intent and potential. We were also "whole" and complete – self-contained – not "bodies without organs" (Deleuze, 1993). But of course several of us processed this material and came out of graduate school as researchers drawing from the works of poststructural and postmodern theorists. We then proceeded to hold seminars in which, then, *our* graduate students similarly did the tapping of the table and the processing of theory that was telling them they probably did not exist. For me, these theories took me back to dilemmas I had encountered in my teenage years when I was reading Upanishads (in their English translation as a dutiful post-but-neo-colonial subject, even though I had claims of having learned Sanskrit), Western Enlightenment ontologies of the body and mind. Round about the same time – exciting 1990s – I also encountered feminist, queer studies, and postcolonial/transnational feminist scholars and philosophers such as Butler, Harraway, Sedgwick, Alcoff, Rubin, Spivak, and Mohanty. We learned then about situated knowledges and epistemological and ontological issues around the body and around knowledge building. Finally, things began to make sense. My body (and mind) – as much as my experience – exists (it has validity!), but it also exists as so much more than the self-contained individual that I had learned I had to become. Yes I was situated and contained, and the assertion of my voice and agency was a continual negotiation within hierarchies around me – but what a relief my body was real.

But while I was reading all the aforementioned scholars in class, I had also encountered this thing called the 'Internet' in my personal time. This thing called the 'Internet' was something I dialed into with a squeaky modem and *entered* via a personal computer. I wrote myself into existence on this Internet space. I eventually developed an online 'self' in variations of 'cyber-diva.' There was simultaneously an elation and an extreme loneliness in living this online persona: the speed of intellectual engagement – that is, when I wasn't being shut down or shouted down by people who felt they owned that space and claimed more technical, intellectual, and social knowledge than I was able to convey in text (and this wasn't necessarily just the self-identified male participants). The elation was based in the ability to extend my 'self' into social spaces of interaction beyond where my physical body could take me – even though the social spaces available through this connectivity were limited by those who had the socioeconomic and technical ability to access the collective Internet spaces. This was more than I had expected to be able to reach out to in my everyday life. Yet because of the promise of access, the lacks, the absences, and the gaps were more visible to me. Sometimes the promise did result in my physical body going to places I might not otherwise have thought to go to, and at other times it lured my physical body away from the physical outside – as I reached 'out' to the Internet-enabled world. It was a jabberwocky situation – all 'brillig' and 'slith toves' (Carroll, 2016). Yet there was a unique loneliness that developed that was akin to what Ellen Ullman describes in the following quote as that experienced by a computer engineer, in her essay "Come in, CQ."

> For an engineer, gaining comfort and skill in using these various bases – and creating the right online persona for each – is a prerequisite for surviving in the profession. Everything happens there: design, technical argument, news, professional visibility; in short, one's working life. Someone who can't survive by e-mail has to find another way to earn a living. If an engineer begins to insist on too many meetings or too many phone calls (woman-ish, interrupting sort of interactions), he or she will soon be seen as a nuisance and a "bad programmer." Early in an engineer's life, one learns to send mail.
>
> *(Ullman, 1996, 4)*

I was experiencing a different kind of loneliness but one that resonated with Ullman's description in some ways nonetheless. It was a renewal – in a different space – of the creative writer's loneliness when she is unable to find time to write or connect with her thoughts well enough to articulate them in the act of writing – when she is unable to visually see her articulations emerge in visual text form either in handwriting or through typing. If anything, the expectation of productivity in writing speeded up – frequency of the need to write and time to write came to be measured in terms of screen space and scrolling cursors and expectations of instant replies to what I was writing. It was also a loneliness of someone who had left her family and friends to come and live in a different country.

Notably, the time rhythm of this sort of loneliness shifted within a few years of my arriving in the United States. The shift from writing long handwritten letters using aerograms or several sheets of letter writing paper stuffed into an envelope and the waiting for replies, waiting for person–person phone calls, or dialing them myself to gradually exchanging emails and calling for longer periods of time happened almost imperceptibly. Suddenly one day – close to eight years after I discovered the Internet – I was no longer sending handwritten letters.

Parallel to my personal experience of encountering and becoming immersed in Internet-mediated everyday life, the socioeconomic scene also had shifted globally. Particularly, in relation to my personal and research life, India found an economic use for the Internet aka "the computer revolution" – the ability to "unbundle" tasks and outsource "hitherto untradeable services" (Gajjala, 2006, 1) involving immaterial and affective work of communication and relational tasks.

A visual rendering in a painting by the artist Vinodini Jayaraman (2000) illustrates the general middle- and upper-class sentiments of celebration around this economic mobility afforded by Internet connectivity. Her painting depicts the body of a kathakali dancer bursting forth through the computer screen. In a caption under the online image of her painting, *India 2000*, she notes,

> One of the best things to happen to India in the nineties was the Computer Revolution. In this picture the Kathakali dancer represents the Indian computer analyst rising out of the blue desktop and pouncing on the international scene like a strong and powerful tiger. It is as if the Gods themselves have showered their blessings on India's one billion people in the form of this computer boom.
>
> *(Jayaraman, 2000)*

This metaphor and even feeling of having been liberated into the outside world – into economic upliftment – is the start of an era of digital-based diasporic formations (Gajjala, 2012) entered into from Global South geographical locations. Formations of digital laborers and service workers – economic subjects – laboring for multinational and transnational corporations mostly headquartered in the Global North. In a manner akin to the engineers that Ullman writes about, these digital laborers carved out leisure spaces within the digital. Simultaneously, the World Wide Web began to turn into a marketplace. Digital laborers connecting from these Global South locations joined leisure users from the Global North in hanging out in leisure spaces. Gaming, instant messaging, and then later social networking sites (SNS) such as Orkut became available to them. Finally, when Facebook opened up to them, there was a mass exodus from other social networking sites to Facebook. Twitter became the tool of both activists and political campaigns.

These workers from the Global South in digital diasporas began to network and connect with free and digital labors in contexts of work and play. Bullying, trolling, and sexual violence through these spaces proliferated.

Material corporeality and digital erasures: Kaitlyn's story

I work through questions of material embodiment and corporeality a lot. Most often, I look to critical disability scholarship to consider my responses to those questions I am asking. I wonder how bodies situated in material space are differently defined at different junctures and contexts. As disability scholarship suggests, disability is a social construction that holds different meanings in diverse temporal and geopolitical contexts. However, disability scholars like Rosemarie Garland-Thomson (2009) and Tobin Siebers (2008) suggest that disability is not just a politically defined identity group; instead, the condition/s of the impairment/s inextricably affects disabled people's lived experiences. Impairments bring to a person's life sensations, behaviors, choices, desires, perspectives, actions, inactions, and reactions that exist along a continuum between (and potentially beyond) pain and pleasure. How do our political and economic systems make these impairments visible or invisible? How do we build an understanding of corporeality that centers impairment and disability as core to our conceptualization of the self and ourselves? And, relevant to our chapter here, how does this material corporeality transfer onto our digital selves?

Because I think about the ways our Western, Global North society imagines impairment and disability as fixed, as the binary opposite of 'able-bodied' (note: I prefer using the term nondisabled to trouble the social constructions reinforced by the term 'able-bodied'), as a problem to be cured, as an aberrant way of being that should be avoided at all costs, I think of how I have hesitated to 'make real' my digital self, to fully immerse myself in digital communities, to digitally come into being. At the same time, I fully realize the privilege that allows me to remain noncommittal in my process of becoming – that allows me to remain a digital specter of my material self.

Despite firmly identifying as part of the 'digital native' generation, online identity-making always seemed so far away from the groundedness of what I understood to be someone's subjectivity. Sure, I was making (and continue making) avatars on *The Sims* that imagined a heteronormative, nondisabled, neoliberal capitalist future for myself, but I kept those desires private, never joining online communities to test out these desires on others. I had a haphazard presence on MySpace, never fully realizing its use in my daily life. I made my obligatory profile, but never set an intentionality for my presence, opting to wait and see if anyone noticed me first. Of course, this was never a very effective strategy toward becoming the idealized version of myself that I imagined on *The Sims*. I was okay with remaining invisible, because it meant avoiding the negative attention I so frequently felt I attracted in material space.

My passivity online is a privilege of invisibility that I don't have in physical space. Throughout my life, I have been hyper-visible in most public spaces I enter. As a fat woman, I incur all the signifiers of fatness – undisciplined, transgressive, unfeminine – and I internalize those signifiers often, falling into neoliberal practices of self-control and consumer-driven solutions to my fatness, all the while knowing of neoliberalism's complex problematic that reinforces misogynistic control of women's bodies. For most of my childhood, I occupied collective space with a severely disabled sibling whose embodiment of her impairments laid bare her corporeal difference. We would become objects that possessed a "to-be-looked-at-ness," Rosemarie Garland-Thomson's (2002, 57) conceptualization of staring as a process that "creates disability as a state of absolute difference." To be hailed as the unknown – the incomprehensible – resulted in an affective reaction of not belonging, of intruding, in spaces not meant (and literally not designed) for my family. While my sister was the impetus for people's stares, our whole family was designated as the unknown as stares were displaced from my sister and onto our bodies, often mine.

I return to what I assert previously: that an ontology of a digital self has often seemed so far removed from my own subjectivity because of the ways in which materialized corporeal embodiment has dominated my understanding of myself and others. And so I have often discredited the meaning-making practices I engage in digital spaces. In my reluctance to fully flesh out my social media and online networking profiles and self-representations, I enact an agency that is born from my intersectional subject-position in material space. I have the privileges of whiteness – a knapsack of associated socioeconomic privileges that off-set my embodied differences. I am cisgendered, straight, married; English is my first language; I am a citizen of the country in which I reside. My chronic illnesses are, for the most part, invisible. And I was covered by health insurance up and until the Affordable Care Act required insurance companies to cover people who have preexisting conditions so that I can live with my illnesses in a way that

I choose. I extend these material privileges onto my digital self as I keep my self-representations to an almost apathetic minimum. These choices for myself conflict often with how I respond to the agency that is taken from others in the representative practices that emerge in textual and visual stagings like those we describe in this chapter.

Like Radhika, I notice gaps in who gets to control their digital presence and how their corporeality, and therefore, their subjectivity, is imagined and circulated. My sister's only digital presence, for example, is her obituary and the representations I create of her. Even her obituary is circulated by a search for my name. Because I am the person with the largest digital presence in my family, and the only one who uses social media to craft my own subjectivity – even as limited as it is – I curate her story for others so that she has a digital record that tells of her life, not just of her death. I have to be careful to work against the assumption that her death was the natural consequence of her disability – that death is a better state of being because of how much pain she lived with. I also don't want to mobilize affective connections that translate into pity for her or myself. In working on my dissertation, I have extended this process to think about how digital systems of representation intersect with the material embodiment of disability in relation to the analytic site of the Make-A-Wish Foundation of America. In talking with people who have been labeled 'sick kids' and/or their family members, I am working to complicate these digital stagings, so that the experiences of disabled people in material spaces align more readily with those online. I want to trouble the representation of the homogenized poster child that so effectively creates philanthropic networks whereby individuals become an idealized altruistic donor online.

Staging of the subaltern

The conceptual discussion in the previous section of this chapter was grounded in what it means to produce an embodied subjectivity/presence in relation and through the digital and how this shifts our ontological view of the body in general. In this section of the chapter, we engage in a description of online microfinance platforms and how they stage digital subaltern bodies. The conceptual discussion in the last section therefore frames the analysis in this part.

In earlier work, Radhika and collaborators have noted how the agency (the 'speaking') of the subaltern represented in such spaces is virtualized on platforms such as Kiva not because the digital is not 'real,' but because the digital subaltern is staged. Yet the presence and impact of the present on subaltern lives are real. Thus, her team argued that the virtual and real are interwoven but not mutually exclusive binaries (Gajjala, 2012). This interweaving happens through different sorts of offline and online labor and networking. Significantly, offline, the NGO labor force, micro-lending organizations, and infrastructures shape both the visual staging and socio-financial access for the staged subaltern. In more recent work (Gajjala, 2017), they noted how the staging of subalternity in such online microfinance platforms is also predicated on layers of affective labor done through feminized sociality from Global North geographies and urban, economically well-off Global South spaces. In all these instances, there is implicit a subtle differentiation between digital access and digital inclusion. Further, through these examples of the 'digital subaltern 2.0,' Radhika and her coauthors distinguished between the notions of 'voicings' and 'stagings' from 'voice' and 'performativity' (Gajjala & Birzescu, 2010). The distinction is based in the interplay of visible and invisible socioeconomic hierarchies at play across the continuum between building and enactment in spaces of digital globalization.

Digital bodies therefore emerge through highly contextualized situations; we understand the resulting stagings, then, as ways to interrogate digital financial infrastructures. We do this to better understand the different ways economic subjectivities (and linked, value-laden formations like citizenship and producer/consumer) are produced online and still have very real effects in material space. Staging bodies on these sites extend their voices into global spaces that are otherwise exclusive and inaccessible; however, the ways Kiva and other microfinancing sites control digital embodiment work in support of global economic power structures. The staging of subaltern bodies in new spaces (and through new mediums) becomes a way of entering subaltern populations into the neoliberal economic frameworks of individualism, self-control, and the linkage of private behaviors (including reproductive labor) to evaluations of an individual's credit worthiness (Federici, 2014).

As we suggested previously, Kiva is an illustrative analytical site for understanding microfinancing platforms' textual and visual stagings. It is a microfinancing philanthropy platform whose ostensible mission is to create mutually beneficial financial relationships between entrepreneurial business owners. In 2005, Matt Flannery and Jessica Jackley cofounded Kiva as "an online lending platform that allows individuals in the developed world to loan to small business people in the developing world" (Flannery, 2007, 31). Kiva's platform uses stagings like the ones we discuss next to support affective networks among Global North lender groups active on its site. With the tagline "Loans that save lives" (kiva.org), Kiva appeals to a neoliberal ethos that prevails in the Global North and suggests that lenders' financial investments make a significant impact by replicating neoliberal capitalism in the Global South. Kiva continues to expand its operations, and US-based borrowers have had a growing presence on the platform in recent years. These diverse borrower populations from both the Global North and the Global South provide us with the opportunity to compare the different ways these borrowers are presented as digital subjects. We consider in this chapter the formation of digital embodiments and the ways Kiva's stagings differently position these borrowers within the global economy.

In order to persuade lenders-in-waiting to donate money (that borrowers intend to repay), Kiva's home page links to popular lending categories so that lenders can identify particular borrower populations or industries that appeal to them. Bright and colorful pictures distinguish each of the links. For example, the category 'Women,' as of this chapter's writing, features an image of two women smiling in front of a neutral building. They wear vividly colored clothing and head coverings, and they emit warmth and openness in their postures and expressions. As we navigate to the borrower profiles of women, we see dozens of images of women framed in much the same way. In the following passage, we compare the profiles of women living in the Global South to those living in the Global North to illustrate how Kiva brings subaltern bodies into digital being in service of digital financialization. We identify elements of agency and interpretation, labor, and geopolitical mobility to think about how Kiva produces digital embodiments for its borrowers.

One of the ways we see digital embodiment differently emerge on Kiva for borrowers from the Global North compared to those from the Global South is the way in which Kiva staff intervene in the making of borrower profiles (i.e., stagings). Kiva contracts fieldworkers to interact with potential borrowers across the Global South. Their journals become the foundation of these borrowers' profiles. Kiva staff create verbal and visual content about borrowers in these profiles: this is the most critical aspect of Kiva's strategy to create authority and credibility within the world microfinance system. Not only is this a means to persuade prospective lenders of the viability of person-to-person microloans, to assure the transparency of the impact of the loans on clients' livelihood, and to foster a degree of immediacy between lenders and borrowers, but it also produces specific subjectivities that are informed by the general objectives of the organization. The profiles include biographical information about the borrowers and details about their businesses or business plans so that the overall content makes a strong case that facilitates website viewers' decisions to start lending.

The symbolic functions of the visuals are highly relevant to the degree that the contrast between absence and presence in the discourse produces othered subjectivities characterized by powerlessness, poverty, and piteousness. While the profile photos might remind visitors of social media pages, the photos of Global South borrowers are usually serious and stationary. The mise-en-scène is simple so that lenders focus on the figure of the borrower. The lighting is harsh and the photos are sometimes blurry. These are photos that Kiva staff chose to stage the borrower for lenders, not photos that the borrower would necessarily choose to represent herself. For example, Roziya's (2018) profile photo ("Roziya") shows her sitting in front of a window, bright light streaming in from the window behind her and shadows cast across her face. The room is simple and her clothing's neutral tones suggest maturity and an unassuming presence. While her cardigan has an intricate design, it does not showcase "the beautiful national dresses" her profile asserts that Roziya makes. Kiva staff are central to the making of her profile, and visitors learn that Kendra Thorogood was the Kiva fellow assigned to profile Roziya. Kendra's name and headshot appear in the center of the profile under the section explaining why this loan is special. Readers are led to understand that Kendra also wrote the profile's textual narrative – written in third person – and possibly even took the photograph. Her presence offers an authentic, first-hand approach to Kiva's outreach program; however, it also illustrates how much Kiva controls Roziya's access and embodiment on the site.[3]

We also see the ways in which discourses of labor, leisure, and mobility indicate how a person's digital entry links back to their movement, or lack thereof, in material space. Visitors to Roziya's profile learn that "she is married and has four children," for example. She is a seamstress and makes traditional Tajikistani dresses. She wants a loan to support her daughter's education. All of these biographical details suggest that Roziya labors in her home space and that this feminized and reproductive labor is valuable to her community. We also learn that Roziya is in her mid-forties and has worked hard "for more than 18 years" ("Roziya"), indicating that Roziya has been productive and responsible. However, her narrative begins and ends with her identity as a mother who needs lenders' help sending her daughter to university. In no way does the textual narrative suggest a future subjectivity for Roziya that extends her into spaces beyond the home. These elements indicate that Roziya's inclusion on Kiva is predicated on her reproductive success and good mothering. She is not going to use this money to leave her community or enter into new spaces.

Comparatively, Judi Rosen's (2018) profile ("Judi") suggests a different subjectivity and digital entry as a Kiva borrower. Conspicuous differences abound in the profiles of women located in the United States and those of women from the Global South. For example, Judi's profile is written in the first person. There is no mention of a Kiva staff member who developed the profile's narrative either in consultation with Judi or on her behalf, suggesting that Judi had more control over her staging than did Roziya. Additionally, and something noteworthy, Judi's profile includes her last name, making it easier for a potential lender to search for Judi elsewhere online. In doing so, we find that Judi has her own website that provides a more complex understanding of her life, business, and subjectivity. Her profile photo appears to be a selfie, further showing that Judi was able to control her staging in ways that Roziya was not. Lenders can identify with Judi in ways that extend beyond a financial transaction. She approaches them on a digital level playing field with a digital presence that preexists and extends beyond her Kiva profile.

Important to note, too, is that Judi's startup business fits well within a neoliberal economic framework. She is a self-described, size-inclusive denim designer.[4] Her work helps others use clothes as an element of corporeal subjectivity in material and digital space. She writes that her loan will help expand opportunities at her brick-and-mortar store to "truly showcase the lifestyle attached to the collection" ("Judi"). This illustrates how Judi's Kiva profile interweaves with her offline subjectivity: both corporealized identities coalesce within the formation of a pro-sumer neoliberal economic subject. Because Judi already presents herself as a neoliberal subject (she is white and thin, she consumes and appreciates fashion, and she produces consumer goods for others who also understand that a person's consumption practices link to their personal economic value), lenders can see her in themselves. Kiva does not have to work to modify her digital staging on their platform; she already stages herself digitally as a neoliberal subject at all her digital entry points.

Conclusion

This chapter worked toward an understanding of digitized embodiment and its interplay with material embodiment by examining the coauthors' digital entry stories and illustrative microfinancing stagings on Kiva's digital platform. Concepts of agency, geopolitical mobility, affect, and labor emerge as central concerns in our analysis of corporeality as it exists in both digital and material spaces. While our personal narratives suggest that digital spaces are a way that we control our process of becoming through our corporealized identities, our discussion of Kiva's stagings of subaltern women reveals that these presentations of self are crafted in support of global microfinancing infrastructures: the stagings align with neoliberal economic frameworks of self-control, feminized labor, and the formation of ostensibly inextricable linkages between private behaviors/actions and economic creditworthiness. Overall, Kiva's stagings (even those ostensibly controlled by borrowers themselves like Judi) provide an analytical site for exploring digital financial infrastructures and their investments in modes of digital embodiment.

Notes

1 The question of the subaltern that emerged in postcolonial scholarship (following Gramsci's [Hoare & Smith, 1999] articulation of the term in "Prison notebooks") returns in regard to Web 2.0 formations. Specifically, the Web 2.0 rhetoric of "inclusivity" that microfinancing platforms and non-profits integrate into their corporate models has become a new site of investigation into the questions originally posed by subaltern studies scholars in regard to academic representation the development of histories and herstories through "writing in reverse" (Beverley, 1999).
2 Original text reads, "Ces theories soulignent également l'implication directe des activités et des biens immatériels, tels que les l'affect et l'attention, dans les calculs économiques du capital" (Jarrett, 2017, 14).
3 Interestingly, during the course of this chapter's writing, Roziya's loan was fully funded and Kendra's name and photo were removed from the profile. This suggests to us that Kiva uses the authority of its westernized and majority white fellows to build lenders' trust in borrowers, but then removes their visible presence to later indicate that the borrower succeeded on her own to secure these loans.
4 Other US-based borrowers also market their startups that perpetuate neoliberal economic values – other clothing designers, makeup artists, skincare experts, and (health) food service entrepreneurs represent a visible majority among these borrowers. US-based borrower profiles that more closely resemble those common among Global South borrowers often highlight their immigrant stories. For example, Guille (2018) (no last name provided) emigrated from Mexico and wants to expand her toy business ("Guille").

References

Beverley, J. (1999). *Subalternity and Representation: Arguments in Cultural Theory*. Durham: Duke University Press.

Blackman, L. (2008). *The Body: The Key Concepts*. London and New York: Berg.

Blackman, L. (2012). *Immaterial Bodies: Affect, Embodiment, Mediation*. London: Sage.

Carroll, L. (2016). *Alice's Adventures in Wonderland and Through the Looking-Glass*. Ballingslöv: Wisehouse Classics.

Cheney-Lippold, J. (2011). A New Algorithmic Identity: Soft Biopolitics and the Modulation of Control. *Theory, Culture & Society*, 28(6), 164–181. https://doi.org/10.1177/0263276411424420.

Deleuze, G. (1993). *The Logic of Sense*. New York: Columbia University Press.

Derrida, J. (1996). *Deconstruction in a Nutshell: A Conversation with Jacques Derrida*. Edited by J. D. Caputo. New York: Fordham University Press.

Federici, S. (2014). From Commoning to Debt: Financialization, Microcredit, and the Changing Architecture of Capital Accumulation. *South Atlantic Quarterly*, 113(2), 231–244. https://doi.org/10.1215/00382876-2643585.

Ferner, A. M., and Pradeu, T. (2017). Ontologies of Living Beings: Introduction. *Philosophy, Theory, and Practice in Biology*, 9(4), 1–4. doi:10.3998/ptb.6959004.0009.004.

Flannery, M. (2007). Kiva and the Birth of Person-to-Person Microfinance. *Innovations*, 2(1–2), 31–56.

Foucault, M. (1977). What Is an Author? (Translated by D. F. Bouchard and S. Simon). In D. F. Bouchard (ed.), *Language, Counter-Memory, Practice: Selected Essays and Interviews by Michel Foucault*. Oxford: Blackwell, pp. 113–138.

Garland-Thomson, R. (2002). The Politics of Staring: Visual Rhetorics of Disability in Popular Photography. In S. L. Snyder, B. J. Brueggemann, and R. Garland-Thomson (eds.), *Disability Studies: Enabling the Humanities*. New York: The Modern Language Association of America, pp. 56–75.

Garland-Thomson, R. (2009). *Staring: How We Look*. Oxford: Oxford University Press.

Gajjala, R. (2012). *Cyberculture and the Subaltern: Weavings of the Virtual and Real*. London: Lexington Press.

Gajjala, R. (2017). *Online Philanthropy in the Global North and South: Connecting, Microfinancing, and Gaming for Change*. London: Lexington Books.

Gajjala, R., and Birzescu, A. (2010). Voicing and Placement in Online Networks. In M. Levina and G. Kien (eds.), *Denoting Danger, Connoting Freedom: Everyday Life in the [Post]Global Network*. New York: Peter Lang, pp. 73–91.

Gajjala, V. (2006). The Role of Information and Communication Technologies in Enhancing Processes of Entrepreneurship and Globalization in Indian Software Companies. *The Electronic Journal on Information Systems in Developing Countries EJISDC*, 26, 1–20.

Guille. (2018). *Kiva*. www.kiva.org/lend/1451225 (Accessed February 14, 2018).

Grosz, E. (1994). *Volatile Bodies: Towards a Corporeal Feminism*. Bloomington: Indiana University Press.

Hoare, G., and Smith, G. N. (1999). *Selections from the Prison Notebooks of Antonio Gramsci*. London: The Electronic Book Company.

Jayaraman, V. (2000). *India 2000 [Acrylic on Canvas]*. Ms. Jayaraman's Private Collection. Vinodini Jayaraman, 2002. www.silkepics.com/index.html.

Jarrett, K. (2016). *Feminism, Labour and Digital Media: The Digital Housewife*. New York: Routledge.

Jarrett, K. (2017). Le travail immatériel dan l'usine sociale: Une critique féministe. *Poli: Politique de l'image*, 13, 12–25.

Judi. (2018). *Kiva*. www.kiva.org/lend/1447769 (Accessed February 13, 2018).

Lessig, L. (2006). *Code: Version 2.0*. New York: Basic Books.

Nakamura, L. (1995). Race In/For Cyberspace: Identity Tourism and Racial Passing on the Internet. *Work and Days*, 13(1–2), 181–193.

Roziya. (2018). *Kiva*. www.kiva.org/lend/1467155 (Accessed February 12, 2018).

Siebers, T. (2008). *Disability Theory*. Ann Arbor: The University of Michigan Press.

Ullman, E. (1996). Come in, CQ: The Body on the Wire. In L. Cherny and E. R. Weise (Eds.), *Wired Women: Gender and the New Realities of Cyberspace*. Seattle: Seal Press, pp. 3–23.

4

Ubiquity

Paul Dourish

The term 'ubiquitous computing' names a program of computer science–based research that originated in a fabled Silicon Valley research laboratory located in California, USA, in the late 1980s. Articulating a singular and compelling vision of an alternative to then-dominant paradigms of personal computing, Mark Weiser, who directed the Computer Science Laboratory at Xerox's Palo Alto Research Center (PARC), published in *Scientific American* an article that was partly a manifesto and partly a progress report (Weiser, 1991). Weiser noted that early computing efforts had been characterized by large-scale mainframe computers that were shared by many users through so-called time-sharing technologies. In the 1970s, the time-sharing paradigm began to be displaced by a new paradigm of 'personal computing,' in which each person could use a computer on their desk that was dedicated entirely to their own use. Given the trend-lines of both computing capacity and digital communications, Weiser suggested that a third 'era' of computing might be just around the corner, an era of what he called 'ubiquitous computing,' in which a single user's needs might be met not by a single computer but by a whole host of computational devices – some large, some small, some encountered in the environment, some worn or carried on the body, some broad in purpose, some narrow in scope, and all communicating together in order to create a rich computational experience that might displace and update the vision of personal computing.

Weiser was remarkably prescient. Many of the technical advances that he envisioned have come to pass – and, indeed, many have been directly enabled by the programs of research that Weiser himself initiated. I am sitting in my office at home writing this document on a laptop computer that is communicating wirelessly with peripheral devices (keyboard and trackpad) and which sits beside an iPad and a smartphone, all of which communicate and share information with each other. Nearby, a small white box connects wirelessly to my home's 'smart' electricity meter, alerting me to sudden spikes in my energy use at home. Just outside the office, attached to the ceiling, another computational device monitors for smoke and, when it detects any, signals this over the Internet to my phone. The heating and cooling in my house and the irrigation system in the yard are all digital devices that maintain a pattern of connectivity and integrated signaling, not to mention wireless-connected bathroom scales, the way my phone tracks my steps, and the wireless-connected speakers through which I listen to music. From smartphones to embedded sensors, Weiser would seem to have anticipated (or caused) major shifts in our technological landscape. On the other hand, the world he outlined seems quite different than ours in many ways. It is a world without Google, but perhaps more importantly without Uber, click-work, and the gig economy, without the 'walled gardens' of Facebook and Apple's App Store, without unintelligible terms-of-service agreements and mind-bending data plans, without the Digital Millennium Copyright Act, Instagram spam, and Pokemon Go. At the same time, both the technical and the rhetorical strategies at the heart of Weiser's program reframed 'ubiquity' as a topic for computer scientists, communication scholars, designers, entrepreneurs, and cultural commentators for decades.

In this chapter, I will explore two related questions. Taking the topic of 'ubiquity' as the central one, my first question examines the contexts of those things that Weiser got right. What were the contexts within which Weiser was operating, and within which ubiquitous computing research came to develop, that helped Weiser to be right about those things that he anticipated? The second inquires into the contexts of those things that Weiser got wrong. In what ways are his vision of computational ubiquity and our experience of it dissonant? What was missing, and with what consequence?

I will take up these topics here through a series of thematic lenses – participation, fragmentation, data flows, and cultural ubiquity.

Ubiquity and the limits of participation

One of the anchors for Weiser's article – and a well-spring of ideas for researchers who turned his vision into an agenda for their own research – is the 'day-in-the-life' scenario of Sal, a fictional inhabitant of a world of ubiquitous computing. In stepping us through the details of Sal's day, Weiser demonstrates aspects of ubicomp's program and the potential for impact in daily life. By complementing his accounts of prototype ubicomp technologies already in development at Xerox PARC, the recourse to a fictional scenario allows Weiser to describe the scope of the program without being limited by available technologies, short-term solutions, or technological constraints. So, he can propose a world in which multimedia communication is already integrated into homes, artificial intelligence is integrated into cars, and the technologies that suffuse an office environment are already fully integrated and interoperable. All of these and more are parts of the digital environment that supports Sal's day, from getting her kids off to school to collaborating productively with her colleagues at work.

Given that the fictional setting releases Weiser from the bonds of conventional practicality, it is interesting to ponder those familiar elements that remain – like meetings, commutes, and email. Ubicomp is transformative, we are being told, but within limits. Indeed, one gets the impression that ubicomp may be transformative, but it is so primarily for a particular group of people: middle-class professionals in full-time, long-term employment, doing project-based work in high-tech workplaces, with a high degree of autonomy, self-direction, and responsibility for planning and executing their work – for people, in other words, like the researchers at Xerox PARC. The fictional flight-of-fancy that Sal's scenario represents might be a way to overcome the technological limitations of contemporary technology that constrain Weiser's account of his lab's work to date, but they seem not to push many other limits.

There are at least three possible readings of this reassertion of convention, and they're not mutually exclusive. One is that Weiser sought, as many futurists might do, to spotlight his particular concerns by placing them in a setting that would be conventionally familiar and legible to his audience. Another is that, influenced by the Participatory Design (PD) researchers working down the corridor, Weiser felt that he could only really speak to likely future scenarios quite close to home, ones in which he, as a regular participant, felt that he could have a voice.

A third is simply that the needs that ubicomp set out to address, at least in its early stages, were largely those of Weiser, his colleagues, and people like them. Turning their own lab into the prototype ubicomp environment – much as his predecessors in the PARC of the 1970s had widely adopted their own networked personal computing prototype, the Alto system, in order to explore its limits and capacities – meant that the problems which ubicomp would address itself were largely the problems that might manifest themselves to the researchers in their own daily lives. And yet the extent to which Sal's scenario is very much 'at home' for researchers at a place like PARC is striking.

Let me return briefly to that program of PD research. It's important to distinguish PD from the broader program of user-centered design, which is a staple of human–computer interaction research and of development settings like PARC. PD originates in the 1970s in the work of a network of Scandinavian information systems researchers who recognized that information technology was poised to have an ever-increasing importance in the workplace and who argued that, consequently, legislation that required the participation of factory workers and labor organizations in shaping workplace conditions meant that digital design efforts demanded similar forms of participation. They were motivated by concerns of social justice, equitable workplace governance, and cooperative engagement between management and workers, largely in industrial settings, and pioneered a set of techniques by which workers could be engaged directly in the design process. As technology, workplaces, and labor politics evolved, so did PD, but at its heart, PD goes beyond calls for user-centeredness to argue for the moral, ethical, and political importance of questions of representation and participation in technological design processes. From its roots in Scandinavia, PD had also developed into an international program, one in which a number of people at PARC, colleagues and interlocutors of Weiser's, played a leading role. Weiser was by no means unfamiliar with this work, although not deeply grounded in its nuance or practices, and doubtless saw the ubicomp program, as implemented at PARC, as engaged in a different sort of development. Still, the juxtaposition of PD and ubicomp turns our attention to the nature of participation in a ubicomp world. What does it take to be involved in the design of these environments? What forms of participation are sought or are possible? Who is represented, and how? What barriers to participation exist and how are they navigated or overcome?

These are always important questions to ask, but they seem, with the benefit of hindsight, to be more important than ever. If Weiser imagined that at some point in the future, once the basic technology had been developed and the problems shaken out, that PD-style efforts might help to introduce ubicomp technologies to workplaces in ways that took workers' concerns seriously, then reality has left his imagination behind in at least two ways. The first is that while Weiser's ubicomp was one in which a singular design vision could be worked through, today's ubicomp is brought to you by Apple, AT&T, Ericsson, Microsoft, Facebook, Google, Cisco, and Amazon. In other words, there are no singular authorities or design movers crafting the experience, nor any single site at which we might expect participation or representation to be concentrated. Similarly, while workplaces were the primary sites at which Weiser imagined ubicomp taking hold, the contemporary ubicomp experience spans domains – work, home, civic life, health care, media consumption, politics, education, law and justice, and family communication, to name a few – over which no singular authority operates. It is not that in this disparate and distributed environment, we have no point of leverage, or no place at which we might demand adequate representation and participation – it is that there are all too many, each of which affects only a sliver of the experience that ubicomp technologies bring for us. Finally, here, it seems important to note those elements of our current ubicomp experience that seem to have been curiously outside of the design focus for ubicomp altogether, including the institutional and regulative contexts within which these technologies would operate – the relationship between different network providers, for example, or the ownership considerations for data to be generated in our interaction with ubicomp devices, or even the jurisdictional arrangements for cloud-based computing services. It is almost impossible to find these issues discussed in the design-oriented ubicomp literature, despite the centrality of these arrangements to our daily experience of ubicomp in practice.

Ubiquity and fragmentation

This latter concern takes us to our second broad theme under the umbrella of 'ubiquity,' that of seamlessness, seamfulness, and fragmentation. The term 'ubiquity' carries with it claims to universality, to the erasure of boundaries, and to the leveling of access to information and services, technically, spatially, and perhaps also economically and politically. Indeed, these erasures and leveling would seem to be fundamental to the project and are manifested not least in the prominence and prevalence of appeals to 'seamless' interoperation, both in the research literature (e.g., Su et al., 2007; Dancu & Marshall, 2015) and in advertising copies from technology organizations. That said, Weiser himself was always conscious of the importance of seams and boundaries as elements around which social life is organized. Just as in everyday space, thresholds, boundaries, and transitions mark distinctions that matter for social life, so too in informational spaces might we need to be able to mark the difference between areas of administrative control, jurisdictions of influence, and transitions between one domain and another.

There are many different objects and units that manifest themselves in Weiser's writings and in those of his immediate contemporaries and successors – devices, notifications, icons, connections, servers, services, views, and more. Singularly absent, though, is one that has come to play a significant role in our contemporary experience of digital ubiquity: 'app.'

On my phone, I have well over 100 apps installed. Each provides some specific piece of functionality (some, redundantly). While the apps coexist on the device, the technical boundaries between them are distinct and hard to cross. Partly, that is because each app was designed in isolation; the designers of one app had no access to the thinking, expectations, or activities of the designers of the others. Partly, it is a consequence of the restricted resources available on a phone, where the operating system seeks to maintain the illusion of simultaneous execution but rarely allows multiple apps to coexist at the same time. Partly, it is a technical decision, made to improve the security of the device; by making it hard for apps to interact, the designers of the phone's operating system sought to minimize the impact that a malicious app could have on other apps or their data.

More importantly, though, while from a technical perspective apps are highly isolated from each other, they are experienced as a set from the perspective of a user of the device. Some of the apps installed on my phone come with the operating system; some others are well-known and widespread, while yet more are highly specialized or obscure. As a set, though, they might well be entirely unique; that is, it is quite possible that, despite the billions of similar phones deployed in the world, no other phone has exactly the combination of apps that I have on mine. The same might also be said of most other phones; in their capacities, they are generic, but in their configurations, they are highly specific. Here, then, is the second site of fragmentation: between the experiences of users of ubiquitous devices.

The flipside of any account of fragmentation here, though, is the question of how those fragments are reassembled into differently coherent wholes. A metaphor I find particularly productive here is that offered by Arjun Appadurai (1996) in his writings on globalization, where he introduces the metaphor of 'scapes.' Just as a landscape, when viewed from a particular vantage point, brings disparate elements (a mountain there, a stand of trees here) into alignment as a singular whole, so other elements of our experience arise independently but are fused together into 'scapes' through which we encounter them – mediascapes, financescapes, ethnoscapes, and more. At the same time, just as there is only one vantage point from which a particular landscape can be seen, each of these other scapes similarly acts to position those who perceive it. Appadurai's work gives us a different way of thinking about the questions of ubiquity and uniformity. It argues, first, that we need to see digital and other objects within a broader context in which different objects contextualize each other (different apps, different media forms, and so on); second, that unique positionings arise in consequence of these arrangements; and, third, that scales of the production of and encounter with media objects may be of quite different sorts. A notion of app-scapes balances our concern with fragmentation by recontextualizing individual apps or app experiences within a scape, a positioning whole. The varieties of ways in which a phone user might communicate with others, then, is not bounded by a single app but smeared across a set of them, but the set of apps that make up the individual app-scape is congruent with the broader contexts of communicative action.

Fragmentation, seams, and wholeness then take on a different form than that originally imagined. Weiser framed the problems of seams largely in terms of devices. In setting out a vision of computing "by the inch, by the foot, and by the yard," he argued that future computing environments would be characterized by the interoperation of multiple devices at different spatial scales. In this, he certainly seemed to anticipate accurately important aspects of our current computational experience. However, the issues of seams, seamfulness, and fragmentation operate almost orthogonally to these dimensions. Integration between phone, tablet, and laptop or desktop computer seems much less problematic than they might have been – as long as I operate within the boundaries of a particular corporate ecosystem or a particular app. I edit this file on my laptop, and it is instantly available to review or transmit from my phone; I turn off the lights in my home from my phone, and my tablet updates its display in coordination. At the same time, interoperation between components on the same device may be much more problematic; I may use my phone to connect to three different cloud storage services, but, supported as they are by independent infrastructures operated by competing corporations, there are no routes to coordination or interoperability there. The greatest degree of their cooperation is that they are available on the same device. It turns out to be the app-scape, not the device-scape, that poses challenges.

Ubiquity and the flows of data

Consideration of the app-scape and its corporate topology also draws our attention to a series of concerns about the flows of information and data that are part of the contemporary experience of ubiquity, if not visible in Weiser's futurist writings. This is, perhaps, a consequence of the dual nature of Weiser's key article, as both manifesto and progress report. As a manifesto, it attempts to enroll its readers for the vision that it portrays; as a progress report, it seeks to validate the directions that it outlines by discussing the prototype technologies already in use in Weiser's lab at Xerox. The fact that the first practical efforts in ubiquitous computing were roll-your-own prototypes developed inside a singular organization means that the kinds of organizational boundaries discussed earlier were never particularly visible; in consequence, the potential flows of information and data across such boundaries, and the problems of privacy, security, and access management that might be encountered at those boundaries, are similarly never visible.

Indeed, they remain largely hidden from view by the user interface models. In the interests of simplicity and smoothness of interaction, manufacturers prevent us from inquiring too far into how those problems are resolved. When I use my phone to turn my living room lights on, what communicative patterns have taken place, and which organizational boundaries have been traversed? Did my phone 'talk' directly to the lights across my network? Or did my phone send a message to a corporate data center, which in turn signaled the Internet-connected light switch? Which of these communications are secured or encrypted? How much personally identifying information flows along with them? No absolute answers can be given to these questions; the current marketplace for so-called Internet of Things devices includes products that have made almost any conceivable design decision in response to each of these questions. In that marketplace, video-based home security devices are perhaps those that make the boundaries most visible. Since most of these devices do not have the storage capacity necessary to preserve long-term video archives, it becomes clear that the data captured by the devices must be stored somewhere else, on the manufacturer's servers; and indeed, the business model of these devices depends on the idea that clients will pay a subscription in order to access the remotely archived video streams of their own activity. As the artist collective Telekommunisten phrases it, "there's no such thing as the Internet of Things; there's just other people's computers in your home."

Again, here, Weiser's view of ubiquity is a ubiquity of devices; our contemporary experience, though, is more of the ubiquity of data. It is data that can be monetized and that holds commercial value; devices and services are sold at discounted rates or given away for free in exchange for access to the data streams that our encounters with them produce. Advertising and the ability to target messages on the basis of highly specific and deeply segmented data sets have become the core value proposition but are entirely absent from Weiser's narrative. One might wonder whether this should not have been clearer at some point to researchers at Xerox, which for long produced printers and copiers but reaped the majority of its revenues from paper and toner, although in fact advertising and the monetization of accessible data streams remain almost entirely overlooked in the computer science research literature on ubiquitous computing even today.

The notion of data flows construed not as ways of getting work done but as revenue streams in themselves is one of a number of topics that gives rise to contemporary concerns about information privacy in the context of digital ubiquity. Digital ubiquity – not just wireless networks but social media and the move of services from offline to online – is often imagined here to inevitably erode long-established principles of information privacy for individuals and groups. The term 'privacy,' though, often obscures as much as it reveals. It is more useful, perhaps, to think about information practices, and the ways in which our many different orientations toward information – as something that we might share with particular others, as a means by which we might cement social relationships, as something we collectively recognize as off-limits, as a resource for navigating everyday life, or as a means to demonstrate our competence in different social arenas – will tend to situate us in social and cultural contexts (Dourish & Anderson, 2006). Think, for example, of the ways in which the recognition of a certain kind of information as being potentially sensitive (e.g., salaries) while other information is public (e.g., job titles) marks our competent cultural membership in different places. Helen Nissenbaum has reconceptualized privacy in terms of our ability to manage "contextually-appropriate information flows" (2009), pointing to the importance of context, of management, and of conscious action as elements of an account of privacy. The question in the context of ubiquity, then, is the extent to which the ways in which information flows between different sites and across different boundaries might become visible to those who participate in those flows.

Ubiquity and cultural presence

Ubiquity, for Weiser, and for those who have taken up aspects of the agenda that he set out, has manifested itself in three ways. One is a spatial ubiquity: a notion that computational services might be made pervasively available, distributed through the world, and available 'any time, any place.' A second is a technological ubiquity: the idea that interactive computational experiences might be coherently crafted out of the interoperation of many small devices and interconnected components, brought together to act in concert. The third is a phenomenological ubiquity: an experiential focus on the encounter with technology-in-use whose constant presence and availability renders it "ready-to-hand" in Heidegger's sense (Heidegger's writings had a strong influence on Weiser's thinking).

Any contemporary reckoning with digital ubiquity, though, must incorporate a fourth understanding, which is a cultural ubiquity. Computationally advanced and wirelessly connected devices are to be found not simply in many people's hands, pockets, and bags but also in our conversations, in our movies and television shows, and in our expectations. Only in the rarest of occasions (and with apologies for the fact that 'reception' is really bad around here) do we find ourselves these days giving visitors directions to our homes or offices; GPS wayfinding is merely expected. Or again, it is interesting to witness filmmakers struggling with the best ways to incorporate the ubiquity of phone-based text messaging into the visual narrative of films and television shows; while many of the strategies they adopt are awkward and intrusive, the alternative – to attempt to tell, say, an hour-long story about contemporary human connection in which digital devices play no part in mediating communication – is even more difficult to imagine. Early studies of text messaging among teens (teens then, office workers now), such as those of Grinter and Eldridge (2001), made clear just how quickly and how thoroughly novel communication modalities were incorporated into everyday practice and especially into the rituals of communication (so that, e.g., the absence of a 'goodnight' message between intimate partners would need to be excused). This is a ubiquity of a radically different sort.

Cultural ubiquity speaks first to the role that different sorts of technology and technological interaction might play in the cultural narratives or scripts that shape everyday interaction. As an illustration, consider an example from my recent personal experience. During a recent sabbatical, I spent two months in Australia, where credit cards are based on contactless technology. My US-based bank does not offer a contactless credit card, but my mobile phone does support the technology, and so my phone became my primary payment device, somewhat to people's amazement (since Australian banks were not yet, at the time of my stay, participating in programs like Apple Pay). However, the technological switch was not yet smoothly incorporated into everyday cultural practice. When one sits at a restaurant table after finishing a meal, with a credit card in one's hand or sitting on the table, it is visible and clear to the wait staff that it's time to bring the bill. Holding a phone in one's hand at that same moment, though, sends none of the same signals. Or, again, when the location-based game Pokemon Go was first launched, it provided a new interpretive frame for the behavior of children jumping around on the sidewalk looking at their phones and pointing them at walls, tables, and street furniture.

Where Weiser's picture and our own experience fail to match up is that, for Weiser, ubiquity was primarily spatial, while in the contemporary technological landscape it needs to be understood as cultural. It is not simply that technological mediation has spread throughout the spaces that we occupy but that it has come to pervade so many different spheres of life, from intimate communication in families to encounters with government and urban services. In many ways, the challenges for this form of ubiquity are greater than those of a spatial ubiquity and more diffuse; similarly, solutions, work-arounds, and adaptations arise more diffusely and with less coordination and coherence. Here, again, seamfulness and fragmentation seemingly arise in inevitable partnership with ubiquity, reconfiguring social relations through the uneven and splintered spread of patterns of action and conventions of practice – payment rituals, communicative routines, patterns of information sharing, adaptations, accommodations, and local arrangements.

Conclusions

The contemporary experience of ubiquity as a topic of interest for media and communication scholars arises in no small part as a consequence of programs of engineering research over the last several decades. This is not a technologically determinist argument by any means, because in many ways, I want to argue, it was the marshaling of rhetorical and cultural resources, rather than the birthing of technological ones, that has played the dominant role, in particular around the formulation of ubiquity itself – ubiquitous access, ubiquitous availability, ubiquitous connection – as a problem and as a goal.

A critical investigation of this program, both in its original framings and in its subsequent influences, might take up the question of the assumed boundaries of ubiquity – in terms of the groups invited to participate, or the nature of access, or indeed the switch from a technological framing to a cultural framing. Ubiquity turns out in these situations to operate within very specific contexts and spaces. Indeed, a focus on ubiquity tends in practice to mask a somewhat different process of reconfiguration, one that inscribes new boundaries and divisions and is characterized not so much by the development of seamless accessibility but rather by the creation and management of new forms of seamfulness. Examining these processes of reconfiguration at work provides an empirical foundation for unpacking the contexts of ubiquity in contemporary communication and media.

References

Appadurai, A. (1996). *Modernity at Large: Cultural Dimensions of Globalization.* Minneapolis: University of Minnesota Press.

Dancu, A., and Marshall, J. (2015). *Designing Seamless Displays for Interaction in Motion.* Proceedings of International Conference on Human-Computer Interaction with Mobile Devices and Services (Adjunct), pp. 1076–1081.

Dourish, P., and Anderson, K. (2006). Collective Information Practice: Exploring Privacy and Security as Social and Cultural Phenomena. *Human-Computer Interaction*, 21(3), 319–342.

Grinter, R. E., and Eldridge, M. (2001). *Y Do Tngrs Luv 2 Txt Msg?* Proceedings of 7th European Conference on Computer Supported Cooperative Work ECSCW '01, Bonn, Germany, pp. 219–238.

Nissenbaum, H. (2009). *Privacy in Context: Technology, Policy, and the Integrity of Social Life.* Stanford: Stanford University Press.

Su, J., Scott, J., Hui, P., Crowcroft, J., De Lara, E., Diot, C., Goel, A., Lim, M., and Upton, E. (2007). *Haggle: Seamless Networking for Mobile Applications.* Proceedings of 9th International Conference on Ubiquitous Computing (UbiComp '07), pp. 391–408.

Weiser, M. (1991). The Computer for the 21st Century. *Scientific American*, 256(30), 94–104.

5

Interfaces and affordances

Matt Ratto, Curtis McCord, Dawn Walker, and Gabby Resch

Design is increasingly part of the modus of social science and humanities disciplines, including communication and new media studies. On the surface, the fit appears straightforward. Design, like many interpretive fields, is deeply interested in the status of the human. It adopts and extends holistic methods like ethnography and phenomenological analysis to make sense of how humans and built and natural environments fit together. Equally, design can act as a 'third way' (Nelson & Stolterman, 2012), a go-between for interpretivist and pragmatic positions in the study of human society. For communication and new media studies in particular, disciplines in which production has featured as part of the pedagogy, design is particularly attractive. Among other benefits, it offers a potential bridge between the concrete technical skilling and pedagogies that are key to educational experiences in these disciplines, while simultaneously providing a rich theoretical and conceptual landscape from which to draw insight. Whether leveraged by communication scholars doing media archaeology to engage with the complex relations between past and current forms of media (Parikka, 2012), or by STS scholars to recover the agency of human decision-making in the production of seemingly natural 'facts' (Latour, 2008; Latour & Weibel, 2005), design concepts and methods find ever more purchase.

However, there are implicit normative commitments from the world of design that are at risk of being reproduced when an otherwise more critical stance should be maintained. In this chapter, we focus on one such commitment and its consequences: design's reliance on the 'user' as a primary point of focus/concern/attention. Specifically, we look at how the user has often been construed within design as the site through which 'the social' is encountered and addressed. The often unintended results of this construction can include individualistic and micro-transactional accounts of human behavior and, importantly, a reductive understanding of the 'interface' as a passive, static site where users and technologies meet. Such perspectives do not match well with deeply held concepts from communication and new media studies such as 'mediation' (Mcluhan, 1994; Bolter & Grusin, 1999) and 'mutual shaping' (Lievrouw, 2014). These ideas hold that the relations between humans and environments are complex, shifting zones of potential action where the boundaries of the human and the environment are co-constructed in the moments of use and engagement. This idea is not essentially at odds in design theory – in fact, design scholars have posited similar notions (Nelson & Stolterman, 2012). However, it is clear that design methods and practices, including such tools as the design 'persona' and related conceptual models, often unintentionally import a more reductive understanding.

Here, we argue that this is in part due to an initial mis-apprehension of a core concept – James Gibson's (1986[1979]) notion of the *affordance* – into design as the theory for human–environment relations. The affordance first entered into design practice not as a relation between entity and environment but as a property of things (Norman, 1988). While this generated an easy-to-implement way to think about the fit between humans and environments, such a reductive understanding does not fit well with the ideas of mediation and mutual shaping that remain core concepts within media theory. We argue that when taken to be 'simple,' the use of the concept of affordance can end up considering subject–object relations as simply involving sets of properties that need to be matched. This reifying move both denies a role for culture and is incommensurate with the deeper commitments of interpretivist fields to a more complex and dynamic understanding of human–environment relations.

Therefore, in the following sections we explore these moves and advance some claims about the value of a more reflexive approach to the incorporation of design into media studies and communication.[1] Ultimately, we describe the value of a reciprocal approach whereby as design is brought into media and communication, so too can media and communication be brought productively into design. First, we survey how design has been brought into fields like communication and new media, providing more explicit details of the potential mismatch noted earlier. Second, we unpack these ideas and reopen a notion of the interface as dynamic and relational. We focus on how the concept of affordance figures in contemporary design practice, starting with a genealogy of affordance theory that takes as its root Gibsonian ecological psychology. Third, we use examples from design itself and our own work to demonstrate how a fulsome idea of interface that can be gleaned from Gibson provides a more useful and appropriate concept to engaging with design within interpretivist fields. We highlight crucial considerations for any framework that reorganizes concepts from design in order to reposition the user and account for the complexity of culture and context. We propose a simple mechanism that can leverage these insights to reopen some of the often under-addressed considerations involved in nature–culture relations.

Finally, it is important to note that the problems we described previously are based not on design per se but on an inadequate understanding of design method brought without reflection into interpretivist fields. In fact, design's recent expansions, from a focus on products to a renewed emphasis on services and systems, entail heightened attention to challenges of social scale. Design often leverages deep knowledge and analyses of the materiality of our built environments in order to think through and across social relations. So too has media and communication studies begun to focus on infrastructures, maintenance, and materiality as a way of moving beyond individualistic accounts. Too great a focus on a semiotic and transactional understanding of affordances can encourage us to lose sight of their commensurate materialities. This does a disservice to both designers and media scholars.

Design and interpretive scholarship

 # design can produce individualistic notions of user

    # need to recognize that this is only design understood in a reductive way, making sure to show that design scholarship does indeed recognize and include more complex understandings of broader social relations.

    # highlight the incompatibility between reductive design and theories from communication (e.g., mediation, mutual shaping)

In this section we identify some cases where design is used as a method in communication and media studies, and other social science research. We elaborate on potential pitfalls that may be presented to interpretive scholars. In particular, we highlight commitments that emerge from contemporary design's understanding of 'the user' as a focal point to engage with societal concerns.

Design is a lens increasingly used within social science and humanities contexts. Digital humanities scholars, for example, attend to design when they create visualizations for data-driven humanistic inquiry (e.g., *Mapping the Republic of Letters*, a collection of interactive data visualizations, datasets, and published articles researched collaboratively; Ceserani & DeArmond, 2015), forcing humanities disciplines to directly engage with questions about the commitments underlying graphical design choices (Drucker, 2011). Communication and media scholars draw on design in attempts to overcome prior concepts of audience studies or non-mediational accounts of human-technology use (Nagy & Neff, 2015; Schrock, 2015). STS scholars use design as a lens through which to reconceive environments, moving from constructing by "matters of fact" toward shaping by "matters of concern" (Latour, 2008).

On the surface, design refers to practices of production and intervention. Through explicit action, design makes use of methods of inquiry for problem-setting and problem-solving. Design scholarship has frequently been guided by an understanding of design in this sense. Papenek, for example, describes design as "the conscious and intuitive effort to impose meaningful order," with the "ultimate job of. . . [transforming] man's environment and tools and, by extension, man himself" (1972, 4). Herbert Simon (1981, 129) proposes the activity of design as "[devising] courses of action aimed at changing existing situations into preferred ones." However, design *in practice* stretches how it is normatively and theoretically conceived. The dominant, modernist practice of design in the 20th century was rooted in the manufacture of products for markets regulated by consumer demand. In the context of consumer capitalism, the design of objects is heavily professionalized into discrete roles, including industrial designers, graphic designers, and interaction designers. The scope of design in this sense is extensive: almost all of the objects we encounter in our everyday environments are the result of industrialized processes of design, relying upon individuals in a professionally legitimated designer role.

Within professionalized spaces, designers create sharp distinctions between practitioners as "insiders" and purchasers as "outsiders." These distinctions are constructed along binary lines separating designer from user and expert from nonexpert. Similarly, Steve Woolgar and Jonathan Grudin have each traced how "the user" is (socially) constructed as a generalized other to stand in for a heterogeneous multitude of actual users, a tendency most clearly manifested in HCI's attention to this generic/abstract figure. Woolgar highlights how design is bound/undergirded by activities and practices which "attempt to define and delimit the user's possible actions" (1990, 57). Grudin's initial work in this area considers how the user is specified in HCI and traces the changing "levels" of interface design over time, from more system-centric to more user-centric (Grudin, 1990, 2017). Design approaches can therefore produce individualistic views, often predicated on the user as a particular site for attention, and interfaces as the site where users are constructed as a set of specific properties. Within design scholarship there is an acknowledgment of the tendency in product-oriented practices to build for individual consumers (Dourish, 2010).

However, contemporary design scholarship has identified the limitations of individualistic approaches. Within HCI, professional design has been criticized for reifying a logic in which "large scale phenomena can be reduced to the aggregated effects of decisions made by rational actors acting in the light of informed self-interest" (Dourish, 2010, 2). Scholars link this mechanistic depiction of individual users to neoliberal market pressures and capitalistic cost-benefit decisions: the technology market's structure and product release cycles lead to design for rapid obsolescence and cyclical purchasing (DiSalvo, 2012). Recent work in HCI and interaction design asks how, and whether, the user should be reconfigured, decentered, or more thoroughly integrated with their machine (e.g., Bardzell et al., 2012; Suchman, 2014; Forlano, 2016).

We turn our attention to what we identify as one of the root historical sources of the reductive and transactional configuration of the interface: the way that a misreading of the concept of 'affordance' from the ecological psychology of perception came to define the way that humans interacted with designed objects – through individualized and discrete transactions. To fit design practices into interpretive scholarship and to resource more socially and contextually informed concepts of design, we first critically reread the uptake of affordance into design, before returning again to Gibson's concept to rehabilitate a more ecological notion of affordance.

Affordance, design, and use in communication

This section provides an overview of the term 'affordance' with an emphasis on its canonical use in design. First, we review the history of affordance as a concept in ecological theories of perception, from its inception in the work of James Gibson – most notably in his 1978 work *An Ecological Theory of Perception*. This first cursory glance leads us to the notion of affordance as it came into the field of design, gaining purchase with Norman's translation of the concept from psychology to design in the late 1980s, before finding wide application amidst an early 2000s paradigm shift in HCI (Harrison et al., 2007; Norman, 1988). In this way, the contributions of affordance to the problems of design treated previously are demonstrated. As we argue that affordance can be productively rehabilitated rather than discarded, we return to Gibson's work to show how affordance can feature in a design framework that does not naturalize a transactional relationship between people (*qua* users) and objects but rather provides opportunities to expand our scope to the mutual shaping of people, technologies, and their environments.

Affordance has pulled a lot of weight for design theory and practice – why might this be? The most plausible answer is that affordance relates agents and their environments in a way that has been useful for design. What designers can find in this articulation of affordance is a language that goes beyond mere properties, focusing instead on how people respond to the design of encountered objects. While this has been extremely productive, we argue that this initial articulation has directly fed into the problems of individuation and transactionalism discussed earlier. This is not a problem with the concept of affordance *as such* but merely reflects the incompleteness of the received view of affordance in design. Affordance, we argue, is a concept that can make objects communicative and usable, allowing one to consider how objects relate to actions, while thinking about how those actions in turn configure larger environments.

Gibson, Norman, and the affordance

#Norman didn't get Gibson's idea of the affordance quite right!

In 1979, James Gibson's influential book *The Ecological Approach to Visual Perception* elaborated an ontological category of "affordance" and marked a phenomenological shift in the theory of perception away from "cognitivist" theories of perception (Gibson, 1986[1979]; Jenkins, 2008). In cognitivist theories, agents/animals interact with their worlds by abstracting from sensory data and creating mental models of their surroundings, projecting their conceptions back onto the world to create directives for action. Here, environments are immanent to perceptive agents and perception is a process of rational, or mental, computation.

By contrast, Gibson situates affordances within an "ecological" frame, explicitly treating perception as mutually constituted by the perceiving agent and their environment. Jenkins calls this blurring of the subject/object distinction "an operationalized presentation of ethology's fundamental principle: reciprocity between an organism and its environment" (Jenkins, 2008, 34). Relying on this reciprocity allows Gibson to step around certain prejudices that humans have about animals. In short, he believes that we can consider the perception of animals and humans in the same way because we do not have to refer to cognitive models – in all cases they perceive their environments in terms of affordances, which are readily apparent to them (Gibson, 1986[1979]).

The foundational articulation of affordance in design studies is popularly attributed to Donald Norman's book *The Psychology Of Everyday Things* (Norman, 1988, republished in several editions; see also Gaver, 1991; Jenkins, 2008). Here, Norman deploys a concept of affordance as "the perceived and actual properties of things . . . that determine just how the thing can possibly be used" (1988, 9). This articulation is middling in its fidelity to Gibson: it is goal-oriented (whereas Gibsonian affordances are simply possibilities), prioritizes a relation between perceiving subject and a perceived object, and describes a property possessed by a single object, rather than a relationship between subject and environment.

Norman's evocation of properties and functions belies his focus on design. He argues that although the "human mind" is already well suited to making sense of and acting in its environment, design should be especially concerned with making affordances obvious: "well-designed objects are easy to interpret and understand. . . [they] contain visible clues to their operation" (1988, 2). In this way, Norman places affordance directly into the matrix of design work: designers who fail to "signal" the proper use of a thing are to blame for difficulties, not those who would use them.

The conceptual motifs of the user-centric and transactional design practice are readily visible in this construal of affordance. Already we have the concept of a user – one who perceives an intentionally placed affordance that suggests a proper use. Affordance ensures that the object itself addresses the capacities of the user directly to disambiguate the object, which is defined in terms of a specific set of functions. Additionally, this notion of affordance recapitulates a cognitivist psychology: it sees affordances as a subject–object relationship where perception occurs against a framework of use, intention, or goals. While Gibsonian affordances are indeed the objects of perception, and do play important parts in the purposeful action of agents, an ecological theory must sharply distinguish the conditions for the existence of affordances from their perception, as well as from any notion of usefulness.

As this concept of affordance rapidly spread through design practice, Norman recognized and lamented these limitations. Speaking specifically about interface design, he argued that too much focus on the needs and abilities of imagined "users" (a term he would seek to do away with altogether) leads to paradoxically complex design. For Norman, the next step was to move from a functional task-oriented "human-centered design" (HCD) paradigm to a more context-aware "activity centered design" (ACD) (Norman, 2005). He saw HCD as too focused on adapting technology to user needs, meaning that not only those users with capacities differing from those imagined would be excluded but even if designs functioned well at the transactional static screen interface, they often failed to adequately support the overarching tasks, the activities, that people were trying to accomplish. Norman recognized that functionality was not something that could determine design, because functionality cannot be reduced to the aggregate of discrete tasks. Design could be more effective if it was distanced from tasks, allowing people to adapt to technologies, rather than vice versa.

The later development of Norman's thought has also touched back on the concept of affordance. In subsequent editions of his book, retitled *The Design of Everyday Things* (Norman, 2002, 2013), Norman addresses previous misconstruals of affordance, and attempts to separate the designed, communicative aspects of affordance from their original concept of a relation of subjunctive possibility between entity and environment (Norman, 2013, 11). To do this, he introduces the term "signifier," whereby "affordances determine what actions are possible . . . signifiers specify how people discover these possibilities" (Norman, 2013, xv).

Norman's call for a focus on activities and his return to Gibsonian affordance are both well taken. The concepts of activities and affordances both point the way to design vocabularies that abet a union between people, tools, and environments. Moreover, we agree that this shift does not entail a complete break with affordance as property or HCD and, as we show, can be based on a rereading of Gibson that specifically addresses the mutuality of subject and object.

#some of the ways that cognitivism presents itself in affordance can prevent us from transcending instrumentalist and transactional design paradigms.

Norman's return to a more Gibsonian affordance has not prevented his cognitivist interpretation of affordance from persisting and circulating – including in contemporary communications scholarship. One way to read this incorporation of affordance into media and communication scholarship is as a way of addressing pernicious issues within this domain. For example, the relational character of affordances skirts the object- versus human-centric focuses of the persistent determinist/constructivist dichotomy in favor of frameworks that seem to embrace mutual shaping (Nagy & Neff, 2015). "In other words, within technology studies, affordance has had to carry a weight counterbalanced to technological determinism" (Nagy & Neff, 2015, 2). However, the more cognitivist tradition is not always so easy to overcome.

Building on Jeffrey Treem and Paul Leonardi's interpretation of affordances as unique to "particular ways in which an actor, or a set of actors, perceives and uses [an] object" (Treem & Leonardi, 2013, 145), Schrock (2015) seeks to explicate "communicative affordances" as a way to hold a middle position between technologically determinate and social shaping perspectives in communications, particularly mobile communications. Acknowledging a different formation from Ruston (2012), Schrock advocates for "empirical communications research" enabled by formalizing affordances through technology-specific typologies (in his case of mobile media affordances). He proposes, for example, affordances such as portability, availability, locatability, and multimediality (2015, 1234). His view of affordance, which draws upon Gibson, is tied to "perceptions of the utility of an object" that are "triggered" by "environmental cues" (2015, 1230). Linking affordance to perceived utility places the perceived object in an instrumental and immanent relation to the goals of the perceiver, the goal being a cognitive entity that causes an affordance to exist, separating it from other, less useful environmental features. Schrock is correct to link the perception of affordance to intention, because this potentially helps move us away from naturalized accounts of perception as wholly determined by 'hard-wired' human biology. However, Schrock's sophisticated understanding still assumes the origin of any affordance lies in the agency of a human thinker. Such notions of affordance are therefore somewhat in tension with the more complex relations depicted in mediational theories of mutual shaping (cf. Lievrouw, 2014).

Return to Gibson

The aforementioned examples demonstrate a need to turn back to a concept of affordance more in line with the mediational theories core to communication and allied fields. One way to do this is to replace the implicit cognitivist theory of perception embedded in Norman's definitions of affordance with the more ecological view originally proposed by Gibson.

Norman views affordances as a way of mediating between a designer's understanding of an object, their "conceptual model," and the user's "mental" model of how the object can be used. Contrasted to cognitivist theories, ecological theories stress the situatedness of perception and, most importantly, the reality of relations between animals and their environment. For Gibson, affordances are those relations: they are what the environment "offers," "provides," or "furnishes" for organisms. Affordances are not simply facts or properties in the world; instead, they are relations between any given animal's capabilities and their environment. Recalling Darwin's finches, we see that environmental affordances differ as the birds themselves differ; affordances, although they are defined in terms of subjects and things, cannot be reduced either to a property of things *or* to some agent's ideas of their world.

Affordances are relationships between animals and their environments that describe the range of potential interactions between the two. For Gibson, an animal's environment is its "surroundings" and is distinct from the "physical world" as such. Environments themselves take on the character of affordances, limited by the perceptive capabilities of agents; the most tangible elements of this mesoscale are landscapes, rooms, and objects. In this way even the perception of affordances is afforded, for example, by sufficient ambient light (Gibson, 1986[1979]). Environment is a foil for any perceptive entity: animals perceive their environment, and their environment is just what that animal perceives – Gibson calls this "mutuality" (Gibson, 1986[1979], 8). Even still, as a noncognitivist relation unlike Norman's affordances, perceived affordances, and signifiers, Gibsonian affordances are sensible to agents not because of an understanding overlaid onto the world but rather *just because* of their own sensory capacities: "to perceive the world is to coperceive oneself . . . awareness of the world and of one's complementary relations to the world are not separable" (Gibson, 1986[1979], 141).

If environments are those things that surround animals, do two animals live in the same environment or each in their own? Gibson sees this as a serious ambiguity for ecological perception but wants to reject the idea that individuals stand at the center of their own private worlds. Gibson tries to reconcile this tension by claiming environments are shared because all individuals have the potential to observe it from any point:

> Insofar as the habitat has a persisting substantial layout, therefore, all its inhabitants have an equal opportunity to explore it. In this sense the environment surrounds all observers in the same way that it surrounds a single observer.
>
> *(Gibson, 1986[1979], 43)*

While this geometric solution provides an impetus for moving beyond an individualistic perspective of affordance, it also highlights a key ambiguity within Gibson's own account. Specifically, it remains unclear how individuals meaningfully share environments. Therefore, while Gibson goes to great effort to put the individual and environment on mutual terms, his conception of affordance remains somewhat bounded. If environments are understood to exist within the gaze of individuals, then objects are defined instrumentally. This extends to other people and animals as well; Gibson's idea of social encounters is as an experience of "one sequence of action being suited to the other in a kind of behavioral loop. All social interaction is of this sort – sexual, maternal, competitive, cooperative – or it may be social grooming, play, and even human conversation" (Gibson, 1986[1979], 42). We believe that this move, within the framework of affordances, reduces culture to a property of individuals conceived in aggregate. It is therefore not enough to simply reject Norman's reworking of affordance and replace it with a more Gibsonian ecological formulation. This then remains to be addressed, not just theoretically but also pragmatically – how can a notion of affordance be extended beyond both Norman and Gibson's to more fully account for the sociocultural context of mutual environments?

Alternative design starting points – decentering the human within theories of affordance

#The move away from an individually centered affordance, that reconsiders the relation of people and environments, also allows us to question the extent to which the concept of affordance locates culture as a property of individuals.

Recent moves within social theory toward the posthuman (Hayles, 2008) and nonhuman (Grusin, 2015) have theorized from relational and hybrid modes of engagement with the world. In this work there is a general emphasis on decentering the human to not have to "go through" the human as the obligatory passage when theorizing about our social world. In these theories, the human features as an implicit part of the environment, rather than the site through which the environment is produced (a view that to some extent echoes Grudin's (1990) early observations about the notion of "user"). Such a move seems particularly fruitful given the issues noted previously with both Norman's and Gibson's more human-centric theories.

Within design studies there are preliminary conversations about how forms of hybrid thinking that account for nonhumans might suggest new methods and practice. Laura Forlano (2017) begins to tease out new considerations through representative cases. These include Perdue reforming their 640 million chicken factory farming operation with the chickens in mind, the Whanganui River in New Zealand being granted legal rights as if it were human in order to recognize its status as an ancestor for a nearby Māori tribe after years of advocacy, and a number of robots increasingly taking on professional designations, including law firm partner. Forlano uses these cases to identify new questions that arise when what/who counts as 'the user' is rethought according to a hybrid mode. Her examples suggest opportunities to decenter the user from the focus of design activity. For example, Forlano (2016) speculates about the potentials for decentering the human in urban "smart city" contexts. Using concepts from STS such as the assemblage (Suchman, 2007), the cyborg (Haraway, 1991), and the hyperobject (Morton, 2013) to challenge assumptions within HCD, Forlano highlights the limits of design work that overly structures relations between human subjects and material infrastructures. Instead, she notes that design work that goes beyond simple solutions for 'human needs' allows an enhanced capacity to engage ethically with the socio-material complexities of the city.

 # Extending from the examples above, there are additional trends of the decentering of the user/ person: Haraway's cyborg (1991), Dumit's Writing the Implosion (2014) Barad's 'agential realism' (2007).

Similarly, Erik Rietveld and Julian Kiverstein explore the possibilities for social interaction offered by the environment through their work on "social affordances," explicitly framed as "relations between aspects of a material environment and abilities available in a form of life" (Rietveld & Kiverstein, 2014, 335). They argue for making a wider range of affordances available to humans and nonhumans. Drawing on Gibson's acknowledgment "that affordances include the whole domain of social significance" (Gibson, 1986[1979], quoted in Rietveld & Kiverstein, 2014, 343), they attempt to design for culture rather than for individuals. With this relational and expansive account of affordances, Rietveld and Kiverstien suggest that environments count *only* in relation to available abilities for that life (p. 339). For humans, this also opens affordances to include the abilities and sociocultural practices within which we are socialized.

For example, in their 2014 installation, *The End of Sitting* (RAAAF, 2015), Rietveld and Kiverstein materially engage this enhanced concept of affordance. Investigating possibilities for radically changing the work environment, the two design a "standing office" rather than "standing desk," sculpting a landscape of "uncompromising materiality" marked by excavated spaces and sloping paths to accommodate bodies held in different positions for moments over space. They see this work as inviting affordances or "solicitations" for skillful engagement in the situation (see https://erikreitveld.com/2014/12/09/enactive-art-installation-the-end-of-sitting/). While these affordances are still designed by Reitveld and Kiverstein to solicit action and response by individuals at work, their intent is to produce a potential for action rather than a 'fit' between individual and environment. Specifically, they redirect our attention away from a simple understanding of 'mutuality' as a relation between physical environmental resources and material properties of the human body. Instead, they posit that affordances link "skillful activities in sociocultural practices and the material resources exploited in those practices" (Rietveld & Kiverstein, 2014, 326.). Rietveld and Kiverstein go further, situating skill within a broader context rather than as an attribute of an individual. Here, skill becomes the capacity to reform one's own behavior according to the specific socio-material context in which one's activity is bound. Affordances, then,

> are not relative to the abilities of a particular individual who actually perceives or detects the affordance. . . [they are] . . . relative to the skills available in the practice . . . to the abilities available in a form of life as a whole.
>
> *(2014, 337)*

We find these two moves particularly evocative for rethinking the affordance in ways that better situate it within interpretive social sciences and humanities generally and media studies specifically.

Conclusion

Design approaches that decenter the human or those that focus more intently on the links between sociocultural practice and materiality both offer an alternative to the more individualistic and binary subject/object relations described by many traditional accounts of affordance.

As we have elaborated previously, the key problem with a theory of design centered on affordance is the way in which the relational structure of affordance requires a direct apprehension of the object by a subject. Despite efforts to skirt the need for a "cognitivist" companion to the phenomenological character of affordance (Jenkins, 2008), its use within the context of design makes the affordance itself seemingly about the object, recalling closely the almost intentional essence of objects signified by parent concepts like *afforderungscharacter* (demand characteristic).

We made a claim that affordance and design have been well linked because both affordance and design require/are generated by transactional accounts of subject–object relations, and this underlying synergy makes affordance a particularly appealing concept for designers. Undoubtedly, design was well served by an individualistic account of users and objects for a time. There is a need to widen the scope of what is included in the ambit of designers. This is not a new call; we see it in the works of those from within design who have struggled with its reductive, often market-driven requirements (e.g., Papanek, 1972; Gaver, 1991; Dunne & Raby, 2013; Forlano, 2016) as well as in the work of many of the other scholars we have cited here.

Scholars who wish to engage with design approaches can and should do so. There is much to value in the combination of design approaches and concepts and those from media studies. We do not need to discard the notion of affordance but reground it in a theory of culture that places humans within a system of culturally communicated affordances that mediate interactions. This regrounding of affordance requires only that we reincorporate culture by disregarding the naive realist undertones in classic notions of affordance.

> # the problem isn't that affordance is merely individualistic, but that it/we tend to naturalize cultural difference/diversity of environments. Mediational theories help insulate us against this inclination. S-O [self and other] are natural vs S-O are mediated by tools/cultural. Being is Absolutely Mediated!

Note

1 Editor's Note: In this chapter, Ratto and his colleagues offer a series of reflections on the growing role of design in mediated communication, especially via digital platforms and systems. They explore pivotal concepts (e.g., the interface and the affordance) and methods that have been imported from design studies into analyses of digital media and communication. These have brought often-unexamined assumptions with them about the nature of communication (such as human actors as 'users') and the implications for the material conditions and socio-technical systems that support them (i.e., communication infrastructure; see Slota et al., this volume). The chapter takes an unconventional form, alternating between scholarly argument and annotations, probes or 'sidebars' (noted with hashmarks and boxed) which – in line with the design studies approach – suggest alternate topics or points for further development.

References

Barad, K. (2007). *Meeting the Universe Halfway: Quantum Physics and the Entanglement of Matter and Meaning.* Durham: Duke University Press.

Bardzell, S., Bardzell, J., Forlizzi, J., Zimmerman, J., and Antanitis, J. (2012). *Critical Design and Critical Theory: The Challenge of Designing for Provocation.* Conference on Designing Interactive Systems.

Bolter, J. D., and Grusin, R. (1999). *Remediation: Understanding New Media.* Cambridge, MA: MIT Press.

Ceserani, G., and DeArmond, T. (2015). *British Architects on the Grand Tour in Eighteenth-Century Italy: Travels, People, Places* [Palladio Components, HTML, CSS, Javascript, JSON, and Markdown files]. Stanford Digital Repository. http://purl.stanford.edu/ct765rs0222.

DiSalvo, C. (2012). *Adversarial Design.* Cambridge, MA: MIT Press.

Dourish, P. (2010). HCI and Environmental Sustainability: The Politics of Design and the Design of Politics. In K. Halskov and M. G. Petersen (eds.), *DIS 2010: Proceedings of the 8th ACM Conference on Designing Interactive Systems.* Århus, Denmark. New York: Association for Computing Machinery, pp. 1–10, August 16–20.

Drucker, J. (2011). Humanities Approaches to Graphical Display. *Digital Humanities Quarterly,* 5(1), 1–21.

Dumit, J. (2014). Writing the Implosion: Teaching the World One Thing at a Time. *Cultural Anthropology*, 29(2), 344–362.

Dunne, A., and Raby, F. (2013). *Speculative Everything: Design, Fiction, and Social Dreaming*. Cambridge, MA: MIT Press.

Forlano, L. (2016). Decentering the Human in the Design of Collaborative Cities. *Design Issues*, 32(3), 42–54.

Forlano, L. (2017). Posthumanism and Design. *She Ji: Journal of Design, Economics and Innovation*, 3(1), 16–29, Spring.

Gaver, W. W. (1991). *Technology Affordances*. Edited by S. P. Robertson, G. M. Olson, and J. S. Olson. CHI '91: Proceedings of the SIGCHI Conference on Human Factors in Computing Systems. Association for Computing Machinery, New Orleans, LA and New York, pp. 79–84, April 27–May 2.

Gibson, J. J. (1986[1979]). *The Ecological Approach to Visual Perception* (Reprint ed.). Hillsdale, NJ and London: Lawrence Erlbaum Associates (Originally published by Houghton Mifflin, Boston, MA).

Grudin, J. (1990). *The Computer Reaches Out: The Historical Continuity of Interface Design*. CHI '90: Proceedings of the SIGCHI Conference on Human Factors in Computing Systems, Association for Computing Machinery, Seattle, WA and New York, pp. 261–268, April 1–5.

Grudin, J. (2017). *From Tool to Partner: The Evolution of Human-Computer Interaction*. San Rafael, CA: Morgan & Claypool.

Grusin, R. (ed.). (2015). *The Nonhuman Turn*. Minneapolis: University of Minnesota Press.

Haraway, D. (1991). A Cyborg Manifesto: Science, Technology, and Socialist-Feminism in the Late Twentieth Century. In *Simians, Cyborgs and Women: The Reinvention of Nature*. New York: Routledge.

Harrison, S., Tatar, D., and Sengers, P. (2007). *The Three Paradigms of Human-Computer Interaction*. CHI 2007: Reach Beyond. Proceedings of the Conference on Human Factors in Computing Systems. Association for Computing Machinery, San Jose, CA, April 28–May 3.

Hayles, N. K. (2008). *How We Became Posthuman: Virtual Bodies in Cybernetics, Literature, and Informatics*. Chicago: University of Chicago Press.

Jenkins, H. S. (2008). Gibson's 'Affordances': Evolution of a Pivotal Concept. *Journal of Scientific Psychology*, 12, 34–45, December.

Latour, B. (2008). *A Cautious Prometheus? A Few Steps Toward a Philosophy of Design (with Special Attention to Peter Sloterdijk)*. Networks of Design: Proceedings of the 2008 Annual International Conference of the Design History Society (UK), University College Falmouth, Universal-Publishers, Boca Raton, FL, pp. 2–10, September 3–6.

Latour, B., and Weibel, P. (eds.). (2005). *Making Things Public: Atmospheres of Democracy*. Cambridge, MA and Karlsruhe: MIT Press.

Lievrouw, L. A. (2014). Materiality and Media in Communication and Technology Studies: An Unfinished Project. In T. Gillespie, P. J. Boczkowski, and K. A. Foot (eds.), *Media Technologies: Essays on Communication, Materiality, and Society*. Cambridge, MA: MIT Press, pp. 21–51.

McLuhan, M., and Lapham, L. H. (1994). *Understanding Media: The Extensions of Man* (Reprint ed.). Cambridge, MA: MIT Press.

Morton, T. (2013). *Hyperobjects: Philosophy and Ecology After the End of the World*. Minneapolis: University of Minnesota Press.

Nagy, P., and Neff, G. (2015). Imagined Affordance: Reconstructing a Keyword for Communication Theory. *Social Media & Society*, 1(2), 1–9, July–December.

Nelson, H., and Stolterman, E. (2012). *The Design Way: Intentional Change in an Unpredictable World*. Cambridge, MA: MIT Press.

Norman, D. A. (1988). *The Psychology of Everyday Things*. New York: Basic Books.

Norman, D. A. (2002). *The Design of Everyday Things* (1st paperback ed.). New York: Basic Books.

Norman, D. A. (2005). Human-Centered Design Considered Harmful. *Interactions*, 12(4), 14–19, July–August.

Norman, D. A. (2013). *The Design of Everyday Things* (revised and expanded ed.). New York: Basic Books.

Papanek, V. (1972). *Design for the Real World: Human Ecology and Social Change*. London: Thames and Hudson.

Parikka, J. (2012). *What Is Media Archaeology?* Cambridge and Maldon, MA: Polity Press.

RAAAF (Rietveld-Architecture-Art-Affordance). (2015). The End of Sitting. *Harvard Design Magazine*, 40, 180–181.

Rietveld, E., and Kiverstein, J. (2014). A Rich Landscape of Affordances. *Ecological Psychology*, 26(4), 325–352.

Ruston, S. W. (2012). Calling Ahead: Cinematic Imaginations of Mobile Media's Critical Affordances. In N. Arceneaux and A. P. Kavoori (eds.), *The Mobile Media Reader*. New York: Peter Lang, pp. 23–39.

Schrock, A. R. (2015). Communicative Affordances of Mobile Media: Portability, Availability, Locatability, and Multimediality. *International Journal of Communication*, 9, 1229–1246.

Simon, H. (1981). *The Sciences of the Artificial* (2nd ed., revised and enlarged ed.). Cambridge, MA: MIT Press.

Suchman, L. (2007). Feminist STS and the Sciences of the Artificial. In *New Handbook of Science and Technology Studies*. Cambridge, MA: MIT Press.

Suchman, L. (2014). Mediations and Their Others. In T. Gillespie, P. J. Boczkowski, and K. A. Foot (eds.), *Media Technologies: Essays on Communication, Materiality, and Society*. Cambridge, MA: MIT Press, pp. 129–137.

Treem, J. W., and Leonardi, P. (2013). Social Media Use in Organizations: Exploring the Affordances of Visibility, Editability, Persistence and Association. *Annals of the International Communication Association (Communication Yearbook 36)*, 36(1), 143–189.

Woolgar, S. (1990). Configuring the User: The Case of Usability Trials. *The Sociological Review*, 38(1 supp), 58–99.

6

Hacking

Finn Brunton

Hack. The word is a noun, a verb, an adjective. It is a professional title and a criminal indictment and a celebration and a pejorative. It is applied to developing software, exploiting software, collecting data, manipulating social networks, working for and against companies, for and against governments, making nice things and being the reason we can't have nice things. Obama dismissively referred to Edward Snowden as 'some hacker' – an outsider exfiltrating data by exploiting technology, without the moral role of the whistleblower – while his administration hosted 'civic hackathons' and promoted a 'culture of hacking.' Facebook fought the threat of 'hacking Facebook' (manipulating metrics or collecting information on their users) while hiring 'hackers' (virtuosic, inventive coders) and celebrating 'the Hacker Way': 'an approach to building that involves continuous improvement and iteration' (Zuckerberg, 2012). A hack can colloquially mean a brilliant, elegant, lateral solution to a programming challenge, or a crude, good-enough fix in the context of constant development – 'move fast and break things,' to take another Facebook credo. Hacking has been closely connected with the creation of the culture, technology, and philosophy of free and open-source software, and with the secretive manipulation of national elections. How can these many meanings be reconciled?

In this chapter, I will assemble what I argue are the most significant meanings of this term through a vocabulary of *actions*. Using both accounts of self-professed hackers, and assembling the literature of the study of hacking, I argue that hacking is best understood as a distinct technological way of being in the world, which we can see most clearly in a set of practices around the making, breaking, and sharing of tools, machines, communities, and systems.

Following this structure of actions avoids the confusion of this overapplied term, sidestepping the merely pejorative or vacuously positive, and helps us see what it is that hacking consistently means. By identifying and grouping research into hacking by types of action we can see hacking outside computing and telecommunications: in biotechnology, law and policy, the creation and management of spaces and communities, even philosophy and cooking. The rest of this chapter will organize our approach to hacking around eight different components of the hacker vocabulary of action: getting and giving access; tinkering and reverse engineering; recursive tooling; commoning; making nonstandard things; performing virtuosity; defining and policing hackerdom; and social engineering. Not every hacker engages in every one or even most of these forms of action. Some were more prevalent at one time than another. Some blur a bit from one to the next but have unique, distinctive traits. Together, these constitute the action, the doing, that makes hacking what it is.

Getting and giving access

This is arguably the foundational act of hacking; the other possibility, which has to do with pranks, is part of the last of the eight actions. A thread that runs through popular, scholarly, and personal accounts of being a hacker is the act of *getting access:* to computers, to telecommunications systems, to knowledge, to source code, to tools, to the inner workings of machines and networks, to accounts with escalated privileges, to secrets and classified information. This thread is everywhere intertwined with *giving access:* with sharing, circulating, and further distributing one's access – providing passwords, how-to guides, commented code, phone numbers, files, specs, standards, and specialized screwdrivers and spatulas for getting inside the cases and containers of the technology.

Many seemingly disparate elements that are recognizably part of hacker culture come together in this fundamental action. The first point of Steven Levy's summary of the 'hacker ethic' as he described it in the early days of hacking at the Massachusetts Institute of Technology (MIT) is: 'Access to computers – and anything which might teach you something about the way the world works – should be unlimited and total. Always yield to the Hands-on Imperative!' (Levy, 1984, 28). As with all of the entries in our vocabulary of hacker action, *getting and giving access* fuses abstract beliefs with practical goals and activities (see also Thomas, 2006, on hackers and getting access to secrets). The hands-on imperative can explain the popularity of locksport – competitive lock-picking – in the hacker community. One of the liveliest corners of the biannual Hackers on Planet Earth conference is the area devoted to picking locks, where participants can get training and face challenges from padlocks to an entire payphone (personal observation). Locks are very sophisticated technological puzzles – riddles in manufactured form – that reward cleverness, persistence, logical problem-solving, and focus; they also happened to often prevent access to computers, telephone equipment, and other interesting gear. The same nascent hackers interested in picking locks in the 1970s were also interested in the pre-Internet Bulletin Board System (BBS), where 'discourses and texts about hacking were ubiquitous' (Coleman, 2013, 30; see also Driscoll, 2016). BBSs were likewise about getting and giving access: to information, including information about getting further information, with the fundamentals of hacking into remote systems, phone numbers for other more distant BBSs, typed-up *samizdat* textfiles of science fiction stories and conspiracy documents – and instructions in lockpicking. For the subculture of phone phreaks (Lapsley, 2013) – another fecund space for what hacking would become – the practical benefit of free long-distance phone calls, which enabled 'party line' communities to form among far-flung proto-hackers, was secondary to the act of *getting access*, not just to the phone network itself but to knowledge about it: they knew AT&T's system even better than her own engineers.

This fundamental action had an essential moral dimension (Coleman puts it in the context of the political history of liberalism [2013, 116–122]): from access, from the hands-on imperative, came knowledge and understanding – and with them, the responsibility of sharing knowledge with others in turn even if one faces legal consequences for doing so. One of the foundational objects of hacker inquiry, the Unix operating system ('our Gilgamesh epic,' Neal Stephenson called it in his essay on hackers and the design of operating systems [1999, 88]), was the property of Bell Labs. It circulated through generations of photocopies of an educational commentary on the source code: *Lions' Commentary on UNIX*, very likely the most copied book in the history of computer science – you would make one copy for yourself and another for your friends (Lions, 1977). (Unix and the work of giving access will come up again later, in 'Commoning,' in the context of free, libre, and open-source software.) The act, and the conviction, of giving and getting access has far-reaching consequences; it can be found even in very early and hacker-adjacent documents and projects, like the *Whole Earth Catalog* and the cyberculture movement chronicled by Fred Turner, which was premised on 'access to tools' (Turner, 2008). It appears in latter-day initiatives, like the One Laptop Per Child (OLPC) project, which sought to manufacture a cheap laptop whose design – built for tinkering and creating one's own software in an open-source framework – was explicitly meant to foster a new generation of hackers. Begun at MIT, like the word 'hacking' itself, it was a vision, combining hubris and altruism: that giving access was all you needed to start children on the path to hacking.

Tinkering and reverse engineering

The OLPC was a dream of giving access: not only to computing as such, or some suite of applications, or the Internet, but to a machine that invited *tinkering*. This is the second of the eight parts of the hacker vocabulary, and one that can be described more briefly than the first. It is two faces of the same phenomenon, a hands-on facet of getting access: the drive to take apart, to fiddle, to modify, to take pre-existing technologies and figure out how they work and how they can be made to work differently. It is a category of action we can partially observe in negative, through all the components developed and deployed by manufacturers and corporations to keep people out. The hacker drive to tinker and reverse engineer, particularly with electronics and digital technologies, is reflected in the prevalence of esoteric screws – pentalobe, hexaloblular – glued-down (rather than screwed-in) panels, holographic tape and other 'tamper-evident' details, warnings of 'no user-serviceable parts inside,' nonstandard connectors and proprietary drivers, and encrypting the traffic between chips on a device. Whether used to protect a digital rights management (DRM) scheme to control the circulation of content, or to prevent competitors from cheaply duplicating a device, hackers often take these components as an affront and a challenge. What could be more interesting than out-thinking an entire company's worth of engineers and security specialists?

Bunnie Huang is one of the preeminent examples of this area of hacker activity: among other exploits, he famously hacked the Microsoft Xbox – figuring out and unlocking how it secured its internal communications – and has produced close analysis of the vulnerabilities of digital storage systems like microSD cards. 'Without the right to tinker and explore,' Huang wrote, 'we risk becoming enslaved by technology; and the more we exercise the right to hack, the harder it will be to take that right away' (2013, np). Huang makes clear throughout his work how intertwined these two activities are. Many hacker stories begin with tinkering, trying to fix some minor problem, or get a device or program to do what it wasn't exactly built to do, and in pursuit of that goal end up reverse engineering the whole of the object's operations; others involve a massive project of 'undesigning' and reverse engineering some elaborate apparatus so it can be playfully tinkered with. The tinkering can sometimes be for the sake of straightforward goals, like 'overclocking,' making chips and computing architectures deliver faster and more powerful performance than their specifications suggest. But often it can be for more quixotic goals – complex for the sake of being complex, impressing other hackers who understand how demanding such a trick was to pull off. A classic example of the latter is getting the classic video game *Doom* running on some ridiculously inappropriate and unlikely platform: on a Kodak digital camera from the early 2000s, an ATM, a seatback in-flight entertainment system, the screen of an MP3 player, even a printer's display.

To take a light-hearted example, consider hacker Natalie Silvanovich, who has done a series of in-depth projects to document and completely understand tamagotchis – yes, the keychain-sized 'artificial pets' that live on LCD screens, fed and pampered through a few buttons (Silvanovich, n.d.). Silvanovich's reverse engineering efforts including using nitric acid, microscopes, ROM dumps, and painstaking analysis to access and decode the tamagotchi hardware and software to 'answer the "deeper questions" of Tamagotchi life.' Her project entails applying a full toolkit (literally and figuratively) of hacker training and techniques to a deliberately fun and silly goal – but one with serious implications, a part of the cultural continuity of hacking, from the phone phreaks mapping out Bell Telephone's network to the people who got Linux running on the Nintendo Switch handheld gaming console earlier this year (Julie Cohen has analyzed the question of a limited right to self-help this raises: 'freedom to tinker,' or 'the right to hack' [2012, 219]). To be able to reverse engineer, and to open devices and systems to tinkering, is to expand the spaces where hackers can take action and where future hackers will emerge.

Recursive tooling

Bunnie Huang has also worked as a manufacturer, focusing on producing 'open hardware' products which encourage their own user modification, reinvention, and development. One of the best examples of this kind of product, Huang's Novena laptop, leads us into the third part of the hacker vocabulary of actions: the reflective project of making the tools you need to make the tools you need for the creation, modification, and tinkering you want to do. Where most laptops are sealed and inaccessible to the user, Huang's is an open box of components: to tilt the screen, you have to expose all the internals. To get it to do anything you have to install parts and an operating system and figure out how to get the components to interoperate: to get to the stage where you could, for instance, compose an email, you would have to develop expertise and install the systems to get the box on the Internet with a working mail client; to get it on the Internet, you would have to get the operating system transmitting over an antenna or an Ethernet jack; to get the operating system working; and so on. A recurring theme in hacker stories is a breakthrough that happened in the course of trying to develop better tools for some other purpose, whether an improved programming language, a versioning system to reconcile different parts of a project, or a whole operating system, in the case of Unix, created with an eye to making the creation of future tools faster and easier.

Like tinkering and reverse engineering, this element of the hacker approach has both smaller everyday and larger abstract aspects. Recursive tooling appears as jokes in the hacker lexicon around things like 'yak-shaving': 'some stupid, fiddly little task that bears no obvious relationship to what you're supposed to be working on, but yet a chain of twelve causal relations links what you're doing to the original meta-task' (Brown, 2000). You started out trying to update a dependency and ended up learning a new programming language. The legendary computer scientist Donald Knuth, for instance – adopted as a hacker patron saint – became frustrated at the inferior quality of the typesetting and design tools available for publishing his work in the 1970s. He ended up creating a complete, immensely complex layout system, TeX, which became the basis for LaTeX, the default standard for mathematical notation and publishing in the sciences to this day (Knuth, 1986). In classic yak-shaving style, to get TeX to work, Knuth developed not only his own programming language for it, by an entirely new theory of how programming could work – and a custom digital font, still in wide use.

On a broader scale, recursive tooling appears as the political arrangement Christopher Kelty identified as the *recursive public:*

> this kind of public includes the activities of making, maintaining, and modifying software and networks, as well as the more conventional discourse that is thereby enabled. . . [a]

series of technical and legal layers – from applications to protocols to the physical infrastructures of waves and wires – that are the subject of this making, maintaining, and modifying.

(Kelty, 2008, 29)

He continues:

[G]eeks use technology as a kind of argument, for a specific kind of order: they argue about technology, but they also argue through it. . . . They express ideas, but they also express infrastructures through which ideas can be expressed (and circulated) in new ways.

(ibid)

Hackers understand themselves as larger communities in terms of the tools that enable their communities, tools they themselves design, develop, and deploy. Arguments over a messaging or versioning system or the software of a mailing list can work on several levels at once: personal, political, technical, infrastructural. The hacker activity of recursive tooling also plays out as the hacker community of the recursive public.

Commoning

Of course, it also plays out in the question of whether and how to circulate and share those tools. Kelty (2008) was writing about the Free Software movement, as was Coleman (2013, 2014), earlier. It is a source of considerable public and scholarly interest: a new way of making things, social and technical at once, that Yochai Benkler terms 'commons-based peer production.' Benkler summarizes the idea of a commons:

a particular institutional form of structuring the rights to access, use, and control resources. . . [R]esources governed by commons may be used or disposed of by anyone among some (more or less well-defined) number of persons, under rules that may range from "anything goes" to quite crisply articulated formal rules that are effectively enforced.

(Benkler, 2006, 61)

I want to identify 'commoning' as a particular form of action we've seen before in this chapter and will see again. In its most general, generic form, this is another facet of getting and giving access (Johns, 2009, 463–496). Often what is being put into commons is the information necessary for tinkering or developing one's own tools – or information that is being leaked or exposed, as will be discussed later. Commoning is distinct, however, as the most conceptually rigorous version of this related set of actions. In a sense it is the most meta-level kind of recursive tooling, creating a legal, political, economic, and cultural environment as well as a set of technical tools for formalizing the getting and giving of access.

Commoning, then, is a verb that takes us beyond giving or sharing. Dumping a bunch of digital media into some online repository is not commoning, as such. Commoning is making use of things like the GNU Public License (GPL), 'copyleft' provisions, Creative Commons licenses, and other open-source frameworks. (If you are reading this digitally, the screen you read it on very likely includes some of these frameworks somewhere in its software.) Commoning is, more tangentially, the creation of open data, open access, open publishing, open hardware, and open standards. Commoning is engagement in ongoing debate about what one means by these very terms: 'open' or 'free' as in whether you have to pay, or whether you can do anything you want? As in transparency? As in having to participate in the commons in turn, with what you produce? 'Open' as a canny business decision, or as a philosophical commitment to a specific understanding of knowledge and society? Android, the mobile phone operating system initially produced by Google, exemplifies the former; Richard Stallman, founder of the Free Software Movement, who exemplifies the latter, described putting together a collection of free software necessities '[s]o that I can continue to use computers without dishonor . . . I refuse to break solidarity with other users' (Stallman, 1985). Rational, righteous, or both?

As with the other components of hacker action, commoning can cover many degrees of action for an array of goals. One can engage in commoning by posting a picture under a Creative Commons license, by making a contribution to a free/libre/open-source project, by running Linux or teaching others to use it, by designing and manufacturing an open-source piece of hardware which can become the basis for other devices (like the famous Arduino platform), by sharing exfiltrated data with the public for a specific end, by engaging in what Aaron Swartz called 'guerilla open access,' moving large bodies of knowledge into the commons even if the project is unsanctioned or illegal: 'We need to take information, wherever it is stored, make our copies and share them with the world' (Swartz, 2008). (Swartz faced disproportionate legal penalties for his guerilla open access downloading of a massive set of academic journal articles, leading to his suicide in 2013.)

This final aspect of commoning has taken on a new significance in the last decade and a half as more and more social and political institutions have moved their operations online. There were prior cases of hacking for disclosure – to share concealed information – but the formal role the hacker occupies as whistleblower has changed: 'the politically engaged geek family continues to grow – in size and significance,' wrote Coleman in her study of Anonymous (Coleman, 2014, 382). Edward Snowden's release of NSA materials to journalists, the creation of the WikiLeaks model by Julian Assange and his collaborators for online publication, the attacks on Sony's movie division and the Ashley Madison site by unknown hacker teams – both of which involved dumping massive caches of documents online for the public to comb through – suggest the scale of this transformation in what it can mean to be a 'hacker.' As Benkler explains in his study of the release of emails related to vulnerabilities in the Diebold company's voting machines, hacking as commoning creates its own infrastructure of sharing, including 'the initial observations of the whistle-blower or the hacker; the materials made available on a "see for yourself" and "come analyze this and share your insights" model; the distribution by students; and the fallback option when their server was shut down of replication around the network' (Benkler, 2006, 262).

As even this brief list suggests, the act of commoning can take place in a mix legally sanctioned frameworks (themselves often the product of hackers and lawyers and journalists formalizing hacker commitments), or as appeals to a higher moral authority: Stallman's 'solidarity,' Swartz's call for informational 'justice.' Finally, like many of the actions outlined here, commoning is reciprocal, to do with both giving and getting – one puts things into the commons, but also draws on them: the other part of Benkler's 'commons-based peer production.' This brings us back to tools, hardware, and software. You need components and data offering the kind of privileges that commoned objects do in order to make many hacker things. What kind of making – what kind of production, what kind of labor – needs that level of access?

Making nonstandard things

McKenzie Wark identified what she called 'the hacker class' as a way to talk about two things. The first was a larger question she identified as 'the nature of information itself as something inimical to property and necessarily existing only as something shared' (2017, 306). It is an issue that should feel familiar to us now as a part of the toolkit of hacker action, a question that builds on her earlier *Hacker Manifesto* (Wark, 2004). The second was to have a way to talk about the people engaged in '(non-)labor practices that make *nonstandard things*,' 'new things' (2017, 9). There are many aspects of this idea, including the very hacker-ish question of the blurring between labor and play, experiment, art, science, and performance (see the next action), with implications for how we discuss issues from compensation, to economics, to unionization in the tech industry (see also Scholz, 2012; Liu, 2004; Neff, 2015).

However, I would like to highlight a different aspect of the fifth of the eight hacker actions: a culture of craft, with a specific aesthetic – one that connects the previous set of actions with the one that follows next. While their work may have widespread effects, appearing in templates, libraries, dependencies, and other widely reproduced, standardized formats and components, a hallmark of hacker production is 'nonstandard things': bespoke tools and products, modified versions, idiosyncratic designs, one-off fixes and solutions whether elegant or crude. As hacker Rodney Folz put it, 'We do things that don't scale. It's in our blood' (Folz, 2015). That last thing, the ugly but effective and expedient fix to an immediate problem, even has its own hacker jargon: a 'kludge' – 'an improvised, spontaneous, seat-of-the-pants way of getting something done,' as Lisa Nakamura put it, which was sometimes also called a 'hack' in the early days of the term (Nakamura, 2006, 318). As the specialized terminology suggests, these kinds of fixes are commonplace, in the spirit of tinkering and developing one's own tools: sometimes the goal might be logical, clean-slate perfection (a recurring hacker temptation) but more often is just to get something working well enough for now.

This nonstandard making can be seen in many aspects of hacker labor but I'll mention two that I believe to be particularly pertinent. The first is in comments and documentation for code. These written materials are intended to provide guidance to the person who is using, reviewing, or modifying the code. They can include text explaining a program and its commands – like the pages one receives for a 'man' (for 'manual') request in the Unix or Linux command line – and text written into the program itself, bracketed out so the computer won't try to interpret or execute it, and the human can read it. One would assume that such technical documentation would be dry, impersonal, the expression of a standardized approach to a standardized product – akin to the owner's and mechanic's manuals printed for cars, for instance, a canonical standardized assembly line machine. But hacker documentation is a textual culture of its own, delightfully personal, sometimes sardonic, frustrated, or gnomic, filled with in-jokes and reflections on the work itself. Sometimes documentation and comments are agreeably ragged: admitting the code could be better, noting an unfinished feature, an experiment that never panned out, a kludgy fix that the programmer will come back to one day. Sometimes they reflect pride in craft – including the warning not to mess with part of a design that you probably don't understand. (Coleman has written extensively about the culture of commented code [2013, 100–120].) Famously, *Lions' Commentary on UNIX* included a comment on a very weird mechanism on line 2238: 'You are not expected to understand this.' Though meant as 'this won't be on the test,' it was often interpreted and playfully riffed on in other code as a challenge – 'don't even try.' The page of text you get for 'man rsh,' the manual for a Unix program, includes this explanatory line for a command: 'this is arguably wrong, but currently hard to fix for reasons too complicated to explain here.' These kinds of notes reflect code that is made by people in personal, inventive, nonstandard, crafty ways – one stitch at a time – and code made with the expectation it will be tinkered with, studied, and further modified.

The second, which I will touch on only briefly, is *how* hacker production often happens: using heavily modified, nonstandard systems and environments. This is closely related to the activity of recursive tooling, making the tools with which to make the tools. A classic hacker rite of passage is not just installing an open-source operating system, but installing that system and then modifying it until it breaks, and then fixing it again. From choosing window managers to customizing text editors to remapping keyboards, nonstandard objects are made with nonstandard tools: a minor but telling detail of hacker life is developing and sharing one's own 'dotfiles,' the configuration files normally hidden from the user, with which you can specify your own preferences for how work is done. Over time, each hacker's production environment will become unique, engineered for their particular, nonstandard practices.

Performing virtuosity

One consequence of making nonstandard objects is that there are individual creators and craftspeople and groups to be celebrated (or castigated) – rather than anonymous systems where interchangeable human crank out interchangeable parts. The questions of attribution and authorship in hacker production are much more complex that we can cover here, but through them runs another distinct form of hacker action: the performance of virtuosity – in some cases for functional ends, as with a brilliant fix, but often as an end in itself, to be appreciated by other hackers who can understand what you've accomplished. This goes back to the tricks pulled off by phone phreaks, like routing calls from relay to relay, across the phone network, around the world. This served no functional purpose – in the sense of getting free long distance, for instance – but was instead a trick that demonstrated extraordinary technical competence: the legendary phone phreak Captain Crunch would set it up to route a call from one handset around the world to another handset in the same room, putting his voice on a planet-size time delay (Rosenbaum, 1971).

This is the purest expression of the making of nonstandard things, the least inflected by the quotidian demands of industries, managers, and end-users, and a crucial action in the hacker lexicon: the performance of technical virtuosity more or less for its own sake. Such accomplishments don't just garner prestige; they reflect a larger community that can admire the extreme difficulty (often self-imposed), and deep insight into the technologies and tools that they reflect. Hackers dub themselves and one another as 'wizards,' 'Jedi,' and 'ninjas,' all groups whose membership is limited by very demanding thresholds of dedication, training, and skill. (Much has been made in geek discussion of how the Jedi from the *Star Wars* universe mark their progress in training by making their own lightsabers from scratch – a cultural fantasy of recursive tooling if ever there was one [Brunton, 2013, 18].) Understanding the implications of this virtuosity is likewise limited to those in the know.

In fact, one of the most extreme expressions of the hacker performance of virtuosity produces the least impressive result: a program that outputs the string 'Hello, world' or various other traditional phrases, like 'Just another Perl hacker,' (the comma is traditional). To write a command that will return this result is the most basic, introductory act of many computer language lessons. The goal of hacker virtuosity is to produce it using the most mind-smashingly opaque, complex, counterintuitive means, which other hackers will delight in picking apart and trying to understand, for events like the International Obfuscated C Code Contest. There are numerous contests for different languages, as well as 'esoteric' languages designed to be challenges in themselves, like Brainfuck, Grass – whose code, built entirely from 'W,' 'w,' and 'v,' looks like grass – and Malbolge, named for the eighth circle of Hell. (The related phenomenon of the 'demoscene' seeks to produce visual and sonic performances out of deliberately constrained programming tools, sometimes pulling off astonishingly rich displays out of only a few lines of exquisitely composed code; part of the pleasure of demoscene events is understanding the ingenuity with which the effect was produced.) As Nick Monfort put it, obfuscated code "darkens the usually 'clear box' of source code into something that is difficult to trace through and puzzle out, but by doing this, it makes code more enticing, inviting the attention and close reading of programmers" (Monfort, 2009, 198; see also Mateas & Monfort, 2005). It speaks to the aesthetic and craft pleasures of hacking expressed as its own set of actions and productions.

Policing and defining hackerdom

Of course, part of the activity around those demoscene competitions is to separate those who really understand and appreciate the technological feats from those who don't, or who fail to appreciate them on the appropriate level – a process of policing and defining the 'elite' and the varieties of non-elite 'lamers.' The seventh of the eight actions and the most self-referential will also be the briefest to describe, because it is the least technically particular: a recurring activity in the hacking community is discussion and debate over the meaning of 'hacker' itself – what are the criteria, who really gets to be one, what you should be doing to qualify, and who has been excluded.

There are many debates and internal conversations to this question that lie beyond the brief scope of our work here. A few brief examples will suffice. Eric S. Raymond, a notable open-source software developer (and author of the landmark open-source development manifesto, *The Cathedral and the Bazaar*) maintains a lengthy document for those who have written to him seeking to develop 'wizardly hacker' expertise: 'How to Become a Hacker' (Raymond, n.d.). 'Hackers build things,' he writes, and provides a blend of mindsets ('No problem should ever have to be solved twice'), particular skills and tools ('Get one of the open-source Unixes and learn to use and run it'), and social capital ('Help test and debug open-source software'). This document, periodically expanded and refined since 1996, perfectly exemplifies a particular hacker type – outside the formal recommendations, Raymond advocates for other practices to find one's way more easily in the hacker scene, like reading science fiction and cultivating a fondness for puns. Raymond subsequently disgraced himself with increasingly bizarre, con-spiratorial, racist and misogynist personal positions which in retrospect colored this document. It implied another requirement to be a hacker in some circles, unstated but seemingly evident: to be an abrasive but thin-skinned, competent but deeply insecure, white guy who likes arguing on the Internet, and assumes other hackers must be more or less like him. The 'flamewar' cul-ture of name-calling, abuse, and insults, and the casual sexism and racism, which result from this culture have killed many an open-source project, or reduced it to only the most high-blood-pressure personalities – who are not necessarily the best developers.

In contrast to this, a wave of new groups, events (including hackathons and workshops) and publications are explicitly trying to renegotiate who gets to be called a hacker and what a hacker is assumed to be. The !!Con, for example, tries to foster not only a more diverse array of hack-ers but also a different culture of hacker engagement – one that is less language and platform focused, and instead emphasizes 'the joy, excitement, and surprise of programming,' an ethos in many ways much closer to the historical roots of hacking as a vocation than the intensely monetized, product-first, overworked-at-a-big-company approach that characterizes the hacker in contexts like Silicon Valley today. Sumana Harihareswara describes !!Con's breadth of techni-cal and engineering talks as an assumption: 'every attendee has the capability of being curious about everything' (Harihareswara, 2016). Or, as Raymond phrased the first requirement for being a hacker almost twenty years earlier, you must believe that 'the world is full of fascinating problems waiting to be solved' (Raymond, n.d.).

Social engineering

This final entry in the hacker vocabulary of actions echoes the earliest days of hacking, but has a new contemporary resonance. With it, we close the loop and conclude this chapter: from the earliest pranks and collegiate 'hacks' to the discussion around 'hacking the election' in the United States and other countries over the last two years – and future mutations of the term 'hacking' and the actions that constitute it.

The earliest 'hacks' identified with that verb were often in the service of sophisticated, complex pranks: the technological ingenuity and access needed to surreptitiously put a car on top of the Great Dome of MIT, or inflate a weather balloon at the fifty-yard-line in the middle of a football game. Pulling off these pranks often involved not only material engineering but 'social engineering': a security-focused version of confidence trickery (Peterson, 2003). Larry Wall, the legendary developer of the Perl programming language, said great programmers possess laziness, impatience, and hubris: they are wildly ambitious, but have no patience for what Eric Raymond's guide to hacking terms 'boredom and drudgery.' This means that – along with automating away repetitive tasks – hackers are always in search of the optimal, efficient shortcut around the seemingly intractable problem. If getting access to a closed building or a phone network needs a code, why not fast-talk someone with the password into giving it to you in a few minutes instead of various time-consuming and perhaps unsuccessful technical approaches? One under-recognized component of the hacker toolkit evolved from this: the accumulated lore of social engineering, from interpersonal activities like cold-calling and looking over someone's shoulder as they type in a password ('shoulder surfing'), to going through a company's trash ('trashing') in search of useful intrusion information, to now-commonplace phishing emails that fool the recipient into logging into an account and thereby giving up a password.

It was a phishing attack that originally gained access to the email account belonging to John Podesta, the chairman of Hillary Clinton's 2016 presidential campaign. The emails, subsequently published on WikiLeaks, played a part (their exact consequences still debated) in the failure of the Clinton campaign and the election of Donald Trump, along with the likewise uncertain effect of social network manipulation through bots and the circulation of false stories and images. This has been widely referred to in the American media as 'hacking' the election, though, arguably, the only part that resembles the history of hacking to this point was the acquisition and leak of the Podesta emails. But it raises a useful question for us: the popular meaning of 'hacking' continues to evolve. Social engineering has always been a part of hacking, back to the phone phreaks getting access to Ma Bell's network and proto-hackers finagling parts and computing system time from their universities and institutions. Etymologically, many of the earliest projects of 'hackers' getting and giving access were in the service of stunts and pranks. Can this be plausibly explained as a single, coherent thread in the history of hacking that began to blur into the space of trolling, doxxing, Rita Raley's 'tactical media,' and prankish weirdness that has become a vector for political disruption – 'social engineering' on a much larger scale (Raley, 2009; see also Phillips, 2015; Coleman, 2014)? At what point does the expansion of the concept of hacking become meaningless?

I hope this chapter has demonstrated that the answer to these contemporary questions lies not in an abstract definition or redefinition, but in studying the particulars of actions that the people involved think of as 'hacking.' Will a distinct, new category of action be added to this collection? Will one of these forms of activity drop away as a salient part of the spectrum of hacking? Getting and giving access; tinkering and reverse engineering; recursive tooling; commoning; making nonstandard things; performing virtuosity; policing and defining hackerdom; social engineering: the eight forms of action described here will change in their subjects and implications, but their continuity throughout the history and transformations of hacking so far argues for their persistence in the future, as components in a technologically specific way of living and working.

References

Benkler, Y. (2006). *The Wealth of Networks: How Social Production Transforms Markets and Freedom*. New Haven: Yale University Press.

Brown, J. (2000). *Yak-Shaving*. www.mit.edu/~xela/yakshaving.html.

Brunton, F. (2013). *Spam: A Shadow History of the Internet*. Cambridge, MA: MIT Press.

Cohen, J. (2012). *Configuring the Networked Self: Law, Code, and the Play of Everyday Practice*. New Haven: Yale University Press.

Coleman, G. (2013). *Coding Freedom: The Ethics and Aesthetics of Hacking*. Princeton, NJ: Princeton University Press.

Coleman, G. (2014). *Hacker, Hoaxer, Whistleblower, Spy: The Many Faces of Anonymous*. New York: Verso.

Driscoll, K. (2016). Social Media's Dial-Up Roots. *IEEE Spectrum*, 53(11), 54–60, November.

Folz, R. (2015). *Selling Out and the Death of Hacker Culture*. https://medium.com/@folz/selling-out-and-the-death-of-hacker-culture-fec1f101b138.

Harihareswara, S. (2016). Towards a !!Con Aesthetic. *The Recompiler*. https://recompilermag.com/issues/extras/toward-a-bangbangcon-aesthetic/.

Huang, B. (2013). *Hacking the Xbox: An Introduction to Reverse Engineering*. San Francisco: No Starch.

Johns, A. (2009). *Piracy: The Intellectual Property Wars from Gutenberg to Gates*. Chicago: University of Chicago Press.

Kelty, C. (2008). *Two Bits: The Cultural Significance of Free Software*. Durham: Duke University Press.

Knuth, D. (1986). *Computers & Typesetting, Volume A: The TeXbook*. Reading, MA: Addison-Wesley.

Lapsley, P. (2013). *Exploding the Phone: The Untold Story of the Teenagers and Outlaws Who Hacked Ma Bell*. New York: Grove Press.

Levy, S. (1984). *Hackers: Heroes of the Computer Revolution*. New York: Anchor, Doubleday.

Lions, J. (1977). *Lions' Commentary on Unix 6th Edition with Source Code: Peer to Peer Communications*. Kensington: University of New South Wales.

Liu, A. (2004). *The Laws of Cool: Knowledge Work and the Culture of Information*. Chicago: University of Chicago Press.

Mateas, M., and Monfort, N. (2005). *A Box, Darkly: Obfuscation, Weird Languages, and Code Aesthetics*. Proceedings of the 6th Digital Arts and Culture Conference, IT University of Copenhagen, December 1–3.

Monfort, N. (2009). Obfuscated Code. In M. Fuller (ed.), *Software Studies: A Lexicon*. Cambridge, MA: MIT Press.

Nakamura, L. (2006). Cybertyping and the Work of Race in the Age of Digital Reproduction. In K. Chun and T. Keenan (eds.), *New Media, Old Media: A History and Theory Reader*. London: Routledge.

Neff, G. (2015). *Venture Labor: Work and the Burden of Risk in Innovative Industries*. Cambridge, MA: MIT Press.

Peterson, T. F. (2003). *Nightwork: A History of Hacks and Pranks at MIT*. Cambridge, MA: MIT Press.

Phillips, W. (2015). *This Is Why We Can't Have Nice Things: Mapping the Relationship Between Online Trolling and Mainstream Culture*. Cambridge, MA: MIT Press.

Raley, R. (2009). *Tactical Media*. Minneapolis: University of Minnesota Press.

Raymond, E. S. (n.d.). *How to Become a Hacker*. www.catb.org/~esr/faqs/hacker-howto.html.

Rosenbaum, R. (1971). Secrets of the Little Blue Box. *Esquire Magazine*, October. http://classic.esquire.com/secrets-of-the-blue-box/.

Scholz, T. (ed.). (2012). *Digital Labor: The Internet as Playground and Factory*. London: Routledge.

Silvanovich, N. (n.d.). *Many Tamagotchis Were Harmed in Making This Presentation*. http://natashenka.ca.

Stallman, R. (1985). *The GNU Manifesto*. www.gnu.org/gnu/manifesto.en.html.

Stephenson, N. (1999). *In the Beginning Was the Command Line*. New York: Avon Books.

Swartz, A. (2008). *Guerilla Open Access Manifesto.* https://archive.org/stream/GuerillaOpenAccessMani-festo/Goamjuly2008_djvu.txt.

Thomas, D. (2006). *Hacker Culture.* Minneapolis: University of Minnesota Press.

Turner, F. (2008). *From Counterculture to Cyberculture: Stewart Brand, the Whole Earth Network, and the Rise of Digital Utopianism.* Chicago: University of Chicago Press.

Wark, M. (2004). *A Hacker Manifesto.* Cambridge, MA: Harvard University Press.

Wark, M. (2017). *General Intellects: Twenty-One Thinkers for the Twenty-First Century.* London: Verso.

Zuckerberg, M. (2012). Mark Zuckerberg's Letter to Investors: 'The Hacker Way'. *WIRED* [online]. www.wired.com/2012/02/zuck-letter/.

7

(Big) data and algorithms

Looking for meaningful patterns

Taina Bucher

In the 1670s the Dutch businessman and scientist Antonie van Leeuwenhoek discovered the hitherto unknown microscopic world. Using his handcrafted microscope, he was the first to observe and describe bacteria and other microorganisms. Equipped with a lifetime of microscopic experimentation and technical refinement, making over 500 optical lenses and creating 25 single-lens microscopes, van Leeuwenhoek is considered not just the father of microbiology but a pioneer in revealing the unseen world using his self-made microscopes (Lane, 2015). Fast forward to our own day and age and there is an entirely different unseen world that engages scientists and business people alike. The future, or more precisely the prediction of what is to come based on what is and has been, is the unseen that people want to discover today. If the men and women of the Golden Age of Dutch science and technology discovered the unseen world through microscopes, the world today is increasingly 'discovered' through large datasets and predictive analytics.[1]

Let's stay in the world of biology for just a little while longer. This time not bacteria but data. Not miniscule worlds but large ones. Not microscopes but Google. When launching Google Flu Trends in 2008 the public health tracking system was hailed as a potential new innovation in epidemiology. By mining the millions of search queries of web users, the idea was that the flu tracker would be able to estimate flu activity even before the official Centers for Disease Control and Prevention (CDC) had the chance to register any outbreaks. Traditional flu monitoring, overseen by the CDA in the case of the United States, depends on national networks of physicians reporting patient cases with Influenza-like symptoms. However, to classify as sick, patients first have to be diagnosed by a doctor and by then it is often too late, they are already sick and have already had plenty of opportunity to infect others. At first, Google Flu Trends seemed remarkably successful. The predictive models created based on CDC data from between 2003 and 2007 proved to be "consistently one to two weeks ahead of the CDC surveillance reports" (Butler, 2008). Yet when Google Flu Trends provided estimates double that of the CDC during the 2012 flu season, the wonders of big data started to fade (Butler, 2013). As Cheney-Lippold writes, it wasn't that Google had "missed the forest for the trees. It missed the sick tree for all the other trees who'd been frantically Googling ways to help the sick tree" (2017, 123). No technique of observation and measurement, whether microscopic nor macroscopic, is ever immune to bias or failure.

While new technical terrains often provide new ways of understanding and measuring the world, as in the aforementioned cases, revealing the worlds of the previously unseen or unmeasurable, these techniques are only half the story. In this chapter on data and algorithms, it is therefore important to highlight a technical as well as historical, cultural, political and economic understanding of the 'datafied' and algorithmically constructed present. One of the biggest truisms about big data is the "end of theory" thesis famously articulated by former Wired editor Chris Anderson in 2008. According to Anderson, we now live in a 'Petabyte Age,' or as Barnes puts it: "an age of ten to the power of 15, binary 2 to the power of 50, bytes" (2013, 298). The point is that the petabyte age is not just big but different "because more is different" (Anderson, 2008). More is supposedly different because we no longer need to hypothesize what things mean, just follow the data. Despite this lingering techno-optimism of the 'big data revolution,' which is particularly evident in the business world and tech industry, much critical scholarship on big data and algorithms have consistently scrutinized such overly simplified notions of 'data as the new oil' (see, e.g., Amoore & Piotukh, 2015; boyd & Crawford, 2012; Crawford et al., 2014; Kitchin, 2014; Neff et al., 2017). Indeed, as Hargittai suggests in relation to the methodological challenges of using big data, "bigger is not always better; size is not all that matters when it comes to datasets" (2015, 74). There is more to big data than its petabyte. As Crawford et al. argue, big data does not constitute the end of theory; it *is* theory (2014, 1664). To understand how big data has become a *Weltanschauung* as Crawford et al. (2014) put it, some necessary grounds will have to be covered first.

This chapter begins by defining some of the key terms, including data and big data, before moving on to historical and technical background in terms of databases, the rise of statistical society, and what Hacking (1990) has termed an "avalanche of numbers." Next, the chapter considers the broader 'datafication' of society, understood as the "process of rendering into data aspects of the world not previously quantified" (Kennedy et al., 2015, 1). The second part of the chapter moves more specifically into the terrain of 'algorithms,' providing some definitional clarity to key terms and contextual understanding in terms of exemplifying how algorithms (and data, big data, and all the related terms) need to be seen as part and parcel of larger socio-technical systems and assemblages.

Data: given, taken, and made

When asked to write about data and algorithms in 2018, there is an implicit understanding of relating the discussion to the ways in which data have assumed such a significant role in society today with the advent of very large datasets – more commonly described under the banner of "big data" – and its supporting and enabling technologies. A decade ago, writing about data may have meant something quite different. That said, a decade ago there would probably not have been a chapter on data and algorithms in a digital media and communications handbook. This does not mean, however, that data or algorithms are anything new. Data are basic forms of enumeration and encodings of the phenomena they represent or describe (Barocas et al., 2014). What is new is the scale and proliferation of these enumerated and encoded phenomena that are increasingly used to drive and support all kinds of decision-making processes in society. But let's not get ahead of ourselves. Why were data and algorithms not taken-for-granted concepts in media and communications a decade ago when these concepts have been around for longer than the discipline has existed? After all, the term 'data' has been part of the English language at least since Antonie van Leeuwenhoek's time. While relatively new in its rhetorical and discursive significance, data understood more narrowly as the classification and quantification of observations need to be understood in a much longer historical context of quantification, documentation, and archiving: the question of why data, now, may be the same as for other disciplines. Before the advent of what is now commonly referred to as "big data," the word "data" did not assert itself in the same way as it does today. Today, we have become accustomed to data driving something, as in data-driven businesses and data-driven organizations. Data have taken on a more active role as cheaper and easier to use technologies support both the collection and the scalability of data in new ways. Add to this the fact that most dominant media outlets, including social media platforms, the entertainment industry, and news organizations, are increasingly relying on data-driven and algorithmically processed insights, and the (renewed) relevance of these terms for media and communication scholars should be quite evident.

Not only has the past decade seen the explosive rise of terms previously tucked down in a computer science textbook or statistical bureau, but the related terms have multiplied as well (at least in regards to the scholarly discussions on them). We not only have data and big data, but we also have social media data, open data, personal data, structured data, unstructured data, small data, thick data, primary data, secondary data, metadata, mundane data, log data, and so forth. All of these terms connote different kinds of data, with their own histories, questions and problems, only some of which will be discussed as part of this chapter. Etymologically the word 'data' is derived from the Latin *dare*, meaning 'to give.' In general use, however, "data refer to those elements that *are* taken; extracted through observations, computations, experiments, and record keeping" (Kitchin, 2014, 2). Moreover, data are always *made*. That is, as Barocas et al. point out, "they are artifacts of human intervention, not facts imparted by nature itself" (2014, 2). As Helles (2013) exemplifies, "the Web server log file that we find online does not become data before we begin to conceptualize it within the context of a research project," or the context of a business model for that matter. As such, data are representative in nature as they provide information on certain aspects of the phenomena we are interested in studying or knowing. As Kitchin points out, data need not be explicit in its representative nature but can also be "implied (e.g., through an absence rather than presence) or derived (e.g., data that are produced from other data, such as percentage change over time calculated by comparing data from two time periods)" (2014, 1).

Ultimately, data need to be processed, analyzed, and made sense of. Whether it is made sense of by humans or machines, or most likely, a combination of both, the process of making data always involves multiple agents (Helles & Jensen, 2013). Data are never simply raw nor do they exist in a vacuum, but they are stored, recorded, collected, processed, analyzed, and employed by a complex ecosystem of users, digital infrastructure, databases, businesses, public and private institutions, algorithms, policy makers, and governments alike. Researchers, for instance, use data to advance the state of knowledge. They may rely on primary data that they have themselves collected, secondary data others have made available to them, or tertiary data, which are derived forms of data that also include someone else's interpretations, such as statistical results. Authorities too not only use but depend on data, including hospitals, where patient records are essential to their service, schools that keep track of their students' performance, and government agencies that meticulously record information about their populations, most notably through the Census Bureau responsible for producing data about a nation's people and economy. While the data points these authorities use and collect may vary, the idea is the same: store, process, and assemble, it will be useful for making decisions.

Database technologies

In order for data to be useful, they need to be organized and kept in databases. While data can be lost, forgotten, or simply overlooked, most data thought valuable are usually collected and classified so that it later can be retrieved for analytical or informational purposes. Understanding database technologies, both analogue and digital, is therefore essential if we want to understand how data are made available for analysis. In the most basic understanding of the term, a phone book could be a database, because it provides a structured list of a few data points such as name and associated phone numbers. A database, broadly conceived, is a record-keeping and information-retrieval system. Its origins predate the computer, going back to libraries, archives, and other government, business, and medical record-keeping. In this broad definition, books, libraries, and archives can be conceived of as databases: they provide a way to store and maintain data. Through a description of its own structure, a database also provides the means for finding and retrieving the data it contains. Books contain a table of contents and, in many cases, an index at the back; libraries include a catalog that is organized according to a specific classification system; and archives likewise depend on indexical and other systems of organization. More specifically, the term 'database' is most commonly used to describe how computers store, manage, and organize data. A database is a collection of data that is encoded and arranged according to a common format. The term is also used interchangeably about systems that manage collections of data and about the tools and techniques that support the manipulation and operation of these data.

In the context of computing, the term 'database' is used more narrowly to describe how computers store, describe, and organize data. Here we might distinguish between three levels at which the term database is used (Dourish, 2014). At the most general level, database is used to merely denote a collection of data. More specifically, database refers to a collection of data that is encoded and arranged according to a common format. This common format, importantly, makes data amenable to a common set of operations, including sorting, comparing, and processing the data in consistent and reliable ways. At a third level, database refers to software management systems that implement the relationship between data formats and data. At this level, database is often used interchangeably with the systems that manage collections of data (e.g., Oracle) and the tools and techniques that support the manipulation and operation of these data (e.g., SQL).

Importantly, databases are constructed artifacts that are designed to "hold certain kinds of data and enable certain kinds of analysis, and how they are structured has profound consequences as to what queries and analysis can be performed" (Kitchin, 2014, 21–22). In the case of relational databases, which is still the most common way of digitally storing and structuring data, data are organized into one or more tables of columns and rows, each with a uniquely identifiable key. Relations between tables are established on the basis of their interactions. Pioneered by E. F. Codd in the early 1970s, relational databases became a de facto standard for digital storage and retrieval when the development of the Structured Query Language (SQL), an English-like syntax for interacting with a relational database, enabled easier management of the data contained in the relational database. Although relational databases have been around for more than 40 years, their position has changed as new database models have done away with the tabular schema. With the steady increase in available data and web services with greater workloads, there have been new demands for data storage and processing. As a result, new kinds of data models and database management systems have evolved, collectively known as post-relational or NoSQL databases. It should be pointed out, however, that these terms do not refer to "a single implementation or conceptual model, but rather to a range of designs that in different ways responds to problems with the relational model" (Dourish, 2017, 123). These databases are typically used to store and retrieve data from web server logs and social media platforms. Unlike relational databases, which can mainly cope with *structured data* (i.e., data that are easily organized and stored in a defined data model), NoSQL databases are useful for operating on *unstructured data* (i.e., data that do not have a pre-defined data model or is not organized in a pre-defined model) too, as they do not require that fields be specified in advance. In NoSQL databases, Kitchin points out, "data are typically distributed and replicated across many machines rather than centralised into one location" (2014, 86).

This move into vast data territories and the development of new storage and processing technologies in parallel is precisely what some scholars have identified as the key characteristic of the big data age, understood as the "transformation in what can be collected or sampled as data, and how it can be rendered analysable" (Amoore & Piotukh, 2015, 345). On the one hand, Amoore and Piotukh suggest that the big in big data refers to the notion that big data pushes at the limits of traditional relational databases, and on the other hand, which is also the more common understanding of big data, the data are considered big because "it exceeds and changes human capacities to read and make sense of it" (2015, 343). The shift from relational databases designed for structured data to post-relational databases built for the capacity to hold unstructured data implies an expansion of the kinds of data forms that can be parsed and detaches analysis from a specific index to allow for analysis to be deterritorialized and conducted across jurisdictions (Amoore & Piotukh, 2015). The advent, then, of post-relational databases that hinge not only on distributed processing but also on new important hardware changes in processor designs and improved memory, as Dourish points out (2017), has contributed to the fact that "we can now collect information that we couldn't before, be it relationships revealed by phone calls or sentiments unveiled through tweets" (Mayer-Schoenberger & Cukier, 2013, 30). In other words, understanding the technical changes in both software and hardware is essential for an understanding of the ideological, political, and social grounds of datafication, the idea of harnessing (big) data and algorithms to analyze social behavior.

Datafication

The exponential growth in available data generated from user interactions in online systems has led not only to more data being collected and stored but also to what scholars have termed *datafication*, the "widespread *belief* in the objective quantification and potential tracking of all kinds of human behaviour and sociality through online media technologies" (van Dijck, 2014, 198). As Kennedy et al. suggest, "datafication refers to the process of rendering into data aspects of the world not previously quantified" (2015, 1). Central to this (re)newed belief in the power of quantification is a type of data, which, as van Dijck suggests, "not too long ago was considered worthless by-products of platform-mediated services" (2014, 199). *Metadata*, or data about data, is essential to the utilization of big data. These are the kind of data that provide additional and associative information to whatever data point one is interested in. In the case of a single email, for example, the metadata provides information about who the receiver and sender is, the time and date of the message, the length and amount of words contained in the message, and so on. Or, when scrolling down your Facebook feed, pretty much every additional information is being logged, from when you log in, which device you are using, what you click on, location, through to the duration of your activities (Facebook Data Policy, 2016). While these kinds of data may not be as interesting in and of themselves, in the aggregate, however, the patterns generated with the help of metadata may be invaluable.

The widespread belief in datafication has been embraced by a number of institutions, private and public, businesses, and researchers alike, where data and metadata are commonly treated as traces of human behavior, or so-called digital footprints. The availability and ease of collecting huge datasets have led to a rush of collecting data for its own sake, oftentimes without a clear purpose in sight. The amount of business and trade press literature on big data are simply overwhelming. The general advice seems to be somewhere along the lines of 'collect as much as possible, even the things you don't think are useful, and worry about analysis later,' thinking that more information is always better. A common critique leveled at social media research, for example, is that it has privileged the study of Twitter, simply because of its publicly available data. As Lomborg writes, "research too often gets seduced by the sheer availability and abundance of data" (2017, 7), while overlooking or turning a blind eye to the messiness and unrepresentativeness of the data collected. Researchers, however, are not alone in being seduced by the abundance in data. As boyd and Crawford argue, there is a "deep government and industrial drive toward gathering and extracting maximal value from data, be it information that will lead to more targeted advertising, product design, traffic planning, or criminal policing" (2012, 675).

In one of the first critical assessments of the term big data in media and communication studies, boyd and Crawford define *big data* as "a cultural, technological, and scholarly phenomenon that rests on the interplay of: Technology, Analysis and Mythology" (2012). Big data, the authors suggest, is no more a technical phenomenon than it is a social and epistemic one. It changes not just how we might collect and analyze data but how we think about objects of knowledge in and of themselves. According to Anderson's 'Petabyte vision,' we no longer start from theories or prior knowledge data will generate it for us. But do numbers speak for themselves, boyd and Crawford rhetorically ask, warning that data will lose its meaning and value if we lose sight of its context (2012, 670). Context means knowing more about the kinds of data that are being generated, who gets to access data, and to what end data are deployed. Context means understanding not just the possibilities but, more importantly, the limitations of big data analytics. To evoke the Google Flu Trends experiment, context means understanding that the device was "better at using browser data to trace the spread of worries about the symptoms of flu than it was at predicting the spread of the virus itself" (Halford & Savage, 2017, 3). It would, however, be a mistake to assume that big data does not *have* context. As Seaver nicely puts it, "the nice thing about context is that everyone has it" (2015). Drawing on fieldwork among data scientists and developers working on music recommender systems, Seaver points out how practitioners are very much geared toward the question of context, as knowing more about individual users is key to providing personalized content and recommendations. Neff et al. further point out how data, whether big or small, are "always already context-rich because of how people imagine data and construct, produce, or define the dataset" (2017, 89).

If boyd and Crawford paved the way for a critical discourse on big data with their six provocative questions about the meaning and governance of data, many more questions and concerns have since been added to the list by scholars and practitioners alike. Some of the recurring issues have to do with the significance of big data for governments (Rieder & Simon, 2016), the health sector (Ruckenstein & Dow Schüll, 2017), surveillance (Lyon, 2014), and privacy and personal integrity (Crawford & Schultz, 2014) to name but a few. Discussions around ethics and methods have been prevailing too, with scholars advocating for ethical data sharing practices (Zook et al., 2017; Zwitter, 2014), attending to the specificities of digital devices themselves (Ruppert et al., 2013) and for more *data-activist research practices* (Milan & Velden, 2016). As so-called big data has come of age, there is also a growing need to account for the concept in historical and sociological terms (Beer, 2016). As mechanisms of quantification, classification, measurement, and prediction, data and algorithms are as much imbued in the history of computation and software engineering as they are in the history of statistics, accounting, and bureaucratization. As such, the historical and cultural contexts of the big data era intersect with the social history of calculation and ordering of various types, including the history and politics of statistical reasoning and large numbers (Desrosières & Naish, 2002; Foucault, 2007; Hacking, 2006; Power, 2004), practices of quantification, numbering and valuation (Callon & Law, 2005;

Espeland & Stevens, 2008; Verran, 2001), the cultural logic of rankings and ratings (Espeland & Sauder, 2007; Sauder & Espeland, 2009), and ideas of critical accounting and auditing (Power, 1999; Strathern, 2000).

The question is not just, as Beer puts is, "how we should do the history of big data" (2016) but also to recognize, as Barnes suggests, there is no single history but rather a "conjuncture of different elements, each with their own history, coming together at this our present moment" (2013, 298). While many scholars have rightfully focused on the lineage of calculation, statistics, and numbers when accounting for the history of big data, the specifics matter. The "avalanche of numbers" (Hacking, 1991), which occurred as nation-states started to classify and count their populations in the 19th century, certainly forms a general backdrop for an understanding of what is at stake today. But in order to arrive at the present moment, we must also acknowledge the complex and disjunctive route it takes to get there, via, but not limited to, the social history of census, punch cards, bureaucratization, wartime machinery, the rise of computers, automated management of populations, biopolitics, machine learning techniques, and so much more.

Data subjects

Consider this advertisement for Spotify's Premium subscription model distributed through various social media platforms during Christmas 2017. Above a bright colored background, the message reads quite simply: "Data has feelings too. Hold it for longer with offline listening Premium." Against the background, the ad mimics a New Year's resolution encouraging consumers to "Spend more time with your data." Not only does this ad anthropomorphize data, showing how music is not necessarily the most important part of the streaming service's business model, but it also shows how data has become part of the social imaginary. The datafication of society has made data mundane in the sense that not only people image data in particular ways but also data have become part of how people image their social existence through software-mediated practices of consumption. The fact that Spotify can run an ad campaign framing data as a friend that needs attention and care is only possible because data have become part of people's everyday practices and contexts.

Data are not part of people's lives; people also actively make data on a daily basis. Online services and social media platforms no longer produce content through the educated guesses of expert individuals trained in trend forecasting, gut feelings based on decades of experience from the industry, or academic educations in film theory or musicology. Not only, at least. Today, content production is supported and driven by the explicit and implicit emission of user-generated data. Companies like Spotify, Netflix, Facebook, and Google provide information and recommendations based on what they think we want, predictions derived by aggregated user data. As *data subjects* (Ruppert, 2011) humans have in a sense themselves *become* data. People's actions and interactions with online services serve as inputs for the construction of personal profiles, or what Cheney-Lippold (2017) calls 'measurable types.' Whether we are speaking of "soccer moms in Florida that are really passionate about action films" or a "female college educated Scandinavian who listens to hip hop and jazz," measurable types are used to classify and filter what we get to see online. As Cheney-Lippold argues, traditional categories like gender are never absolute, you are never just 'male' or 'female.' Rather, based on statistical confidence and probability, you might be 92% confidently 'male' and 32% confidently 'female' (2017, 34). Based on further inputs, such as clicks, purchase behavior, and other actions, these measures may subsequently either rise or fall. In other words, while you may be 92% confidently male today, tomorrow the confidence score may have dropped to 70%. Thus, the data subject is generated through a malleable and changing 'algorithmic identity' (Cheney-Lippold, 2017), emerging in and through data.

Such is the work of 'profiling machines' (Elmer, 2004) that seek to produce a sense of identity through detailed consumer profiles, which are geared toward anticipating future needs. Based on statistical inferences and inductive reasoning, profiling algorithms do "not necessarily have any rational grounds and can lead to irrational stereotyping and discrimination" (de Vries, 2010, 80). Still, the question of whether 'correct' identifications are being constructed may be beside the point. As de Vries (2010) argues, misidentification is not simply a mismatch or something that should be considered inappropriate. Misidentifications may also give some leeway for thinking about how identity construction is experienced. Experiencing algorithmic landscapes is as much about what the algorithm does in terms of making certain connections as it is about people's personal engagements. A particular landscape, the anthropologist Ingold (1993) suggests, owes its character to the experiences it affords to the ones that spend time there – to their observations and expectations. In my research on how people encounter algorithms online, several participants reported the limits to algorithmic identity construction (Bucher, 2017). One of the interviewees, who identified as transgender, described how she felt there was no obvious space for her in Amazon's purchasing recommendations. Either there were suggestions for makeup or power tools, but never anything in between. To Amazon you are still either male or female although the degree to which you may be one or the other may differ. As a person in transition, she felt her queer subject-position became too much. Amazon seemed willing to try and categorize people according to fluid demographic buckets, just not the ones that might endanger their profits and risk offending someone. More than simply describing strange feelings, experiences like these describe some of the many mundane moments in which people variously encounter the algorithmic realities and principles underlying contemporary media platforms.

While Spotify wants us to believe that "data have feelings," making sense of how people have feelings for data is important too (Kennedy & Hill, 2017). If we turn to the phenomenon of self-tracking, understood as an individual's use of technology to record, monitor, and reflect upon features of daily life (Lomborg & Frandsen, 2016), we may see how data "only make sense in the context in which people decide to collect their data and the social relationships and expectations, places and spaces in which they do so" (Lupton, 2017, 10). Whether someone is monitoring his or her heart rate or keeping track of calories burnt during physical exercise, these metrics can only tell limited details about the body. Without interpretation and additional contextual information, the result of these digital tracking devices means very little. As Lupton points out, "when people review their data, they actively relate them to the contexts in which they were generated. People consider such aspects as the time of day, the weather, how their bodies felt, whether they were lacking sleep, were hungry," and so on (2017, 11). Whether we are talking about large technical systems such as the Google Flu tracker or individual's fitness trackers, big data or small data, what we cannot lose sight of in our datafied age is the importance of interpretation and the need to contextualize data in everyday practices.

Algorithms: making sense of data

While the significant power and potential of big data (the quantity of information produced by people, things, and their interactions) cannot be denied, its value derives not so much from the data itself but from the ways in which it has been brought together into new forms of meaningfulness by the associational infrastructure of the respective software systems in which algorithms play a key role.[2] In the standard computer science understanding of the term, an algorithm refers to a set of instructions for solving a problem or completing a task following a carefully planned sequential order. Perhaps, the most common way to define an algorithm is to describe it as a recipe, understood as a step-by-step guide that prescribes how to obtain a certain goal, given specific parameters. Understood as a procedure or method for processing data, the algorithm as recipe would be analogous to the operational logic for making a cake out of flour, water, and eggs. Without the specific instructions for *how* to mix the eggs and flour or *when* to add the sugar or water, for instance, these ingredients would remain just that. For someone who has never baked a cake, step-by-step instructions would be pivotal if they wanted to bake one. For any computational process to be operational, the algorithm must be rigorously defined, that is, specified in such a way that it applies in all possible circumstances. A program will execute a certain section of code only if certain conditions are met. Otherwise, it takes an alternative route, which implies that particular future circumstances are already anticipated by the conditional construct of the 'if . . . then statement' upon which most algorithms depend.

Programmers usually control the flow by specifying certain procedures and parameters through a programming language. In principle, the algorithm is "independent of programming languages and independent of the machines that execute the programs" (Goffey, 2008, 15). The same type of instructions can be written in the languages C, C#, or Python, and still be the same algorithm. This makes the concept of the 'algorithm' particularly powerful, given that what an algorithm signifies is an inherent assumption in all software design about order, sequence, and sorting. The actual steps are what is important, not the wording per se. Designing an algorithm to perform a certain task implies a simplification of the problem at hand. From an engineering perspective, the specific operation of an algorithm depends largely not only on technical considerations, including efficiency, processing time, and reduction of memory load, but also on the elegance of the code written (Fuller, 2008; Knuth, 1984). The operation of algorithms depends on a variety of other elements – most fundamentally, on *data structures*. To be actually operational, algorithms work in tandem not only with data structures but also with a whole assemblage of elements, including data types, databases, compilers, hardware, CPU, and so forth.

An important distinction needs to be made between algorithms that are pre-programmed and behave more or less deterministically and algorithms that have the ability to "learn" or improve in performance over time. Given a particular input, a deterministic algorithm will always produce the same output by passing through the same sequence of steps. The learning kind, however, will learn to predict outputs based on previous examples of relationships between input data and outputs. Unlike a deterministic algorithm that correctly sorts an alphabetized list, many of the algorithms that run the Internet today do not necessarily have one easily definable, correct result. The kinds of algorithms and techniques to which I am referring here are called *machine learning*, which is essentially the notion that we can now program a computer to learn by itself (Domingos, 2015). In contrast to the strict logical rules of traditional programming, machine learning is about writing programs that learn to solve the problem from examples. Whereas a programmer previously had to write all the 'if . . . then' statements in anticipation of an outcome herself, machine learning algorithms let the computer learn the rules from a large number of training examples without being explicitly programmed to do so. In order to help reach a target goal, algorithms are 'trained' on a *corpus* of data from which they may 'learn' to make certain kinds of decisions without human oversight.

Just like rule-based algorithms, machine learning algorithms come in many different flavors. Similar to humans, the machine itself learns in different ways. One of the most common ways in which algorithms learn is called *supervised learning*. Essentially an inductive approach to learning, algorithms are given a training set comprising the characteristics that engineers want the algorithm to detect and compare with new data (Flach, 2012). Importantly, the training set includes data about the desired output. When the training data do *not* include data about desired outputs, the approach is called *unsupervised learning*. Often, machine learning algorithms may fall somewhere in between: the data only contain a few desired outputs, which is also called semi-supervised learning (Domingos, 2015). Before an algorithm can be applied to learn from data, *models* have to be constructed that formalize the task and goals, so that it can be processed by a computer. For instance, before an algorithm can perform the task of finding the most important news feed stories, models have to be created to represent the relationship between news and relevance.

In data-intensive environments such as social media, machine learning algorithms have become a standard way of learning to recognize patterns in the data, to discover knowledge, and to predict the likelihood of user actions and tastes. Another way to put this is to say that machine learning is largely enabled by proliferating data from which models may learn. In the age of so-called big data, having the biggest pool of data available from which to detect patterns is often seen as a competitive necessity. The bigger the database, the better the conditions for algorithms to detect relevant patterns. Commercial application of machine learning is commonly called *data mining*, which basically refers to the routinized and automated processes of discovering patterns from models (Barocas et al., 2014, 6). Though data mining has become somewhat of a contemporary buzzword, the concept has been around for over 25 years, pioneered by IBM research fellow Rakesh Agrawal in a paper demonstrating the utility of consumer algorithms coupled with retail data (Agrawal et al., 1993). However, the world has moved way beyond analyzing patterns in Marks & Spencer's retail data as was the case with the aforementioned research paper. Today, data mining has become a standardized way of collecting and saving traces of human activity, whether these data subjects are consumers, citizens, criminals or 'users.' What is important is that we do not lose sight of what data mining is for, or whom and in what situations. Beyond simply collecting, storing, and analyzing data, the critical task is to interrogate the purposes and processes of data mining in a broader perspective. As van Dijck asks: "why do we look for certain patterns in piles of metadata, in whose interests, and for what purposes?" (2014, 202). It is when data mining becomes an argument for even more data mining – more data to make borders secure or more data to make more effective business decisions – that we need to be particularly alert (Vaidhyanathan, 2017). As we confront the world of increased enumeration, quantification, and prediction, there is also a need to ask what the possibilities are to remain invisible, silent, indeed, undiscoverable? Notwithstanding the men and women of the Golden Age of Dutch science and technology or the epidemiologists of Google, sometimes the unseen should remain just that.

Notes

1 I borrow the opening story from an article published in The Atlantic: see Brynjolfsson and Mcafee (2011).
2 Portions of the section on algorithms are adapted from Bucher 2018.

References

Agrawal, R., Imieliński, T., and Swami, A. (1993). *Mining Association Rules Between Sets of Items in Large Databases*. Paper presented at the ACM Sigmod Record.
Amoore, L., and Piotukh, V. (2015). Life Beyond Big Data: Governing with Little Analytics. *Economy and Society*, 44(3), 341–366.

Anderson, C. (2008). The end of theory: The data deluge makes the scientific method obsolete. *Wired magazine*, 16(7), 16–07.

Barnes, T. J. (2013). Big data, little history. *Dialogues in Human Geography*, 3(3), 297–302.

Barocas, S., Rosenblat, A., boyd, d., Gangadharan, S. P., and Yu, C. (2014). Data & Civil Rights: Technology Primer. *Data & Society*. www.datacivilrights.org/.

Beer, D. (2016). How Should We Do the History of Big Data? *Big Data & Society*, 3(1), 1–10. doi:2053951716646135.

Boyd, D., and Crawford, K. (2012). Critical Questions for Big Data: Provocations for a Cultural, Technological, and Scholarly Phenomenon. *Information, Communication & Society*, 15(5), 662–679.

Brynjolfsson, E., and Mcafee, A. (2011). The Big Data Boom Is the Innovation Story of Our Time. *The Atlantic*. www.theatlantic.com/business/archive/2011/11/the-big-data-boom-is-the-innovation-story-of-our-time/248215.

Bucher, T. (2017). The Algorithmic Imaginary: Exploring the Ordinary Affects of Facebook Algorithms. *Information, Communication & Society*, 20(1), 30–44.

Bucher, T. (2018). *IF . . . THEN: Algorithmic Power and Politics*. New York: Oxford University Press.

Butler, D. (2008). Web Data Predict Flu. *Nature*, 456, 287–288.

Butler, D. (2013). When Google Got Flu Wrong. *Nature*, 494(7436), 155.

Callon, M., and Law, J. (2005). On Qualculation, Agency, and Otherness. *Environment and Planning D: Society and Space*, 23(5), 717–733.

Cheney-Lippold, J. (2017). *We Are Data: Algorithms and The Making of Our Digital Selves*. New York: New York University Press.

Crawford, K., Miltner, K., and Gray, M. L. (2014). Critiquing Big Data: Politics, Ethics, Epistemology. *International Journal of Communication (19328036)*, 8.

Crawford, K., and Schultz, J. (2014). Big Data and Due Process: Toward a Framework to Redress Predictive Privacy Harms. *Boston College Law Review*, 55, 93.

Desrosières, A., and Naish, C. (2002). *The Politics of Large Numbers: A History of Statistical Reasoning*. Cambridge, MA: Harvard University Press.

De Vries, K. (2010). Identity, Profiling Algorithms and a World of Ambient Intelligence. *Ethics and Information Technology*, 12(1), 71–85.

Domingos, P. (2015). *The Master Algorithm: How the Quest for the Ultimate Learning Machine Will Remake Our World*. New York: Basic Books.

Dourish, P. (2014). NoSQL: The Shifting Materialities of Database Technology. *Computational Culture*, 4.

Dourish, P. (2017). *The Stuff of Bits: An Essay on the Materialities of Information*. Cambridge, MA: MIT Press.

Elmer, G. (2004). *Profiling Machines*. Cambridge, MA: MIT Press.

Espeland, W. N., and Sauder, M. (2007). Rankings and Reactivity: How Public Measures Recreate Social Worlds. *American Journal of Sociology*, 113(1), 1–40.

Espeland, W. N., & Stevens, M. L. (2008). A sociology of quantification. *European Journal of Sociology*, 49(03), 401–436.

Facebook. (2016). *Data Policy*. www.facebook.com/full_data_use_policy.

Flach, P. (2012). *Machine Learning: The Art and Science of Algorithms That Make Sense of Data*. Cambridge: Cambridge University Press.

Foucault, M. (2007). *Security, Territory, Population*. New York: Palgrave Macmillan.

Fuller, M. (2008). *Software Studies: A Lexicon*. Cambridge, MA: MIT Press.

Goffey, A. (2008). Algorithm. In M. Fuller (ed.), *Software Studies: A Lexicon*. Cambridge, MA: MIT Press.

Hacking, I. (1990). *The Taming of Chance*. Cambridge: Cambridge University Press.

Hacking, I. (1991). How Should We Do the History of Statistics? In G. Burchell, C. Gordon, and P. Miller (eds.), *The Foucault Effect – Studies in Governmentality*. London: Harvester, Wheatsheaf.

Hacking, I. (2006). *The Emergence of Probability: A Philosophical Study of Early Ideas About Probability, Induction and Statistical Inference*. Cambridge: Cambridge University Press.

Halford, S., and Savage, M. (2017). Speaking Sociologically with Big Data: Symphonic Social Science and the Future for Big Data Research. *Sociology*. doi:10.1177/0038038517698639.

Hargittai, E. (2015). Is Bigger Always Better? Potential Biases of Big Data Derived from Social Network Sites. *The Annals of the American Academy of Political and Social Science*, 659(1), 63–76.

Helles, R. (2013). The Big Head and the Long Tail: An Illustration of Explanatory Strategies for Big Data Internet Studies. *First Monday*, 18(10).

Helles, R., and Jensen, K. B. (2013). Introduction to the Special Issue: Making Data–Big Data and Beyond. *First Monday*, 18(10).

Ingold, T. (1993). The Temporality of the Landscape. *World Archaeology*, 25(2), 152–174.

Kennedy, H., and Hill, R. L. (2017). The Feeling of Numbers: Emotions in Everyday Engagements with Data and Their Visualisation. *Sociology*. doi:10.1177/0038038516674675.

Kennedy, H., Poell, T., and van Dijck, J. (2015). Introduction: Special issue on Data and agency. *Data & Society* 2.

Kitchin, R. (2014). *The Data Revolution: Big Data, Open Data, Data Infrastructures and Their Consequences*. Thousand Oaks, CA: Sage.

Knuth, D. E. (1984). Literate Programming. *The Computer Journal*, 27(2), 97–111.

Lane, N. (2015). The Unseen World: Reflections on Leeuwenhoek (1677), Concerning Little Animals. *Philosophical Transactions of the Royal Society B*, 370(1666), 20140344.

Lomborg, S. (2017). A state of flux: Histories of social media research. *European Journal of Communication*, 32(1), 6–15.

Lomborg, S., and Frandsen, K. (2016). Self-Tracking as Communication. *Information, Communication & Society*, 19(7), 1015–1027.

Lupton, D. (2017). Data Thing-Power: How Do Personal Digital Data Come to Matter? *Available at SSRN 2998571*.

Lyon, D. (2014). Surveillance, Snowden, and Big Data: Capacities, Consequences, Critique. *Big Data & Society*, 1(2). doi:10.1177/2053951714541861.

Mayer-Schönberger, V., & Cukier, K. (2013). *Big data: A revolution that will transform how we live, work, and think*. Houghton Mifflin Harcourt.

Milan, S., and Velden, L. V. D. (2016). The Alternative Epistemologies of Data Activism. *Digital Culture & Society*, 2(2), 57–74.

Neff, G., Tanweer, A., Fiore-Gartland, B., and Osburn, L. (2017). Critique and Contribute: A Practice-Based Framework for Improving Critical Data Studies and Data Science. *Big Data*, 5(2), 85–97.

Power, M. (2004). Counting, Control and Calculation: Reflections on Measuring and Management. *Human Relations*, 57(6), 765–783.

Power, M. (1999). *The audit society: Rituals of verification*. Oxford: Oxford University Press.

Rieder, G., and Simon, J. (2016). Datatrust: Or, the Political Quest for Numerical Evidence and the Epistemologies of Big Data. *Big Data & Society*, 3(1). doi:10.1177/2053951716649398.

Ruckenstein, M., and Schüll, N. D. (2017). The Datafication of Health. *Annual Review of Anthropology*, 46, 261–278.

Ruppert, E. (2011). Population Objects: Interpassive Subjects. *Sociology*, 45(2), 218–233.

Ruppert, E., Law, J., and Savage, M. (2013). Reassembling Social Science Methods: The Challenge of Digital Devices. *Theory, Culture & Society*, 30(4), 22–46.

Sauder, M., and Espeland, W. N. (2009). The Discipline of Rankings: Tight Coupling and Organizational Change. *American Sociological Review*, 74(1), 63–82.

Seaver, N. (2015). The Nice Thing About Context Is That Everyone Has It. *Media, Culture & Society*, 37(7), 1101–1109.

Strathern, M. (2000). *Audit cultures: Anthropological studies in accountability, ethics, and the academy*. London: Routledge.

Vaidhyanathan, S. (2017). The Incomplete Political Economy of Social Media. *The Sage Handbook of Social Media*, 213.

Van Dijck, J. (2014). Datafication, Dataism and Dataveillance: Big Data Between Scientific Paradigm and Ideology. *Surveillance & Society*, 12(2), 197.

Verran, H. (2001). *Science and an African Logic*. Chicago: University of Chicago Press.

Zook, M. et al. (2017). Ten Simple Rules for Responsible Big Data Research. *PLoS Computational Biology*, 13(3), e1005399.

Zwitter, A. (2014). Big Data Ethics. *Big Data & Society*, 1(2). doi:10.1177/2053951714559253.

8

Archive Fever revisited

Algorithmic archons and the ordering of social media

David Beer

When attempting to understand contemporary media and the power of data, Jacques Derrida's book *Archive Fever* (1996) may not seem like an obvious place to turn. Originally delivered as a lecture on the June 5, 1994,[1] he was largely concerned with returning to Freud and responding to the contemporaneous work of Yosef Hayim Yerushalmi. As a result, *Archive Fever* is largely occupied with important political questions about remembrance. On top of this, Derrida's lecture also predates many of the developments that we have come to associate with contemporary media. We might also be surprised of the utility of the lecture when we consider that Derrida used a typewriter for most of his career. Yet, in 1986, when 56 years old, he enthusiastically switched to a computer. He encountered some initial difficulties and even lost a number of files – suggesting his own careful archiving practices were disrupted, if only briefly, by this technology (see Peeters, 2013, 424–425). So, although *Archive Fever* isn't directly about computation, he had been using a computer in his working life for around 8 years before delivering this lecture.[2] Indeed, in this lecture he even briefly alludes to his "little portable Macintosh on which [he has] begun to write" (Derrida, 1996, 25). This momentary reflection causes him to wonder if the archive is indeed changing.

The pressing problem that we face today, I would suggest, is with understanding the power dynamics and ordering processes that underpin contemporary media and data circulations of different types. In trying to understand these power dynamics, and especially the new forms of social ordering and governance that they bring, it is helpful to revisit certain conceptual ideas that might enable us to cast new light upon the social and cultural formations that we see today (for a similar revisiting of concepts, see Fuchs, 2013). Derrida's (1996) *Archive Fever: A Freudian Impression*, or *Mal d'Archive: une impression freudienne* in the original French (see Derrida, 1995) is one such text from which this type of conceptual inspiration might be derived.

More specifically then, this chapter is concerned with attempting to conceptualize the implicit ordering structures within social media and 'the big data revolution' (Kitchin, 2014). By treating social media as a kind of archival media form, building upon my earlier work (see particularly Beer, 2013, 40–62; as well as Beer & Burrows, 2013; Gane & Beer, 2008), this chapter uses Derrida's text to further open-up the political dimensions of these archives. It explores the potential the concept of the archive holds for helping us to think about the organization, ordering, classification, storage, and retrieval of data as captured within social media (see also Featherstone, 2000). *Archive Fever* is used here to explore in what ways these media forms are archival and what this means for how they are organized and ordered. Approaching social media through Derrida's text encourages an examination of the underpinning processes of accumulation, classification, and retrieval (features that are shown to be crucial to understanding contemporary media by Day, 2014). Throughout the chapter asks: If social media are archives then what can they be used to say about the lives that they record?

The concept of the archive and the role of the archon

Derrida begins his lecture with some reflections on the etymology of the archive. This, the following passage intimates, gives us some scope for reflecting on the dynamics of the archive:

> *Arkhē*, we recall, names at once the *commencement* and the *commandment*. This name apparently coordinates two principles in one: the principle according to nature or history, *there* where things *commence* – physical, historical, or ontological principle – but also the principle according to the law, *there* where men and gods *command*, *there* where authority, social order are exercised, *in this place* from which *order* is given – nomological principle.
>
> *(Derrida, 1996, 1)*[3]

We see then, from the aforementioned, that the roots of the term 'archive' might reveal something of the archive itself. It is both a way of establishing and then accumulating, while also providing the platform from which orders and pronouncements can be made. In short then, it is the basis for deciding what data are captured and is then the means by which things can be said using those data. The roots of the term suggest that the archive is where things begin, where they start to accumulate into memory, while also then becoming the source from which commandments are made. The archive, based on this reflection upon its lines of origin, is a source of power for establishing certain regimes of ordering along with being the source from which social ordering can then be performed. In this formulation the archive is the source of authority. Archives are where power can be exercised in the form of social ordering. The archive is the place of knowledge and expertise, a spatial resource for exercising power through ordering. As we see then reflected in Foucault's (2002, 145) point that the archive dictates what can be said or Featherstone's (2006, 594) point that the archive is a resource for making or reworking memory. This is a point that has been picked up more recently with what Long et al. (2017) have referred to as 'affective archives,' in which social media like YouTube allow people to connect with their past and engage in collective do-it-yourself memory making. This is where power works through the archives' ability to capture and then to enable the deployment of knowledge to make statements or to rework memory.

Derrida's point is that this power is in some way concealed or secreted away in the archive, we forget that it carries such power. As he puts it, the 'the concept of the archive shelters in itself, of course, this memory of the name *arkhē*. But it also *shelters* itself from this memory which it shelters: Which comes down to saying that it also forgets it' (Derrida, 1996, 2). Not only do we forget the origins of the term but at the same time the archive works to conceal such a set of power connections. It reinforces and hides its own powers to shape knowledge and craft memory. Part of the power of the archive then, we might conclude, is in its appearance as neutral and disinterested. As Derrida puts it, there is a concept hidden within a concept, or 'the concept archived in this word "archive"' (Derrida, 1996, 90).

Derrida's important opening analysis of the origins of the archive does not end there. He adds:

> As is the case for the Latin *archivum* or *archium* (. . .), the meaning of "archive," its only meaning, comes to it from the Greek *arkheion*: initially a house, a domicile, an address, the residence of the superior magistrates, the *archons*, those who commanded.
>
> *(Derrida, 1996, 2)*

The archive then has these origins within a spatial setting, which might need to be rethought as social media come to enable us to archive our everyday lives (see Beer & Burrows, 2013) or to place the archive at the center of everyday life (Featherstone, 2000). The broader point though is that the archive is spatially contained. It has limits and boundaries – these boundaries perform the role of demarcating what is in the archive from what is not. The 'archons' were responsible for maintaining those boundaries and for controlling the archive. As such, they were responsible for drawing imper-meable lines around the archive, lines that made the archive internally coherent. They maintained the archive's boundary walls. The archons and the archive carry with them a 'publicly recognized authority' (Derrida, 1996, 2) that is spatially defined. As Derrida further explains:

> The archons are first of all the documents' guardians. They do not only ensure the physical security of what is deposited and of the substrate. They are also accorded the hermeneutic right and competence. They have the power to interpret the archives. Entrusted to such archons, these documents in effect speak the law: they recall the law and call upon or impose the law.
>
> *(Derrida, 1996, 2)*

In Derrida's accounts then the archons are crucial to understanding the archive. Understanding the role of the archon is necessary to understanding the archival practices and structures and to understanding what the archive is used to say or to capture. The archons are the guardians of the archive's limits and scope, they protect that knowledge and the archive's documents. They protect and control the substrate, the deposits in the archive. They protect the viability, coher-ence, and validity of the archive. More than this though they have what Derrida refers to as the 'hermeneutic right,' that is to say that they have the right and power to impose meaning upon the documents contained in the archive. This 'hermeneutic right' is the right to attach meaning to the documents and, crucially, to decide what can be said with them. As this indicates, the archons do not just collate and classify documents, they also decide what meanings and knowl-edge can then be extracted from that archive.

As this would suggest, the archons are the ones who are deemed to have the right and competence to decide what the archive can be used to say. It is the archons that have the role of interpreting the documents. Thus they mediate between the material documents and the assertions that can be made from those documents. Derrida's point is that these documents are spoken as law through the mediating figures of the archons. The archons take the role of gate-keeping, protecting and interpreting the archive – managing its integrity and coherence. They are there to both stop the data being hacked, to make decisions about what is documented, but also then to define what the archive is used to reveal. To ensure the authority of the archive it needs both to be secure and to have a material presence. As Derrida claims, 'the jurisdiction of this speaking the law' needs both a 'guardian and a localization'; it needs both a 'substrate' and a 'residence' (Derrida, 1996, 2). The archive, in other words, needs both limits and active figures who protect those limits. By protecting those limits the archive can be used to speak the law or to reinforce meanings, interpretations, and, possibly, memories.

The authority of the archive and its pledge to the future

The archive then derives its authority through a combination of its documents, its location, and its interpreters. But it also gains its authority from its ability to reform the relations between the public and the private, something that we know is now a common thread in understandings of the broadcasting of lives in social media (see, for one example, Bauman, 2007). Indeed, for Derrida, the archive marks a shift in a transition in privacy. For Derrida, 'the dwelling, this place where they dwell permanently, marks the institutional passage from the private to the public, which does not always mean from the secret to the non-secret' (Derrida, 1996, 2–3). The archival space enables a shift in the relations between the public and the private as it opens the individual life up to being recorded. But there is an interesting subtlety here concerning the notion of *the public*. To make public here, is to house documents about that individual life in the archive. Thus it is not to make that life entirely public, but rather it is to document it within the archive. Privacy may be reconfigured in social media archives, but the data they hold are rarely entirely open or public – which is an echo we may need to explore. Instead the power relations are to be found in the control of access to documents and in the tensions around privacy. This is about making private lives into public documents, but not necessarily for the purposes of transparency – Clare Birchall's work provides a superb insight into the intricacies of notions of transparency (see, for example, Birchall, 2015). Becoming public is not then the same as becoming open or non-secretive. Rather, that publicized knowledge is used or deployed within the power structures represented by the archive. Instead, documents are captured in the archive 'by virtue of a privileged topology' (Derrida, 1996, 3). This, Derrida is suggesting, is a place where 'law and singularity intersect in privilege' (Derrida, 1996, 3). There is a hierarchy to both accumulation and access. Consider here how privacy settings limit the archival access to the detail of social media profiles. Or, more significantly, how the background data produced by social media usage is captured in the recesses of the archival structures rather than being broadcast – to later be used for commercial targeted advertising and the like. Privacy and changing notions of privacy is clearly important but is nonetheless a complex issue in social media (as discussed by Fuchs, 2013, 156–159). Clearly, it is not as straightforward as social media profiles creating spaces for private lives to become. Derrida's account of the role of secrecy in archives can help to disrupt any simple notions of the social media archive as public. The opacity of archive systems is worth reflecting on when we think of the scale of social media, a point that has been picked up by Ronald Day (2014, 4) in some wide-ranging reflections on the indexing of documents:

> With increasing recursivity, scale, and ubiquity in sociotechnical infrastructures, algorithms and indexes have become both more opaque and more mobile, hiding the logical and psychological assumptions that once were very clear in traditional top-down and universal classification and taxonomic structures, as well as in other professional information techniques and technologies.

The volume and scale contribute to the opacity, as do the changing properties of the infrastructures. This role of secrecy is something that has recently been explored in some detail in Frank Pasquale's (2015) work, especially through his notion of a 'black box society,' in which secrecy around data and algorithmic processes is central to the performance of contemporary capitalism. In the black box society envisioned by Pasquale, secrecy is part of how value is protected and managed. This would suggest that with social media archives, we might expect there to be some secrecy.

The archive's role in both making public and managing its secrets is important in the power it holds or facilitates. This might remind us of the way in which the modern state is based upon the knowledge of its populations; a form of knowledge that Foucault suggests is central to forms of liberal and neoliberal governance (see Foucault, 2007, 2008). Derrida attempts to take us inside the functioning of this archival facilitated power by reflecting on the way that the archive enables the parameters of knowledge to be set. As Derrida puts it, 'the archontic power, which also gathers the functions of unification, of identification, of classification, must be paired with what we call the power of *consignation*' (Derrida, 1996, 3). So, this archival power is based upon the bringing together of documents, it relies on the identification of people and things, and it is structured through the categories and classifications that are used to house those documents – which exposes social media archives to the broader politics and prejudices of classification (Tyler, 2015; MacMillan Cottom, 2017, 218–220). But there is a further process here, for Derrida, a process in which the archive's limits and tenor are established. When he speaks of 'consignation' he is talking of gathering together and assigning of residence to documents and traces; but there is something a little more than this. As he then adds, 'It is not only the traditional *consignatio*, that is, the written proof, but what all *consignatio* begins by presupposing' (Derrida, 1996, 3). The archive then is based upon presuppositions that define what is captured. The gathering together of documents is based upon an understanding of what is suitable for the archive, and thus sets the rules of what is to be included and what is not. This is about the pre-set ideas of the archive, its purpose and the type of information it should hold. The archive then has aims that influence what is gathered together. The archive has an established framework from which accumulation of documents begins. We will reflect on this in terms of the relations we have with an imagined future in a moment, but we can think here about how presuppositions and pre-set ideas about social media archives come to shape what is gathered together in the user's profiles. This is also about how, over the years, various presuppositions about these archives have, gradually, morphed into norms about what is appropriate and desirable information to be held in a profile – which we might now be seeing in the particular forms of 'impression management' on social media specific profiles (as discussed by Ward, 2017; Ravenelle, 2017). The balance of sharing without oversharing is one such question that social media users often ponder. In other words, reflecting on Derrida's points about consignation forces us to reflect on how presuppositions come to determine the shape of the social media profile and of the archiving processes that occur within social media spaces. These presuppositions are based on a kind of modeling or understanding of the world and the role of the archive within it. This is about an imagination of what the archive should capture, which then translates into the form it takes and the types of materials that are then pursued.

The discussion of consignation does not end there though. Derrida continues by suggesting:

> *Consignation* aims to coordinate a single corpus, in a system or a synchrony in which all the elements articulate the unity of an ideal configuration. In an archive there should not be any absolute dissociation, any heterogeneity or *secret* which could separate (*secernere*), or partition, in an absolute manner. The archontic principle of the archive is also a principle of consignation, that is, of gathering together.
>
> *(Derrida, 1996, 3)*

The pursuit here is of a notion of unity. A gathering together of sources that lend unity to the subjects covered. It is about finding connections and linkages between materials to make them feel connected and coherent. It is an attempt to gather materials together in a unified way. That notion of coherence and unification require, for Derrida, some pre-set ideas. In the case of a social media profile, we can imagine how the archive is used to suggest the unity and coherence of the life being captured. The tagging of people in photos is perhaps one visible instance of how the documents are selected to enable the connections to be made, with the right photos classified in the right ways to give a sense of connectivity (for a discussion see Hand, 2012, 143–184). We can think here of how a profile on social media is an attempt to try to assemble or consign bits to create a single coherent corpus of information about us. If this formulation is fitting for social media then the ideal would be the configuration of a coherent profile, even if this might not ultimately be achieved. Applying Derrida's point here is to think about how that gathering together of a Facebook or Instagram profile is an act that requires pre-set ideas and presuppositions about what the archive is for and how it will depict that life. Thus, consignation in a social media archive is actively shaping what that archive captures and how. This is why Derrida (1996, 4) argues that a 'science of the archive must include the theory of this institutionalization, that is to say, the theory both of the law which begins by inscribing itself there and of the right which authorizes it.' It is at the moment of institutionalization that the rules begin to form, rules that are based on ideas about what the archive is for and how it will be used. The archive then becomes a producer of our attempts to capture the present or the past for the purposes of an imagined future.

The aforementioned suggests that the archive is a powerful and active presence in shaping what is known. For Derrida, the archive

> is not only the place for stocking and for conserving an archivable content *of the past* which would exist in any case, such as, without the archive, one still believes it was or will have been. No, the technical structure of the *archiving* archive also determines the structure of the *archivable* content even in its very coming into existence and in its relationship to the future. The archivization produces as much as it records the event.
>
> *(Derrida, 1996, 17)*

The archive, Derrida contends, is a process that produces and creates rather than simply recording and capturing. This is not just about what is included in the archive, it is also about the way that the captured materials are ordered and organized. The structures of the archive dictate the way those materials are interpreted. So, understanding the productive power of the archive is to understand the choices made about content while also appreciating the categorization and classification processes that feed into that content. Derrida's point here is that the choices about inclusion and classification pitch the archive into a set of relations with imagined futures. In terms of classification, Derrida's (1996, 40) point is that 'there could be no archiving without titles (hence without names and without the archontic principle of legitimization, without laws, without criteria of classification and of hierarchization, without order and without order, in the double sense of the word).' Classifications or titles are needed for the archive's content to be retrievable, but these classifications are as much about this relation to the future as the content that is selected for inclusion. Categorizations are based on how it is imagined that the archive will be searched in the future. This is why Derrida sees the establishment of the archive as being crucial in understanding the politics of that archive. Especially as it is in the early stages that the rules are set and when the relations to the future are originally orientated. As Derrida explains:

> The first archivist institutes the archive as it should be, that is to say, not only in exhibiting the document but in *establishing* it. He reads it, interprets it, classes it. In this case what is at play is all the more serious, as the document turns out to keep this inscription.
>
> *(Derrida, 1996, 55)*

These early stages then are seminal in shaping the later conventions that are to be followed and the visions of future interpretation that shape classification and selection. Social media have really been widely used since 2006, over the last decade or so we might be able to reflect on how the rules of those archives were established by the first population of social media archivists. More than this though, Derrida's point might cause us to reflect on the importance of the hashtag as a cross cutting classification within social media. By linking content together from diverse users the hashtag performs a powerful classificatory role, such as in hashtag activism, and can thus have some powerful political dynamics that are only just becoming apparent (as discussed in Highfield, 2016, 106–114). A hashtag is likely to be created or reused with a sense of an imagined future in which others use or through which the associated content is discovered. This is a little like what has been described as the 'game' (Seiffert-Brockman et al., 2017) of memes, in which future activity around that meme is imagined during its creation – with the meme as an invitation formulated to provoke future adaptation of the content (Shifman, 2014, 341). Social media, it would seem, however instant they appear, are often concerned with an imagined future use of the content in mind.

Derrida's claim is that archiving is concerned with capturing the past and present but in the context of an imagined future – a future in which those documents will be deployed for certain predicted purposes. Thus the form of the archive and the materials it contains are a product of how it is imagined that those materials will be accessed and retrieved in the future and who they might be used by. This is why Derrida claims that 'the archive as an irreducible experience of the future' (Derrida, 1996, 68). And that when the archive is forming, accumulating, and classifying its documents we can see 'the future as *specter*' (Derrida, 1996, 84). The future reception and use of the archive materials mean that these imagined futures are a part of the archival processes and practices as they happen – with the future then shaping how the archive develops and what it might be used to say.

In this formulation we might imagine that social media archives produce as well as record events. All of these events and traces of life are not just captured but are produced in response to the presence of social media archives. In short then, the form that these archival social media take, produces and shapes the events that they capture and the way that people understand, respond and memorialize those events. Knowledge and memory are changed as the archival structures within which we live change. As Derrida put it, 'archival technology no longer determines, will never have determined, merely the moment of the conservational recording, but rather the very institution of the archivable event.' (Derrida, 1996, 18). The future, via the archive, finds its way into the actual events that they capture – bringing an imagined future into the processes of archiving lives.

The archive, for Derrida, 'ties knowledge and memory to the promise' (Derrida, 1996, 30). This is a promise of what the archive might in the future be used to reveal. So the archive is concerned with a notion of the past, but one that is captured in line with the promises of the future. In social media we can imagine that lives are archived in profiles with potential futures in mind. These are rapid environments, so the promises and pledges are often aligned to a more immediate sense of the future – will people react, like, and share this picture, status update, or observation, for example. Yet they may also be shaped by individuals reflecting on how they might want to look back on events in the future and how they may wish to remember certain times in their lives. This is especially the case now as social media platforms tell users what they were doing on the date in previous years and with year in review products and the like, meaning that there are constant reminders that this is also an archive of their lives. Memories are not a part of the imaginary of social media (Bucher, 2017, 38). As with more established archives, for archival social media '[i]t is a question of the future, the question of the future itself, the question of a response, of a promise and of a responsibility for tomorrow' (Derrida, 1996, 36). With these developments in social media it is likely that the use of social media archives will also be shaped by an imagined future-self using the archive to revisit and remember moments within that life. This would suggest that social media archives are used in ways that have such an imagined future stimulation of memories in mind. The content added to the archive is likely to be shaped by the way we imagine that we might wish to remember in the future.

So it is not just about the way the event is captured in the archive; rather, it is that it shapes the events that happen in the first place. In the case of social media, we might imagine how life events are shaped or cultivated to suit the particularities of the social media archive in which it will be captured. The archive's existence and form provokes events and actions. We might reflect here on how people shape their practices, behaviors, and the events in their life in order to create the right type of content for their social media archive. From creating the right kinds of photographs that we know will circulate, to the engagement in extreme activities or unusual practices, such as urban exploration, to create striking images. This is based, for Derrida (1996, 18), on a kind of 'anticipation of the future' – which might be based on how the event will be captured and received by the archive, or responded to in the future. Derrida speaks of this relation to the future as a kind of 'pledge.' The archive, according to Derrida (1996, 18), 'has always been a *pledge*, and like every pledge, a token of the future.' There is a sense of a pledge in archival acts. In the case of social media, this would require us to reflect on how a profile, as an archive of an individual life nested within a vast archive of lives, is a product of such pledges – where the notion of how the profile will be consumed, read and interpreted shapes what goes into the profile and how that content is tagged and classified. More than this though, it also forces us to reflect on how that life is lived differently as a result of the archive shaping the life events themselves. In other words, we have to reflect on how the presence of archival social media actually change how life is lived and how lives adapt to the need for the right type of social media content. We can turn again to Derrida on this point, he argues that 'what is no longer archived in the same way is no longer lived in the same way' (Derrida, 1996, 18). If we follow this logic it might lead us to think that everyday life is not just recorded differently by archival social media forms, but that it is also lived differently as a result of the presence of these archives. In other words, everyday life might well then be designed to suit the archival forms and the pledges to the future that they are built around. With social media our lives are no longer archived in the same way, so, if Derrida is correct, they will no longer be lived in the same way either. Archives don't just capture lives; they alter the way that they are lived.

Politics and memory

All of this hints at their being a politics of the archive that operates on very different scales. On this point Derrida's position is unequivocal. His contention is:

> There is no political power without control of the archive, if not of memory. Effective democratization can always be measured by this essential criterion: the participation in and the access to the archive, its constitution, and its interpretation.
>
> *(Derrida, 1996, 4 n1)*[4]

Again we see that the archive is placed at the center of power structures. This time though it is through a focus on memory that the power of the archive can be elaborated more fully. The archive can be seen to dictate what is remembered and how. The archive may be formulated through a sense of the future but when that future arrives those earlier decisions dictate the insights that can be drawn from the archive in the form of memories, pasts and biographies. One issue here is that absences in the archive can't be proven (Derrida, 1996, 64), so decisions about inclusion are powerful and dictate what is known and what cannot be known. So the decisions about what pictures are included in a social media profile, for instance, might then dictate directly what is remembered – with the photos being left out leaving gaps or alternative narratives aside. Thus, with the shaping of memory, Derrida notes in a phrase that is likely to be influenced by the type of remembrance with which he was primarily concerned, there is a 'violence of the archive itself, *as archive, as archival violence*' (Derrida, 1996, 7). This is because, he continues, every archive is 'at once institutive and conservative. Revolutionary and traditional. An *eco-nomic* archive in this double sense: it keeps, it puts in reserve, it saves, but in an unnatural fashion, that is to say in making the law (*nomos*) or in making people respect the law.' (Derrida, 1996, 7). The act of conserving, Derrida is suggesting here, is innately conservative. It carries a sense of risk, through which judgments are made. And the exclusions and inclusions can be violent in the consequences that they have for people.

As we consider what this means for the laws and rules of contemporary media, we can note that Derrida was himself starting to reflect on what computer technologies might mean for archiving. In particular he reflected on what computers might mean for the relation between internal and external memory – a point that resonates with Hayles (2006) much later claims about the presence of a 'cognisphere' in which cognitive processes stretch out across media. Derrida does not take these considerations very far; he instead seems to concentrate on a narrower focus on more established archival forms. But he does wonder what changing computerized media might mean for archival memory. At one point, reflecting on email and computers he asks: 'Do these archival machines change anything? Do they affect the essentials of Freud's discourse?' (Derrida, 1996, 14). He doesn't then provide any direct answer to this but there seems an implicit assumption that they will reconfigure memory by introducing new types of archives into everyday spaces. Derrida offers some further clues in this regard. Or at least he offers a further more detailed formulation of the same question. This time he asks:

> Is the psychic apparatus *better represented* or is it *affected differently* by all the technical mechanisms for archivization and for reproduction, for prostheses of the so-called live memory, for simulacrums of living things which already are, and will increasingly be, more refined, complicated, powerful than the "mystic pad" (microcomputing, electonization, computerization, etc.)?
>
> *(Derrida, 1996, 15)*

This question reveals Derrida's interest in the implications of archival technologies for the understanding of the individual and their memory – while also suggesting his uncertainty about what the implications will be. There is this hint here at a computerized prosthesis of memory. It would seem that his uncertainty is coupled with a sense of a significant change to come. This would be a change, he suspects, that is not just a change to speed, temporality, architectures, and representation, it would be a question of 'an entirely different logic' (Derrida, 1996, 15). Perhaps with social media we are seeing something of that different logic at work in these archival spaces – with social media being archives but with a very different logic to the archives of the past.

One change, it would seem, is the potential for these media to create an 'archival earthquake' (Derrida, 1996, 16). If we think of social media as being archival, then we might have seen the vibrating ruptures of this kind. The archive is no longer contained or containable, but rather archiving through social media appears spatially limitless in its capacity due to its unanchored geography and its apparent lack of walls. The 'archive drive' (Derrida, 1996, 19) certainly goes well beyond the state, with archiving now a pastime that reaches a vast population of users in both scale and in the detail of the archives produced. These are commercial rather than state-controlled archives and they have a very different materiality to the archives imagined by Derrida. The social media archive may have a materiality, in data centers, cabling, and servers, but this materiality no longer limits what is placed within it or how its internal coherence is managed. The materiality of our data environment has been brilliantly articulated in a short film called points of presence created by Adam Fish and Bradley Garrett (2017). That film shows the movement of apparently immaterial data through cables, storage centers and geographic environments. This shifting materiality is one issue, but another is that social media archives are certainly less routed in a locality. If the locality was a source of the archives coherence and credibility, it is now finding a new coherence in social media spaces.

Further developing the concept of the archive for social media

Derrida's essay on the archive is a quite rich resource for reflecting on social media. If we are to think of social media as archival, then Derrida's piece creates a wide range of questions to consider. We have the questions of classification and categorization, but we also have his points on the questions of privacy and secrecy. Similarly, he might force us to think about how social media activity is a kind of pledge to an imagined future in which that content is retrieved from the archive in different ways – hence *Archive Fever* suggests to us that there are presuppositions about the archive that will drive the content that is added to social media. Clearly there is much here to consider about the role of social media in memory and remembrance, especially as we have now been living with social media forms for over a decade and greater proportions of people's biographies are captured within them.

It is hard to tell if this fits with Derrida's idea that this archiving is fuelled by a combination of a 'destruction drive' and a 'conservation drive' – which is the 'internal contradiction' that he refers to as 'archive fever' (Derrida, 1996, 19). It would seem that these competing archival drives flourish within social media, especially as ordinary and 'demotic' aspects of life are turned into media content (Turner, 2010). The key symptom of Derrida's archive fever 'is to have a compulsive, repetitive, and nostalgic desire for the archive' (Derrida, 1996, 91). It would seem that this desire is rife as people record the events, tastes and relationships that define their lives. Social media archiving is certainly feverish.

We might initially conclude that social media users have become the archons of these new archives. They decide on their profile's content and therefore they decide what goes into the archive and the meanings attached to those documents – as they go about building profiles and classifying content. But what does this mean for political power? And can we really assume that people have now gained a 'hermeneutic right' over their own lives as a result of the social media archives? Perhaps the way forward here is to reflect on how the role of archon is changed by social media. What we find is a kind of archonic division of labor. As well as the individual user acting as a kind of archon of their own profile, there are also the archons of commercial archives – that is, those archiving data generated from the use of our media and devices. So the power dynamics at play here become more complex if we focus on the archon as well as upon the archive.

With these decentralized archival media typical of contemporary social media, we cannot simply say that we have all become archons or that we all now are able to shape the data and metadata of these social media archives. We have not been granted the sole right to speak from these archives or to narrate the content about our lives. Nor are we in a position to control what is captured and what those documents are used to say. Rather we need to look at the interplay of different types of archival structures in our lives to see how each then shapes our lives, our memories and the information we have available and retrievable to us. Alongside this we might reflect on the role of the archon as it has been mutated in social media. It is important to reflect on the structures of these archives to think about how their architecture is a product of commercial and individual interests. This pushes us to reflect on how social media are organized, moderated, and controlled, and, crucially, how systems of classification and categorization are deployed in these spaces. Using the concept of the archive allows us to do this, but it is the concept of the archon that might help us to understand the power dynamics of social media. It is not only about who can capture what in these archival media that matters, but how that content is then organized and rendered retrievable.

Considering the role of the social media archon will help us to explore if the ordinary social media user has the same recognized authority to create and interpret the archive as those archons of the centralized official archival spaces of the past? Although we fill these social media archives with content about our everyday lives and that of our social networks, we might still ask who has the right and authority to say something based on those archives. Social media algorithms present the archives to us in neatly packaged forms, based upon predictions about what we want to know or what we want to remember. Perhaps reducing the social media user to the role of the archon is misleading – or, more accurately, perhaps treating the social media user as the *sole* archon is the mistake. In the aforementioned it is suggested that the labor is divided between the user or the ordinary archon and I kind of commercial archon, who we might understand to be the actors who shape social media platforms, analyze the data, and who own and use the profiles to generate value. Alongside the ordinary and commercial archon, there may be another presence exercising their hermeneutic right. Perhaps archons are also residing in the structures of the archives themselves – with algorithms making decisions about what is visible, how items are ranked or sorted and what is retrieved and encountered (for an overview, see Kitchin, 2017). In social media the data being produced and held in the archive are not only interpreted by human actors; the scale is too great. Instead we can see the processes of archival speaking as being led by *algorithmic archons* – machines that mine and read the data and then produce inferences and predictions. These would take the form of things like the Facebook Edgerank algorithm, which defines the news feed of each individual and therefore constantly decides what is being said with the archive (Bucher, 2012). These predictions often take the form of newsfeeds or prioritized highlights of content that you missed while you were away, and so on. In a context of social media and data analytics the 'hermeneutic right' moves to the hands of the algorithmic archon. With social media the archive may be compiled by the routine practices of accumulation in the individual profiles, with people adding their own content, but it is being filtered by algorithmic archons aimed at commercial enhancement and value generation that is shaping what is visible. Social media archives may be built by people, but they are searched and filtered by algorithms. It could be that it is these algorithmic archons that decide what can be said from the archive's content. As such, the archon here becomes a kind of blend of human and machine, of our cognitive interpretation of the archive and its classifications, combined with active forms of algorithmic sorting, recommendation, prioritizing, filtering, visibility, and retrieval. This is where the social media user is not the only guardian or interpreter of their own archives, and nor is the commercial actor. Rather they are in flux with the archival structures. Hence a focus on the archon as well as the archive may lead to further understanding of the dynamics of social media. The interplay of this triumvirate of archons – ordinary, commercial and algorithmic – may provide one way of exploring the way that meaning, memory and knowledge are created within and through the social media archives.

David Beer

Notes

1 Of course, there is a dialogue with Freud that is going on here, plus there is a wider political context for Derrida's lecture (see Peeters, 2013). Because of the focus of this essay, I've have concentrated centrally upon the conceptualization of the archive rather than reading the broader theoretical context and network of connections into this piece.
2 In terms of personal circumstances, we might also wonder if Derrida's accounts of archives might have been shaped by the ongoing sense of anxiety and the legal complexities that accompanied the archiving of Derrida's own personal papers in California and Paris (see Peeters, 2013).
3 Derrida frequently uses italics in his work. Rather than keep repeating that the italics are taken from the original, instead throughout this article I have left the italicized the quotes as they are in the original source.
4 In this passage Derrida refers directly and appears to be influenced by Sonia Combe's book *Archives interdites: Les peurs françaises face à l'histoire contemporaine* which was published in the same year that Derrida gave his lecture.

References

Bauman, Z. (2007). *Consuming Life*. Cambridge: Polity Press.
Beer, D. (2013). *Popular Culture and New Media: The Politics of Circulation*. Basingstoke: Palgrave Macmillan.
Beer, D., and Burrows, R. (2013). Popular Culture, Digital Archives and the New Social Life of Data. *Theory, Culture & Society*, 30(4), 47–71.
Birchall, C. (2015). 'Data.Gov-in-a-Box': Delimiting Transparency. *European Journal of Social Theory*, 18(2), 185–202.
Bucher, T. (2012). Want to Be on Top? Algorithmic Power and the Threat of Invisibility on Facebook. *New Media & Society*, 14(7), 1164–1180.
Bucher, T. (2017). The Algorithmic Imaginary: Exploring the Ordinary Affects of Facebook Algorithms. *Information, Communication & Society*, 20(1), 30–44.
Day, R. E. (2014). *Indexing It All: The Subject in the Age of Documentation, Information, and Data*. Cambridge, MA: MIT Press.
Derrida, J. (1995). *Mal d'Archive: une impression freudienne*. Paris: Galilée.
Derrida, J. (1996). *Archive Fever: A Freudian Impression*. Chicago and London: University of Chicago Press.
Featherstone, M. (2000). Archiving Cultures. *British Journal of Sociology*, 51(1), 168–184.
Featherstone, M. (2006). Archive. *Theory, Culture & Society*, 23(2–3), 591–596.
Fish, A., and Garrett, B. (2017). *Points of Presence*. https://vimeo.com/217078305 (Accessed December 10, 2017).
Foucault, M. (2002). *The Archaeology of Knowledge*. London: Routledge.
Foucault, M. (2007). *Security, Territory, Population: Lectures at the Collège de France 1977–1978*. Basingstoke: Palgrave Macmillan.
Foucault, M. (2008). *The Birth of Biopolitics: Lectures at the Collège de France 1978–1979*. Basingstoke: Palgrave Macmillan.
Fuchs, C. (2013). *Social Media: A Critical Introduction*. London: Sage.
Gane, N., and Beer, D. (2008). *New Media: The Key Concepts*. Oxford: Berg.
Hand, M. (2012). *Ubiquitous Photography*. Cambridge: Polity Press.
Hayles, N. K. (2006). Unfinished Work: From Cyborg to Cognisphere. *Theory, Culture & Society*, 23(7–8), 159–166.
Highfield, T. (2016). *Social Media and Everyday Politics*. Cambridge: Polity Press.
Kitchin, R. (2014). *The Data Revolution: Big Data, Open Data, Data Infrastructures & Their Consequences*. London: Sage.
Kitchin, R. (2017). Thinking Critically About and Researching Algorithms. *Information, Communication & Society*, 20(1), 14–29.
Long, P., Baker, S., Istvandity, L., and Collins, J. (2017). The Labour of Love: The Affective Archives of Popular Music Culture. *Archives and Records*, 38(1), 61–79.

Macmillan Cottom, T. (2017). Black Cyberfeminism: Ways Forward for Intersectionality and Digital Sociology. In J. Daniels, K. Gregory, and T. McMillan Cottom (eds.), *Digital Sociologies*. Bristol: Policy Press, pp. 211–231.

Pasquale, F. (2015). *The Black Box Society: The Secret Algorithms That Control Money and Information*. Cambridge, MA: Harvard University Press.

Peeters, B. (2013). *Derrida: A Biography*. Cambridge: Polity Press.

Ravenelle, A. J. (2017). A Return to Gemeinschaft: Digital Impression Management and the Sharing Economy. In J. Daniels, K. Gregory, and T. McMillan Cottom (eds.), *Digital Sociologies*. Bristol: Policy Press, pp. 27–46.

Seiffert-Brockman, J., Diehl, T., and Dobusch, L. (2017). Memes as Games: The Evolution of a Digital Discourse Online. *New Media & Society*. https://doi.org/10.1177/1461444817735334.

Shifman, L. (2014). The Cultural Logic of Photo-Based Meme Genres. *Journal of Visual Culture*, 13(3), 340–358.

Turner, G. (2010). *Ordinary People and the Media*. London: Sage.

Tyler, I. (2015). Classificatory Struggles: Class, Culture and Inequality in Neoliberal Times. *The Sociological Review*, 63(2), 493–511.

Ward, J. (2017). What Are You Doing on Tinder? Impression Management on Matchmaking Mobile App. *Information, Communication & Society*, 20(11), 1644–1659.

Part II
Practices

9

The practice of identity

Development, expression, performance, form

Mary Chayko

Our sense of being a person can come from being drawn into a wider social unit; our sense of selfhood can arise through the little ways in which we resist the pull. Our status is backed by the solid buildings of the world, while our sense of personal identity often resides in the cracks.

(Erving Goffman, 1968, 320)

Modern individuals are often engaged in the critical, often quite creative, practice of constructing a personal identity. Groups and organizations – even macro structures like nations – construct identities, as well. Digital media and communication technologies, including social media, are, for many, indispensable to these processes, as they help people locate one another, learn about one another, form networks, and exchange information and social capital, all of which are paramount in the exploration of self and identity.

The individual *self* is one's conception of being a person. It is constituted of characteristics and traits, mental and physical, and is presented in a variety of ways to the world. The self can be further broken down into the 'actual self' or 'empirical self' (one's most enduring traits – see James, 1983/1890); the 'ideal self' (the type of person one aspires to be); and the 'ought self' or 'possible selves' (the type of person one 'should' be and may be some day – see Higgins, 1987; Markus & Nurius, 1986).

Identity is the internal definition of, and internal conversation regarding, the ever-developing self, as actions are taken and choices are made regarding the presentation of the self or of a group in social roles and situations. These actions can be tacit, rote, or quite strategic, and undertaken in many types of contexts, for groups and organizations seek to develop *shared identities*, or *group identities*, as well. While both individuals and organizations frequently engage in reflection and debate as to how to best express, shape, brand, and share their identities, this essay will focus on individualist notions of self and identity.

As individuals learn the ways of society and how to participate in it via the process of *socialization*, the individual self comes into being. Self and identity develop as this process unfolds. In learning about the world and how others operate within it, and interacting with others, some of what is experienced becomes incorporated into a way of viewing the world. Gradually, the self – physical, psychological, emotional, social – comes into being and continues to evolve.

This is a never-ending process, continuing until the day we die, in which we learn what it is to be a person and a self, how to play out social roles and what it means to have a personal identity. It is a highly complex, fluid process in the digital age. But it was not always such.

As of the late 18th century, most people still tended to view themselves more as exemplars of more general categories, such as religion, class, profession, or family, than as an individualized self. People had the characteristics of personality and temperament that are now considered central to personal identity, of course, but such qualities were not highlighted when one thought about one's place in the world. Rather, one's membership in categories contributed most substantially to one's sense of identity and became equated with one's definition of 'personhood,' and as these categories were likely not seen as particularly mutable, so the self was not seen as changeable or specialized. This was especially the case in cultures that were not predominantly literate, complex, or specialized (Chayko, 2002).

Certain aspects and consequences of this process continue today. Identifying with the groups and categories to which we belong is common practice; it provides us with needed community and the sense of pride, self-esteem, and belonging that can derive from group membership. Many of the organizations, teams, nations, schools, interest groups, and the like that we feel an affiliation with are found and followed on the Internet and mass and digital media. We also locate others with whom we feel group affiliations on the basis of social characteristics such as gender, sexuality race, ethnicity, age or generation, socioeconomic class, level of education, physical or intellectual abilities and challenges, and the like. Stereotypical "us vs. them" thinking can then arise, and people can come to see their group as superior to the "out-group" to which they do not belong (Tajfel & Turner, 1979).

Newer, digital media afford additional countless opportunities to affiliate with different and diverse networks and groups and to form the relationships and communities so essential to the formation of identities. Even if the people have never met and may never meet, they can consider themselves close – closer, even, than those who see one another regularly face-to-face (Chayko, 2002; McKenna et al., 2002). Colleagues separated by distance can come to feel the same level of shared identity and sense of cognitive and affective closeness as those who work together in the same location (O'Leary et al., 2014). As a result, individual and group identities can be developed and shaped near constantly.

The development of identity

We develop our individual selves in concert with others. We 'try on' the behaviors, roles, and attitudes of those around us (Mead, 2009/1934), and those others then become, in effect, 'mirrors' that reflect back to us how we appear to and are received by the outside world (Cooley, 1964/1922). Perpetually, subtly, we develop a sense of who we are and who we want to be, using others as points of reference and reference group around which we pivot, developing and adjusting our identities accordingly all the while (Shibutani, 1955).

In a technology-rich society there are countless 'others' to whom we can compare ourselves at every turn. In my early work on mass media effects, I argued that in television and radio use, actual, legitimate primary groups are generated, because mass media enable people to get to know others and form groupings with them in such a personal, meaningful way (Cerulo et al., 1992). In Internet and social media use, this is even more apparent. People routinely form connections and communities that have deep significance for them, whether or not they have much (or any) face-to-face contact with them.

People are constantly aware of others' presence online and of their connection to them. In the 'attention economy' of online society (Davenport & Beck, 2002), it is easy to become invested in getting 'likes,' followers, and comments that represent attention and approval; we may even create content solely with an eye toward such reception. We can respond to these metrics and indicators of approval (or disapproval) quite emotionally, because we see them as indicators of how we are perceived and of our own popularity and identity. Our sense of self can be affected just as profoundly as when receiving such feedback face-to-face.

Just as the physical body is in a constant state of replenishment (e.g., on the cellular level), the self is in a constant state of development, redevelopment, and replenishment. Children and teens, we know, often envision themselves as young adults, trying out and testing who they are and who they want to be. This often takes place in casual, playful activities and spaces, online and offline, as opposed to those in which more formal learning takes place (indeed, the relaxed kind of learning that takes place during play is critical to the creation of self – Mead, 2009/1934). As freedom from authority can enhance the development of maturity and identity (especially sexual identity) in teens, social media and smartphones are often used to create and spend time in digital spaces in which they can move about and interact more freely (boyd, 2014).

Adults, too, shape their identities in part in online, digital spaces. Sometimes, identity construction takes on heightened importance for adults. They may be taking on new roles and challenges, such as when one moves, changes jobs, or has a change in relationship status. New roles arise and existing roles (partner, spouse, parent, colleague) change. The structures that supported past identities may no longer be there, or an individual may simply feel that it is time to make a change – to develop new skills, interests, friends, and so on. Online groups can serve as a needed resource and support at such times and as an opportunity to see how others respond to and interpret such life developments (Hormuth, 1990; Iyer et al., 2008; McCall & Simmons, 1978).

People may find that an aspect of identity that they might have assumed was "fixed" in some way is actually more "fluid" or changeable, whether physically or mentally. These can range from those that are relatively incidental to one's identity – enjoying a certain type of popular culture, for example – to those that are more fundamental. Gender identity, racial identity, sexual orientation – these and other aspects of identity can come to be considered in a different way over time, by an individual and by a culture.

Some aspects of identity are fluid and mutable across a lifetime, or even day to day, and might best be understood as existing along a spectrum rather than with a system of binary or strict categorization (such as gender or sexuality; see Budd-Cording, 2017). Online support groups and resources for those looking to deepen their understanding of identity as fluid and changeable have proven to be of enormous benefit, even a lifesaver, for many. Social support is perhaps never as important as when a pronounced change in identity is being considered or the acceptance of a non-mainstream, possibly confusing, aspect of identity is being sought. Such support can often be found in online communities (Chayko, 2008).

At the same time, threats, incidents of harm, and harassment of those claiming non-mainstream identities (gay, transgender, queer, atheist, differently abled) are common on social media and in digital tech spaces. Indeed, hate and harassment are rampant online and are often targeted toward those who are members of non-mainstream groups and populations. Sharing opinions and speaking openly about their experiences are often met with hate and harassment online (Duggan, 2017).

Digital technology can now be used to evaluate and assess one's behavior on a constant and detailed basis, especially in the area of health and fitness. Digital, often wearable, technology can help a person keep track of calories expended or miles run, increasing the likelihood that goals will be met. In the *quantified self* movement, people apply this practice to numerous aspects of their lives. They might measure time spent studying, watching TV, or sleeping (perhaps even tracking quality of sleep). They might receive feedback as to stress or hormonal or vitamin deficiencies. The data can then be interpreted and lifestyle changes made accordingly so as to enhance one's health, progress toward a goal, and self-development.

Technology now permits the capture, documentation, and archiving of nearly everything about our lives. This kind of *lifelogging* can result in a great deal of highly specific, searchable data made available and potentially made public (Rainie & Wellman, 2012, 285–287). This renders much about a life potentially searchable and hackable, opening it up where both help and harm can be rampant. According to Bell and Gemmell (2009), the self-knowledge that can result can be revelatory and life-changing. It can provide psychological benefits and social support and can contribute to the overall understanding of how selfhood develops (and might even more optimally develop). On the other hand, in the event that personal data were to be made public, a host of problems, from embarrassment and surveillance to harassment, could follow. The long-term effects of having nearly every moment of one's life documented and recorded – even if self-documented – are difficult to predict (Chayko, 2018).

The expression of identity

The strong human need for self-expression is at the heart of our search for and development of identity. We communicate aspects of our identities as we express and display our tastes in clothing, food, pop culture, and politics. We affiliate with groups (and individuals) with whom we share interests and adapt our interests to those of other groups (and individuals) that have an attraction for us.

The Internet and digital technology have opened up countless such opportunities for expressing and declaring our identities and sharing our journeys of affiliation and identity exploration. Online communicators select and create avatars, memes, nicknames, photos, videos, music, accounts and profiles, and even distinct linguistic and writing styles (abbreviations, emojis, and the like). They remix and integrate others' work with their own to create new hybrid forms of culture. They also customize the tech itself – devices, cases, ringtones, wallpaper, and so on – expressing themselves as distinctively as possible.

Digital technology and social media in particular rely on, and commodify, such expressions and declarations of identity. Social networking sites like Facebook, Twitter, Pinterest, Instagram, Snapchat, and YouTube encourage the near-continuous practice of personal expression through text, photos, videos, and so on as part of their business model. The same is true of blogs and the various blogging platforms that enable the activity (Blogger, WordPress, Wix, Tumblr, etc.). By establishing and incentivizing a participatory culture of easy sharing, consuming, and commenting, these sites and business models have encouraged an explosion of creative expression, the possible negative impacts of which (surveillance, data mining, hacking) may not always be discerned. When engaged in the 'rush,' or intimacy, of the experience itself, the longer-term consequences may not be apparent (Chayko, 2018).

Additionally, the anonymity or partial anonymity often possible in online engagement can result in somewhat freer, more open, and sometimes coarser forms of self-expression. Disinhibition and the loosening of norms are not uncommon in digital settings (Suler, 2004). People are often not bound by face-to-face accountability and physical restrictions when they are online. In my research, individuals tell me that they feel more playful, free, and bold when they are online (Chayko, 2008). Such attitudes can easily result in ill-advised behaviors and decisions.

Churning out endless streams of communication, information, and creative expression, the identities of individuals, groups, and organizations continuously evolve and can be highly distinctive. Special words, phrases, nicknames, modes of speaking, symbols, colors, logos, and the like form a kind of boundary around "in-groups" of those who understand the symbols and are "in the know," separating them from the "out-groups" who are not. It feels good and is important to live life as part of meaningful groups, and so the affiliation with meaningful groups is highly desired. It only makes sense that people would use the technologies constantly at their disposal to create and sustain such affiliations and express such identities.

According to sociologist Anthony Giddens, we all create narratives that constitute our "self-identity . . . the ongoing story of the self" (1991, 56). We tell others (and ourselves) stories about who we are and why we do what we do. In so doing, a narrative of our life emerges that imputes a kind of logic to our life decisions and events. Viewed as episodes in a larger story, past and future events are imbued with meaning and coherence. Our lives, and others', can be better understood (Chayko, 2018).

The telling and re-telling of stories is critical to the establishment of groups, as well. It gives a group definition and creates solidarity among members. It also heightens social presence among dispersed community members and supplies the detail and images that populate and shape the mental 'space' that the group inhabits. The more detailed, resonant, and serialized the story, the more 'personal' these spaces can become and the more vividly the people in them can come to life for one another (see Chayko, 2008, 159–182, for more on self-expression and storytelling online). Social media and other digital spaces are perfectly situated to inspire (indeed, incentivize) the act of telling stories that express the self.

If the Internet offers "a unique opportunity for self-expression," as psychologist John Bargh and his coauthors point out, "then we would expect a person to use it first and foremost to express those aspects of self that he or she has the strongest need to express" (2002, 34). Racial and ethnic minorities, women, the gay community, the disabled, lonely, shy, or those with non-mainstream identities and lifestyles can discover avenues for self-expression online that may be denied them offline (Chayko, 2018; Mehra et al., 2004; Mitra, 2004, 2005; Lin, 2006; Baker, 2005). As we have seen, the responses to such expression often include hate, harm, and harassment. Those who have been targeted for harassment, though, have also found communities online that have helped them deal with it. In the process, their group and individual identities can be further bolstered (Chayko, 2018).

For people who have physical and/or perceptual difficulties accessing online content, the Internet and digital media can feel like a 'closed club' that they have difficulty entering. While technological advancements are making it easier for people with visual and aural impairments to access and use these technologies, for many, it can still be difficult. When such barriers are overcome, though, the gains can be substantial, as identities can be expressed in environments where their impairments are unknown, irrelevant, or supported by others. Networking with those in similar situations, they can gather needed information and resources and express themselves more fully and spontaneously.

Both challenges and opportunities in expressing one's identity online abound. Offline power differentials migrate to the online realm; social inequalities and problems are amplified and find greater visibility online. But when those with reduced social power find and support one another, create communities that may become safe spaces, and unite and organize to make a difference, it gives rise to hope that we are creating the conditions for identities to be more safely expressed. Regulation of social media companies, who may need to take responsibility for that which is expressed on their platforms, may be forthcoming.

The performance of identity

This dramaturgical perspective of social interaction, famously theorized by Erving Goffman (1959), holds that individuals carefully manage the behaviors and the impressions they are making on others ('impression management') almost as though they are putting on a show. They stage and rehearse these impressions privately (in the 'back stage' of society) and then perform them publicly (on the 'front stage'). The objective is to produce a successful "show" in which one is shown in the desired light.

In the creation of these 'shows' and the practicing and playing of these 'parts,' Goffman says, the self is 'performed' into being. Writing in a pre-Internet era, he could surely not have imagined the implications of his work for a digital ICT future. But digital tech and social media platforms provide a wide variety of spaces and 'stages' – some more open and accessible than others – within which people practice and present the performances that help to shape who they are.

Plays and shows take place in front of audiences, and digital performances are no exception. Multiple audiences converge, constantly, publicly, and invisibly, on the Internet and social media. Individuals, groups, and organizations must at some level take these audiences into account as they post and create content that represents aspects of identity. Many of those who will encounter our content online, though, are unknown and unknowable. Having multiple, diverse, invisible, often imagined audiences and contexts encounter one's content differently sets up the conditions for 'context collapse,' in which the various interpretations of these different audiences must be addressed and dealt with (Marwick & boyd, 2011). This is just one of the challenges of expressing identity in this public, performative way.

It is sometimes said that when we are online we are not being 'authentic'; that identities are highly and perhaps deceptively edited online. But identity can develop in all kinds of settings, whenever people enter one another's lives and consciousnesses. We all imagine, edit, practice, perform. We try things out and see how others react. We act a bit differently in different settings. We take note of how others react and make identity adjustments accordingly.

To be sure, some aspects of the self are more easily altered or experimented with online. When interaction is text-based, many social markers are invisible, and so gender, race, nationality, age, appearance, and so on can be disguised or altered. People can alter their identities in ways that would be impossible offline, exploring different (or potential) aspects of their selves in the process. But this does not happen as often as one might think. Deeply ingrained social characteristics are difficult to disguise, especially over the long term. Mostly, people don't separate into different, distinct identities, online or offline (Chayko 2008, 169, 2018).

Of course, people select and edit photos and text online so as to appear in a more positive, more flattering, light. We do this offline, too, all the time. We select clothing purposefully, style ourselves carefully, and purchase particular accessories and accoutrements, designing our lives for others' gaze and consumption. We do the same with technology devices, platforms, and apps, including dating sites. We stage our lives to perform identities that reflect who we are while communicating who we want to be.

We construct these fairly complex performances, accommodating audiences, situations, and our own impulses casually and constantly, both online and offline. Online identity 'performances' are really best understood as by-products of the authentic human need to connect, to form networks and communities and multifaceted identities. In modern technology-rich societies, a good portion of this identity work happens to take place in the digital realm, but it is best, I argue, to view the digital and the physical as one single, enmeshed, reality in which a techno-social life is lived (Chayko, 2014, 2018).

What, then, of authenticity? Most of us wish for our social connections and relationships to have a genuine core, to be as 'real' as possible as often as possible (Chayko, 2014, 2008, 2002). (Having said that, human beings lie to and deceive others as a matter of course as well, but often simply out of expediency or as a kind of social lubricant – see DePaulo, 2004.) Pressures to highlight our positive attributes are "experienced in tandem with the need to present one's true (or authentic) self to others, especially in significant relationships" (Ellison et al., 2006). People manage impressions strategically so as to resolve this tension.

Having a core of authenticity to our lives and experiences matters to human beings, and just as with relationships in the physical realm, connections and communities made and maintained online provide that reality for us. As my research suggests, relationships that exist predominantly online are routinely described as 'real' or 'just as real' as those that exist predominantly face-to-face and are experienced as such (Chayko, 2014, 2008, 2002). Digital media provide the means to craft a self-presentation so that it highlights positive one's attributes yet is generally experienced as real. And while the presentation of self may often be a performance, it is one that is geared toward honest ends: it is necessary for the establishment of an orderly society, Goffman reminds us, for which we all must take responsibility (1959).

Modern forms of identity

The Internet is in many ways a laboratory in which experiments in identity development constantly take place (Palfrey & Gasser, 2008). Some scholars claim that a 'postmodern self' has emerged in which separate, distinct selves never quite merge together into a singular and unitary self. Feminist technology scholar Donna Haraway claims that the self is always partial, consisting of pieces or fragments, and that this is necessary so that we can understand different viewpoints (in Kennedy, 2006; see Haraway, 1998). Some conjecture that when online, people 'cycle through' a number of segmented selves (Turkle, 1995; Kennedy, 2006; Higgins, 1987; Markus & Kunda, 1986). As cultural sociologist Samuel Hall sums up this position, the modern identity is "never singular but multiply constructed across different, often intersecting and antagonistic, discourses, practices and positions" (1996, 4; see Chayko, 2018).

While identity is undoubtedly intersectional, with one's various roles and aspects of identity overlapping and experienced 'together,' some scholars disagree with the idea of it as 'multiple' (Kendall, 2002; Huffaker & Calvert, 2005; Chayko, 2008). They point out that individuals are 'anchored' in a single body and tend to speak more or less consistently online with a single voice. Identity is better understood as singular than multiple or fractured, they argue.

It may be helpful, I submit, to think of identity as consisting of intersecting and overlapping components, each of which can be developed, expressed, and performed, than to think of it as consisting of multiple distinct entities. It may make sense to think of the aspects of the self that are expressed online as interpenetrating those articulated face-to-face – or, in short, to think of all of these combined aspects as, simply, the self. While the self is certainly fluid and multidimensional, it can also be seen as unitary, one self with many aspects, moods, colors, and textures, rather than necessarily as separate, distinct, multiple selves (see James (1983/1890) on the continuity of the self).

Georg Simmel (1962[1908]) writes of how we are each situated within a complex 'web' of diverse group affiliations. Taking on a large number of roles, and identifying, at least in part, with numerous groups, modern people often experience not only strain and conflict but also a spectacular kind of freedom and flexibility of self-construction and expression. In the process, we have become more highly differentiated from one another, more different and specialized, than at any time in human history. In coordinating diverse roles and expressing different aspects

121

of ourselves in each group, the modern individual (whom Rainie and Wellman would call the 'networked individual' – 2012) can become deeply complex, utterly unique. This is an exciting, even freeing, proposal, with a darker flip side: we must work harder than ever before to understand how these pieces fit together (see Chayko, 2015). More than at any time in the past, the modern self can become "saturated" and break down, or find itself adrift, in a flood of ever-increasing, ever-demanding electronically mediated interactions (Gergen, 1991).

Identities that are developed and expressed at least in part online are not bound by the limitations of the physical world. Space and time can be transcended. Individuals can be influenced by those who came before them and by the specter of those who will live in the future. In a very real way, the self can outlast and outlive the physical person and can have a social reality of indefinite shape and length.

To some extent this has always been the case. Books and letters have, for centuries, helped people learn or form connections to ancestors and historical figures. Art, photos, telegraphy, telephones, and the mass electronic media similarly provided a means for such connections to be generated and, operating in tandem, to help deepen them. Early research of mine (Chayko, 2002) suggests that people can become deeply and meaningfully bonded to those who are dead, inanimate, or even fictional if they detect sufficient like-mindedness.

Consider the continued *social reality* of a known historical figure such as the author Robert Louis Stevenson:

> Would it not be absurd to deny social reality to Robert Louis Stevenson, who is so much alive in many minds and so potently affects important phases of thought and content? He is certainly more alive in this real practical sense than most of us who have not yet lost our corporeity, more alive, perhaps, than he was before he lost his own, because of his wider influence.
>
> *(Cooley, 1964[1922])*

Stevenson (and by extension, others who lived in the past or who 'live' via mediated storytelling) can be in essence kept alive, even 'more alive,' due to his influence and presence in the hearts and minds of others. With digital ICTs providing countless platforms on which the words and works of others can be preserved, it is but a next step to see these as spaces for a kind of continued existence, a socially real self, identity, and 'personhood' that can transcend space and time (Chayko, 2002, 2018).

The Internet and digital media facilitate the perception and experience of proximity and presence in ways that go beyond the physical. In fact, that is one of their most enticing affordances. When connecting online, those whom we encounter can truly seem to be 'there.' Digital technologies allow people to be cognitively present and to have *perceived proximity* to one another even when they are physically distant (O'Leary et al., 2014) or absent altogether (Chayko, 2002).

The enhanced *social presence* facilitated by these technologies has several consequences for the user, one of which is that physical entities can acquire an enhanced social and mental (i.e., sociomental) lifespan (Short et al., 1976; Chayko, 2002, 2018). Digital technologies and ICTs enable this sense of presence so well and so consistently that they make it possible for selves and identities to linger and persist and have influence well into the future. Advancements in medicine, robotics, and artificial intelligence will, of course, further extend and possibly reimagine the human lifespan and even what it means to be 'alive' and human.

Increasingly, individuals view "death, dying, mourning, grieving, and even mortality itself as a hybrid between the physical and the digital" (Moreman & Lewis, 2014, 2). It has become common to memorialize individuals online after their deaths. Blogs and websites are set up as a repository of photos and testimonials. Many funeral homes have created online spaces for memories to be shared. Those who have died are not only remembered and spoken *of* but often spoken *to* on social media, demonstrating the desire to keep the memory of the deceased alive and for contact with them to be maintained. Social media sometimes seems to have a kind of 'airborne' quality that may encourage the feeling that the deceased can be somehow 'reached' across time and space.

The deceased are now more easily reimagined as an audience with whom one can 'interact.' Messages may be directed to those who have passed away, sometimes on memorial sites that persist for many years, even indefinitely. Photos and videos are widely shared and spread. Social media provides a kind of channel by which the dead are brought more often into physical space and where it can feel like we are encountering them and experiencing a type of interaction with them (Chayko, 2018).

Digitally depicted via video, audio, photos, or even using such technology as holograms, people can even be present to us if they have never truly had corporeal existence (i.e., they are fictional or imagined characters). Digital scenarios can be created in which physical and non-physical others interact. While intellectually the consumer of these images may understand that someone digitally depicted is not truly alive, experiencing it can be so genuine and resonant that the person's impact is that of proximal presence. This is, in fact, why movies, television, and books have such power, because the social world that we are drawn into is temporarily as real as any other and can impact us deeply and emotionally (Davis, 1983).

In such ways, and many more to come, what it means to be present to one another, and to 'have' a self and identity, is changing. To be sure, it requires conceptual flexibility to see the self as indefinitely present, even indefinitely alive. It is a challenge – the scope of which can easily overwhelm and can both seem to have and actually have dark, frightening prospects. But the implications for the understanding of a complex modern self, identity, and even personhood and humanity are tantalizing and require collaborative understandings that cross such disciplinary boundaries as communication, information science, sociology, psychology, computer science, engineering, and all the arts and humanities.

We do not know the long-term effects of constructing selves and identities in a time of such rapid and accelerating technological change as we are experiencing today. Opportunities and challenges rise and fall swiftly. Corporations and regimes gain increased, intensified power. Individuals can easily feel moorless; their identities and selves fragile, vulnerable.

As Erving Goffman reminds us, though, that identity breathes and grows in the 'cracks' of societies' so-called 'solid buildings'. In these interstitial spaces, opportunities for the practice of unique, fluid, creatively developed identities abound. In the modern, digital age, these opportunities become ever more plentiful – indeed, they can multiply infinitely – but we must faithfully and relentlessly apply chisel and resistance to the inexorable strength of structure.

References

Baker, A. J. (2005). *Double Click: Romance and Commitment Among Online Couples*. Creskill, NJ: Hampton Press.

Bargh, J. A., McKenna, K. Y. A., and Fitzsimons, G. M. (2002). Can You See the Real Me? Activation and Expression of the 'True Self' on the Internet. *Journal of Social Issues*, 58(1), 33–48.

Bell, G., and Gemmell, J. (2009). *Total Recall*. New York: Dutton.

boyd, d. (2014). *It's Complicated: The Social Lives of Networked Teens*. New Haven, CT: Yale University Press.

Budd-Cording, G. (2017). *Queeriosity.com* (website).

Cerulo, K. A., Ruane, J. M., and Chayko, M. (1992). Technological Ties That Bind. *Communication Research*, 19(1), 109–129.

Chayko, M. (2002). *Connecting: How We Form Social Bonds and Communities in the Internet Age*. Albany: State University of New York Press.

Chayko, M. (2008). *Portable Communities: The Social Dynamics of Online and Mobile Connectedness*. Albany: State University of New York Press.

Chayko, M. (2014). Techno-Social Life: The Internet, Digital Technology, and Social Connectedness. *Sociology Compass*, 8(7), 976–991.

Chayko, M. (2015). The First Web Theorist? The Legacy of Georg Simmel and 'the Web of Group-Affiliations'. *Information, Communication & Society*. doi:10.1080/1369118X.2015.1042394.

Chayko, M. (2018). *Superconnected: The Internet, Digital Media, and Techno-Social Life* (2nd ed.). Thousand Oaks, CA: Sage.

Cooley, C. H. (1964). *Human Nature and the Social Order*. New York, NY: Schocken (Original work published 1922).

Davenport, T. H., and Beck, J. C. (2002). *The Attention Economy: Understanding the New Currency of Business*. Boston, MA: Harvard Business Review Press.

Davis, M. S. (1983). *Smut: Erotic Reality, Obscene Ideology*. Chicago: University of Chicago Press.

DePaulo, B. M. (2004). The Many Faces of Lies. In A. G. Miller (ed.), *The Social Psychology of Good and Evil*. New York: Guilford Press, pp. 303–326.

Duggan, M. (2017, July 11). Online Harassment, 2017. *Pew Research Center*. www.pewInternat. org/2017/07/11/online-harassment-2017/.

Ellison, N., Heino, R., and Gibbs, J. (2006). Managing Impressions Online: Self-Presentation Processes in the Online Dating Environment. *Journal of Computer-Mediated Communication*, 11(2), 415–441.

Gergen, K. J. (1991). *The Saturated Self: Dilemmas of Identity in Contemporary Life*. New York: Basic Books.

Giddens, A. (1991). *Modernity and Self-Identity*. Stanford, CA: Stanford University Press.

Goffman, E. (1959). *The Presentation of Self in Everyday Life*. New York: Anchor.

Goffman, E. (1968). *Asylums: Essays on the Social Situation of Mental Patients and Other Inmates*. Chicago: AldineTransaction.

Hall, S. (1996). Who Needs Identity? In S. Hall and P. duGay (eds.), *Questions of Cultural Identity*. London, UK: Sage, pp. 1–17.

Haraway, D. (1998). The Persistence of Vision. In N. Mirzoeff (ed.), *The Visual Culture Reader*. London, UK: Routledge, pp. 191–198.

Higgins, E. T. (1987). Self-Discrepancy: A Theory Relating Self and Affect. *Psychological Review*, 94(3), 319–340.

Hormuth, S. E. (1990). *The Ecology of the Self: Relocation and Self-Concept Change*. Cambridge: Cambridge University Press.

Huffaker, D. A., and Calvert, S. L. (2005). Gender, Identity, and Language Use in Teenage Blogs. *Journal of Computer-Mediated Communication*, 10(2).

Iyer, A., Jetten, J., and Tsivrikos, D. (2008). Torn Between Identities: Predictors of Adjustment to Identity Change. In F. Sani (ed.), *Self Continuity: Individual and Collective Perspectives*. New York: Psychology Press, pp. 187–197.

James, W. (1983). *The Principles of Psychology*. Cambridge, MA: Harvard University Press (Original work published 1890).

Kendall, L. (2002). *Hanging Out in the Virtual Pub: Masculinities and Relationships Online*. Berkeley: University of California Press.

Kennedy, H. (2006). Beyond Anonymity: Future Directions for Internet Identity Research. *New Media and Society*, 8(6), 859–876.

Lin, D. C. (2006). Sissies Online: Taiwanese Male Queers Performing Sissinesses in Cyberspaces. *Inter-Asia Cultural Studies*, 7(2), 270–288. doi:10.1080/14649370600673938.

Markus, H., and Kunda, Z. (1986). Stability and Malleability of the Self-Concept. *Journal of Personality and Social Psychology*, 51(4), 858–866.

Markus, H., and Nurius, P. (1986). Possible Selves. *American Psychologist*, 41(9), 954–969.

Marwick, A. E., and boyd, d. (2011). I Tweet Honestly, I Tweet Passionately: Twitter Users, Context Collapse, and the Imagined Audience. *New Media & Society*, 13(1), 114–133.

McCall, G. J., and Simmons, J. L. (1978). *Identities and Interactions*. New York: Free Press.

McKenna, K. Y. A., Green, A. S., and Gleason, M. E. J. (2002). Relationship Formation on the Internet: What's the Big Attraction? *Journal of Social Issues*, 58(1), 9–31.

Mead, G. H. (2009). *Mind, Self, and Society: From the Standpoint of a Social Behaviorist*. Chicago, IL: University of Chicago (Original work published 1934).

Mehra, B., Merkel, C., and Bishop, A. P. (2004). The Internet for Empowerment of Minority and Marginalized Users. *New Media and Society*, 6(6), 781–802. doi:10.1177/146144804047513.

Mitra, A. (2004). Voices of the Marginalized on the Internet: Examples from a Website for Women of South Asia. *Journal of Communication*, 54(3), 492–510.

Mitra, A. (2005). Creating Immigrant Identities in Cybernetic Space: Examples from a Non-Resident Indian Website. *Media, Culture & Society*, 27(3), 371–390.

Moreman, C. M., and Lewis, D. (2014). *Digital Death: Mortality and Beyond in the Online Age*. New York, NY: Praeger.

O'Leary, M. B., Wilson, J. M., and Metiu, A. (2014). Beyond Being There: The Symbolic Role of Communication and Identification in Perceptions of Proximity to Geographically Dispersed Colleagues. *MIS Quarterly*, 38(4), 1219–1243. http://www18.georgetown.edu/data/people/mbo9/publication-77556.pdf.

Palfrey, J. G., and Gasser, U. (2008). *Born Digital: Understanding the First Generation of Digital Natives*. New York: Basic Books.

Rainie, L., and Wellman, B. (2012). *Networked: The New Social Operating System*. Cambridge, MA: MIT Press.

Shibutani, T. (1955). Reference Groups as Perspectives. *American Journal of Sociology*, 60(6), 562–569.

Short, J., Williams, E., and Christie, B. (1976). *The Social Psychology of Telecommunications*. New York: John Wiley & Sons.

Simmel, G. (1962). *Conflict and the Web of Group Affiliations*. New York: Free Press (Original work published 1908).

Suler, J. (2004). The Online Disinhibition Effect. *Cyberpsychology and Behavior*, 7(3), 321–326.

Tajfel, H., and Turner, J. C. (1979). An Integrative Theory of Intergroup Conflict. *The Social Psychology of Intergroup Relations*, 33(47), 74.

Turkle, S. (1995). *Life on the Screen: Identity in the Age of the Internet*. New York: Simon & Schuster.

10

Our digital social life

Irina Shklovski

Well over a decade ago, Nancy Baym (2006) argued that the Internet as a fundamentally social technology is worthy of scrutiny for its role in interpersonal life "online." Since then, the Internet has moved on and moved into social interaction and relational maintenance through smartphones and social media applications, becoming part of the very fabric of social life in much of the world. As mediated modes of communication became accessible to more people and in more situations, the ability to engage each other online has shifted from an interesting but relatively unusual activity to an expected mode of living. It no longer makes sense to speak of interaction online as a particular activity separate from other forms of social interaction. The use of technologies for communication is now a basic assumption of social practice (Bayer et al., 2015). Lievrouw (2009, 313) has called it "the growing ordinariness or 'banalization' of new media." In basic terms human social needs have remained the same. People feel the need for belonging and connectedness (Baumeister & Leary, 1995), they love, worry, argue, and rely on each other in times of need. How we go about these in practice, however, has changed if only because there are so many more ways to achieve social ends.

Ours is the age of sharing in social, economic and rhetorical arenas made possible through the functionality of networked technologies (John, 2016). Interaction with friends or strangers is just a click away, often passively consumed rather than actively engaged in (Burchell, 2015; Shklovski et al., 2015). For some, the perpetual possibility for interaction creates demands for attention and pressures for making the self available to others, where disconnection and moments without social interaction become anomalous (Burchell, 2015). Possibilities for social contact may seem endless but the labor necessary for maintaining relationships has not diminished. Rather, what used to be mundane and expected – phone calls, visits and even postcards – now qualify as effortful communication that can signal particular relational investment and care, having been supplanted by myriad other actions (Sørensen & Shklovski, 2011; Shklovski et al., 2008).

The proliferation of technologies that can facilitate a variety of communication practices has led to an explosion of research on their implications for sociability. Concerns with whether particular forms of social engagement might be better or worse than others, a considerable source of interest and anxiety just a decade ago (Shklovski et al., 2006), are now few and far between. Instead, research has shifted to consider issues such as information overload (LaRose et al., 2014), context collapse and the attendant problem of unintended information disclosure (Binder et al., 2009; Brake, 2014; Laampinen et al., 2011), new forms of social embededness (Shklovski et al., 2015; Bayer et al., 2015), and the ability to leverage social relationships in new ways (Vitak & Ellison, 2013) among others.

This chapter traces the research from early considerations of computer-mediated-communication (CMC) to current concerns and excitement around social network sites and pervasive connectedness, exploring the changing dynamics of social interaction and relational practice. As digital societies leverage networked connectedness where people become increasingly reachable it is important to consider how social interaction and relational practice have become inflected.

Early considerations of CMC

Researchers have been investigating the role of information and communication technologies in social practice for nearly half a century (de Sola Pool, 1977; Fischer, 1994; Kiesler et al., 1984). With the advent of the Internet scholars debated ever more vigorously whether computer-mediated interactions were substituting impoverished modes of relating for much richer in-person engagements (McKenna & Bargh, 2000; Katz & Aspden, 1997; Kraut et al., 2002; Nie & Hillygus, 2002). Premised on the idea that affordances of any media would have consistent and predictable effects, much of the early research focused on group and workplace communication and compared the efficiency and effectiveness of various mediated communication channels with in-person interaction.

Social interaction as a basic action is rooted in moments of communication that are reciprocal (Sigman, 1995). Inherent in this reciprocity is an effort to avoid misunderstanding through practical checks and balances of reaction to each subsequent action. This lead to the idea that richer and more immediate modes of communication would inherently allow for less misunderstanding and smoother interaction. Scholars argued that the richness of the communication channel accounted for the differences in the amount of information that could be transmitted, leading to impoverished results in mediated contexts (Daft & Lengel, 1984; Lea & Spears, 1995). Walther proposed that mediated communication technologies provided affordances that allowed users to craft the image they expected to present in order to enhance social outcomes (Walther, 1995, 2007, Walther et al., 1994). Determining whether the richness or narrowness of the communication channel is important to the success of communication, however, depends on how communication is conceptualized in the first place (Wellman & Gulia, 1999). Peters (2000) writes that communication through any means is a kind of "making do," never perfect but offering opportunities for transmission of information, for communion and emotional engagement, and, ultimately, for possibilities of failure through technical problems, miscommunication or misunderstanding. Success in social interaction is not guaranteed regardless of modality.

The debate about the role of the Internet in informal social interactions and relational practice followed a similar logic. In the late 90's two studies framed the debate about the social impact of the Internet, focusing on how Internet use affected people's social interaction and social involvement with others. Where Katz and Aspden (1997) argued that Internet use augmented traditional communication, Kraut et al. (1998) countered that Internet use could displace time spent with friends and family. This concern with whether the Internet replaced or augmented social practice drove a significant amount of research. Nie and colleagues conducted large-scale surveys, arguing that Internet use reduced the frequency of face-to-face interaction, which was seen as more important (Nie & Hillygus, 2002; Nie, 2001). In contrast, McKenna and Bargh argued that the Internet improved people's ability to form and maintain social relationships because it allowed individuals to better control self-presentation and to overcome problems such as shyness (McKenna & Bargh, 2000). Turkle wrote that mediated communication technologies were beneficial for developing a better sense of self because they offered opportunities to experiment with different identities and self-representations (Turkle, 1995). In an attempt to resolve the debate Shklovski et al. (2006, 262) conducted a meta-analysis of survey research between 1995 and 2003, concluding that "even though the Internet may have changed many habits, the effects of those changes on fundamental relationships and psychological well-being seem to be small or at least slow in emerging." They called for a more differentiated view of the Internet as a "malleable and diverse technology," noting that its effects may differ given the many ways it can be used.

The notion that the use of the Internet and other new media is not monolithic and that studying it as such is misleading because of its individual customizability, was not new (Lievrouw, 2001). Many researchers studied particular effects of the use of email (Stafford et al., 1999), instant messaging (Boneva et al, 2006), online games (McKenna & Bargh, 2000; Parks & Roberts, 1998) and Usenet groups (Parks & Floyd, 1996; Baym, 2000) reporting largely positive outcomes and meaningful interactions. Later research on the role of mediated communication showed that personal relationships tend to be multi-modal, maintained through the use of a number of modalities rather than relying on one particular method of interaction (Baym et al., 2004; Ledbetter, 2008). In fact, the range of modalities used to maintain any relationship is associated with the strength of that relationship and its' perceived importance (Haythornthwaite, 2005).

It is no longer a point of debate that digital forms of communication are important for relational maintenance (Dimmick et al., 2011), but different communication practices can achieve different goals. For example, Shklovski et al. (2008) showed that while email is less effective at promoting relational growth, it can be important for perpetuating relational continuity. After all, any form of social interaction is a particular kind of experience. It is impossible to classify whether one mode of communication is "better" or "worse" than the other ontologically – they are simply different. The use of mediated communication did change how different modalities might be interpreted. For example, with the broad adoption of email the frequency of letter writing has dropped significantly and took on a different relational meaning (Baron, 1998). Yet, as Harper (2010, 21) puts it: "Letters are not an analogue of face to face communication [or email for that matter]; they create a new experience of human bonding." The proliferation of communication technologies has enabled myriad new forms of human bonding, complicating our understanding of the practices involved in accomplishing social interaction.

SNS and pervasive connectedness

Early considerations of interpersonal impact of the Internet focused on dyadic or group forms of communication (Rheingold, 1993; Baym, 2000). There was some attention to the fact that the Internet blurred "the boundary between interpersonal and mass media" (Baym, 2006, 38) and that the ability to broadcast limited how well people could predict their audience (Carnevale & Probst, 1997). Yet discussions of interpersonal processes invariably invoked relations that were clearly bounded. However, as blogs (Brake, 2014) and then social network sites (SNS) became popular, researchers had to contend with an increasing mixing of broadcasting and interpersonal communication across different media. Early research on social network sites identified these sites as "public displays of connection" (Donath & boyd, 2004) that people could use to validate identity information of their connections and as social resumes that served as evidence of their own social abilities (boyd & Ellison, 2007). Later studies explored the presentation of self online through identity performance (Tufekci, 2008), impression management (Barash et al.,

2010) and exhibits of the self (Hogan, 2010). The vast majority of this research has focused on Facebook in particular (Rains & Brunner, 2015; Stoycheff et al., 2017).

People use SNS for many different purposes (Joinson, 2008; Lampe et al., 2006) and might choose to limit or even terminate their use of these technologies for a range of reasons (Vitak & Ellison, 2013). Current research suggests that people derive social, emotional and psychological benefits from the use of SNS and that these sites can also have substantial practical and political significance (Burke et al., 2011; Ellison et al., 2011; Hampton et al., 2011; Valenzuela et al., 2014). At the same time, there is evidence that some ways of using SNS can lead to worse moods (Verduyn et al., 2015) and overall decreases in subjective well-being (Shakya & Christakis, 2017). Similar to early concerns about Internet-based communication replacing face-to-face interactions, researchers have also considered whether sociability via SNS would affect other methods of communication (Brandtzæg & Nov, 2011). The verdict tends to be that SNSs augment the array of modalities that people use for daily social activities (Barkhuus & Tashiro, 2010; Brandtzæg & Nov, 2011). These sites offer elaborate systems for perpetuating relational continuity (Sigman, 1991) through explicit articulations of connections and through a range of communicative functions (Ellison et al., 2011; Young, 2011). SNS communicative functions are typically used for "lightweight" relational maintenance (Lampe et al., 2008; Subrahmanyam et al., 2008), although there is also evidence that people use the site differently for interactions with strong and weak connections (Ellison et al., 2011).

Studies of interpersonal communication on social network sites comprise a significant proportion of research on these technologies (Stoycheff et al., 2017). Many scholars have also investigated whether SNS use facilitates growth of social capital[1] (Ellison et al., 2007), what type of social capital is affected most (Ellison et al., 2011) and which types of uses are most effective in this process (Burke et al., 2010; Ellison & Vitak, 2015). This work took a primarily functional view on social processes, investigating how people "tap" their networks (Vitak & Ellison, 2013) or "cultivate" their social resources (Ellison et al., 2014). Relational maintenance practices evident on SNSs are complex and difficult to disentangle (Ellison et al., 2011), in part because of the problem of context collapse – the undifferentiated colocation of social connections from across disparate life spheres – can cause considerable social tension for social activity (Binder et al., 2009). Surprisingly, fewer studies have investigated the particulars of relational practice – the demands and obligations of maintaining relationships through social network sites (Burchell, 2015). Arguably, it is the labor of relational practice that makes activation of social capital possible. Where most Facebook research has been deeply concerned with whether and how SNS users might leverage their personal networks for personal advantage, it is enactments of relational work that likely comprises the vast majority of activities on these sites.

Leveraging the network

Social relationships lend themselves to thinking of social practice in structural terms and in terms of networks. Social relationships function within a social system and people must reconcile not only their own and their partner's needs, intentions, and demands but also the pressures and expectations of the social system itself. A network perspective improves upon an individual or even a dyadic view of social practice, offering the opportunity to consider effects of interaction in a broader social context. The way people negotiate their position in society, social connections, themselves, identities and meanings is through interaction with relations that comprise their networks. Network scholars have studied social practice as networks at different levels of analysis from societies (Castells, 1996) to communities (Wellman et al., 2003) to individual-focused analyses of ego-networks (Feld, 1991). The talk of networks is the talk of structure.

Early social network research produced romantic notions of infinite connectedness, powered by Milgram's "Small World Problem" (Travers & Milgram, 1969). It is tempting to conceive of networks as infinite and unbounded, but, as Strathern (1996) points out, what matters is the choice of where to "cut the network" when defining objects of analysis. Although theoretically social networks can extend endlessly, in practice the coherence of these connections varies because the effort to keep them sustained and durable, even if made simpler and easier by technology, nevertheless has limits. Network structure and the content that flows through it are co-determining, but social network analysis focuses primarily on structure as a basis for explaining social practice (Knox et al., 2006). Yet neither groups nor networks are clearly bounded. There are always fuzzy peripheries in social structures that are difficult to document and quantify.

The idea of cutting the network is important for the notion of social capital, used extensively to discuss the potential benefits of SNSs. Networks can be interpreted as collections of assets, implicated in the flows of information, goods or support. Social interaction enables people to build communities, to commit themselves to each other, and to knit together the social fabric that can be captured as a network structure. Concrete experience of social networks can foster a sense of belonging, which relies on relationships of trust, tolerance and mutual aid (Baumeister & Leary, 1995). According to Putnam, such cooperative and mutually supportive relations in communities and nations are facilitated by social capital (Putnam, 2001). Therefore, he argued, social capital is a valuable means of combatting many of the social disorders inherent in modern societies. Putnam distinguished between bonding social capital, reliant on intimate social ties that foster feelings of solidarity, and bridging social capital, reliant on weak and less known relations but important for information about the world and for encouraging a sense of belonging to a broader community.

The concepts of bonding and bridging social capital have featured heavily in SNS research (Ellison et al., 2007). Although Putnam emphasized the importance of social capital for communal outcomes, SNS research has tended to focus more on the benefits that individuals can derive from the web of their social relationships. In this view, activities oriented toward improving social capital would lead to increased personal access to information, to a greater variety of skills sets and to an enhanced ability to achieve goals (Burke et al., 2011; Vitak & Ellison, 2013). Here, social capital is an important resource for individuals to further their own prospects. Such an individualistic conception relies on the idea that social capital is something to be accrued, where individuals can have more or less of it depending on whether they choose to use SNSs and how they might use these technologies. This tends to result in an over-simplification of what constitutes social capital, with more relationships being equated to increases in social capital, often getting boiled down to a two-step description of a problem of leveraging personal networks that can be solved with technology: that (1) our social relationships are some of the most important assets that we own; and (2) that we are inefficient at leveraging these assets.

An alternative conception of social capital sees it as a process rather than a quantity to be obtained. Bourdieu posited that in social groups held together by mutual self-interest 'the profits which accrue from membership in a group are the basis of the solidarity which makes them possible,' emphasizing the importance of inequality and power, as membership in groups is about exclusivity rather than open-ended association (Bourdieu, 1986). Bourdieu's notion of social capital was fundamentally processual, where social capital is enacted in moments of exchange as norms and expectations frame resource-negotiations and define whether and how resources may be given, used or reinvested (Portes, 1998). In other words, leveraging the network is not without costs, but comes with obligations and demands and conforms to the impositions of existing social stratification in society. Social networks are not bottomless repositories of resources to be leveraged. If leveraged too often without upkeep, networks can fatigue and resources can deteriorate (Norris & Kaniasty, 1996).

Where and how networks are cut (Strathern, 1996) to denote boundaries of membership is an important consideration for social capital. How and why information or some other type of support is exchanged depends on the state of the particular relation as well as on the impact that this action may have on other relations. How much of the network must these considerations encompass? How far can a request travel and still remain legitimate? What is necessary for a relation to become a resource?

Enacting relational work

Relationships are both predictable and paradoxical. They are valued assets as much as they are performances, they are a state as much as a process and, by and large, relationships are expected to be predictably consistent, constantly negotiated and redefined in interaction (Khrakhordin, 2005; Blieszner & Adams, 1992). Enactments of social capital on SNS are likely less about extraction of value as they are about expressions of intimacy and vulnerability (Lambert, 2016). Exchanges of social capital are probably less frequent than the proliferation of research might lead us to believe. Most of the time people engage in interaction that is boring, mundane and even entirely contentless (Duck, 1977). In an in-depth analysis of the content of instant messaging conversations, Boneva and colleagues demonstrated that the majority of conversations did not contain much beyond greetings and idle small talk (Boneva et al., 2006). It is unlikely that interactions on social network sites are much more weighty in content. Evidence suggests that the vast majority of social interaction on SNS is light-weight and mostly focused on entertainment, consisting of perusing the content one's relations have produced and occasionally reacting to it (Papacharissi & Mendelson, 2010; Shklovski et al., 2015).

Much research on Facebook has purposefully distinguished between active engagement, such as posting content or directly engaging with people (Burke et al., 2011), and entertainment from observing the content posted by others (Papacharissi & Mendelson, 2010). Shklovski et al. (2015) propose that instead of focusing only on active posting of content or commentary, it is important to consider the relational function of such interactive and non-interactive practices on Facebook. Even if reading friends' content is entertaining and lends itself well to procrastination, being up to date on the goings on of one's social ties is important given the way social network technologies have been integrated into relational practice (Burchell, 2015). The semi-public nature of Facebook requires that individuals always consider the relational meaning of each visible action not only for the particular relationship, which is enacted directly, but also for all other social ties that may or may not observe this interaction (Shklovski et al., 2015). This is made more complicated given the fact that most Facebook users tend to under-estimate the size of the audience for the content they produce on the site (Bernstein et al., 2013). As a result people have developed a range of mechanisms for managing this sort of relational quandary. These are social steganography to ensure that true meaning is known only to the intended audience (boyd & Marwick, 2011), self-censorship (Shklovski et al., 2015; Das & Kramer, 2013), or carefully managed visibility of interactions (Bazarova et al., 2015). The forethought and care such interactions require is a form of never-ending and constantly demanding relational labor.

Despite the delight with the possibilities new technologies offer for social interaction people also at times harbor resentment for the demands these possibilities place on them. No matter how easy it is to click a button, to express support or to answer a question, each of these actions takes time. Managing communication practices is an increasingly demanding process because the volume of actual and possible communication continues to grow (Burchell, 2015). Time then, is an essential expression of care in this digital environment and time is key to being able to maintain relationships and to respond to requests for support. It is the relational work embedded in interactions between people that can create the perception of social assets being "leveraged." Social interactions, no matter how minor and inconsequential, still require time investments and, as Nowotny writes, "technologies alone can never manufacture time, any more than clocks" (c.f. Burchell, 2015, 48).

Reconnecting and disconnecting

Social network sites may not manufacture time, but they occasionally allow people to reach into the past. As sites for enactment and maintenance of existing active relationships, SNS allow people to retain connection through life changes and residential mobility. SNS also provide ways for people to locate those with whom they had previously lost touch. Although opinions on the function of the "people you may know" feature of many SNS vary (Hill, 2017), the ability to locate old classmates or friends is something many appreciate out of curiosity or because of the pleasure of revisiting the past together (Quinn, 2013). SNS can not only potentially mitigate or prevent loss of current connections, they also encourage reconnection with lapsed ties, something that could be construed as a way to broaden networks (Levin et al., 2010).

What does reconnection with long lost contacts result in? Do these people become friends again and can they also be included into accounting as social resources? My own research in Russia and Kazakhstan found reconnection to be one of the most popular reasons for the use of SNS in the region (Shklovski, 2012). I found that reconnection had more to do with re-activating and re-living memories associated with particular social ties. For many this was an emotional experience but reconnected relationships rarely remained active for long despite being connected on SNS. Rather people commented how their obligations for holiday and birthday greetings simply extended the reconnected ties on these platforms. The obligatory congratulations and well wishes on holidays and birthdays are what Dindia and colleagues (2004) called "hygienic factors" that can keep relationships from disappearing completely.

Well before the advent of SNS, Stafford observed that long distance relationships often fell apart when people were able to meet in person after a long separation (Stafford, 2004). For most people in my study, SNS use remained a form of remembering and then re-archiving old relationships that were important but were no longer immediately relevant to daily life. The experience of reconnecting in most cases satisfied the need for remembrances and fed the curiosity borne of simple interest in seeing where someone from the past had ended up in their life. Among my respondents, reconnected ties rarely translated into deep and long lasting relationships, but became a different although potentially more accessible social archive of the past.

At the same time, reconnected ties represented memories and for some such memories were not those that they wanted to revisit. Ties from the past could become a liability where emotional costs of revisiting that past were high. Relationships that have lapsed, are encumbered with memories of a different time. Yet even if people do not reconnect to their past, the relationships they actively engage with on SNS right now are likely to remain connected regardless of the routes lives take in the future. What does it mean for a person's future, if their current ties remain more connected to them than was possible before? What happens if such social memory is made more durable than ever?

Social memory and forgetting

Social technologies generally and SNS in particular emphasize elaborate cataloguing of friendships and acquaintances, business partners and family ties – in order to organize them, to make them accessible and to lower the cognitive load of remembering the relevant details about everyone. The insistence of SNS on promoting self-disclosure leads to a neat cataloguing of our own actions, needs, wants and likes, thus making these available to our ties in the event they had forgotten some relevant detail necessary for further interaction. The social feed can be a memory-aid for social relationships, a way to simplify social management and access. SNS create a seductive promise of being able to manage myriad relationships through lightweight relational work at just the right moments in time. What are the effects of such cataloguing on sociality?

If we consider SNS as both a container and an archive for our social relationships, then what happens to those of our relationships that stubbornly refuse to participate? What about those that do not want to have a digital identity of this sort, those that are not allowed to join for whatever reason, or those that simply cannot? Our social ties themselves create the reality of their presence inside the SNS and they (along with their connections) collaboratively create the image that can be accessed as a reminder. Non-use of technology can have many reasons (Selwyn, 2003; Satchell & Dourish, 2009). The difference is in how these reasons are accommodated by the immediate social relationships. Where those that engage in what Satchell and Dourish (2009) term 'active resistance' are typically supported by their immediate social network in this act, those that a disenfranchised of particular social arrangements will likely experience significant problems. For example, Baumer and colleagues have demonstrated that leaving Facebook could have significant consequences such as losing social contact and potentially productivity from the loss of access to social information resources (Baumer et al., 2013). In his study of scientific memory practices Bowker notes that that which is not allowed to become part of the archive is eventually forgotten (Bowker, 2005). This exclusion is the source of power of the archive – and it is an imperative, commanding power. In a regime where every social action is automatically remembered, where curation has been flipped to determine what might need to be forgotten instead of determining what to remember, absence can be difficult to keep in mind.

The ability to remember is an important problem that computing has been trying to solve for decades. When Google introduced its Gmail service in 2004, it advocated the idea that deleting is unnecessary (Dalsgaard et al., 2005). To combat the limitations of human memory prone to forgetfulness (Bell & Gemmell, 2009), current technical infrastructures and systems preserve without effort data that people produce everyday in what can be described as the default of saving. Development of data management software tends to concentrate on improving tools to avoid accidental information loss as a particularly pernicious problem (Kalnikaité & Whittaker, 2011). Not only can these tools store and help us share important documents, photos or other media, they are even more crucial for helping us fulfill our social obligations of birthday greetings and anniversary congratulations.

Although there is plenty of discussion about the long memory of the Internet, there is also a lot of concern about the attendant lack of longevity of digital objects. The kinds of digital objects that people may want to preserve, such as photographs, diaries, or other keepsakes and artifacts, may in fact be difficult to preserve for two reasons. First, given the speed of technological development old formats can quickly become difficult to access if these formats are no longer supported by newer technologies (Lievrouw, 2000; Hoorens & Rothenberg, 2008). Second, as Lievrouw (2000, 12) warns: "digital media degrade much more quickly than do relatively stable formats like print, analog audio recording . . . or art media." Ironically, the rhetoric about whether or not to delete or preserve digital traces tends to overlook what appears to be a paradox of digital memories. The digital traces that people leave behind, collected by platforms and sensors, shared via social media or posted on a webpage, can be very difficult to remove or forget when those that create such content lose control of its distribution and storage (Woodruff, 2014). The digital objects and traces that people create and would like to preserve, however, may not actually get preserved as well as expected (Lievrouw, 2000).

Intentional ephemerality

Ephemerality in communication has been the expected default prior to the broad adoption of online media. In-person interactions and phone calls can potentially be recorded (whether with or without our knowledge) but the basic expectation is that the record of these interactions remains for only as long as the faults of human memory can sustain for those who are directly involved. Bannon (2006) argues that forgetting is not merely a failure of memory that ought to be corrected but an active process that is a central feature of life. He points to the idea that the inability to forget can be as problematic as the inability to remember through examples coming from studies of neurological disturbances of the function of forgetting (Bannon, 2006). What does it mean then that the vast majority of social technologies people use everyday make it difficult to forget the details of interactions that occur digitally?

Recent and increasing popularity of applications, such as Snapchat, Telegram, Frankly and many others, that offer erasure of shared media after a short period of time by default, suggests that there is an important function to ephemerality in interaction. The relative newness of these technologies means that there has been limited research on how and why they are used. Most research so far has focused on Snapchat – an application that allows users to exchange annotated photos that are erased after a period of time pre-set by the sender (up to 10 seconds) from both sender and receiver devices – as the most commonly used application in Europe and North America. Snapchat is a zero-history application which offers a list of contacts but no history of interaction with these contacts is available. There is considerable agreement that Snapchat use tends to focus on small and meticulously selected sets of relations (Kotfila, 2014; Piwek & Joinson, 2016). Playful and intimate messages are sent to a trusted audience (Bayer et al., 2016) in an attempt to share 'in the moment' (Billings et al., 2017). How are these interactions different when the digital objects produced and exchanged are expected to be deleted by default?

When my students and I first began studying Snapchat, we were surprised by the fact that people we spoke to almost uniformly rejected the idea that Snapchat had anything to do with photography. The fact that the pictures exchanged via Snapchat "don't really exist" (Shklovski & Bruun Hervik, 2016) made the whole interaction worthwhile. Bayer and colleagues also found that although their participants agreed they were sending messages in the form of a picture they were resolute that these messages were not photos (Bayer et al., 2015). Snapchat is used alongside other media such as Facebook, SMS and media messaging, but seems to perform different functions (Bayer et al., 2015). The content exchanged via Snapchat is often playful and at times a little risqué (Piwek & Joinson, 2016) but definitely deemed not worth saving (Bayer et al., 2015; Shklovski & Bruun Hervik, 2016; Shein, 2013).

Most everyday conversations are neither meaningful nor deep. Rather the random chitchat is necessary because of its existence for the pleasure of company and this is an important form of relational maintenance (Canary & Stafford, 1994). The digital objects composed of such chitchat (e.g., chat transcripts, Facebook comments or text messages) may not retain much meaning or value if re-encountered later. Our own research suggests that people are quite mindful of cluttering up each other's media devices, acknowledging that deleting takes extra time and effort. After all, not every interaction needs to produce memorable content. At the same time, there is vulnerability involved in sending funny, ugly or potentially incomprehensible missives to trusted relations and this is an important part of closeness and relational growth. The ability to send such content via an ephemeral medium removes the tinge of guilt associated with being silly and allows greater margins for play and for misinterpretation.

Ephemerality in social media conflicts with the way collection of digital content and its endless multiplication have become the basic building blocks of social technologies. People communicate about things "small" and "not important" but the default of saving in most digital media can make the "small" and "not important" potentially dangerous, resulting in privacy violations or embarrassments in future interactions (Laampinen et al., 2011). After all, play isn't play if the details of its performance can be remembered and shared out of context.

Play is an important way people explore the boundaries of their social worlds. Nippert-Eng terms this boundary play: "the visible, imaginative manipulation of shared cultural-cognitive categories for the purpose of amusement" (Nippert-Eng, 2005, 302). She argues that when conceptualizing play as exploration, people play with boundaries in the gray areas of definitions, rules and protocols, whether these are related to interactions with physical artifacts or social relations. The default of ephemerality that Snapchat and its ilk is well suited to enable boundary play – a kind of "feeling out" of relationships and their boundaries and edges – a test of confidences.

Snapchat allows for easy explicit targeting of communication, the ephemerality enabling a kind of relational play impossible in the formalization imposed on content through the default of saving. The expectation of erasure allows experimentation, offering protection for the future self from the playful actions and transgressions of the past – something that the default of saving constantly threatens. Ephemerality enables relational work that play invites, but such relational work cannot be conducted at scale. Relational boundary play presumes a trusted audience, which explains the repeated finding that Snapchat involves a small number of select relations (Utz et al., 2015; Piwek & Joinson, 2016; Shklovski & Hervik, 2016). Ephemeral communication simply does not make sense to audiences that are typical of Facebook, which is much more useful for leveraging networks rather than engaging in tricky and intimate relational work.

No technology can guarantee erasure. The ephemeral functions of Snapchat and its ilk can be easily circumvented with screenshots and third-party software (Kotfila, 2014). Here the technical defaults matter and the emphasis on the idea that "this picture doesn't really exist" (Shklovski & Bruun Hervik, 2016) suggests that the default of ephemerality of content presumes a relational expectation of forgetting and assigns meaning to acts of deliberate remembrance. Saving a Snapchat communiqué is an intentional act, in the same way as deleting a Facebook post can only be intentional. These acts communicate succinctly that the sender and the recipient disagree about the value of the content. When the image is saved on Snapchat the intentions of the sender are denied but, in saving an image that was intended to be ephemeral, the receiver declares that what wasn't deemed worth saving actually is. The opposite message is communicated when content on Facebook is intentionally deleted and what is deemed worth saving is explicitly discarded. Both actions can have relational consequences if discovered.

The rise of ephemeral social media suggests that perhaps there is no need to remember everything even if we might regret forgetting later. Interpersonal communication involves more than one person's intentions and meanings. For relations and individuals to explore each other and to grow they must be allowed to push boundaries, make mistakes and be foolish in a way that gives space and opportunity for forgetting. Snapchat use seems to be about intentional data loss that allows carelessness in a digital world where every action could be saved and catalogued, requiring far too much forethought and care.

Looking forward

Social interactions of any kind need places and tools to be enacted. Spending time with a friend is an enactment of friendship but it must happen somewhere. The Internet and the social technologies it powers offer myriad options for relational enactment. These 'personal communication systems' (Boase, 2008) have grown in complexity and concerns of the research conducted just a decade ago now seem somewhat naive and limited. As computer mediated communication moved from a curiosity to an integral part of how people manage their daily lives, being "connected" through social media shifted from an affectation to a requirement. Burchell (2015) calls this "need for networked connection" a necessity for participation in the contemporary digital society. This necessity brings with it demands and pressures strong enough that "digital detox" and "disconnection" retreats are becoming a common practice.

Scholars may no longer debate the importance of online social practice, but they continue to argue about the effects that extensive adoption and use of social media might have on individuals, their relationships and the society at large. Peters (2000) writes that in the early 20th century in scholarly debates "communication was a term without specifications of scale." The extent of reach became an important distinction in the 1930s when interest in the effects of new technologies such as radio emerged. Information and communication technologies, as they have evolved, first created an opportunity for the distinction between mass and interpersonal communication and then eventually removed the possibility of it. What used to be distinctly dyadic and interpersonal communication can now slip into scaled mass communication, sometimes unexpectedly as statements become viral memes or get broadcast beyond the intended audience. The outcomes of such communication can be vast and unpredictable. Communication on Facebook in general can hardly be conceived as "small scale" or interpersonal in the same way – the direct visibility of dyadic interactions to broader networks creates a kind of medium scale of communication, located somewhere between the traditional notions of mass and interpersonal. The reach of our interaction efforts is ironically more than we may expect, as we under-estimate our Facebook audiences (Bernstein et al., 2013) and less than we may hope, as we fail to gain the attention we would like (Marwick & boyd, 2010).

As people become more reachable, and, by extension more digitally archivable, what does this mean for the future, for the ability to move beyond the past and to be allowed to grow apart and to become different? The maxim of connectivity presumes that social connections will remain despite upheaval, minor changes or major life events. Moving to a new location no longer means losing touch with friends and family. Yet relationships fade for a reason, sometimes good and sometimes bad, but for a reason none-the-less and many people experience growth and find value in creating new relationships. What if loosing contact becomes a conscious choice, a requirement of cutting the connection on Facebook? As people go through life, some parts of their past might be ones that they want to lose, the memories that they want to forget and the people who are involved with that past, are the ones with whom they would not want to remain in touch. However, such sentiment may not be shared by all parties equally. Social ties are encumbered by past memories in a particular period of a past life. In that sense they are a way to compare ourselves to possible other outcomes but mostly perhaps to note that all survived sufficiently. Yet the reality of current selves may be abruptly questioned and even sabotaged by those who cannot help but see these selves from a point some place in the past.

Social lives, relations and interactions are extensively catalogued and archived, but the people that produce these data often retain little control over whether and how it may be preserved. In response some seek spaces where interaction can remain ephemeral, free from the burden of generating content that is worth saving. Being social is a necessity and a commitment. Yet the dictum of social connection, sharing and communion is often accepted as an unquestionably positive concept. Peters argues that this is problematic, suggesting that instead communication ought to be considered as: "the project of reconciling self and other. The mistake is to think that communications will solve the problems of communication, that better wiring will eliminate the ghosts" (Peters, 2000, 9). More ways of communicating is not necessarily better because reaching an understanding remains difficult. Transmission of information, after all, is not the same as reaching an emotional resonance. To be social is equivalent to the act of interaction, constitutive of the social world – consequential in an ongoing process of meaning making that is simultaneously individual and collaborative (Sigman, 1991). It may be convenient to conceptualize interaction as a purely functional process of transmitting information and grooming social connections, yet such conceptualizations will always remain deficient if they do not recognize the labor involved and perhaps include a bit of play and wonder.

Note

1 The concept of "social capital" has been defined in many different ways by many social theorists. The particular definition that Ellison et al. use in their work conceptualizes social capital as the sum of resources available to an individual from other members of the networks to which said individual belongs (Ellison et al., 2007).

References

Bannon, L. J. (2006). Forgetting as a Feature, not a Bug: The Duality of Memory and Implications for Ubiquitous Computing. *CoDesign*, 2(01), 3–15.

Barash, V., Ducheneaut, N., Isaacs, E., and Bellotti, V. (2010). *Faceplant: Impression (Mis) Management in Facebook Status Updates*. ICWSM, International AAAI Conference on Web and Social Media.

Barkhuus, L., and Tashiro, J. (2010). *Student Socialization in the Age of Facebook*. Proceedings of the SIGCHI Conference on Human Factors in Computing Systems, ACM, pp. 133–142.

Baron, N. S. (1998). Letters by Phone or Speech by Other Means: The Linguistics of Email. *Language & Communication*, 18(2), 133–170.

Bayer, J. B., Campbell, S. W., and Ling, R. (2015). Connection Cues: Activating the Norms and Habits of Social Connectedness. *Communication Theory*, 26(2), 128–149.

Bayer, J. B., Ellison, N. B., Schoenebeck, S. Y., and Falk, E. B. (2016). Sharing the Small Moments: Ephemeral Social Interaction on Snapchat. *Information, Communication & Society*, 19(7), 956–977.

Baym, N. K. (2000). *Tune in, Log on: Soaps, Fandom, and Online Community*. Thousand Oaks: Sage.

Baym, N. (2006). Interpersonal Life Online. In L. A. Lievrouw & S. Livingstone (Eds.), *Handbook of New Media: Student Edition* (pp. 35–54). London: Sage.

Baym, N. K., Zhang, Y. B., and Lin, M. C. (2004). Social Interactions Across Media: Interpersonal Communication on the Internet, Telephone and Face-to-Face. *New Media & Society*, 6(3), 299–318.

Baumeister, R. F., and Leary, M. R. (1995). The Need to Belong: Desire for Interpersonal Attachments as a Fundamental Human Motivation. *Psychological Bulletin*, 117(3), 497.

Baumer, E. P., Adams, P., Khovanskaya, V. D., Liao, T. C., Smith, M. E., Schwanda Sosik, V., and Williams, K. (2013). *Limiting, Leaving, and (Re)lapsing: An Exploration of Facebook Non-Use Practices and Experiences*. Proceedings of the SIGCHI Conference on Human Factors in Computing Systems, ACM, pp. 3257–3266, April.

Bazarova, N. N., Choi, Y. H., Schwanda Sosik, V., Cosley, D., and Whitlock, J. (2015). *Social Sharing of Emotions on Facebook: Channel Differences, Satisfaction, and Replies*. Proceedings of the 18th ACM Conference on Computer Supported Cooperative Work & Social Computing, ACM, pp. 154–164.

Bell, C., and Gemmell, J. (2009). *Total Recall: How the E-Memory Revolution Will Change Everything*. New York: Dutton.

Bernstein, M. S., Bakshy, E., Burke, M., and Karrer, B. (2013). *Quantifying the Invisible Audience in Social Networks*. Proceedings of the SIGCHI Conference on Human Factors in Computing Systems, pp. 21–30.

Billings, A. C., Qiao, F., Conlin, L., and Nie, T. (2017). Permanently Desiring the Temporary? Snapchat, Social Media, and the Shifting Motivations of Sports Fans. *Communication & Sport*, 5(1), 10–26.

Binder, J., Howes, A., and Sutcliffe, A. (2009). *The Problem of Conflicting Social Spheres: Effects of Network Structure on Experienced Tension in Social Network Sites*. Proceedings of the SIGCHI Conference on Human Factors in Computing Systems, ACM, pp. 965–974.

Blieszner, R., and Adams, R. G. (1992). *Adult Friendship*. Newbury Park: Sage.

Boase, J. (2008). Personal Networks and the Personal Communication System. *Information, Communication & Society*, 11(4), 490–508.

Boneva, B. S., Quinn, A., Kraut, R., Kiesler, S., and Shklovski, I. (2006). Teenage Communication in the Instant Messaging Era. In R. Kraut, M. Brynin, and S. Kiesler (eds.) *Computers, Phones, and the Internet: Domesticating Information Technology*. New York: Oxford University Press, pp. 201–218.

Bourdieu, P. (1986). The Forms of Capital. In J. Richardson (ed.), *Handbook of Theory and Research for the Sociology of Education*. New York, Greenwood, pp. 241–256.

boyd, d., and Ellison, N. B. (2007). Social Network Sites: Definition, History, and Scholarship. *Journal of Computer-Mediated Communication*, 13(1), 210–230.

boyd, d., and Marwick, A. (2011). Social Privacy in Networked Publics: Teens' Attitudes, Practices, and Strategies. In *A Decade in Internet Time*. Oxford: Oxford University Press.

Bowker, G. C. (2005). *Memory Practices in the Sciences* (vol. 205). Cambridge, MA: MIT Press.

Brake, D. (2014). *Sharing Our Lives Online: Risks and Exposure in Social Media*. Berlin: Springer.

Brandtzæg, P. B., and Nov, O. (2011). Facebook Use and Social Capital – A Longitudinal Study. *Age*, 15(30), 31–40.

Burchell, K. (2015). Tasking the Everyday: Where Mobile and Online Communication Take Time. *Mobile Media & Communication*, 3(1), 36–52.

Brandtzæg, P. B., and Nov, O. (2011). Facebook Use and Social Capital – a Longitudinal Study. *Age*, 15(30), 31–40.

Burke, M., Kraut, R., and Marlow, C. (2011). *Social Capital on Facebook: Differentiating Uses and Users*. Proceedings of the 2011 Annual Conference on Human Factors in Computing Systems, Vancouver, BC.

Castells, M. (1996). *The Rise of the Network Society: The Information Age: Economy, Society, and Culture*. New York: John Wiley & Sons.

Canary, D., and Stafford, L. (1994). Maintaining Relationships Through Strategic & Routine Interaction. In D. Canary and L. Stafford (eds.), *Communication & Relational Maintenance*. San Diego, CA: Academic Press.

Carnevale, P. J., and Probst, T. M. (1997). Conflict on the Internet. *Culture of the Internet*, 233–255.

Daft, R. L., and Lengel, R. H. (1984). Information Richness: A New Approach to Managerial Behaviour and Organizational Design. *Research in Organizational Behaviour*, 6, 191–233.

Dalsgaard, P., Eriksson, E., and Hansen, L. K. (2005). *Rethinking Information Handling: Designing for Information Offload*. Proceedings of the 4th Decennial Conference on Critical Computing: Between Sense and Sensibility, ACM, pp. 161–164.

Das, S., and Kramer, A. (2013). *Self-Censorship on Facebook*. Proceedings of International AAAI Conference on Weblogs and Social Media.

de Sola Pool, I. (ed.). (1977). *The Social Impact of the Telephone* (vol. 1). Cambridge, MA: MIT Press.

Dimmick, J., Feaster, J. C., and Ramirez Jr, A. (2011). The Niches of Interpersonal Media: Relationships in Time and Space. *New Media & Society*, 13(8), 1265–1282.

Dindia, K., Timmerman, L., Langan, E., Sahlstein, E. M., and Quandt, J. (2004). The Function of Holiday Greetings in Maintaining Relationships. *Journal of Social and Personal Relationships*, 21(5), 577–593.

Donath, J., and Boyd, D. (2004). Public Displays of Connection. *BT Technology Journal*, 22(4), 71–82.

Duck, S. W. (1977). *The Study of Acquaintance*. Farnborough: Teakfield-Saxon House.

Ellison, N., Steinfield, C., and Lampe, C. (2007). The Benefits of Facebook 'Friends': Social Capital and College Students' Use of Online Social Network Sites. *Journal of Computer-Mediated Communication*, 12(4), 1143–1168.

Ellison, N. B., Steinfield, C., and Lampe, C. (2011). Connection Strategies: Social Capital Implications of Facebook-Enabled Communication Practices. *New Media & Society*, 13(6), 873–892.

Ellison, N. B., Vitak, J., Gray, R., and Lampe, C. (2014). Cultivating Social Resources on Social Network Sites: Facebook Relationship Maintenance Behaviors and Their Role in Social Capital Processes. *Journal of Computer-Mediated Communication*, 19(4), 855–870.

Ellison, N. B., and Vitak, J. (2015). Social Network Site Affordances and Their Relationship to Social Capital Processes. *The Handbook of the Psychology of Communication Technology*, 32, 205–228.

Feld, S. L. (1991). Why Your Friends Have More Friends Than You Do. *American Journal of Sociology*, 96(6), 1464–1477.

Fischer, C. S. (1994). *America Calling: A Social History of the Telephone to 1940*. Stanford: University of California Press.

Hampton, K., Goulet, L. S., Rainie, L., and Purcell, K. (2011). Social Networking Sites and Our Lives. *Pew Internet & American Life Project*, 16, 1–85.

Harper, R. H. (2010). *Texture: Human Expression in the Age of Communications Overload*. Cambridge, MA: MIT Press.

Haythornthwaite, C. (2005). Social Networks and Internet Connectivity Effects. *Information, Community & Society*, 8(2), 125–147.

Hill, K. (2017). *Facebook Figured Out My Family Secrets, And It Won't Tell Me How*. Gizmodo. https://gizmodo.com/facebook-figured-out-my-family-secrets-and-it-wont-tel-1797696163.

Hogan, B. (2010). The Presentation of Self in the Age of Social Media: Distinguishing Performances and Exhibitions Online. *Bulletin of Science, Technology & Society*, 30(6), 377–386.

Hoorens, S., and Rothenberg, J. (2008). *Digital Preservation: The Uncertain Future of Saving the Past*. Report. RAND Corporation.

John, N. A. (2016). *The Age of Sharing*. New York: John Wiley & Sons.

Joinson, A. N. (2008). *Looking at, Looking Up or Keeping Up with People? Motives and Use of Facebook*. Proceedings of the Twenty-Sixth Annual SIGCHI Conference on Human Factors in Computing Systems, Florence, Italy.

Kalnikaitė, V., and Whittaker, S. (2011). A Saunter Down Memory Lane: Digital Reflection on Personal Mementos. *International Journal of Human-Computer Studies*, 69(5), 298–310.

Katz, J. E., and Aspden, P. (1997). A Nation of Strangers? *Communications of the ACM*, 40(12), 81–86.

Kharkhordin, O. (2005). *Main Concepts of Russian Politics*. Lanham, MD: UP.

Kiesler, S., Siegel, J., and McGuire, T. W. (1984). Social Psychological Aspects of Computer-Mediated Communication. *American Psychologist*, 39(10), 1123.

Knox, H., Savage, M., and Harvey, P. (2006). Social Networks and the Study of Relations: Networks as Method, Metaphor and Form. *Economy and Society*, 35, 113–140.

Kotfila, C. (2014). This Message Will Self-Destruct: The Growing Role of Obscurity and Self-Destructing Data in Digital Communication. *Bulletin of the American Society for Information Science and Technology*, 40(2), 12–16.

Kraut, R., Kiesler, S., Boneva, B., Cummings, J., Helgeson, V., and Crawford, A. (2002). Internet Paradox Revisited. *Journal of Social Issues*, 58(1), 49–74.

Kraut, R., Patterson, M., Lundmark, V., Kiesler, S., Mukophadhyay, T., and Scherlis, W. (1998). Internet Paradox: A Social Technology That Reduces Social Involvement and Psychological Well-Being? *American Psychologist*, 53(9), 1017.

Laampinen, A., Lehtinen, V., Lehmuskallio, A., and Tamminen, S. (2011). *We're in It Together: Interpersonal Management of Disclosure in Social Network Services*. Proceedings of CHI, Vancouver, Canada.

LaRose, R., Connolly, R., Lee, H., Li, K., and Hales, K. D. (2014). Connection Overload? A Cross Cultural Study of the Consequences of Social Media Connection. *Information Systems Management*, 31(1), 59–73.

Lambert, A. (2016). Intimacy and Social Capital on Facebook: Beyond the Psychological Perspective. *New Media & Society*, 18(11), 2559–2575.

Lampe, C., Ellison, N., and Steinfield, C. (2006). *A Face(book) in the Crowd: Social Searching vs. Social Browsing*. In Proceedings of the 2006 Conference on Computer Supported Cooperative Work. http://doi.acm.org/10.1145/1180875.1180901.

Lampe, C., Ellison, N. B., and Steinfield, C. (2008). *Changes in Use and Perception of Facebook*. Proceedings of the 2008 ACM Conference on Computer Supported Cooperative Work, pp. 721–730. https://doi.org/10.1145/1460563.1460675.

Lea, M., Spears, R. (1995). Love at First Byte. In S. Duck and J. T. Wood (eds.), *Understudied Relationships: Off the Beaten Track*. Thousand Oaks: Sage, pp. 197–233.

Ledbetter, A. M. (2008). Media Use and Relational Closeness in Long-Term Friendships: Interpreting Patterns of Multimodality. *New Media & Society*, 10(4), 547–564.

Levin, D. Z., Walter, J., and Murnighan, J. K. (2010). Dormant Ties: The Value of Reconnecting. *Organization Science*, 22(4), 923–939. doi:10.1287/orsc.1100.0576.

Lievriouw, L. A. (2000) Nonobvious Things About New Media: "Dead Media" and the Loss of Electronic Cultural Heritage. *ICA Newsletter*, 28(1), January, 12–13.

Lievrouw, L. A. (2001). New Media and the 'Pluralization of Life-Worlds': A Role for Information in Social Differentiation. *New Media & Society*, 3(1), 7–28.

Lievrouw, L. A. (2009). New Media, Mediation, and Communication Study. *Information, Communication & Society*, 12(3), 303–325.

Marwick, A. E., and boyd, d. (2011). I Tweet Honestly, I Tweet Passionately: Twitter Users, Context Collapse, and the Imagined Audience. *New Media & Society*, 13(1), 114–133.

McKenna, K. Y., and Bargh, J. A. (2000). Plan 9 from Cyberspace: The Implications of the Internet for Personality and Social Psychology. *Personality and Social Psychology Review*, 4(1), 57–75.

Nie, N. H. (2001). Sociability, Interpersonal Relations, and the Internet: Reconciling Conflicting Findings. *American Behavioral Scientist*, 45(3), 420–435.

Nie, N. H., and Hillygus, D. S. (2002). The Impact of Internet Use on Sociability: Time-Diary Findings. *IT & Society*, 1(1), 1–20.

Nippert-Eng, C. (2005). Boundary Play. *Space and Culture*, 8(3), 302–324.

Norris, F. H., and Kaniasty, K. (1996). Received and Perceived Social Support in Times of Stress: A Test of the Social Support Deterioration Deterrence Model. *Journal of Personality and Social Psychology*, 71(3), 498.

Papacharissi, Z., and Mendelson, A. (2010). 12 Toward a New(er) Sociability: Uses, Gratifications and Social Capital on Facebook. In S. Papathanassopoulos (ed.), *Media Perspectives for the 21st Century*. New York: Routledge, pp. 212–230.

Parks, M. R., and Floyd, K. (1996). Making Friends in Cyberspace. *Journal of Computer-Mediated Communication*, 1(4).

Parks, M. R., and Roberts, L. D. (1998). Making MOOsic': The Development of Personal Relationships on Line and a Comparison to Their Off-Line Counterparts. *Journal of Social and Personal Relationships*, 15(4), 517–537.

Peters, J. D. (2000). *Speaking Into the Air: A History of the Idea of Communication*. Chicago: University of Chicago Press.

Piwek, L., and Joinson, A. (2016). 'What Do They Snapchat About?' Patterns of Use in Time-Limited Instant Messaging Service. *Computers in Human Behavior*, 54, 358–367.

Portes, A. (1998). Social Capital: Its Origins and Applications in Modern Sociology. *Annual Review of Sociology*, 24(1), 1–24.

Putnam, R. (2001). *Bowling Alone: The Collapse and Revival of American Community*. New York: Simon & Schuster.

Quinn, K. (2013). We Haven't Talked in 30 Years! *Information, Communication & Society*, 16(3), 397–420.

Rains, S. A., and Brunner, S. R. (2015). What Can We Learn About Social Network Sites by Studying Facebook? A Call and Recommendations for Research on Social Network Sites. *New Media & Society*, 17(1), 114–131.

Rheingold, H. (1993). *The Virtual Community: Finding Connection in a Computerized World*. Boston, MA: Addison-Wesley Longman Publishing Co.

Satchell, C., and Dourish, P. (2009). *Beyond the User: Use and Non-Use in HCI*. Proceedings of the 21st Annual Conference of the Australian Computer-Human Interaction, ACM, pp. 9–16, November.

Selwyn, N. (2003). Apart from Technology: Understanding People's Non-use of Information and Communication Technologies in Everyday Life. *Technology in Society*, 25(1), 99–116.

Shakya, H. B., and Christakis, N. A. (2017). Association of Facebook Use with Compromised Well-Being: A Longitudinal Study. *American Journal of Epidemiology*, 185(3), 203–211.

Shein, E. (2013). Ephemeral Data. *Communications of the ACM*, 56(9), 20–22.

Shklovski, I. (2012). *Social Network Sites: Indispensable or Optional Social Tools?* Proceedings of the International Conference on Weblogs and Social Media, 20 (ICWSM 2012), AAAI Press.

Shklovski, I., Barkhuus, L., Bornoe, N., and Kaye, J. J. (2015). *Friendship Maintenance in the Digital Age: Applying a Relational Lens to Online Social Interaction*. Proceedings of the 18th ACM Conference on Computer Supported Cooperative Work & Social Computing, ACM, pp. 1477–1487.

Shklovski, I., and Bruun Hervik, S. (2016). 'The Silly Pictures Disappear': Ephemeral Social Media as Boundary Play. *AoIR Selected Papers of Internet Research*, 5.

Shklovski, I., Kiesler, S., and Kraut, R. (2006). The Internet and Social Interaction: A Meta-Analysis and Critique of Studies, 1995–2003. In R. Kraut, M. Brynin, and S. Kiesler (eds.), *Computers, Phones, and the Internet. Domesticating Information Technology*. Oxford: Oxford University Press.

Shklovski, I., Kraut, R., and Cummings, J. (2008). *Keeping in Touch by Technology: Maintaining Friendships After a Residential Move*. Proceedings of the SIGCHI Conference on Human Factors in Computing Systems, ACM, pp. 807–816.

Sigman, S. J. (1991). Handling the Discontinuous Aspects of Continuous Social Relationships: Toward Research on the Persistence of Social Forms. *Communication Theory*, 1(2), 106–127.

Sigman, S. J. (ed.). (1995). *The Consequentiality of Communication*. London: Psychology Press.

Sørensen, A. T., and Shklovski, I. (2011). *The Hugging Team: The Role of Technology in Business Networking Practices*. ECSCW 2011: Proceedings of the 12th European Conference on Computer Supported Cooperative Work, Aarhus Denmark, Springer, London, pp. 333–352.

Stafford, L. (2004). *Maintaining Long-Distance and Cross-Residential Relationships*. London: Routledge.

Stafford, L., Kline, S. L., and Dimmick, J. (1999). Home E-Mail: Relational Maintenance and Gratification Opportunities. *Journal of Broadcasting & Electronic Media*, 43(4), 659–669.

Stoycheff, E., Liu, J., Wibowo, K. A., and Nanni, D. P. (2017). What Have We Learned About Social Media by Studying Facebook? A Decade in Review. *New Media & Society*, 19(6), 968–980.

Strathern, M. (1996). Cutting the Network. *Journal of the Royal Anthropological Institute*, 517–535.

Subrahmanyam, K., Reich, S. M., Waechter, N., and Espinoza, G. (2008). Online and Offline Social Networks: Use of Social Networking Sites by Emerging Adults. *Journal of Applied Developmental Psychology*, 29(6), 420–433.

Sørensen, A. T., and Shklovski, I. (2011). The Hugging Team: The Role of Technology in Business Networking Practices. In S. Bødker, N. O. Bouvin, V. Wulf, L. Ciolfi, and W. Lutters (eds.), *ECSCW 2011: Proceedings of the 12th European Conference on Computer Supported Cooperative Work*, 24–28 September 2011. Aarhus, Denmark: Springer, pp. 333–352.

Travers, J., and Milgram, S. (1969). An Experimental Study of the Small World Problem. *Sociometry*, 425–443.

Tufekci, Z. (2008). Grooming, Gossip, Facebook and MySpace: What Can We Learn About These Sites from Those Who Won't Assimilate? *Information, Communication & Society*, 11(4), 544–564.

Turkle, S. (1995). *Life on the Screen: Identity in the Age of the Internet*. New York: Touchstone.

Utz, S., Muscanell, N., and Khalid, C. (2015). Snapchat Elicits More Jealousy Than Facebook: A Comparison of Snapchat and Facebook Use. *Cyberpsychology, Behavior, and Social Networking*, 18(3), 141–146.

Valenzuela, S., Arriagada, A., and Scherman, A. (2014). Facebook, Twitter, and Youth Engagement: A Quasi-experimental Study of Social Media Use and Protest Behavior Using Propensity Score Matching. *International Journal of Communication*, 8, 25.

Vaterlaus, J. M., Barnett, K., Roche, C., and Young, J. A. (2016). "Snapchat Is More Personal": An Exploratory Study on Snapchat Behaviors and Young Adult Interpersonal Relationships. *Computers in Human Behavior*, 62(Supplement C), 594–601.

Verduyn, P. et al. (2015). Passive Facebook Usage Undermines Affective Well-Being: Experimental and Longitudinal Evidence. *Journal of Experimental Psychology*, 144(2), 480–488. http://dx.doi.org/10.1037/xge0000057.

Vitak, J., and Ellison, N. B. (2013). 'There's a Network Out There You Might as Well Tap': Exploring the Benefits of and Barriers to Exchanging Informational and Support-Based Resources on Facebook. *New Media & Society*, 15(2), 243–259.

Walther, J. B., Anderson, J. E., and Park, D. W. (1994). Interpersonal Antisocial Communication. *Communication Research*, 21, 460–487.

Walther, J. B. (1995). Relational Aspects of Computer-Mediated Communication: Experimental Observations Over Time. *Organization Science*, 6(2), 186–203.

Walther, J. B. (2007). Selective Self-Presentation in Computer-Mediated Communication: Hyperpersonal Dimensions of Technology, Language, and Cognition. *Computers in Human Behavior*, 23(5), 2538–2557.

Wellman, B., and Gulia, M. (1999). Net Surfers Don't Ride Alone: Virtual Communities as Communities. *Networks in the Global Village*, 331–366.

Wellman, B., Quan-Haase, A., Boase, J., Chen, W., Hampton, K., Díaz, I., and Miyata, K. (2003). The Social Affordances of the Internet for Networked Individualism. *Journal of Computer-Mediated Communication*, 8(3).

Woodruff, A. (2014). *Necessary, Unpleasant, and Disempowering: Reputation Management in the Internet Age*. In Proceedings of the SIGCHI Conference on Human Factors in Computing Systems, ACM, pp. 149–158.

Young, K. (2011). Social Ties, Social Networks and the Facebook Experience. *International Journal of Emerging Technologies and Society*, 9(1), 20–34.

11

Digital literacies in a wireless world

Antero Garcia

The past two decades have seen a significant shift in what counts as literacies research and where such literacies are found, enacted, engaged. Primarily rising as a field alongside mainstream use of the Internet (Lankshear & Knobel, 2008), digital literacy has come to signal a widespread set of interdisciplinary, social, scholarly, and business-related practices. First providing some foundational grounding, this chapter presents several guidelines for how the field of digital literacy is changing. Throughout this chapter, I define the field of literacy research as the broader study of how different communities develop, enact, and produce through the varied literacies practices they engage in. This framing of literacy as community-based points to a key tenet that will be developed across this chapter: literacies live within specific cultural practices and historical contexts. As such, the framing of digital literacies in this chapter is offered from a sociocultural and sometimes socio*critical* (Gutiérrez, 2008) understanding of the field of literacy.

Rather than simply describe where research on digital literacies is headed, I identify three fundamental and interlinked principles that are shaping the direction of literacies research. These principles – that literacies are *connected, embodied*, and *platform-dependent* – offer a 'layered' (Abrams & Russo, 2015; Garcia, 2017a) perspective of the field and contextualize how literacies function at different levels. Such a lens ultimately resists the processes of digital enclosure that can shape one perspective of digital communications throughout this volume.

Recognizing the consequences of digital technologies in our current globalized world, digital literacies shape issues of equity, pedagogy, and power in society today (e.g., New London Group, 1996; Penuel & O'Connor, 2018). This chapter offers a contemporary review of what literacy means in light of recent technological and cultural advances. Grounding this work in how digital and multimodal literacies have shifted the landscape of learning, pedagogy, and engagement, this chapter focuses on how individuals enact literacies in and across virtual and physical environments. In doing so, this understanding of digital literacies demonstrates how scrutinizing digital literacies individually often leads to occluding a broader ecology of interaction.

Considering that, for a relatively long period of time, the Internet was accessed through 'dialing up' services from garishly large devices anchored to walls, the shift to a *wireless* set of digital literacies is recent. Though the history of digital literacies is covered later, it is with a recognition that the environments through which digital practices occur blend more fluidly into the everyday lives of individuals across the globe. With this porousness of digital literacies in today's wireless world is a need to re-define how multimodal and diverse communicative practices are understood in the 21st century.

Toward definition of digital and of literacies

Long before the study of litera*cies* became a pluralized field, literacy research highlighted how practices of reading, writing, and communicating were tied to personhood and civics (Kintgen et al., 1988). Habermas (1991) explains how language frames and mediates participation within the "public sphere." Similarly, McLuhan (1962) contended that print-based culture helped shape national identities; a uniformity of book culture dictated principles for state-based power and control. This emphasis on how literacy practices are tied to issues of power remains pertinent as digital technologies encroach on the everyday work and social activities in society today. At the same time, to explain 'literacy' as a singular phenomenon has long been seen as insufficient for both researchers and educators (Kintgen et al., 1988, v).

Recognizing advances in technology before the turn of the 21st century, a sociocultural approach to understanding literacies significantly broadened the field. James Gee describes how a focus on 'new' literacies studies in the 1990s expanded the field intentionally to consider advances in technology: "new literacies studies is about studying new types of literacy beyond print literacy, especially digital literacies and literacy practices embedded in popular culture" (2010, 31). As he further explains, researchers like Brian Street (1994) emphasize how literacy practices changed over different cultural, temporal, and spatial contexts. In this sense, a radical shift just prior to the 21st century occurred within the literacy field with "the recognition of multiple literacies, varying according to time and space, but also contested in relations of power" (Street, 1994, 77).

Multiliteracies

Connecting the notion of multiple literacies to technology, power, and culture, a collective of ten literacy researchers – under the name the New London Group – released a formative document in the mid-1990s that drew together these key ideas and introduced the notion of 'multiliteracies' (1996). Titled "A Pedagogy of Multiliteracies: Designing Social Futures," the New London Group's theoretical work emphasized that multimodal communication and linguistic diversity were rapidly expanding the kinds of literacies enacted in the world. At the same time, these advances were happening at a time of increasing globalization and tightening of capitalist power. As the title of their paper alludes, the New London Group's emphasis was on the pedagogical considerations related to multiliteracies, particularly as related to issues of equity and power:

> The changing technological and organizational shape of working life provides some with access to lifestyles of unprecedented affluence, while excluding others in ways that are increasingly related to the outcomes of education and training. It may well be that we have to rethink what we are teaching, and, in particular, what new learning needs literacy pedagogy might now address.
>
> (The New London Group, 1996, 61).

As a multifaceted approach, multiliteracies points to the role of identity, technology, and power in human communication. Kress – one of the New London Group members – focused on the role of technology and modality. Explaining the role of 'multi' in multiliteracies, Kress argues for various theoretical pathways:

> "multi-" lay in the multiplicities of socially distinct uses of language – whether seen as discourses or as a multiplicity of socially shaped differences in what might be seen as one language. Or it might have lain in the multiplicities of factors that constitute the social domain itself – culturally, linguistically, in terms of class, of gender, of age as generation and so on.
>
> *(Kress, 2009, 207)*

Kress highlights how new technologies shift readers' relationships with authors has from "unidirectional into bidirectionality" (Kress, 2003, 6). Acknowledging that the "power of the author . . . is lessened and diffused" (ibid), Kress hints at how shifts in technology continue to redefine what kind of "social futures" (New London Group, 1996) can be designed.

In the twenty years since the New London Group's description of multiliteracies, the field of literacy has expanded, clarified, and debated the term; it has been the bedrock of sociocultural perspectives of digital literacies for several generations of scholarship at this point. As described later in this chapter, this has been expanded beyond the 'ocularcentrism' of the initial New London Group document: "the emphasis on what can be seen with the eyes over what is perceived through other senses" (Mills, 2016, 79). Further, the spatial dimensions of literacies have been connected even more aptly to issues of global power as Lam and Warriner have noted. They explain that "examining literacy across social and geographical spaces is especially relevant to the practices of people of migrant backgrounds as they develop and maintain relationships that often spread across territorial boundaries" (2012, 191). A prescient and forward-looking document, the New London Group's articulation of multiliteracies remains foundational to how the field of literacies research and education identify, communicate, and teach about and with digital tools today. At the same time, little in the way of literacies research has updated this foundational text for an era filled with hashtags, mainstream virtual reality platforms, and an 'Internet of Things' as explored later.

Not a singular field

The foundational emphasis on multiliteracies is not to occlude other trends that have developed outside of the field of literacy over the past two decades. Rather, an understanding of how new literacies studies and multiliteracies have progressed in tandem with advances in cultural studies and explorations of participatory culture (Jenkins et al., 2009) have only broadened how we understand literacies in an era of digital culture today. Admittedly, the overview of how digital literacies are studied previously is one that is shared from a sociocultural stance. There are other approaches to understanding digital literacies – particularly a grounding of literacy in the fields of psychology and cognition. However, as an emphasis of how individuals, communities, and history change, the work that has been formatively shaped around the New London Group is a useful grounding for understanding how literacies shape meaning making today. At the same time, this definition points only to a general grounding for the field. Various critical offshoots, such as media literacies (Hobbs, 2011), *critical* digital literacies (Avila & Pandya, 2012; Morrell, 2008), and computational literacies (Lee & Soep, 2016; Lynch, 2015) illustrate nuanced pathways that digital literacies have taken. Though each emerging field is an extension, clarification, and re-shaping of how specific literacies practices are developed and enacted, the remainder of this chapter is aimed at addressing the broader shifts that the field of literacies is facing. Across these expansive notions of digital literacies, how researchers study these literacies must be considered. The units of analysis and the kinds of discursive 'turns' (Sacks et al., 1974) that are made in newly emerging digital literacies will continue to evolve.

As the role of digital literacies continues to blur with the role of literacies writ large in an era of Internet-connected, 'smart' devices, and as digital tools continue to be aligned with globalized enactments of Western capitalism as identified two decades ago by the New London Group, several emergent trends are shaping the direction of digital literacy research. Much of the remaining chapter explores how this confluence of digital advances are redefining the field and how these understandings reshape what literacies *mean* for broader contexts of learning and research. By digging into each of these, I hope to offer an overview of where empirical and theoretical understandings of digital literacies are headed, how these are shaping the processes of communicating, learning, and socializing, and how such shifts impact literacy research.

Broadening digital literacy research and practice

As explained earlier, the nature of literacies is multiple and fluid across varied contexts of learning, commerce, labor, and socialization today. At the same time, I want to caution that – while plausible – labeling *any* communicative practice as a unique kind of literacy is fraught. The emphasis on specific forms of literacies – digital (Coiro, 2012; Knobel & Lankshear, 2007), civic (Garcia & Mirra, 2019; Mirra & Garcia, 2017), media (Hobbs, 2011; Share, 2015) – should be intentional and useful in guiding how research and practitioner communities approach their work. With this recognition, rather than highlight and name new forms of digital literacies I focus next on three guidelines for what digital literacies can *mean* and how the present moment of digital literacies research is shifting. Further, while the tenets of literacies as connected, embodied, and platform-dependent are described individually, I also point to how they are intertwined as well.

Literacies are connected

In considering literacies as 'connected,' I emphasize two different aspects of what shapes contemporary literacies understanding. On the one hand, understanding how meaning is shaped in informal learning contexts of play, making, and remix illustrates what Ito et al. (2013) have referred to as 'connected learning.' This framework describes how individuals engage in practices that are "socially embedded, interest-driven, and oriented toward educational, economic, or political opportunity" (Ito et al., 2013, 6). Focusing on gaming and maker communities that run the gamut of participant engagement from "hanging out" to "geeking out" (Ito et al., 2009), connected learning casts new light on primarily informal learning activities often happening outside of school settings.

The fluidity of how individuals collaborate, distribute leadership, and offer meaningful feedback highlight the *connected literacies* that are particularly abundant in the digitally mediated contexts of participation today. Primarily, connected learning research has focused on the practices of young people – designing and playing video games (Rafalow & Tekinbas, 2014), writing fan fiction (Hellekson & Busse, 2014), and communicating in online fan communities (Pfister, 2014) for instance. However, a connected learning and connected literacies framework is exemplary of adult and youth learning contexts and can be particularly useful in considering classroom digital literacies practices for teachers today (Garcia, 2014, 2017b). Literacies guide and link interactions across the spaces of connected learning. When collaborating with peers while building model rockets (Azevedo, 2011) or while collaborating on a youth-driven magazine (in Mirra, 2014), literacies link the communicative and social activities that are at the foundation of connected learning. These practices move fluidly across digital and analog contexts, just as much of our participation in contemporary society does.

At the same time that literacies that are connected point to a specific set of learning principles that have emerged in today's participatory culture, this same descriptor highlights how literacies are tied to practices, domains, and fields specific to unique audiences and cultures. That is, literacies do not live abstractly and discretely separate from how individuals participate in society. Even traditional literacy practices like reading and writing are tied to particular contexts: we read and write *for* specific purposes and *to* specific audiences (even if those audiences are ourselves). In this sense, literacies both glue together conglomerations of individuals across space and time and are continually redefined by the use and technological advances in which communities leverage literacies for specific purposes. For example, looking back on archaic instances of technology, White (1962) highlights how technologies that seem mundane today such as stirrups for riding horses transform individuals' relationship to land, to nature, and to one another. Being able to leverage new tools re-connects society to newly mediated literacy practices. Similarly, in describing the cultural history of the chair as form of technology, Cranz notes that, "What is true of the chair is true of all the artifacts we create. We design them; but once built, they shape us" (1998, 15). Though literacies connect us to meaning, they also maintain the cultural contexts we imbue them with over time.

In considering the role of technology in shaping how communities are connected and redefine literacies "from narratives that are floating around" (Sfard & Prusak, 2005, 18), it is necessary to recognize that digital literacies blur space and time in ways previous technological advances have been inching toward. By allowing asynchronous and distant forms of multimodal deliberation, socialization, and collaboration, digital technologies bring the practices of connected literacies closer to one another. Literacies in today's digital epoch connect individuals across space, across time, and in both physical and virtual world settings.

Literacies are embodied

Building from the recognition that literacies are constructed and given meaning within connected contexts, it is important to recognize that literacies are *embodied*. Pushing the literacy field's understanding of multiliteracies, Leander and Boldt, closely trace the actions of a young manga fan across his day-to-day activities. They ultimately note that this young man's "experience of the world around him is enacted through his body; text – in this case, manga – joins the flow or movement of multiple sensations and experiences as he sits, reads, performs, later searches the Internet, looks at trading cards, and engages in sword play" (2012, 29). As Leander and Boldt emphasize, literacies are not simply performed or – as the New London Group (1996) urges – *designed* but are experienced within one's body. Expanding on this principle, Leander and Boldt write:

> This body is both material and incorporeal. Materially, we move within time and space as bodies. As bodies, we perceive and register, consciously or unconsciously, some of the infinite patterns and variations in our environment. It is in the body that we locate the affective sensations of those registrations that are available to our consciousness, often making meaning of them by giving them form and significance as emotion, physical sensation, response, or energy.
>
> *(2012, 29)*

Though this may feel theoretically distant from this chapter's emphasis on digital literacies, it is important to recognize that any digital activity is parsed and given meaning within individual bodies. It is the physical actions of moving eyes, swiping screens, gesturing in virtual worlds that ultimately allow digital material to be produced and understood. *Digital literacies begin within the bodies of individuals.*

In describing multimodal literacies research with children, Mills emphasizes how digital literacies remain foundationally grounded in embodied principles:

> We allowed the children to take video cameras home to film life in their homes and communities, and walked with cameras in the local area beyond the school for the students to understand the world perceived through their sensing bodies. Filming, as a literacy experience, was embodied because the students represented their sensory experiences of the places they visited in tangible ways. Physical experiences were central to the story. The filmmakers' bodies and the bodies of their peers were not peripheral, but central to their knowing and representing the world to others.
>
> *(2016, 154).*

Mills draws together the key ways that literacies that are embodied and experienced individually in the bodies and minds of young people are distilled into digital literacy performance. Likewise, we can imagine viewers of these young people's films feeling the energy (perhaps even a touch of nausea!) as cameras sway and move with the rhythms of young people frolicking through the processes of production.

Considering the embodied nature of *all* literacies, the work of literacies researchers like Leander and Boldt (2012) and Mills (2016) harken back to foundational tenets of sociocultural literacy practices. As Freire and Macedo (1987) explain, reading print-based texts must first begin by "reading the world." The ways we understand texts in digital and non-digital environments first begins with how our bodies sense and make meaning of the images, sounds, and other produced ephemera. Further, as Freire and Macedo allude, this meaning is grounded in the cultural understandings we carry with us.

Literacies are platform-dependent

Moving from an emphasis on individuals as embodying literacies, I want to turn to the digital tools, systems, and mechanisms on which these literacy acts are conveyed and processed. By turning to *platforms*, it is important to consider how one platform conveys different kinds of meanings than others. For example, the paratextual features (Genette, 1997) of a printed book – its margins, its title page, its unique ISBN code – are substantially different from the features surrounding a post read and consumed on an online social network, or on the interface of a control stick digitally manipulating a flying drone, or on the interface that sends information to a nearby 3d printer. The platforms of digital literacies are abundant and the acts that they mediate differ substantially.

Bogost and Monfort explain that "A platform is a computing system of any sort upon which further computing development can be done. It can be implemented entirely in hardware, entirely in software (which runs on any of several hardware platforms), or in some combination of the two" (2009, 1). Building on this definition Bogost and Monfort have been curating the "Platform Studies" book series through MIT Press, focusing on the meaning and possibilities of individual gaming platforms to highlight how cultural and technical epochs shape what happened on a Nintendo gaming system or on Atari's first home gaming system.

Though Leorke (2012) highlights that the field of platform studies has primarily focused on the technical aspects of platforms like videogaming consoles, the emphasis on platforms also broadens a discourse about how platforms mediate the kinds of literacy practices enacted by both users and designers. As Leorke notes, platform studies "provides a framework for analyzing the culture within which platforms are created, taking into account the development of their material, technical components as well as broader social and cultural concerns" (2012, 259). From a literacies stance, focusing on how literacies transpire on specific platforms shapes the scope of how communicative practices are understood. A tweet, for instance, conveys specific kinds of communicative constraints. Knowing a message is sent via Twitter highlights how one platform's intended meaning shapes what literacy practices are engaged on it. At the same time, these constraints also point to possibilities: "the technical limitations and constraints of platforms are not inhibitors to creativity, but rather shape and often generate the creative labour that is produced by them" (ibid).

One critique of platform studies is that the nascent field may overly focus on the technical and computational aspects of what platforms afford and constrain. Though the initial volumes in the "Platform Studies" series focus on individual gaming consoles, Bogost and Monfort note that the field is not simply about technical studies. Rather, "Platform studies is about the connection between technical specifics and culture" (2009, 4). While an emphasis on the technical aspects of literacy production can help shape how platforms imbue meaning in the communicative practices in today's society, a broader connection of platforms to their sociocultural roots is useful. Pointing back to the tenets of literacies as connected, the sociotechnical histories of non-digital tools like chairs (Cranz, 1998) and stirrups (White, 1962) illustrate how tools and the societies in which they are developed ascribe meaning to what literacies are enacted and for whom. Connecting this to the continuing discussion of platform studies, Apperley and Jayemane explain, "The materiality of platforms can be turned inwards to examine the individual components of a platform, and just as easily outwards to focus on the organizational structure that allows the platform to be produced" (2012, 12). This explanation also aligns with Flanagan's description of game-based tools as "social technologies" (2009, 9), broadening the scope of what *counts* as a platform and what kinds of literacies may be enacted on them. Further, by expanding the meaning of platforms to non-digital contexts such as card games (Svelch, 2016) and roleplaying games (Garcia, 2017c), the role of platforms in literacy studies helps illustrate how individuals mediate meaning across different kinds of contexts.

Synthesis: a layered approach

The three aforementioned principles help recast the landscape of digital literacies as one that is found *between* individuals, *within* bodies, and *across* specific platforms. At the same time, it is important to underscore that these guidelines are not definitive. As the tendrils of digital technologies trickle further into the practices of everyday life in ever more seamless ways, the scope and contexts will change as well. That being said, it is also necessary to recognize that the aforementioned three tenets are not discrete, separate principles. Rather, in following with recent literacies scholarship, the tenets that literacies are connected, embodied, and platform-specific illustrate a broader, *layered* (Abrams & Russo, 2015, Garcia, 2017a) understanding of the field.

Recognizing that literacies function across these systems seamlessly points to the various actors interchanging meaning and understanding in today's society. An individual participating in a fandom community comprehends and gestures toward meaning; her literacy practices are *embodied*. At the same time these literacies are conveyed and understood within the specific cultural vernacular of peers interested in the same topic; these are literacies that are *connected*. Further, these communicative practices are disseminated through the designed constraints of specific technological and cultural platforms; these literacies are *platform-dependent*. In considering this network of literacy practices, researchers should consider at what level their work examines. By focusing on individuals, for example, what literacy practices are overly emphasized? Left out? Further, across *all* of the layers of digital literacies, the role of culture and of power cannot be underplayed. How individuals and groups understand meaning is dependent on the cultural values at work. Likewise, recognizing that platforms are developed by individuals can point to how implicit bias can lead to a Google-owned algorithm identifying black people as 'gorillas' (Barr, 2015; Jackyalcine, 2015).

Recognizing that digital literacies are instantiated long before and after a digital medium conveys them repositions the role of technology in literacy studies and should broaden how digital communication is understood in the lives of individuals. At the same time, this layered approach highlights that literacies are interwoven into the individuals, groups, and tools that enact and rely upon them. This mutual existence of a literacy and its practice highlights an ongoing updating as technology progresses ever forward.

More than enclosure

Some contemporary studies related to digital literacies tend to emphasize the possibilities of specific tools – a social platform, a media production program, a curriculum. However, while these kinds of studies can highlight singular examples of innovative uses or contexts of learning tied to digital tools, they also point to the fencing of new, digital media into cordoned spaces of continued use. *Enclosure*, when tied to digital literacies leads to emphasizing the value of singular tools as examples of expansive technology. This closing off of practices implicitly shifts a perspective of literacies as individually tool-based rather than as part of a set of shifting contexts that emerge in the layered ecosystem described earlier. Further, in considering how literacies can be platform-dependent, one can read this as a condemnation of the processes of enclosure that have been discussed across this volume. However, as part of a broader, layered approach to understanding digital literacies, platform-based literacy practices emphasize how individuals mediate, design, and communicate across settings rather than how tools construct discrete ecosystems.

In previous work (Garcia, 2017b; Philip & Garcia, 2014), I have emphasized that in studying learning and technology educators must focus on the 'context' rather than on specific 'tools.' The pedagogies of reading beyond singular tools is one way of seeing possibilities where capitalist constraints often feel omnipresent.

In considering the intersection of digital literacies with research on critical cyberculture (Silver & Massanari, 2006), enclosure is not tied simply to capitalist constraining of Internet and digital environments. Rather issues of racism, inequality, and systemic power (e.g., Daniels, 2013; Noble, 2018) are topics are part of the sociocultural fabric at the heart of *reading* digital literacies today.

Finally, it is important to consider enclosure from the stance of the original New London Group's (1996) framework: as an extension of the intertwining of globalization and technological innovation. In terms of studying shifts in digital literacies over time, enclosure can be read as part of a broader understanding of critical media literacy in an era of participatory culture (Garcia et al., 2013). Likewise, enclosure reinforces a broader legacy of digital technology reinforcing power structures of inequality in offline settings (e.g., Cuban, 1986; Silver & Massanari, 2006). Creating awareness around digital enclosure can be one way of becoming 'net smart' (Rheingold, 2012). However, simply developing resiliency related to enclosure is not enough. By focusing on reading, teaching, and working *across* contexts, educators and researchers can traverse digital enclosure.

Conclusion

Looking closely at the state of digital literacy illustrates a historical trend that has moved toward broadening the field in several distinct ways. As noted earlier in the chapter, literacies have multiplied. What *counts* as literacies and for what purpose remains a continually expansive conversation. Likewise, the 'digital' in digital literacy continues to be redefined every few years. As digital practices blend seamlessly with the ways we work, learn, interact, *live*, the labeling of these specific literacies becomes a challenging moniker. When nearly all aspects of our lives can be mediated by digital tools – from cooking to hailing local transportation to engaging in forms of activism – the literacies of contemporary society are continually challenging what we mean when we discuss digital and literacies. Throughout this chapter, rather than hone in on the individual and *enclosed* tools that often drive analyses of literacies practices today, I've highlighted the layered principles that literacies *connect* "communities of practice" (Lave & Wenger, 1991), are *embodied* by individuals, and are often dependent on the affordances of specific *platforms*.

As Robyn Seglem and I described in a recent look back on the contributions of the New London Group more than 20 years ago (2018), what digital technologies meant then, have shifted substantially; the New London Group's 1996 document was written long before the existence of online social networks like YouTube, Facebook, MySpace, Friendster, Instagram, Snapchat, TikTok, and Twitter. Technical advances from smart phones to Internet-enabled thermostats, doorbells, and fitness trackers had not yet redefined our relationships to stuff at the time that multiliteracies outlined new modes of communication and understanding. Though advances in technology were still seen as central to the hopes of educational reform in the United States (Cuban, 1986), entire ways of interacting and communicating with one another and mediating the comfort of middle class lives did not exist.

Strikingly, though written before many of the resources and contexts through which individuals learn and interact today, the New London Group's broad analysis of digital literacy remains a lasting anchor point for digital literacies today. However, as described throughout this chapter, researchers and educators are now in a place of taking the analysis of power and technology at the heart of the 'social futures' that the New London Group wrote about and applying it to an era that includes the Internet of Things, neoliberal engagement of cryptocurrencies (Golumbia, 2016), and an ever broadening set of practices that oppress online identities just as much as technological research speaks to their advances (e.g., Hurley, 2016; Quinn, 2017).

The historic changes to the field of digital literacies illustrate how cultural and technological shifts redefine both what and where literacies transpire. How individuals interact with and through technology in the coming years will point to new methodological challenges for digital literacies researchers. Two generations ago, ours was largely a wireless society. As more of our technologies rely on wireless Internet, long-lasting battery charges, and interfaces that may not require traditional screens, we are entering yet another phase of 'wireless' life. The literacies of digital technology that appear all but invisible – perhaps 'magical' from today's vantage (Clarke, 1962) – point to the ongoing expansion of the field of digital literacy.

References

Abrams, S. S., and Russo, M. P. (2015). Layering Literacies and Contemporary Learning. *Journal of Adolescent & Adult Literacy*, 59(2), 131–135.

Apperley, T., and Jayemane, D. (2012). Game Studies' Material Turn. *Westminster Papers in Communication and Culture*, 9(1), 5–26.

Avila, J., and Pandya, J. Z. (2012). *Critical Digital Literacies as Social Praxis: Intersections and Challenges*. New York: Peter Lang Publishing.

Azevedo, F. S. (2011). Lines of Practice: A Practice-Centered Theory of Interest Relationships. *Cognition and Instruction*, 29(2), 147–184.

Barr, A. (2015). Google Mistakenly Tags Black People as 'Gorillas,' Showing Limits of Algorithms. *The Wall Street Journal*. http://blogs.wsj.com/digits/2015/07/01/google-mistakenly-tags-black-people-as-gorillas-showing-limits-of-algorithms/.

Bogost, I., and Montfort, N. (2009). *Platform Studies: Frequently Questioned Answers.* Proceedings of the Digital Arts and Culture Conference. Retrieved from http://escholarship.org/uc/item/01r0k9br.pdf

Clarke, A. C. (1962). *Profiles of the Future: An Inquiry into the Limits of the Possible.* London: Victor Gollancz.

Coiro, J. (2012). Understanding Dispositions Toward Reading on the Internet. *Journal of Adolescent & Adult Literacy,* 55(7), 645–648.

Cranz, G. (1998). *The Chair: Rethinking Culture, Body, and Design.* New York: W.W. Norton & Company.

Cuban, L. (1986). *Teachers and Machines: The Classroom Use of Technology Since 1920.* New York: Teachers College Press.

Daniels, J. (2013). Race, Racism & Internet Studies: A Review and Critique. *New Media & Society,* 15(5), 695–719. doi:10.1177/1461444812462849.

Flanagan, M. (2009). *Critical Play: Radical Game Design.* Cambridge, MA: MIT Press.

Freire, P., and Macedo, D. (1987). *Literacy: Reading the Word and the World.* Westport, CT: Bergin & Garvey.

Garcia, A. (ed.). (2014). *Teaching in the Connected Learning Classroom.* Irvine, CA: Digital Media and Learning Research Hub.

Garcia, A. (2017a). Space, Time, and Production: Games and the New Frontier of Digital Literacies. In K. A. Mills, A. Stornaiuolo, A. Smith, and J. Z. Pandya (eds.), *Handbook of Writing, Literacies, and Education in Digital Cultures.* New York: Routledge, pp. 198–209.

Garcia, A. (2017b). *Good Reception: Teens, Teachers, and Mobile Media in a Los Angeles High School.* Cambridge, MA: MIT Press.

Garcia, A. (2017c). Privilege, Power, and Dungeons & Dragons: How Systems Shape Racial and Gender Identities in Tabletop Role-Playing Games. *Mind, Culture, and Activity.* doi:10.1080/10749039.2017. 1293691.

Garcia, A., and Mirra, N. (2019). 'Signifying Nothing': Identifying Conceptions of Youth Civic Identity in the English Language Arts Common Core State Standards and the National Assessment of Educational Progress' Reading Framework. *Berkeley Review of Education,* 8(2), 195–223.

Garcia, A., and Seglem, R. (2018). This Issue. *Theory Into Practice,* 56(1), 1–4.

Garcia, A., Seglem, R., and Share, J. (2013). Transforming Teaching and Learning Through Critical Media Literacy Pedagogy. *Learning Landscapes,* 6(2), 109–123.

Genette, G. (1997). *Paratexts: Thresholds of Interpretation.* Cambridge: Cambridge University Press.

Gee, J. P. (2010). *New Digital Media and Learning as an Emerging Area and "Worked Examples" as One Way Forward.* Cambridge, MA: MIT Press.

Golumbia, D. (2016). *The Politics of Bitcoin: Software as Right-Wing Extremism.* Minneapolis: University of Minnesota Press.

Gutiérrez, K. (2008). Developing Sociocritical Literacy in the Third Space. *Reading Research Quarterly,* 43(2), 148–164.

Habermas, J. (1991). *The Structural Transformation of the Public Sphere: An Inquiry into a Category of Bourgeois Society.* Cambridge, MA: MIT Press.

Hellekson, K., and Busse, K. (2014). *The Fan Fiction Studies Reader.* Iowa City: University of Iowa Press.

Hobbs, R. (2011). *Digital and Media Literacy: Connecting Culture and Classroom.* Thousand Oaks, CA: Corwin.

Hurley, K. (2016). *The Geek Feminist Revolution.* New York: Tor Books.

Ito et al., (2009). *Hanging Out, Messing Around, and Geeking Out: Kids Living and Learning with New Media.* Cambridge, MA: MIT Press.

Ito, M. et al. (2013). *Connected Learning: An Agenda for Research and Design.* Irvine, CA: Digital Media and Learning Research Hub.

Jackyalcine. (2015). *Google Photos, y'all Fucked Up: My Friend's Not a Gorilla* [Tweet]. https://mobile. twitter.com/jackyalcine/status/615329515909156865.

Jenkins, H., Clinton, K., Purushotma, R., Robison, A. J., and Weigel, M. (2009). *Confronting the Challenges of Participatory Culture: Media Education for the 21st Century.* Chicago: MacArthur Foundation.

Kintgen, E. R., Kroll, B. M., and Rose, M. (eds.) (1988). *Perspectives on Literacy.* Carbondale, IL: Southern Illinois University Press.

Knobel, M., and Lankshear, C. (2007). *A New Literacies Sampler.* New York: Peter Lang.

Kress, G. (2003). *Literacy in the New Media Age.* London: Routledge.

Kress, G. (2009). *Multimodality: A Social Semiotic Approach to Contemporary Communication*. New York: Routledge.

Lam, W. S. E., and Warriner, D. S. (2012). Transnationalism and Literacy: Investigating the Mobility of People, Languages, Texts, and Practices in Contexts of Migration. *Reading Research Quarterly*, 47(2), 191–215.

Lankshear, C., and Knobel, M. (2008). *Digital Literacies: Concepts, Policies and Practices*. New York: Peter Lang.

Lave, J., and Wenger, E. (1991). *Situated Learning: Legitimate Peripheral Participation*. Cambridge: Cambridge University Press.

Leander, K., and Boldt, G. (2012). Rereading 'a Pedagogy of Multiliteracies' Bodies, Texts, and Emergence. *Journal of Literacy Research*, 45, 22–46.

Lee, C. H., and Soep, E. (2016). None but Ourselves Can Free Our Minds: Critical Computational Literacy as a Pedagogy of Resistance. *Equity & Excellence in Education*, 49(4), 480–492.

Leorke, D. (2012). Rebranding the Platform: The Limitations of 'Platform Studies'. *Digital Culture & Education*, 4(3), 257–268.

Lynch, T. L. (2015). Software's Smile: A Critical Software Analysis of an Educational Technology Specialist Program. *Contemporary Issues in Technology and Teacher Education*, 15(4), 600–616.

McLuhan, M. (1962). *The Gutenberg Galaxy: The Making of Typographic Man*. Toronto: University of Toronto Press.

Mills, K. A. (2016). *Literacy Theories for the Digital Age: Social, Critical, Multimodal, Spatial, Material and Sensory Lenses*. Bristol: Multilingual Matters.

Mirra, N. (2014). Interest-Driven Learning. In A. Garcia (ed.), *Teaching in the Connected Learning Classroom*. Irvine, CA: Digital Media and Learning Research Hub, pp. 10–23.

Mirra, N., and Garcia, A. (2017). Re-Imagining Civic Participation: Youth Interrogating and Innovating in the Multimodal Public Sphere. *Review of Research in Education*, 31.

Morrell, E. (2008). *Critical Literacy and Urban Youth: Pedagogies of Access, Dissent, and Liberation*. New York: Routledge.

New London Group. (1996). A Pedagogy of Multiliteracies: Designing Social Futures. *Harvard Educational Review*, 66, 60–92.

Noble, S. U. (2018). *Algorithms of Oppression: How Search Engines Reinforce Racism*. New York: New York University Press.

Penuel, W. R., and O'Connor, K. (2018). From Designing to Organizing New Social Futures: Multiliteracies Pedagogies for Today. *Theory Into Practice*, 57(1), 64–71.

Pfister, R. C. (2014). *Hats for House Elves: Connected Learning and Civic Engagement in Hogwarts at Ravelry*. Irvine, CA: Digital Media and Learning Research Hub.

Philip, T. M., and Garcia, A. (2014). Schooling Mobile Phones: Assumptions About Proximal Benefits, the Challenges of Shifting Meanings, and the Politics of Teaching. *Educational Policy*. doi:10.1177/0895904813518105.

Quinn, Z. (2017). *Crash Override: How Gamergate (Nearly) Destroyed My Life and How We Can Win the Fight Against Online Hate*. New York: Public Affairs.

Rafalow, M. H., and Tekinbas, K. S. (2014). *Welcome to Sackboy Planet: Connected Learning Among LittleBigPlanet 2 Players*. Irvine, CA: Digital Media and Learning Research Hub.

Rheingold, H. (2012). *Net Smart: How to Thrive Online*. Cambridge, MA: MIT Press.

Silver, D., and Massanari, A. (2006). *Critical Cyberculture Studies*. New York: New York University Press.

Sacks, H., Schegloff, E. A., and Jefferson, G. (1974). A Simplest Systematics for the Organization of Turn-Taking for Conversation. *Language*, 50, 696–735.

Sfard, A., and Prusak, A. (2005). Telling Identities: In Search of an Analytic Tool for Investigating Learning as a Culturally Shaped Activity. *Educational Researcher*, 34(4), 14–22.

Share, J. (2015). *Media Literacy Is Elementary: Teaching Youth to Critically Read and Create Media* (2nd ed.). New York, NY: Peter Lang.

Street, B. (1994). What's 'New' in New Literacy Studies? Critical Approaches to Literacy in Theory and Practice. *Current Issues in Comparative Education*, 5(2), 77–91.

Svelch, S. (2016). Platform studies, computational essentialism, and Magic: The Gathering. *Analog Game Studies*, 3(4).

White Jr., L. (1962). *Medieval Technology and Social Change*. London: Oxford University Press.

12

Family practices and digital technology

Nancy Jennings

Digital technologies are increasingly becoming a larger part of family life and family practices.[1] Wired singles use dating apps to find their soulmate, and couples announce their intention to marry on social media and YouTube wedding proposals. Even before birth, parents establish their child's digital footprint by sharing sonogram pictures through social media. New terms have been developed to label different behaviors and family practices related to digital technologies such as 'Pphubbing' and 'sharenting.' As such, it is increasingly important to know about the role of digital technologies in the lives of families. How successful are marriages that began with online dating? Does mobile technology enhance or distract from family communication practices? How do teens cope with the digital footprint established by their parents? These are just a few of the many questions about the implications of digital technology on the family that will be explored in this chapter.

Different theoretical approaches have been used to understand practices of media and technology in families. Watt and White (1999) utilize family development theory to focus on the role of technology on different family stages and the sequencing and timing of transitions between stages. In their discussion of seven stages of family development (mate selection, early marriages, preschool children, elementary school children, adolescents, post-parenting, and retirement families), they suggest that technological innovations influence the ways in which family members communicate, work, and recreate. Jordan (2003) suggests that a family structure framework provides a mechanism by which to assess how media use (and in this case uses of technology) "'fit' with the norms, values, and beliefs that define the family system" (p. 143). As such, scholars have used this paradigm to distinguish the impact of digital technologies on structural components of the family system such as family boundaries and family cohesion. More recently, Jennings and Wartella (2013) employed the life course paradigm as a complement to the family structures framework and family development theory to capture the pathways of human development in and across historical time of the structures and stages of family life. This chapter will integrate these approaches to examine the practices of technology within and across these different stages and structures as a means to understand the role technology plays in family interactions and personal identity within the family over the past two decades.

Partnering practices

As suggested by Watt and White (1999), the first stage of family development involves mate selection. Contemporary technology has made a substantial contribution to this partnering practice through online dating websites and apps. In the United States, online dating has grown into a $2.2 billion industry and has become "the bedrock of the American love life" (Harwell, 2015, n.d.). A total of 15% of Americans have used online dating site or apps, 41% know someone who uses online dating, and 29% know someone who has met a spouse or long-term partner through online dating (Pew Research Center, 2016). The largest growth in users of online dating has been among 18- to 24-year-olds and 55- to 64-year-olds, rising from 10% and 6%, respectively, in 2013 to 27% and 12% in 2015 (Pew Research Center, 2016). However, online dating is not just an American phenomenon. Valkenburg and Peter (2007) examined online dating among Dutch adults and discovered that 43% of 367 Dutch respondents had visited a dating site, 33.2% had posted an online profile on a dating site, and that online dating was not related to education or income levels. Moreover, people low in dating anxiety were more likely to participate in online dating than those high in dating anxiety, suggesting that those low in dating anxiety see the Internet as just another way to find a potential partner (Valkenburg & Peter, 2007). Similarly, an online dater in Australia expressed a desire for an intimate relationship and explained, "I just wanted to find someone who wanted to live the rest of their life with me! That sounds old-fashioned. I don't really care what anyone else thinks. I just wanted to meet someone" (Henry-Waring & Barraket, 2008, 17). In an ever-increasingly busy and complicated world, individuals want a more straightforward way to find a mate, and these apps and online dating provide the means to do so. As a reflection of the acceptance of this means to find a mate, stigma associated with using these online resources has reduced with more people reporting that online dating is a good way to meet people and fewer people reporting that people who use online dating sites are desperate (Smith & Anderson, 2016). While only 5% of Americans who are married or in a long-term relationship met their partner online, this is likely to change given the increased use and acceptance of online dating apps, particularly among young adults (Smith & Duggan, 2013).

Shifts in the nature of online sites and apps may have implications for the future of online dating. First, one of the early online sites, known as *eHarmony.com*, employs a very systematic and calculated form of matching of couples based on an extensive questionnaire. When *eHarmony* first launched in 2000, the questionnaire consisted of 450 questions but has now been reduced to 150 questions (Marinova, 2014). More recently, "swipe friendly" apps based on location to identify local singles available for dating have emerged, suggesting a shift to "more visual, faster, 'gamification' of dating, versus the profile matching of eHarmony," according to industry analyst Kerry Rice (Harwell, 2015). Second, the online dating industry has been segmented into different target markets or "specialized communities" (peoplemedia.com). There has been a rise in niche online dating sites that claim to connect singles of specific backgrounds, unique interests, and stages of life: for example, sites that specialize in connecting African-American singles (BlackPeopleMeet.com), Jewish singles (JDate), plus-size singles (BBPeopleMeet.com), single parents (SingleParentMeet.com), singles over the age of 50 years (OurTime.com), conservative singles (RepublicanPeopleMeet.com), and even pet lovers (PetPeopleMeet.com) (People Media, 2017; Davidson, 2014). Among these specialized sites, poachers have been using these sites to find a partner of a particular group even though they personally do not belong to that group – thin singles seeking plus-sized partners or younger people looking for older partners. JDate has capitalized on this trend by offering options of "willing to convert" to appeal to those not already Jewish (Davidson, 2014). Finally, not all partnering sites are for heterosexual couples. The Grindr app claims to bring together "gay, bi, curious, and queer men" (Grindr, 2017), and PinkCupid.com helps "thousands of lesbian singles find their match" (PinkCupid, n.d.). As such, digital technology has become a growing part of contemporary partnering practices employing focused searches to find love and connect with others.

Once couples find a partner, use of digital technology continues in the form of relational maintenance. Hall and Baym (2012) offer a model of mobile maintenance expectations which are grounded in friendship expectations of inclusion and in mundane maintenance via media. These may also be applied to romantic relationships as suggested by Tong and Walther (2011) in three ways: (1) presence, (2) sign ties, and (3) mundane conversation. Communication technologies allow for a sense of emotional connection to the other partner, even when they are not physically present. Moreover, many social networking sites allow individuals to express their relationship status, thus serving as a sign tie to their partner. Tong and Walther (2011) suggest that texting and social networking sites such as Twitter are particularly well suited for everyday exchange of routine activities and mundane observations that are an essential element of relationship maintenance, thus allowing for mundane conversation to occur.

Indeed, digital communication technologies have been reported as having an impact on relationships of individuals in married or long-term relationships. According to the Pew Research Center, of the individuals in married or long-term relationships that indicated the Internet had an impact on their relationship, the vast majority (74%) indicated that the effect was positive, particularly younger adults (Lenhart & Duggan, 2014). Moreover, as expected, online daters were the most likely to report that the Internet had an impact on their relationship, with 38% indicating a major impact and 26% indicating a minor impact. Primarily, Internet users in a committed relationship indicate that technology has been used as a source of support and communication with their partner. Nearly a quarter (21%) of committed Internet users reported that they have felt closer to their partner because of exchanges they have had online or via text, and 9% reported that they have been able to resolve a conflict online or via text that they were not able to accomplish in face-to-face communication (Lenhart & Duggan, 2014). The numbers rise dramatically for young adults aged 18–29, with 41% reporting feeling closer to their partner and 21% being able to resolve a conflict (Lenhart & Duggan, 2014). In fact, Internet users in a committed relationship even share digital communication tools and logistics such as a shared email account (27%), an online calendar (11%), and even social media profiles (11%) (Lenhart & Duggan, 2014). As such, it would appear that the Internet and social media in particular are useful to partnered couples, particularly young adults, to maintain presence, inclusion, and mundane conversation feeling supported and loved.

However, not all uses of communication technology benefit couples. Indeed, 20% of Internet users in committed relationships indicated that the Internet resulted in negative effects on their relationship (Lenhart & Duggan, 2014). Technology has also been seen as a source of tension for partners. Interestingly, most of the tension seems to be the result of using digital devices while in the presence of one another. A quarter (25%) of Internet users in a committed relationship indicated that they were upset with their partner when they seemed distracted by a digital device in the presence of one another (Lenhart & Duggan, 2014). This behavior has become so common that it has been labeled as "phubbing" – "to be snubbed by someone using their cell phone when in your company" (Roberts & David, 2015, 134). When phubbing is committed in the presence of a romantic partner, this behavior is referred to as "partner phubbing (Pphubbing)" (Roberts & David, 2015, 134). This behavior can be detrimental to partnership satisfaction as a result of conflict incurred through interruptions and distractions caused by Pphubbing, and this is heightened for individuals with highly anxious attachment styles (Roberts & David, 2015). Moreover, Halpern and Katz (2017) confirm the rise in conflict in couples that engage in pphubing, but also note a sense of diminished intimacy as a result of displaced focus on the romantic partner, concluding that technology which is intended to bring people together may interfere with relationship maintenance if used in the presence of each other. The everyday practice of constant connection with the phone can lead to detrimental implications for relationships.

As such, rules and expectations about technology use may be necessary to be negotiated among partners. Miller-Ott and colleagues (2012) discovered that rules about cell phone use can be related to relational satisfaction among romantic couples. As such, partners were happier and more satisfied with their relationship when they had rules about limiting relational talk via cell phone (Relational Issues), did not restrict how frequently they could text each other (Repetitive Contact), and did not have rules prohibiting each other from checking and reading each other's text messages (Monitoring Partner Usage). Moreover, when expectations of digital behaviors are violated, tensions may occur. Overall, digital behaviors with intimate partners fall into two sets of expectations: (1) Expected Undivided Attention and (2) Expected and Acceptable Divided Attention (Miller-Ott & Kelly, 2015). Certain contexts such as formal dates and intimate moments in private are considered times for expected undivided attention to the partner. When partners violated this with Pphubbing, the partner was considered rude or annoying. However, in informal situations such as "hanging out" with partners, using a cell phone was expected and acceptable divided attention from the partner, unless the use was considered excessive.

Parenting practices

Once a child enters the family system, a new stage of family development begins, parenting. As children can become part of a family at different times, it is valuable to consider parenting practices of children of different ages from infancy to adolescents. Even before children are born, expectant parents are using digital technologies to announce the baby's impending arrival, track the baby's development in utero, seeking pregnancy advice and solutions to discomforts, pains, and joys, and sharing photos of sonograms, tummies, and even birthing experiences. Uses of technology change as children develop, and as a result, parenting practices change as well (Jennings & Wartella, 2013). Lupton and colleagues (2016) reviewed research and parenting practices involving digital technologies beginning with parenting websites in the 1990s through contemporary use of social media and apps. These practices include information seeking, support seeking, sharing experiences, lifelogging or baby-logging, and life caching to track and digitally record aspects of a baby's life. One of the most substantial areas of research with parents and children is about parental monitoring and mediation of their children's media use. While technology can provide a whole new means of monitoring children's behaviors, it also raises questions of surveillance. Moreover, the practice of phubbing that occurs between partners can also carry over into parenting practices, resulting in a level of disengagement between parent and child. The next section focuses on two of the more pervasive and challenging technological parenting practices, lifelogging and sharing experiences.

Lifelogging, baby-logging, and life caching

Modern digital technologies allow for rapid and expanded recording and saving of pictures, messages, text, and more to document and track our lives. While keeping a diary and taking photographs of family events is not a new practice, digitization has made it easier by removing barriers to archive life moments such as incompatible formats of items (e.g., 35 mm slides, 8 mm film, VHS, printed photos, written pages), fragility of documents and film that deteriorates and may become lost over time, and limited storage of physical documents and materials. The two practices of digital lifelogging and life caching have become an active part of family life, although life caching may be more common. Doherty and his colleagues (2011) describe lifelogging as "the process of automatically recording aspects of one's life in digital form" (p. 1948). Hundreds of apps, various wearable cameras, and biosensor tools have become a resource to assist with the lifelogging process. Life caching refers to not only capturing life's moments but sharing these moments with others (Beagrie, 2008). The explosion of social media provides ample ways in which to share life's moments with others.

Family life provides ample opportunity for lifelogging and life caching. As noted by Lupton and her colleagues (2016), there are a multitude of apps for tracking various parenting life moments, including ovulation and fertility tracking apps, pregnancy tracking apps to track fetal growth, heart rate, and movements, and a variety of ways to track and monitor infant feeding, sleeping, growth, and development. Biosensors that can be attached to smartphones to allow for fetal monitoring for expectant mothers, wearable devices, or sensor-embedded clothing can measure infant biometrics such as their movements and heart rate while sleeping, and livestream images of infants and toddlers can be watched from smartphones. Johnson (2014) cautions that the "device-ification" of mothering can "turn it into an administrative and calculable activity, valuing data over subjective experiences and changing the meaning of what it is to mother and be a mother" (p. 346). However, this "device-ification" of mothering supports the dominant and "proper" ideology of motherhood in North America known as "intensive mothering" – an ideology that suggests mothering is "child-centered, expert-guided, emotionally absorbing, labor-intensive, and financially expensive" (Hays, 1996, 8). As such, these apps provide mothers with resources at their fingertips to practice child-centered logging and tracking of life moments such as tracking naps, feedings, diaper changes, and more from pre-conception and beyond. Moreover, these apps allow mothers to receive expert advice from apps that push information about child development in daily or weekly texts or emailed newsletters or serve as a database for health, safety, and parenting tips that can be searched at a moment's notice. These resources may put some mothers at ease knowing they are being a "good mother" by tracking their child's development and being able to provide fine details to pediatricians at wellness and sick visits. However, it may raise the anxiety and concerns of other women who cannot keep up with the tracking systems and expectations set by these systems or whose children do not meet the milestones prescribed by these apps.

To date, there has been very limited research on lifelogging and life caching by parents. The limited research on the use of apps for lifelogging focuses on women who track their pregnancy and suggests that pregnant women use apps to seek additional information about their pregnancy between prenatal visits, track baby development progress and pregnancy-related health issues such as their weight gain during pregnancy, and prefer apps and Internet resources to traditional pamphlets, books, and other reading materials for ease and accessibility for finding information (Kraschnewski et al., 2014; Rodger et al., 2013). Moreover, some expressed relief at having information pushed to them such as a Facebook plug-in that posts automatically on the mother's wall to show progression of their baby's development while others expressed concern about oversharing of information (Kraschnewski et al., 2014). Indeed, social media provides a means not only to collect and track information but to share it with others. Research suggests that parents are actively life caching (or "sharenting") as their family grows, using Facebook (and to a lesser extent Instagram), to make baby announcements, provide details about the mother's pregnancy, and post updates and pictures of their children (Lupton et al., 2016). According to a British study, parents of children from birth to 13 years share on average 1,498 photos by a child's fifth birthday, with the top three social media sites including Facebook (54%), Instagram (16%), and Twitter (12%) (Nominet, 2016).

However, sharenting raises questions about identity and privacy of both the parent and the child. New parents seem to post pictures and information about their new child on social media such as Facebook as both a means of "social nesting" to bring family and friends closer to them and as a way to build and maintain social capital with weak-tie connections (Bartholomew et al., 2012). Moreover, higher amounts of Facebook use among new mothers were associated with higher levels of maternal identity confirmation and societal-oriented parenting perfectionism among new mothers (Schoppe-Sullivan et al., 2017). While social media may reinforce and represent their new parental identity, it is also creating an identity for the child. This becomes particularly problematic as children become teens and want to create and shape their own unique identity. Blum-Ross and Livingstone (2017) submit that parents face a digital dilemma in regard to sharing parenting moments because they must negotiate

> the twin truths that to represent one's own identity as a parent means making public aspects of a (potentially vulnerable) child's life and yet because they are the parent, they are precisely the person primarily responsible for protecting that child's privacy.
>
> *(p. 112)*

The very pictures and posts that represent the parent's identity reveal and shape the child's identity. This raises the question of the construction of the self, the other, and the blending of the two. As Blum-Ross and Livingstone (2017) submit, " 'user generated content' . . . is taken to refer to a singular individual. But when we represent ourselves through our relationships, this is not straightforward" (p. 121). In this case, the identity constructed by parents of children at early stages of family development (preschool and elementary school children) has an impact on the child's identity construction as an adolescent via the changes experienced over the life course. While there is no clear resolution, teens and parents need to negotiate best practices to navigate identity and family dynamics with regard to the sharing of family information.

Mediating, monitoring, and modeling

Parenting practices and rules about media use are rooted in coping strategies for television use in the household. Amy Nathanson (1999) conceptualized television mediation as a three-dimensional construct: (1) active mediation (talking about television content with children), (2) restrictive mediation (setting rules about children's television viewing), and (3) co-viewing (watching television together with children). More recently, other parenting practices have been added to the mix of these mediation techniques with digital technologies. Sarah Vaala and Amy Bleakley (2015) examine parental monitoring and parental modeling of digital media use, specifically computer and Internet use. Parents who "are aware of their adolescents' whereabouts, peers, and activities" (Vaala & Bleakley, 2015, 41) engage in parental monitoring. With parental modeling, parents function as a social referent for their children and, as such, model, teach, and normalize behaviors through their own actions.

Parents engage in a variety of ways to monitor the online lives of their teens, including checking the websites their teen visits, checking their teen's social media profiles and following/friending them on those social media sites where the teen has a profile, and looking through their teen's texts and messages (Andersen, 2016). Although few online parents report using digital monitoring tools to track their teens (Andersen, 2016), apps and software have been developed to track teens' location via GPS, monitor and send notifications for their social media activities, review incoming and outgoing texts from their phone, and even send an alert when they are driving too fast (Singer, n.d.). This form of monitoring may be an extension of the intensive mothering mentioned earlier, applied only to older children – rather than tracking baby's dirty diapers, mothers can now track their teen's driving speed. What was a "normalized" practice as an infant has now become a form of surveillance for older children.

Interestingly, while devices like smartphones can be a source of surveillance or monitoring, they can also be a means to feel safe and secure – just a text away – from parents. Ribak (2009) suggests that cell phones operate as a transitional object, allowing for intergenerational distance while maintaining intimacy when needed. Parents can feel reassured of the safety and well-being of their teen when they hear their voice, while teens express appreciation of the independence that this "lifeline" can provide (Devitt & Roker, 2009). Cell phone ownership can be a marker of breaking away from home for teens while providing a sense that their parents are "absent-though-ever-present" (Ribak, 2009, 191).

While smartphones may provide a lifeline for teens, they may be a distractor for parents of younger children. Behaviors of phubbing that were associated with partnering practices also reappear in child–parent interactions. Jenny Radesky and colleagues (2014) observed caregivers eating with one or more children in fast-food restaurants to study their uses of electronic devices during their meal. Nearly three-fourths of the 55 caregivers observed (73%) used their cellphone during the meal, with a primary behavior of cellphone absorption, "defined as the extent to which the primary focus of the caregiver's attention and engagement was with the device rather than the child" (Radesky et al., 2014, e845). While 15 observed caregivers did not bring a device out during the meal, slightly more caregivers (16) used a device almost constantly throughout the meal, with the remaining caregivers ranging from having a device on the table but not using it to brief uses such as responding to a text or taking a phone call (Radesky et al., 2014). Child phone snubbing, "cphubbing," can be harmful and dangerous, particularly in the presence of young children, yet it reflects the routinization of smartphone use. Not only can it be physically harmful, but parents that cphub their children are also modeling smartphone use and practices that their children may learn and practice themselves. This becomes a vicious circle of placing value on the interaction with the device over interpersonal interaction with those in your physical space. With the rapid spread and increased use of digital devices, parental media monitoring, medication, and modeling should continue to be explored as a part of parenting media practices.

Playmate practices

With the arrival of a second child in a family structure, a sibling subsystem is developed and provides a space where children can learn about peer relations through negotiation, cooperation, and competition (Minuchin, 1974). As such, sibling relationships can be "the most intimate, enduring, troubling, and conflictual relationships" experienced (Hindle & Sherwin-White, 2014, 4). However, very little attention has been given to these relationships and interactions as they relate to digital media, and what research has been conducted focuses primarily on play, particularly video game play.

Siblings can be playmates with each other and, with digital technology, play can occur through video games. Early qualitative research revealed that video game playing provided an even playing field for children of different ages and sizes, making it a place where younger and older siblings can play together (Mitchell, 1985). However, as children's skill levels increased at differing paces, cooperative play began to be replaced with sibling rivalry (Mitchell, 1985).

More recently, Coyne and her colleagues (2016) found that in households with siblings video game play was more likely to be a same-sex activity, with boys playing more video games with brothers and girls playing more video games with girls. Time spent playing video games alone for adolescents was associated with not only lower levels of sibling affection but also lower levels of sibling conflict. Finally, playing video games together was related to increased sibling affection for both boys and girls (Coyne et al., 2016). A recent phenomenon of a sandbox video game known as *Minecraft* has created a space for sibling play where once again the playing field is leveled, and they can co-create together (Livingstone et al., 2014).

Digital platforms and smartphones also provide a space for siblings to monitor and track one another, similar to parental monitoring, which also may be a reflection of modeling the parents' behaviors. Livingstone and her colleagues (2014) found that for younger children under the age of eight years, older siblings provided oversight for monitoring their younger sibling's access to websites, and older siblings both explained and played with younger siblings on mobile devices. Recently, news reports suggest that older siblings engage in digital monitoring or surveillance of their younger siblings, acting as helicopter siblings (Wells, 2015). Siblings may follow each other on social media and learn about their friends, activities, and whereabouts through these connections. Moreover, older siblings may report information collected through digital monitoring back to their parents, resulting in "digital tattling" (Wells, 2015). Just as with digital parenting, siblings negotiate various roles and interactions with digital technologies, from playmate to protector.

Practices across generations

Although slower to adopt to new technologies than younger adults, increasingly, seniors have been using more technology in their lives. A recent study of American adults ages 65 and older shows a dramatic increase in Internet use from 12% in 2000 to 67% in 2016, a 55 percentage increase in just under two decades (Anderson & Perrin, 2017). How they use technology is important to consider, particularly in the family context. According to the AARP research in the United States, 94% of Americans aged 50 and older say that technology helps them keep in touch with friends and family (Kakulla, 2019). These are important trends to consider for intergenerational communication and family practices, and recent research has begun to explore these implications.

Several factors contribute to the use of different modes of communication by grandparents and between grandparents and grandchildren. Among older adults, Carpenter and Buday (2007) found that computer users tended to be younger, more educated, have a higher average income, and had a better self-rated health than non-users. Interestingly, computer users reported fewer depressive symptoms, less loneliness, and had better overall social resources than non-users (Carpenter & Buday, 2007). Hurme et al. (2010) discovered that the physical distance between grandparents and grandchildren has an impact on the ways in which they communicate with one another, such that the farther away the generations live, the fewer face-to-face contacts, landline phone contacts, and mobile phone contacts were made, but more letters and/ or cards were sent between generations. Age of the grandchild also plays an important role in the choice of connectivity between grandparent and grandchild. Quadrello et al. (2005) found that grandparents were more likely to use new technology in their communication with older grandchildren, even though SMS was the preferred form of contact among younger grandchildren. A particularly important outcome of these new ways to communicate across generations is the potential for better relationships between grandparents and grandchildren. According to Bangerter and Waldron (2014), grandparents perceived the use of Skype, Facebook, and text messaging as a means to increase their closeness with their grandchildren by enhancing experiences and conversations. Moreover, grandparents reported more frequent and versatile communication with their grandchildren as a result of technology use and that they felt more involved in their grandchildren's lives (Bangerter & Waldron, 2014).

While most of the research concerning intergenerational technology use has focused on tweens, teens, and emerging adults and their grandparents, other research has focused on young, pre-literate children and their shared technology experiences with their grandparents. Digital tools such as email and SMS are of little use when communicating with young children who cannot read, do not have their own phones, and do not have an email address. Video conferencing technologies, however, provide a more accessible way for both young and old to connect without a heavy reliance on text-based messages. Ames and colleagues (2010) observed differences in family conversations held between young grandchildren (between the ages of one to nine years) and their grandparents by phone call and by video chat. Younger children had difficulty with phone (audio-only) conversations and encountered such problems as using non-verbal cues to communicate, having difficulty holding the phone in the correct position, and parents experiencing more difficulty supporting the conversation because they could not hear each other communicate while the child was on the phone. Although video chats require work and facilitation by parents, the video chat was preferred by parents and grandparents alike to overcome physical distance between families, provide a stronger connection with one another, provide an affordable choice to keep in contact, and have a sense of "being there" to see their grandchildren grow (Ames et al., 2010). As an extension of video chat, grandparents, parents, and grandchildren have also used video conferencing to read children's story books together over a distance (Raffle et al., 2011; Ballagas et al., 2010; Raffle et al., 2010). Video chat, mobile devices, and SMS/texting all serve as ways to enhance intergenerational communication and family practices.

Conclusion

The rapid pace of change in media and digital technologies raises challenges for families and for researchers. Over the years, families and policy makers have transitioned from finding ways to limit media use to learning strategies to cope with and navigate media in our lives as digital technologies become more pervasive and acceptable. Even the American Academy of Pediatrics has come to a new understanding of media as "just another environment" in a "world where 'screen time' is becoming simply 'time'" (Brown et al., 2015, 54). Digital technologies have also become more individualized, shifting from family time in front of the big screen to me time with the device in one's lap. These changes have implications for family life and family practices. Households have become increasingly quieter when the television no longer dominates the media use within the home, booming its sound even as background noise throughout the family living space. Tracking and monitoring each other have become possible in ways never imagined. The Internet allows parents and caregivers to find support and network when it seems like no one nearby shares the same experience.

However, as with most uses of technology, access and use may be indicators of privilege and technology competency, suggesting that information and communication technologies "may be *one* way to help *some*" (Madge & O'Connor, 2006, 215) people in parenting support and practices. There are still issues of digital divides not only in terms of the haves and the have-nots but also in the competency levels of individuals with digital tools. Parents who may not understand the nuances of their smartphone may rely on the digital tattling of older siblings. As such, digital technology may serve the needs of some but not all families.

Continued research needs to be conducted with families and digital technologies. Gaps in the research are still prevalent, particularly with siblings. The emerging practice of " 'transcendent parenting' which goes beyond traditional, physical concepts of parenting, to incorporate virtual and online parenting and how these all intersect" (Lim, 2016, 21) needs to be explored. Further understanding of the implications of phubbing needs to be addressed as this practice extends in different ways within the family in parent–child interactions as well as partner interactions. Moreover, new technologies and new uses of existing technologies will continue to occur and provide new questions to be answered. Working together, families and researchers can explore these questions and discover the opportunities and challenges of digital technologies on family practices.

Note

1 For the purposes of this chapter, family will have a broad definition to incorporate many of the complex as well as traditional constructions of family. As suggested by Andreasen (2001), a family is a system "bound by ties of blood, law, or affection and, like all systems, they require cohesiveness and adaptability for their survival" (p. 10). As such, a wide variety of family structures, contexts, and interactions will be considered.

References

Ames, M. G., Go, J., Kaye, J. J., and Spasojevic, M. (2010). *Making Love in the Network Closet: The Benefits and Work of Family Videochat*. Proceedings of the 2010 ACM Conference on Computer Supported Cooperative Work, ACM, pp. 145–154, February.

Andersen, M. (2016). *Parents, Teens and Digital Monitoring*. www.pewInternat.org/2016/01/07/parents-teens-and-digital-monitoring/.

Anderson, M., and Perrin, A. (2017). *Tech Adoption Climbs Among Older Adults*. www.pewInternat.org/2017/05/17/tech-adoption-climbs-among-older-adults/.

Andreasen, M. (2001). Evolution in the Family's Use of Television: An Overview. In J. Bryant and J. A. Bryant (eds.), *Television and the American Family* (2nd ed.). Mahwah, NJ: Lawrence Erlbaum, pp. 3–30.

Ballagas, R. et al. (2010). Story Time for the 21st Century. *IEEE Pervasive Computing*, 9(3), 28–36.

Bangerter, L. R., and Waldron, V. R. (2014). Turning Points in Long Distance Grandparent – Grandchild Relationships. *Journal of Aging Studies*, 29, 88–97. doi:10.1016/j.jaging.2014.01.004.

Bartholomew, M. K., Schoppe-Sullivan, S. J., Glassman, M., Kamp Dush, C. M., and Sullivan, J. M. (2012). New Parents' Facebook Use at the Transition to Parenthood. *Family Relations*, 61(3), 455–469.

Beagrie, N. (2008). Digital Curation for Science, Digital Libraries, and Individuals. *International Journal of Digital Curation*, 1(1), 3–16.

Blum-Ross, A., and Livingstone, S. (2017). 'Sharenting', Parent Blogging, and the Boundaries of the Digital Self. *Popular Communication*, 15(2), 110–125. doi:10.1080/15405702.2016.1223300.

Brown, A., Shifrin, D. L., and Hill, D. L. (2015). Beyond 'Turn It Off': How to Advise Families on Media Use. *AAP News*, 36(10), 54. www.aappublications.org/content/36/10/54.

Carpenter, B. D., and Buday, S. (2007). Computer Use Among Older Adults in a Naturally Occurring Retirement Community. *Computers in Human Behavior*, 23(6), 3012–3024. doi:10.1016/j.chb.2006.08.015.

Coyne, S. M., Jensen, A. C., Smith, N. J., and Erickson, D. H. (2016). Super Mario Brothers and Sisters: Associations Between Coplaying Video Games and Sibling Conflict and Affection. *Journal of Adolescence*, 47, 48–59. doi:10.1016/j.adolescence.2015.12.001.

Davidson, L. (2014). The Problem of Trespassing on Niche Dating Sites. *The Atlantic*, March 19. www.theatlantic.com/health/archive/2014/03/the-problem-of-trespassing-on-niche-dating-sites/283988/.

Devitt, K., and Roker, D. (2009). The Role of Mobile Phones in Family Communication. *Children & Society*, 23, 189–202. doi:10.1111/j.1099-0860.2008.00166.x.

Doherty, A. R., Caprani, N., Conaire, C. Ó., Kalnikaite, V., Gurrin, C., Smeaton, A. F., and O'Connor, N. E. (2011). Passively Recognising Human Activities Through Lifelogging. *Computers in Human Behavior*, 27(5), 1948–1958. doi:10.1016/j.chb.2011.05.002.

Grindr. (2017). *About*. www.grindr.com/.

Hall, J. A., and Baym, N. K. (2012). Calling and Texting (too much): Mobile Maintenance Expectations (over), Dependence, Entrapment, and Friendship Satisfaction. *New Media & Society*, 14(2), 316–331. doi:10.1177/1461444811415047.

Halpern, D., and Katz, J. E. (2017). Texting's Consequences for Romantic Relationships: A Cross-Lagged Analysis Highlights Its Risks. *Computers in Human Behavior*, 71, 386–394. doi:10.1016/j.chb.2017.01.051.

Harwell, D. (2015). *Online Dating's Age Wars: Inside Tinder and eHarmony's Fight for Our Love Lives*, April 6. www.washingtonpost.com/news/business/wp/2015/04/06/online-datings-age-wars-inside-tinder-and-eharmonys-fight-for-our-love-lives/?utm_term=.5a9e8bd0a562.

Hays, S. (1996). *The Cultural Contradictions of Motherhood*. New Haven: Yale University Press.

Henry-Waring, M., and Barraket, J. (2008). Dating & Intimacy in the 21st Century: The Use of Online Dating Sites in Australia. *International Journal of Emerging Technologies & Society*, 6(1), 14–33. www.swin.edu.au/ijets.

Hindle, D., and Sherwin-White, S. (eds.). (2014). *Sibling Matters: A Psychoanalytic, Developmental, and Systemic Approach*. London: Karnac Books.

Hurme, H., Westerback, S., and Quadrello, T. (2010). Traditional and New Forms of Contact Between Grandparents and Grandchildren. *Journal of Intergenerational Relationships*, 8(3), 264–280. doi:10.1080/15350770.2010.498739.

Jennings, N., and Wartella, E. (2013). Technology and the Family. In A. Vangelisti (Ed.), *The Handbook of Family Communication* (2nd ed.). Mahwah, NJ: Lawrence Erlbaum Associates, pp. 448–462.

Johnson, S. A. (2014). 'Maternal Devices' Social Media and the Self-Management of Pregnancy, Mothering and Child Health. *Societies*, 4(2), 330–350.

Jordan, A. B. (2003). A Family Systems Approach to Examining the Role of the Internet in the Home. In J. Turow and A. L. Kavanaugh (eds.), *The Wired Homestead: An MIT Press Sourcebook on the Internet and the Family*. Cambridge, MA: MIT Press, pp. 141–160.

Kakulla, B. N. (2019). *2019 Tech Trends and the 50+*. Washington, DC: AARP Research. https://doi.org/10.26419/res.00269.001.

Kraschnewski, L. J. et al. (2014). Paging 'Dr. Google': Does Technology Fill the Gap Created by the Prenatal Care Visit Structure? Qualitative Focus Group Study with Pregnant Women. *Journal of Medical Internet Research*, 16, e147. doi:10.2196/jmir.3385.

Lenhart, A., and Duggan, M. (2014). *Couples, the Internet, and Social Media*, February 11. www.pewInternat.org/2014/02/11/couples-the-Internat-and-social-media/.

Lim, S. S. (2016). Through the Tablet Glass: Transcendent Parenting in an Era of Mobile Media and Cloud Computing. *Journal of Children and Media*, 10(1), 21–29. doi:10.1080/17482798.2015.1121896.

Livingstone, S., Marsh, J., Plowman, L., Ottovordemgentschenfelde, S., and Fletcher-Watson, B. (2014). *Young Children (0–8) and Digital Technology: A Qualitative Exploratory Study – National Report – UK*. Luxembourg: Joint Research Centre, European Commission. http://eprints.lse.ac.uk/60799/.

Lupton, D., Pedersen, S., and Thomas, G. M. (2016). Parenting and Digital Media: From the Early Web to Contemporary Digital Society. *Sociology Compass*, 10(8), 730–743. doi:10.1111/soc4.12398.

Madge, C., and O'Connor, H. (2006). Parenting Gone Wired: Empowerment of New Mothers on the Internet? *Social & Cultural Geography*, 7, 199–220. doi:10.1080/14649360600600528.

Marinova, P. (2014). How Dating Site eHarmony Uses Machine Learning to Help You Find Love. *Fortune*, February 14. http://fortune.com/2017/02/14/eharmony-dating-machine-learning/.

Miller-Ott, A., and Kelly, L. (2015). The Presence of Cell Phones in Romantic Partner Face-to-Face Interactions: An Expectancy Violation Theory Approach. *Southern Communication Journal*, 80(4), 253–270. doi:10.1080/1041794X.2015.1055371.

Miller-Ott, A. E., Kelly, L., and Duran, R. L. (2012). The Effects of Cell Phone Usage Rules on Satisfaction in Romantic Relationships. *Communication Quarterly*, 60(1), 17–34. doi:10.1080/01463373.2012.642263.

Minuchin, S. (1974). *Families and Family Therapy*. Cambridge, MA: Harvard University Press.

Mitchell, E. (1985). The Dynamics of Family Interaction Around Home Video Games. In M. B. Sussman (ed.), *Personal Computers and the Family*. New York, NY: Haworth Press, pp. 121–136.

Nathanson, A. I. (1999). Identifying and Explaining the Relationship Between Parental Mediation and Children's Aggression. *Communication Research*, 26, 124–143. doi:10.1177/009365099026002002.

Nominet. (2016). *Parents 'Oversharing' Family Photos Online, but Lack Basic Privacy Know-How*. www.nominet.uk/parents-oversharing-family-photos-online-lack-basic-privacy-know/.

People Media. (2017). *Home*. www.peoplemedia.com/.

Pew Research Center. (2016). *15% of American Adults Have Used Online Dating Sites or Mobile Dating Apps*, February. www.pewInternat.org/2016/02/11/15-percent-of-american-adults-have-used-online-dating-sites-or-mobile-dating-apps/.

PinkCupid. (n.d.). *Meet Your Lesbian Match*. www.pinkcupid.com/.

Quadrello, T., Hurme, H., Menzinger, J., Smith, P. K., Veisson, M., Vidal, S., and Westerback, S. (2005). Grandparents' Use of New Communication Technology in a European Perspective. *European Journal of Ageing*, 2, 200–2007.

Radesky, J. S. et al. (2014). Patterns of Mobile Device Use by Caregivers and Children During Meals in Fast Food Restaurants. *Pediatrics*, 133, e843–e849. doi:10.1542/peds.2013-3703.

Raffle, H. et al. (2010). *Family Story Play: Reading with Young Children (and Elmo) Over a Distance*. In Proceedings of the SIGCHI Conference on Human Factors in Computing Systems, ACM, pp. 1583–1592, April.

Raffle, H. et al. (2011). *Hello, Is Grandma There? Let's Read! StoryVisit: Family Video Chat and Connected E-Books*. Proceedings of the SIGCHI Conference on Human Factors in Computing Systems, ACM, pp. 1195–1204, May.

Ribak, R. (2009). Remote Control, Umbilical Cord and Beyond: The Mobile Phone as a Transitional Object. *British Journal of Developmental Psychology*, 27, 183–196.

Roberts, J. A., and David, M. E. (2016). My Life Has Become a Major Distraction from My Cell Phone: Partner Phubbing and Relationship Satisfaction Among Romantic Partners. *Computers in Human Behavior*, 54, 134–141. doi:10.1016/j.chb.2015.07.058.

Rodger, D., Skuse, A., Wilmore, M., Humphreys, S., Dalton, J., Flabouris, M., and Clifton, V. L. (2013). Pregnant Women's Use of Information and Communications Technologies to Access Pregnancy-Related Health Information in South Australia. *Australian Journal of Primary Health*, 19, 308–312. doi:10.1071/PY13029.

Schoppe-Sullivan, S. J., Yavorsky, J. E., Bartholomew, M. K., Sullivan, J. M., Lee, M. A., Dush, C. M. K., and Glassman, M. (2017). Doing Gender Online: New Mothers' Psychological Characteristics, Facebook Use, and Depressive Symptoms. *Sex Roles*, 76(5–6), 276–289.

Singer, B. (n.d.). 10 Best Apps for Paranoid Parents. *Parents*. www.parents.com/parenting/technology/best-apps-for-paranoid-parents/.

Smith, A., and Anderson, M. (2016). *5 Facts About Online Dating*, February 29. www.pewresearch.org/fact-tank/2016/02/29/5-facts-about-online-dating/.

Smith, A., and Duggan, M. (2013). *Online Dating & Relationships*. www.pewInternat.org/files/old-media//Files/Reports/2013/PIP_Online%20Dating%202013.pdf.

Tong, S. T., and Walther, J. B. (2011). Relational Maintenance and CMC. In K. B. Wright and L. M. Webb (eds.), *Computer-Mediated Communication in Personal Relationships*. New York: Peter Lang, pp. 98–118.

Vaala, S. E., and Bleakley, A. (2015). Monitoring, Mediating, and Modeling: Parental Influence on Adolescent Computer and Internet Use in the United States. *Journal of Children and Media*, 9, 40–57. doi: 10.1080/17482798.2015.997103.

Valkenburg, P. M., and Peter, J. (2007). Who Visits Online Dating Sites? Exploring Some Characteristics of Online Daters. *CyberPsychology & Behavior*, 10(6), 849–852. doi:10.1089/cpb.2007.9941.

Watt, D., and White, J. M. (1999). Computers and the Family Life: A Family Development Perspective. *Journal of Comparative Family Studies*, 30(1), 1–15. https://search.proquest.com/docview/232574405?accountid=2909.

Wells, C. (2015). Helicopter Siblings Use Social Media to Watch Over Sisters and Brothers. *Wall Street Journal*, June 23. www.wsj.com/articles/helicopter-siblings-use-social-media-to-watch-over-sisters-and-brothers-1435079344.

13

Youth, algorithms, and the problem of political data

Veronica Barassi

On September 27, 2018, a young activist and aid worker was found guilty by a French court in Boulogne-sur-Mer in northern France of defamation for a tweet he had posted earlier in the year. The tweet showed the picture of two police officers standing over a man who appears to be a migrant sitting on his sleeping bag. In the tweet the 21-year-old suggests the officers are about to take away his sleeping bag, and the caption reads "but, we are the French nation, sir." With the tweet the young-aid worker wanted to raise awareness on the refugee crisis in Europe and mock the French President Emmanuel Macron who used the phrase "but, we are the French nation, sir" in a speech about overcoming adversity in 2017. The court ordered the 21-year-old to pay €500 to the officers, as well as €475 in court fees. Despite an outcry from organizations such as Human Rights Watch and Amnesty International – who believed that such a conviction could set up a problematic and dangerous precedent and have an impact on people's right to freedom of expression on social media – the news went largely unreported by mainstream media, and will probably be forgotten by public opinion. When I read the news I wondered how the young activist and aid worker would see the incident in the future. Will he forget the event? Will he feel proud? Will he regret it? There is no way to know how things will develop for him. Yet this example, I believe, speaks greatly about the historical moment we are living in. We live at an historical time where people use social media to express their opinion, to show their outrage, and participate to society. We also live at a time where everything we post on social media becomes a data trace that can be used against us.

In this chapter I want to explore the complex relationship between youth, political participation and data traces. The first part of the chapter will argue that in the last 20 years youth cultures have been defined by the emergence of new forms of political participation, which were often self-centered, networked, and flexible. These new forms of political participation were made possible by two simultaneous changes: a change in the political repertoires of social movements on the one hand and the development of new media technologies and later social media on the other. In fact, it will be shown that while the movements of the 1990s and 2000s reformulated understandings of political identity and belonging by relying on ideas autonomy and networked affinity, the rise of new media first and social media later enabled the development of new forms of online self-enactment and participation.

The second section of the chapter will thus turn attention to these forms of self-enactment, participation and performance online by analyzing the relationship between digital storytelling and self-construction. The third section of the chapter will focus on the current techno-historical transformation. It will argue that after more than a decade in which youths have been constructing themselves online and sharing important political and personal data, we have reached an historical moment in which individuals are no longer only digital citizens because they participate and self-enact online, they are datafied citizens because their data speaks for and about them. In this context, the chapter will conclude that we need to look at what is happening to new generations and the multiple and complex ways in which they are being datafied from the moment of conception. Only by doing so we can start addressing the democratic challenges and implications of allowing data traces and algorithms to talk for and about our public self.

New media and the making of digital citizens: identity, performance, and citizen rights

Youth, identity and civic engagement: a brief history from the 1990s to 2018

During the 1990s and early 2000s, especially in Europe and the United States, it started to become clear that we were witnessing a sharp decline in youth participation in traditional forms of political engagement (Norris, 2003). While public opinion and mainstream media emphasized the problem of 'political apathy' in younger generations, social researchers argued that focusing on notions of apathy and political disengagement overlooked an important dimension in forms of youth participation (Loader, 2007; Henn et al., 2005). In fact, the decline of youth engagement in institutional politics needed to be understood with reference to the rise of other types of civic based political participation and 'extra-institutional' forms of activism (Meyer & Tarrow, 1998).

This latter point became particularly evident if researchers considered the new political imaginations and repertoires of action that emerged during the global justice movements of the late 1990s. One of the distinctive features of these movements was precisely that they challenged classical understandings of institutional politics and representative democracy. Influenced by the teachings of the Zapatista Movement and Deleuze and Guattari's (2004) understanding that the state is a form of relationship, the movements for global justice acted on the logic of autonomy. In a similar line to the classical anarchists of the 19th century, such as Kropotkin and Laundauer, these movements argued that state relationships 'capture' and 'control' minorities (Day, 2005). Hence their aim was to enact forms of communitarianism and non-hierarchical relationships through direct action and participatory democracy. The way in which they organized themselves collectively and non-hierarchically, therefore, became not only a practice but, as Graeber (2002) suggested, a form of ideology, an ideology which is based on anarchism and autonomism.

The autonomous discourses of the movements for global justice have created the basis for a new reformulation of political identity and belonging. During the 1980s, scholars, such as Laclau and Mouffe (2001), suggested that there was no longer a whole vision of society but only multiple and conflicting political identities (2001, 34–39), and others – like Touraine – contended that society was not a system but a field of action, and that conflicts occurred over the control of the cultural, social, and political means of self-production (2001, 750–754). Identity was therefore a key word in any debate that related to social and political struggle. In the late 1990s, according to Day (2005), the 'politics of demand' that was fostered by new social movements had gradually been replaced by an understanding that the emancipations of political identities are constantly in-strumentalized by power forces. Social movements were no longer interested in achieving recognition through the state for their marginal 'identities,' because they no longer believed that the state could be perceived as a neutral arbiter. On the contrary, these movements saw state relationships as the very reason behind social inequality. Among the movements for global justice, therefore, political identity was no longer a reason for struggle or the very ground for cohesion. It was replaced by more hybrid and 'nomadic' understandings of engagement and participation, which focus on a politics of 'affinity' rather than politics of 'identity'

In order to better understand the characteristics of these forms of belonging that have emerged in the political imaginations of the networked movements for global justice, it is important to rely on the work of the Italian philosopher Agamben (1993), and his model of community: *the coming community*. According to Agamben, the coming communities were composed by different singularities; they were neither universal nor common subjects, nor do they work for the construction of collective belonging (1993, 17–23). They are brought together spontaneously by relations of affinity. The coming communities have many dividing lines but are interconnected and united by values and shared ethico-political commitments (1993, 43–47). They rely on a politics of affinity, which is based on an understanding of 'groundless solidarity' (solidarity that is not based on identity) and 'infinite responsibility' (Day, 2005).

The financial crisis of 2008 brought about a fundamental transformation in repertoires of political action. The new movements emerging especially between 2011 and 2013, which have been labeled the 'movements of the squares' because of their practice of occupation and assembly in public squares (Juris, 2012; Gerbaudo, 2012) shared many understandings with the global justice movements as far as participatory democracy and networked belonging was concerned. Yet they were also influenced by populist ideologies, by the shared understanding that all governmental elites were corrupted, inadequate and were moved only by neoliberal concerns and interests and that the people needed to take control of institutions (della Porta, 2015; Gerbaudo, 2017). It is thanks to these ideologies that we have seen the rise of new political parties, such as Podemos in Spain or the 5 Star Movement in Italy as well as a renewed youth participation in party politics in general (e.g., Labour Party in the United Kingdom). What is fascinating about these political parties, is not only their staggering success and the fact that they have come to dominate key institutional positions, but also the fact that they built their success on an 'ideology of the movement' (Treré & Barassi, 2015). The overall assumption was that these parties were not hierarchical but grassroots and horizontal in nature, and were there to challenge the status quo.

A lot can be said about these latest political constellations, and the multiple ways in which party and movement politics have come to intersect. A lot can also be said about the fact that the new forms of flexible political belonging and networked identity which found their roots in the global justice movements and have come to dominate also the so called 'movements of the squares' have created the ground for complex political alliances such as the one of the 5 Star Movement with the xenophobic extreme right party Lega Nord, which – at the time of writing – is in power in Italy. Yet this is not the concern of this chapter. Here, I want to focus on the relationship between the rise of networked and flexible forms of belonging, especially amongst younger generations, and digital technologies.

From new media to social media: the networked self, youth and the new forms of belonging

When we think about the rise of new forms of networked political participation and identity amongst younger generations, we cannot overlook the central role played by new media technologies in the movements of the 1990s and by social media in the 'movements of the squares.'

In the 1990s, new media technologies became the material support not only of new forms of collective (transnational) organizing practices but also the means through which the global justice movements could imagine transantional solidarity (Castells, 1997). Research on youth engagement after the 1990s thus has shown that new technologies enabled individuals to create loose networks of community action, and actualize themselves as citizens (Bennett, 2008). They also enabled them to engage in community life without impinging on one's desired openness and changeability of one's life course (Vinken, 2007). With the advent of social media these perspectives have been further extended, as it became clear that these platforms reinforced the logic of connective action, a form of networked politics that was based on individual networks of communication and action (Bennett & Segerberg, 2012). They also enabled the rise of a new logic of aggregation and assembly in public spaces (Juris, 2012; Gerbaudo, 2012).

The understanding that new media and social media technologies enabled the making of more flexible and networking forms of political participation and action emerged very vividly from my very first ethnographic fieldwork. In 2007/2008, I was carrying out an ethnographic research on the impact of social media on international solidarity organizations within the British Labour movement. During fieldwork many participants expressed their concerns about the fact that their type of politics was no longer appealing to younger generations. At times, especially when I was talking to older members, they started to show distress with the idea that their 'world was dying.' When confronted with the question of why they thought that trade union politics was no longer appealing to young activists, most of the people talked about the fact that younger generations were not interested in 'joining' political organizations. In this regard, particularly insightful is the following interview with Matt (a full-time employee of the Venezuelan Information Centre) who at the time of fieldwork was in his early twenties.

V: why do you think there is little interest from younger generations in Labour politics?
M: . . . most of our friends are involved with campaigning organizations, but we are a group which is not representative at all because we come from the student movement. But in general there is a bit of a culture around young people and their relationship with politics. You know some people keep on saying "oh I don't join anything" and that is a bit of a culture. . .

After my interview with Matt and Sian, I had the pleasure to interview Rob, who at the time of my fieldwork led the Cuba solidarity campaign. Like Matt, Rob also believed that part of the problem for the lack of participation in the Labour movement needed to be found in the youth culture of the time:

R: Young people tend to not join anything really. They don't want to feel part. It seems as if there is a shared anti-culture of any kind of membership. But I don't know why that is. The idea of individualism, perhaps. I think Thatcher is to blame and the eighties. I don't know. Even environmentalism is pretty much an individual exercise. But doing something collectively with other people, getting involved and organized . . . no they just don't organize, they just float around.

During fieldwork I carried out semi-structured interviews and had regular contact with 35 people between 19 and 28 years of age, who would participate in events, conferences, or summer work holidays despite not being active members of any particular organization. When questioned on how they defined themselves politically or what they understood as political participation, a great majority of them suggested that although they believed in the values of labor politics, they did not believe in the idea of joining a campaigning organizations or political parties. What I realized during fieldwork was that there was a gap between the way in which young people thought and experienced political belonging, and the ideas of political identity and affiliation that were constantly reinforced by trade unions and campaigning organizations. This latter point emerges particularly well in an extract of an interview with Mark[1] – a 22-year-old sociology student who volunteered for a short period for the Cuba solidarity Campaign while not wanting to become a member.

V: How do you define yourself politically?
M: I don't know. I think you have to identify a common ground, an issue to tackle. But, you see, here is the difficult thing. I don't want to say when people ask who is your enemy for instance, I don't want to identify my enemies and my friends or my enemies' enemies or things like that . . . I don't think it's getting the world anywhere this sort of thing . . . this constant drawing a line. Political solidarity can come in many shapes and forms.

Mark believed in collective action. What he did not believe was the idea of "defining enemies or friends," of drawing lines and boundaries and associating to a particular political organization. Defining enemies and friends – or in other words establishing sameness and difference – constitutes the very basis for the construction of collective identity. Therefore, despite believing in political involvement he seems to be rejecting the classical understanding of political identity, as a relational concept which is defined by the constant construction of 'us' and 'them.' Similar to Mark, the young activists that I encountered during fieldwork – although believing in labor values and gravitating around the social world of international solidarity organizations – had replaced the idea of 'membership politics' promoted by the Labour movement with more flexible and networked understanding of 'affinity' and 'belonging.'

As argued elsewhere (Barassi, 2013), one fascinating finding that emerged during fieldwork is the fact that many of the young participants I met believed that online technologies were a great way of contributing to a campaign without belonging to it. What transpired from the informal conversations with them was that digital media (in contrast to other media such as printed magazines) enabled them to act fast on specific issues, and organize large communities of action, without being 'pinned down' to a specific group or organization. They felt that they could 'be part of something' without being a member.

During my research I came to the conclusion that as different scholars had effectively pointed out (Loader, 2007; Dahlgren & Olsson, 2007, Bennett, 2008) new media were in fact enabling a form of political participation that was more networked, flexible, and based on self-interest, and that this was particularly important for younger generations of activists. Of course, the scholars have also shown that when we think about youth participation, we need to be aware of the fact that the relationship between new media technologies and political engagement is far from obvious, and that it is important not to jump to conclusions or over-estimate new media's potential for the engagement of younger generations. Online political engagement is often dependent upon offline factors and the link between online participation and offline part-taking is not so obvious. In fact, as Livingstone et al. (2007) have argued with their research on young people in the United Kingdom, the fact of simply providing Internet access or developing more civic websites does not guarantee political engagement (2007).

When we think about youth, political participation, and digital technologies it is essential that we avoid techno-deterministic perspectives. Yet we cannot fail to appreciate the fact that these technologies have become the space for the enactment of a new type of self-actualized citizenship that distanced itself from traditional forms of political association and action. According to Castells (2001, 2009), this form of self-actualized citizenship was the product of 'networked-individualism,' a social pattern that enables individuals to build their networks online and offline on the basis of their interests, values, and affinities. In this way networked individualism organizes around communities of choice that are flexible, fluid, and ever changing (2001, 131).

In the past I focused on the limits of networked individualism and have shown how the networked-self impacts the collective creativity of groups (Fenton & Barassi, 2011; Barassi, 2015). In the next two setions, however, I want to shed light on a different dimension. At first I want to explore how the networked self has given rise to the enactment and performance of the digital citizen, a subject that performs its digital citizenship online through processes of digital storytelling (Isin & Ruppert, 2015; Couldry et al., 2014). Afterwards, I want to take the argument a bit further. I will argue that on the one hand the very self-centered nature of civic engagement and digital storytelling online has led to the production of vast archives of personal and political data about people's lives, and not only the lives of the people who produced that data but also the lives of the others who happen to be associated with specific digital citizens. I will also argue that, with the advent of big data, once this data has started to become aggregated with other data traces to profile individuals, we witnessed a radical transformation to the very notion of networked self. In fact today, the networked self is no longer only a digital citizen able to participate to society through practices of self-performance and enactment (Isin & Ruppert, 2015) but is a datafied citizen coerced into participating to society through data traces that speak for and about her (Barassi, 2016, 2017, 2018; Hintz et al., 2017, 2018). This is particularly true if we think about younger generations who have grown up or have been born in these new data environments.

From digital to datafied citizens: data traces and the problem of political data

The networked self and the performance of the digital citizen

The understanding that digital technologies enabled a new form of self-enactment and political participation online led different scholars to turn their attention to the notion of digital citizenship. The concept of digital citizenship has been used to explore how digital technologies have transformed the pre-conditions of citizens' participation in the public realm (Dahlgren, 2009) as citizens participate in society via digital technologies (Mossberger et al., 2007). Yet in recent years it became evident that online self-enactment and civic engagement was much more complex than simple 'participation' in society via digital media. In fact as Isin and Ruppert (2015) have shown the focus on 'participation' alone leaves out too much in the analysis of how the Internet has impacted on the figure of the citizen. According to the scholars, 'digital acts' are complex 'speech acts' which enable digital citizens not only to make rights claim on the Internet (2015, 69) but to self-perform and enact of one's own position in society (2015, 25).

Isin and Ruppert's work (2015) is important because it enables us to appreciate that if people (and especially youth) participate to society through online technologies, they do so through complex processes of self-enactment and performance. One of the complex ways in which digital citizenship is 'performed' is through *digital storytelling* (Couldry et al., 2014). Here the work of Vivienne (2011, 2016) among political activists is particularly revealing. Drawing on qualitative interviews, discourse analysis and ethnographic methodologies amongst queer activists, Vivienne makes a powerful claim about the importance of understanding the complex relationship between digital storytelling, activism and processes of self-construction. One of the main merits of her work is represented by the fact that – drawing on philosophical and postmodern thought – she understands self-construction as a contradictory and messy process, which is tightly linked to performance, and hence storytelling. In this framework, she demonstrates that digital media (and she is broad in her definition) are the spaces for people to carry out – through digital story-telling – the work of constructing one's own 'networked identity' by building bridges between multiple, co-existent, understandings of self, family and community (2016, 132–173).

When I read Vivienne's (2016) work I was reminded of my own ethnographic findings. A few years after my first research in the Labour movement in the United Kingdom, I found myself researching a very different political movement: the autonomous movement in Italy. The new field of research was not only different because activists shared very different politi-cal ideologies and practices to the ones I had encountered amongst the UK trade unions and international organizations, but also because the activists I worked with were mostly young, between 16 and 25 years of age, with a few exceptions in their early thirties. It was while I was working with the Italian movement that I realized the complexity of processes of political self-construction. What I realized during fieldwork was that, as argued elsewhere (Barassi, 2017), activists often talked about their political self through messy and complex processes of narrative construction, which entailed forms of self-recognition and self-distancing from specific rela-tionships (from family life to the different groups one had belonged to).

Hence I questioned whether these messy processes of self-construction translated on social media. In 2015, thus, I launched a short digital ethnography of activists' social media pro-files, and analyzed how activists' engaged in digital storytelling and self-construction. As argued elsewhere (Barassi, 2017, 2018), the research revealed that – like Vivienne (2016) had rightly noted – social media were becoming important platforms for self-construction and performance through digital narratives. What fascinated me most about these narratives was that they were largely complex, open-ended, contradictory, multifaceted and incoherent. At times individual activists traced connections with their family and their childhood memories and provided these relationships and memories with political meanings (see Barassi, 2017). Other times they re-affirmed their sense of belonging to specific collectives, groups or shared past events (Barassi, 2018; Barassi & Zamponi, 2020).

The datafication of citizens and the question about political profiling

As I was carrying out my research, however, I started to become more and more aware of the fact that what I was analyzing was large amounts of *political data*. Through their practices of digital storytelling, activists built a wide variety of political data that was directly traceable to individual, groups and networks. Through the sharing of highly political social media posts and memories, the activists that I researched, were not only constructing a complex, contradictory identity nar-rative but, as argued elsewhere Barassi (2018), they were also constructing a *political biography* on social media: a digital and widely public auto-biographical story of their political self. These biog-raphies were becoming digital artifacts which defined not only activists' political identities but also the people, networks, and groups that were associated with them. What I found particularly prob-lematic to notice was that – because the activists that I studied had been on social media for almost ten years – one could find a long history of political activities and beliefs. Of course, social media posts can be deleted or edited, but what I noticed during the research was that this is seldom done.

In addition, the technological developments of the last five years combined with the re-structuring of the political economy of big data have radically transformed the digital environ-ments in which this political data is stored. Years before my digital ethnographic project took place, for instance, when I was still carrying out my field research in Italy, I had the pleasure to interview Pietro[2] a 24 -year-old student and activist. During the interview, Pietro talked about the fact that within the political group he belonged to, activists were really concerned about privacy and surveillance on Facebook. He told me that for this reason they established the common rule that if an individual posted a group photo on Facebook he could not tag the other members of the group. Since the launch of Facebook's DeepFace facial recognition technology in 2014, Pietro's and other activists' precaution would be completely useless.

Today Pietro is in his early thirties, and not only he has a long political biography on Facebook which is constructed out of all the different political data traces that he built through his posts, but these traces are now aggregated with a plurality of other traces to profile him. This understanding made me come to the conclusion that – with the advent and establishment of big data and its political economy – we can no longer understand the networked self and the digital citizen merely as a form of self-enactment and performance online, but we need to take into account how data traces are being used to profile and identify individuals, to discriminate them and set them out from others. Of course, the more data is out there about an individual's life, the greater the impact. This is particularly true if we consider young and new generations.

Increasingly more, younger and younger generations are no longer only digital citizens who self-enactment and perform online through digital storytelling they are all becoming datafied citizens because the *data traces are made to speak for and about their lives*. It is for this reason that in the last couple of years I have moved away from the study of political participation to focus on the study of digital participation in broader terms. The project that I have been working on is called Child | Data | Citizen. The project explored the impact of big data on family life and investigated how children's data traces relate to new understandings of digital citizenship. Methodologically, the project was based on the belief that in order to understand the multiple and complex ways in which the cultural phenomenon of big data is transforming family life we need to consider the relationship between UK and US ethnographic contexts. Therefore, I work with families in London and Los Angeles, with children between 0 and 13 years of age, whose personal information online is ruled by the Children's Online Privacy Protection Act (1998). The research relied on a multi-method approach, which combined 50 semi-structured in-depth interviews, 2 years of auto-ethnographic participant observation, 9 months of digital ethnography of the social media of 8 families, 2 focus groups, and the qualitative platform analysis of the technologies that collected and shared children's data (Barassi, 2020).

The project revealed that – in contrast to the generation of those who grew up before the advent of big data, children are today *coerced* into digitally participating from before they are born through a variety of data traces (Barassi, 2019). From the moment in which a child is conceived, important biometric information is uploaded on social media or pregnancy apps. As children grow up most of their health and educational data is digitized, archived and sold by privately owned corporations. All these different forms of data monitoring and processing are just the tip of the iceberg, and the picture becomes much more complex if we consider the role played by home hubs, artificial intelligence systems, facial recognition technologies and genetic mapping. One of the most interesting aspects of children's data is that more often than not this data is produced, shared and processed thanks to the digital practices and choices of others: the parents, the friends, the educators, the healthcare providers, the state officials, and the business developers. Children's data is in most cases more collective than personal, and is the product of complex social relationships and messy digital practices. It is by looking at children's data, I believe, that we can start appreciating the pervasiveness and ubiquity of the datafication of citizens, and we can highlight some of the most problematic implications of our data environments.

This latter point is particularly clear if we take into account the issue of *political data*. As argued elsewhere (Barassi, 2017), during my digital ethnographic research on activists social media profiles and digital storytelling, I realized that activists Facebook timelines were filled with images of their own children or the children of other family members and friends. By sharing images and personal identifying information of these children, activists constructed their political profiles by making visible their family history and the political values of the family. In addition to this, activists discursively constructed these children as political agents. On the Facebook profile of Paul,[3] an activist involved in the British Trade Union Movement, for instance, there is a picture of his toddler son sitting on the floor together with another boy. The caption of the image reads: 'discussing the details of their vanguard party.' This example is not isolated. During my research, I came across posts of children at demonstrations holding banners and flags, children playing together and being described as 'plotting the next revolution,' children with signs openly criticizing the current government or supporting specific political campaigns. It is clear that there is a playful and joking dimension in the posts. However, critical questions emerge on the ways in which political data could be used in the future.

The 2018 Cambridge Analytica/Facebook scandal is perhaps the very first example in the public domain of the multiple ways in which political data is being used. What the Cambridge Analytica scandal revealed, was that individuals were being profiled for their political views and sent specific information aimed at having an emotional impact and influencing their electoral choices. Another example comes from the United Kingdom when it transpired that the Labour Party recently bought the data of new mothers or mothers to be, to politically profile them. All these uses and misuses of political data are just the tip of the iceberg when we think about the data traces collected from youth and children, and a darker scenario emerges if we start exploring other types of data use, such as biometric data or home life data (Barassi, 2018).

What is becoming clear is that data broking and digital profiling is not only impacting on our consumers' rights (e.g., determining the price we get for things, or the access we have to specific products such as insurances) it is impacting on our civic and democratic rights (e.g., impacting on the right to express our political views without being judged and framed). The line between citizen and consumer data subject is becoming so blurred that at present we are seeing the emergence of new public debates, lawsuits and regulations that are aimed at addressing this societal transformation. In the EU, the implementation of the General Data Protection Regulations in May 2018 is holding businesses, organizations and institutions accountable for protecting individual privacy (with a special attention to the data of children). In the United States, over the last year, we witnessed the first lawsuits that address the problem of inaccurate profiling and data harm. What we need to understand is that at the moment the datafied futures of youth and children are being negotiated piece by piece and that the datafication of citizens does not have to be an inevitable future.

Conclusion

Over the last twenty years, the rise of new media (and social media) together with the emergence of new political imaginations and repertoires have brought about a more networked, self-centered and flexible understanding of civic engagement and identity construction amongst youth cultures. This chapter has analyzed this historical transformation and has argued that – in the last two decades – different generations of activists have grown up using digital technologies as platforms for civic engagement and self-construction through digital storytelling. These platforms enabled them to voice their opinions, feel part of specific groups, make sense of their own experiences and perform their own public self.

When we think about youth, participation and new media therefore it is important to understand the social significance of practices of self-enactment, civic participation and performance online. Yet it is also important to explore the complex ways in which, in the last decade, the data produced through practices of digital storytelling has been embedded into complex political economic and techno-social environments. With the advent of big data and its profoundly problematic political economic structures, data traces are constantly collected, aggregated and processed in such a way that they end up talking for and about individuals.

While this transformation is affecting everyone in one way or another, youth and younger generations are being more exposed, simply because more data is being collected from their lives. We live at an historical time when the data of children is being produced, collected, shared, and processed by a variety of human and nonhuman agents from before they are born. In this context, we are creating entire generations of citizens that are no longer digital citizens because they decided to participate to society through online technologies but are datafied citizens because they are coerced into digitally participating to society through data traces that are produced, collected and profiled for them by others. This techno-historical transformation, as this chapter has argued, can have serious implications for our democratic futures and for the lives of the generations to come. Starting to question this transformation by looking at what brought us here, and what changed is of central importance. As it can enable us to shift contemporary debates on data traces and youth from the focus on privacy and surveillance to a critical analysis on freedom of expression, self-representation and data justice.

Notes

1 Fictional name to protect participant's choice of anonymity.
2 Fictional name to protect participant's choice of anonymity.
3 Fictional Name to protect the participant's anonymity.

References

Agamben, G. (1993). *The Coming Community*. Translated by M. Hardt. Minneapolis: University of Minnesota Press.

Barassi, V. (2013). When Materiality Counts: The Social and Political Importance of Activist Magazines in Europe. *Global Media and Communication*, 9(2), 135–151. https://doi.org/10.1177/1742766513479717.

Barassi, V. (2015). *Activism on the Web: Everyday Struggles Against Digital Capitalism*. New York, NY: Routledge.

Barassi, V. (2016). Datafied Citizens? Social Media Activism, Digital Traces and the Question About Political Profiling. *Communication and the Public*. https://doi.org/10.1177/2057047316683200.

Barassi, V. (2017). Digital Citizens? Data Traces and Family Life. *Contemporary Social Science*, 12(1–2), 84–95. https://doi.org/10.1080/21582041.2017.1338353.

Barassi, V. (2018). Social Media Activism, Self-Representation and the Construction of Political Biographies. In G. Meikle (ed.), *The Routledge Companion to Media and Activism* (1st ed.). Abingdon, Oxon and New York: Routledge, pp. 142–151.

Barassi, V. (2019). Datafied Citizens in the Age of Coerced Digital Participation. *Sociological Research Online*. https://doi.org/10.1177/1360780419857734.

Barassi, V. (2020). *Child Data Citizen: How Tech Companies Are Profiling Us from Before Birth*. Cambridge, MA: The MIT Press.

Barassi, V., and Zamponi, L. (2020). Social Media Time, Identity Narratives and the Construction of Political Biographies. *Social Movement Studies*, 0(0), 1–17. https://doi.org/10.1080/14742837.2020.1718489.

Bennett, W. L. (2008). Changing Citizenship in the Digital Age. In W. L. Bennett (ed.), *Civic Life Online: Learning How Digital Media Can Engage Youth*. Cambridge, MA: MIT Press.

Bennett, W. L., and Segerberg, A. (2012). The Logic of Connective Action. *Information, Communication & Society*, 15(5), 739–768. https://doi.org/10.1080/1369118X.2012.670661.

Castells, M. (1997). *The Power of Identity: The Information Age – Economy, Society, and Culture: 2*. Malden, MA: Wiley-Blackwell.

Castells, M. (2001). *The Internet Galaxy: Reflections on the Internet, Business, and Society*. Oxford: Oxford University Press.

Castells, M. (2009). *Communication Power*. Oxford: Oxford University Press.

Couldry, N., Stephansen, H., Fotopoulou, A., MacDonald, R., Clark, W., and Dickens, L. (2014). Digital Citizenship? Narrative Exchange and the Changing Terms of Civic Culture. *Citizenship Studies*, 18(6–7), 615–629. https://doi.org/10.1080/13621025.2013.865903.

Dahlgren, P. (2009). *Media and Political Engagement: Citizens, Communication and Democracy*. Cambridge: Cambridge University Press.

Dahlgren, P., and Olsson, T. (2007). Young Activists, Political Horizons and the Internet: Adapting the Net to One's Purposes. In B. D. Loader (ed.), *Young Citizens in the Digital Age: Political Engagement, Young People and New Media* (1st ed.). London and New York: Routledge, pp. 68–81.

Day, R. J. F. (2005). *Gramsci Is Dead: Anarchist Currents in the Newest Social Movements*. London, Ann Arbor, MI and Toronto: Pluto Press.

Deleuze, G., and Guattari, F. (2004). *A Thousand Plateaus: Capitalism and Schizophrenia* (New ed.). London: Continuum International Publishing Group Ltd.

Della Porta, D. (2015). *Social Movements in Times of Austerity: Bringing Capitalism Back Into Protest Analysis*. New York: John Wiley & Sons.

Fenton, N., and Barassi, V. (2011). Alternative Media and Social Networking Sites: The Politics of Individuation and Political Participation. *The Communication Review*, 14(3), 179–196. https://doi.org/10.1080/10714421.2011.597245.

Gerbaudo, P. (2012). *Tweets and the Streets: Social Media and Contemporary Activism*. London: Pluto Press.

Gerbaudo, P. (2017). *The Mask and the Flag: Populism, Citizenism and Global Protest*. London: Hurst.

Graeber, D. (2002). The New Anarchists. *New Left Review*, 13, 61–73.

Henn, M., Weinstein, M., & Forrest, S. (2005). Uninterested Youth? Young People's Attitudes towards Party Politics in Britain. *Political Studies*, 53(3), 556–578. https://doi.org/10.1111/j.1467-9248.2005.00544.x

Hintz, A., Dencik, L., and Wahl-Jorgensen, K. (2017). Digital Citizenship and Surveillance| Digital Citizenship and Surveillance Society – Introduction. *International Journal of Communication*, 11, 9.

Hintz, A., Dencik, L., and Wahl-Jorgensen, K. (2018). *Digital Citizenship in a Datafied Society*. Cambridge: Polity Press.

Isin, E. F., and Ruppert, E. S. (2015). *Being Digital Citizens*. London: Rowman & Littlefield.

Juris, J. S. (2012). Reflections on #Occupy Everywhere: Social Media, Public Space, and Emerging Logics of Aggregation. *American Ethnologist*, 39(2), 259–279. https://doi.org/10.1111/j.1548-1425.2012.01362.x.

Laclau, E., and Mouffe, C. (2001). *Hegemony and Socialist Strategy: Towards a Radical Democratic Politics*. London: Verso.

Livingstone, S. and Helsper, E. (2007). Gradations in Digital Inclusion: Children, young people and the digital divide, *New Media & Society*, 9:4, pp. 671–696.

Loader, B. D. (2007). Introduction: Young Citizens in the Digital Age: Disaffected or Displaced? In B. D. Loader (ed.), *Young Citizens in the Digital Age: Political Engagement, Young People and New Media* (1st ed.). London and New York: Routledge.

Meyer, D. S., and Tarrow, S. G. (1998). *The Social Movement Society: Contentious Politics for a New Century*. Lanham: Rowman & Littlefield.

Mossberger, K., Tolbert, C. J., and McNeal, R. S. (2007). *Digital Citizenship: The Internet, Society, and Participation*. Bellingham: MIT Press.

Norris, P. (2003). 'Young people and democratic institutions: from disillusionment to participation' Report for the Council of Europe Symposium, Strasbourg, 27–28th November.

Treré, E., and Barassi, V. (2015). Net-Authoritarianism? How Web Ideologies Reinforce Political Hierarchies in the Italian 5 Star Movement. *Journal of Italian Cinema & Media Studies*, 3(3), 287–304. https://doi.org/10.1386/jicms.3.3.287_1.

Vinken, H. (2007). Changing Life Courses, Citizenship and New Media: The Impact of Reflexive Biographization. In P. Dahlgren (ed.), *Young Citizens and New Media: Learning for Democratic Participation*. London: Routledge, pp. 41–59.

Vivienne, S. (2011). Mediating Identity Narratives : A Case Study in Queer Digital Storytelling as Everyday Activism. In S. Fragoso (ed.), *AOIR Selected Papers of Internet Research (IR 12.0) : Performance and Participation* (vol. IR12.0). Seattle, WA: Association of Internet Researchers (AoIR), pp. 1–19. http://spir.aoir.org/index.php/spir/article/view/37.

Vivienne, S. (2016). *Digital Identity and Everyday Activism: Sharing Private Stories with Networked Publics*. New York: Springer.

14

What remains of digital democracy? Contemporary political cleavages and democratic practices

Brian D. Loader

Once regarded as the savior of the democratic polity, digital media and communications have more recently come to be seen as its nemesis. The disruptive capacity of the Internet has in the past been variously championed for undermining authoritarian regimes, providing alternative independent media channels, enabling citizen journalism, as well as offering the prospect of casting a transparent light into our darkened representative chambers through a new dawn of participatory democracy. In recent times however it seems as if these turbulent digital affordances have opened a Pandora's box of anti-democratic forces. It is claimed that both the outcomes of the UK referendum on membership of the European Union (EU) and the 2016 US presidential election may have been influenced by disinformation, and, even by malicious hacking by foreign agencies. In the hands of populist parties and leaders, social media has been effectively used to spread propaganda, create public fear and target potentially gullible supporters. Moreover, the monopolistic and unaccountable power of the giant commercial organizations that own the digital infrastructure, and thereby control much of the collection, processing and use of big data, is seen as further evidence of the dangers posed by the digital media ecology to democratic politics. So, what now remains of the promise of digital democracy?

I want to argue in this chapter that we keep making the same mistake by thinking that digital media is somehow inherently democratic and then blaming it when it fails to realize our desires. This repeat offending is not only a theoretical flaw but more crucially prevents us from both recognizing the contested nature of digital communications technologies and the need to politically engage in their ownership, development, and regulation in order to pursue democratic governance. Furthermore, this misconception of digital media is compounded by its reliance upon essentialist models of democracy. Instead of regarding democracy as an independent variable, set apart as a measure for the Internet's capacity for empowering citizens, we should see their emancipatory potential as interdependent. It is precisely the contingent, contested and changing nature of both digital media *and* democracy that makes them inexorably bound together. The problem with much mainstream debate is that it assumes that democracy and digital media are stable entities, outside of social relations of power and thereby curiously non-political.

I want to propose instead that we see digital media and democracy as interdependent variables that are mutually subject to flexible development, intelligibility and outcomes. Indeed, we may decide that they are so intimately related that little remains of the need to prefix the term digital to democracy. But then again, perhaps it still remains helpful as term to foreground a distinctive round of political battles in the long history of democratic politics. Its value is to remind us of contemporary historicity. That accusations of fake news, populist narratives, clandestine citizen targeting, and the counter arguments for twitter revolutions, virtual states and Facebook elections, are all part of the contested attempts by individuals, and groups to shape social relations of power through digital media and the contingent factors that in turn act to mitigate such attempts.

Democratic practices

Despite the many attempts to define democracy and the resultant typologies of various ideal types identified or proposed (Barber, 2003; Hartley, 2010; Held, 2006), it is somewhat remarkable how little attention is paid to the contingent nature of these abstractions. Both time and place have repeatedly shaped the possibilities and manifestations of democratic politics in such ways as to make any natural or universal explanations for its development seem erroneous (Keane, 2009). The interplay of geography and history that mark democracy's episodic entrances and exits upon the world's political stages should make us very weary of those (primarily) Western notions of taken-for-granted citizen rights enshrined in laws, institutions, elections and public spheres. Instead of seeing democracy as solid structures that characterize progressive modern societies capable of being replicated by developing countries, it might be more helpful to understand it as something closer to the periodic outcomes of the ongoing and newly emerging claims by competing social groups. Democracy is not something bestowed upon us by some higher reasoning and cultural superiority. It is certainly not solid or static, although it includes attempts by those most advantaged at any one time to make us think that it is. Rather than something outside of the social it is better to see it as an assemblage of cultural practices. It is enacted and repeatedly brought into existence by action, habit and performance. Communication is at the heart of these democratic practices.

I want therefore to define the illusive concept of democracy as a set of *cultural practices* undertaken by and to groups of citizens, that manifest themselves through institutions (Parliaments, embassies, elections, etc.), social structures (bounded communities, social movements, political parties and the like), symbolic narratives (such as histories, music, art, flags), social action (voting, protesting, campaigning, etc.) discourses (ideologies, language, social control for example) and communication technologies (such as a free press, social media, etc.), that are both historically and geographically contingent, and are inherently contested and vulnerable.

Such an approach has the advantage of capturing the dynamic yet precarious nature of democratic politics wherever and whenever it emerges. It is also capable of encompassing the wide variety of democratic practices that emanate from the socially diverse everyday lived experiences of peoples all over the planet. It is further helpful for several other reasons I believe. First, seen as social activities, it enables us to understand democratic practices as relational, spatial, networked, connective and collective. This is in marked contrast to those models of democracy, such as rational choice theory, that reduce all political engagement to the aggregate sum of individual self-interested cost-benefit calculations (Downs, 1957). Democratic practices are developed through social interaction and communication within and between different social groups that have different perspectives and interests. That is, they are not developed and enacted in isolation from the particular social and cultural contexts within which citizens live their lives. People's sense of political self or identity is achieved in conditions of unequal social and political relations that shape their values, expectations and thereby the kinds of democratic practices that are available to them.

Second, democratic practices are comprised of everyday routines, conventions and habits. Thus, they provide the basis for political engagement in situations requiring action. Routinized interaction thereby structures democratic practices. They are somewhat akin to Bourdieu's notion of *habitus* (Bourdieu, 1977) in that everyday interaction with oneself, other people or physical environment, gives rise to personal deportments – attitudes, values, emotions and feelings – that are expressed, performed and enacted through a variety of communicative forms (talk, text, video, images, body language, fashion, etc.). Often everyday situations require little more than existing democratic practices. However, the concept of democratic practices encompasses both *stability* through well-established routines and *change* where socioeconomic or cultural conditions manifest failure or invite re-interpretations. Democratic practices thereby enable us to explore repetition of everyday political habits but within a context of environmental change that can give rise to new forms civic engagement. They thereby possess the capacity for innovative actions that may structure future practices that reinvent democracy.

Third, and central to our concern here, the concept of democratic practices enables us to include physical spaces and artifacts in our understanding of how engagement is manifested and restricted. Computers, mobile phones, cameras, streets, public spaces, for example, can be conceptualized as constituent aspects of democratic practices. The physical interaction of groups with familiar localities (Parkinson, 2012) or their everyday use of social networks can shape the routine repertoires of political action. Often neglected in studies of political participation, these physical relations can influence enabling and/or inhibiting factors shaping action.

But it should also be recognized, however, that a further consequence of this approach is its revelation of the darker side of democratic politics. In times of austerity, crises (pandemics, climate) and rapidly growing social inequality, it may be deemed more appropriate by some groups to adopt political practices that are neither emancipatory nor conducive to positive outcomes for democracy. The recent and pernicious use of social media and digital communication by religious fundamentalists, extremist groups, xenophobes and populist parties bears testimony to such threats. Yet democracy must always harbor the forces which threaten its own destruction if it is to be inclusive in ways that facilitate voices of descent. It is thereby always unstable. Open to challenge by its enemies, who are often intent upon laying bear its tendency to prevarication, bureaucracy, indecision, and compromise. Nonetheless, its sustainability cannot be guaranteed by excluding those voices or ignoring their claims. Democracy must always succor the serpents willing its destruction and rely instead upon those who engage in fostering democratic practices best suited to meet the contingencies of the times. The crucial point is that such practices are not naturally progressive, universal or stable. They emerge from the contested claims of competing social groups living in a variety of social and historical contexts.

Digital democratic practices

Once we adopt a contingent and open view of democratic politics and understand digital media as a constituent part of the formation of the practices necessary for its realization, it becomes possible for us to understand digital media as political culture. Let me be clear. To say that digital media are political is not the same thing as saying they are inherently democratic or authoritarian in nature. But it does mean that digital media are designed, developed and diffused in particular social contexts that both facilitate or deny certain forms of democratic practice.

Yet this is a difficult point for many people to concede. While they might accept that digital media can have political consequences, they would still baulk at the idea that digital media are themselves political. Surely the technology is value-neutral they would say. People are political, not technologies. Thus social media, for example, is often portrayed as free open networks offering us opportunities to network with friends, share with others and access unlimited information. It is thereby not the fault of the technology if people use it for identity theft, cyber bullying, pornography or disinformation. But we seldom ask if there are motives and values, other than those proclaimed, built into the design of digital media technologies. At least since Langdon Winner's seminal article 'do artefacts have politics?'(Winner, 1985) there has been a powerful argument that technologies are not value-free. Indeed, a well-established school of social scientists working within the field of science and technology studies (STS) have been at pains to make the case that technologies are socially shaped and capable of 'flexible interpretation' by competing social groups (Bijker, 1995; Bijker et al., 1987; MacKenzie & Wacjman, 1999). The history of the Internet itself provides ample examples of different interests (military, countercultural hippies, neoliberal entrepreneurs) actively attempting to shape its use in ways that reflect their respective political values (Abbate, 1999; Castells, 2001; Mosco, 2005; Streeter, 2011). While these may not always be overt, they can nonetheless be revealed behind the value-neutral scientific claims for business competitiveness, increasing GDP, economic efficiency, or the more naturalizing perspective that digital networking acts for the good of humanity. The point here is that digital media do not just have unintended political consequences. But rather that the very social activities of defining problems, objectives, solutions, technical requirements, and ethical choices by those groups involved in the development, use and diffusion of digital media are themselves shaped by political values. It is to recognize that some political consequences may be built into the design, objectives, and use of networked communication technologies.

Caution is required at this stage to avoid the erroneous conclusion that the intended (or unintended for that matter) political consequences of digital technology are determinate. But the fact that political intentions to shape digital media may not always produce their desired effect, should not distract us from recognizing that political values are often consciously or otherwise informing the visions and deliberations of those social groups intent upon shaping the outcomes. Moreover, in relation to democratic practices these contestations over flexible interpretations of design and adoption take place within social conditions of unequal relations of power, access to resources and competing discourses. The value of the work of those STS scholars who painstakingly chart how technologies are flexibility interpreted and socially shaped, is not only to challenge notions of technological determinism but also to foreground the power struggles that have been played out between different actors and agents in the process of design, construction and marketing of products. Alternative outcomes were frequently possible but the actual power relations and specific intentions of the unequal contests are seldom revealed in detail or made transparent until after the event. By this time the early flexibility is replaced by stabilization and the phenomenon of 'closure' or 'lock down,' discussed elsewhere in this book, becomes prevalent.

By recognizing the development and diffusion of digital media as an intrinsic part of the contestations over democratic practices, both shaping them and being in turn shaped by them, it becomes possible to move beyond the value-neutral depictions of digital media and question the political assumptions that inform the discourses promoting their adoption. It thereby also enables us to form theoretical bridges between macro level discussions of political values and micro level investigations into digital media communication. Such a flexible interpretation of digital media, and the contingent nature of democratic practices, surely reveal the futility of seeking a single universal model of *digital democracy*. Instead, we have to examine digital democratic practices within specific historical, cultural and geographical contexts. Each will produce variants of digitally informed democratic politics. But what might these political cultural contexts look like and how may contemporary democratic practices of digital media play out within them?

Contemporary political cultural cleavages

I want to suggest that one way it is possible to understand the contestations over digital media is to place them within the broader context of the current political landscape. Inevitably such a process can only be an abstract interpretation of complex factors and not everyone would agree with them. Nonetheless, it enables us to reveal how competing perspectives produce different narratives over digital media that in turn invoke the performance of diverse democratic practices.

Traditionally, political scientists and commentators have adopted a one-dimensional scale to analyze political values along a left-right axis. These respective 'wings' have become shorthand for describing attitudes to business, taxation, social welfare, immigration, wealth distribution, regulation and other issues. But there has been a growing consensus that a left-right continuum is no longer sufficient to understand contemporary political norms. Surveying the backdrop to recent political events it is possible instead to discern the emergence of a significant cultural cleavage between what we might describe as internationalism and nationalism that cuts across and disrupts these older ideologies and party dichotomies. Many late-modern societies have been profoundly challenged by processes of economic and political internationalization that have increasingly divided the attitudes and lived experiences of their populations. In crude terms it is possible to discern a growing cultural divide between that portion of the electorate who are comfortable with the processes of internationalization and those, sometimes condescendingly described as the 'left behind' (Ford & Goodwin, 2014), who fear the consequences of such developments. The former may broadly be characterized as more 'outward looking' and open to other cultures; typically more egalitarian and meritocratic in their views about social diversity; have a weak affiliation to traditional group identities such as class, nation or party; and prize self-realization and autonomy. The latter, by contrast, privilege community, cultural tradition and bounded territories; they are often nostalgic for a lost past; are suspicious of multiculturalism that they believe undermines national identity; and, consequently, appeal to nationalism and the primacy of the nation-state to mitigate the effects of internationalism. The election of President Trump, the results of the UK referendum on leaving the EU, and the dramatic rise of populist parties and leaders across Europe can all be regarded as manifestations of the discontent of millions of citizens with globalization and the mainstream politicians and media who they regard as its mouthpiece.

While this international/national cultural divide can be identified in polling surveys it should not be overdrawn as some social commentators have attempted to do (Goodhart, 2017). The picture is instead complicated by the continuing existence of traditional left-right divides, between those favoring political models that prioritize strong democratic welfare states over economic markets and those perspectives privileging the role of business over a limited role for the democratic state. The intersection of the emerging national-international axis by the left-right dimension produces what appears as something like the two-dimensional representation of contemporary political values depicted in Figure 14.1, which outlines these cleavages as a simple matrix of four broad political formations. To repeat, this is a crude abstraction that is useful only as a means to identify four major perspectives, each of which has a different narrative. We should not regard the segments as equal in reality, with some perspectives (e.g., neoliberal globalization) more dominant than others. Moreover, as stated earlier, some groups may adopt positions that have no need for democracy – authoritarian markets or state-run economies for example. There is not time to discuss each in any detail but my point here is that they provide different narratives and values that shape the design and diffusion of digital media for democratic practices. Digital democracy is not formed outside these kinds of perspectives. It is a constituent part of

Figure 14.1 Contemporary political cultural cleavages

their attempts to shape democratic practices that are consistent with their political views. In what follows we will consider, in very simplified form, the narratives of each of these competing perspectives and the potential digital democratic practices that are privileged by their adherents.

Neoliberal globalization

The emergence of neoliberal globalization as the most dominant political-economic doctrine of the last four decades (Figure 14.1, top-right quadrant) has been crucially facilitated by the transforming capacities of the Internet. Indeed following the 'big bang' in 1981 when the deregulation of the London Stock Exchange ushered in the international global finance market, networked communications have facilitated and accelerated the process of globalization. (Castells, 1996, 2001). Digital media technologies have not only been at the forefront of globalization but they have also had a curious elective affinity with the cyberlibertarian narrative championing the development of the Internet (Loader, 1997). With the more widespread diffusion of the Internet in the 1990s a dominant countercultural political narrative emerged that privileged individual freedom, weakened democratic states, privatized media infrastructure, deregulated markets and liberalized finance. An early example of the rhetoric can be found in John Perry Barlow's call to 'think locally and act globally,' where he stated that the Internet heralded:

> The promise of a new social space, global and anti-sovereign, within which anybody, anywhere can express to the rest of humanity whatever he or she believes without fear. There is in these new media a foreshadowing of the intellectual and economic liberty that might undo all the authoritarian powers on earth.
>
> *(Barlow, 1996)*

In these kinds of renditions digital media is almost always a force for good that releases the individual from the chains of political control to pursue their own interests across global markets with networks of friends of their own choosing. In a more recent exposition of the libertarian narrative shaping digital media we see Anthony Mayfield claim that:

> A good way to think about social media is that all of this is actually just about being human beings. Sharing ideas, cooperating and collaborating to create art, thinking and commerce, vigorous debate and discourse, finding people who might be good friends, allies and lovers – it's what our species has built several civilization's on.
>
> *(Mayfield, 2008).*

Who could not be seduced by the exhortations to let the emerging digital media networks work their virtual magic and facilitate the natural sharing, collaboration and personal development that is the human condition as depicted by the counter-cultural creation myth of the Internet? But its comparison with the classical liberal economics belief in the 'invisible hand of the free market,' where the forces of laissez-faire play out without state interference, regulation or direction is purposely illusionary. Despite the public demands of neoliberals for small government, unregulated markets and the primacy of individual freedom, their actions when in power have revealed their hidden political intention to reinvent the state and not abolish it. To use it to intervene in the construction of markets and protection of global corporations, and manage populations though techniques of self-regulation that are at odds with the precepts of libertarians. This apparent contradiction between the emancipatory individualism of libertarianism and neoliberal state intervention is what Mirowski describes as the 'double truth doctrine' of neoliberalism (Mirowski, 2014, 68–69). While lip service is paid to the championing of free markets for public consumption, neoliberals, in their varied guises, have not been prepared to leave things to chance, and instead engage in politically determined aims and directives.

This neoliberal double truth doctrine can be witnessed by the manner in which the libertarian and counter cultural myths about the origins and role of digital media provide a useful cloak for the neoliberal intention to control and shape the technologies for their own political ends. Countercultural depictions may provide a vision of digital media as virtual, benevolent and free, but this only helps disguise the fact that the technologies are actually material, increasingly privately owned and politically shaped by vested interests fostering globalization. They are intended to convince us that digital media corporations, for example, are outside human values and politics and only exist to meet the human need to be free. Thus they not only conceal the material and complex realities of digitally networked neoliberal globalization but also act to frame digital media as non-political and thereby immune to contestation or alternative formulation. Where flexible interpretation is made available to users, to personalize their experiences, it is enabled in ways that capture their data, monitor their activities and make socioeconomic classification and segmentation realizable (Zuboff, 2019).

Politically digital media has been imbricated in the neoliberal project both through the intention to restructure state institutions but also to foster the development of what might be described as the 'customer-citizen.' In the former case digital media has been bound up with strategies to restructure democratic welfare state institutions by facilitating re-regulation, privatization, franchising of public service provision and instigating a culture of 'new public management' (NPM). Models of *e-government* were predicated upon the delivery of public services by using electronic networks to restructure public bureaucracies into core-periphery flexible organizations. NPM techniques were assisted by software designed to de-skill professionals through auditing of performance and ranking of service delivery. Much of the digital media technology and consultancy required to underpin such developments were/are provided by the global commercial sector, thereby enabling the neoliberal pursuit of using public finance to support private sector interests.

The re-wiring of public services (Fountain, 2001) however also requires a complementary transformation of the citizen-state relationship that has profound consequences for democratic practices. In an oft-recited remark the high priest of neoliberalism Frederick Heyek once proclaimed that in "demanding unlimited power of the majority, [democracies] become essentially anti-liberal" (Hayek, 1967, 161). This potential conflict between a strong neoliberal state and the voice of the people is tackled by transforming the enlightenment idea of democratic politics, as the free and equal engagement of citizens in the decisions that affect their lives, to one where it is itself a market-place of competing customer-citizen preferences and desires. Consequently, only very weak models of democracy are required, and the resultant democratic practices performed are more akin to those found in the shopping mall.

Significantly the consumer-citizen is not required to participate or engage in the formulation of collective public opinions. The democratic value of the customer-citizen is expressed not by their labour, property or human needs, but rather by their individual performances and personal preferences that can be read off from their online activities. Engulfed in data that resonates from the individual's performance and is digitally fed back to them continuously, the individual is responsible for monitoring their health, productivity, happiness, image and presentation of self (Davies, 2015). Ignorance is no defense against the charge of failure in the neoliberal life-world.

Social media in this context acts to harvest and aggregate the data of citizens in order to produce rational technocratic policy-making. The democratic practices required of the citizen-consumer amount to the limited option to periodically choose their career politicians and rate their teachers, doctors, civil servants and other public service facilitators. Democratic politics thereby becomes the domain of data analysts, public relations experts, and the biopolitical management of populations to foster neoliberal globalization. Thus, contrary to the liberal proposition that democracy is a prerequisite for a market economy, the neoliberals are keen that the people should not interfere too much in their objectives. As we have already noted the neoliberal doctrine requires a strong but restructured state destined to support the development of global corporations and the maintenance of the myth of the free market. Citizens must be managed by career politicians working closely with professional policy-makers, a compliant media and financially supported by multinational corporations and elites.

For some commentators this can be interpreted as not simply restructuring politics but the emergence of post-democracy (Crouch, 2004) whereby power is concentrated overwhelmingly in the hands of a transnational elite (Robinson, 2012). Confronted with the competitive advantage of global corporations in negotiations, national politicians have frequently conceded to neoliberal requests for market deregulation, privatization of public services, weakening trade union rights, and rolling back the welfare state, as the price to be paid for securing inward investment and financial stability. Nowhere has this been more apparent than where leaders of the political left, such as Schroeder, Clinton and Blair, have complied with the neoliberal global agenda.

In sum, neoliberal globalization can be seen to provide a distinctive set of values, institutional frameworks, and dominant discourses, all of which inform the design and diffusion of digital media to foster democratic practices commensurate with pursuing the neoliberal project. The double truth doctrine of championing individual freedom, small state, and free markets, while actually practicing a politics of data surveillance, strong government, and re-regulated markets, is encoded in the digital network technologies and applications shaping our social world and identities. It is played out through the democratic practices associated with the customer citizen whose digital traces from their online performances reveal their preferences, desires, and fears that enable the datafied state to manage their populations through segmentation, surveillance and self-monitoring.

Nationalist populism

While clearly the most dominant narrative, neoliberal globalization is not the only political perspective, and its socioeconomic consequences have led in recent years to a growing cultural backlash against neoliberal globalization from the political right in the form of populist parties and leaders[1] (Figure 14.1, bottom-right quadrant). Rapid de-industrialization, growing social inequality, cutbacks of public services and rising migration has led to significant social unease. It has also fostered disenchantment with mainstream political parties and the ability of career politicians to address these concerns. In many traditional democracies around the world we have witnessed the rise, often very rapidly, of populist parties, movements and leaders (Mudde & Kaltwasser, 2017). Although different in context populist parties typically share a common concern to 'speak for the people' against both supposedly corrupt elites who advocate globalization and 'others,' often immigrants, who they believe threaten the employment security, welfare benefits and national identity of 'the people.' Populism is less a coherent ideology and more a political narrative, discourse (Aslanidis, 2015) or political style (Moffitt & Tormey, 2014) that invokes the grievances against the negative consequences of globalization and provokes emotional opposition to 'establishment' elites and global institutions like the European Union, United Nations or global trade alliances.

While populist narratives may foreground the contention that elites have defrauded 'the people' of their rightful political authority they do not appear to set out the democratic practices to express their sovereignty beyond protest against 'outside' threats, appeals to common national identity and following those populist parties and leaders. Thus, at best, weak models of democracy underpin populism with leaders speaking for, or on behalf of 'the people,' instead of requiring the people to speak for themselves. At worst, privileging 'the people' may act to undermine democratic governance itself by denying voice or citizenship to groups or individuals that do not meet the increasingly restrictive threshold of national community membership. It is perhaps worth remembering that the history of nation-state formation is typically one of enforcing and expanding boundaries through warfare, colonialism, enslavement and even the attempted genocide of indigenous peoples. The construction of national identities has also often been achieved through the subjugation of regional and minority cultural differences of language, religions, mores and race. As Robert Dadl reminds us, "In the real world, then, answers to the question, what constitutes 'a people' for democratic purposes? are far more likely to come from political action and conflict, which will be accompanied by violence and coercion, than from reasoned inferences from democratic principles and practices"(Dahl, 1989, 209).

In a national populist perspective social media have provided an opportunity to reach out directly to 'the people' and have been central to the rapid growth and organization of populist parties in many countries. By circumventing mainstream media and politics they have, as they see it, enabled the voices of those who feel excluded by elites to express their opinions and concerns. It is perhaps an interesting irony that while it was the political left who championed digital media networks as a means to break the monopolistic control of broadcast media corporations and enable alternative discourses to be aired, in the event it was the populist right parties who seized those opportunities most effectively. Obama's 2008 presidential campaign may plausibly claim to be the first significant Internet election, but it was Donald Trump who used the full potential of social media to speak directly to his support base and circumvent the party machine and media. It was they who exploited the targeted messaging potential of Facebook and Twitter.

But it is the use of big data arising from the mundane everyday use of social media and its algorithmic capacity to identify and secretly target citizens with partisan or disinformation that may be regarded as the biggest threat to democratic practices from right wing populist parties. Such exploitation is, of course, available at present to any political groups or individuals, with the same detrimental prospects for democracy. But to date it is right wing populist movements and parties who seem to have been at the forefront of using data analytics to seek out those citizens most susceptible to their targeted propaganda. Companies such as Cambridge Analytica trawled through the personal data of millions of Facebook users to identity sexual orientation, intelligence, race, gender and much more, all to be gleaned from users profiles and 'likes.' The threat to democratic governance, of course, is that such practices enable populist parties to use such profiling to tailor their political messages in forms congruent with individual prejudice and fears, in order to gain their allegiance. Undertaken covertly and often hidden within the 'recommendations' and ads that appear on YouTube and Facebook pages, such messages are less likely to be subject to rebuttal or opposition in a public domain. Here then, we have clear examples of where digital media and communications technologies are shaped and designed for political advantage in ways which give lie to the notion that social media is value free and dispassionately sharing information and opinions with users. It also, as a consequence, raises questions about whether the self-policing of content by many of the world's largest tech companies, such as Google, Facebook and Twitter, is sufficient to safeguard transparent democratic practices or whether state regulations are also required?

Democratic nationalism

On the left of the political spectrum we also see some reactions to the consequences of neo-liberal globalization expressed through the prism of the nation-state (Figure 14.1, bottom-left quadrant). Here too we see a discourse that foregrounds an organic relationship between political and cultural communities that enable the construction of 'imagined communities' (Anderson, 1983) to be formed by common consciousness, language, history, and so on. Globalization and rapid large-scale immigration are thereby interpreted as a threat to the coherence, solidarity and mutual obligations of these societies. The resulting social inequalities have marginalized particularly working-class communities in deindustrialized areas, who feel they have been abandoned by their political representatives and subject to austerity, precarious employment and public service cuts.

The response from the nationalist democrats is to reaffirm the primacy of welfare states. For them democracy is conducted in a bounded territory with a community of citizens each having rights against, and, obligations to that political community. Consequently, democracy is a stronger variant than the previous narratives. In contrast to either notions of individualism or 'the people,' it is sensitive to the existence of a multiplicity of social groups competing over resources, rights claims and cultural recognition. Yet this is a pluralism bounded by the national political community.

It is perhaps not surprising then that discussions over the shape and diffusion of digital media and communication within this political perspective have been those most closely associated with the Habermassian primacy of the public sphere (Habermas, 1962). Essential for pluralist democracy are the domains where competing social interests, opinions, resistance, innovation, and visions can be played out and formulated through reasoned deliberation. The development of representative democracy has inexorably been bound up with mass media and expanding literacy. From the mass circulation of pamphlets and early broadsheet newspapers through to broadcast radio and television, communications media have informed the citizen and facilitated the formation of public opinion. The arrival of the Internet, for many commentators, simply enabled a further step in the reconfiguration of the public sphere. Developing his earlier work with Michael Gurevitch (Blumler & Gurevitch, 2001), Jay Blumler, for example, championed the idea of a digital 'civic commons' in a book written with Stephen Colemen (Coleman & Blumler, 2009). Inspired by the example of the UK public service broadcaster, the BBC, a national online civic commons could be funded and regulated by the state to facilitate deliberative democracy.

The difficulty with these national digital democratic practices is twofold. First, the degree to which deliberative forums, whether online or not, are capable of facilitating a wide range of voices, ideas and modes of expression has been convincingly questioned by postmodern and feminist theorists. The public sphere, they argue, has been and continues to be largely restricted to the dominant discourses of predominately white, middle class males (Pateman, 1989; Fraser, 1990). Indeed, the BBC, whatever its strengths, can hardly be regarded as a forum for airing political views or lifestyle choices that seriously diverge from the mainstream norms of public opinion. Second, such models of bounded political community deliberation seem at variance with the emerging diverse and different cultures that are characteristic of many contemporary societies.

Transnational democracy

For many citizens, distrustful of the motives or ability of national politicians to represent their interests, what is sought is the displacement of bounded rational deliberative democratic systems by *discursive* models that facilitate multiple and transnational engagement in global public spheres (Dryzek, 2000; Young, 2000).

This leads us to consider the final set of perspectives on democratic governance to arise from the disruption of the left–right political continuum by the national-international cultural cleavage resulting from globalization (Figure 14.1, top-left quadrant).

Again, there is no single coherent template but rather a number of perspectives that can be seen to have some common threads. First, they are international in their orientation and foreground human rights and identity as the grounding principles for democratic governance. Second, while they acknowledge the challenges posed by neoliberal globalization and the resulting social and ecological costs, they do not believe that nation-states acting alone are capable of addressing these challenges; global problems such as the climate crisis, social inequality and poverty, war and conflict, forced migration and risks of health epidemics, require transnational democratic solutions. Third, the identification of global risks to humanity can give rise to transnational solidarity between foreigners and strangers (Beck, 2000, 95).

Transnational democratic practices can manifest themselves through a range of formulations including cosmopolitanism (Held, 2004), international citizenship, global civic spheres (Keane, 2003) and transnational social movements (Porta & Mosca, 2005; Porta della et al., 2006). Again, each constellation will foreground different digital media affordances. For those citizens, especially young people, who have experienced the damaging effects of neoliberal globalization in terms of precarious employment opportunities, austerity cuts in public services, and declining opportunities, digital media have become the communication tool of choice (Loader et al., 2014) to express their outrage and mobilize their opposition (Castells, 2012). The prominence of transnational social movements in the early decades of this century has seen the adoption of digital networked communications to facilitate and organize a wide range of protests. A number of these political actions, such as 15 May in Spain, 5 Star in Italy, the Occupy movements in the United States and the United Kingdom or Gezi Park in Turkey, spread rapidly and haphazardly from country to country, sharing and coordinating their innovatory repertoires using social media such as Facebook, Twitter and YouTube. Typically, these movement protests distanced themselves from national political parties, trades unions or NGOs and instead engaged through digitally mediated loose networks with little or no hierarchy.

Some of the user-centered innovation shaping these digital democratic practices has been revealed through a series of publications drawing upon in-depth empirical investigations of these transnational protest organizations by Lance Bennett and Alex Segerberg (Bennett & Segerberg, 2012, 2013; Bennett et al., 2014). Through the addition of what they describe as 'connective action,' which complement the more familiar collective action, new unconventional democratic practices arise enabling citizens and activists to network through social media and share personalized identity frames. The meme 'we are the 99%,' for example, enabled diverse people around the world to identify personally with concerns and experiences of increasing social inequality. Moreover, such transnational networked spheres also provided the capacity for the rapid scaling up and enactment of large scale offline protests (Bennett & Segerberg, 2012, 742).

The focus upon transnational democratic practices thereby points to an alternative range of flexible interpretations of digital communications media. Here we see social media being creatively used to track human rights abuses, political campaigns and contestations around the world that facilitate the democratic practices described by Schudson (Schudson, 1998) and others (Keane, 2009) as 'monitorial ': depicting the role of citizens as agents keeping a check on states and holding them to account for their actions.

But in other significant ways these emergent democratic practices are characteristic of a deliberate divergence from the stable routines and habits of established mainstream representative political practices. They are shaped in response to the negative socioeconomic effects of the neoliberal globalization environment and represent attempts to both challenge these dominant discourses and search for new modes of democratic engagement. They can thus be regarded as episodes in discursive democracy (Dryzek, 2000) rather than examples of global deliberation.

Of course, as with the previous perspectives considered, transnational democratic practices are also subject to contestation. For democratic or populist nationalists wedded to the primacy of the imagined political communities represented by the state, the necessary bonds of common identity and social obligation simply cannot be replicated at the transnational level. Furthermore, it has been pointed out that transnational democrats may not be socially representative: typically they tend to be more highly educated, middle class and mobile. Consequently, those more socially and economically disadvantaged groups may not only have been politically excluded in many countries but have also been marginalized by many academic social theorists mesmerised by the promise of the global citizen. This neglect by the academe not only prevented many scholars from anticipating the cultural cleavages that underlay Brexit, Trump and the march of national populism, but it has delayed innovative explorations into the conditions required for socially inclusive transnational democratic practices to be effective.

Concluding comments

What then now does remain of *digital democracy*? Well it seems clear from our cursory examination of how digital media is diversely shaped within the context of contemporary political fissures and trends that the notion of a single universal model of digital democracy is an illusion. Instead, what becomes apparent is the flexible manner in which social media informs the development and expression of democratic practices responding to contested political, socioeconomic and cultural objectives. Too often digital media and communication networks are discussed as either politically benign or an inevitable danger to our democracies. Yet consideration of the four distinct but interlinked political perspectives that can be said to characterize contemporary debates reveals the multiple ways that digital media and communications technologies are an inescapable constituent aspect of democratic politics. It seems reasonable therefore to assert that digital communications media are essentially political, but they are not essentially democratic. We need to acknowledge that democratic practices can be either innovatory or restrictive in performance according to competing objectives, interpretations, contestations and adoptions that are informed by and in turn shape unequal social relations of power between different groups and citizens. Digital media and communications are inherently infused in such contestations.

Note

1 While the concept of populism is too general for some commentators and can also include movements and leaders on the political left, I have chosen to adopt it here as presently the only useful description of right wing collective actions of which I am familiar.

References

Abbate, J. (1999). *Inventing the Internet*. Cambridge, MA: MIT Press.

Anderson, B. (1983). *Imagined Communities*. London: Verso.

Aslanidis, P. (2015). Is Populism an Ideology? A Refutation and a New Perspective. *Political Studies*, 1–17. doi:10.1111/1467-9248.12224.

Barber, B. R. (2003). *Strong Democracy: Participatory Politics for a New Age* (20th Anniversary ed.). Berkeley and Los Angeles: University of California Press.

Barlow, J. P. (1996). Thinking Locally, Acting Globally. *EFF*. www.eff.org/pages/thinking-locally-acting-globally.

Beck, U. (2000). The Cosmopolitan Perspective: Sociology of the Second Age of Modernity*. *The British Journal of Sociology*, 51(1), 79–105. doi:10.1080/000713100358444.

Bennett, W. L., and Segerberg, A. (2012). The Logic of Connective Action. *Information, Communication & Society*, 15(5), 739–768. doi:10.1080/1369118X.2012.670661.

Bennett, W. L., and Segerberg, A. (2013). *The Logic of Connective Action: Digital Media and the Personalization of Contentious Politics*. Cambridge: Cambridge University press.

Bennett, W. L., Segerberg, A., and Walker, S. (2014). Organization in the Crowd: Peer Production in Large-Scale Networked Protests. *Information, Communication & Society*, 17(2), 232–260, Taylor & Francis. doi:10.1080/1369118X.2013.870379.

Bijker, W. E. (1995). *Of Bicycles, Bakelites and Bulbs: Toward a Theory of Sociotechnical Change*. Cambridge, MA: MIT Press.

Bijker, W. E., Hughes, T. P., and Pinch, T. (1987). *The Social Construction of Technological Systems: New Directions in the Sociology and History of Technology*. Cambridge, MA: MIT Press.

Blumler, J., and Gurevitch, M. (2001). The New Media and Our Political Communication Discontents: Democratizing Cyberspace. *Information, Communication & Society*, 4(1), 1–13.

Bourdieu, P. (1977). *Outline of a Theory of Practice*. Cambridge: Cambridge University Press.

Castells, M. (1996). *The Rise of the Network Society*. Oxford: Wiley-Blackwell.

Castells, M. (2001). *The Internet Galaxy*. Oxford: Oxford University Press.

Castells, M. (2012). *Networks of Outrage and Hope*. Cambridge: Polity Press.

Coleman, S., and Blumler, J. (2009). *The Internet and Democratic Citizenship: Theory, Practice and Policy*. Cambridge: Cambridge University Press.

Crouch, C. (2004). *Post-Democracy*. Cambridge: Polity Press.

Dahl, R. (1989). *Democracy and Its Critics*. New Haven: Yale University Press.

Davies, W. (2015). *The Happiness Industry: How the Government and Big Business Sold Us Well-Being*. London: Verso.

Downs, A. (1957). *An Economic Theory of Democracy*. New York: Harper and Row.

Dryzek, J. S. (2000). *Deliberative Democracy and Beyond: Liberals, Critics, Contestations*. Oxford: Oxford University Press.

Ford, R., and Goodwin, M. (2014). *Revolt on the Right: Explaining Support for the Radical Right in Britain*. London: Routledge.

Fountain, J. (2001). *Building the Virtual State: Information Technology and Institutional Change*. Washington, DC: Brookings Institution.

Fraser, N. (1990). Rethinking the Public Sphere: A Contribution to the Critique of Actually Existing Democracy. *Social Text*, 25, 56–80.

Goodhart, D. (2017). *The Road to Somewhere: the Populist Revolt and the Future of Politics*. London: C. Hurst & Co.

Habermas, J. (1962). *The Structural Transformation of the Public Sphere: An Inquiry into a Category of Bourgeois Society*. Cambridge: MA: MIT Press.

Hartley, J. (2010). Silly Citizenship. *Critical Discourse Studies*, 7(4), 233–248. doi:10.1080/17405904.2010. 511826.

Hayek, F. (1967). *Studies in Philosophy, Politics and Economics*. New York: Simon & Schuster.

Held, D. (2004). *Global Covenant: The Social Democratic Alternative to the Washington Consensus*. Cambridge: Polity Press.

Held, D. (2006). *Models of Democracy*. Stanford: Stanford University Press.

Keane, J. (2003). *Global Civil Society?* Cambridge: Cambridge University Press.

Keane, J. (2009). *The Life and Death of Democracy*. London: Simon & Schuster.

Loader, B. D. (1997). *The Governance of Cyberspace: Politics, Technology and Global Restructuring*. London: Routledge.

Loader, B. D., Vromen, A., and Xenos, M. A. (2014). *The Networked Young Citizen: Social Media, Political Participation and Civic Engagement*. Edited by B. D. Loader, A. Vromen, and M. A. Xenos. New York: Routledge.

MacKenzie, D., and Wacjman, J. (1999). *The Social Shaping of Technology*. Edited by D. MacKenzie and J. Wacjman. Milton Keynes: Oxford University Press.

Mayfield, A. (2008). What Is Social Media? *iCrossing*. www.icrossing.com/uk/sites/default/files_uk/insight_pdf_files/What is Social Media_iCrossing_ebook.pdf.

Mirowski, P. (2014). *Never Let a Serious Crisis Go to Waste: How Neoliberalism Survived the Financial Meltdown*. New York: Verso.

Moffitt, B., and Tormey, S. (2014). Rethinking Populism: Politics, Mediatisation and Political Style. *Political Studies*, 62(2), 381–397. doi:10.1111/1467-9248.12032.

Mosco, V. (2005). *The Digital Sublime: Myth, Power and Cyberspace*. Cambridge, MA: MIT Press.

Mudde, C., and Kaltwasser, C. (2017). *Populism: A Very Short Introduction*. Oxford: Oxford University Press.

Parkinson, J. R. (2012). *Democracy and Public Space*. Oxford: Oxford University Press.

Pateman, C. (1989). *The Disorder of Women: Democracy, Feminism and Political Theory*. Cambridge: Polity Press.

Porta della., D. et al. (2006). *Globalization from Below: Transnational Activists and Protest Networks*. Minneapolis: University of Minnesota Press.

Porta, D., and Mosca, L. (2005). Global-net for Global Movements? A Netwrok of Neworks for a Movement of Movements. *Journal of Public Policy*, 25(1), 165–190.

Robinson, W. (2012). Global Capitalism Theory and the Emergence of Transnational Elites. *Critical Sociology*, 38(3), 349–463.

Schudson, M. (1998). *The Good Citizen: A History of American Public Life*. New York: Free Press.

Streeter, T. (2011). *The Net Effect: Romantism, Capitalism and the Internet*. New York: New York University Press.

Winner, L. (1985). Do Artefacts Have Politics? In D. MacKenzie and J. Wajcman (eds.), *The Social Shaping of Technology*. Buckingham: Open University Press, pp. 26–38.

Young, I. M. (2000). *Inclusion and Democracy*. Oxford: Oxford University Press.

Zuboff, S. (2019). *The Age of Surveillance Capitalism: The Fight for a Human Future at the New Frontier of Power*. London: Profile Books.

15

Journalism's digital publics
Researching the "visual citizen"

*Stuart Allan and Chris Peters**

Disruptions associated with either financial or technological change have long garnered most of the attention when considering the democratic challenges facing journalism in a digital era (Pavlik, 2000; Picard, 2014; Usher, 2010). The proliferation of media platforms offering repurposed content has fragmented formerly stable audience profiles to varying degrees (Fletcher & Nielsen, 2017); declining advertising and subscription revenues, as well as an elusive business model, has impacted on staffing and resources (Deuze & Witschge, 2018); a multiskilling of roles in the newsroom and field risks compromising news outlets' capacity to produce quality reportage (Bro et al., 2016); and the ease with which digital manipulation and distribution can undermine accuracy and verification on a wide scale makes it ever more difficult to separate the truthful from the deceitful, the 'real' from the 'fake' (Graves, 2016). It is readily apparent issues such as these complicate any easy, straightforward alignment between journalism and civic participation in public life yet also invite further consideration of the very nature of citizenship itself in a digital era.

Set against this backdrop of wider debates about journalism and democratic cultures, this chapter interweaves diverse yet complementary strands of research to help discern, first, the ways in which journalism's digital publics are becoming increasingly image-ready, willing, and able, and, second, the implications for remediations of authority, objectivity, and transparency. It argues there is heuristic value in reversing familiar emphases by adopting bottom-up, citizen-centered perspectives to explore civic modes of seeing, particularly in and through the generation, deployment, and use of digital imagery. To substantiate this claim, this chapter strives to map the broad features of scholarly investigations into the ongoing changes between journalism, citizens, and the politics of digital imagery. Given there is a variety of useful research schematics around citizen witnessing, social movements, audience practices, and Internet cultures (among others), which emphasize the growing importance of the visual, bringing them together offers a valuable holistic, interdisciplinary overview and periodization. Moreover, doing so allows us to clarify image-related technological affordances and constraints, news organizations' interactions with citizens in newsmaking and critique, and the envisioned potentials of news reporting for political engagement.

* We wish to thank the Carlsberg Fund for its financial support, which facilitated a research stay for Chris Peters at Cardiff University to work with Stuart Allan on the writing of this chapter, under grant number CF17–0332.

The first part of this chapter situates this evolving ecosystem in relation to our conception of the 'visual citizen' (Allan & Peters, 2019). Having briefly outlined pertinent technological developments and associated sociopolitical implications for journalism, we pinpoint a guiding research rationale for investigating precipitous civic commitments to creating, curating, sharing, and repurposing vernacular imagery. On this basis, we proceed to assess recent scholarly literatures exploring the visual citizen, namely as news observer and circulator (seeing and sharing news in everyday life through news consumption); 'accidental' news image-maker (citizen witnessing and 'amateur' photojournalism); purposeful news image-maker and activist (visualizing dissent and sousveillance); and creative image-maker and news commentator (GIF and meme culture). We then conclude by highlighting possible trajectories for future research.

Digital imagery's communicative implications for journalism

The reconfiguration of formerly stable patterns of news consumption (or so they may appear in retrospect) has been a recurrent theme occupying many news and journalism studies scholars in recent decades, with increasing attention being placed on the different ways audiences have taken up new media devices (e.g., Newman, 2018; Westlund & Färdigh, 2015). Frequently, the desired metric is 'use' – in terms of device preference, frequency, intensity, levels of interactivity, and so on – that people take with possible ways of engaging with journalism. Similarly, studies of newsroom practice, especially when it comes to the incorporation of analytics and algorithms, present the case that hard data on impressions, views, and the like preoccupy the journalism industry (Tandoc, 2015). In short, the emphasis is on measurability over form, with the changing materiality of news being typically considered in terms of usage-based possibilities. Less prominent, however, is research addressing the shifting processes of socialization that occur for audiences around news consumption and the associated ramifications for norms, values, and forms of political engagement. Capturing such transformations is challenging as "it is often much more difficult for researchers to identify, define, and study situational definitions than it is for the average citizen to navigate them" (Meyrowitz, 1986, 24). In this respect, this chapter makes the case that taking visual engagement as a starting point and contrasting it to what came before offer a valuable heuristic.

One can make the broader case that the wave of visual technologies appearing over recent decades encourages a number of reconsiderations about "why we attend to the things to which we attend" (Comor, 2001, 282), as well as how "changes in communication technology influence what we can concretely create and apprehend" (Carey, 2008, 24). The rise of video camcorders, then personal digital cameras, and now smartphones changes the ease with which 'newsworthy' imagery can be captured by 'ordinary' people ('user-generated content') and, in turn, shapes public expectations of mobile 'amateur' witnessing of events typically relayed before professional journalists arrive on the scene. Similarly, the increased public sharing of photographs via the web and social media means that these documented first-hand experiences can be widely seen, even without news organizations acting as intermediaries. Other examples, such as the emergence of GIF, meme, and emoticon culture as features of connectivity in everyday life, or the generation of witnessing imagery to mobilize resistance, protest, and dissent, are just a few further instances of recent changes that underscore the growing ubiquity of myriad types of imagery in contemporary news landscapes. Indeed, highlighting such lived materialities of visuality invites further reflection on the political implications of their mediation, helping to inspire new questions regarding the ways diverse communities of interest struggle over definitions of what is 'real' and 'meaningful' in ideological terms.

This is evidenced in public disquiet over thorny questions of truth, authenticity, and verification within an 'image-saturated' culture. From discussions surrounding the visible staging of electoral politics in the era of 'fake news' (Boczkowski & Papacharissi, 2018; Happer et al., 2018), to disputes over the acceptable limits of Photoshop where news photography's indexical claim on the real is concerned (Ritchin, 2013; Wheeler, 2005), to the visual surveillance of authorities over publics (and sousveillance of publics over authorities) using video cameras (Ristovska, 2016), and many other debates, ongoing interdisciplinary dialogues around contemporary citizenship and democracy are often inherently bound up with the visual. Even though image-making has always mattered for civic politics, the shifting time-spaces of digitalization throw into sharp relief how everyday practices of seeing are being recast. The confusing, contested political realities of image-circulation and re-inflection disrupt previous understandings, such as when the emotive qualities of violent imagery no longer necessarily claim a purchase on identification, let alone compassion (Mortensen et al., 2017), or the objectivity ascribed to photojournalism is dismissed for being malleable, and as such compromised (Borges-Rey, 2015).

In the sections to follow, we gather together an array of insights drawn from pertinent literatures addressing four of the more significant areas of recent scholarly investigation into visual citizenship. Each of these foci resonates within a different regime of visibility (Chouliaraki & Stolic, 2017) and, as such, helps to equip researchers with an alternative basis from which to rethink journalism's normative relationships with its digital publics.

Visual citizen as news observer and circulator

The creation, processing, curation, and sharing of various types of imagery in the digital media sphere is one of the manifest transformations of everyday communicative practices in recent times. Common social ways of observing and reacting to news stories are becoming bound-up and tied to the visual in emergent ways, while – paradoxically – at the same time mundane practices of news consumption are becoming less visible. Affective reactions about the news, for example, are increasingly expressed on social media through nonverbal emoticons and recommender buttons (e.g., like, favorite), and these markers, along with the algorithmic preferences ascribed to them, influence the persistence of online expressions and spreadability of messages (boyd, 2014). In turn, where news events are concerned, these changes may well impact upon related public forms of democratic engagement (see Larsson, 2018; Messing & Westwood, 2014). Research by Swart et al. (2018), for example, illustrates that many people opt for phatic communication on Facebook to respond to shared news stories, avoiding sharing or commenting explicitly themselves due to the face-threatening nature of the act and possible exposure to criticism or abuse (see also Ksiazek et al., 2016; Larsson, 2017). The increased prominence of social media feeds as informational sources in everyday life (Bakshy et al., 2015; Costera Meijer & Groot Kormelink, 2015; Newman et al., 2018), in which public affairs and personal updates intermingle and interweave, is thus but one prominent example of the evolving interpretive contexts within which news stories are encountered.

In this respect, when it comes to assessing the potential significance of variable news habits, it is illustrative to consider the shifts in visibility of news consumption from the analogue era of traditional broadcast media to today. It has been something of a truism among researchers that news consumption facilitated the creation of collective identity, and with it the potential of shared, communal senses of belonging; that is, journalism prompted a 'national conversation' and, in so doing, staked its claim to be at the center of public life (Anderson, 2011). The cultural history of the newspaper in many countries was closely connected to its status as "a mobile object designed to be carried through the streets and read on trains, platforms, or subway cars, not simply in isolation, but in a connected social space" (Sheller, 2015, 14). In other words, visibility (both actual and imagined) was key to the establishment of journalism's proclaimed status and cultural authority. Moreover, the social formation of news habits was largely predicated on seeing others consume journalism, from the aforementioned newspaper on public transit to radio bulletins in the kitchen, newscasts on the family television, and so forth (Peters, 2012). For researchers striving to anticipate future trends, it remains unclear what impact the continued individualization of media devices will have on future generations' inclination to consume journalism, the forms of engagement these will take, or how new technologies will be 'domesticated' as expedient news devices in everyday routines (see also Haddon, 2006; Livingstone, 2002). Smartphone use renders news consumption as a personally visible but publicly *in*visible practice.

In this regard, then, technologies of observation are crucial resources for future generations to be socialized into understanding not only how but also when and where we culturally expect to 'see' journalism. 'Getting the news' via social media feeds and smartphone apps is a pronounced change in the visuality of news akin to the introduction of the news ticker and multiple screens with cable news in the 1990s. Alongside other visual complexities that have also presented themselves over this timeframe, and continue to do so – from hyperlinks to data visualizations, embedded tweets and videos, and so on – the myriad changes in the visual presentation of journalism indicate that how citizens come to see, potentially share, and socially engage with news is undergoing a radical transformation.

Visual citizen as 'accidental' news image-maker

The way social life is seen, felt, and communicated has become constantly intertwined with these ongoing, emergent, visual potentialities, and in this respect, it is unsurprising that on-the-spot 'amateur' imagery has become an essential part of news coverage. No longer the occasional exception to the general rule, breaking news reporting now routinely relies on the willingness of ordinary people to bear witness to what they see and hear unfolding around them, sometimes at considerable risk to themselves. Such instances point to the potentialities of personal imagery being reappropriated from the lived contingencies of the ordinary (everyday life contexts) into projections of the extraordinary (personal perceptions of – even possible engagement in – citizen photojournalism).

Our everyday image-ready culture may not demand such an elevated sense of civic duty, but it has certainly alerted individuals to the reality that they could potentially be called upon to act as crisis reporting surrogates (Allan & Peters, 2015). Moreover, citizen imagery has been shown to strongly engage citizens around its perceived authenticity and affectivity even if concerns remain about ethics and possible manipulation (Ahva & Hellman, 2015; Reading, 2009; Rentschler, 2009). These developments, along with other experiments in user-generated content (UGC) associated with the digitalization of journalism, have led to a more collaborative ethos for news organizations committed to enhancing audience participation (Peters & Witschge, 2015). Among the pertinent factors here are two largely concurrent developments, namely the rise of first camera phones and then smartphones, and the introduction of image-sharing websites and apps. The successful integration of cameras on personal devices and newfound visual mobility for the public in the mid-2000s led commentators at the time to anticipate startling implications for the fledgling device – 'everyone becomes a photojournalist' – which proved newsworthy in their own right (Allan, 2017; Caple, 2014). These developments, much like the introduction of camcorders in the 1990s, had a similar effect of bringing the possible contributions of 'amateurs' in contact with the journalistic 'needs' of news coverage. Several instances in the years following the early introduction of camera phones, when citizens relayed mobile imagery to document major news events in the absence of journalists on the ground, gradually normalized the role of the 'citizen witness' (Allan, 2013) in generating reportage to such an extent that having access to such imagery is now almost the expected norm. 'Pics or it didn't happen' is "the populist mantra of the social networking age," as Silverman (2015) sums it up. "Show us what you did, so that we may believe and validate it" (see also Alper, 2014; Mortensen, 2014; Wardle et al., 2014).

Diverse forms of public participation in visual newsmaking are flourishing as never before, often neatly sidestepping the mainstream media's professional gatekeepers striving to mediate or, more to the point, regulate and monetize demotic contributions within preferred institutional boundaries. Pessimistic appraisals of photojournalism's future are being readily countered by bold assertions about the promise of citizen-centered coverage, especially the advent of alternative, embodied approaches to visual truth-telling (Madrigal, 2012; Wall & El Zahed, 2015). Tempering this enthusiasm, however, are those expressing their misgivings – commentators and scholars alike – about occasional shortcomings in the quality, fidelity, or credibility of this reportage (Pantti & Sirén, 2015; Tait, 2011). News organizations routinely encounter 'flak' over their choices of visuals, not least by politically motivated media monitoring 'watchdogs' – situated across the political spectrum – increasingly taking it upon themselves to police for perceived misuses of imagery for partisan or commercial advantage. At the same time, many photo editors have adapted, taking elaborate care to cultivate a nuanced relationship with their publics, effectively crediting them with the interpretive skills necessary to differentiate subtle gradations in journalistic authority over contested evidence (Allan, 2017). Tell-tale words such as 'purportedly' or phrases such as 'appears to show,' signal this contingency, the unspoken acknowledgment that sometimes cameras – or, more to the point, the people holding them – cannot always be trusted.

Visual citizen as purposeful news image-maker

Many scholars seeking to move beyond all-encompassing conceptions of 'citizen journalism' recognize the importance of discerning multiple modalities for purposes of closer analysis, three of which can be briefly differentiated across an imagined continuum as follows. At one end is the individual engaged in self-described citizen newsmaking, perhaps enacting a sense of civic duty or obligation by offering their community a form of 'hyper-local' news coverage otherwise unavailable in the absence of professional journalists employed by news organizations. For some researchers, such assumed roles are suggestive of what they describe as a 'fifth estate,' a nascent realm of digitally savvy citizens intent on fashioning alternative forms of reporting actively supplementing – and, in some instances, supplanting – the mainstream news media's fourth-estate commitments (see Cooper, 2006; Dutton, 2009; Williams et al., 2011). At the opposite end of this continuum is the individual who, much to their own surprise, performs the type of impromptu, 'accidental' reportage discussed previously, namely by bearing witness to an unfolding event for the benefit of distant family, friends, or followers, most likely via a social media platform (Allan, 2013; Mortensen, 2015). A third modality, situated in a shifting, even contested (at times) relationship to the other two, is the individual self-reflexively committed to purposeful witnessing. Examples include the activist determined to challenge injustice (Atton, 2015; Greer & McLaughlin, 2011; Martini, 2018), the NGO worker revealing a humanitarian crisis (Chouliaraki & Stolic, 2017; Dencik & Allan, 2017), the combatant recording the grisly realities of violent conflict (Ibrahim, 2014; Kross, 2016; Rodriguez, 2011; Smit et al., 2015), or the whistleblower exposing corruption (Brevini et al., 2013), among other possibilities.

Examinations of this third modality have frequently brought to light frictions besetting the maintenance, repair, and policing of professional-amateur normative boundary-making

(Carlson & Lewis, 2015; Waisbord, 2013). Of particular interest to some scholars concerned with questions of state power in this regard has been the efforts of citizens to wield portable, often wearable personal technologies to gather and share visible evidence in the public interest. In contrast with 'surveillance' (watching over), the term 'sousveillance' (watching from below) has been elaborated in several studies to capture further dimensions of these processes, notably the reverse tactics employed to monitor those in positions of authority "by informal networks of regular people, equipped with little more than cellphone cameras, video blogs and the desire to remain vigilant against the excesses of the powers that be" (Hoffman, 2006; see also Bakir, 2010; Mann, 2002). Such lens-reversal practices, studies have shown, have facilitated concerted efforts by afflicted communities to confront institutions of authority, in part by affording counter-narratives of their lived experience of oppression with the potential to disrupt what can otherwise seem to be a hegemonic politics of visibility in news reporting.

Several pertinent initiatives have attracted academic inquiries over recent years. A formative example is WITNESS, an international nonprofit organization widely perceived to be a leader in a global movement to create change by developing citizen-centered approaches to human rights reportage. Launched in 1992 by a small group led by the pop-star Peter Gabriel (2014), its current website declares its aim to empower "human rights defenders to use video to fight injustice, and to transform personal stories of abuse into powerful tools that can pressure those in power or with power to act." Its initial strategy, namely to provide "people who chose to be in the wrong place at the right time" with video cameras so as to help them document violations and abuses in the field, has evolved to prioritize both activists' and ordinary citizens' engagement in personal reportage with a view to its evidential importance for the advancement of human rights causes. To date, WITNESS has partnered with more than 360 human rights groups in 97 countries, devoting particular effort to supporting the inclusion of citizen video as a 'democratic tool' in human rights campaigns seen by millions of people around the world (see also Allan, 2015; Gregory, 2015; Ristovska, 2016).

A further important strand in scholarship investigates citizens' purposeful uses of visual imagery in the politics of protest and dissent concerning long-standing antagonisms over poverty, injustice, and corruption. Examples include the 'London Riots' of summer 2011, where residents living in some of the city's most deprived areas shared real-time still photographs and video footage over several days. An array of 'haunting images' chronicling the violence 'flooded the Internet,' including on community sites such as Citizenside and The-Latest, among many others, capturing what were frequently poignant visual testimonies of loss and personal hardship (Kalter, 2011; Vis et al., 2013). A relatively small portion of the imagery was shot by the participants themselves, including incriminating 'trophy' snapshots of one another standing in front of ransacked shops (Holehouse & Millward, 2011). Later, the same year in New York, Occupy Wall Street set in motion a fledgling network of activists – symbolized in its rallying cry 'We are the 99%' – intent on refashioning social media platforms to strategic advantage. Live-footage gathered and posted online by 'the army of citizen documenters' (O'Carroll, 2011) galvanized sporadic protests into a movement, leading *The Economist* (2011) to observe: "what's going on in America right now may be the world's first genuine social-media uprising" (see also Penney & Dadas, 2014). Similarly, the Black Lives Matter activist movement has recurrently drawn upon sousveillant documentation in its campaigns against violence and systemic racism toward black people, recognizing the raw power of imagery to focus media – and thereby public – attention on instances of alleged police shootings, brutality, or misconduct (Allan & Dencik, 2017; Bock, 2016). In making such acts visible, nationwide protests resulted, federal investigations were launched, and discussions of policy and attitudes on racial prejudice and discrimination came to the fore on media agendas (Stephen, 2015; Steiner & Waisbord, 2017). Visual citizenship was also shown to be a double-edged sword, however, with those engaging in sousveillance sometimes finding themselves rendered too visible, quite possibly at risk of arrest, violence, or intimidation.

Visual citizen as creative commentator

Research into different aspects of visual citizenship and the impact on journalism is gradually catching up with increasingly common efforts by citizens to transform how everyday political critique is performed online. Once the purview of fan sites, hacker communities, and groups at the vanguard of Internet cultures (see Knobel & Lankshear, 2007; Shifman, 2012), digital visual practices such as the creation and circulation of memes, GIFs, and video remixes are now regularly deployed as forms of news commentary (see also Bayerl & Stoynov, 2016; Eppink, 2014; Milner, 2013a, 2013b). Taking forms ranging from bricolage to repurposing, parody, critique, and subversion, these creative visual reflections on public affairs are no longer merely confined to message boards and 'lonely people in their basements' but have emerged into the mainstream. Indeed, the idea of such communicative practices has become so culturally ingrained that it is now commonplace to assert the controversial nature or absurdity of a political statement by noting it has 'become a meme.'

Native-online forms of image creation potentially impact the relationship the visual citizen has with journalism in terms of facilitating accessible forms of critical engagement – specialist websites like 'Know your Meme' and 'GIFFY' categorize and sort significant examples while easily learned meme and GIF generators abound, welcoming participation. Relying on the power of networks to spread them within the social media ecosystem, engagement with such visualities is, of course "bounded by technical limitations (features and affordances), entrenched social behaviours, and inclusion in (or exclusion from) a shared understanding of the meme" (Leavitt, 2014, 148; see also Miltner, 2014). However, it would be a mistake to underestimate their political and journalistic importance. As Highfield and Leaver note:

> visual content on social media is not necessarily a set of selfies, food porn, memes, and GIFs, marked in their narcissism or frivolousness. Instead, visual social media content can highlight affect, political views, reactions, key information, and scenes of importance.
>
> *(2016, 48: see also Gal et al., 2016; Milner, 2013b)*

There seems to be growing recognition of this on the part of journalists too; creating and curating these visual commentaries is now a common part of news coverage, forming an interpretive loop wherein the visual commentary on the news event folds back into the 'original' story itself.

Such creative visual critique, while attended to in the research literature around social movements and protest (Milner, 2013a) and politics in general (Shifman, 2014), is a somewhat neglected dimension within journalism studies. It demands more sustained scholarly attention going forward. Visual critique in journalism, historically the purview of the political cartoonist (Greenberg, 2002), is now increasingly seen through the lens of these digital commentaries created, shared, and further curated by the public, creating entirely new visual communicative forms and conversational dynamics around public affairs. As Shifman argues:

> human agency should be an integral part of our conceptualization of memes by describing them as dynamic entities that spread in response to technological, cultural and social

choices made by people . . . building blocks of complex cultures, intertwining and interacting with each other.

(2012, 189)

They are 'spreadable media' (Jenkins et al., 2013), in which their movement (through sharing and circulation), combined with ongoing encapsulation of publics (through awareness or active participation around them), strengthens the potential impact of their message (see also Wiggins & Bowers, 2015). Their emergence has led to them becoming an increasingly integral part of political campaigns – grassroots to national – as witnessed in their sustained use as tools of delegitimization (Ross & Rivers, 2017). Similarly pertinent is the increasing presence of 'social media consultants,' who are tasked with the job of trying to create visual messaging via memes, gifs, hashtags, video mixes, and mashups that resonates with desired electors (Bowls, 2018).

Just as scholars endeavored to understand the factors shaping the rise of professional PR consultants in the 1980s and 1990s, today much attention is focused on visualized political communication strategies and their implications for civic engagement. Disputes over imagery open up new fluid spheres of contestation, in both the 'mainstream' and more radical 'fringes' of global newscapes (Massanari, 2017; Nissenbaum & Shifman, 2017). Well-known examples of visual critique in the 2016 US presidential campaign (e.g., Pepe the Frog, #TrumpTapes) and first 100 days of the Trump presidency (Prankster Joe Biden, #AlternativeFacts) are not the exception but the new normal, it would appear. This emergent communicative ethos means that research agendas going forth will need to attend to the significance of 'creative' audience-generated imagery for visual journalism, with critical insights into the role of humor, ironic detachment, and critique in such interactive practices. Intriguing on their own terms, these newfound illustrative techniques also warrant investigation with regard to the modes of citizenship they affirm – and undercut – within broader civic deliberations.

Conclusion

Scholarship concerned with citizen-centered forms of visual reportage brings to light the promise – and, on occasion, the pitfalls – of news organizations' concerted efforts to rethink their relationship with their publics. Coming to terms with "the people formerly known as the audience" (Rosen, 2006) invites ever greater commitments to innovation and experimentation, with a variety of tactics, devices, protocols, and strategies undergoing active, ad hoc revisioning, often under intense pressure in difficult circumstances. When it works, such as in several examples discussed earlier, these types of synergies help to secure first-hand perspectives long before the professional journalist arrives on the scene. They enable news stories to affirm an evidential basis that may be otherwise too dangerous – or, indeed, prohibitively expensive – to cover with sufficient rigor and depth. In other instances, as we have seen, purposeful practices of sousveillance afford vital insights into the experiences of those who may be otherwise ignored, marginalized, or trivialized in media representations. Still, serious shortcomings have also come to the fore. The same visual practices facilitating empathetic spectatorship in response to a newsworthy crisis may simultaneously embolden visual regimes determined to legitimize extremist views or incite hatred against women or minority groups (Carter et al., 2019). Similarly, the playfulness long associated with Internet meme culture is open to the risk of reappropriation to troll, bully, or otherwise undermine others' personal rights to self-expression.

In striving to delve deeper into the sociopolitical significance of such transformative shifts, this chapter's evaluative survey of pertinent new media research has sought to move beyond familiar conceptions of 'citizen journalism,' in part by disentangling civic modes of seeing for closer analysis and critique. Using our formulation of the 'visual citizen' to guide our inquiry, we have attempted to illuminate the contingent, uneven – and politically fraught – nature of these transitional processes of visual connectivity, and also why the civic responsibilities they elucidate are so important. In this way, we have aimed to facilitate efforts to explore pressing questions regarding the visualities of journalistic collaboration and connectivity, and inclusion/ exclusion, within democratic cultures.

This chapter's discussion is intended as a strategic starting point for future investigations, not least as an encouragement for those seeking to attend to complexities frequently glossed over in broader assertions about the challenges facing journalism's continued viability. The uneven, inchoate ways in which visually centered forms of news reporting are evolving in a 'post-truth' environment, where 'alternative facts' abound, warrant urgent attention for news and journalism studies research (see also Allbeson & Allan, 2018). At a time when long-standing assumptions regarding journalism's presumed centrality to public life appear to be in danger of unraveling, laudable platitudes about media and civic empowerment risk seeming anachronistic within a digital networked ecology all but obscured in the swirl of 'fake news' rhetoric (Boczkowski & Papacharissi, 2018; Happer et al., 2018). Critical research, we suggest, must find new ways to assist efforts to secure deliberative spaces for dialogue and debate over the reinvigoration of journalism's reportorial commitments for tomorrow's participatory news cultures.

References

Ahva, L., and Hellman, M. (2015). Citizen Eyewitness Images and Audience Engagement in Crisis Coverage. *International Communication Gazette*, 77(7), 668–681.

Allan, S. (2013). *Citizen Witnessing: Revisioning Journalism in Times of Crisis*. Cambridge: Polity Press.

Allan, S. (2015). Visualising Human Rights: The Video Advocacy of Witness. In S. Cottle and G. Cooper (eds.), *Humanitarianism, Communications and Change*. New York: Peter Lang, pp. 197–210.

Allan, S. (ed) (2017). *Photojournalism and Citizen Journalism: Co-Operation, Collaboration and Connectivity*. London and New York: Routledge.

Allan, S., and Dencik, L. (2017). 'It's Not a Pretty Picture': Visualizing the Baltimore Crisis on Social Media. In L. Steiner and S. Waisbord (eds.), *News of Baltimore: Race, Rage and the City*. London and New York: Routledge, pp. 103–119.

Allan, S., and Peters, C. (2015). Visual Truths of Citizen Reportage: Four Research Problematics *Information, Communication & Society*, 11(3), 237–253.

Allan, S., and Peters, C. (2019). The Visual Citizen in a Digital News Landscape. *Communication Theory*. https://doi.org/10.1093/ct/qtz028.

Allbeson, T., and Allan, S. (2018). The War of Images in the Age of Trump. In C. Happer, A. Hoskins, and W. Merrin (eds.), *Trump's Media War*. London: Palgrave Macmillan, pp. 69–84.

Alper, M. (2014). War on Instagram: Framing Conflict Photojournalism with Mobile Photography Apps. *New Media & Society*, 16(8), 1233–1248.

Anderson, C. W. (2011). Blowing Up the Newsroom: Ethnography in the Age of Distributed Journalism. In D. Domingo and C. Paterson (eds.), *Making Online News*, Volume 2. New York: Peter Lang. pp. 151–160.

Atton, C. (ed.). (2015). *The Routledge Companion to Alternative and Community Media*. London: Routledge.

Bakir, V. (2010). *Sousveillance, Media and Strategic Political Communication*. London: Continuum.

Bakshy, E., Messing, S., and Adamic, L. A. (2015). Exposure to Ideologically Diverse News and Opinion on Facebook. *Science*, 348(6239), 1130–1132.

Bayerl, P. S., and Stoynov, L. (2016). Revenge by Photoshop: Memefying Police Acts in the Public Dialogue About Injustice. *New Media & Society*, 18(6), 1006–1026.

Bock, M. A. (2016). Film the Police! Cop-Watching and Its Embodied Narratives. *Journal of Communication*, 66(1), 12–34.

Boczkowski, P. J., and Papacharissi, Z. (eds.). (2018). *Trump and the Media*. Cambridge, MA: MIT Press.

Borges-Rey, E. (2015). News Images on Instagram: The Paradox of Authenticity in Hyperreal Photo Reportage. *Digital Journalism*, 3(4), 571–593.

Bowls, N. (2018). Welcome to the Post-Text Future: The Mainstreaming of Political Memes Online. *New York Times*, February 14.

boyd, d. (2014). *It's Complicated: The Social lives of Networked Teens*. New Haven: Yale University Press.

Brevini, B., Hintz, A., and McCurdy, P. (eds.). (2013). *Beyond WikiLeaks: Implications for the Future of Communications, Journalism and Society*. Basingstoke: Palgrave MacMillan.

Bro, P., Hansen, K. R., and Andersson, R. (2016). Improving Productivity in the Newsroom? Deskilling, Reskilling and Multiskilling in the News Media. *Journalism Practice*, 10(8), 1005–1018.

Caple, H. (2014). Anyone Can Take a Photo, but: Is There Space for the Professional Photographer in the Twenty-First Century Newsroom? *Digital Journalism*, 2(3), 355–365.

Carey, J. W. (2008). *Communication as Culture, Revised Edition: Essays on Media and Society*. London: Routledge.

Carlson, M., and Lewis, S. C. (eds.). (2015). *Boundaries of Journalism: Professionalism, Practices and Participation*. New York: Routledge.

Carter, C., Steiner, L., and Allan, S. (eds.). (2019). *Journalism, Gender and Power*. London and New York: Routledge.

Chouliaraki, L., and Stolic, T. (2017). Rethinking Media Responsibility in the Refugee 'Crisis': A Visual Typology of European News. *Media, Culture & Society*. doi:10.1177/0163443717726163.

Comor, E. (2001). Harold Innis and The Bias of Communication. *Information, Communication & Society*, 4(2), 274–294.

Cooper, S. D. (2006). *Watching the Watchdog: Bloggers as the Fifth Estate*. Spokane, WA: Marquette Books.

Costera Meijer, I., and Groot Kormelink, T. (2015). Checking, Sharing, Clicking and Linking: Changing Patterns of News Use Between 2004 and 2014. *Digital Journalism*, 3(5), 664–679.

Dencik, L., and Allan, S. (2017). In/visible Conflicts: NGOs and the Visual Politics of Humanitarian Photography. *Media, Culture & Society*, 39(8), 1178–1193.

Deuze, M., and Witschge, T. (2018). Beyond Journalism: Theorizing the Transformation of Journalism. *Journalism*, 19(2), 165–181.

Dutton, W. H. (2009). The Fifth Estate Emerging Through the Network of Networks. *Prometheus*, 27(1), 1–15.

The Economist. (2011). #Occupytheweb Democracy in America Blog. *The Economist*, 11 October.

Eppink, J. (2014). A Brief History of the GIF (so far). *Journal of Visual Culture*, 13(3), 298–306.

Fletcher, R., and Nielsen, R. K. (2017). Are News Audiences Increasingly Fragmented? A Cross-National Comparative Analysis of Cross-Platform News Audience Fragmentation and Duplication. *Journal of Communication*, 67(4), 476–498.

Gabriel, P. (2014). *Peter Gabriel RNR HOF Speech 4–10–14 Rock and Roll Hall of Fame*. Youtube, posted by D. Pastor, April 11. http://youtu.be/yZpTj9YT-IQ.

Gal, N., Shifman, L., and Kampf, Z. (2016). 'It Gets Better': Internet Memes and the Construction of Collective Identity. *New Media & Society*, 18(8), 1698–1714.

Graves, L. (2016). *Deciding What's True: The Rise of Political Fact-Checking in American Journalism*. New York: Columbia University Press.

Greenberg, J. (2002). Framing and Temporality in Political Cartoons: A Critical Analysis of Visual News Discourse. *Canadian Review of Sociology/Revue canadienne de sociologie*, 39(2), 181–198.

Greer, C., and McLaughlin, E. (2011). This Is Not Justice': Ian Tomlinson, Institutional Failure and the Press Politics of Outrage. *British Journal of Criminology*, 52(2), 274–293.

Gregory, S. (2015). Ubiquitous Witnesses: Who Creates the Evidence and the Live(d) Experience of Human Rights Violations? *Information, Communication & Society*, 18(11), 1378–1392.

Haddon, L. (2006). The Contribution of Domestication Research to in-Home Computing and Media Consumption. *The Information Society*, 22(4), 195–203.

Happer, C., Hoskins, A., and Merrin, W. (eds.). (2018). *Trump's Media War*. London: Palgrave Macmillan.

Highfield, T., and Leaver, T. (2016). Instagrammatics and Digital Methods: Studying Visual Social Media, From Selfies and GIFs to Memes and Emoji. *Communication Research and Practice*, 2(1), 47–62.

Hoffman, J. (2006). Sousveillance. *The New York Times*, December 10. www.nytimes.com/2006/12/10/magazine/10section3b.t-3.html.

Holehouse, M., and Millward, D. (2011). How Technology Fuelled Britain's First 21st Century Riot. *The Telegraph*, August 8.

Ibrahim, Y. (2014). Social Media and the Mumbai Terror Attack: The Coming of Age of Twitter. In E. Thorsen and S. Allan (eds.), *Citizen Journalism: Global Perspectives* (vol. 2). New York: Peter Lang, pp. 15–26.

Jenkins, H., Ford, S., and Green, J. (2013). *Spreadable Media: Creating Value and Meaning in a Networked Culture*. New York: New York University Press.

Kalter, L. (2011). Five Websites Where Citizen Journalists Are Documenting Riots in London. *International Journalists' Network, IJNet.org*, August 8. http://ijnet.org/blog/how-london-citizen-journalists-are-using-smart-phones-capture-riots.

Knobel, M., and Lankshear, C. (2007). Online Memes, Affinities, and Cultural Production. In M. Knobel and C. Lankshear (eds.), *A New Literacies Sampler*. New York: Peter Lang, pp. 199–227.

Kross, C. (2016). Memory, Guardianship and the Witnessing Amateur in the Emergence of Citizen Journalism. In M. Baker and B. B. Blaagaard (eds.), *Citizen Media and Public Spaces*. London and New York: Routledge, pp. 225–238.

Ksiazek, T. B., Peer, L., and Lessard, K. (2016). User Engagement with Online News: Conceptualizing Interactivity and Exploring the Relationship Between Online News Videos and User Comments. *New Media & Society*, 18(3), 502–520.

Larsson, A. O. (2017). The News User on Social Media: A Comparative Study of Interacting with Media Organizations on Facebook and Instagram. *Journalism Studies*, 1–18. doi:10.1080/1461670X.2017.1332957.

Larsson, A. O. (2018). Thumbs Up, Thumbs Down? Likes and Dislikes as Popularity Drivers of Political YouTube Videos. *First Monday*, 23(8).

Leavitt, A. (2014). From# FollowFriday to YOlO. In K. Weller et al. (eds.), *Twitter and Society*. New York: Peter Lang, pp. 137–154.

Livingstone, S. (2002). *Young People and New Media: Childhood and the Changing Media Environment*. Thousand Oaks: Sage.

Madrigal, A. (2012). Sorting the Real Sandy Photos from the Fakes. *The Atlantic*, October 29. www.theatlantic.com/technology/archive/2012/10/sorting-the-real-sandy-photos-from-the-fakes/264243/.

Mann, S. (2002). Sousveillance, Not Just Surveillance, in Response to Terrorism. *Metal and Flesh*, 6(1). http://wearcam.org/metalandflesh.htm.

Martini, M. (2018). Online Distant Witnessing and Live-Streaming Activism: Emerging Differences in the Activation of Networked Publics. *New Media & Society*. https://doi.org/10.1177/1461444818766703.

Massanari, A. (2017). # Gamergate and The Fappening: How Reddit's algorithm, governance, and Culture Support Toxic Technocultures. *New Media & Society*, 19(3), 329–346.

Messing, S., and Westwood, S. J. (2014). Selective Exposure in the Age of Social Media: Endorsements Trump Partisan Source Affiliation When Selecting News Online. *Communication Research*, 41(8), 1042–1063.

Meyrowitz, J. (1986). *No Sense of Place*. Oxford: Oxford University Press.

Milner, R. M. (2013a). Pop Polyvocality: Internet Memes, Public Participation, and the Occupy Wall Street movement. *International Journal of Communication*, 7, 2357–2390.

Milner, R. M. (2013b). FCJ-156 Hacking the Social: Internet Memes, Identity Antagonism, and the Logic of Lulz. *The Fibreculture Journal*, 22.

Miltner, K. (2014). 'There's No Place for Lulz on LOLCats': The Role of Genre, Gender, and Group Identity in the Interpretation and Enjoyment of an Internet Meme. *First Monday*, 19(8).

Mortensen, T. M. (2014). Blurry and Centered or Clear and Balanced? Citizen Photojournalists and Professional Photojournalists' Understanding of Each Other's Visual Values. *Journalism Practice* (ahead-of-print), 1–22.

Mortensen, M. (2015). *Journalism and Eyewitness Images*. London: Routledge.

Mortensen, M., Allan, S., and Peters, C. (2017). The Iconic Image in a Digital Age: Editorial Mediations Over the Alan Kurdi Photographs. *Nordicom Review*, 38(2), 71–86.

Nissenbaum, A., and Shifman, L. (2017). Internet Memes as Contested Cultural Capital: The Case of 4chan's/b/board. *New Media & Society*, 19(4), 483–501.

O'Carroll, L. (2011). London Riots: Photographers Targeted by Looters. *Guardian Unlimited*, August 9.

Newman, N. et al. (2018). *Reuters Institute Digital News Report 2018*. Oxford: Oxford University Press.

Pantti, M., and Sirén, S. (2015). The Fragility of Photo-Truth: Verification of Amateur Images in Finnish Newsrooms. *Digital Journalism*, 3(4), 495–512.

Pavlik, J. (2000). The Impact of Technology on Journalism. *Journalism Studies*, 1(2), 229–237.

Penney, J., and Dadas, C. (2014). (Re)Tweeting in the Service of Protest: Digital Composition and Circulation in the Occupy Wall Street Movement. *New Media & Society*, 16(1), 74–90.

Peters, C. (2012). Journalism to Go: The Changing Spaces of News Consumption. *Journalism Studies*, 13(5–6), 695–705.

Peters, C., and Witschge, T. (2015). From Grand Narratives of Democracy to Small Expectations of Participation: Audiences, Citizenship, and Interactive Tools in Digital Journalism. *Journalism Practice*, 9(1), 19–34.

Picard, R. G. (2014). Twilight or New Dawn of Journalism? Evidence from the Changing News Ecosystem. *Journalism Practice*, 8(5), 488–498.

Reading, A. (2009). Mobile Witnessing: Ethics and the Camera Phone in the 'War on Terror'. *Globalizations*, 6(1), 61–76.

Rentschler, C. (2009). From Danger to Trauma: Affective Labor and the Journalistic Discourse of Witnessing. In P. Frosh and A. Pinchevski (eds.), *Media Witnessing: Testimony in the age of Mass Communication*. Basingstoke: Palgrave Macmillan, pp. 158–181.

Ristovska, S. (2016). Strategic Witnessing in an Age of Video Activism. *Media, Culture & Society*, 38(7), 1034–1047.

Ritchin, F. (2013). *Bending the Frame: Photojournalism, Documentary, and the Citizen*. New York: Aperture.

Rodriguez, C. (2011). *Citizens' Media Against Armed Conflict*. Minneapolis: University of Minnesota Press.

Ross, A. S., and Rivers, D. J. (2017). Digital Cultures of Political Participation: Internet Memes and the Discursive Delegitimization of the 2016 US Presidential Candidates. *Discourse, Context & Media*, 16, 1–11.

Rosen, J. (2006). The People Formerly Known as the Audience. *Pressthink.org*, June 27. http://archive.pressthink.org/2006/06/27/ppl_frmr.html.

Sheller, M. (2015). News Now: Interface, Ambience, Flow, and the Disruptive Spatio-tempo- Realities of Mobile News Media, *Journalism Studies*, 16(1), 12–26.

Shifman, L. (2012). An Anatomy of a YouTube Meme. *New Media & Society*, 14(2), 187–203.

Shifman, L. (2014). *Memes in Digital Culture*. Cambridge, MA: MIT Press.

Silverman, J. (2015). Pics or It Didn't Happen – The Mantra of the Instagram Era. *Guardian*, February 26. www.theguardian.com/news/2015/feb/26/pics-or-it-didnt-happen-mantra-instagram-era-facebook-twitter.

Smit, R., Heinrich, A., and Broersma, M. (2015). Witnessing in the New Memory Ecology: Memory Construction of the Syrian Conflict on YouTube. *New Media & Society*, 19(2), 289–307.

Steiner, L., and Waisbord, S. (eds.). (2017). *News of Baltimore: Race, Rage and the City*. London and New York: Routledge.

Stephen, B. (2015). How Black Lives Matter Uses Social Media to Fight the Power. *WIRED*, November.

Swart, J., Peters, C., and Broersma, M. (2018). Shedding Light on the Dark Social: The Connective Role of News and Journalism in Social Media Communities. *New Media & Society*. doi:10.1177/1461444818772063.

Tait, S. (2011). Bearing Witness, Journalism and Moral Responsibility. *Media, Culture & Society*, 33(8), 1220–1235.

Tandoc Jr, E. C. (2015). Why Web Analytics Click: Factors Affecting the Ways Journalists Use Audience Metrics. *Journalism Studies*, 16(6), 782–799.

Usher, N. (2010). Goodbye to the News: How Out-of-Work Journalists Assess Enduring News Values and the New Media Landscape. *New Media & Society*, 12(6), 911–928.

Vis, F., Faulkner, S., Parry, K., Manyukhina, Y., and Evans, L. (2013). Twitpic-ing the Riots: Analysing Images Shared on Twitter During the 2011 UK Riots. In K. Weller et al. (eds.), *Twitter and Society*. New York: Peter Lang, pp. 385–398.

Waisbord, S. (2013). *Reinventing Professionalism*. Cambridge: Polity.

Wall, M., and El Zahed, S. (2015). Embedding Content from Syrian Citizen Journalists: The Rise of the Collaborative News Clip. *Journalism*, 6(2), 163–180.

Wardle, C., Dubberley, S., and Brown, P. (2014). *Amateur Footage: A Global Study of User-Generated Content in TV and Online News Output*. Tow Center for Digital Journalism. New York: Columbia University Press.

Westlund, O., and Färdigh, M. A. (2015). Accessing the News in an Age of Mobile Media: Tracing Displacing and Complementary Effects of Mobile News on Newspapers and Online News. *Mobile Media & Communication*, 3(1), 53–74.

Wheeler, T. H. (2005). *Phototruth or Photofiction?: Ethics and Media Imagery in the Digital Age*. London: Routledge.

Wiggins, B. E., and Bowers, G. B. (2015). Memes as Genre: A Structurational Analysis of the Memescape. *New Media & Society*, 17(11), 1886–1906.

Williams, A., Wardle, C., and Wahl-Jorgensen, K. (2011). Have They Got News for Us? Audience Revolution or Business as Usual at the BBC? *Journalism Practice*, 5(1), 85–99.

16

News curation, war, and conflict

Holly Steel

The role of the Internet in communicating war and conflict has been of increasing academic interest (see Cottle, 2006; Matheson & Allan, 2009; Hoskins & O'Loughlin, 2011; Chouliaraki, 2015). The proliferation of digital networked devices means that today conflicts are saturated with more information than ever before, and this information is transmitted through a wider variety of actors and groups; in other words, there is an increase in the chorus of voices vying to assert their account or narrative of events within the new media ecology.[1] There are those who are physically proximate to conflict (a direct eyewitness regardless of other roles that actor might occupy); those who are actors to the conflict (such as activists, rebels, soldiers, the state involved, who might be external to the event in question); those involved in formal global decisions (States, the UN, NGOs), experts and specialists, diaspora groups, religious organizations, news media; and, finally, local, national, and transnational audiences. Not only can these pieces of user-generated content (UGC) bear tangible witness to events, but they also travel through the media ecology as resources for distant witnessing for those outside the conflict zone (Torchin, 2012; Andén-Papadopoulos, 2014; Chouliaraki, 2015). This potential is heightened through the popularity of global social media platforms, such as Facebook, YouTube and Twitter, which have "further simplified access to publishing tools for ordinary citizens and subsequently increased visibility of demotic voices to both national and global audiences" (Thorsen, 2012, 296). The Internet offers new opportunities for those within the conflict to tell their own stories and has the potential to transform news coverage of conflict (see Beckett, 2008; Cottle, 2009; Chouliaraki, 2010; Allan, 2013; Mortensen, 2015). In this context, curation – whereby content is aggregated and organized from a variety of sources onto a single webpage – emerges as a key tool for news organizations covering events in real time. As Mark Little, cofounder of *Storyful*, argues, journalists need to "get used to being 'curators'; sorting news from the noise on the social web using smart new tools and good old-fashioned reporting skills" (Little, 2011). Curation offers new opportunities for the inclusion of a greater diversity of voices and experiences in news coverage.

This chapter will explore the practice of news curation in the context of coverage of the Syria conflict. First, in order to understand the emergence of curation in the newsroom, this chapter will define news curation as a set of distinctive web-oriented journalistic practices, which produce web-native news texts. Having outlined the emergence and development of news curation, the chapter will then examine the processes of curation by focusing on *The Guardian's* Middle East Live (MEL), a live blog that ran from 2011 to 2014. It will focus on providing a snapshot of how social media content was selected for covering the Syria conflict during this period and the challenges faced by journalists producing such texts. Finally, the chapter will raise critical questions that will need to be addressed in future research in order to understand the continued uses of curation in conflict coverage.

News curation

Curation can be understood as a digital practice whereby content from across the media ecology is aggregated and organized onto a single page. This includes UGC, produced by professional and nonprofessional users, and mainstream media content. Broadly speaking, curation as an online practice can be done by anyone with the relevant access and skills and can be seen in a variety of forms and scales (Zuckerman, 2010). On social media sites such as Facebook, for example, users purposively select content, such as news articles and GIFs, to share as part of a story about themselves and their interests. This chapter will focus on curation on a larger scale, outlining how these processes are enacted within the institutional space of the newsroom. Events are increasingly being communicated from streets to screens around the world, and the practice of curation is one way of navigating the increasingly fragmented and complex media ecology in which they operate, where content can emerge at any moment, from a variety of actors with differing agendas and perspectives (Hoskins & O'Loughlin, 2011). This section will firstly address the different ways in which the role of UGC in the newsroom has been theorized, before focusing on the uses of curation to cover conflict.

Curation is not a completely new practice; instead, it can be considered to be one of the most recent uses of UGC integration within the news (see Matheson, 2004; Beckett, 2008; Hermida & Thurman, 2008; Thorsen, 2013). The processes I am describing as 'curation' have been explained in relation to both 'networked' (Jarvis, 2006; Beckett, 2008) and 'convergent' journalism (Chouliaraki, 2014). In order to situate curation as a distinct theoretical concept, a brief outline of these overlapping concepts is necessary. Firstly, Jarvis contends that networked journalism

> takes into account the collaborative nature of journalism now: professionals and amateurs working together to get the real story, linking to each other across brands and old boundaries to share facts, questions, answers, ideas, perspectives. It recognizes the complex relationships that will make news. And it focuses on the process more than the product.
>
> *(Jarvis, 2006)*

In this iteration, the emphasis is on the networked potential offered by the Internet, which discursively constructs the public as having more input into the news process, who are able to collaborate in order to cover those events that are relevant to them. Crucially, it presents the boundaries between the 'old' and 'new' media as increasingly porous. Networked journalism allows journalists to work across these traditional boundaries to produce content that is up-to-date and relevant to web-savvy audiences (Beckett, 2008). Convergent journalism is similar and places the focus upon convergence as "both a top-down corporate-driven process and a bottom-up consumer-driven process" (Jenkins & Deuze, 2008, 6). In its journalistic form, this results in a "fundamental re-articulation of [news] performativity from the primacy of acts of information to the primacy of acts of deliberation and witnessing," challenging the primacy of journalism through the integration of a wider range of 'ordinary' voices (Chouliaraki, 2013b, 268).

Both networked and convergent journalism explore the relationship between the journalist and the rapidly changing media ecology and use 'curation' as a term within their accounts. However, I argue that curation should be considered as a distinct concept in itself, which builds upon these theories of 'networked' and 'convergent' journalism. Both 'networked' and 'convergent' evoke particular elements of the practice, including the environment with which the information emerges, and the bringing together of different actors within the informational environment. However, I argue that 'curation' is more appropriate in this context as it highlights the informational hierarchies that are enacted through curatorial practices, which reflect existing relationships in terms of both geo-politics and journalistic practice. Crucially, the term 'curation' indicates the relationship between the journalist and the wider media ecology; there is a journalist bringing the pieces of content together, drawing on established journalistic practices, on an institutional platform. As Davis contends, curatorial decisions "are selections of ourselves, selections of others, and selections of the social world" (Davis, 2017, 771). The final curated text will be informed by many sources – each emerging in different ways, with different effects – but it is the journalist curator who will have the final say on what makes it into the text.

This conception of digital curation "metaphorically draws on, but is not equivalent to, the more precise term" (Monroy-Hernández et al., 2013). Curation is a practice most commonly associated with museums, whereby artifacts are selected, brought together, and arranged in order to create displays and narratives about a particular topic. Beckett describes this as being an "unhappy connotation," which he argues does not reflect the "very active, topical act" (2012, 23). Evoking museums as a way of understanding the process of digital curation is helpful in indicating the organizing and narrative principles in play. The commonality between curation and journalism is that they both entail forms of storytelling. Social media curation is about sharing stories through the arrangement of digital artifacts into a coherent narrative; this coherence may be functional, for example, providing updates on an event as it occurs in real time, or it may be about creating a unified story of the event. It shows us that while the technology might be new, the act is embedded in existing practices and ideologies. It also means that the power relationship between the journalist curator and the sources is more transparent in this description. It is important to note that the label 'curator' should not detract from the fact that those undertaking these practices are journalists first and foremost; crucially, the focus on curation marks the *forms of journalistic labor* undertaken in aggregating and contextualizing content, as opposed to reporting directly from the field. What makes curation distinctive is that it relies on the social media ecology for data, be it eyewitness accounts or official responses, in a seemingly more transparent text. Pieces of content are not necessarily directly prompted by the journalists, as in the 'woman on the street' style interview, but rather emerge independently of the newsroom.

In terms of conflict coverage, the proliferation of UGC from the ground raises several challenges for contemporary journalism. In particular, news organizations need to develop tools to help them manage the deluge of information appearing online, while also maintaining their position as a primary intermediary for audiences seeking news content (Beckett, 2008). This role is challenged by the prevalence of social media. Want to know what's happening at a protest? Login to Twitter and follow the activists directly. However, just because there is more information being produced doesn't mean that it is easier to discern what is happening on the ground. It is in this context, Beckett (2012) argues that we need *more* journalism rather than less. Curation as a practice allows journalists to be attentive to social media content emerging from the conflict zone, which can be included in the coverage, while also adding contextualization for their audience. In particular, social media will be curated with additional information about the veracity of the piece – for example, 'this video has been verified' – which lets readers know the perceived trustworthiness of that piece of media in terms of existing journalistic epistemologies

(Matheson, 2004). Curators may also provide translation services, bridging potential language barriers between those producing the content and the organization's audience.[2] These practices – both verification and translation – might be carried out collaboratively with other actors in the field but will appear in the institutional setting of the newspaper website. This highlights the multiple forms of labor the journalist curator must undertake in order to produce curated coverage of events (Guerrini, 2013).

News curation requires journalists to occupy multiple roles in the news process. Guerrini argues that curation reveals how it "is now (theoretically) possible for one person – usually but not necessarily, an editor – to cover all the roles before performed by different professionals" (2013, 8). The journalist curator may edit, verify, and produce coverage in real time as part of their newsgathering and coverage. The primary focal point for the journalist curator is to actively engage with multiple forms of media – including the mainstream and social media – to identify the most relevant content to drive the coverage of that event, and to provide context for that content. This is akin to what Bruns (2005) has termed 'gatewatching,' whereby the journalist follows and observes content published on multiple platforms and media channels. In this sense, journalist curators are not necessarily specialists in the subject being covered, but rather *they specialize in the medium*. Curators in the context of this chapter, therefore, are experts at negotiating social media within the framework of existing journalistic norms. I argue that curation is a unique form of labor that is distinct from other traditional journalistic practices in three key ways: first, the journalist occupies multiple roles as a curator; second, the journalist does not always contribute substantive new journalistic content to the coverage; and, third, journalistic specialism is often focused on the medium rather than the subject matter. These distinctions may vary between and within institutions but are important markers for understanding curation as a practice in the newsroom.

Finally, it is important to address the form that curation takes. These texts can take a number of different forms, and what distinguishes curated news texts from an online news article is that they are inherently *of* the Internet, rather than simply *on* the Internet (Rosen, 2001 quoted in Matheson, 2004), with videos, images, and audio embedded and hyperlinked within the body of the text, which can be continuously updated and added to throughout the required period of time (Thurman & Walters, 2013; Thorsen, 2013; Thurman & Rodgers, 2014). One of the central features of curation, therefore, is the *visible* and/or *transparent* use of web-native media content, in particular social media. Curation as a practice produces a variety of texts dependent upon the aims of the organization, the rationale for curation, and the types of media produced by an event. In the context of this chapter, curated texts take the form of blog-style pages, organized around the logic of the timeline or the narrative of the event, and they are used in order to cover events in real-time.

We will now focus on one of the most prominent forms in news coverage, the live blog, whereby news is navigated through a timeline of events. Live blogs can be defined as "a contextualised, rolling aggregation of spoken and written dispatches" from different actors around the world (Manhire, 2012, xv). The format places emphasis on "the direct relaying of commentary and analysis as events are unfolding, rather than a written-through narrative constructed after the event" (Thurman & Walters, 2013, 83). Content is aggregated and curated onto a single page from a wide selection of sources, including, but not limited to, traditional journalism, press releases, and UGC. This has consequences for the ways in which the story is covered, producing fragmented news narratives, where multiple stories may be covered within the same text. Like hypertexts, live blogs can be characterized as "in flux, impermanent, and designed to change" (Huesca & Dervin, 1999), which is a key strength that makes them adaptable to fast-paced events (Beckett, 2008).

Curating coverage of the Syria conflict

In order to illustrate the practices of news curation, we will look at a case study that focuses on curatorial practices. In 2013, I interviewed two journalists working on *The Guardian's* MEL blog about social media curation in the context of the Syria conflict. This section provides a snapshot of the role social media plays in the newsgathering process.

During the Syrian uprising, social media became "just another front in the conflict" (Harkin et al., 2012, 7; see also Wardle et al., 2014; Lynch et al., 2014), with thousands of videos and accounts uploaded on to the Internet every day. Syria provides an example of a conflict zone that was closed off, with limitations on the ability for journalists to fully report on events from the ground. Information channels were tightly controlled, with high levels of state control and a 'hybrid' private media established by President Assad (Harkin et al., 2012, 3). Journalists within the country faced high risks if they chose to defy the state narrative, including imprisonment and possible death. With the increased crackdown, and other pressures of conflict, an underground media formed which relied on the Internet to disseminate their work (ibid). Eyewitnesses and activists, of all affiliations, used social media sites such as Facebook, Twitter and YouTube to share eyewitness accounts and to try and gain global attention and action on the conflict. As such, the international community has predominantly watched the "conflict unfold via the lens of social media" (Varghese, 2013). These changes to the media ecology, whereby eyewitnesses, activists, and armed groups are now able to produce and disseminate their own accounts, have implications for news organizations who have traditionally acted as gatekeepers in reporting conflict. As discussed previously, news organizations have adapted to these changes through the practice of curation, integrating UGC from the ground, which has the potential to include more diverse voices and experiences from the zone of conflict (Ashuri & Pinchevski, 2011; Allan, 2013; Chouliaraki, 2013a). Given these factors – the limited number of journalists on the ground and the reliance upon accounts circulating on social media – Syria is a significant case study for examining news curation in the context of conflict coverage.

In 2011 *The Guardian* started the live blog MEL, which was a series focused on the Middle Eastern and North African region, and emerged during the so-called Arab Spring as a way of covering the protests and violence in real-time drawing upon social media coming from the ground (see Manhire, 2012). As a text it is structured around the logic of the timeline, with entries appearing in chronological order throughout the day. An entry might include an update from the wires or other news media, an article from the organization, interviews with relevant actors, and pieces of media both 'traditional' and those characterized as UGC. MEL was launched daily with a summary of events occurring within the region, which was developed through reference to the RSS feed of the journalist managing the blog; this is a web-based feed of updates from selected organizations, journalists, state departments, bloggers, and so forth (Interview 1, *The Guardian*). The headline for the piece would be based upon the key points of this summary but was open to change throughout the course of the day should an event occur that requires more specific focus on the coverage. The job of the curator was then to balance the coverage in line with events as they occur, while maintaining a narrative to the text. While UGC allows journalists to access conflict zones from a distance in new ways (Interview 2, *The Guardian*), as MEL covers a large geographical region, maintaining a news narrative requires a high level of data management. As one journalist noted:

> It's particularly difficult if there's lots of things to keep an eye on. If there's something kicking off in Bahrain at the same time as something in Syria and something in Libya, it just becomes really hard to keep on top of. I sort of think of it in my mind as someone spinning

plates, and you've got to keep on wobbling the stalks to keep the thing going, keep the thing present in people's minds, otherwise the narrative sort of disappears.

(Interview 1, The Guardian)

The spinning plates metaphor is apt for describing the variety of journalistic labor undertaken, as the journalist works to aggregate a diversity of material from a large geographic area onto the curated page, while maintaining the overall narrative for the reader and working within the bounds of institutional norms. This quote highlights the sheer amount of information that must be negotiated by the curator – emerging through traditional mainstream media sources and social media – which is negotiated through multiple strategies. This includes identifying a narrow range of sources to follow in relation to the event, which involved curating small-scale lists of Twitter users that were relevant to the coverage, and following relevant activist groups across social media sites. For example, the journalist quoted previously had a list on Twitter of activist accounts and journalists who regularly tweeted from Syria in English and followed groups such as the Local Coordinating Committee of Syria and the Syrian Observatory of Human Rights on Facebook. These strategies were particularly important in the context of the MEL as the journalists had limited resources to identify and verify UGC, and it allowed the journalists to manage the deluge of information by tapping into specialist networks to identify relevant content.

A key issue that shaped curatorial practices in this context was that UGC from Syria was largely in Arabic. Neither of the journalists interviewed were able to speak Arabic, and language barriers, therefore, shaped how the journalist was able to access the conflict zone through social media:

[Twitter is an] unsatisfactory way of doing it because I didn't speak Arabic. I don't speak Arabic. So, by definition, it is a very self-selected bunch of people. It is people who are tweeting about Syria who can speak English, which I was conscious of and uncomfortable at times, that this is a warped sample of people.

(Interview 1, The Guardian)

So on YouTube they had an Arabic title but they would say where it was in English and so that wouldn't be a problem. The dialogue ones would be more, I don't know, when it's people speaking to each other or someone supposedly being interrogated, then if you just put up a video it probably wouldn't make much sense without having a translation. In which case we probably wouldn't put it up unless [an Arabic-speaking colleague] was able to help.

(Interview 2, The Guardian)

This difficulty in accessing Arabic-language content online fed into wider issues of trust about the information being presented to them; the use of English was seen to be targeted at journalists, and this was cause for suspicion. The journalists felt discomfort in having to rely upon English-language media as there was an acknowledgment that it limited the information that could be drawn upon to curate coverage. Here the targeted use of English to direct communication toward the journalist was perceived to manipulate the narrative of events in favor of a pro-democracy narrative. These English-language narratives were perceived to be 'drowning out' other perspectives and obscuring the complexity of the conflict; in particular, the role of Islamic extremism in the anti-government movement (Interview 1, *The Guardian*). These actors were seen to be providing English-language stories for English-speaking Western audiences.

However, while there was discomfort in acknowledging the reliance upon these accounts, English-language witnesses, activists, and commentators were essential for maintaining the live blog. Where translation was necessary, as indicated in the earlier quotes, additional support was sought from colleagues working in other departments or translation software.

Once the live blog has been launched for the day, the journalist in charge needed to ensure there was a mix of media included in the feed, which was verified and newsworthy. First, in terms of verification, journalists had limited resources and were unable to extensively verify all the UGC relevant to the event. This was negotiated by including content that was verified by other trusted organizations, such as *Storyful*, and by using discursive strategies when embedding UGC that had not been verified. This includes statements such as 'video purports to show' and 'we cannot verify' (Interview 2, *The Guardian*). Through these practices, the journalist transparently shows the audience both what is known and what is not known.

Second, the journalist seeks to include content that is newsworthy. The journalists interviewed noted that this could be challenging in relation to the some of the content emerging from Syria. The format of curated texts demands that the conflict be seen through, in part, the integration of UGC, whereas notions of newsworthiness shape what is thought to be relevant to the coverage. The live-blog format, more specifically, is focused on moving the story forward, and there are issues here about how to report a story where the coverage is perceived to be similar on a day-to-day basis. This idea of what constitutes 'newsworthy' UGC is shaped by the sheer amount of UGC emerging from Syria: acts of violence, including extensive bombing campaigns, occur every day across the region, and many of them are filmed and shared online. Violence alone is not newsworthy, and when conflict is mediated to such an extent, the journalists interviewed noted that acts of violence lose impact in terms of mainstream coverage (see also Wardle et al., 2014). In part this is due to the fact that the content often does not fit within the Western media's preexisting narratives – an event-driven model of coverage – for covering warfare. For example, footage of bombings during a period of conflict do not necessarily progress the news narrative. This is coupled with news-cycle fatigue, whereby the footage must increasingly reveal something new to the audience:

> It's so difficult because by the very nature of a live blog you are kind of expected to post a certain number of things. . . . I think Syria is a good example because you try to post something and by the end of it you very much want to post something else that wasn't just in the normal course of things. For example, there were videos every day saying 'shelling in Damascus', so in itself that required input and generally you're trying to find stories that are a bit more human where there's a bit more information rather than just a video of smoke. Or things that you think are significant in the context of the conflict, so diplomatic [issues]. So it's kind of, almost, stuff that does move the story on.
>
> *(Interview 2, The Guardian)*

> The point about a live-blog, it's great for a story that has lots of elements, that has lots of multi-media bits to it, and that has a narrative – there's that narrative drive to it. But you wouldn't choose to write one or read one if that element is not there. There isn't that sort of thirst for breaking news in quite the same way.
>
> *(Interview 1, The Guardian)*

The tension between these two curatorial demands of newsworthiness and UGC integration, therefore, means that journalists may seek out social media content that does not necessarily move the coverage of the event forward but rather indicates the wider violence in the region and adds 'color' to the feed (Interview 2, *The Guardian*). In addition to this, journalists also needed to ensure that graphic and violent content was re-mediated in line with notions of taste and decency. For example, during the August 21, 2013, chemical attack in East Ghouta, while footage of the aftermath of the event was newsworthy it was deemed to be too graphic for the audience. The journalists, therefore, decided to provide a written description of the videos instead, which included links to the relevant footage.

The discussion so far has highlighted the strategies used in terms of both curatorial practices for negotiating the media ecology and making decisions about which UGC to include in the coverage. It is important to note that at the time of the interviews the journalists stated that the newsworthiness of the conflict had declined over time, and this was a significant factor in the decline of the MEL series. This was linked to the shift away from the democratic Arab Spring narrative, as those original protests developed into a fragmented and widespread armed conflict. The journalist describes the decline as follows:

> I think the decision, I'm not sure quite why we decided to switch it . . . but the story had become very stale and repetitive. In a sense, it was no longer news that people were dying in their thousands in Syria, unfortunately. And the sense of momentum and that something was about to happen, something immense was about to happen, disappeared too. You know, for quite a long time it appeared that Assad was on the verge of being toppled. Slowly, we and the rest of the Western media cottoned on to the fact that that was not going to happen any time soon and as a result, the whole imperative of the blog disappeared, the urgency of it, and the readership had dropped off too I think.
>
> *(Interview 1, The Guardian)*

With prolonged conflicts the demands of the story change. When the Syria conflict was relatively new and shaped by the Arab Spring narrative, the fall-out into armed conflict was the story; as this journalist noted, there was a sense of momentum toward an ending, and a democratic narrative of revolution ending in the toppling of Assad. However, this narrative is simplistic and does not reflect the conflict, which includes fragmented groups fighting for different ends, some of whom are affiliated with Islamic extremism, and where human rights violations have been documented on all sides. Concerns relating to this shaped the curatorial strategies in approaching social media, where those producing content were viewed from a position of doubt. In other words, without the resources to translate and verify the content themselves, the journalists often included content with a caveat that the video or image had not been verified. This framing, I argue, protects the news organization in line with existing policies regarding objectivity but marginalizes the voices of activists and eyewitnesses whose media is included.

Conclusion

Drawing upon a case study of *The Guardian*'s MEL, this chapter has highlighted some of the key opportunities and challenges afforded by social media in covering conflict. The curator journalist is, I argue, best understood as a hub within a network, bringing together different knowledge(s) to produce a coherent text. In the context of Syria, curation allows opportunities for the voices of those on the ground to be directly included in the coverage. However, the sheer amount of content being posted online and the limited resources available to the journalist meant that there were limitations to this claim. Curation in the newsroom is ultimately informed by wider journalistic norms and practices which shape the strategies employed for negotiating the media ecology and selecting materials to include in the coverage. Overall, therefore, I argue that we must be cautious in celebrating the potential of UGC produced by those on the ground in shaping the coverage of events.

The use of curation must also be considered alongside the trajectory of the news agenda. The interviews occurred during 2013, when the MEL was producing less live coverage, which was focused on more high-profile events; it stopped producing new live-blog coverage of the region in 2014. While *The Guardian* does continue to use live blogs, I argue that it is used more selectively to cover high-profile news events (e.g., a terrorist attack, an election result), rather than sustained coverage of an ongoing issue (e.g., conflict and humanitarian crises). The 'Arab Spring' represented a moment where social media was seen as having the potential for news organizations to cover events in new and innovative ways. This idea was challenged by the perceived failure of those movements to create democratic change in the region and the development of long-term conflict and civil war.

The presence of social media content produced by those on the ground, therefore, does not necessarily change the hegemonic news narrative. I argue that while UGC is *disruptive*, curation has become an institutional tool for managing that disruption. Once established as a form, the curated text can be used to 'tame' any event where social media is a prominent part of the mediation. The curated text, or live blog, has become a marker of the significance of an event – 'this is happening now, watch it unfold live.' Ultimately, curation has become an institutional tool to manage the flow of data.

Notes

1 I am using the term media ecology to refer to the media environment(s) within which content is produced, circulated and curated. In particular, today's media ecology is characterized by pervasive networked digital technologies and a wider range of actors contributing content to the global media flows around crisis events. These changes have shaped the ways in which mainstream media organizations produce and audiences consume media content.
2 In the context of this chapter, we will be discussing the appearance of Arabic media in English-language news coverage.

Bibliography

Allan, S. (2013). *Citizen Witnessing: Revisioning Journalism in Times of Crisis*. Cambridge: Polity Press.
Andén-Papadopoulos, K. (2014). Citizen Camera-Witnessing: Embodied Political Dissent in the Age of 'Mediated Mass Self-Communication'. *New Media and Society*, 16(5), 753–769.
Ashuri, T., and Pinchevski, A. (2011). Witnessing as a Field. In P. Frosh and A. Pinchevski (eds.), *Media Witnessing: Testimony in the Age of Mass Communication*. Basingstoke: Palgrave Macmillan.
Beckett, C. (2008). *SuperMedia: Saving Journalism so It Can Save the World*. London: Blackwell Publishing.
Beckett, C. (2012). Communicating for Change: Media and Agency in the Networked Public Sphere. In *Polis*. London: London School of Economics.
Bruns, A. (2005). *Gatewatching: Collaborative Online News Production*. New York: Peter Lang.
Chouliaraki, L. (2010). Ordinary Witnessing in Post-Television News: Towards a New Moral Imagination. *Critical Discourse Studies*, 7(4), 305–319.
Chouliaraki, L. (2013a) *The Ironic Spectator: Solidarity in the Age of Post-Humanitarianism*. Cambridge: Polity Press.
Chouliaraki, L. (2013b). Re-Mediation, Inter-Mediation, Trans-Mediation: The Cosmopolitan Trajectories of Convergent Journalism. *Journalism Studies*, 14(2), 267–283.
Chouliaraki, L. (2014). 'I Have a Voice': The Cosmopolitan Ambivalence of Convergent Journalism. In E. Thorsen and S. Allan (eds.), *Citizen Journalism: Global Perspectives* (vol. 2). New York: Peter Lang, pp. 51–66.
Chouliaraki, L. (2015). Digital Witnessing in Conflict Zones: The Politics of Remediation. *Information, Communication & Society*, 18(11), 1362–1377.

Cottle, S. (2006). *Mediatized Conflict*. Maidenhead: Open University Press.

Cottle, S. (2009). *Global Crisis Reporting: Journalism in the Global Age*. Maidenhead: Open University Press.

Davis, J. (2017). Curation: A Theoretical Treatment. *Information, Communication & Society*, 20(5), 770–783.

Guerrini, F. (2013). *Newsroom Curators and Independent Storytellers: Content Curation as a New Form of Journalism*. Reuters Institute Fellowship Paper. Oxford: Reuters Institute for the Study of Journalism.

Harkin, J., Anderson, K., Morgan, L., and Smith, B. (2012). *Deciphering UGC in Transitional Societies: A Syria Coverage Case Study*. Washington, DC: Internews Center for Innovation and Learning.

Hermida, A., and Thurman, N. (2008). A Clash of Cultures. *Journalism Practice*, 2(3), 343–356.

Hoskins, A., and O'Loughlin, B. (2011). *War and Media: The Emergence of Diffused War*. Cambridge: Polity Press.

Huesca, R., and Dervin, B. (1999). Hypertext and Journalism: Audiences Respond to Competing News Narratives. In *Media in Transition*. Cambridge, MA: MIT Press.

Jarvis, J. (2006). Networked Journalism. *BuzzMachine*. http://buzzmachine.com/2006/07/05/networked-journalism/(Accessed April 10, 2019).

Jenkins, H., and Deuze, M. (2008). Convergence Culture. *Convergence: The International Journal of Research into New Media Technologies*, 14(1), 5–12.

Little, M. (2011). The Human Algorithm. *Storyful*, May 20. http://blog.storyful.com/2011/05/20/the-human-algorithm-2/-.UtPbBXmYgds (Accessed January 13, 2014).

Lynch, M., Freelon, D., and Aday, S. (2014). *Syria's Socially Mediated Civil War*. Blogs to Bullets. Washington, DC: United States Institute for Peace.

Manhire, T. (2012). *The Arab Spring: Rebellion, Revolution and a New World Order*. London: Guardian Books.

Matheson, D. (2004). Weblogs and the Epistemology of the News: Some Trends In Online Journalism. *New Media and Society*, 6(4), 443–468.

Matheson, D., and Allan, S. (2009). *Digital War Reporting*. Cambridge: Polity Press.

Monroy-Hernández, A., boyd, d., Kiciman, E., De Choudhury, M., and Counts, S. (2013). *The New War Correspondents: The Rise of Civic Media Curation in Urban Warfare*, Computer Supported Cooperative Work, CSCW '13, Austin, TX.

Mortensen, M. (2015). *Journalism and Eyewitness Images: Digital Media, Participation and Conflict*. New York: Routledge.

Thorsen, E. (2012). Introduction: Online Reporting of Elections. *Journalism Practice*, 6(3), 292–301.

Thorsen, E. (2013). Live Blogging and Social Media Curation: Challenges and Opportunities for Journalism. In K. Fowler-Watt and S. Allan (eds.), *Journalism: New Challenges*. Bournmouth: Centre for Journalism and Communication Research.

Thurman, N., and Rodgers, J. (2014). Citizen Journalism in Real Time? Live Blogging and Crisis Events. In S. Allan and E. Thorsen (eds.), *Citizen Journalism: Global Perspectives* (vol. 2). New York: Peter Lang, pp. 81–95.

Thurman, N., and Walters, A. (2013). Live Blogging – Digital Journalism's Pivotal Platform? *Digital Journalism*, 1(1), 82–101.

Torchin, L. (2012). *Creating the Witness: Documenting Genocide on Film, Video and the Internet*. Minneapolis: University of Minnesota Press.

Varghese, A. (2013). *Social Media Reporting and the Syrian Civil War*. Washington, DC: USIP.

Wardle, C., Dubberley, S., and Brown, P. (2014). *Amateur Footage: A Global Study of User-Generated Content in TV and Online News Output*. Tow Center for Digital Journalism. A Tow/Knight Report. http://towcenter.org/research/amateur-footagea-global-study-of-user-generated-content/.

Zuckerman, E. (2010). Listening to Global Voices. *TED Global*, July. www.ted.com/talks/ethan_zuckerman?language=en (Accessed April 10, 2019).

17

Information, technology, and work
Proletarianism, precarity, piecework

Leah A. Lievrouw and Brittany Paris

The publication of Fritz Machlup's *The Production and Distribution of Knowledge in the United States* (1962), a novel exploration of the role of knowledge in the postwar American economy, marked a turning point in analyses of economic activity and employment. He demonstrated that the most knowledge-intensive sectors in the economy (he counted education, research and development, publishing and other media production, telecommunications, 'conventions,' information machines, professional services, and government) had contributed a surprisingly large and growing amount to the gross national product in the 1950s and employed a correspondingly growing and productive contingent of highly educated, professionalized, white-collar 'knowledge workers.' Knowledge production, he suggested, was poised to rival or even overtake the economic power of industrial manufacturing.

Machlup's findings laid the groundwork for myriad studies of so-called white-collar employment and occupations, especially in developed, affluent societies (e.g., Dizard, 1982; Jonscher, 1983; Nora & Minc, 1980[1978]; Porat & Rubin, 1977; Schement et al., 1983; Schement & Lievrouw, 1984). His work also preceded the elaboration of social theories and policy studies of 'post-industrial society,' the 'information age,' 'network society,' and 'knowledge society,' among other formulations, in the United States and other developed nations, especially their potential to supersede 19th- and 20th-century industrialism (e.g., Bell, 1973; Castells, 1996, 2000; Stehr, 1994; Touraine, 1971[1969]). Meanwhile, social and cultural critics debated the existence, cultural influence, and political power of an ascendant 'new class' of educated professionals and managers (Bruce-Briggs, 1979; Gouldner, 1979; Horowitz, 1979; Wuthnow & Shrum, 1983).

Well into the 21st century, it seems evident that information/knowledge work and the technological systems that support it have indeed become defining features of society and culture in many societies around the globe. It is cast as the pivotal segment of the workforce in most wealthy societies. Economists, politicians, educators, and cultural leaders take as given the necessity of communication skills, facility with information technology, advanced degrees, and professional training (especially in all-important STEM fields – science, technology, engineering, and mathematics) as essential qualifications for economic participation and success in knowledge-driven economies – although some critics argue that this narrow focus diminishes the definition of what constitutes 'education' (Hacker, 2015).

Yet in the decades since Machlup's book and other analyses appeared, a paradox has emerged: information/knowledge work and occupations – the presumed paths to success in a rapidly globalizing, communicating world – have become increasingly piecemeal, part-time, and precarious, with worrying consequences for workers' prosperity and upward mobility.[1] As Manuel Castells has recognized, *"the traditional form of work, based on full-time employment, clear-cut occupational assignments, and a career pattern over the lifecycle is being slowly but surely eroded away"* (1996, 268; emphasis in the original). Or, as Ulrich Beck has put it, "More and more individuals are encouraged to perform as a 'Me & Co.,' selling themselves on the marketplace" (Beck, 2000, 3). Many members of the white-collar workforce can no longer expect stable, progressively advancing careers in the fields or occupations they choose. Instead, they face a lifetime of temporary or on-call employment, freelancing and 'consulting,' repeated moves from job to job and industry to industry, flat or declining wages, reduced or nonexistent employment benefits (health care, pensions, paid holidays), and multiple rounds of redundancy and retraining – an endless future of 'lifelong learning' at their own expense (Economist, 2017a). In an interesting inversion of what Castells (1996) characterized as a bifurcation between the 'core' professional, informational, 'self-programming' labor force and the 'generic,' disposable, service workforce, some are responding to growing precarity by leaving the ranks of white-collar work entirely in favor of skilled craft, personal service, and 'maker' occupations (Ocejo, 2017).

The spread of automation in white-collar and professional occupations and workplaces that were formerly thought to be immune to industrial-style rationalization explains some of these changes – for example, as the production of documents and media content has been converted into digital piecework. But the speed with which technology has been applied to impose a rationalized, fragmented, 'crowd-sourced' model suggests a more fundamental shift in the logic and organization of information- or knowledge-based work, from creative or expert professional practice to extractive enterprise. To use a bleaker metaphor, growing precarity "threatens to turn millions of people into casual workers who eat only what they can kill" (Economist, 2017b, 52).

The present chapter surveys this 60-year arc of the ways that information/knowledge work has been understood and theorized, from prized, powerful new class to the most highly educated faction of the 'precariat' in today's casual, 'gig' economy (Frassanito Network, 2006; Standing, 2011).[2]

As suggested earlier, several prominent social theorists have taken different perspectives on these changes, and we highlight several examples in the following discussion. Notably, beginning with his analyses of the events of May 1968 in France and his original theorization of new social movements, Alain Touraine has argued that individual and collective *actors*, not abstract social forces, functions, systems, structures, power, or classes, are the true agents of social change; they participate in, and contest control over, shifts in the totality of society's patterns of knowledge production and culture. In what he was the first to call *post-industrial* or *programmed* societies (Touraine came to prefer the latter term), he asserted that such shifts directly implicate the nature of work, and of information infrastructures, technology, and media as the means of production. Crucially, he argued that the nature of work itself and of knowledge production were becoming the central sites of social and political contestation, struggle, and change in advanced post-war societies (Touraine, 1971[1969], 1977[1973]).

We begin with an overview of how information/knowledge work has been measured, theorized, and understood since that earlier period.[3] We propose a basic conceptual framing for these changes adapted from Touraine's theorization and conclude with a discussion of journalism as an archetypal example of modern knowledge work whose conditions, technologies, practices, and status have reflected the contestation over knowledge production and culture.

Information/knowledge work over time

Definitions and measurement

Historically, the terms information work and knowledge work emerged as distinct occupational and analytic categories alongside changes in economic activity and employment in developed nations after World War II. In affluent societies, declining employment in the extractive industries (agriculture, mining, fishing/hunting, timber, etc.), and to a lesser extent in manufacturing, in parallel with rising employment among professional and white-collar occupations, were viewed by many as "the most striking changes to have taken place in the economy over the course of this century" (Jonscher, 1983, 14). The conventional three-sector analytic scheme (extractive, manufacturing, services) was originally developed as a way to characterize 20th-century industrial economies, particularly the shift from agriculture and other commodity production toward goods manufacturing as the principal source of economic activity and wealth (Clark, 1940). By the 1940s US manufacturing employment had eclipsed that in the extractive sector, due in part to after effects of the Depression (which had driven many farmers off the land and sparked waves of migration and urbanization in search of wage work), and the increased productivity gained by applying industrial-style production methods and machinery to commodity production for the war effort (Castells, 1996; Jonscher, 1983; Porat & Rubin, 1977). Twenty years later, analysts like Machlup, Daniel Bell (1973), Eli Ginzberg (Ginzberg & Vojta, 1981), Marc Porat, Simon Nora and Alain Minc, and Peter Drucker (1969) would observe new patterns of growth in the services sector and suggest a similar displacement of occupations and employment from manufacturing to services.

The difficulty, however, was that the tertiary (services) sector had long been considered something of a residual category for 'not elsewhere classified' economic activities thought merely to support or contribute to the 'real' productivity of commodity production and goods manufacturing, rather than being productive in themselves (Castells & Aoyama, 1994; Gershuny & Miles, 1983). Activities ranging from law, finance, government, education, research, religion, health care, and communications to food service, housekeeping, maintenance and repair, utilities, entertainment, transportation, and personal services were seen as ancillary – social costs to be counted against the price and circulation of commodities and goods production (Bell, 1973). Thus, one of the first moves among early information society scholars was an attempt to disentangle information/knowledge work from the looser category of 'services' and consider it as productive in its own right.

Different writers approached redefinition differently. Some categorized all high-status, educated professions, and white-collar work *a priori* as information work (Machlup, 1962). Others included any occupation whose main output or product was information (e.g., lawyers, teachers, engineers), or those working with high-value information or information and communication technologies (ICT) (e.g., programmers, librarians, media producers, telecommunications workers; Jonscher, 1983). Some counted all occupations in industries that produced informational products, such as publishing, broadcasting, education, government, or finance.

Critics noted the obvious elitism of including only highly paid professionals with advanced education as knowledge workers, or only high-status fields like law, research, education, media, and finance as information industries. A worker's main job activities and responsibilities, they said, should define whether an occupation counts as information work or not, so it was possible to find information and non-information workers in every sector and industry of the economy (Schement & Lievrouw, 1984). Moreover, information/knowledge work-like activities (like the larger class of services) had been part of every society throughout history. Thus, the growing presence and significance of information/knowledge work could be seen more as a matter of historical degree than an entirely new development.

Whatever the approach, by the 1980s research findings had become relatively consistent. Whether counted as economic inputs/investment, industrial outputs or work products, employment figures, activities on the job, use of information and communication technologies, gross national product, or proliferation of new occupations, information-related work and industries had grown to account for anywhere from around one-third to just over half of economic activity and/or employment in many developed, industrialized societies – although the exact patterns varied considerably by country (Castells, 1996; OECD, 1981).

On the other hand, much of this effort to delineate the extent and contours of information/knowledge work or post-industrial/information society was dismissed by some left-critical sociologists and communication scholars who considered it historically uninformed and critically unengaged (e.g., Elliott, 1982; Lyon, 1988; Mosco, 1982; D. Schiller, 1982; H. I. Schiller, 1981; Slack, 1984; Webster & Robins, 1989). The whole idea of post-industrialism or information society, they said, served only to advance and obscure the interests of capitalist markets and ideology; at best, it was a passing technocratic craze promulgated by managerialist boosters and futurists like Alvin Toffler and John Naisbitt or fashionable neoconservative intellectuals like Daniel Bell. For these critics, the power of any purported 'new' economic system or occupational group was negligible compared to that of established, cross-national industrial production and the mass media industries. Indeed, they said, the supposed information industries and occupations were themselves organized, controlled, and automated according to the same logic of industrial capitalism and served the same economic and political interests, as industrialism had been before them.

Still, the sheer number, proliferation, and heterogeneity of information occupations and industries prompted analysts to develop new frameworks and classifications – for example, to separate the information sector from the rest of the economy as a whole (Jonscher, 1983, 1988). Some called for the tertiary sector to be split into two parts (Porat & Rubin, 1977), or even three: Daniel Bell (1973, 1979a) argued that the traditional three-sector framework should be expanded to five, including primary (extractive), secondary (fabrication), tertiary (transportation and utilities), quaternary (trade and finance), and quinary (education, research, government, recreation, and health). Some years later, urbanist Richard Florida would revisit the definitions of the US Department of Labor's Standard Occupational Classifications (SOC) system and identify what he called a small 'creative class' of workers with outsized cultural impact and economic power in the arts, sciences, engineering, and media (Florida, 2002).

The 'new class'

Meanwhile, public intellectuals and cultural critics – some of whom had been acute observers of industrial-style, consumption-driven 'mass society' and 'mass media' in the mid-20th century – entered into debates about the rising social and cultural significance and consequences of college-educated, white-collar professional work and bureaucracy and its relation to new information technologies and media. For example, David Riesman, renowned for his 1950 book *The Lonely Crowd*, wondered whether the growing presence of white-collar work would create more time for leisure and cultural pursuits in society at large (Riesman, 1964[1958]). In *The Technological Society*, French philosopher Jacques Ellul (1964[1954]) worried that the substitution of technocratic rationality and data for humanistic knowledge would erode social values, individual autonomy, and critical judgment. Marshall McLuhan saw automation and information retrieval transforming work:

> Under electric technology the entire business of man becomes learning and knowing . . . all forms of employment become 'paid learning,' and all forms of wealth result from the movement of information. The problem of discovering occupations or employment may prove as difficult as wealth is easy.
>
> *(McLuhan, 1964, 65).*

By the 1970s, such views had crystallized around the idea of an ascendant 'New Class' of intellectuals and technocrats.[4] For these affluent, educated professionals – neither proletarian nor capitalist, salaried employees rather than owners of capital – social and cultural interests and political engagement seemed to matter more than basic economic and material security concerns or traditional class solidarities (Bruce-Briggs, 1979; Inglehart, 1971; Wuthnow & Shrum, 1983). For example, in the face of considerable criticism, Alvin Gouldner (1979) theorized the role and cultural influence of the new class as an essential, and in some ways more powerful, formation than the historical capitalist class: capital increasingly depended on the knowledge and creativity of the new class, as wealth production shifted toward knowledge-based information industries and media.

The New Class notion certainly had its detractors, particularly among neo-Marxist scholars who rejected the suggestion that bureaucrats and intellectuals could usurp the economic power of capital joined with the 'cultural industries,' or that any new class could exist without its own distinctive, coherent ideology, collective consciousness, class interests, or program of collective action. In the definitive collection, *The New Class?*, Michael Harrington contended that "the very concept of the new class is about as solid as jello" (Harrington, 1979, 123). Andrew Hacker memorably called members of the New Class "bit players who do not even choose their own lines" (Hacker, 1979, 167). Even Daniel Bell acknowledged basic problems with the idea, titling his chapter "The New Class: A Muddled Concept" (Bell, 1979b,169). Nonetheless, in a review essay commenting on *The New Class?*, Irving Louis Horowitz – himself a new-class skeptic – also argued for a thorough reassessment of 'old-class theory' and theorists who "continue to act as if nothing really has happened in the past 100 years except the increasing decadence of world capitalism" (Horowitz, 1979, 61).

Theories of society and knowledge work: Beck and Castells

By the late 1980s the persistent disagreements between 'discontinuity' views, which interpreted changes in employment and economic output as watershed economic, social, and cultural transformations, and 'continuity' views, which insisted that those changes were simply the latest extension of industrial capitalism, had settled into a sort of stalemate (Schement & Lievrouw, 1987). Yet many scholars also recognized that as an empirical matter some novel patterns of economic activity, technological development, institutional formation, and cultural practice had indeed emerged, from micro-scale interpersonal, workplace, and family relations and identity to macro-scale, globalized flows of money, people, and knowledge. They sought to theorize the changes without falling prey either to celebratory techno-futurism or anachronistic, teleological, or ideological assumptions about power, social structures, or value.

As noted previously, Alain Touraine and Daniel Bell both advanced early formulations of post-industrial society focused on work and occupations (Touraine's theorization is explored at more length later in this chapter). Other important theorists also proposed accounts of broad-based, knowledge- and information-driven social change, including Anthony Giddens, Scott Lash, Niklas Luhmann, Antonio Negri, and Nico Stehr. However, the social theories of Ulrich Beck and Manuel Castells in the 1990s and early 2000s stand out for their emphasis on work. Beck (who died in 2015) and Castells are famously prolific writers; a full consideration of their respective contributions and related commentary is beyond the scope of this chapter. For the present discussion, however, it is useful to review a few of the most relevant points and parallels in their theorizations.

For example, both Beck and Castells reject simple claims of a wholly new post-industrial or postmodern society superseding industrialism, of wholesale shifts in employment from manufacturing to poorly defined services, or that knowledge work and industries thrive only in developed nations while manufacturing is relegated to the global periphery. Rather, conditions have changed more organically and idiosyncratically, based not only in enduring cultural and industrial forms and dynamics but also in introducing new arrangements that challenge the established order.

Both writers see current societies as the outcome of two critical periods of change rather than a singular, irruptive revolution. For Beck, a 'first modernity' associated with the transition from agriculture/commodity extraction to industrialism has been followed by a 'second modernity' marked by more informational, networked, and extensive modes of social and economic organization. In this second modernity, society is more globalized and transnational in scope *and* more reflexive, self-aware, and individualized in focus; it must "face unintended and unwanted consequences of its own success" (Beck, 2000, 21). Beck considers the combination of greater actual risk (environmental, technological, economic, etc.) and the social awareness of that risk as the defining feature of contemporary informationalized society.

Similarly, Castells sees the first and second halves of the 20th century as two distinct episodes of modernity and industrialism, the first of which becomes 'post-agricultural' and the second more 'post-industrial.' Each generates tremendous increases in scientific and technological knowledge. However, the latter is distinguished by the rise of complex, networked information technologies that have shifted perceptions of space and time, expanded the potential arena of action to a more extensive global scale, and become powerful tools for creating, organizing, and deploying knowledge as a resource or product in itself. Thus, both Castells and Beck contend that information technology has played a pivotal role in recent social and cultural change as well as economics.

Both argue that networked information/communication technologies and forms of social organization and action have fostered individualization.[5] People's lives and experiences are increasingly self-created, discarded, and re-created as circumstances require. The "individual rather than the class is becoming the basic unit of social reproduction" (Beck & Willms, 2004, 101). Recalling Touraine's 'programmed society' concept, Castells argues that knowledge work becomes "self-programmable," that is, workers "retrain [themselves], and adapt to new tasks, new processes and new sources of information, as technology, demand, and management speed up their rate of change" (Castells, 2000, 12). Individualization particularly suits educated, white-collar workers, who combine technical expertise and relational and communication skills with a strong sense of professional identity and personal autonomy.

This adaptability has encouraged firms to reorganize work, supplanting stable organizational hierarchies with constantly reorganizing network forms that rely on outsourcing and globalized, contingent labor forces and supply chains.[6] Beck puts it simply: "capital is global, work is local" (2000, 27). But flexibility also creates new problems of control over radically dispersed production processes and increasingly individualized workforces. Here, both Beck and Castells identify a fundamental transformation in the relation between employer and employed. As employers demand more 'flexibilization' of work, the basic social contract that underpinned industrial societies – the assurance of standard full-time, stable employment, wages, benefits, and work roles through the life cycle – is abandoned. The result is what Beck terms "flexible and pluralized underemployment" (1992[1986], 140), and Castells calls the "disintegration of the workforce" (1996, 62). Even high-status professionals and knowledge workers are expected to assume ever more of the expense and risk of employment, as precarity, retraining ('self-programming'), layoffs and job search, and multiple part-time 'gigs' ('underemployment') become the norm. "It is not the end of paid work but the end of full employment which is at issue" (Beck, 2000, 38); "work society is becoming risk society" (2000, 67).

This dialectic tension between globalization and individualization, where network forms, processes, and sensibilities have extended 'up' to global-scale technology infrastructures and 'down' to individual experience and interaction, has had a number of consequences. In some cases it has eroded the primacy and sovereignty of nation-states (the defining institutional formation of modernity), blurred national and cultural boundaries, and encouraged destabilizing, cross-border 'flows' of people, resources, and information. Taken together, these phenomena foster what today has become a familiar form of backlash, which Castells calls 'resistance identity,' among "actors that are in positions/conditions devalued and/or stigmatized . . . on the basis of principles different from, or opposed to, those permeating the institutions of society" (Castells, 1997, 8; see also Stalder, 2006). Beck takes a darker view: "the desire for relief from the pressure to individuate can lead to all kinds of fundamentalism" (Beck & Willms, 2004, 67), particularly a new 'postmodern nationalism,' which provides

> a new basis for ethnic identity that is compatible with the new conditions . . . the result is a paradoxical mixture of relativism and fundamentalism. Its proponents seek to draw a line separating [their] identity from all others . . . Over time this model is being extended to cover not only minorities but all possible identities.
>
> *(2004, 91–92)*

Cultural/critical perspectives

Studies measuring and theorizing the nature, extent, and consequences of information/knowledge work have been paralleled by work that critiques its influence on the quality and sensibility of culture and everyday life. An early example is found in J. W. Freiburg's introduction to Alain Touraine's analysis of the May 1968 events in France, in which he describes the protesters:

> What do students have in common with workers in aerospace, radio and television technicians, and managerial circles in industry? All are – or will be in the future – highly trained, white-collar workers who share an opposition to those who direct and exploit their expertise.
>
> *(Freiburg, 1971, 7)*

Arlie Russell Hochschild's fieldwork studies (1983) showed that 'feeling rules,' that is, the management of emotional self-presentation and relational communication, are essential to the successful performance of routine white-collar work, from back-office bill collectors to bank tellers and airline flight attendants; for these workers, such 'emotion work' constitutes a major source of workplace stress and alienation. Tessa Morris-Suzuki presciently foresaw the "private appropriation of accumulated social knowledge" (1986, 89) as a hallmark of the digital age: in information/knowledge economies, personal expressions, relationships, cultural practices, folkways, and traditions would be recast as commodities from which value, including labor value, might be extracted.

As the introduction of browsers, natural-language search engines, and the World Wide Web made the Internet broadly accessible to non-technical users in the mid-1990s, and especially after the collapse of the dot-com bubble around 2000 (itself fostered by the 'land rush'-style commercialization of the Internet in the post-browser period), some scholars and critics began to reexamine notions of class and cooperative work through the lens of everyday culture online. Richard Barbrook, for example, argued that post-industrial and information-society studies and theorizing had neglected the cultural implications of information sharing and the circulation of free and open-source information among Internet users and online workers, a phenomenon he called the 'hi-tech gift economy' (Barbrook, 1998). Yochai Benkler (2002) contended that 'commons-based peer production' – nonprofit, cooperative modes of information/knowledge work that can enlist thousands of workers online, such as open-source software development or the volunteer-driven Wikipedia project – is ethically preferable to work dictated by the profit-driven priorities of either firms or markets. Mackenzie Wark (2004) identified new strains of class tension between information/knowledge workers – creative 'hackers' who produce value through 'abstraction' (i.e., creating "the possibility of new things entering the world"; Wark, 2004, §02, p. xx) – and the interests of a 'vectoralist' class intent on appropriating, commodifying, and monetizing hacker creativity.

The tradition of Autonomous Marxism has been an important perspective in this arena. Its focus on worker capacity and autonomy, and the inclusion of unwaged service work and 'immaterial labor' (including unpaid 'abstract' and 'affective' labor such as housework, volunteer work, or family care) within the working class defies orthodox Marxist and labor-movement views of working-class victimization (Dyer-Witheford, 2001; Lazzarato, n.d.; Scholz, 2008). Leading Autonomist thinkers, notably Antonio Negri and Michael Hardt, argue that globalization and the Internet have facilitated the extension of capitalist power and production into every aspect of everyday life, social relations, and individual subjectivity, a phenomenon that they and their colleagues have dubbed 'factory society' (Hardt & Negri, 2000; see also Gill & Pratt, 2008). At the same time, they argue, the dynamics of globalized digital networks can also create new opportunities for worker-driven, self-active modes of resistance to capital, especially local, improvised, and emergent micro-scale actions and cooperation, in contrast to older, grander visions of totalizing revolution led by party vanguards.

Some Autonomist writers have been less optimistic, however. Tiziana Terranova has critiqued the "glamorization of digital labor. . . [its] continuities with the modern sweatshop and . . . the increasing degradation of knowledge work" (Terranova, 2000, 33). She identifies 'free labor' as an integral element of digital capitalism, including common online activities such as "building Web sites, modifying software packages, reading and participating in mailing lists, and building virtual spaces on MUDs and MOOs" (ibid.). Free labor, she argues, is the defining feature of the 'social factory.' "Such labor is not exclusive to so-called knowledge workers, but is a pervasive feature of the postindustrial economy" (2000, 35).

Similarly, Andrew Ross (2001) has pointed out the considerable ironies of informal high-tech workplaces, where the "office was re-imagined as a giant, multi-purpose playroom" that reinforces a 24/7 work-life culture. These and the rise of contingent and part-time work and 'consultants' in the 1990s "are the ultimate physical embodiment of all the 'flexibility' talk that has dominated corporate culture for the last twenty years" (Ross, 2001, 78). They encourage information/knowledge workers to think of themselves as 'creatives' like artists or academics, whose 'sacrificial labor' – rewarded by professional satisfaction or peer recognition rather than a commensurate wage – is accepted as the price of (ostensible) creative freedom.

Cultural critic Trebor Scholz holds that both free and sacrificial labor have become more pronounced with the growth of social and algorithmic media (Scholz, 2008, 2017). Like Terranova, he argues that by playing games, posting photos or videos, blogging or tweeting, recommending sites or products to friends, or selecting content, people are not just producing content but actually performing unpaid labor that adds to the market value of those sites, games, products, or content without compensation, and generating surplus value in the form of data streams.

Gina Neff (2012) has proposed an insightful analysis of the rise of unpaid information/knowledge work. Professional and white-collar workers are now often expected to adopt an entrepreneurial approach to job searching and employment, investing time, effort and skills in the form of what Neff calls (in an allusion to venture capital) uncompensated 'venture labor,' to promote their personal 'brands' and compete for piecework or temporary employment. The dynamic of venture labor extends unwaged, 'on spec' work into ever more areas of traditional white-collar and professional fields, including law, technology, media, the arts, and the academy.

The technological exploitation of information/knowledge workers has become an increasingly visible theme in both popular media and the academic literature. Reporters, researchers and essayists have documented the precarity, isolation, and alienation of crowd-sourced piecework (Hodson, 2013; Irani, 2015; Katz, 2017) and 'content serfs' (Timberg, 2016); the declining productivity, exhaustion, and burnout resulting from 'hyperemployment,' as employers impose multiple jobs and workloads on each worker (Bogost, 2013); the absence of basic benefits and workplace protections for freelancers (Horowitz, 2011); and the cooptation of human knowledge and creativity as they are harnessed to algorithmic work-control processes (Kushner, 2013). Hamid Ekbia and Bonnie Nardi argue that 'heteromation,' defined as the "extraction of economic value from low-cost or free labor" (2017, 1), has become the dominant logic of computationally or algorithmically regulated information work, and propose five types of heteromated labor, including communicative, cognitive, creative, emotional, and organizing labor. Writing about crowd-sourcing, one team of computer scientists has posed a question that could apply just as well to the future of information/knowledge work more broadly: "*Can we foresee a future crowd workplace in which we would want our children to participate?*" (Kittur et al., 2013, 1301, emphasis in the original).

Measurement, revisited

These issues, and a surprising absence of reliable employment data, have prompted a recent resurgence of interest among policy makers, economists, and sociologists in measuring and quantifying the extent and significance of information/knowledge work in its new, precarious incarnation.

Historically, contingent employment of all types has been inconsistently defined and measured, particularly in the United States. Of necessity, studies often rely on industry data, private investment analyses, or small-scale academic research rather than systematic, long-term data gathered at the national level. Nor are definitions of contingent, nonstandard, or alternative work consistent across analyses, countries, or regions. In a recent overview of 'new forms of work' across its member states and the United States, the Organization for Economic Cooperation and Development (OECD, 2016) notes these disparities and the urgent need for better measurement and data about all aspects of 'nonstandard work' (NSW), especially in 'platform service markets' where the connection between employers and workers is mediated and governed online. The OECD paper also distinguishes between platform-mediated 'services delivered physically,' such as transportation, lodging, deliveries, or maintenance/repair work, and 'services delivered digitally,' which is more clearly the domain of information/knowledge work, for example, design, writing, marketing, video production, accounting, translation, software development, and so on (see Note 2).

In the United States, the US Bureau of Labor Statistics (BLS) conducted the Contingent Work Supplement (CWS) study every two years between 1995 and 2005 in conjunction with its regular Current Population Survey. The CWS survey interviews members of a sample of US households to estimate the extent of 'contingent and alternative employment arrangements' (historical CWS data and findings are available at www.bls.gov/bls/news.release/home. htm#CONEMP). BLS found minimal change in the proportion of the workforce so employed over the period. Contingent employment (workers without contracts for standard, long-term employment, whether or not they worked full-time) declined slightly, from 4.9% in 1995 to 4.1% in 2005; alternative employment arrangements (nonstandard relationships with employers, including independent contractors, on-call workers and day laborers, and workers provided by temp agencies and contract firms) increased slightly, from 9.9% to 10.7%.

However, funding for the CWS was cut from the BLS budget after 2005 and not reinstated until 2017, a period which included the Great Recession and the emergence of platform-mediated online work.[7] Thus, while there was growing anecdotal evidence of the prevalence and risks of contingent, part-time, temporary, or 'gig' work, particularly online, after 2005 (and especially after the economic crisis of 2008), the BLS could provide no systematic data about its incidence, including work performed or controlled via online platforms. Subsequently, US Senators Patty Murray (D-Washington) and Kirsten Gillibrand (D-New York), both members of the Senate Committee on Health, Education, Labor and Pensions, requested that the US Government Accountability Office (U.S. GAO) audit existing CWS data and analyze more recent data from other sources to assess the extent and implications of contingent employment before and after the Great Recession. Using somewhat more inclusive definitions than the CWS, the GAO found that even in 1995, contingent and alternative work arrangements appeared to comprise about 32% of all employment. Consistent with the trend in the BLS data, that figure fell moderately by 2005, to 30.6%. However, according to the GAO, post-2005 data showed a dramatic rise in contingent and alternative work arrangements, to 35.3% of US employment in 2006 and a remarkable 40.4% in 2010 (U.S. GAO, 2015).

These findings attracted considerable attention in the general and business press but had the disadvantage of not being strictly comparable with the original BLS studies. Economists Lawrence Katz and Alan Krueger thus set out to estimate the prevalence, wages, and hours of alternative work arrangements in the United States over time (again, using alternative data in the absence of the CWS) with methods designed to be more comparable with the original CWS studies (Katz & Krueger, 2016). Like the CWS, they found a small increase in alternative work arrangements between 1995 and 2005 (from 9.3% to 10.7%). But from 2005 to 2015 that figure grew to 15.8% of total US employment – an increase of more than 50% in a decade. Moreover, according to their estimates, "*94% of the net employment growth in the U.S. economy from 2005 to 2015 appears to have occurred in alternative work*" (Katz & Krueger, 2016, 7; emphasis in the original). The proportion of workers describing themselves as self-employed also declined during the period, while the proportion employed by contract firms or temp-work agencies rose. With respect to information/knowledge work in particular, Katz and Krueger observed the largest increase in alternative work arrangements in education and health services between 2005 and 2015; they also found sharp increases in the information fields, public administration, leisure and hospitality, and other services (although not in finance, professions, or business).

The OECD's data on NSW is somewhat more extensive, given its greater (though not complete) consistency of definitions, collection over time, and comparability across member countries – although the OECD too supplements member data with private-sector financial and industrial sources (OECD, 2016). They find a substantial and increasing proportion of NSW in its member economies, ranging in 2013 from roughly 15% (Estonia) to nearly 60% (The Netherlands), with a mean of 33% across the EU 29 countries. When permanent part-time work is excluded, that average drops to 22%, still a major fraction of the EU 29 workforce. The OECD analysis also finds evidence that workers often accept NSW arrangements due to a lack of available full-time employment. They tend to earn less, receive less employer-sponsored training, and are more likely to hold multiple jobs at once, than workers in full-time, permanent employment. The OECD concludes that several issues require better and more extensive research and may warrant regulation, from worker rights and potential de-skilling, to workers' reputational and privacy risks, to the asymmetric power of platforms themselves to regulate and enforce work standards and expectations.

As a final note on measurement, in June 2018 the US Bureau of Labor Statistics did release selected, long-awaited findings from the May 2017 Contingent Work Supplement survey, the first conducted since 2005 (see Note 7). Remarkably, and contrary to the GAO, Katz and Krueger, and OECD analyses, the BLS reported that the US picture for contingent and alternative work arrangements was almost unchanged from 2005. The percentage of employees in contingent work declined slightly, from 4.1% in 2005 to 3.8% in 2017. Alternative work arrangements accounted for 10.1% of employment in 2017, barely different from 10.7% in 2005.

In sum, though the measurement picture is incomplete and somewhat contradictory, what data there are do seem to suggest the basic outlines of a new, challenging, and more precarious era of information/knowledge work.

Struggles over information/knowledge work: a framework

As the preceding discussion suggests, the concept of information/knowledge work has inspired an array of theoretical perspectives, measurement techniques, and social and policy debates over the last 60 years. If there is one 'throughline,' however, it may be a rising tension between visions of information/knowledge work as the keystone of prosperity and social well-being in developed, 'good' societies, and the impending realities of increasingly fragmented, isolated, de-skilled, and precarious white-collar work life. A framework for characterizing this tension and its dynamics over time could help put these contending visions and realities into perspective without resorting to technocratic hype on the one hand, or purely anecdotal accounts of exploitation on the other, that are proliferating in popular discourse on the topic.

For this, we can return to Alain Touraine's early insight that post-industrial or programmed societies are distinguished by 'struggles over the totality of cultural patterns and knowledge production,' more than struggles over the distribution of material resources in themselves. From this perspective, information/knowledge work can be considered as both the manifestation of those struggles and their product. Writing in the 1960s and 1970s, Touraine observed that educated, white-collar workers' agency, action, self-expression, creativity, and control over the production and sharing of knowledge – ultimately, what he saw as their subjectivity – constituted a more powerful mainspring of contestation than the abstract class structures, social forces, and functions advanced by classical industrial-era theories of modernity and collective action (Touraine, 1981[1978]). With this as a point of departure, we can ask how such workers' prospects, agency, and control over knowledge production have fared since that earlier period.

Touraine's sociology has been studied and debated at length over his long career, but several writers have proposed that it spans several periods or thematic moments (e.g., Ballantyne, 2007; McDonald, 1994). These correspond roughly to different moments of contestation over the totality of knowledge and culture, with different implications for information/knowledge work, though some trends or dynamics may persist across them.

The first moment, associated with Touraine's original theorizing of post-industrial society and new social movements, places elite professionals, students, and bureaucracy at the center of social critique and change after World War II. This framing of their role departs from both the Marxist view of the working-class proletariat as the prime agent of historical change, and from structural-functionalist accounts of integrative social roles and relations (Touraine, 1971[1969], 1977[1973], 1981[1979]). New telecommunications, broadcast, and computing systems, and expanded access to higher education create large new workforces, audiences, and markets for information, media, and communications. This new contingent of information/knowledge workers seeks ways to articulate its occupational priorities and values, creative and personal experiences, and lifestyles. They are less tied to material/economic gain than to their ability to live and work on their own terms and to express themselves as the basis of a new politics, distinct from (if alongside) the market and dominant social institutions. Here, the struggle over the totality of cultural patterns takes the form of contested control over the nature of work, creativity, and the production of culture and knowledge; put simply, it is a struggle over whose knowledge and/or experience 'counts' as a legitimate basis for power. These tensions not only echo some of the 'new class' themes reviewed earlier but also produce 'new social movements,' collective actors that differ in fundamental ways from those associated with the industrial-era labor movement (e.g., types of grievances; modes of collective action, protest, and political activism).

In the second moment – roughly, 1980 to the turn of the century – Touraine's thinking turns toward what he calls the 'post-social.' The new social movements of the 1960s and 1970s have become the standard model (e.g., feminism, environmentalism, anti-globalization, gender, and ethnic identity), but the sense of rupture between people's lifestyles, experience, and cultures, and the globalized circulation of information, cultural products, capital, and power becomes more acute. With the end of the post-war economic boom, private-sector industries and markets are deregulated and social-democratic safety nets are dismantled. Women and minority groups begin to enter the growing white-collar workforce, particularly in routine, but information-intensive, 'service industries' where relational and communicative skills are essential qualifications, though such occupations are recast as low-status and paid less than executive or professional jobs. Mediating institutions and the information/knowledge workers whose expertise constitutes them are similarly marginalized and undermined by the rise of globalized, neoliberal markets (especially markets in information transmitted through world-wide digital networks, which undermine local expertise) and their neoconservative political champions (Touraine, 1995[1992], 2000[1997]). Law, education, media, the arts, politics, and government, and even the nation-state, all struggle for legitimacy. Thanks to the proliferation of computing and telecommunications networks in the workplace and for personal use, everyday experience, expression, and work life become at once more intensive – focused on local identities, communities, and relationships – and more extensive: individual communication and identity, creative expression, and information seeking become global in scale, scope, and consequences.

Thus, in this moment struggles over the totality of cultural patterns take the form of what Touraine calls 'de-modernization' – that is, some communities turn away from the disruptive and oppressive institutional, cultural, and political structures of modernity. Here, pluralism, the 'social contract,' and broad-based collective action and solidarity across community interests – indeed the modern notion of society – are rejected in favor of individual and local interests that privilege cultural and ethnic identity, the private sphere, and personal relationships/exchange networks (Touraine 2000[1997], 2013).[8] Contestation arises between this growing sensibility

225

and the looming risks and loss of autonomy associated with surging technological and economic globalization (here, we see parallels with Beck and Castells). And, as Touraine warns, where there is no arena or civil space in which diverse groups can negotiate their interests or possibilities for change in the face of globalized power, "*Society no longer exists*" (Touraine, 2014[2010], 54; emphasis in the original).

Touraine's third, most current moment has been marked by a chronic sense of global economic and political crisis. On the economic side, it extends roughly from the dot-com bust of 2000 to the global collapse of deregulated, speculative financial markets in 2007–08, the 'Great Recession' and subsequent austerity measures imposed in societies most disrupted by the crash, and the persistent wage stagnation, un- and under-employment, and gaping disparities of income, wealth and power that have persisted in the aftermath. Politically, the same period begins with a terrifying surge of spectacular, sophisticated, and often suicidal attacks waged by radicalized ethnic, political, and religious insurgents throughout the world, from Brussels and Boston to Bali and Beslan, but especially against developed, multicultural states and societies. These campaigns of 'asymmetric' warfare by non-state actors and local provocateurs induce a permanent 'global war on terror,' stalemated regional military conflicts, pervasive state surveillance and security regimes, and new limits on civil liberties and basic freedoms.

Economic and political crisis have launched enormous waves of migration, with refugees fleeing genocidal conflict and economic desperation throughout the world; they are met by increasingly xenophobic hostility and nationalist reaction (notably the recent Brexit vote in the United Kingdom and swings toward authoritarian, right-wing politics in many affluent nations, including some in Europe and the United States). Alongside specters of terrorism, economic, environmental, and epidemiological crisis, reactionary nationalism, and autocracy, the moment has also been defined by dramatic growth in worldwide Internet access, mobile technologies, and social and algorithmic media, which has fostered the emergence of 'platform capitalism' (Srnicek, 2016), the routinization of robotics, artificial intelligence and machine learning, and the nascent 'Internet of Things' (IoT) in commerce, state security, the workplace, and even the home – all of which require enormous, extractive data capture systems that are increasingly opaque and resistant to social or legal regulation. At the same time, as the Internet has grown into a global-scale platform for even the most arcane interests, viewpoints, desires, impulses, and resentments, it has lost its early promise as a new, democratic frontier for interaction, deliberation, tolerance, and innovation, and is increasingly seen as a mean world rife with fraud, violence, misinformation and lies, exploitation, conflict, and cultural pollution (Lievrouw, 2012). Online risk and danger prompt the creation of private 'firewalls,' 'ecosystems,' or 'walled gardens' that effectively govern and filter people's exposure to unfamiliar information sources, strange people, or undesirable (or unpaid-for) ideas. People accept the routine, intrusive, and pervasive monitoring and surveillance of their activities and communications by state security agencies and commercial enterprises as the price of safety, or at least of 'free' access to essential digital networks and services.

Touraine is particularly concerned by two consequences of these developments. The first is the limited ability of progressive, inclusive, or emancipatory social movements, even those that mobilize and gain global visibility and popular legitimacy via sophisticated digital networks and social media, to gain significant political power or lasting reform, even as authoritarian and nationalist regimes co-opt the same systems to repress and subvert movement aims and organizing. The second is the turn to extremism and violence, not only among more traditional or ideologically rigid cultural, political, and ethnic communities but also (and more recently) in ordinary political discourse and activism in modernized, affluent societies. In both contexts such tactics are used to reinforce group particularity, identity and norms, draw stark boundaries between those who 'belong' and those who don't, and to defy cultural tolerance, political pluralism, and modern values – notably, supposed universals like reason, speech rights, the rule of (secular) law, human rights, and the advancement of women.

Thus, Touraine argues that the challenges of the new century revolve around accelerating processes of individuation and separatism, and the de-legitimation of pluralist, democratic politics in favor of other more authoritarian forms of power. Struggles over the totality of cultural patterns and knowledge production focus on risk, contingency, and insecurity; contestation becomes a search for identity, security, and shelter against that risk, and the creation of separate 'safe' arenas for group solidarity and interaction, including a suspicion or rejection of majoritarian or pluralist views and institutions. Taken together, these conditions may push the most vulnerable groups toward identity-driven or neo-communitarian social separatism and political segregation, resurgent nationalism, and, in extreme cases, autocracy (Touraine, 2007[2005], 2014[2010]).

Touraine sees little prospect for reviving the kind of idealized, mass-mediated public sphere or civil society theorized by Jürgen Habermas, among others, as the defining institutional feature of modern democracies, or as sites for launching broad-based, heterogeneous social movements. Rather, he suggests that analysts must adopt a distinctly cultural perspective on contemporary social change, shifting their theoretical focus from social systems and structures to actors and agency. Inspired by feminism, he sees 'subjectivation' as the best possibility for understanding and fostering civil discourse, 'living together,' and effective collective action. Subjectivation is the cultivation of an individual's capacities in ways that not only support her own autonomy and competence as an actor but also allows her to recognize and appreciate the different subjectivities of others and to engage across those differences as different *and* equal. "[W]hat takes the place of the hierarchy [of social categories and classes] on which the old world was based is the capacity (present or absent) of each individual to respect the subject in themselves and others" (Touraine, 2014[2010], 55).

Of course, the preceding outline is a very schematic gloss on Touraine's sophisticated and evolving theorization of social change over recent decades, and his thinking continues to evolve in his recent work (e.g., Touraine, 2013). However, in the remainder of this chapter, a brief overview of journalism since the post-industrial period is presented to consider whether, and to what extent, Touraine's 'moments' may be a useful way to understand the changing conditions, nature, and experience of information/knowledge occupations over time – particularly the transition from high-status, professional 'new class' to highly educated yet insecure, 'precariat.'

Journalism and moments in information/knowledge work

The post-industrial moment

By the time that the idea of post-industrial society, and of information/knowledge work, emerged as distinct concepts in social theory and research in the 1960s and 1970s, journalism was already a well-established, relatively prestigious occupation. In the 20th century, American journalism had shed its more freewheeling past (including the jingoistic yellow journalism hawked by press barons like Joseph Pulitzer and William Randolph Hearst in the late 19th century, and the sensationalist, crime-, sex-, and scandal-obsessed tabloid journalism) in favor of the more professionalized, technocratic, and genteel pursuit advocated by cultural arbiters like Walter Lippmann (1922) and practiced in the 'quality press' and 'serious' broadcast media in the United States, the United Kingdom, and Europe. By the 1960s, pressrooms and newsrooms had long been unionized; in the United States, major universities offered journalism degree programs accredited by academic associations like the Association for Education in Journalism (now Association for Education in Journalism and Mass Communication). Although formal journalism education was slower to develop in Europe, even in the mid-19th century a substantial number of European (especially German) university graduates facing an "overpopulation of the literary market" had turned to journalism to make a living; in 1900, 78.5% of German journalists had university degrees (Wilke, 2013, para. 31:48).

Professional societies and organizations, such as the American Society of Newspaper (now News) Editors, and Sigma Delta Chi (now Society for Professional Journalists) in the United States, the Association of European Journalists, and the National Union of Journalists (UK), had formulated ethical and conduct codes and gave awards and prizes for outstanding journalistic accomplishments. As the 20th century proceeded, 'objectivity' became a core professional norm, particularly in the United States, as journalists sought to distinguish their work from political spin, advertising, public relations (Schudson, 2001), and governments seeking to co-opt or 'instrumentalise' them as propagandists (Wilke, 2013, para. 53–57). 'Precision journalism' (a forerunner of today's 'data journalism') was advanced in the 1970s to bring the rigor of the social and behavioral sciences to the coverage of complex social and policy issues (Meyer, 1973). In this 'global village' era, the introduction of computers, video, electronic news-gathering (ENG) technologies, and global telecommunications and satellite networks accelerated the news cycle and required journalists to master new technical skills and production routines.

All of these developments contributed to demands for well-educated journalists with specialized training and high standards of professional conduct. Indeed, in the United States employment in the occupational category of 'reporters and editors' witnessed a substantial rise beginning in 1950 (U.S. Census Bureau, 1975, 1990, 2000, 2010). In a real sense, the 1960s and 1970s marked a high point for the power and prestige of professional journalism: in the United States, investigative reporting on the Watergate scandal and revelations of the government's failing Vietnam War effort were credited with changing the course of American politics and foreign policy, for example. News media had become cultural institutions whose power to set policy agendas and shape the public sphere rivaled the law, politics, and the academy. No longer mere observers and reporters of events, journalists were also influential economic, political, and cultural analysts and critics.

This picture is obviously painted in broad strokes. But it does suggest some parallels between the practice of journalism (at least, at its more elite levels) and Touraine's theorizing of the post-industrial moment. Journalists, now part of the institutional elite, were neither proletarians in the classic sense nor wealthy owners of capital (although many of their employers might be). The news organizations that employed them were powerful defenders of their institutional and occupational priorities and privileges. The traditional watchdog function of the press had expanded into a wide-ranging, critical, and agenda-setting mission across politics, culture, economics, and the most pressing social problems of the day (in the United States, some compared the period to the reformist campaigns of the 'muckraking' journalists of the Progressive Era). Some journalists took an increasingly skeptical view of mainstream politics and culture. They became sought-after experts and advocates for communities and causes, including civil rights, the anti-war movement, environmentalism, feminism, and the counterculture; many senior reporters and editors moved readily from the newsroom to foundations, think tanks, and university faculties of journalism and public policy.

The post-social moment

In the late 1970s and 1980s, however, news organizations began to encounter technological and economic pressures that would ultimately transform their industry. Journalists faced a paradox: on the one hand, the post-Watergate, post-Vietnam period was a high-water mark for their prestige and cultural power and that of their news organizations – young journalists, including women and ethnic and cultural minorities, were attracted to the field in greater numbers than ever before. Although the advent of television in the 1950s had pressured newspaper revenues, new telecommunications networks and computerization had radically extended the reach of news coverage to a global scale and accelerated the daily news cycle. On the other hand, the global economic recession of the mid-1970s also opened the way for neoconservative political movements (such as those that brought US President Ronald Reagan and Britain's Prime Minister Margaret Thatcher to power) that championed global free trade regimes and the rollback of corporate regulation and antitrust and consumer protections – and were openly hostile to press power. Audiences migrated to free, over-the-air broadcast news and to new pay-television news channels, reducing demand for local coverage and general-interest economic and political news, and punishing print circulation and advertising revenues. In terms of contestation over cultural patterns and knowledge, journalists and the press moved from the vanguard of those struggles to having their own elite roles and knowledge challenged.

In this climate, around 1980, the number of daily newspapers in the United States began a slow decline (Kamarck & Gabriele, 2015). Some papers trimmed 'hard' news coverage in favor of features and entertainment, or introduced splashy images and layout in an effort to compete with the visual appeal of video (perhaps the most notable example being the launch of *USA Today* in 1982). Some news organizations reduced their production support staffs, for example, fact-checkers, rewrite desks, and morgues, shifting those tasks onto reporters and editors themselves. Even the influx of young journalists helped to suppress wages and job security for all but the most senior staff.

Under competitive pressures from insurgent media rivals and shareholders' steeply increasing demands for profit, news ownership (like media ownership more broadly) consolidated into fewer and fewer hands, particularly in the United States (Bagdikian, 2004). Privately- (often, family-) owned publications and broadcasters resorted to public stock offerings, mergers with entertainment and telecommunications firms, rounds of sell-offs and layoffs, and experiments with management consultants and new cost-saving digital technologies to rationalize the reporting and production process.

> The result of all these consultants and computers was that between 1975 and 1990, corporate newspaper chains [in the United States] reduced their production costs by 50 percent, nearly a decade and a half before the widespread adoption of broadband Internet.
>
> *(Saval, 2018, 35)*

Many American cities were reduced to a single daily paper, despite earlier efforts to prop up competition with the Newspaper Preservation Act of 1970. The Act exempted local newspapers from anti-trust laws through extraordinary 'joint operating agreements' (JOAs) that permitted rival papers to operate separately while sharing production and distribution costs and facilities – but also secured their market power and protected against new competitors (Busterna & Picard, 1993; Gross, 2003). Meanwhile, in the 1980s the US Federal Communications Commission (comprised mainly of Reagan appointees) rescinded long-standing rules requiring broadcast licensees to air minimum amounts of non-commercial, public affairs programming, as well as standards for program diversity, localism, and compliance with the public interest (*Charting the Digital Broadcasting Future*, 1998). Many local radio and television stations radically cut back or abandoned hard news coverage entirely, or entered into 'news share agreements' in which a single outlet (typically one affiliated with a 'major' national broadcast network) produced and distributed a set package of news content to other local stations.

The news business also faced challenges from new subscription-based, 'interactive' digital information services such as DIALOG, LEXIS, Prodigy, and CompuServe (Bourne & Hahn, 2003), as well as fledgling videotex systems delivering information to the home via broadcast sidebands, telephone lines, or cable (Case, 1994; Lievrouw, 2006; Mosco, 1982).[9] Global-scale telecommunications and data networks also generated new markets in information and 'electronic publishing' (Dordick et al., 1981; Greenberger, 1985) and incentives for the privatization of government reference or technical information, or data from government-funded research, which previously had been produced and distributed by public-sector services and agencies (H.I. Schiller, 1981). In the same spirit, control of nonprofit education and research networks, that is, the fledgling Internet, began to be transferred from the National Science Foundation and university research alliances to a handful of private-sector telecommunications firms in the late 1980s and early 1990s. Together, these shifts contributed to a 'Wild West' wave of investment and speculation in early Internet-based start-up firms (so-called dot-coms, from their .com domain names), which culminated in the dot-com bust of 2000 (*Here & Now*, 2017; Lewis, 1994; see also Wikipedia, https://en.wikipedia.org/wiki/Commercialization_of_the_Internet).

Journalists' occupational roles and status were thus assailed from all sides. The economics of news, particularly local and 'hard,' watchdog news, was increasingly shaky. News operations were among the least profitable units within large, conglomerated media firms, while entertainment – sports, movies, television, recorded music, fashion, celebrity news, and special-interest cable channels – was far more appealing to audiences, advertisers, and stockholders. With little commitment to the traditional public service responsibilities of the press, corporate owners readily cut back news reporting and production operations to improve profitability.

At the same time, a wave of conservative reaction and *laissez-faire* policies governing corporate power and profitability encouraged politicians to frame traditional news media as self-serving, remote, technocratic, elite institutions, alongside their supposed allies in the academy and government bureaucracies, and disconnected from the communities whose interests they claimed to uphold. Journalists' prerogatives and values – speech and press rights, protection and confidentiality of sources, objectivity – were cast as so many cynical covers for powerful media industry and government interests. For their part, journalists lamented what they saw as the public's declining interest in complex social and political issues, 'news literacy,' and poor 'news judgment' (Gans, 1979).

Local papers and broadcasters reduced staff (especially the most experienced, expensive reporters and editors), focused on more lucrative content and programming, and devoted more space and time to cross-promoting their owners' other media and entertainment properties. Recent US Bureau of Labor Statistics figures show that total newspaper employment peaked around 1990 in the United States, and then began a decade of slow decline (see www.bls.gov/opub/ted/2016/employment-trends-in-newspaper-publishing-and-other-media-1990-2016.htm). This trend is broadly consistent with figures for 'newsroom employment' for the same period compiled by the American Society of News Editors (Kamarck & Gabriele, 2015). Meanwhile, employment in other traditional media industries either remained flat (radio and television broadcasting) or showed only modest increases (periodical publishing) between 1990 and 1999. In contrast, employment in some industries enjoyed extraordinary growth, notably motion picture and video production (up roughly 83% in the decade), and cable and other subscription television programming (up about 59%). Employment in the new category of 'Internet publishing and broadcasting' increased by an astonishing 190% in the same period, although from a very low base.[10]

A more narrowly focused series of studies conducted by David Weaver and his colleagues since the 1980s (Weaver et al., 2018) shows a similar pattern. Based on a random sample of full-time journalists selected from a similarly randomized sample of 'mainstream' American news organizations, they estimated the size of the US editorial workforce across print publications, broadcast outlets, news services, and online news sites at roughly ten-year intervals. Their estimates show an overall increase of nearly 76% for the total editorial workforce between 1971 and 1992 (with the greatest increase occurring between 1971 and 1982), followed by a mild decline of about 5% between 1992 and 2002.

As the preceding discussion suggests, in this second moment major economic, political, and technological changes in society at large helped realign struggles over the totality of cultural patterns, particularly the production of knowledge – in this case, news. The economic downturn and stagnation of the late 1970s prompted the deregulation of media industries – increasing consolidation, concentration, and globalization of ownership – and unprecedented demands for profit, along with a resurgent, neoconservative individualism and entrepreneurialism that attacked the news media's supposed 1960s-era liberal biases. New, high-bandwidth transmission technologies – satellites, cable, microwave networks, telecommunications, and computing – provided the infrastructural foundations for new globalized markets in data, information services, and content precisely tailored to audiences' narrowing concerns and worldviews. Ultimately those audiences shifted their spending and time away from traditional, in-depth, investigative, and local news (and the advertising that supported them) and toward new electronic media that provided non-stop entertainment, pop culture, consumption, and lifestyle content. Journalists found themselves cast as the same kind of institutional elites they had previously criticized.

Despite some news organizations' attempts to meet these challenges, their efforts could not halt journalism's reversal of fortune in the last quarter of the 20th century. A stagnant economy; the derogation of professional journalists and news organizations by corporate media conglomerates, neoconservative politicians, and communities feeling patronized or neglected; as well as increasingly globalized, digital technological platforms, all depressed news circulation, advertising revenues, and, ultimately, the status of, and demand for, professional journalists.

The present moment: sociology of the subject

In the first of Touraine's moments, struggles over the totality of cultural patterns and knowledge production opposed two visions of modernity: the growing ranks of educated information/knowledge workers challenged the dominance of industrial-era political and cultural institutions and power. In the second moment, as globalization accelerated, that push against institutional power spread beyond white-collar elites to communities and groups at every level of society who saw the emerging global order – and its institutional scaffolding in law, politics, education, the arts and sciences, and media – as threats to their particular interests, autonomy, identity, and ways of life. With the third moment, these struggles have crystallized into a persistent sense of crisis and irreconcilable conflict among fragmented, polarized communities and interest groups, while the mediating institutions of modern society often seem unable or unwilling to intervene. The question of whose knowledge 'counts' as a legitimate basis for power is more fraught than ever and mirrored in a similarly fragmented, partisan, and multi-platform media and news landscape.

The slow decline of the traditional news business that began around 1990 went into something of a free-fall after 2000, coincident with the introduction of social media and ubiquitous mobile devices and advertisers' moves online. New ranks of bloggers and amateur 'citizen journalists' built their reputations and readership as vehement, often crude critics of mainstream news media (in the United States many of the most popular early bloggers were political or religious conservatives; see Massing, 2005). By the middle of the first decade of the 20th century, obituaries for the newspaper business were already appearing (e.g., Economist, 2006). Technology was widely blamed as the cause of the crisis, although as we have seen the news industry was undergoing economic and technological upheaval well before the Internet was widely available or an important part of news production.

Since then, like other white-collar workers, journalists have seen their work conditions erode and career prospects fade, especially in the post-recession period. Although a handful of the largest operations have recently enjoyed rising profitability with pared-down staffs (many hired away from failing digital competitors) and high-priced paywalls (Smith, 2020), many smaller news organizations have endured severe cutbacks and staff reductions, particularly in the United States and Europe.[11] The press's cherished values are under continual attack. According to the 2018 World Press Freedom Index compiled by Reporters without Borders, in many parts of the world the press itself is increasingly subject to political control, censorship, or harassment (even as an 'enemy of the people,' in the notorious phrase of the current US administration). More journalists are being jailed or killed than at any time in recent decades (see https://rsf.org/en/rsf-index-2018-hatred-journalism-threatens-democracies).

The consequences seem clear enough in employment statistics (US figures are used here and are rounded to the closest whole number; see Note 3). Industry figures published by the US Bureau of Labor Statistics in 2016, cited earlier, show that US newspaper employment dropped more than 40% between 2000 and 2010, and a further 39% between 2010 and the first quarter of 2016 (or −56% over the 16-year period). Employment for print periodicals fell more than 44%, and by 26% for radio production in the same period. Employment in television production declined about 14% from 2000 to 2010 but recovered most of that loss by early 2016; employment in the motion picture industry (2010–16) actually grew by about 28%. But the most striking pattern in the BLS data is seen in 'Internet broadcasting and publishing,' which rose by 42% in just one year (1999–2000) and then slid about 17% over the next decade (perhaps in the wake of the dot-com bust). However, between 2010 and 2016 it resumed its upward trajectory, rising by 112%. Indeed, BLS figures show that by 2016 Internet-based media organizations employed more people in the United States (~196,000) than newspapers did (~184,000).

The data reported by Weaver et al. (2018), based on their sample surveys of American journalists and editors at mainstream news organizations, document employment for that segment of journalists who are employed full-time. Their estimate of total editorial employment (all media) decreased by about 28% between 2002 and 2013. The cuts varied substantially across different media; however, while the total news workforce for all types of print publications declined by about 30% from 2002 to 2013, the drop was most pronounced for news magazines (−54%) and daily newspapers (−44%). Weekly papers, in contrast, enjoyed a modest employment gain (+9%), continuing a trend that began with the 1992 survey. Estimated employment in broadcast news overall declined a little more than 31% in the same period, but radio employment plummeted by nearly 69%, while television employment declined only modestly, about 7%.[12]

The now-defunct *Paper Cuts* blog, written by journalist Erica Smith, kept a running tally and mapped all US newspaper layoffs and buyouts (early retirements and other inducements to resign) between 2007 and April 2012, based on available news reports and (sometimes anonymous) tips from journalist colleagues in newsrooms around the country. The blog (selected pages are archived at the Internet Archive's Wayback Machine, https://web.archive.org) gives a sense of the frustration and discouragement many journalists experienced as the industry struggled. Layoffs and buyouts ballooned from about 2,300 in 2007 to nearly 16,000 in 2008 and a little less than 15,000 in 2009. The number fell off sharply in 2010, to around 2,900, but increased again to 4,000 in 2011. The count for 2012 was over 1,800 and still growing when Smith discontinued the project in April that year.

Neither BLS data nor other official sources provide easily accessible details about the extent of freelance, part-time, temporary, or other alternative work arrangements among American journalists and editors. However, the entry for 'reporters, correspondents and broadcast news analysts' in the BLS's most recent *Occupational Outlook Handbook* paints a negative picture of current median pay and employment prospects for the decade to 2028, forecasting a 10% decrease (www.bls.org/ooh/media-and-communication/reporters-correspondents-and-broadcast-news-analysts.htm). The US Census Bureau's last 'industry snapshot' for newspaper publishers shows a 12.5% decline in the number of publishers between 1997 and 2012, and a decline of 41.9% in the number of people they employed during the same period, with the biggest drop between 2007 and 2012. The decline continued between 2012 and 2017, with a further 5.4% drop in the number of publishers and the number of employees decreasing by 17.2%.[13]

These figures parallel numerous discussions of the employment struggles and stresses that journalists commonly experience today. For example, the spring/summer 2018 issue of the *Columbia Journalism Review* gives a sobering account of possible career paths and the personal and professional strategies journalists must adopt to make a living. The burnout and insecurity associated with online news production and 'news as process' (Lievrouw, 2015; Robinson, 2011) have been well documented (Örnebring, 2010; Paulussen, 2012; Peters, 2010; Reinardy, 2011; Richtel, 2008). Journalism educators are acutely aware that they must teach graduates to cope with routine job precarity (Nygren, 2011).

Concluding remarks: piecework, precarity, proletarianization?

To recap the main points of the preceding discussion, we have seen how the conceptualization and measurement of information/knowledge work developed between the introduction of the concept in the 1960s and today. We have suggested that this trajectory can be usefully framed according to moments in Alain Touraine's social theory, which argues that change in post-industrial knowledge societies takes the form of struggles over cultural patterns and knowledge production, in contrast to struggles over the distribution of material resources and wealth. And we have traced journalism over the same period to propose that shifts in journalistic practice and employment correspond broadly to Touraine's moments in recent social change, from the post-industrial or programmed society, to the post-social period, and now to the sociology of the subject.

On the whole, the Tourainian framing seems to suggest that as an occupation, journalism has moved from the center of cultural influence to the periphery. Its practitioners have less and less control over the nature and ethos of their work, or its standards of performance. They benefit less and less from the market shelter that comes with professional qualifications and institutional influence. Technologies and networks have enabled increased automation and 'heteromation' (Ekbia & Nardi, 2017), as digital media and information systems set the priorities and pace of work and rationalize whole creative pursuits into ever smaller tasks.

It is important to point out that even though journalism may be an archetypal example, it may also face special challenges (or have greater ability to resist these pressures) due to its role as a cultural gatekeeper and check on political power as well as its market position within highly profitable media industries. Nonetheless, the patterns identified here may apply as well to other traditionally high-status information/knowledge occupations, from education and health care to law, design, finance, administration, government, and other fields that may be subject to automation in the form of data capture and algorithmic analysis.

What may we conclude about information/knowledge work, its current conditions, and its future prospects? Clearly, myriad factors have influenced the development of information/knowledge work, both as a concept and as a core productive activity of post-industrial modernity. But based on the analyses and literatures covered here, we would highlight three particular features of information/knowledge work that seem to be emerging as sites of cultural contention over knowledge production, in Touraine's sense.

The first is 'proletarianization,' as observed by various Autonomous Marxist scholars as well as other contemporary theorists (e.g., Stigler, 2010). Here, the classical processes of rationalization, de-skilling, and declining social status associated with industrial labor are extended to creative knowledge production as well, as professionals' expertise is externalized and appropriated into commodity form as information through various combinations of bureaucratic, technological, and/or institutional systems. This is by no means a new process: various perspectives on deprofessionalization and proletarianization of white-collar work were collected into a special supplemental issue of *The Sociological Review* as early as 1972, for example (see Haug, 1972; Oppenheimer, 1972). However, proletarianization of information/knowledge work has surely accelerated and become more prevalent and disruptive with the growth of digital platforms and algorithmic media.

A second, widely noted feature of information/knowledge work has been its growing 'precarity,' in the form of temporary, short-term, or part-time work, alternative work arrangements, self-employment or freelancing, and so on. As discussed earlier, this aspect has been amply documented by prominent social theorists like Beck and Castells, cultural critics, and in the popular media as well. Indeed, precarity has become something of a 'new normal' for well-educated, white-collar workers today, a situation that may explain persistently flat or declining wages and productivity in even the wealthiest economies with the highest proportion of information/knowledge workers.

The third notable feature is the progressive reorganization – indeed, rationalization – of information/knowledge work itself into 'piecework.' There is more than a touch of irony in bringing the logic of industrial mass production to creative work and knowledge production, rather than investing workers with more control over their work and responsibility for entire projects (once the occupational promise of post-industrial societies). Digital communication and information technologies have been systematically designed and applied to reduce workers' judgment and autonomy, whether framed in terms of supply chains, outsourcing, flexibilization, gig work, 'microwork' (Ekbia & Nardi, 2017; Irani, 2015), or the algorithmically micromanaged division of informational and creative tasks (the most celebrated example being platform-based work like Mechanical Turk).

Together, these features paint a discouraging picture of the types of work that were once heralded as the centerpiece of modern, affluent, 'good' societies. However, it is important to acknowledge that none of these aspects of contemporary information/knowledge work are final or uncontested. Indeed, Touraine's notion of subjectivation (the central concept of his 'sociology of the subject') suggests a more affirmative possibility for ways ahead. In this view, people draw on personal experience and perspectives to bridge differences and recognize the subjectivity of others and to regain their autonomy as actors and workers, rather than rely on the intervention of larger collective movements or institutions to set standards for practice or to maintain equitable working conditions. For example, recent employee protests within major technology firms like Google, Microsoft, and Salesforce may be a prefigurative indicator of this process. Elite, highly skilled, highly paid professional staff have launched actions like petitions and walkouts against their employers over gender equity in hiring, workplace sexual harassment, military contracting, and product development tailored for law enforcement surveillance or repressive political regimes. As one senior employee-activist at Google put it, "People who signed up to be tech heroes don't want to be implicated in human rights abuses" (Tiku, 2018, n.p.).

To return to the example of journalism, signs of subjectivation as a basis for contestation and change might also be seen in the growing rejection of the ideology of objectivity among journalists and news organizations. Many publishers are foregrounding the voices of experienced reporters and editors from diverse communities, cultures, and backgrounds as part of an ethical framework emphasizing fairness, accuracy, authenticity, reliability, and community engagement (Lievrouw, 2015). The remote, omniscient 'news from nowhere' derided by critics of the mainstream press and mass media may eventually give way to a more active, personal, credible journalism practice that is faithful to the facts as well as the contexts and conditions that produce them, perhaps making journalists and news organizations better able to play the crucial ethical, cultural, and political roles required to support effective democracies and tolerant, informed citizenries.

In sum, then, although information/knowledge work today offers more of a cautionary tale than the sunny visions that heralded its rise in the late 20th century, its history is still being written. It remains as crucial an arena of contestation over the 'totality of cultural patterns' and knowledge production as it was for students at the Paris barricades in 1968 or the 'new class' critics of the 1970s and 80s. The question today is whether those patterns and production will ultimately be defined and governed by educated, creative workers and professionals themselves or by the pervasive data capture and algorithmic automation of platform capitalism – or indeed whether new, unanticipated patterns may yet emerge.

Notes

1 We have deliberately emphasized the term *work* here instead of *labor*, to foreground the nature and experience of work and occupations and the worker's point of view. The term also emphasizes the creative or "making" character of work in contrast to labor as a more basic activity necessary to sustain life and consumption, a distinction most notably associated with Hannah Arendt (1998). The word 'labor' can also carry connotations of simple economic inputs, on the one hand, or institutional forms associated with industrialism, rationalization, Taylorism, and so on. These broader considerations would warrant a further essay as a useful complement to the present discussion.

2 We would point out that many types of services, not just those considered informational or knowledge work, are subject to crowdsource-style rationalization and exploitation in the *sharing economy* or *gig economy* (Heller, 2017). However, we distinguish between platform-mediated physical services, such as ride hailing (Uber, Lyft), hiring someone to run one's errands or do household repairs (Taskrabbit), or booking lodging in someone else's home rather than a hotel (AirBnB), and tasks that are primarily information- or knowledge-based, such as copyediting or translating a document, taking legal depositions, designing a logo, or writing computer code. (This distinction is also made in a recent OECD report [2016].) All these use online platforms to connect persons seeking someone to perform a service with those with the time, skills, or material resources to provide it. But the relevant question for the present discussion, as it has been for decades, is definitional: what activities may be defined as information/knowledge *work*, versus the use of technological platforms to provide other types of services?

3 Of course, information/knowledge work is a feature of many types of economies and societies. However, in the present discussion we draw primarily (though not exclusively) from the US case, primarily because of the authors' greater familiarity with the relevant literature and statistical sources.

4 The term *new class* was coined by Milovan Djilas (1957), a high-ranking Yugoslav Communist Party official, in a critique of the rise of bureaucratic Party elites who, he charged, had assumed the role of a new ruling class – a view for which he was subsequently purged and imprisoned. The term was later adopted by liberal and neo-conservative American intellectuals, including David Bazelon, J.K. Galbraith, Irving Kristol, Daniel Patrick Moynihan, and Norman Podhoretz, to describe an emerging white-collar professional and bureaucratic elite in post-war US culture and politics.

5 Both Castells and Beck acknowledge and build on Anthony Giddens's theorization of individualization in modernity, including its tension with globalization, although they take a more collective perspective, in contrast to Giddens's greater focus on individuals (Giddens, 1991).

6 This might be seen as a reversion to markets from Coase's (1937) notion of the firm, an organizational form that internalizes and minimizes the transaction costs ordinarily incurred in open markets. Globalized technology networks and flows of people and resources may have lowered market transaction costs sufficiently to "re-externalize" them beyond the firm (Katz & Krueger, 2016). Yochai Benkler (2002) also advances a version of this argument in his analysis of commons-based peer production.

7 In 2016, BLS Commissioner Erica Groshen announced that the US Department of Labor had provided funding for a one-time update of the CWS, which was subsequently conducted in May 2017 (Groshen, 2016). However, Groshen stepped down as Commissioner at the start of the Trump administration in January 2017 and former BLS Deputy Commissioner William Wiatrowski was named as Acting Commissioner. The main May 2017 supplemental findings were summarized in a BLS news release in early June 2018, but excluded data from four new questions designed "to identify individuals who found short tasks or jobs through an app or website and were paid through the same app or website" (see BLS *Labor Force Characteristics*, www.bls.gov/cps/lfcharacteristics.htm#contingent). BLS published those findings in the *Monthly Labor Review* in September 2018, including data from new questions on "electronically mediated work," which BLS reported "did not work as intended" and yielded a large number of incorrect 'yes' answers. Instead, the BLS used confidntial 'microdata' gathered in individual interviews, which found that electronically mediated work amount to just 1.0% of total US employment in May 2017. See www.bls.gov/opub/mlr/2018/article/electronically-mediated-work-new-question-in-the-contingent-worker-supplement.htm.

8 Indeed, Touraine finds the most troubling evidence of de-modernization in the genocidal conflicts and "ethnic cleansing" associated with the upheavals of 1989, in the modern societies of Central and Eastern Europe (Touraine, 2000[1997]).

9 Similar systems were already successful elsewhere in the world, for example the BBC's Ceefax, France Télécom's Minitel, the Canadian Communications Research Centre's Telidon, and the UK Post Office's Prestel. Some major American news chains and broadcasters, such as Knight-Ridder, the Times-Mirror Company, Time/Life, and CBS conducted videotex trials in various US markets using some of these technologies. However, critics contended that these trials were never intended to succeed since such so-called "information utilities" posed a direct challenge to the news organizations' existing business models (see Lievrouw, 2006).

10 All figures are averages for the years cited, calculated by the authors from the BLS data provided at the URL cited.

11 However, the economic pain is unevenly distributed. For example, while major newspapers in the United States, Europe, and Australia have experienced severe cuts, closures, and layoffs, their counterparts in developing regions of the world enjoy strong circulation and remain broadly profitable, notably in India, Brazil, and China. Many major news organizations in these areas are state-controlled or party organs, however, and thus not subject to the same competitive pressures (Economist, 2011).

12 The Weaver et al. study (2018) does not report comparable data for cable/subscription news channels. Online news organizations were first included in the 2013 survey, when they were estimated to have employed just over 2% of the total full-time editorial workforce, or about 2000 workers.

13 The Census Bureau's 'industry snapshots,' its periodic *Hot Reports* on industry employment prospects, and the Bureau's Industry Statistics Portal where they were available, are no longer supported and went offline at the end of March 2020. The figures for 2012-17 were calculated from Census datasets that were downloaded and are available from the first author.

References

Arendt, H. (1998). *The Human Condition*. Introduction by M. Canovan (2nd ed.). Chicago and London: University of Chicago Press.

Bagdikian, B. H. (2004). *The New Media Monopoly* (20th ed.). Boston, MA: Beacon Press.

Ballantyne, G. (2007). *Creativity and Critique: Subjectivity and Agency in Touraine and Ricoeur*. Leiden and Boston, MA: Brill.

Barbrook, R. (1998). The Hi-Tech Gift Economy. *First Monday*, 3(12), December 7. http://firstmonday.org/ojs/index.php/fm/article/view/631/552/.

Beck, U. (1992). *Risk Society: Towards a New Modernity*. Translated by M. Ritter. London and Thousand Oaks, CA: Sage (Originally published as *Risikogesellschaft: Auf dem Weg in eine andere Moderne*. Frankfurt am Main: Surbkamp Verlag, 1986).

Beck, U. (2000). *The Brave New World of Work*. Cambridge: Polity Press.

Beck, U., and Willms, J. (2004). *Conversations with Ulrich Beck*. Translated by M. Pollak. Cambridge: Polity Press.

Bell, D. (1973). *The Coming of Post-Industrial Society: A Venture in Social Forecasting*. New York: Basic Books.

Bell, D. (1979a). The Social Framework of the Information Society. In M. L. Dertouzos and J. Moses (eds.), *The Computer Age: A Twenty-Year View.* Cambridge, MA: MIT Press, pp. 163–211.

Bell, D. (1979b). The New Class: A Muddled Concept. In B. Bruce-Briggs (ed.), *The New Class?.* New York: McGraw-Hill, pp. 169–190.

Benkler, Y. (2002). Coase's Penguin, or, Linux and *The Nature of the Firm. Yale Law Journal,* 112(3), 369–446, December.

Bogost, I. (2013). Hyperemployment, or the Exhausting Work of the Technology User. *The Atlantic,* November 8. www.theatlantic.com/technology/archive/2013/11/hyperemployment-or-the-exhausting-work-of-the-technology-user/281149/.

Bourne, C. P., and Hahn, T. B. (2003). *A History of Online Information Services, 1963–1976.* Cambridge, MA: MIT Press.

Bruce-Briggs, B. (ed.) (1979). *The New Class?* New York: McGraw-Hill.

Busterna, J. C., and Picard, R. G. (1993). *Joint Operating Agreements: The Newspaper Preservation Act and Its Application.* Norwood, NJ: Ablex.

Case, D. O. (1994). The Social Shaping of Videotex: How Information Services for the Public Have Evolved. *Journal of the American Society for Information Science,* 45(7), 483–497.

Castells, M. (1996). *The Rise of the Network Society* (The Information Age: Economy, Society and Culture, vol. 1.) Oxford: Wiley-Blackwell.

Castells, M. (1997). *The Power of Identity* (The Information Age: Economy, Society and Culture, vol. II.) Oxford: Wiley-Blackwell.

Castells, M. (2000). Materials for an Exploratory Theory of the Network Society. *British Journal of Sociology,* 51(1), 5–24.

Castells, M., and Aoyama, Y. (1994). Paths Towards the Informational Society: Employment Structure in G-7 Countries, 1920–90. *International Labour Review,* 133(1), 5–33.

Charting the Digital Broadcasting Future. (1998). Final Report of the Advisory Committee on Public Interest Obligations of Digital Television Broadcasters (pursuant to Section 2 of Executive Order No. 13038, March 11, 1997). Washington, DC: U.S. Department of Commerce, National Telecommunications and Information Administration. Available from the Benton Foundation. www.benton.org/initiatives/obligations/charting_the_digital_broadcasting_future and in PDF format from the CyberCemetery Archive of the U.S. Government Printing Office and the University of North Texas Libraries, https://govinfo.library.unt.edu/piac/piacreport.pdf.

Clark, C. (1940). *The Conditions of Economic Progress.* London: Palgrave Macmillan.

Coase, R. H. (1937). The Nature of the Firm. *Economica,* 4(16), 386–405, November.

Dizard, W. P. (1982). *The Coming Information Age: An Overview of Technology, Economy and Policy.* New York: Longman.

Djilas, M. (1957). *The New Class: An Analysis of the Communist System.* New York: Praeger.

Dordick, H. S., Bradley, H. G., and Nanus, B. (1981). *The Emerging Network Marketplace.* Norwood, NJ: Ablex.

Drucker, P. F. (1969). *The Age of Discontinuity: Guidelines to Our Changing Society.* New York: Harper & Row.

Dyer-Witheford, N. (2001). Empire, Immaterial Labor, the New Combinations, and the Global Worker. *Rethinking Marxism,* 13(3–4), 70–80, Fall–Winter.

The Economist. (2006). Who Killed the Newspaper? *The Economist,* 9, 52–54, August 26.

The Economist. (2011). Bulletins from the Future (Special Report on the News Industry). *The Economist,* July 9.

The Economist. (2017a). Learning and Earning (Special Report on Lifelong Education). *The Economist,* January 14.

The Economist. (2017b). The Marxist Moment. *The Economist,* 52, May 13.

Ekbia, H., and Nardi, B. (2017). *Heteromation and Other Stories of Computing and Capitalism.* Cambridge, MA: MIT Press.

Elliott, P. (1982). Intellectuals, the 'Information Society' and the Disappearance of the Public Sphere. *Media, Culture & Society,* 4, 243–253.

Ellul, J. (1964[1954]). *The Technological Society*. New York: Alfred A. Knopf (Originally published as *La Technique ou l'enjeu du siècle*. Paris: Librairie Armand Colin, 1954.).

Florida, R. (2002). *Rise of the Creative Class: and How It's Transforming Work, Leisure, Community and Everyday Life*. New York: Perseus.

Frassanito Network. (2006). Precarious, Precarisation, Precariat? *Mute*, January 8. www.metamute.org/editorial/articles/precarious-precarisation-precariat.

Freiburg, J. W. (1971). A View from California. In A. Touraine (ed.), L. F. X. Mayhew (trans.), *The May Movement: Revolt and Reform*. New York: Random House (Originally published as *Le Mouvement de mai ou le communism utopique*. Paris: Editions du Seuil, 1968).

Gans, H. J. (1979). *Deciding What's News: A Study of CBS Evening News, NBC Nightly News, Newsweek, and Time*. New York: Pantheon.

Gershuny, J. I., and Miles, I. D. (1983). *The New Service Economy: The Transformation of Employment in Industrial Societies*. London: Pinter.

Giddens, A. (1991). *Modernity and Self-Identity*. Cambridge: Polity Press.

Gill, R., and Pratt, A. (2008). In the Social Factory? Immaterial Labour, Precariousness and Cultural Work. *Theory, Culture & Society*, 25(7–8), 1–30. doi:10.1177/0263276408097794.

Ginzberg, E., and Vojta, G. J. (1981). The Service Sector of the U.S. Economy. *Scientific American*, 244(3), 48–55, March.

Gouldner, A. W. (1979). *The Future of Intellectuals and the Rise of the New Class*. New York: Seabury Press.

Greenberger, M. (ed.). (1985). *Electronic Publishing Plus*. White Plains, NY: Knowledge Industry.

Groshen, E. (2016). Why This Counts: Measuring 'Gig' Work. *Commissioner's Corner* (blog), March 3. Bureau of Labor Statistics, U.S. Department of Labor. https://beta.bls.gov/labs/blogs/2016/03/03/what-this-counts-measuring-gig-work/.

Gross, D. (2003). JOA DOA? *Slate*, May 8. www.slate.com/articles/business/moneybox/2003/05/joa_doa.html.

Hacker, A. (1979). Two 'New Classes' or None? In B. Bruce-Briggs (ed.), *The New Class?*. New York: McGraw-Hill, pp. 155–168.

Hacker, A. (2015). The Frenzy About High-Tech Talent. *New York Review of Books*, 33–35, July 9.

Hardt, M., and Negri, A. (2000). *Empire*. Cambridge, MA and London: Harvard University Press.

Harrington, M. (1979). The New Class and the Left. In B. Bruce-Briggs (ed.), *The New Class?*. New York: McGraw-Hill, pp. 123–138.

Haug, M. R. (1972). Deprofessionalization: An Alternate Hypothesis for the Future. *Sociological Review*, 20(suppl. 1), 195–211.

Heller, N. (2017). Is the Gig Economy Working? *The New Yorker*, May 15. www.newyorker.com/magazine/2017/05/15/is-the-gig-ecnomy-working?.

Here & Now. (2017). How Private Companies Came to Control so Much of the Internet: A Conversation with Jaron Lanier and Jeremy Hobson (audio, 10:38), May 12. Boston, MA: WBUR-FM. www.wbur.org/hereandnow/2017/05/12/private-companies-Internat.

Hochschild, A. R. (1983). *The Managed Heart: Commercialization of Human Feeling*. Berkeley, CA: University of California Press.

Hodson, H. (2013). Crowdsourcing Grows Up as Online Workers Unite. *New Scientist*, 2903, February 6. www.newscientist.com/article/mg21719036.200-crowdsourcing-grows-up-as-online-workers-unite/.

Horowitz, I. L. (1979). On the Expansion of New Theories and the Withering Away of Old Classes. *Society*, 55–62, January–February.

Horowitz, S. (2011). A Jobs Plan for the Post-Cubicle Economy. *The Atlantic*, September 5. www.theatlantic.com/business/archive/2011/09/a-jobs-plan-for-the-post-cubicle-economy/244549/.

Inglehart, R. (1971). The Silent Revolution in Europe: Intergenerational Change in Post-Industrial Societies. *American Political Science Review*, 65(4), 991–1017, December.

Irani, L. (2015). The Cultural Work of Microwork. *New Media & Society*, 17(5), 720–739.

Jonscher, C. (1983). Information Resources and Economic Productivity. *Information Economics and Policy*, 1, 13–35.

Jonscher, C. (1988). Rejoiner to Nightingale Paper. *Information Economics and Policy*, 3, 69–73.

Kamarck, E. C., and Gabriele, A. (2015). *The News Today: 7 Trends in Old and New Media.* Washington, DC: Center for Effective Public Management, The Brookings Institution, November. www.brookings.edu/wp-content/uploads/2016/07/new-media.pdf.

Katz, L. F., and Krueger, A. B. (2016). *The Rise and Nature of Alternative Work Arrangements in the United States, 1995–2015.* NBER Working Paper 22667. Cambridge, MA: National Bureau of Economic Research, September. www.nber.org/papers/w22667.pdf.

Katz, M. (2017). Amazon's Turker Crowd Has Had Enough. *WIRED*, August 23. www.wired.com/story/amazons-turker-crowd-has-had-enough/.

Kittur, A., Nickerson, J. V., Bernstein, M. S., Gerber, E. M., Shaw, A., Zimmerman, J., Lease, M., and Horton, J. J. (2013). *The Future of Crowd Work.* Proceedings of the 2013 Conference on Computer Supported Cooperative Work, CSCW '13, San Antonio, TX, pp. 1301–1317, February 23–27. Sponsored by SIGCHI, ACM Special Interest Group on Computer-Human Interaction. New York: Association for Computing Machinery.

Kushner, S. (2013). The Freelance Translation Machine: Algorithmic Culture and the Invisible Industry. *New Media & Society*, 15(8), 1241–1258. doi:10.1177/1461444812469597.

Lazzarato, M. (n.d.). Immaterial Labor. *Generation Online* (website). www.generation-online.org/c/fcimmateriallabour3.htm.

Lewis, P. L. (1994). U.S. Begins Privatizing Internet Operations. *New York Times*, p. D1, October 24. https://nyti.ms/2GnIp2X.

Lievrouw, L. A. (2006). New Media Design and Development: Diffusion of Innovations v Social Shaping of Technology. In L. A. Lievrouw and S. Livingstone (eds.), *The Handbook of New Media* (updated student ed.). London: Sage, pp. 246–265.

Lievrouw, L. A. (2012). The Next Decade in Internet Time: Ways Ahead for New Media Studies. *Information, Communication & Society*, 15(5), 616–638.

Lievrouw, L. A. (2015). Digital media and news. In C. Atton (ed.), *The Routledge Companion to Alternative and Community Media.* London and New York: Routledge, pp. 301–312.

Lippmann, W. (1922). *Public Opinion.* New York: Harcourt, Brace & Co.

Lyon, D. (1988). *The Information Society: Issues and Illusions.* Cambridge: Polity Press.

Machlup, F. (1962). *The Production and Distribution of Knowledge in the United States.* Princeton, NJ: Princeton University Press.

Massing, M. (2005). The End of News? *New York Review of Books*, 52(19), 23–27.

McDonald, K. (1994). Alain Touraine's Sociology of the Subject. *Thesis Eleven*, 38, 46–60.

McLuhan, M. (1964). *Understanding Media: The Extensions of Man.* New York: McGraw-Hill.

Meyer, P. (1973). *Precision Journalism: A Reporter's Introduction to Social Science Methods.* Bloomington: Indiana University Press.

Morris-Suzuki, T. (1986). Capitalism in the Computer Age. *New Left Review*, I(160), 81–91, November–December.

Mosco, V. (1982). *Pushbutton Fantasies: Critical Perspectives on Videotex and Information Technology.* Norwood, NJ: Ablex.

Neff, G. (2012). *Venture Labor: Work and the Burden of Risk in Innovative Industries.* Cambridge, MA: MIT Press.

Nora, S., and Minc, A. (1980[1978]). *The Computerization of Society: A Report to the President of France.* Cambridge, MA: MIT Press (Originally published as *Informatisation de la société: rapport à M. le Président de la République.* Paris: La Documentation française, 1978).

Nygren, G. (2011). Passing Through Journalism? Journalism as a Temporary Job and Professional Institutions in Decline. In B. Franklin and D. Mensing (eds.), *Journalism Education, Training and Employment.* London and New York: Routledge, pp. 207–221.

Ocejo, R. E. (2017). *Masters of Craft: Old Jobs in the New Urban Economy.* Princeton, NJ: Princeton University Press.

OECD. (1981). *Information Activities, Electronics, and Telecommunication Technologies: Vol. 1, Impact on Employment, Growth and Trade.* Directorate for Science, Technology and Industry, Committee for Information, Computer and Communications Policy, Publication No. 6. Paris: Organization for Economic Co-operation and Development.

OECD. (2016). *New Forms of Work in the Digital Economy*. Directorate for Science, Technology and Innovation, Committee on Digital Economy Policy, Working Party on Measurement and Analysis of the Digital Economy. Report no. DSTI/ICCP/IIS(2015)13/FINAL. Paris: Organization for Economic Co-operation and Development.

Oppenheimer, M. (1972). The Proletarianization of the Professional. *Sociological Review*, 20(suppl. 1), 213–227.

Örnebring, H. (2010). Technology and Journalism-as-Labor: Historical Perspectives. *Journalism*, 11(1), 57–74.

Paulussen, S. (2012). Technology and the Transformation of News Work: Are Labor Conditions in (online) Journalism Changing? In E. Siapera and A. Veglis (eds.), *The Handbook of Global Online Journalism*. New York: John Wiley & Sons, pp. 192–208.

Peters, J. W. (2010). In a World of Online News, Burnout Starts Younger. *New York Times*, p. B1, July 18. www.nytimes.com/2010/07/19/business/media/19press.html.

Porat, M. U., and Rubin, M. R. (1977). *The Information Economy* (vols. 1–8). Washington, DC: U.S. Department of Commerce, Office of Telecommunications. OT Special Publication 77–12.

Reinardy, S. (2011). Newspaper Journalism in Crisis: Burnout on the Rise, Eroding Young Journalists' Career Advancement. *Journalism*, 12(1), 33–50.

Richtel, M. (2008). In the Web World of 24/7 Stress, Writers Blog Till They Drop. *New York Times*, p. A1, A23, April 6. www.nytimes.com/2008/04/06/technology/06sweat.html.

Riesman, D. (1964[1958]). Leisure and Work in Postindustrial Society. In *Abundance for What? and Other Essays*. Garden City, NY: Doubleday, pp. 162–183.

Robinson, S. (2011). 'News as Process': The Organizational Implications of Participatory Online News. *Journalism & Communication Monographs*, 13(3), 137–210.

Ross, A. (2001). No-Collar Labour in America's 'New Economy'. *Socialist Register*, 37, 77–87. https://socialistregister.com/index.php/srv/article/view/5756.

Saval, N. (2018). Productivity. *Columbia Journalism Review*, 32–39, Spring–Summer.

Schement, J. R., and Lievrouw, L. A. (1984). A Behavioural Measure of Information Work. *Telecommunications Policy*, 8(4), 321–334, December.

Schement, J. R., and Lievrouw, L. A. (eds.). (1987). *Competing Visions, Complex Realities: Social Aspects of the Information Society*. Norwood, NJ: Ablex.

Schement, J. R., Lievrouw, L. A., and Dordick, H. I. (1983). The Information Society in California: Social Factors Influencing Its Emergence. *Telecommunications Policy*, 7(1), 64–72, March.

Schiller, D. (1982). *Telematics and Government*. Norwood, NJ: Ablex.

Schiller, H. I. (1981). *Who Knows: Information in the Age of the Fortune 500*. Norwood, NJ: Ablex.

Scholz, T. (2008). Market Ideology and the Myths of Web 2.0. *First Monday*, 13(3), March 3.

Scholz, T. (2017). *Uberworked and Underpaid: How Workers are Disrupting the Digital Economy*. Cambridge: Polity Press.

Schudson, M. (2001). The Objectivity Norm in American Journalism. *Journalism*, 2(2), 149–170.

Smith, B. (2020). Why the Success of the New York Times May Be Bad News for Journalism. New York Times, p. B1, March 1. www.nytimes.com/2020/03/01/business/media/ben-smith-journalism-news-publishers-local.html.

Slack, J. D. (1984). The Information Revolution as Ideology. *Media, Culture & Society*, 6, 247–256.

Srnicek, N. (2016). *Platform Capitalism*. Cambridge: Polity Press.

Stalder, F. (2006). *Manuel Castells: The Theory of the Network Society*. Cambridge: Polity Press.

Standing, G. (2011). *The Precariat: The Dangerous New Class*. London and New York: Bloomsbury.

Stehr, N. (1994). *Knowledge Societies*. London and Thousand Oaks, CA: Sage.

Stigler, B. (2010). *New Critique of Political Economy*. Translated by D. Ross. Cambridge and Malden, MA: Polity Press.

Terranova, T. (2000). Free Labor: Producing Culture for the Digital Economy. *Social Text 63*, 18(2), 33–58, Summer.

Tiku, N. (2018). Why tech worker dissent is going viral. *WIRED*, June 29. www.wired.com/story/why-tech-worker-dissent-is-going-viral/.

Timberg, S. (2016). *Culture Crash: The Killing of the Creative Class* (with a new preface). New Haven and London: Yale University Press.

Touraine, A. (1971). *The Post-Industrial Society*. Translated by L. F. X. Mayhew. New York: Random House (Originally published as *La Société post-industrielle*. Paris: Editions Denoël S.A.R.L., 1969).

Touraine, A. (1977). *The Self-Production of Society*. Translated by D. Coltman. Chicago: University of Chicago Press (Originally published as *Production de la société*. Paris: Éditions du Seuil, 1973).

Touraine, A. (1981). *The Voice and the Eye: An Analysis of Social Movements*. Translated by A. Duff, with a foreword by R. Sennett. Cambridge: Cambridge University Press and Editions de la Maison des Sciences de l'Homme (Originally published as *Le Voix et le Regard*. Paris: Editions du Seuil, 1978).

Touraine, A. (1995). *Critique of Modernity*. Translated by D. Macey. Oxford: Blackwell (Originally published as *Une Critique de la Modernité*. Paris: Librarie Arthème Fayard, 1992).

Touraine, A. (2000). *Can We Live Together? Equality and Difference*. Translated by D. Macey. Stanford, CA: Stanford University Press, and Cambridge: Polity, in association with Blackwell (Originally published as *Pourrons-nous vivre ensemble? Egaux et Différents*. Paris: Librarie Arthème Fayard, 1997).

Touraine, A. (2007). *A New Paradigm for Understanding Today's World*. Translated by G. Elliott. Cambridge: Polity (Originally published as *Un Nouveau Paradigme pour comprendre le monde d'aujourd'hui*. Paris: Librarie Arthème Fayard, 2005).

Touraine, A. (2013). *La fin des societies*. Paris: Éditions du Seuil.

Touraine, A. (2014). *After the Crisis*. Translated by H. Morrison. Cambridge: Polity (Originally published as *Après la Crise*. Paris: Editions du Seuil, 2010).

U.S. Census Bureau. (1975). *Historical Statistics of the United States, Colonial Times to 1970* (Bicentennial ed.). Washington, DC: U.S. Census Bureau. www.census.gov/library/publications/1975/compendia/hist_stats_colonial-1970.html.

U.S. Census Bureau. (1990). *Statistical Abstract of the United States: 1990*. Washington, DC: U.S. Census Bureau. www.census.gov/library/publications/1990/compendia/statab/110ed.html.

U.S. Census Bureau. (2000). *Statistical Abstract of the United States: 2000*. Washington, DC: U.S. Census Bureau. www.census.gov/library/publications/2000/compendia/statab/120ed.html.

U.S. Census Bureau. (2010). *Statistical Abstract of the United States: 2010*. Washington, DC: U.S. Census Bureau. www.census.gov/library/publications/2009/compendia/statab/129ed.html.

U.S. Government Accountability Office. (2015). *Contingent Workforce: Size, Characteristics, Earnings, and Benefits*. GAO Report GAO-15–168R. Washington, DC: GAO. www.gao.gov/products/GAO-15-168R.

Wark, M. (2004). *A Hacker Manifesto*. Cambridge, MA: Harvard University Press.

Weaver, D. H., Willnat, L., and Wilhoit, G. C. (2018). The American Journalist in the Digital Age: Another Look at U.S. News People. *Journalism & Mass Communication Quarterly*, 1–30.

Webster, F., and Robins, K. (1989). Plan and Control: Towards a Cultural History of the Information Society. *Theory & Society*, 18, 323–351.

Wilke, J. (2013). Journalism. *European History Online* (EGO), published by the Leibniz Institute of European History (IEG), Mainz, August 6. www.ieg-ego.eu/wilkej-2013b-en.

Wuthnow, R., and Shrum, W. (1983). Knowledge Workers as a 'New Class': Structural and Ideological Convergences Among Professional-Technical Workers and Managers. *Work and Occupations*, 10, 471–487.

18

Automated surveillance

Mark Andrejevic

Surveillance no longer refers solely to the work of covert agencies and their spies or police and CCTV networks. In recent decades it has become a central component of the burgeoning online economy, as evidenced by the ready invocation in popular mainstream media of the so-called 'surveillance economy.' *The Wall Street Journal*, for example, ran a series of stories in 2012 about the growing range of digital surveillance technologies, ranging from automated license plate readers to online tracking, that it grouped under the rubric of the 'surveillance economy' (WSJ, Sept. 29, 2012). It is becoming increasingly clear that a large segment of the digital media economy is based on comprehensive and extensive forms of data collection about everyone and everything that can be measured. As the sociologist David Lyon has observed,

> Surveillance . . . now occurs routinely, locally and globally as an unavoidable feature of everyday life in contemporary societies. Organizations of all kinds engage in surveillance and citizens, consumers, and employees generally comply with that surveillance (with some noteworthy exceptions).
>
> *(2003, 1)*

The networked digital infrastructure continues to serve as the rapidly expanding foundation for this data-driven economy, and the advent of the so-called Internet of Things promises to transform our lived environment into a fully monitored one. While it is true that not all forms of information collection qualify as 'surveillance,' the development of this sensor-permeated infrastructure enables new logics of surveillance to emerge and take hold. This chapter explores the emerging logic of surveillance in the era of automated digital data collection, which transforms the scope, scale, and goals of surveillance practices and institutions.

A key feature of the so-called surveillance economy is that data collection piggybacks on a growing range of activities. Many new forms of efficiency and convenience enabled by digital devices and platforms come at the price of routine submission to increasingly comprehensive forms of data collection. We can immediately access all kinds of information online, we can remain in constant contact over networked systems, but all of these activities are simultaneously redoubled in the form of information about ourselves. The interactive overlay that increasingly characterizes our mediated activities acts as a historically unprecedented monitoring system empowering those who control commercial platforms and apps. Moreover the decisions we have made about how best to fund the online economy have facilitated the rapid accumulation of huge quantities of data. There are many ways to support a media platform or function, including public support and direct subscription, but targeted advertising has developed as a way of providing seemingly 'free' access to commercial platforms, and targeted advertising relies upon comprehensive data collection about those who use the platform. The development of this commercial model has, as Frank Pasquale has argued and the Snowden leaks revealed, created huge troves that have been used not just for commerce but also for state surveillance: "Government agencies want data that they can't legally or constitutionally collect for themselves; data brokers have it and want to sell it" (2015, 49). Even if the data is not sold, intelligence agencies have relied on both overt and covert strategies for obtaining it from commercial entities. At the same time, these agencies have imported not just databases but also models of data collection and data processing from the commercial sector. The former Chief Technology Officer for the CIA has cited Google's approach to data analytics as a model for approaching the process of intelligence gathering: "We have these astounding commercial capabilities that have emerged in the market space that allow us to do things with information we've never been able to do before" ("CIA's Chief Tech Officer . . .": 2013).

The blurring of the boundary between commercial and state surveillance corresponds to a de-differentiation of monitoring from surveillance – a claim that begs the question of the difference between the two. Surveillance connotes a metaphorical view from above, which is to say that it implies a power hierarchy of watcher over watched. It is possible to monitor from a variety of power positions for a range of purposes. Activist groups might monitor campaign finance contributions, for example, but we likely would not think of this as a form of surveillance. The pioneering surveillance studies scholar David Lyon has described surveillance as, "Any collection and processing of personal data, whether identifiable or not, for the purposes of influencing or managing those whose data have been garnered" (2001, 32). This is a broad definition that does not necessarily imply a power hierarchy: even activist monitoring of corporate or state activity might be characterized, in these terms, as a form of surveillance. The critical theorist Christian Fuchs offers what he describes as a more 'negative' take on surveillance as, "the collection of data on individuals or groups that are used so that control and discipline of behaviour can be exercised by the threat of being targeted by violence" (2011, 136). This is a definition that would exclude activities we are likely to think of as forming the basis of the 'surveillance economy,' such as Facebook determining when teenagers are feeling anxious or insecure and therefore vulnerable to particular marketing appeals. There are forms of control and coercion that fall short of violence but still reflect and reinforce hierarchical power relations.

Thus, for the purposes of this chapter, surveillance can be understood as a form of monitoring that takes place within a context of asymmetrical power relations, wherein the watchers are in the privileged position. This is a broad definition that might also include, for example, parental oversight, but it captures an element that seems central to a discussion of surveillance: the fact that it takes place from 'above.' We might add the further qualification that the interests of the watchers and the watched do not coincide – and that those of the former are privileged by the unequal power relations that characterize the surveillance process. Such a formulation helps distinguish between forms of monitoring that might be termed care and those that entail some level of coercion and can thus be understood as surveillance. With this in mind, the remainder of the chapter explores the reconfiguration of surveillance practices enabled by digital infrastructures that facilitate large scale, passive data collection and automated data processing. It seeks to identify emerging logics of automated forms of surveillance that, in their relationship to one another, constitute a distinct configuration without entirely displacing previous surveillance practices. In particular, the chapter argues that digital surveillance dispenses with the disciplinary logics associated with the classic model of surveillance – the Panopticon. Rather than disciplining subjects by getting them to internalize the imperatives of the monitoring gaze, emerging surveillance practices are linked to forms of prediction that legitimize active external intervention. This intervention typically takes place in the register of pre-emption and relies upon increasingly comprehensive forms of information collection as well as the ongoing attempt to govern via what Foucault once described as "environmental" forms of regulation (2008, 271): "a governmentality which will act on the environment and systematically modify its variables" (Massumi, 2009, 155). This is a mode of governance well suited to the incunabulum of the 'Internet of Things' and its hyper-mediated complement: virtual/augmented reality. Both envision the automated malleability of the environment as a mode of feedback-based response and control. They also envision the convergence of mediation, surveillance, and response: an environment that anticipates and reacts to those who inhabit it. If smart spaces, for example, may someday predict when someone is going to fall and inflate an airbag to cushion the fall, virtual reality will deform in response to users in ways that reflect the imperatives of the platform upon which it relies. On the one hand, we might view this form of control as a promise of liberation from the obduracy and resistance of the material world; on the other hand it amounts to the combination of total surveillance with enhanced forms of social control. As Slavoj Žižek puts it in his discussion of the two complementary aspects of virtual reality: "on the one hand, reduction of reality to a virtual domain regulated by arbitrary rules that can be suspended; on the other hand, the concealed truth of this freedom, the reduction of the subject to an utter instrumentalized passivity" (Žižek, 2006, 1551).

From investigation to intelligence

In his work on automated decision-making, the critical legal scholar Frank Pasquale identifies a characteristic shift of the logic of surveillance in the digital era: from targeted monitoring of suspects to anticipatory monitoring of entire populations. As he puts it, as opposed to standard models of investigation, " 'intelligence' work is anticipatory" (2015, 47). Thanks to the advent of digital, interactive technology, the work of surveillance can be offloaded onto automated systems. Once upon a time, it was costly, time intensive work to track the minute-by-minute movements of a particular individual. Thanks to the ubiquity of mobile telephony, such tracking becomes an automated by-product of using the technology. When surveillance resources are limited, there is a need for parsimony in its deployment – both in terms of information collection and information processing. Tracking half of the population would require the efforts of the other half. The great innovation of that prototypically utilitarian invention, *the Panopticon*, was its promise to generalize surveillance without having to enlist half the population to watch the other half. Bentham's hope was that the technology would train individuals to become reflexive spies, relentlessly monitoring their own activity to ensure that it was in line with the priorities of power. The internalization of the monitoring gaze made it possible to envision the possibility that everyone could be monitored all the time – on the condition that they did so themselves. Thus, for Bentham, the function of the 'inspector' in the central tower of the panoptic prison (or hospital, or barracks, or schoolyard) was a symbolic one, in the precise sense that it represented an absent referent: the all-seeing eye of power. This 'eye' had to remain hidden precisely to produce the illusion of total vision, just as surveillance cameras now operate behind smoked glass to signify that they could be casting their gaze in any direction. Once the Panopticon started to function properly, the figure of the inspector would no longer be needed because subjects would become self-disciplining: the symbol of power would fill in for the absence of omniscience. As Foucault put it, being watched all the time is, in the panoptic model, "at once too much and too little" for the purposes of disciplinary control of the prisoner: "too little, for what matters is that he knows himself to be observed; too much, because he has no need in fact of being so" (1977, 201).

By contrast, digital surveillance operates in the register of full expenditure and total information collection. In the interactive era, the formula is flipped: Panoptic forms of surveillance are at once too much and not enough; too much because in the post-panoptic model there is no need for the target to be aware of the reach and depth of surveillance or even that it is taking place; too little because the emerging model relies on total information collection: amassing all the information that can be captured and holding on to it forever. In this respect, digital surveillance operates in a post-disciplinary register. This shift was foreshadowed by Oscar Gandy's (1993) formulation of the "Panoptic Sort" – which relied more on external categorization of individuals than on their internalization of normalized forms of behavior. Gandy's seminal work, which described data mining as "a difference machine that sorts individuals into categories and classes on the basis of routine measurements" (p. 2), anticipated the rise of mass customization and the forms of automated data processing that drive the online economy. Post-disciplinarity has several characteristic consequences for the surveillance process: deterrence is displaced by pre-emption; surveillance no longer relies upon symbolic efficiency; and the target of surveillance becomes neither the subject nor the population, but the pattern.

Beyond the frame

The characteristic attribute of this reconfigured form of surveillance can be described as 'frame-lessness' – there is no delimitation to the amount or type of information to be collected. By contrast, from a panoptic perspective, surveillance is limited to the level that results in the internalization of the monitoring gaze. According to conventional search-and-winnow models, surveillance is focused on designated targets and relevant information. Extraneous information can be discarded. From the perspective of either commerce or security, targets can be sorted into high and low value, with many falling below the monitoring threshold. All of this changes with the rise of automated, digital data collection and processing, which hold out the promise of total information collection: the redoubling of the world in informational form so that it can be fully mined, stored, and processed. This shift has sometimes been described as a change in emphasis from monitoring individuals to tracking groups and eventually the entire population. However, in the era of automated surveillance it is neither the individual nor the population that is at stake, but the pattern. When the pattern is the target, all information is potentially relevant and none can be discarded until the full picture emerges (i.e. – never, although the picture never stops emerging: from the perspective of the monitoring apparatus all response is data, even non-response). An additional piece of information may allow a previously un-discerned pattern to emerge – one that would have been impossible to detect without the entirety of already compiled data. The goal is not simply to monitor populations, as in the biopolitical mode of governance described by Foucault in his lectures at the College de France (2003), but to reconstruct entire environments, and therefore to anticipate discrete, emergent events. If Foucault's version of biopower exerted itself at the level of overarching statistical trends, emerging strategies of comprehensive surveillance returns to the level of individual actions and events. Consider, for example, the framing of so-called predictive policing, which uses data-driven predictive analytics to send police to the site of potential emergence of particular crimes. The paradigmatic example, frequently cited in early articles about predictive policing, recounts the case of an officer positioned just in the right place to catch criminals in the act:

> A Santa Cruz beat cop . . . was eating his lunch in his patrol car in a downtown parking lot because it was on that shift's predictive list. He spotted two women trying to break into cars and arrested them.
>
> *(Baxter, 2013, 1)*

Pre-emption, in this context, remains short term – almost instantaneous. As the opening of one article on predictive policing put it, "What if police could detect a crime before it happened? Say they could nab a burglar before he's even broken a window? Or stop a fight before the first punch has even been thrown?" (O'Donoghue, 2016). Such examples invoke the temporal reconfiguration described by Pasquale: from tracking identified suspects to gathering predictive intelligence.

Pre-emption versus prevention

In this regard, digital era surveillance embraces the anticipatory logic of pre-emption, which is a more active, interventionist model than panoptic logics of deterrence. Whereas the Panopticon envisioned the possibility of the absence of intervention when individuals have become fully self-regulating, total monitoring anticipates a world of ongoing, targeted forms of external intervention. If no police are needed in the perfected panoptic state, an increasingly intrusive and automated policing presence is the hallmark of pre-emptive monitoring. To the extent that each act can be anticipated in advance, it can be acted upon prior to its emergence. But this requires increased policing resources and inaugurates what might be described as a logic of automation whereby automated data collection leads to automated information processing and, eventually, automated response. If the Panoptic model turns each subject into its own self-policing officer, post-Panopticism externalizes the policing process once again, returning it to the active intervention of the authorities. What makes possible the fantasy of ongoing external intervention is the promise of automation, for there are not enough human resources available to keep up with the ongoing need for intervention once subjects are no longer relied upon to internalize the monitoring gaze. We should not be surprised, then, that the growing interest in predictive policing is coupled with the return of the fantasy of automated policing: the rise of networked systems of 'robocops.'

To put it in somewhat different terms, we might describe the ambition of total surveillance as post-disciplinary in the sense that it does not rely on the self-disciplined subject. The spectacle of panoptic discipline is a familiar one: we are surrounded by monitoring mechanisms that signify their own presence in order to shape our behavior. Recall, for example, the familiar 'smile, you're on camera' signs in shops, or the speed camera signs alongside highways. This model of surveillance relies on the combination of symbolic efficiency with self-disciplining subjects: if I see the symbol of surveillance, I will internalize its imperatives and behave accordingly. In such a model, symbolic efficiency – the power of the representation of surveillance (in the form of the tower or the CCTV camera, for example) goes hand-in-hand with the disciplinable subject. By contrast, total surveillance dispenses with reliance on such a subject. It may still perhaps have a deterrent effect, but this need not be counted upon. In the world of total surveillance, the fantasy of automation is that future acts can be anticipated with an accuracy that allows them to be acted upon directly, in the present. As Brian Massumi puts it, this form of governance "must work through the 'regulation of effects' rather than of causes" (2009, 153). It projects into the future to anticipate eventual effects (the radicalization of an individual or the eruption of criminal activity) before they take place – acting upon them as if they are so certain to happen that it is as if, for all practical purposes, they already have.

There is a certain resonance of this version of surveillance within the post-9/11 era, which takes as its defining figure, not the disciplined subject of Foucault's prison enclosure, but the undisciplinable, irrational, and a-subjective figure of the terrorist. Media theorist Elayne Rapping traces this shift in her comparison of conventional detective dramas with the reality TV show *Cops* (which is based on actual footage of policing activity). She argues that whereas conventional crime dramas such as *Colombo* (which typically unfolds a narrative around criminal motives and their detection) portray criminals as subjects, albeit malfunctioning ones, *Cops* marks a shift to the portrayal of criminals as post-subjective, and thus inaccessible to disciplinary practices. They are framed, she argues, as, "incorrigibly 'other' and 'alien;' incapable of internalizing or abiding by the norms and values of a liberal democracy, for they are far too irrational, uncontrollable, and inscrutable for such measures to be effective" (2004, 227). The criminals portrayed on *Cops* are not figures who participate in the rational calculus inspired by the threat of surveillance and the specter of punishment: they come to represent the resurgence of the category of the un-disciplinable. The very staging of the show emphasizes the obliviousness of the alleged criminals it portrays to the power of the monitoring gaze. They are on TV yet unable or unwilling to 'behave.' The paradigmatic representative of a non-narrativizable, ubiquitous criminal threat is the terrorist: "Terrorists are irrational, inscrutable, and inherently violent . . . And they cannot be 'reformed' or 'rehabilitated'" (2004, 225). Instead, their actions must be detected in advance and thwarted before they can take shape: they must be pre-empted. Such an approach retains what might be described as an actuarial approach, insofar as criminality is taken for granted as a recurring, regular and predictable tendency in the population. However, instead of attempting to manage this tendency in preventative fashion by focusing on underlying causes, post-disciplinary approaches target behavior at its point of emergence.

This is a familiar model from the Global War on Terror, which identifies high-risk individuals and targets them with drone strikes before they can act. The goal is not to 'understand' criminal motivation – because motivation becomes inaccessible in allegedly undisciplinable subjects – but to detect it and act first. If disciplinary surveillance retains a utilitarian aversion to violence (taken to the limit, generalized self-regulation could dispense with punishment altogether), post-disciplinary surveillance envisions perpetual, ongoing, intervention: violence without end. In the Cold War model described by Jean Baudrillard information-based simulation is associated with the frozen stasis of deterrence. By contrast, the data-driven simulations of the war on terror anticipate a process of ongoing violent pre-emption. The difference is a result of asymmetry and the 'frontierless' character of conflict (strikes can happen, from both sides, anywhere without warning) as well as of the imagined capabilities of comprehensive monitoring to predict behavior in advance. A generalized sense of distributed risk serves as a warrant for surveillance without limit. As Ben Anderson puts it, in his discussion of counter-insurgency: strategies of pre-emption, including surveillance, "must also extend throughout life without limit . . . Dangerousness exists as a potential distributed everywhere and conditioned by anything and everything" (2011, 221).

Beyond the Panopticon

Taken together, the emergent character of risk and the dissolution of the model of the disciplinable subject contribute to the imperative of framelessness – understood as information collection without limits. It is telling, in this regard, that contemporary media increasingly embrace the aesthetic dimension of framelessness, such as 360- degree video and virtual reality. Such forms remain nominally within the ambit of representation, but their tendency pushes further into what might be described as the realm of the 'operational' image. Conventional surveillance relied upon the creation of information portraits to be interpreted by human analysts. Digital era surveillance generates databases that extend far beyond the capacity of human interpretation. If the panoptic model of surveillance invokes the figure of all-too human surveillance in the form of the superintendent; that of digital era surveillance relies upon the automated perfection of an all-seeing presence. If the superintendent served as a symbolic stand-in for an omniscient gaze, automated surveillance envisions the construction of omniscience in reality. If the former symbolizes the deity, the latter replaces it. Panopticism relies upon the *symbols* of surveillance: tower, camera, microphone, one-way glass, and so on, whereas automated surveillance no longer needs to represent itself – to make itself present to targets – precisely because it is everywhere, and so it recedes into the environment. This 'becoming ambient' of monitoring is the model of the 'Internet of Things': all of the objects in our lives, including the spaces through which we move, become redoubled as sensors. We still experience them as the components of our environment: the toaster, the refrigerator, the door; but in the world of ubiquitous computing they will also 'see' us – or rather 'sense' us in every register for which sensors can be developed. Their symbolic presence is no longer necessary because the goal is no longer to provide a constant reminder of the prospect of a monitoring gaze. Nor is it to instill the productive uncertainty of the Panopticon: the question of whether, at any given moment I am being watched. All doubt is removed in a context of environmental surveillance: there is no question about whether I am watched. Nor is this knowledge meant to be productive or disciplinary. For the purposes of comprehensive surveillance, the goal is not that activity is reformed through the process of being watched, but rather that conduct is anticipated. The objective becomes the normalization of surveillance to the extent that even the awareness that it is taking place fades into the background, so that surveillance no longer modifies activity. Comprehensive monitoring systems rely precisely on forms of ignoring/ignorance that allow for unconstrained behavior to be accurately documented. The sensors seek to catch us as we are – not as we should be – in order to police (and market) more efficiently. The reality TV cast member who recounts becoming so accustomed to the surrounding cameras that she no longer notices them – and thus behaves 'more naturally,' unconstrained by any attempt to perform for the absent other – models the prescribed attitude for always-on surveillance (Andrejevic, 2004).

Automated surveillance turns out to be even more productive than its Panoptic predecessor. For Foucault, the Panopticon embodied the productive imperative of capitalism, not to waste potentially productive bodies by damaging them or leaving them to be forgotten in dungeons, but to render them "docile and useful" (1977, 231). But the Panopticon also embodied the paradox of parsimonious power: the incitation to productivity was coupled with an economy of force characteristic of industrial mass production. Utility and conformity conspired to produce homogeneity: the submission to a unified standard of disciplined behavior, whether in the prison, factory, or classroom. Moreover, the monitoring apparatus's goal might be described as self-subtraction or self-disintegration: not more and more surveillance, but less and less. As Foucault puts it, the Panopticon's inventor, Jeremy Bentham, "was surprised that panoptic institutions could be so light" (1977, 202). The internalization of the monitoring gaze meant that, "external power may throw off its physical weight" (1977, 203). This economy of force renders the need for actual surveillance, along with its infrastructures and processors, its watchers and enforcers superfluous, resulting in a contraction that complements the increased productivity of the docile bodies it produces.

The lightness of the panoptic apparatus corresponds with the homogeneity of its disciplining power – a fact attested to by the role of the tower as the unified site of centralized control. As Deleuze's (1992) work on the rise of 'societies of control' suggests, the imperative of capitalist productivity runs headlong into the parsimony and homogeneity of industrial mass society. The advent of automated, computerized control enabled the burgeoning differentiation, individualization, and de-homogenization of mass customized production. If, as Deleuze puts it, industrial capitalism is "a capitalism of concentration," digital capitalism is "essentially dispersive" (1992, 6). Bursting the limits of mass production means unleashing a growing diversity of options, choices, lifestyles, and behaviors. The simulation of surveillance that produced the static behavioral template of the Panopticon gives way to surveillance as simulation: the attempt to model and predict the multiplying array of activities, desires, and risks unleashed by post-mass society (Bogard, 1996). The excessive hyper-productivity of post-panoptic surveillance displaces the parsimony of the Panopticon. The withering away of the surveillance apparatus envisioned by the perfection of discipline is superseded by the infinite productivity of surveillance capitalism: more sensors, more data, and endless intervention.

Convergent surveillance and environmentality

Here again, we might mark the affinity between market and state surveillance. In the post-panoptic era, both embrace the logic of data collection without limits – and of accelerating processes of external intervention. The example of Amazon.com's anticipatory shipping patent models the datafied acceleration that collapses the future into the present. Based on detailed user profile, the company imagines the possibility of knowing what consumers want better than – and before – they do themselves in order to ship products to them without waiting for consumers to order what they don't yet know they want. As one press account of the patent put it, "The company crunches its streams of data to forecast generally where a certain item might be wanted, [and] sends it on its way . . . On the off chance that the item doesn't actually get ordered, Amazon might discount it to the person at the place it arrived, or even give it away for free" (DePillis, 2014). This model for product delivery replicates the anticipatory logic of the drone strike: in both cases, a delivery is made before the target can act: whether in the realm of violence or that of consumption. Tellingly, both forms of 'anticipatory shipping' rely on drone delivery. Amazon has patented a floating mother-ship warehouse blimp that would hover over cities, launching deliver drones to individual houses below. Both logics raise questions of temporality: how far ahead can a future be compressed into the present? How many packages can Amazon deliver as it anticipates a future trajectory of consumption? How far ahead can state surveillance anticipate eventual acts of insurgency and terror? We can see these logics at play, for example, in the attempt to use genetic analysis to predict both consumption and criminality. At first glance we might imagine that the two forms of drone delivery are opposed: one anticipates an ongoing lifecycle of consumption, the other ends this cycle abruptly and definitively. But there is perhaps an underlying affinity: in each case the perfection of surveillance is redoubled in the form of pre-emption: desires are acted upon before they emerge. To the extent that life manifests itself in the unfolding of desire, it is thwarted. Umbilicular consumption projects backward to the pre-subjective state of the unborn; pre-emptive strikes project forward to a post-subjective version of stasis. Both rely on the proliferation of surveillance to extinguish desire: its death-grip upon life in all dimensions.

We might, then describe the automation of surveillance in terms of its becoming both 'environmental' and 'operational.' Brian Massumi draws on Foucault's lectures at the College de France to describe "a contemporary regime of power, coincident with the rise of neoliberalism, as 'environmental': a governmentality which will act on the environment and systematically modify its variables" (2009, 155). This is a suggestive formulation in the era of the convergent interactivity of physical and virtual environments. To speak of a power that can modulate the variables of our surroundings is to invoke a process that has become increasingly familiar. We know that the online environment is infinitely malleable, constantly in the process of varying itself to conduct experiments on consumers and provide them with a targeted, customized interface. The 'Internet of Things' redoubles this process of modulation in physical space. In both cases, environmental modulation goes hand-in-hand with what might be described as environmental surveillance: not just the redoubling of the environment as sensor but also the attempt to capture and simulate entire environments in digital form. The imperative of environmental surveillance is driven by the double logic of ubiquitous risk and opportunity. We might describe these as the double-edged sword of post-disciplinary society: on the one hand the infinite productivity of post-homogeneity; on the other, the threat of undisciplined subjects. As Massumi puts it, "The shift in the figure of the environment has moved it out of reach of normalization. It asserts its own normality, of crisis: the anywhere, anytime potential for the emergence of the abnormal" (2009, 160).

From representation to operation

The becoming environmental of surveillance reconfigures the logic of representation that underpins surveillance by generating an avalanche of information unprocessable without the aid of automation. This is the cascading logic of automated interactivity: automated data collection leads to automated data processing and, eventually automated response. Consider, for example, the transitional model of 'cortically coupled vision.' Developed to accelerate human image processing for drone imagery, the system capitalizes on the fact that the brains of people searching through images for anomalies register a physiological response prior to the viewing subject consciously noticing any anomaly. The brain 'notices' something before the thinking subject is aware of it. To speed up image processing, researchers use electroencephalography (EEG) to determine when viewers' brains respond to particular images – prior to their conscious registration of this response (Gerson et al., 2006). That is, brains are treated as sensors that, when connected to a monitoring infrastructure, allow viewers, "to find meaningful objects in mountains of images up to 10 times faster than they normally could" (Discover, 2011, 1). This is just a transitional phase: the researchers plan to use the data to train machines to respond even more rapidly to the same anomalies that triggered brain response in humans. This process of prosthetic automation is become a common characteristic of our interactive devices: they assist us in processing information, noting the patterns of our response and eventually automating the information sorting process. Texting allows us to respond in real time to a growing range of contacts faster and more efficiently – and new platforms promise to automate our text responses to speed things up even more. The systems learn from our activity and then replicate it. The increasing range and sensitivity of our interactive interfaces generate more information than we could hope to manage and then help configure the spaces through which we move, the information to which we are exposed, and our social contacts. Environmental monitoring and environmental modulation go hand-in-hand.

The quantity of information collected and the speed with which it is processed surpass the limits of representation. Consider, once again, the example of cortically coupled vision. Once machines are trained to respond to the anomalies that trigger a human reaction, they can process images at speeds and levels of complexity far surpassing those achieved by humans. This process will correspond with the obliteration of the image itself, as sensor signals (of all kinds of information: visual, auditory, etc.) are fed directly into automated systems. Drawing on the work of Harun Farocki, the artist Trevor Paglen (2014) describes this obliteration of the image as its becoming 'operational.' Farocki made a series of films about images made neither to entertain nor to inform, but as a way of representing how machines process information. As he put it, "I called such images. . . 'operative images.' These are images that do not represent an object, but rather are part of an operation" (2004, 17). Since the machines can convey information directly to one another, the production of an image for human viewers becomes irrelevant and superfluous. At work here is an anaesthetics of disappearance – not the screenic dematerialization explored by Paul Virilio (1980), but the obliteration of the screen altogether, along with its associated aesthetics. In this regard, the operational image is post-representational (although not in the 'affective' sense), post-screen, and post-aesthetic. As operations become automatic, they disappear into the machinic apparatus. Thus, when Paglen attempted to update Farocki's work more than a decade later, he discovered, "that machines rarely even bother making the meat-eye interpretable versions of their operational images that we saw in [Farocki's] *Eye/Machine*. There's really no point. Meat-eyes are far too inefficient to see what's going on anyway" (Paglen, 2014, 3). Just as the sensors fade into the environment, the images they generate dissipate into the atmosphere of invisible electro-magnetic communication. The 'images' they create are beyond human access and comprehension, comprised of multi-dimensional and multisensory inputs merged into the convergent language of bits. It comes as no surprise that 'transparency' becomes the rallying cry for accountability at a time when there is nothing left to see: we want to see precisely what we cannot: the complex interactions between millions of variables and the reasons behind the emergent decisions they make. The public secret of comprehensive surveillance is that there is nothing left for those who watch the watchers to *see*. Even if the databases were to be thrown open by force, the decision-making process has retreated into the black box of neural nets and emergent processes of data mining and machine learning.

Operational surveillance does not just raise important issues of accountability; it also collapses the space of representation and thus for politics. Taken to its limit the endpoint of data-driven decision-making is the automation of judgment. In practical terms the goal is to develop automated systems that make decisions that govern life, liberty, and opportunity. In this respect automation, as suggested earlier, embraces the logic of immediation that parallels the promise of virtual reality. Both partake of what the philosopher Slavoj Žižek describes as, "the dream of a language which no longer acts upon the subject merely through the intermediate sphere of meaning, but has direct effects in the real" (1996, 196). This is precisely the promise of machine language – which differs from human language precisely because it is non-representational. For the machine there is no space between sign and referent: there is no 'lack' in a language that is complete unto itself. In this respect, machine language is 'psychotic' in the precise sense that Žižek uses to describe virtual reality:

> If, in 'normal' symbolic communication, we are dealing with the distance (between 'things' and 'words') which opens up the space for the domain of Sense and, within it, for symbolic engagement, in the case of virtual reality, on the contrary, the very over-proximity (of the sign and the designated content) disengages us, closes up the space for symbolic engagement.
>
> *(1996, 196)*

Symbolic language, in Žižek's terms, opens up the space for interpretation, politics, and judgment, precisely because of its gaps, its incompleteness. Total surveillance via digital media promises to fill in all the gaps: not just those associated with incomplete knowledge but also that between things and words. That these are both unbridgeable gaps does not change the fact that the pursuit of automation proceeds according to an impossible fantasy of completeness. This impossibility is unlikely to stop the progression of the automation of surveillance to incorporate that of decision-making and response. However, it does provide an entry point for critique: what passes itself off as complete and totalized is always only partial – and this partiality is shaped by the priorities of those who design the sensors and program the databases. Representation re-enters in the form of narratives about the incompleteness of the database and the uses to which it is put: the goals that are prioritized and the ends these serve. Information will never be total and the machine borrows its priorities from those who program it. The peril posed by automated surveillance is not that it will be perfected, but that we will act as if it could be, developing increasingly comprehensive sensing networks to feed into automated sorting and decision-making systems, displacing the language of politics with that of the operation.

References

Anderson, B. (2011). Facing the Future Enemy: US Counterinsurgency Doctrine and the Pre-Insurgent. *Theory, Culture & Society*, 28(7–8), 216–240.

Andrejevic, M. (2004). *Reality TV: The Work of Being Watched*. Lanham: Rowman & Littlefield.

Baxter, S. (2013). Santa Cruz Predictive Policing Adds Tool for Cops, Neighbors. *Santa Cruz Sentinel*, August 14. www.santacruzsentinel.com/article/zz/20130814/NEWS/130817547.

Bogard, W. (1996). *The Simulation of Surveillance: Hyper-Control in Telematic Societies*. Cambridge: Press Syndicate of the University of Cambridge.

Deleuze, G. (1992). Postscript on the Societies of Control. *October*, 59, 3–7.

DePillis, L. (2014). Amazon Wants to Send Stuff Before You Order It: Are Other Retailers Doomed? *The Washington Post*, January 30. www.washingtonpost.com/news/wonk/wp/2014/01/30/amazon-wants-to-send-stuff-before-you-order-it-are-other-retailers-doomed/?utm_term=.cd5abb0e135c (Accessed March 1, 2018).

Discover. (2011). *How to Fix Our Most Vexing Problems*, October. http://discovermagazine.com/2011/oct/21-how-to-fix-problems-mosquitoes-potholes-corpses.

Farocki, H. (2004). Phantom Images. *Public*, 29.

Foucault, M. (1977). *Discipline and Punish*. New York: Pantheon.

Foucault, M. (2003). *'Society Must Be Defended': Lectures at the Collège de France, 1975–1976* (vol. 1). New York: Palgrave Macmillan.

Foucault, M. (2008). *'The Birth of Biopolitics': Lectures at the Collège de France 1978–1979*. Translated by Graham Burchell. New York: Palgrave Macmillan.

Fuchs, C. (2011). New Media, Web 2.0 and Surveillance. *Sociology Compass*, 5(2), 134–147.

Gandy Jr, O. H. (1993). *The Panoptic Sort: A Political Economy of Personal Information. Critical Studies in Communication and in the Cultural Industries*. Boulder, CO: Westview Press.

Gerson, A. D., Parra, L. C., and Sajda, P. (2006). Cortically Coupled Computer Vision for Rapid Image Search. *Neural Systems and Rehabilitation Engineering, IEEE Transactions on*, 14(2), 174–179.

Lyon, D. (2001). *Surveillance Society: Monitoring Everyday Life*. London: Open University Press.

Lyon, D. (ed.). (2003). *Surveillance as Social Sorting: Privacy, Risk, and Digital Discrimination*. London: Psychology Press.

Massumi, B. (2009). National Enterprise Emergency: Steps Toward an Ecology of Powers. *Theory, Culture & Society*, 26(6), 153–185.

O'Donoghue, R. (2016). Is Kent's Predictive Policing Project the Future of Crime Prevention? *Kent Online*, April 5. Retrieved 10 July, 2020. http://www.kentonline.co.uk/sheerness/news/what-if-police-could-detect-93715 (Accessed July 10, 2020).

Paglen, T. (2014). Operational Images. *E-Flux*, 59, 1–3.

Pasquale, F. (2015). *The Black Box Society: The Secret Algorithms That Control Money and Information*. Cambridge, MA: Harvard University Press.

Rapping, E. (2004). *Aliens, Nomads, Mad Dogs, and Road Warriors: The Changing Face of Criminal Violence on TV*. CIA's Chief Tech Officer on Big Data: We Try to Collect Everything and Hang Onto It Forever, YouTube.com. Video. www.youtube.com/watch?v=GUPd2uMiXXg (Accessed August 1, 2018).

Virilio, P. (1980). *The Aesthetics of Disappearance*. New York: SemioText(e).

Žižek, S. (1996). *The Indivisible Remainder: An Essay on Schelling and Related Matters*. London: Verso.

Žižek, S. (2006). The Matrix, or, the Two Sides of Perversion. In *The International Handbook of Virtual Learning Environments*. Dordrecht: Springer, pp. 1549–1569.

Part III

Arrangements

19

Deep mediatization

Media institutions' changing relations to the social

Nick Couldry

Media are ways of organizing communication. The relationship between media in this broad sense and the very possibility of *social order* is so basic that it is hard to see: its operations are almost entirely naturalized. The key institutions of modernity (corporations and trade unions, communities and churches, civil society organizations and governments) have been organized on the basis of a particular set of relations between media and everyday life (social, economic, political). But what if those relations are changing? What if those relations are now being disrupted by a new and distinct pattern of institutionalization through 'media'? Under conditions of intensified production and circulation of communication – and radically transformed market competition – the set of institutions we still call 'media' demand a reinterpretation of how social life is ordered through media, indeed of the role that institutional concentrations of power such as media now play in social order itself. This chapter hopes to unpack this deep transformation that is under way today.

This requires uncovering the role that communications have *always* played in the emergence of the coordinated spaces of exchange and interaction intrinsic to modernity. Markets throughout history have been spaces of communication, but the national and regional market economies that characterized modernity required a more organized flow of communications across space and time than the market square allowed. Not only do economic transactions now require many layers of communication at a distance (e.g., the operations of national stock markets or the credit card system) but, more indirectly, a large economy relies on a transportation system, and that transportation system, if it is not to quickly break down, relies in turn on faster, more coordinated flows of communication (Beniger, 1987). Yet, because human beings are animals who construct reality through communication, communication is so basic to human life that has often in the past been *effaced* in accounts of how organizations and economies have been transformed. Institutional analysis often seems to 'see through' the organization of communication to focus on supposedly 'harder' structures underlying it, forgetting precisely the fundamental role that media, understood as the organization of communication, plays in making those very structures possible. But recent far-reaching changes in the organization of communication make inadequate any attempt to 'see through' communications' role in forming today's institutions (what we might call 'institution*alization*'); media in the broad sense are changing the basic ways in which people and resources can be organized to form anything like a 'social order' (Wrong,

1994). In developing the theme of institutionalization, I will build on the argument of a recent book that tried to think in new ways about the contributions of media to the very possibility of social order (Couldry & Hepp, 2016).

The late 20th and early 21st centuries have seen the digitization of most communicational content, the construction of a global space of communicative exchange called 'the Internet,' and the embedding in daily life of connections across that space that have begun to transform social relations. While a first wave of social theory (Giddens, 1990; Appadurai, 1996) drew key insights from an earlier stage in the globalization of media (live broadcasting, cable and satellite television, the increasing banality of global telecommunications), those insights predated the establishment of high-speed, high-bandwidth, many-directional digital communications as a *basic fact* in the everyday lives of billions of people. The particular way that this intensification has been funded (the basic model of *free* content and *free* infrastructure) has come at a price: our access to these important new forms of connection become conditional on accepting the gathering, processing, evaluating and selling of data generated by our acts of communication. The result is an emerging regime of continuous tracking primarily for corporate benefit, but also with huge benefits for political power. Markets and states, indeed all social forms of institution building, are becoming increasingly dependent on an infrastructure of continuous connection *and* monitoring that changes the terms on which individuals now relate to institutions and infrastructure.

Put more bluntly, this shift in the nature of institutionalization has altered media's 'deal' with modernity, making that deal increasingly tense and paradoxical. In response, leading commentators such as computer security expert Bruce Schneier note that "the primary business model of the Internet is built on mass surveillance" (Schneier, 2013), while legal scholar Tim Wu recently asked whether our increasing attention to what reaches us through infrastructures of connection requires us to "reclaim ownership of the very experience of living" (Wu, 2016, 353). The basic fit between media and modernity that has been a foundational principle in communications research (e.g., Thompson, 1995) can no longer be taken for granted. This is the higher-dimensional disruption of the *possibilities for* social order to which the term 'deep mediatization' (Couldry & Hepp, 2016) refers.

Media institutions and the possibility of social order

To appreciate the problem, we need, first, a little history.

The role of the printing press in the social and political transformations of early modern Europe is well known; so too is the role of books and pamphlets in early moves toward democracy and political representation that emergenced in the United Kingdom, France, and elsewhere, and in the longer term the building of modern civil society (Wuthnow, 1989). Newspapers, although their origin derived from the need for the circulation of market information (Rantanen, 2009), became over time essential fora for democratic deliberation (Tocqueville, 1961). Mass newspapers helped make possible the emergence of the more intensely connected national publics of the 20th century (Tarde, 1969). This history of mass printed media within modernity has been frequently celebrated.[1]

Less often celebrated have been broader infrastructures for distributing communications in all directions which was essential to market and state, for example, the modern postal service. As a general system for distributing content *from anywhere to anywhere*, the postal service was crucial to the emergence of modern markets (both networks of producers and an interconnected mass of consumers). Once we focus on many-to-many communications, other media – equally important in modernity's history – come into view, such as mass transportation. It is useful in fact to think of media's relation to modernity *not* from the perspective of specific media innovations, but at the broadest institutional level: the development of the modern state, modern economy, and, through both, the emergence of a 'world system' (Wallerstein, 2011). That means emphasizing changes in how communications technologies of all sorts became embedded in wider patterns of *organizing everything*. Corporations were part of this, but so too were new configurations of interpersonal communication. As Craig Calhoun pointed out for the 19th century:

> State power could grow because the new forms of organization and the improved transportation and communications infrastructure (based partly on new technologies but, at first, more on heavy investments in the extension of old methods) enabled the spread of increasingly effective administration throughout the various territories of a country . . . But [recognizing this, NC] is not sufficient. A full account needs to recognize . . . that the growth of the state, like the capitalist economy, developed infrastructures that could be used by ordinary people to 'develop connections with each other.'
>
> *(Calhoun, 1992, 214).*

The gradual development of those connections, not just among 'ordinary people,' but in people's interactions with corporations, was to install a 'tertiary' (i.e., institutionally mediated) level to social relations over and above the two basic levels of primary and secondary relations (whole-person relations versus relations mediated by roles) that Charles Cooley (1962) had theorized at the start of the 20th century.

James Beniger's book *The Control Revolution* (1987) thought through this transformation in terms of the changing role in social order of 'information processing' and 'communication' (1987, 8). This broader focus enabled him to see an underlying dynamic of 19th century modernity which he called 'a crisis of control.' Because the Industrial Revolution speeded up certain forms of production and circulation, it precipitated 'a crisis of control' in which information processing and communications practices lagged behind other processes such as energy production, manufacturing and transportation (1987, vii). This lag created very important local problems. Beniger's most vivid example is a US rail crash in 1841 in which two Western US railroad trains crashed head on, simply because (unknown to each other) they were traveling down the same track at the same time in the opposite direction (Beniger, 1987, 221–226). The resulting crisis created by this and other local problems of coordination required integrative solutions across many diverse domains, for example, transportation *and* media, product standardization *and* advertising, in order to enhance the overall predictability of social life. Everyday interaction in any one locality, because its communicative relations with other localities had changed profoundly, now acquired a new risk profile: the banal possibility of transporting distant goods and people into that locality within a few hours required the development of a communications ecology that linked localities *everywhere* in new ways, with profound implications for the nature of economies and states.

Such an account takes us some way from centralizing narratives concerning media's role in the imagining of community (Anderson, 1990) to emphasize the key role of coordinated communication in the development of market *and* state *and* state/market relations: the primary issue becomes not the integration of nations through media, but the emergence of new forms of social interdependency (Elias, 1994) in which media institutions are profoundly involved. Similar stories can be told about the role of communications technologies in the 20th century, linked together in Raymond Williams's (1990) classic narrative of 'mobile privatization': radio and television became the means for instant communication of symbolic content to populations of hundreds of millions; the telephone became a means for instant one-to-one communication across local, national, and international networks; and radical changes in transportation – the car over shorter distances, the plane for long-distance travel – enabled the increased movement of people between the sites where media were produced and received.

The increasing presence of daily and, by the second half of the 20th century, hourly media flows in everyday life helped transform wider norms of sociability, mutual recognition and engagement with the state-focused political system (Scannell & Cardiff, 1991; Starr, 2004). Notwithstanding some cases of social and political disintegration linked to the same basic infrastructural transformation (for example, Nazism (Kershaw, 1987); the disintegration of former Yugoslavia (Smith, 1995)), there is plausibility to the general claim that the continuous daily operations of media institutions ('the media') contributed overall to the stabilization of the institutional frameworks associated with modernity across the world. 'The media' were institutions without which inherited forms of social and political organization society are barely imaginable.

This history can be developed too at the level of representation. Media are institutions with particular power over the means for representing shared reality, reality that, over time and through that power, becomes recognized as 'ours.' Media institutions, in modernity, acquired what Pierre Bourdieu, for earlier religious institutions, called 'the power of constructing reality' (Bourdieu, 1991, 166). To grasp how this power works, we need to follow the larger stories about the 'social world' that get told through our everyday uses of media. What I have called *the myth of the mediated center* (Couldry, 2012) is the way of organizing things, people and resources, and their interrelations, around a practical 'center' of communications, 'the media.' This myth has various beneficiaries: media institutions themselves, and ultimately government (which needs large media to provide the means for assuming that it can still talk to its population) as well as advertisers, or least those advertisers still interested in buying access to whole populations or segments of them. The social importance of this myth goes beyond particular media contents and production processes to involve the shaping of media's role in the stories we tell about ourselves, as members of a social domain. Through the myth of the mediated center, media institutions became increasingly implicated in the languages, practices and organizational logics of whole societies. The myth tells us that society *has* a 'center' of value, knowledge, and meaning, and that particular institutions, those we call 'media,' *have* a privileged role in giving us access to that supposed 'center.'

At least until the early years of the 21st century, the myth of the mediated center enabled modernity's pressures toward centralization and decentralization to be resolved in a set of stable forms that installed certain media institutions as narrators of the "reality" of the nation (Schlesinger, 1980). Other institutions organized themselves around this narrative power. But in the past 15 years, forces have emerged within the expanded media industries which potentially are disrupting the interlocking arrangement of modern institutions.

What Sonia Livingstone called 'the mediation of everything' (2009) that results from the ever deeper embedding of media in every aspect of daily life constitutes, a different type of social order in *every element* of which media are involved. The resulting change in *the nature* of social order is what Andreas Hepp and I call 'deep mediatization' (Couldry & Hepp, 2016, chapter 4). Deep mediatization refers not to a specific set of processes, but is rather a meta-concept that points to a change in *how* processes become social at all, and media's role in that. Without getting into the long debate about the term 'mediatization' (Lundby, 2009), let us explore what deep mediatization might mean for how media institutions contribute to social order, in other words, for the institutionalization of the social.

The Internet and media's changing role as social institutions

Something in media's relations to social order has changed. It is not that 'media' have disappeared (most traditional media remain, although hardcopy newspapers are under pressure in most countries), or that media institutions' claims to be central have diminished – arguably those claims have become *more* insistent. It is rather that media's *whole* set of possibilities for organizing communications have been reshaped by what Rainie and Wellman (2012, ix) call the 'triple revolution': the Internat, mobile devices giving continuous access to communication (interpersonal or mass, often online) while on the move, and the rise of online social networking via digital platforms. Social media are important to the myth of the mediated center, because they offer a new *form* of centrality, a new *social* 'liveness,' mediated apparently *by us* rather than by content-producing media institutions, generating perhaps a new 'myth of us' (Couldry, 2014, compare Couldry, 2004). But it is the implications of deep mediatization for our relations with media as social institutions that are most profound. It is not just that we cannot sharply separate any more 'media' infrastructure (for the centralized distribution of institutional content) from 'communications' infrastructure (for distributed, interpersonal forms of communication), because now both flow into and over each other and across the same platforms. Underway now also is a change in the conditions under which communications flows become centralized, with profound implications for the institutional basis of modernity.

At the turn of the century, when Internet services were only just beginning to become consistently available, their significance was framed primarily in terms of whether the Internet would replace television as the reference medium of contemporary life. This was the wrong question. Television viewing has not disappeared, but *increased* in many countries, as Internet use has established itself (Miller, 2010); television remains a dominant form of news and entertainment, even if the physical device for watching television may, for many, have changed from a non-networked analogue television set to a digital television, laptop or tablet that can interface with a range of Internet-based content streams. The better question concerns the role that the *connective infrastructure* of 'the Internet' is playing in the institutional transformations of late modernity. And here the picture is dramatically changing.

It is well known that 'the Internet' emerged from the research arm of the United States' military establishment, through its connections with university research labs; as such it exemplifies how developments for which 'the market' claims credit usually derive from underlying subsidies by the state and other public institutions (Mazzucatto, 2013). But that is only the beginning. More important are the steps (some state-led, some driven by markets) as a result of which in 2015 a small number of corporations loosely called 'media' – Google, Facebook, Apple, Amazon and in China Alibaba – gained the ability, through their 'platforms,' to *act directly* on the world of consumption and the world of everyday social interaction.

How did this happen? By the early 1990s, the publicly subsidized development of the Internet and World Wide Web had produced the skeleton of a connective infrastructure, that in principle could link every computer on the planet, but this was not yet linked to everyday commercial activity, or even non-specialist everyday use. The deeply commercialized Internet that we know in the late 2010s developed through a number of discrete moves: the handing over of the Internat's operations by the US government to commercial providers; the first commercial web browsers; the diffusion of small desktop computers and then laptops as means for accessing the Internet easily. Particularly important was the emergence of Google's *algorithmically* based model of indexing web-pages based on a hierarchy ordered through counting the number of *links in* to each Internet page (Keen, 2015, 54). Building on the huge success of its Google search engine, Google bolted on to it a new commercial infrastructure for the Internet:

a new model for advertising tied to terms searched through Google ('Google Adwords') and a system of live-auction advertising ('Adsense'), which provided a new basis for the *marketization* of online 'space' (Wu, 2016, 263–264). Meanwhile 'smart' mobile phones were developed that could access not just phone functions but also the World Wide Web, increasingly through 'apps,' so providing easy access to particular domains of web data. In addition, a new type of web architecture (the 'platform') emerged that enabled over time billions of users to network with each other, but within the parameters designed by that platform's owners (Gillespie, 2010).

We have seen a strikingly complete transformation of 'the Internet' from a closed, publicly funded and publicly oriented network for discrete forms of specialist communication into a deeply commercialized, pervasively linked space for the *conduct* of increasingly many aspects of social life. So how do we make sense of this transformation of 'media' (as infrastructures of connection)[2] for social order more generally?

Institutional adjustments

Many-to-many communications space was already inherent in the small networks which began to be set up between computers in the 1960s, but then it benefited only elite communicators. Diffusing the possibility of networked transmission and networked reception across large percentages of the population changed the *basic resources* of everyday social action. 'Mass self-communication' (Castells, 2009) from the mid-2000s, unimaginable even a decade before, had become by the end of the 2000s banal in many countries. This is the 21st century replaying the role of lateral communications which Calhoun (1992, 214) noticed for the 19th century, but harnessed to a global and fully commercial domain of communications. As a result, the space of social action ceased to be one in which the possibility of action-at-a-distance could from time to time be 'loaded' by the use of particular technologies (phone, radio, email) and it has become a space that is permanently 'sprung' with the potential for acting, and being acted upon, at/from multiple distances/directions, and in multiple modalities of communication. In rich countries at least, people take for granted the possibility of being continually 'online.'

This new 'sprung' potential of social action – always at least two-way (in the simplest case, the capacity to send an SMS while on the move, saying you are late *and* the capacity to receive an SMS, indicating that there is no point going on, because your meeting is canceled) – encompasses not just actions between individuals but actions by corporations *on* individuals. But corporations can act more continuously across time and space than individuals. Social space-time, accordingly, becomes permanently open to saturation by corporate communication: communication directed at exclusively instrumental ends, whether the making of profit (for corporations) or (for governments) the regulation of action.

Yet corporations (in fact, any entity that needs to communicate to larger audiences) face a deep challenge. Since all actors now have hugely increased capacities to send messages in all directions, the exponential increase in the volume of messages in circulation creates two problems: the need to filter out most messages (regardless of their value), and the need for ever more tools to search for particular messages. Each person comes increasingly therefore to engage with the world through technologies of filtering, which, in turn, increases the difficulty of generalized communicators such as advertisers and governments reaching individuals with any *one* message. In response, advertisers (Turow, 2011) have evolved their own set of solutions: in the United States and the United Kingdom at least, they try increasingly to reach audiences through continuous tracking, wherever individuals are online and whatever they are doing.

This in turn has fuelled the rise of generalized communication interfaces (so-called 'platforms': Gillespie, 2010) whose goal is to ensure that people spend as much time as possible *just there*, while performing as many actions as possible. Platforms are an institutional device optimizing the overlap between social interaction and the domain of profit. The simple name 'platform' belies a dramatic shift from a world (until the mid-2000s) of largely non-networked social action concentrated nowhere in particular to a world (from the mid-2000s) of pervasively networked social action (Van Dijck 2013). This is the infrastructure on which everyday actions (from arranging a meeting to paying for a service to finding out what's going on in the world) now rely.

What are the implications of these developments for social order?

A new more intimate institutionalization of the social

I have argued so far that media institutions have always played an important role in the constitution of social order in modernity. In the 18th to 20th centuries, that role had two basic modalities, whose shape became particularly clear from the late 19th century onwards: the centralized circulation of mass-produced content and the sustaining of infrastructures for extending interpersonal communications across space and time. The first modality provided a layer of circulating common knowledge in support of everyday life and reframed the broader narratives of social action in the exercise of symbolic power already discussed. The second modality provided the means for everyday social action to be extended in space and time. These roles that media played in social order implied a distinctive form of relationship between individuals and media institutions. Whereas the second modality was sunk, like all infrastructures (Star & Ruhleder, 1996), into the background of everyday life, the first modality was anything but invisible: on the contrary, it provided a privileged, at times spectacular, means for representing the social. Media contributed to social order according to two 'settings': as distant transmitters or forgotten infrastructures, occasionally both.

While those older modalities of course continue, today's media institutions are implicated in daily life in new and distinctive ways. Deep mediatization brings in what elsewhere with Andreas Hepp I have called an 'expanded institutionalization' in which all sorts of actors and other elements of social life "become dependent for their basic operations and functioning on a wider media infrastructure that is supplied and controlled by [the] new types of institutional power" described earlier (Couldry & Hepp, 2016, 217–218). Social actors accordingly become repositioned in relation to the institutions we go on calling 'media': instead of needing media only for common knowledge and for the means to interact with others at a distance, media become the institutions on which every person and organization relies to go on acting in ordinary ways wherever they are. From being (merely, but that was already a lot!) an infrastructure for embedding individuals within society's larger scale, media became the intimate and insistently necessary means to live out one's life anywhere. This affects also the forms of power exercised *through* media. As Bruce Schneier puts it, our surveillance today is 'a very intimate form of surveillance' (Schneier, 2014, 1). Intimate too is the character of our increasing dependence on Internet connection for the forms of exchange that seem basic to life, for the access to work systems through which we act in the world, and for the commercial interfaces through which we gather resources for those actions.

This growing intimization of media institutions and their infrastructural role is echoed in the language of marketers and media providers. Because it is now standard to send marketing messages to people's personal devices, marketers argue that those messages need to be 'personalized,' precisely targeted to what available data suggests that person wants right here and now. The new form of social knowledge provides both long-term goal and short-term pretext for an expansion of surveillance without social limits. By contrast, marketers describe personalization in terms of 'one-to-one communication' and 'one-to-one dialogue.'[3] The sellers of the online learning system BlackBoard Learn boast that the software enables teachers as they monitor pupils online to 'immediately intervene in a highly personalized way.'[4] The notion of personalization can be expressed as a democratization of knowledge, as in the use of self-tracking devices to generate information for one's medical professionals (Topol, 2016). But, paradoxically, this increasingly intimate mode of institutionalization through media involves processes of tracking, categorization and behavioral nudging that until recently were associated not with intimacy, but with the violation of intimacy: such interventions in daily life were once regarded as surveillance, the heavy hand of the authoritarian state.

I must leave aside the wider implications of these new developments for democracy and freedom[5] and concentrate here narrowly on what all this means for the role that media infrastructures and institutions are now playing in social order. Four points are striking.

First, social life in all its fluidity and open-endedness becomes, under this new arrangement, the object of commercial targeting and, potentially, state awareness. On the state's perspective, the CIA's Chief Technology Officer said "since you can't connect dots you don't have, it drives us [the CIA] into a mode of, we fundamentally try to collect everything and hang onto it forever" (quoted in Kennedy, 2016, 46). This operationalization of everyday life for capital and more broadly for power would have been unimaginable without the connective infrastructure of the Internet, but now it is becoming banal. Two frontiers of this development are wearable tracking devices (soon to be implantables?) and the 'Internet of Things.' Why not, as Price Waterhouse Coopers note in their report on 'The Future of Wearables,' imagine a world of universal wearable processors, linked up to a commercial tracking and messaging system, where 'brands could even tap body cues to tailor messages'?[6] Meanwhile a report about 'The Internet of Things: Opportunities for Insurers' noted that insurers could 'use IoT-*enriched* relationships to connect more holistically to customers and influence their behaviours.'[7]

Second, because the social is being operationalized increasingly in commercial processes, a special advantage accrues to the media sites where the social appears to gather, such as Facebook with its two billion users worldwide. This has huge implications not only for political economy – the new forms of monopoly buying or receiving power, or monopsony (Mejias, 2013) which are capturing the flow of everyday communications – but for social order itself. Suddenly – across a decade or little more – the social world, having been diffusely present, becomes imagined as cohering on particular corporate platforms, creating new and probably unwelcome forms of responsibility for the operators of those platforms. Mark Zuckerberg's message to the global 'Facebook community' in February 2017 was a document which confronted uneasily that new situation, straddling the domains of economy and society (Zuckerberg, 2017).

Third, the extraordinary new forms of institutional concentration that flow from platforms' role within the new infrastructures of connection create new forms of dependence: individuals have little option but to accept platform terms, to follow instructions, and to opt in to their power, or so it seems. The resulting relation between infrastructure and individual becomes, as legal scholar Julie Cohen notes, 'authoritarian' (Cohen, 2012, 188–189), a system-based authoritarianism that rules across huge swathes of everyday life. Government meanwhile does not stand aside from these developments but itself looks to rely on the new accessibility of the social domain for permanent automated surveillance (see Andrejevic this volume; Couldry & Mejias, 2019). The possibility of asymmetrical monitoring of the social is not in itself new and was already theorized by Calhoun (1992, 219) as a 'quaternary' relationship to supplement the 'tertiary' level of communications noted earlier. But, while Calhoun (compare Gandy, 1993) noted the growth of data collection for commercial purposes, the extent, depth, and connective power of today's data collection was not predictable in the early 1990s, because it depends precisely on the Internet's development as an interconnected domain for social life (Amoore, 2013; Turow, 2011).

These new relations between individual and commercial power – indeed, between individual and state power – amount, fourth, to a different type of social order, with new centers of gravity, new rigidities, new vulnerabilities. These new patterns are structured around a highly consequential ambiguity between private ownership and public consequences: the merging of privately owned platforms such as Facebook increasingly into infrastructure, and the operationalization of infrastructure (including that of the state) increasingly through the controlled interfaces of platforms (Plantin et al., 2016). This larger cycle of infrastructure/platform/infrastructure captures the distinctive mode of institutionalizing power in contemporary societies and contemporary media's distinctive contribution to social order.

Conclusion

In this chapter, I have tried to find a social-theoretical language to bring out the deeper significance of two things: the recent transformation of media institutions, and their relations, as institutions, with social order. I began the chapter with a historical comparison via James Beniger's analysis of how communications technologies contributed to *solving* the 19th century's 'crisis of control' generated by simultaneous fast development of economy, society and technology. Is the situation analogous today? Is it plausible to see communications technologies as solving such problems, or are they rather generating new problems?

In terms of business models, there is no doubt that the Internet and the new architecture of platforms provide new opportunities for creating economic value and restructuring commercial operations. But how about the social consequences? Here the balance of advantage is much less clear. We need to ask what are the long-term implications of such transformations for the legitimacy of the institutions (from governments to corporations to civil society organizations) on which modernity has depended? Can the institutional arrangements of modernity endure when their precondition appears to be a regime of total surveillance under the guise of freedom? Are we, as a result, at the beginning of a new 'crisis of control' focused not (as Beniger saw for the 19th century) on the complexities of risk management but, more fundamentally, on the very compatibility of system effectiveness and normative legitimacy in the evolving institutional orders we call modernity?

If so, we may begin to turn for guidance to a different commentator on the 19th century, the economic historian Karl Polanyi, whose focus was on the transition from the crisis generated by unrestrained industrial capitalism in the early 19th century, with its huge social costs, and the attempts from the mid-19th century onwards to adjust those consequences: that is, to 'tame' the full destructiveness of capitalism (see Cohen this volume). The outcome was gradually and partially, over time, to regulate the forces of capitalism. On this model, we can look forward to a long period of adjustment in which media institutions, as the distinctive social faces of capitalism's new dynamics,[8] face increasing social and political resistance. What if, far from being the sustainer of modernity, media institutions come increasingly to be seen as the forces that disrupt modernity? What would happen then to our standard narratives of media and modernity?

Notes

1 For fuller histories, see Thompson (1995), Starr (2004), Mattelart (1994).
2 For the term 'infrastructures of connection,' see Couldry et al. (2017).
3 Turow (2017, 179, 180, 185).
4 See website of Blackboard. www.blackboard.com/(US) and http://uki.blackboard.com/(UK)
5 But see Couldry and Mejias (2019), Couldry and Yu (2018).

6 Price Waterhouse Coopers (2014, 22, cited Turow (2017, 226).
7 Cited in Christl and Spiekermann (2016, 71).
8 See for example Zuboff (2015).

References

Amoore, L. (2013). *The Politics of Possibility*. Durham, NC: Duke University Press.

Anderson, B. (1990). *Imagined Communities* (2nd ed.). London: Verso.

Appadurai, A. (1996). *Modernity at Large*. Minneapolis: University of Minnesota Press.

Beniger, J. (1987). *The Control Revolution*. Cambridge, MA: Harvard University Press.

Bourdieu, P. (1991). *Language and Symbolic Power*. Cambridge: Polity Press.

Calhoun, C. (1992). The Infrastructure of Modernity: Indirect social Relationships, Information Technology, and Social Integration. In H. Haferkamp and N. Smelser (eds.), *Social Change and Modernity*. Berkeley: University of California Press, pp. 205–236.

Castells, M. (2009). *Communication Power*. Oxford: Oxford University Press.

Christl, W., and Spiekermann, S. (2016). *Networks of Control: A Report on Corporate Surveillance, Digital Tracking, Big Data & Privacy*. www.privacylab.ay=t/wp-content/uploads/2016/09/Crhistl-Networks_K_o.pdf.

Cohen, J. (2012). *Configuring the Networked Self*. New Haven: Yale University Press.

Cooley, C. (1962)[1902]. *Social Organization*. New York: Schocken.

Couldry, N. (2004). Liveness 'Reality', and the Mediated Habitus: From Television to the Mobile Phone. *The Communication Review*, 7(4), 353–362.

Couldry, N. (2012). *Media Society World*. Cambridge: Polity Press.

Couldry, N. (2014). The Myth of Us: Digital Networks, Political Change and the Production of Collectivity. *Information Communication and Society*, 18(6), 608–626.

Couldry, N., and Mejias, U. (2019). *The Costs of Connection: How Data Colonizes Human Life and Appropriates It for Capitalism*. Stanford: Stanford University Press.

Couldry, N. et al. (2017). *International Panel on Social Progress*. Chapter 13 on Media and Communications. www.ipsp.org/download/chapter-13.

Couldry, N., and Hepp, A. (2016). *The Mediated Construction of Reality*. Cambridge: Polity Press.

Couldry, N., and Yu, J. (2018). Deconstructing Datafication's Brave New World. *New Media & Society*. doi:10.1177/1461444818775968.

Elias, N. (1994)[1939]. *The Civilizing Process*. Oxford: Blackwell.

Gandy, O. (1993). *The Panoptic Sort*. Boulder: Westview Press.

Giddens, A. (1990). *The Consequences of Modernity*. Cambridge: Polity Press.

Gillespie, T. (2010). The Politics of 'Platforms'. *New Media & Society*, 12(3), 347–364.

Keen, A. (2015). *The Internet Is Not the Answer*. London: Atlantic Books.

Kennedy, H. (2016). *Post Mine Repeat*. Basingstoke: Palgrave Macmillan.

Kershaw, I. (1987). *The Hitler Myth*. Oxford: Oxford University Press.

Livingstone, S. (2009). The Mediation of Everything. *Journal of Communication*, 59(1), 1–18.

Lundby, K. (ed.). (2009). *Mediatization*. New York: Peter Lang.

Mattelart, A. (1994). *The Invention of Communication*. Minneapolis: Minnesota University Press.

Mazzucatto, M. (2013). *The Entrepreneurial State*. London: Anthem.

Mejias, U. (2013). *Off the Network*. Minneapolis: University of Minnesota Press.

Miller, T. (2010). *Television Studies: The Basics*. London: Routledge.

Plantin, J.-C., Lagoze, C., Edwards, P., and Sandvig, C. (2016). Infrastructure Studies Meet Platform Studies in the Age of Google and Facebook. *New Media & Society*, 20(1), 293–310.

Price Waterhouse Coopers. (2014). *The Wearable Future*, November. www.pwc.com/mx/es/industrias/archivo/2014-11-pwc-the-wearable-future.pdf (Accessed September 18, 2017).

Rainie, L., and Wellman, B. (2012). *Networked: The New Social Operating System*. Cambridge, MA: MIT Press.

Rantanen, T. (2009). *When News Was New*. Malden, MA: Wiley-Blackwell.

Scannell, P., and Cardiff, D. (1991). *A Social History of British Broadcasting* (vol. 1). Oxford: Blackwell.

Schlesinger, P. (1980). *Putting 'Reality' Together*. London: Methuen.

Schneier, B. (2013). The Public-Private Surveillance Partnership. *Bloomberg Business Week*, July 31.

Schneier, B. (2014). *Data and Goliath*. New York: WW Norton.

Smith, A. (1995). *Nations and Nationalism in a Global Era*. Cambridge: Polity Press.

Star, S., and Ruhleder, K. (1996). Steps Toward an Ecology of Infrastructure: Design, Access for Large Information Space. *Information System Research*, 7, 111–134.

Starr, P. (2004). *The Creation of the Media*. New York: Basic Books.

Tarde, G. (1969)[1922]. *Communication and Social Opinion*. Chicago: Chicago University Press.

Thompson, J. (1995). *The Media and Modernity*. Cambridge: Polity Press.

Tocqueville, A. de (1961)[1835–1840]. *Democracy in America* (vol. 1). New York: Schocken.

Topol, E. (2016). *The Doctor Will See You Now*. New York: Basic Books.

Turow, J. (2011). *The Daily You*. New Haven: Yale University Press.

Turow, J. (2017). *The Aisles Have Eyes*. New Haven: Yale University Press.

Van Dijck, J. (2013). *The Culture of Connectivity*. Oxford: Oxford University Press.

Wallerstein, I. (2011). *The Modern World System* (vol. 1). Berkeley: University of California Press.

Williams, R. (1990). *Television: Technology and Cultural Form*. London: Routledge.

Wrong, D. (1994). *The Problem of Order*. New York: Free Press.

Wu, T. (2016). *The Attention Merchants*. New York: Vintage.

Wuthnow, R. (1989). *Communities of Discourse*. Cambridge, MA: Harvard University Press.

Zuboff, S. (2015). Big Other: Surveillance Capitalism and the Prospects of an Information Civilization. *Journal of Information Technology*, 30, 75–89.

Zuckerberg, M. (2017). *Building Global Community*, February 16. www.facebook.com/notes/mark-zuckerberg/building-global-community/10154544292806634/.

20

Fluid hybridity

Organizational form and formlessness in the digital age

Shiv Ganesh and Cynthia Stohl

The powerful relationship between technological change and organizing practices has been recognized throughout the modern study of formal organizations. In the 20th century, most research on technology and organizing focused on the study of organizational forms. More than 50 years ago, Burns and Stalker (1961, 6) noted, "Technical progress and development of new organizational forms proceed in tandem; advancement in either field augurs movement in the other field." Early in the digital era as well, scholars were prone to say the affordances of digital technologies caused the emergence of new organizational forms. Beniger (1986) argued that designing information technology and designing organization were virtually the same task, each creating new opportunities for the development of the other. Gerstein et al. reflected, "perhaps the largest single influence on organizational architecture and design has been the evolution of information technology" (1992, 5). And in a special issue of *Organization Science*, Fulk and De Sanctis (1995) highlighted the interplay between communication technology and form: "Electronic communication technologies are enablers of changed forms by offering capabilities to overcome constraints on time and distance, key barriers around which organizational forms traditionally have been designed " (1995, 337). Overall, as the digital era unfolded, research on emerging organizational forms made clear that digitization and automation not only upended core assumptions about jobs and employees, labor, and capital but were also linked to key organizing dimensions of coordination, control, communication, and in-group and interorganizational linkages.

More recently, however, research on organizing practices in the digitally ubiquitous era has been prone to emphasizing *formlessness* rather than form, with researchers arguing that digital environments can enable organizing practices that do not take on specific forms but are instead fluid, volatile, shapeless, ephemeral, short-lived, and fast-paced (e.g., Introna & Petrakaki, 2007). Indeed, fluidity has become an increasingly prominent metaphor for contemporary life. Bauman's highly influential work on liquid modernity, for example, features fluidity as a central descriptor in a world where structures are precarious, the only certainty is uncertainty, social orders are unsettled, and individuals are radically autonomous. This fluidity extends into the organizational domain: as he says, "today's business organization has an element of disorganization deliberately built into it; the less solid and more fluid it is, the better" (Bauman, 2012, 59). Contemporary fluid organizing, then, involves not only flexibility and ad-hocness but constant movement and flux; enacting membership without the constraints of formal membership rituals and procedures; producing permeable boundaries that transcend traditional private/public/work/personal distinctions; and constantly inventing and reinventing new work and organizing practices. The underlying assumption that the digital world brings with it chaotic forms of organizing is also captured in any number of popular discourses, ranging from corporate discussions about disruptive innovation, journalistic commentary on contemporary populist politics, or community organizers' laments about increasingly isolated and disconnected individuals.

Our chapter brings together contemporary work on both organizational form and fluid organizing to illustrate how digital ubiquity simultaneously may produce both form and formlessness in contemporary organizing. In doing so, we neither embrace a deterministic view of technology whereby actions are caused by technological forces independent of individual behavior, nor argue for completely discrete and voluntaristic distinctions among organizational forms, whereby humans shape their environments by relying upon norms, values, ideologies, and beliefs to drive organizational action (for a discussion of determinism versus voluntarism, see Leonardi & Barley, 2008). We argue that the changes from bureaucracy to post-bureaucracy, bounded organizations to networks, and unitary to hybrid structures are neither unified nor conclusive but are instead a mixture of opposing tendencies and human activities of both form and formlessness.

Contemporary organizations function within an environment of digital ubiquity, which we define as an information-rich environment in which digital technology is no longer exotic, remarkable, nor scare but rather mundane, expected, and seamlessly integrated into everyday practices (Bimber et al., 2012). As we shall see, digital ubiquity does not suggest the inevitable replacement of traditional or network forms with fluid organizing practice but rather transforms communicative dynamics and needed competencies in the digital era to produce both fluid organizing and hybrid forms of organization. This suggestion also implies that contemporary organizational forms are no longer tied to one ideal type, whether that be in terms of coordination (e.g., markets, network, or organizations), hierarchical control arrangements (e.g., flat/tall organizations), or sectoral positioning. Rather, we show how contemporary organizations typically combine characteristics of these ideal forms through a set of four archetypes, not so much in a static finite manner but through organizing processes that ebb and flow, borrowing from multiple forms and structures, inventing and recreating communicative practice and competence across a range of institutional contexts and sectors, and both crafting new identities and preserving legacy ones.

Accordingly, we begin by first reviewing work on technology and organizational forms that have established networks as a quintessential organizational form in the digital era, arguing that we need to reconsider the central place given to the network form in an era of digital ubiquity. To further animate such reconsideration, we turn to a discussion of the digitally ubiquitous communication environment, identifying a range of features that produce both fluid organizing and hybrid organizing forms. We then provide an overview of contemporary research on hybrid forms and fluidity, focusing on four key organizational aspects: structure, institutions, agency, and identity. We conclude the chapter by outlining a set of four organizing archetypes that bring together hybridity and fluidity in different ways and highlight the need for coherence management as a central communication concern in an era of digital ubiquity.

Technology and organizational forms

Historically, the study of organizational form has been grounded in the notion of "fit" among environmental contingencies, technological affordances, and the communicative demands of the context. Tracing the moves from bureaucratic, mechanistic, and technocratic forms of organization to organic, post-bureaucratic structures, organizational scholars have focused on the ways that organizations have adjusted to the contingencies and communicative demands of an increasingly interconnected world where boundaries are highly permeable and emergent technologies enable new forms of interactivity (Bimber et al.,2012). Not surprisingly, over the past several decades, the intersection of globalization dynamics and digital expansion has accelerated the emergence and study of new forms. The hypercompetitive, highly interconnected, volatile, information-rich global environment, coupled with the compression of time and space, the decreasing cost of information transmission, and the increasing speed, breadth, and depth of digital communication, has produced greater demands and more opportunities for organizational transformation. Along with this we have seen a significant amount of attention paid to network forms of organization. In fact, the 2002 *Handbook of New Media* identified the move from "organizations as networks" to "networks as organizations" as a major research concern in studies of new media and organizing (Contractor, 2002).

Among the most influential work linking global dynamics, technological development, and organizational form is that of Manuel Castells. His (1996) opus on the network society highlights the transformation of social structure that results from interactions between the new digital paradigm and social organizing writ large. Indeed, since the 1980s networks have come to be seen as the quintessential organizational form. Network forms embody a set of distinct norms, organizing logics and types of interactivity that cannot be classified as either markets or hierarchies. A considerable amount of work continues to conceptualize contemporary life in the digital era in terms of networks. Benkler's (2006) influential work, the *Wealth of Networks*, for example, argues that networked information economies are transformational because they significantly enhance individual autonomy, create networked public spheres that undermine centralized and hierarchical media systems, and enable sharing-based, critical, and self-reflective cultures. In a similar vein, Rainie and Wellman (2012) coined the term "networked individualism" to highlight how digital technologies facilitate highly individualized and personalized networks that allow individuals to act *sans* organizations.

The power of networks became so ingrained in organizational thinking that just as Francis Fukuyama (1992) mistakenly saw the rise of Western liberal democracy to signal the "end of history," that is the endpoint of humanity's sociocultural evolution, pundits started to herald the digital era and the rise of the networks as "the end of organizations as we know them" (Powers, 2012). Perhaps the most extreme version of this network fetishism is found in Clay Shirkey's 2008 best seller *Here Comes Everybody, the Power of Organizing without Organization*. Shirkey captured the popular imagination as he described a world in which digital affordances, the Internat, and mobile computing would enable us to come together, organize and get things done, breaking our dependence on formal organizations and our increasing reliance on emergent networking.

The conceptual centrality of networks as the quintessential organizational form of the digital era reached its height around the turn of the millennium and the years immediately succeeding it, so it is not surprising, for instance, that networks were a central term in scholarly treatments of the evocative term "digital enclosure" when it was first coined (Andrejevic, 2004, 2007). For Andrejevic, digital enclosure is an integral function of privatized communication networks and describes the process by which networks gather data about every communicative act of the individuals in those networks. However, a latent aspect of Andrejevic's initial work on the subject has to do with the very concerns that motivated the concept of enclosure: the centralization of power and the privatization of information. Both centralization and privatization make sense not in a context where organizations have dissolved into networks but in one where more formal bureaucratic and technocratic organizational forms continue to assert themselves. Under these circumstances, formal organizations are not abruptly replaced by individualized networks with the onset of the digital era: indeed, organizational fecundity abounded in the 1990s and onward (see Bimber et al., 2012). Consequently, contemporary networks themselves need to be seen not as organization-less entities but as multi-level forms that implicate individuals, groups, and entire organizations (Monge & Contractor, 2004).

Over the last decade, scholars have done precisely this, recognizing that formal public and private sector organizations have continued to thrive but do so by mixing elements, value systems, and organizational/institutional logics from various sectors of society. It is in this way that organizational hybridity is beginning to replace the central conceptual place of networks in organizational analysis. Simultaneously, scholars are also turning to the notion of digital ubiquity to better describe the fluid communicative conditions in which hybridic organizing and its consequences, including enclosure, realize themselves.

Digital ubiquity and the contemporary organizing environment

We use the term "digital ubiquity" to describe the extensive, seamless, and unremarkable integration of digital technologies into everyday life (Bimber et al., 2012). Because technologies are so widely diffused and embedded in social practice, digital media use can no longer be conceptualized as a variable that may or may not impact organizing or organizational forms; instead, it must be considered part of the ground upon which organizing itself occurs (Bimber, 2017). Digital ubiquity has resulted in conditions of communication abundance (Blumler & Coleman, 2015). Opportunities for communication are both extensive and readily available; consequently, the communicative reach of individuals has expanded exponentially and, in turn, the amount we communicate and the ways we communicate (both technically and relationally) are no longer bound by rigid hierarchies or inflexible routines.

Scholars have used the acronym VUCA (volatility, uncertainty, complexity and ambiguity), first coined by the US Army War College to describe post cold-war multilateral politics, as a shorthand for the communicative conditions in which contemporary organizing occurs (Mack et al., 2016). VUCA captures some fundamental spatio-temporal dynamics of the organizing and communication environment: it presumes that the organizing world is both highly interconnected and differentiated, and changes quickly and rapidly, resulting in both highly unpredictable and precarious outcomes and confusion, disorder, and chaos, Organizational theorists have suggested these characteristics enable fluidity, whereby organizations can shift shape seamlessly and rapidly. As Jackson (2007) put it, in a VUCA environment, communication itself has become more promiscuous, connecting people with issues, objects, and each other quickly and oftentimes in unpredictable, random, and chaotic ways.

It is clear how VUCA, as a central feature of a digitally ubiquitous communication environment, produces fluidity in organizing practices. However, there are several other features of the contemporary environment that one might consider, especially as it pertains to the production of hybrid organizational forms. For one, it is what one might call *intemperate*, inasmuch as minor problems and issues related to organizing might become misleadingly and unpredictably inflated, immoderate, and urgent. Riach and Kelly (2015) colorfully use the term "vampiric" to underscore the fascination with newness and "virality" that prompts managers and organizers to treat some organizing problems with disproportionate focus. Berger and Milkman (2012) note that within the affective sharing culture associated with digital ubiquity, online content that evokes emotions characterized by high arousal tends to be more viral. The fact that organizations have to deal with issues, controversies, and demands for accountability that are far beyond their wheelhouse creates an urgency to be responsive in ways that transcend their normative routines. This exigence creates conditions for hybrid organizational forms because it requires borrowing, crafting, and reshaping practices and structures from organizational archetypes in other structures and settings.

Second, the organizing environment becomes *amnesiac*, because, despite the immoderate potential and power of digital archiving and the possibility for instant recall, the transient quality of communication results in digital memory being fallible, forgetful, and disembedded. Not only are tweets, instant messaging, or Snapchat messages fleeting insofar as they are rarely inscribed in ways that do not require a great deal of effort to retrieve, but the sheer amount of available information overloads the organizing environment (Stohl et al., 2016). The result is that often organizers reinvent the wheel when it comes to organizing techniques and tactics without recognizing connections or tensions with earlier organizing practices, in the process preserving seemingly archaic ways of doing things.

Third, *visibility* becomes a master trope for organizing (Brighenti, 2007) in that organizing processes themselves become increasingly noticeable, accessible, knowable, and monitorable. It is no coincidence that organizational transparency has become a central idealized and mythical part of our contemporary world (Christensen & Cheney, 2015), or that surveillance, the dark other of transparency, has become such a prevalent issue. Heightened visibility makes it impossible for different organizing forms to not "see" each other in the organizing environment; consequently, the velocity and scale of organizational mimesis is likely to increase, resulting in increasingly hybrid organizing forms across sectors. Consequently, as Flyverbom (2016) argues, managing visibility is a key issue for contemporary organizing.

Finally, and following from heightened visibility, *proximity* is an important feature of the digitally ubiquitous organizing environment. Precisely because both space and time are so highly compressed, that which seemed distant now becomes close. Digital proximity makes it possible for multiple kinds of organizations – formal or informal, large or small, hierarchical or flat – to share resources and work together on the same task, regardless of whether that task might be organizing a protest, solving a social problem, working on a wicked community issue, or creating new public goods in a sharing economy.

Fluid hybridity

We argue that taken together the features of digital ubiquity create conditions for fluid hybridity to emerge as the quintessential organizational dynamic. Fluid hybridity infuses both traditional and new organizational archetypes, structures, and forms, having important implications for the types of communicative competencies, relationship, and identities that are inscribed in contemporary organizations. We discuss the two key elements of this dynamic next.

Organizational hybridity

The term 'hybridity' became widespread alongside the growth of biology as a natural science in the 19th century, referring to the selective breeding of plants to produce new varieties with specific qualities of improved performances. Hybridity, the fusion of relatively distinct forms, was, within the discourse of colonialism, perceived as a stigma in association with notions of racial purity and the horror of miscegenation (Kraidy, 2002). It was also embedded in language, food, and other aspects of culture. Before its appropriation into the lexicon of cultural studies, the term 'creole' was initially used, for example, in the Spanish and French Caribbean, to describe inferior 'mixtures' of European and African culture.

In the last 30 years, alongside the explosion of work on globalization, hybridity has received extensive scholarly attention in multiple disciplines related to communication, including media and cultural studies (Bhabha, 1994), literary studies (Bakhtin, 1981), organizational studies (e.g., Makadok & Coff, 2009), and political communication (Chadwick, 2017). We are, of course, particularly concerned with treatments of hybrid forms that emphasize organizations, organizing, and digital technologies. We observe that scholars in organization studies, unsurprisingly, tend to take an organization-first approach to hybridity, using structures and institutions as their analytical starting points, whereas scholars of political communication tend to highlight communicative activities and agency as starting points in their consideration of hybrid forms. It is useful, then, to conceive of hybridity using Denis, Ferlie and Van Gestel's (2015) fourfold analytical framework of hybridity that implicates structure, institutions, identity, and agency. We note that this framework covers a broad swathe of organizational communication processes. Its relative completeness is evident in its similarity to Stohl and Cheney's (2001) comprehensive account of organizational communication paradoxes related to participation: they argue that the majority of paradoxes associated with communication and organizing are related to structure, power, agency, and identity. The framework is also similar to McPhee and Zaug's (2000) treatment of four message flows that constitute organizations themselves, which they label "organizational self-structuring," "institutional positioning," "membership negotiation," and "activity coordination."

Scholars who approach hybridity in terms of structure have tended to draw from Ouchi's (1979) distinction between hierarchies, networks, and markets, positioning hybrid forms as intermingling elements of all three structural forms. Makadok and Coff (2009), for example, identify six prototypical hybrids that combine elements of hierarchies and markets to create hybrids such as empowering hierarchies, consortiums, and franchises. Others have located hybridity as a fundamental structural aspect of organizing. Brown and Duguid (2000), for example, pointed out nearly two decades ago that all formal organizational structures are hybrid in some manner, and such hybridity was likely to be accentuated by new information and communication technologies.

Other organizational scholars take institutions as the starting point for their treatment of hybrid forms. The place of institutional orders in producing hybridity has long been recognized. "Institutional environments are often pluralistic . . . As a result organizations in search of external support and stability incorporate all sorts of incompatible structural elements" (Meyer & Rowan, 1977, 356). This recognition carries over into the digital age, with many organizational studies scholars examining the foundational role of multiple institutional logics in the organizing environment (Besharov & Smith, 2014). Ganesh and Stohl (2013), for example, identified how institutional and digitized logics of networking interacted with logics of aggregation to create nascent organizational forms in the Occupy movement.

Several communication scholars have also focused on agency, in the form of an emphasis on activity, and action in their analyses of organizational hybridity as a new form of organizing. For example Bennett and Segerberg in their highly influential typology of collective and connective action highlight how different organizing structures are implicated in the creation of three "ideal types of action involving digital media" (2013, 13), but their emphasis is on the *nature* of action in large-scale networks of contentious politics. They understand hybridity in terms of action that features formal organizations whose identities are not salient in performance of the protest but may help coordinate and provide technology in concert with informal, crowd-based methods of organizing, that is, self-organizing networks. Chadwick's work on hybridity is also activity oriented. He understands contemporary political organizations as a product of "a process of hybridization based on the selective transplantation and adaptation of digital network repertoires previously considered typical of social movements," produced by the "spatial and temporal interactions" facilitated by the Internet (2007, 284).

Finally, some communication studies of digital organizing focus on identity and membership as central aspects of hybrid organizational forms. This is true not only of studies that trace how multiple organizational affiliations of members in collective action groups result in transformations in the organizational form of those groups (e.g., Norton, 2009) but also of studies that trace the changing meanings of membership in the collective action environment itself (Bimber et al., 2012). Ganesh and Stohl argue that studying how organizations manage members is key to unpacking how formal and informal organizational forms intermingle and interact, maintaining that the increasing expansion and dilution of organizational membership throws into relief broader questions of how organizations are embedded in their environment and how large formal organizations "are likely to be affected by and take on the organizing dynamics of smaller and more transient digital groups" (2014, 753).

Fluid organizing

As we have suggested previously, hybridity is not merely a new organizational form. Rather in the ubiquitous digital environment, hybridity is coupled with the principle of fluidity. We observe with some irony that theorists of fluid organizing appear to have operated with fluid definitions of fluidity itself. It follows from our discussion of VUCA earlier that we understand the principle of fluidity comprehensively, as the seamless and dynamic movement of communication that serves to dissolve organizing structures, institutions, activities, and identities. Framing fluidity in this way makes it apparent, as Schreyögg and Sydow (2010) have pointed out, that fluidity is akin to formlessness and thus in many respects antithetical to the idea of organization itself. Organizations, after all, require at least some measure of form and solidity to exist because they need to simplify, manage, and control environmental uncertainty; in Weick's (1979) famous terms, they are consensually validated grammars for reducing equivocality. Schreyögg and Sydow argued: "Reacting in a turbulent environment to any new event by improvisation and without any pattern implies giving up the distinction between inside and outside. Organizations would merge with their environment – or never emerge in the first place" (2010, 1254).

Fluid organizing itself, then, should be understood as a set of organizing practices that moves organizations toward fluidity without actually getting them there – or conversely, carving nascent organizations out of fluid environments. Dobusch and Schoeneborn (2015) define fluid organizing as implicating contested membership and open boundaries, and other scholars have associated fluid organizing with self-organizing systems (Bennett & Segerberg, 2013) and with ideas of seamlessness, speed, and flexibility (Introna & Petrakaki, 2007). Empirically, fluid organizing encompasses as broad a swathe of organizational communication phenomena as hybridity, implicating structure, institutions, identity, and agency.

So, structural fluidity in organizing practice has represented the move away from formal, hierarchical, specialized, and differentiated departments and staff units to horizontal, improvised processes and temporary groups (Glance & Huberman, 1993). Sheller and Urry (2006), for example, refer to fluid structures as involving ambiguously defined relationships among groups of people such that change and flux become normative. Likewise, institutional fluidity has implied the movement from stable and ordered institutional environments and interorganizational relationships and partnerships to pluralistic, constantly changing institutional orders and temporary cross-sectoral connections (Hensmans, 2005; Granqvist & Gustafsson, 2013).

Fluid agency has involved the movement from activity contained within ongoing programs and coordination structures toward ad hoc projects and spontaneous, short-lived and opportunistic ventures (Kuhn et al., 2017). Hickson and his colleagues (Hickson et al., 2001) relatedly identify a mode of decision-making that they call fluid, involving steady and rapid flows, in contradistinction to constricted or sporadic modes of decision-making. Finally, fluid organizational identity involves the movement from clearly identifiable members, employees, and participants to loose and unstable and even impersonal coalitions of individuals and crowds (Stohl, 2011). Recent work on debranding, for example, traces how large organizations can more easily decouple themselves from pre-established identities in digital environments, working either under new identities or *sans* strong identities – in some cases, even anonymously (Kear et al., 2013).

Four archetypes of digital organizing

So far we have argued that the digitally ubiquitous organizing environment is comprised of a distinct set of characteristics that serve to produce both hybrid organizational forms and fluid organizing. Here, we shed more light on how fluid organizing and hybrid forms might come together in the digital environment by presenting a set of four organizing archetypes in the digital environment. Unlike other taxonomies or ideal types of organizing in the digital environment that position fluidity and hybridity at different points on the organizing spectrum (e.g., Bennett & Segerberg, 2013), or treat some forms of organizing as more digitized than others (Kitchin & Dodge, 2013), we assume that both fluid organizing and hybridity stretch across the spectrum of organizing and need to be conceptualized as such. So, our taxonomy is based on the relative emphasis in each archetype on the relationship between form and fluidity. This in turn helps us assess how communication competencies coalesce around issues of coherence within and across each organizing archetype. We present four organizing archetypes that embody fluid hybridity: organizationally driven, organizationally enabled, organizationally light, and organizationally embryonic.

In the *organizationally driven archetype*, a single organizational structure and logic is dominant, despite mingling with other logics and structures. Styhre's (2007) analysis of bureaucratic structures that incorporate more fluid principles of innovation is a case in point. Organizationally driven archetypes are also identifiably embedded in specified institutional fields and environments, despite having to deal with institutional contradictions and flux. Organizing activities themselves are based on historically grounded expectations, with clearly defined impacts and outcomes. And while organizational identity tends to be singular, and is often understood in "legacy" or pre-digital terms (Karpf, 2012), this archetype embodies particular forms of fluid hybridity. In their work on collective action in organizations in an era of technological change, for example, Bimber et al. (2012) showed how in the new information environment, organizational members' participatory styles were entangled with organizational structures creating a complex "collective action space" in which the organizational form became multifaceted and more complex. Members had fewer constraints and greater opportunity and individual choice in how organizing dynamics were enacted.

To illustrate the fluid hybridity embedded within the organizationally driven archetype, we point to the findings of Bimber et al.'s (2012) study of AARP. The results showed how the professionally managed advocacy organization, which for almost 100 years embraced the dynamics of a classic interest group (i.e., an organization where people share a common general interest but members are personally unknown to one another, pay dues levied by the organization, and respond to calls for specific action by leaders who make operational and tactical decisions), morphed into a vibrant multifaceted organization that developed new protocols such as online community tools. These tools weakened organizational boundaries and personalized and transformed patterns of engagement and interaction among their members. AARP was still driven by its large bureaucratic form, but as members' personal idiosyncrasies and differing styles of online participation were interwoven within traditional routines, new and sometimes transient structures and routines emerged as members were able to seamlessly move between institutional and entrepreneurial modes of engagement and personal and impersonal involvement. Despite the changes in organizing practices, however, as Delli Carpini observed, "the result is not the death of formal organizations but a shift in power and agency from leaders to members" (2012, Back Cover).

In the *organizationally enabled archetype*, two or more organizing structures and logics intermingle in organizing efforts that require a significant amount of communicative labor as organizational actors strive to make sense of the fluid movements from one form to another. The institutional order is visibly multisectoral and the identity of the organizing effort is shaped jointly by multiple parties; nonetheless, legacy identities of various parties persist in the effort. As a result, the impact of organizational activity becomes more difficult to calibrate, measure and evaluate. A campaign by several civil society groups to highlight mercury poisoning around the hill town of Kodaikkanal as a result of pollution by Hindustan Lever, Uniliver's India subsidiary, provides an interesting illustration of this archetype. *Jhatkaa*, a digital platform designed to put pressure on government and corporate bodies in India, coordinated a petition collaboratively with the Unilever Employee Welfare Association and a Chennai-based activist group. They leveraged Jhatkaa's connections with the entertainment industry in Mumbai and helped create and promote a video by Sofia Ashraf, a Mumbai-based rapper, which subsequently went viral, with many millions of views on YouTube and other platforms; the hashtag #wontbuyunilever trended on Twitter, and consequently, several million people signed the petition. The movement also attracted the support of 38 Degrees, a UK-based activist group, and their efforts resulted in a statement on the subject by Paul Polman, Unilever's Global CEO. However, Jhatkaa is still in an ongoing and difficult process of assessing how it can measure the success of its digital petitions in a broader environment where petitions may or may not carry significant rhetorical force. The cleanup has yet to occur, despite the visibility accorded to the issue and initially positive responses by both Unilever and the Indian government, as well as compensation given to ex UniLever employees who were affected by the poisoning.

The organizationally light archetype features organizational structures that are improvisational and easily changeable. The institutional environment in which organizing occurs is volatile, complex, and highly multisectoral. Legacy identities are absent; instead, identities emerge from coordinated activity. Organizing activity itself is volatile and unstable, and is difficult to establish and measure. The fluid hybridity of this archetype is exemplified in two distinct ways. In the first organizing-centric point of view there is an emergent entity in which creative inventiveness and impulsiveness are built directly into the DNA of the archetype. The Occupy movement in New Zealand, for example, resulted in the formation of a social collective called Loomio, designed to help activists make better decisions together using digital technologies. Second, as Ganesh and Stohl (2013) show, from a movement-centric point of view, movements such as Occupy themselves embody the types of emergent activities, loosely coupled communicative routines and transitional identities that are encapsulated in this archetype, enabling them to go global almost instantly and orchestrate similar, if broad and ambiguous, messages around the world. The multiple and heterogeneous social processes embedded in this type of collective action is captured by Melucci's (1996) notion of 'identization' rather than 'identity.' The inevitable confusion and the consequences of the acceleration of speed by digital media create an incoherence that gets played out, as the collective identity ebbs and flows, and organizational routines emerge, disappear only to reemerge in new ways.

Finally, in the *organizationally embryonic archetype*, organizing structures are nascent and on the verge of emergence. The institutional context is as yet unformed, and there is no impact or outcome of activity beyond digital visibility. Organizational identity and the meaning of organizing activity are still in the early stages of negotiation and, therefore, relatively unformed and unassigned and could take such forms as hashtags, discursive constructions, or material symbols, including buttons and clothing choices. Take, for example, the #metoo movement that emerged in 2017, not from a predetermined campaign strategy but spontaneously, as individual women found their voices. As time passed, this loose and fluid "network of outrage" (Castells, 2012) morphed into informal groups, such as Times Up. This coalition of over 300 women in the entertainment industry still does not have the accoutrements of one or many organizations and now faces the challenge of crafting a collective identity, developing relationships between members, and reaching out beyond the entertainment industry to vulnerable women in other sectors and industries who need legal, emotional, and social support in making their harassment experiences visible. Times Up may well turn into an organizationally light archetype, but it may well not; in either instance, it vividly illustrates the fluid dynamics of ebb and flow, and the coming together and coming apart of individuals, groups, and communities over time in the digital environment.

Conclusion: communication and coherence

In this chapter we have argued that archetypes embody both the form and formlessness of contemporary organizing in the context of digital ubiquity and implicate a variety of communication dynamics. Indeed, the fluid hybridity embodied in each of these archetypes has led to a great deal of speculation regarding the sorts of communicative skills and organizational competencies that are needed in this context. For example, Kuhn, Ashcraft, and Cooren argue that such an environment privileges communication skills that "lend themselves to effortless adaptability, inquiry, enthusiasm and self-promotion" (2017, 10). Management scholars argue that organizations need to develop new abilities that enable fluid shifts in organizational gears. Kanter argues, for example, that managers "must both standardize and innovate, endeavoring to prevent consistency from becoming stifling conformity. . . [and] have a strong reliance on partners, whom they collaborate with but do not control" (Kanter, 2008, 49).

Regardless of the nature of appropriate communication or the context or archetype of organizing, we suggest coherence management as a foundational communication skill in the contemporary era of fluid hybridity. Coherence is traditionally regarded as a structural property of organizing – where agency, activity, and identity come together as connectedness in action. Under those conditions coherence management means resolving the contradictory demands and expectations within the organizational environment. However, in the age of fluid hybridity, coherence management goes beyond organizational alignment and congruence or the resolution of contradiction and implicates the constant negotiation between form and formlessness, text and discourse, meaning and action.

In emphasizing its importance, we are therefore not endorsing a bias toward coherence; instead, we wish to further emphasize that the act of communicative cohering is much more problematic now than it ever has been. That is, sensemaking and intelligibility are as primary a concern now as the audiences for communication. Managing coherence has at least three qualities: it is *recursive*, involving a constant looking back and clarifying the content and flow of communication; it is *multilevel*, implicating individuals, groups, organizations, and communities simultaneously; and it is temporally, structurally, and contextually *ambidextrous*, involving "the ability to both use and refine existing knowledge (exploitation) while also creating new knowledge to overcome knowledge deficiencies or absences identified within the execution of the work (exploration)" (Turner et al., 2013).

Further, the shape of coherence management itself varies depending on the organizing archetype. For example, popular rhetoric of disruptive innovation implicitly frames appropriate communication as immediate and revolutionary responses to organizing challenges, captured in the adage "disrupt or be disrupted." Lepore (2014) argues, however, that scholars who privilege disruptive innovation ignore the fact that long-term sustainable success for organizers has historically involved incremental, thoughtful, and gradual response to what appear to be change imperatives rather than sudden, risky, and disruptive responses. From our standpoint, what counts is not so much the legitimacy of the adage "disrupt or be disrupted" as it is the fact that it emerges as a cohering challenge in an organizationally driven archetype but not necessarily in any of the others.

We have presented our ideas on digital ubiquity, fluid hybridity, and the four archetypes as provocations, designed much more to spark thought, discussion, and examination, than as any kind of final word on the organizing arrangements possible in the digital era. Two things are clear: first, that we need more empirical studies of the fascinating range of organizing archetypes that are emerging in the digitally ubiquitous environment, to establish their prevalence, to understand how organizing practices might switch, duplicate, reinvent, or reverse archetypes, and to trace the emergence of new ones. We are not proposing a stage model of organizational development in the digital era; indeed, we believe that organizations can flip and reverse forms; however, this requires much more empirical study. Second, and finally, it is already clear to us that digitially ubiquitous environments are volatile enough that even archtypes such as the ones we have presented, which seem to cover all available ranges, may in fact become an incomplete set, as what counts as ubiquity itself continues to morph, spread, and transform. This sort of indeterminacy is, in fact, a defining feature of our times.

References

Andrejevic, M. (2004). The Work of Watching One Another: Lateral Surveillance, Risk, and Governance. *Surveillance & Society*, 2(4), 479–497.

Andrejevic, M. (2007). Surveillance in the Digital Enclosure. *The Communication Review*, 10(4), 295–317.

Bakhtin, M. (1981). Discourse in the Novel In M. Holquist (ed.), *The Dialogic Imagination*. Austin: University of Texas, pp. 259–422.

Bauman, Z. (2012). *Liquid Modernity*. Cambridge: Polity Press.

Beniger, J. R. (1986). *The Control Revolution: Technological and Economic Origins of the Information Society*. Cambridge, MA: Harvard University Press.

Benkler, Y. (2006). *The Wealth of Networks: How Social Production Transforms Markets and Freedom*. New Haven: Yale University Press.

Bennett, L., and Segerberg, A. (2013). *The Logic of Connective Action: Digital Media and the Personalization of Contentious Politics*. Cambridge: Cambridge University Press.

Berger, J., and Milkman, K. (2012). What Makes Online Content Viral? *Journal of Marketing Research*, 49(2), 192–205, April.

Besharov, M. L., and Smith, W. K. (2014). Multiple Institutional Logics in Organizations: Explaining Their Varied Nature and Implications. *Academy of Management Review*, 43(1), 87–109.

Bhabha, H. K. (1994). *The Location of Culture*. London: Routledge.

Bimber, B. (2017). Three Prompts for Collective Action in the Context of Digital Media. *Political Communication*, 34(1), 6–20.

Bimber, B., Flanagin, A., and Stohl, C. (2012). *Collective Action in Organizations: Interaction and Engagement in an Era of Technological Change*. Cambridge: Cambridge University Press.

Blumler, J. G., and Coleman, S. (2015). Democracy and the Media – Revisited. *Javnost*, 22, 111–128.

Brighenti, A. (2007). Visibility: A Category for the Social Sciences. *Current Sociology*, 55(3), 323–342.

Brown, J. S., and Duguid, P. (2000). *The Social Life of Information*. Boston, MA: Harvard Business School Press.

Castells, M. (1996). *The Rise of the Network Society*. Oxford: Wiley-Blackwell.

Castells, M. (2012). *Networks of Outrage and Hope: Social Movements in the Internet Age*. Cambridge: Polity Press.

Chadwick, A. (2007). Digital Network Repertoires and Organizational Hybridity. *Political Communication*, 24, 283–301.

Chadwick, A. (2017). *The Hybrid Media System: Politics and Power* (2nd ed.). Oxford: Oxford University Press.

Christensen, L. T., and Cheney, G. (2015). Peering into Transparency: Challenging Ideals, Proxies, and Organizational Practices. *Communication Theory*, 25, 70–90.

Contractor, N. (2002). Introduction. In L. A. Lievrouw and S. Livingstone (eds.), *Handbook of New Media: Social Shaping and Consequences of ICTs*. Newbury Park: Sage.

Delli Carpini, M. (2012). Backcover. In Bimber, B., Flanagin, A., and Stohl, C. (eds.), *Collective Action in Organizations: Interaction and Engagement in an Era of Technological Change*. Cambridge: Cambridge University Press, p 225.

Denis, J.-L., Ferlie, E., and van Gestel, N. (2015). Understanding Hybridity in Public Organizations. *Public Administration*, 93(2), 273–289.

Dobusch, L., and Schoeneborn, D. (2015). Fluidity, Identity, and Organizationality: The Communicative Constitution of Anonymous. *Journal of Management Studies*, 52(8), 1005–1035.

Flyverbom, M. (2016). Transparency: Mediation and the Management of Visibilities. *International Journal of Communication*, 10, 110–122.

Fukuyama, F. (1992). *The End of History and the Last Man London*. Hamish Hamilton.

Fulk, J. and DeSanctis, G. (1995). Electronic Communication and Changing Organizational Forms. *Organization Science*, 6, 337–349.

Ganesh, S., and Stohl, C. (2013). From Wall Street to Wellington: Protests in an Era of Digital Ubiquity. *Communication Monographs*, 80(4), 425–451. doi:10.1080/03637751.2013.828156.

Ganesh, S., and Stohl, C. (2014). Collective Action, Community Organizing and Social Movements. In D. K. Mumby and L. L. Putnam (eds.), *Sage Handbook of Organizational Communication* (3rd ed.). Newbury Park, CA: Sage, pp. 743–765.

Gerstein, M., Nadler, D., and Shaw, R. (1992). *Organizational Architecture*. San Francisco: Jossey-Bass Publishers.

Glance, N. S., and Huberman, B. A. (1993). Social Dilemmas and Fluid Organizations. In K. Carley and M. Prietula (eds.), *Computational Organizational Theory*. London: Lawrence Erlbaum, pp. 217–240.

Granqvist, N., and Gustafsson, R. (2013). *Fluidity in Institutional Embedding of Proto-Institutions*. Paper presented at the Academy of Management Proceedings.

Hensmans, M. (2005). Social Movement Organizations: A Metaphor for Strategic Actors in Institutional Fields. *Organization Studies*, 24(3), 355–381.

Hickson, D. J., Butler, R. J., Cray, D., and Wilson, D. C. (2001). *The Bradford Studies of Strategic Decision Making*. London: Ashgate.

Introna, L. D., and Petrakaki, D. (2007). Defining the Virtual Organization. In D. Barnes (ed.), *E-Commerce and V-Business* (2nd ed.) Butterworth: Heinemann.

Jackson, M. (2007). Fluidity, Promiscuity, and Mash-Ups: New Concepts for the Study of Mobility and Communication. *Communication Monographs*, 74(3), 408–413.

Kanter, R. M. (2008). Transforming Giants. *Harvard Business Review*, 86(1), 43–52.

Karpf, D. (2012). *The Move on Effect: The Unexpected Transformation of American Political Advocacy*. Oxford: Oxford University Press.

Kear, A., Bown, G. R., and Christidi, S. (2013). Debranding in Fantasy Realms: Perceived Marketing Opportunities Within the Virtual World *International Journal of Advanced Computer Science and Applications*, 4(8), 111–117.

Kitchin, R., and Dodge, M. (2013). *Code/Space: Software and Everyday Life*. Boston, MA: MIT Press.

Kraidy, M. M. (2002). Hybridity in Cultural Globalization. *Communication Theory*, 12(3), 316–339. https://doci.org/10.1111/cj.1468-2885.2002.ctb00272.

Kuhn, T., Ashcraft, K., and Cooren, F. (2017). *The Work of Communication: Relational Perspectives on Working and Organizing in Contemporary Capitalism*. New York: Routledge.

Leonardi, P., and Barley, S. (2008). Materiality and Change: Challenges to Building Better Theory About Technology and Organizing. *Information and Organization*, 18, 159–176.

Lepore, J. (2014). The Disruption Machine. *The New Yorker*, 23, 30–36.

Mack, O., Khare, A., Krämer, A., and Burgartz, T. (eds.). (2016). *Managing in a VUCA World*. New York: Springer.

Makadok, R., and Coff, R. (2009). Both Market and Hierarchy: An Incentive-System Theory of Hybrid Governance Forms. *Academy of Management Review*, 34(2), 297–319.

McPhee, R., and Zaug, P. (2000). The Communicative Constitution of Organizations. *Electronic Journal of Communication*, 10(1), 1–17.

Melucci, A. (1996). *Challenging Codes: Collective Action in the Information Age*. Cambridge: Cambridge University Press.

Meyer, J. W., and Rowan, B. (1977). Institutionalized Organizations: Formal Structure as Myth and Ceremony. *American Journal of Sociology*, 83(2), 340–363.

Monge, P., and Contractor, N. (2004). *Theories of Communication Networks*. Oxford: Oxford University Press.

Nadler, D., Gerstein, M. S., and Shaw, R. B. (1992). *Organizational Architecture: Designs for Changing Organizations* (Vol. 192). San Francisco, CA: Jossey-Bass Inc.

Norton, T. (2009). Situating Organizations in Politics: A Diachronic View of Control-Resistance Dialectics. *Management Communication Quarterly*, 22(4), 525–554.

Ouchi, W. G. (1979). A Conceptual Framework for the Design of Organizational Control Mechanisms. *Management Science*, 25(9), 833–848.

Powers, T. (2012). The End of Organizations as We Know Them. *TEDx Maastricht*. www.youtube.com/watch?v=OcCcssS-lrQ.

Rainie, L., and Wellman, B. (2012). *Networked Individualism: The New Social Operating System*. Boston, MA: MIT Press.

Riach, K., and Kelly, S. (2015). The Need for Fresh Blood: Understanding Age Inequality Through a Vampiric Lens. *Organization*, 22(3), 287–305.

Schreyögg, G., and Sydow, J. (2010). Organizing for Fluidity? Dilemmas of New Organizational Forms. *Organization Science*, 21(6), 1251–1262.

Sheller, M., and Urry, J. (eds.). (2006). *Mobile Technologies of the City*. London, UK: Routledge.

Stohl, C. (2011). Paradoxes of Connectivity: Boundary Permeability, Technological Variability, and Organisational Durability. *Australian Journal of Communication*, 38, 123–139.

Stohl, C., and Cheney, G. E. (2001). Participatory Processes, Paradoxical Practices: Communication and the Dilemmas of Workplace Democracy. *Management Communication Quarterly*, 14(3), 349–407.

Stohl, C. Stohl, M., & Leonardi, P. (2016). Managing opacity: Information visibility and the paradox of transparency in the digital age. *International Journal of Communication*, 10, 123–137.

Styhre, A. (2007). *The Innovative Bureaucracy: Bureaucracy in an Age of Fluidity*. New York: Routledge.

Turner, N., Swart, J., and Maylor, H. (2013). Mechanisms for Managing Ambidexterity: A Review and Research Agenda. *International Journal of Management Reviews*, 15(3), 317–332.

Weick, K. (1979). *The Social Psychology of Organizing*. Reading, MA: Addison-Wesley.

21

All the lonely people?

The continuing lament about the loss of community

Keith N. Hampton and Barry Wellman *

"All the lonely people: where do they all come from?" the Beatles wondered, singing in particular about Eleanor Rigby (Lennon & McCartney, 1965). When we look back, we find that many generations – perhaps each generation – have feared that community has disappeared (Image 21.1). The most recent examples can be found in the response that commentators have had to the rise of social media, mobile phones, and related digital technologies (Turkle, 2011, 2015; Twenge, 2017). Why does every generation believe that relationships were stronger and community better in the recent past?

Each generation thinks this, and each generation is wrong. We trace here the long history of misplaced grieving for a supposedly lost community – a fear that has always been misplaced – and examine how communication technologies are now transforming communities into persistent, pervasive networks. Our discussion is largely based on observations about the structure of community in North America and Europe, but our historical account has been observed in many countries (Drouhot, 2017; Xu & Chan, 2011). The changes to community structure that we describe likely apply to diverse societal contexts, although at different points in time.

Some of the current alarm about the loss of community is in the recognition that the structure of community is changing as technologies change. Another part of the unease comes from a selective perception of the present. There is nostalgia for a perfect pastoral past that never was (see the critique in Laslett, 1965). This longing for a time when the grass was ever greener dims an awareness of the powerful stresses and cleavages that have always pervaded human society. "Fings ain't wot they used to be" (Bart & Norman, 1959), according to the English nostalgic song – but then again, they never were. In people's haste to bemoan what has been lost and focus on what is absent from contemporary community, they have neglected to recognize those aspects of traditional community that are returning and changing everyday lives.

When North Americans reflect on the 18th century or even earlier, they perceive a different type of community: a different organization of relationships with friends, relatives, neighbors,

* A version of this paper, significantly revised, updated, and expanded here, was previously published as: Hampton, K., and Wellman, B. (2018). Lost and Saved . . . Again: The Moral Panic About the Loss of Community Takes Hold of Social Media. *Contemporary Sociology*, 47(6), 643–651.

Image 21.1   Statue by Tommy Steele of Eleanor Rigby, Stanley Street, Liverpool, sitting alone on a park bench and dedicated to "All the Lonely People." Open-source image copyright Peter Tarleton. https://commons.wikimedia.org/wiki/File:Eleanor_Rigby_Statue_Liverpool.JPG

and workmates. Before the rise of the Industrial Revolution in Europe and the growth of urbanization in America, a person's community generally consisted of a relatively small number of social ties, densely connected and organized around the home and small town life. People spent most of their lives surrounded by relatives, neighbors, and friends who not only shared similar backgrounds and beliefs but also did similar tasks and daily labor. The vast majority of connections were to strong ties with whom they were in regular, often daily, contact and with whom they had much in common. Indeed, this type of community structure can be ideal for providing certain types of social support: Companionship and aid could be abundant; in an emergency, everyone knew who was in need; and people could reliably expect help when it was needed. For a lack of a better term, we call this 'traditional community.'

Much about the relations typical of traditional community has been idealized. Yet the structure of community in olden days had its drawbacks. The density of relations afforded a high degree of conformity. Similar beliefs, backgrounds, and daily labor were the norm. Rigid hierarchies governed who could communicate with whom. Adopting a term more commonly associated with social media, the structure of traditional community created "echo chambers" (Sunstein, 2009). Information was not filtered by algorithms; rather, the primordial "filter bubble" (Pariser, 2012) consisted of tradition, church, and kin, all of which worked to limit exposure to external information. Beliefs were amplified through interactions that were largely confined to a closed social system. There was little maneuverability in situations when everyone kept an often critical eye on everyone else. Informal watchfulness was high. When individuals did not conform, there were strong repressive sanctions. Offenses were crimes against society and were met with rapid, organized, and passionate punishment. For better or worse, people were born into and died as members of the local community that they had inherited at birth.

Although such a community structure is no longer widespread in developed countries and has largely ceased to exist in developing nations, some lament its loss as if it existed only yesterday. They are grieving primarily for the supposed loss of social solidarity while ignoring parallel costs to the flow of information and personal freedoms.

Since the disappearance of traditional community, networks of supportive relations have undergone two major shifts. The first shift was a result of increased mobility. It began with the Industrial Revolution and urbanization and culminated with the introduction of the Internet and mobile phone. Wellman has called this "networked individualism" (Rainie & Wellman, 2012; Wellman, 2001). The second, a shift that has only begun to become apparent, is a result of what Hampton (2016) calls "relational persistence" and "pervasive awareness." This latest shift is being afforded through the increasing permanence of email addresses and mobile phone numbers, technologies such as social media that allow for the articulation of social ties, the persistence of contact over time, and high levels of awareness of the opinions and daily activities of community members. The result is that once again people are becoming embedded in a community structure that provides informal watchfulness and awareness of an enduring set of relations. Community has not been lost but has profoundly changed.

Ongoing fears of the loss of community

Old World Fears: Although the lyrics vary, the loss of community is not a new alarm. Pundits continue to sing an old refrain in a new language, part of a long-lived line of thought that posits that the only good relationships are those nestled in rural villages or their urban imitations – neighborhoods. Their writing reflects the continuing belief that primordial village-like bonds are the ideal for a good society. They also show the recurrent worries that the shift away from villages to big cities and ultimately to relationships maintained online are resulting in disconnection, isolation, and social unrest. Literary scholars call this "pastoralism": nostalgia for an idealized, mutually supportive, rural past that rarely was.

Perhaps the earliest scholarly reference can be found in the works of the North African scholar Ibn Khaldun (1377[2015]), who contended in the *Kitāb al-'Ibar* (*Book of Lessons*) that as societies progressed on a continuum from tribal to urban life, social solidarity (*asabiyah*) grew weaker and civilizations declined. In the Western world, the warnings go back to at least the 17th century, when philosopher Thomas Hobbes warned in 1651 that rapid social change in England was creating loneliness and alienation and leading to a "war of all against all" (Chapter 1, Para.13).

As with today's concerns about social media, mobile phones, and the Internet, many commentators wrestled to understand the ways in which large-scale social changes associated with the Industrial Revolution may have affected the composition, structure, and operation of communities. Their analyses have reflected the unease with which 19th-century pundits faced the impacts on relations with kith and kin of industrialization, bureaucratization, capitalism, imperialism, and technological developments. Although religion, locality, and kinship group had some integrative claims on such relations, the shift to mobile, market societies now has the potential to disconnect individuals from the strengths and constraints of tradition (Marx, 1964; Smith, 1979; White & White, 1962; Williams, 1973).

Ferdinand Tönnies set the prevailing tone in 1887 by asserting there were fundamental differences between the communally organized societies of yesteryear (which he called 'gemeinschaft') and the contractually organized societies ('gesellschaft') of the Industrial Revolution. Tönnies asserted that communally organized societies, supposedly characteristic of rural areas and underdeveloped states, had densely interconnected relationships composed principally of neighbors and kin. By contrast, contractually organized societies, supposedly characteristic of industrial bureaucratic cities, had more sparsely knit relationships composed principally of ties between friends and acquaintances. Tönnies argued that the lack of cohesion in such gesellschaft societies was leading to specialized contractual exchanges that were replacing communally enforced norms of mutual support.

This was not only an isolated, nostalgic lament for the supposed loss of the mythical pastoral past where happy villagers knew their place. Tönnies' vision was part of a particularly European debate about the transformation of societies: aristocrats, intellectuals, and parvenus coming to terms with the transformation of ordered hierarchical societies of peasants and landowners, workers and merchants. Many analysts shared Tönnies' fears about the supposed contemporary loss of community, although they offered different reasons for why it was happening, including industrialization, urbanization, bureaucratization, capitalism, socialism, and technological change.

With a radically different tone but a similar premise, Karl Marx (1852) and Friedrich Engels (1885[1970]) made the loss of community a centerpiece of their communist analyses, asserting that industrial capitalism had created new types of interpersonal exploitation that drove people apart. They claimed that capitalism had alienated workers not only from their work but from each other. Taking yet another tack, the late 19th-century sociologist Émile Durkheim (1897[1951]) feared that the loss of solidarity had weakened communal support and fostered social pathology. Shortly afterward, sociologist Max Weber (1946, 1958) extolled modern rationality but nonetheless feared that bureaucratization and urbanization were weakening communal bonds and traditional authority.

On the other hand, some commentators noted that the large-scale reorganization of production had created new opportunities for community relations. Thus, Marx acknowledged that industrialization had reduced poverty, and Engels realized that working-class home ownership would heighten local communal bonds. Weber argued that bureaucracy and urbanization would liberate many from the traditional, stultifying bases of community, and Durkheim (1893[1993]) argued that the new complex divisions of labor were binding people together in networks of interdependent "organic solidarity." German sociologist Georg Simmel celebrated urban liberation but also worried that the new individualism would lead to superficial relationships (1903[1950], 1922[1955]). He recognized that the move from villages to cities meant that people were no longer totally enmeshed in one all-encompassing community but could maneuver more freely through their partial social attachments.

New World Fears: Despite different social conditions, American politicians, pundits, and social scientists carried forward European concerns about the loss of community. Near the end of the American Revolution, Thomas Jefferson followed up on a key preoccupation of two 18th-century British philosophers, John Locke and David Hume: their quest to understand how primordial community relations underpinned the social basis of large-scale societies (see also Wills, 1978). Based at his Monticello plantation, Jefferson's *Notes on the State of Virginia* gave the issue a clear anti-urban cast – communal bonds are not viable in industrial, commercial cities. He asserted:

> The mobs of great cities add just so much to the support of pure government, as sores do to the strength of the human body.

(1787)

Through the US Constitution, written soon afterward in 1787, Jefferson's agrarian model of America gave more political weight to small rural states, and this rural bias has continued to shape the American political landscape. Although these small rural states now contain just 17% of the population, they can elect a Senate majority (Lee & Oppenheimer, 1999).

Moreover, American states – even those that are more urban, such as California, Florida, Illinois, Michigan, New York, and Pennsylvania – have often located their capitals away from big cities (Engstrom et al., 2013).

Americans wrestled with Tönnies' concerns, debating whether modern times have occasioned the loss of community in developed Western societies (e.g., Berger, 1960; Grant, 1969; Nisbet, 1962; Parsons, 1943; Slater, 1970). They, too, decried the loss of traditional communities bound together by custom and tradition, but they recognized the constraints of traditional community. Some analyses reflected the continuing American tension between individualism and communalism originally put forward by the influential historian Frederick Jackson Turner (1893). Focusing on the populace's march westward to settle the supposedly empty frontier, Turner argued that frequent mobility left little opportunity for community to develop. He maintained that what little community there was in the West consisted of transient groups of settlers helping each other, with instrumental aid overshadowing emotional support, companionship, or a sense of communal belonging. Even the cities were filled with migrants: floating proletarians who were constantly on the move, seeking work that would push them up the ladder (Chudacoff, 1972; Katz et al., 1982; Thernstrom, 1964, 1973). The rural settlers and urban migrants embodied the Turnerian spirit of individualism and practicality. In shedding stability and embracing mobility, they had avoided being embedded in traditional community bonds (Starr, 1985, 1990).

Although the urban-industrial community freed the individual from the constraints of a densely knit local network, many pundits viewed this new structure of relations with suspicion. They looked to the mythical pastoralism epitomized in Thornton Wilder's "Our Town" (1938). Echoing Jefferson, they demonized urban life. Well before the advent of Facebook, scholars questioned the value of having a large number of ties with people who were not family and with whom one was not especially close – a characteristic of urban life. The city was the manifestation of the mobility afforded by the telephone, railway, and related technologies. After all, as founding member of the "Chicago School" of sociology, Ernest Burgess, recognized:

> Mobility may be measured not only by these changes of movement, but also by increase of contacts. While the increase of population of Chicago in 1912–22 was less than 25 percent (23.6 percent), the increase of letters delivered to Chicagoans was double that . . . The number of telephone calls in Chicago increased from 606,131,928 in 2014 to 944,010,586 in 1922, an increase of 55.7 per cent, while the population increased only 13.4 per cent.
>
> *(1925, 60–61)*

Surely such heightened levels of communication would lead to the breakdown of social control. Would families not be destroyed as outside contact took the place of relations with immediate kin, local friends, and neighbors? As sociologist Maurice Stein argued a generation later in *The Eclipse of Community*:

> The old feeling of solidarity based on a sense that everyone in town belongs to a common community gives way to sub-communities with hostile attitudes toward each other (1960, 92) . . . . Community ties become increasingly dispensable, finally extending even into the nuclear family, and we are forced to watch children dispensing with their parents at an even earlier age in suburbia,
>
> *(1960, 329)*

Stein's sociological contemporary, Robert Nisbet, had similar thoughts in his *Community and Power*:

> The traditional primary relationships of men have become functionally irrelevant to our State and economy and meaningless to the moral inspirations of individuals.
>
> *(1962, 49)*

Although such armchair lamentations were laced with anecdotes, the lamenters rarely supported their arguments with systematic research. Starting in the 1960s, scholars such as Herbert Gans (1962) countered laments with actual documentation of the supportive nature of social ties in the city, while urbanists such as Jane Jacobs (1961) contrasted the diversity and security of cities with the alienation of suburbs. By the mid-1960s, the irony had not been lost on some observers. For example, S.D. Clark – himself a product of rural Saskatchewan and then at the peak of his career in the metropolitan University of Toronto – noted:

> A generation ago, the student of American society, then in background truly a man of the country, could find in the big city all that was evil, depraved, and corrupt in the American way of life. . . . In the quarter century or so that has since passed, the student of American society has learned to love the city in the manner that he has long loved the country, and now it is suburbia, portrayed in terms of slavish conformity, fetish of togetherness, and craze for organization, which is set over against a romantic image of the city.
>
> *(1966, 4–5)*

Each generation has looked back longingly and nostalgically and supposed that the previous generation had better relationships. Different generations point to different sources for the supposed loss of community. This is the perennial "Community Question" debate that Wellman first identified in 1979. It has been a cyclical argument that rises in unison with major social and technological changes, with the Community Question again becoming a major issue in how people interpret change as they ponder how quickening technological change is affecting the structure of community.

Technology in the mix

Since the Industrial Revolution, technology has been a visible suspect in the death of community (Levitt, 2012). Consider George Inness' 1855 painting of a steam locomotive chugging through green fields in Pennsylvania's "The Lackawanna Valley" (Image 21.2). Although the

Image 21.2 'The Lackawanna Valley' c. 1856. Painting by George Inness
Washington: National Gallery of Art

train might be carrying people to visit distant relatives, the image is of a monstrous interloper – a steam-puffing Godzilla – destroying bucolic country life.

Even things we now take for granted have been singled out. Thus, one of America's first sociologists, Charles H. Cooley, noted:

> What a strange practice it is, when you think of it, that a man should sit down to his break-fast table and, instead of conversing with his wife, and children, hold before his face a sort of screen on which is inscribed a world-wide gossip!
>
> *(1909, 105)*

A century ago, Cooley was talking about the introduction of the daily newspaper. That, too, was a time of rapid technological change associated with transformations in community. Cooley observed that new technologies – railroads, telegraphs, telephones, and a national postal system – were overcoming the constraints of time and space, creating new permanence through recorded communication, and emboldening democracy through universal access to information and debate.

Like the Devil, *Technology the Destroyer* has appeared in many aspects. For example, there are the soulless giant factory machines made famous in Charlie Chaplin's (1936) *Modern Times* movie, and the selfish privatism about which the scholar Robert Bellah complained in *Habits of the Heart* (Bellah et al., 1985), as did TV news anchor Tom Brokaw in *The Greatest Generation* (1998). In addition, there is the social disconnection that Robert Putnam (2000) deplored in *Bowling Alone* – worrying that people were staying home watching TV instead of going to the local community's bowling or civic club.

Computerization and its extension into new digital media are often the *bêtes noirs*. As early as the 1970s, futurist Alvin Toffler (1970) argued that the rise of computers would extend human mobility to the point that community would collapse. As expressed by narrator Orson Welles in the documentary about Toffler's *Future Shock* book (Grasshoff, 1972), there is a

> feeling that nothing is permanent anymore . . . man's relationship to things is increasingly temporary . . . the telephone directory is rewritten every day to keep track of the mobile society . . . as we breed a new race of nomads.

The public, media commentators, and even some scholars worry that people in developed societies have become so immersed in digital media – the Internet and mobile devices – that they have become socially isolated (e.g., Harmon, 1998; Turkle, 2011). They blame such digital media for pulling people away from spending quality, in-person time with their friends, neighbors, and relatives. They wonder how people can have meaningful relationships through a computer or phone screen. Thus *Globe and Mail* columnist Douglas Cornish worried:

> Will this glow [from the Internat] produce a closed generation of socially challenged individuals; humans who are more comfortable with machines than anything else?
>
> *(2006)*

Or, as columnist Stephen Marche (2012) proclaimed in *The Atlantic*:

> We are living in an isolation that would have been unimaginable to our ancestors, and yet we have never been more accessible . . . Within this world of instant and absolute communication, unbounded by limits of time or space, we suffer from unprecedented alienation.

We have never been more detached from one another, or lonelier. In a world consumed by ever more novel modes of socializing, we have less and less actual society. We live in an accelerating contradiction: the more connected we become, the lonelier we are. We were promised a global village; instead, we inhabit the drab cul-de-sacs and endless freeways of a vast suburb of information.

(2012)

Parallels to earlier alarms about the loss of community could not be clearer. However, while the alarm is unfounded, something *has* changed – community is not what it used to be.

Networks rather than groups

Much of the misunderstanding about the changing nature of community stems from the assumption that people have always belonged to village-like community groups. In reality, people have always belonged to various configurations of social networks. One such network structure is idealized by the image of traditional community, as depicted in Figure 21.1: a social network that is densely interconnected, with many local, strong ties.

As with variation in how people interact with the physical design of objects (Gibson, 1979) and between people and technologies (Norman, 1988), variation in community structure affords different outcomes. The structure of community is variable and malleable only to the

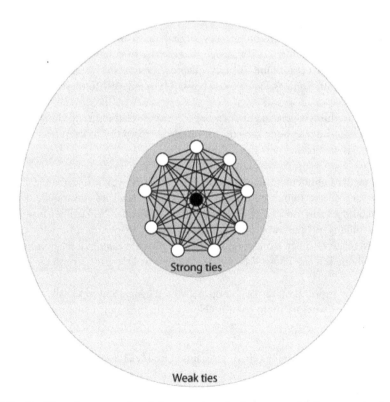

Figure 21.1 Traditional community: A dense network of closer social ties organized around a single focus of activity, such as the home and neighborhood

extent afforded by communication and transportation technologies. While outcomes might still vary based on people's traits, skills, culture, and the role of institutions such as religion and government, the configuration of people's community networks fundamentally constrains and affords different outcomes. Just as a chair offers most people a poor affordance for sleeping, at least in comparison to the opportunities provided by a bed, a dense, closed community network affords much less diversity than one that is loosely knit. Thus, traditional community structure, and in turn what it could afford, was a product of the constraints of the technology of the day. In a traditional community, people were often born into and died as part of the same network because they mostly could only move and communicate easily across short distances. The technology afforded only local, dense networks that persisted over an individual's lifetime.

Yet community never fully resembled the structure of a traditional community as the early scholars had idealized it. People have been part of far-flung, mobile networks for much longer than is usually recognized. Some people migrated between localities while keeping connections with kin near and far (Wellman & Wetherell, 1996; Wetherell et al., 1994). This was particularly true for soldiers and their camp followers, and elites and their servants. By the late 18th century, the European and North American worlds were already mobile and well on their way to becoming industrialized (Tilly, 1988). Even the scale of European villages was changing. There was a significant decrease in the population involved in agricultural production and an increase in the scale of manufacturing. Although the household remained the typical production unit, the scale of production was shifting to networks of households that produced cheap goods, particularly textiles, for national markets and international trade. The seasonal nature of agricultural production freed segments of the population to travel from village to village in search of agricultural and industrial labor. A steady flow of migrants traveled between Europe and abroad. In the 18th century alone, an estimated 45 million Europeans migrated out of Europe – the majority to the Americas – whereas 10 million returned home (Tilly, 1988).

The introduction of new technologies affords different network structures, which can transform how people form and maintain relationships as well as gain access to information and support (Hampton, 2016). Technologies that facilitated contact at a distance – telephones, steamships, railroads, cars, and planes – allowed people to escape the bonds of encapsulated social ties of kinship, locality, and occupation. Such technologies afforded opportunities to form supportive social relations in multiple contexts that did not strongly overlap – family at home; colleagues in the workplace; and friends in the neighborhood, church, and voluntary associations (Rainie & Wellman, 2012). They were able to escape the control of tradition and hierarchy and maneuver around the insular minds of densely knit networks: the original filter bubbles and echo chambers.

Wellman (1979) was one of the first to articulate that community was not necessarily "lost" or "saved" as a result of the transformations afforded by mobility (see also Webber, 1963). Mobility has liberated people from the dense bonds of traditional community, but they have continued to find companionship and support in sparsely knit networks (Lu & Hampton, 2017). Throughout their life course, people moved from one neighborhood to another, from one job to another, and from one interest to another. Necessitated by mobility, they severed ties in one context only to form new, supportive ties in another. As people and information moved more freely through time and space, the structure of community became less densely knit, less local, less tightly bounded, more diverse, and more fragmented. Such a structure no longer afforded social control through informal watchfulness alone, and social control became facilitated through formalized institutional surveillance and the rule of law, with well-defined sanctions and prescribed punishments. Such is the structure of community depicted in Figure 21.2 that is a part of modern urban life. Few individuals are socially isolated, but there is little mutual awareness of daily

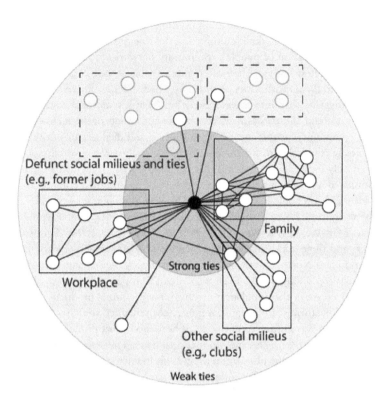

Figure 21.2   Urban-industrial community: A loosely knit network with a small number of strong ties and many weaker ties from multiple social milieus that may be active, dormant, and replaced over the life course

activities. As networked individuals, their community extends to social ties that are both local and distant (Rainie & Wellman, 2012; Wang & Wellman, 2010; Wellman, 2001).

Home computing, Internet technologies, and, later, mobile phones amplified the trend toward networked individualism. Indeed, sociologist Manuel Castells (1996) argued that new information and communication technologies allowed people to overcome historical limits on interaction. These limits were the natural boundaries of interaction that were possible within the spatial organization of the traditional realm of community. Castells calls this the "space of places." Castells suggested that in the networked society, the "space of flows" had superseded the space of places; interaction was even less constrained by place than in the urban condition. Mobile phones take this trend to the extreme by allowing individuals to overcome the limits of interaction that once required them to maintain community by traipsing door-to-door or staying rooted to their desktop Internet (Hampton & Wellman, 2003; Rainie & Wellman, 2012). Few individuals are socially isolated, but, as networked individuals, their community extends to social ties that are both local and distant (Kraut & Burke, 2015).

Although previous technologies had afforded mobility, they did not support two key characteristics of a traditional community: the persistence and sustained awareness of social ties. Even during the rise of the Internet, the lack of persistence has meant that in an urban-industrial community, social ties were often lost at key life-course events, such as moving, graduation, changing jobs, marriage, parenthood, and divorce (Hampton & Wellman, 2003; Wellman et al.,

1997). The absence of relational persistence has contributed to a "nostalgia epidemic" (Bauman, 2017): the perception that more relationships are transitory and disposable and therefore less meaningful than in the past. Although lower levels of network awareness provided an escape from insularity and control, they limit people's knowledge of the opinions and activities of those in their network.

Hampton (2016) suggests that this may no longer be the case. Recent communication technologies better afford persistent contact by allowing people to articulate their association and maintain contact over time (Figure 21.3) Examples of these technologies include Facebook's "friends" lists and other social media that contain ties formed over a lifetime. These technologies allow people to sustain contact without substantially drawing from the time and resources required to maintain ties through other channels of communication. The persistence of ties is a counterforce to mobility and has the potential to link lives across generations and over a lifetime in ways that resemble the structure of affiliation found in preindustrial communities (Quan-Haase et al., 2017; Yuan et al., 2016). Yet, unlike preindustrial communities, mobility still affords opportunities for partial commitments to different social milieus.

Another contemporary affordance, pervasive awareness, results from the ambient nature of digital communication technologies to share information and indicate the attentiveness and availability of social ties. Although the content of messages that contribute to pervasive awareness

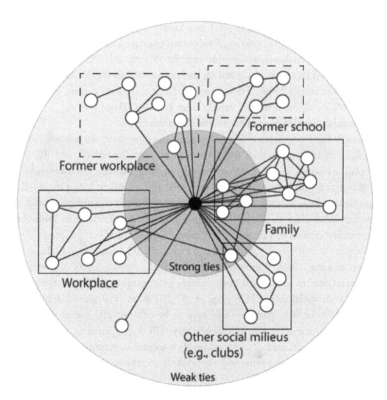

Figure 21.3   Persistent-pervasive community: A hybrid of traditional and urban-industrial community structures. Organized around multiple social milieus that persist over the life course, ties are not as loosely knit as in the urban-industrial community, ties are more persistent over time, and dormant ties are visible through chains of affiliation

may appear trivial – for example, a photograph of a meal or presence at an event – they can also convey subtle knowledge of the interests, locations, opinions, and activities embedded in the everyday lives of one's social ties. Heightened awareness of network life events – stressful activities in others' lives – might even increase the cost of caring (Hampton et al., 2016). Although it is tempting to equate persistent contact and pervasive awareness with formal surveillance, they have more in common with the informal watchfulness that traditional community structure afforded. They resemble the shared daily experiences and gossip of traditional community networks, but in a partial, more limited way. Indeed, a persistent-pervasive community represents a hybrid of traditional and urban-industrial community structures (Hampton, 2016).

Natural by-products of pervasive awareness and persistent contact are higher levels of awareness of diversity within one's social network (Chen, 2013; Hampton et al., 2011). Network diversity can be related to improved access to information and resources. Such awareness may counter the loss of social capital that earlier scholars feared (Putnam, 2000). However, because persistence and awareness reduce tie dormancy and dissolution from established friends and family, it is not clear how much new social capital will be created. The increased visibility between network members from different social milieus – flattened into a single audience on social media such as Facebook – may even close structural holes that provide bridges to information and resources (Burt, 1992; Granovetter, 1973). In this way, persistent and pervasive community may make visible those resources, diversity, and activities that were always present but overlooked as a result of a lack of visibility and a tendency to assume similarity with community (Goel et al., 2010). An awareness of newfound diversity could increase access to (and possibly understanding of) diverse points of view and counter a natural tendency to form echo chambers. Indeed, individuals remain highly mobile (Rainie & Wellman, 2019), involved in multiple social milieus (Hampton et al., 2011), and connected through multiple channels online and offline (Hampton et al., 2009). Hence, any self-selection into online echo chambers (Del Vicario et al., 2016) or algorithmically driven filter bubbles (Bakshy et al., 2015) pale in comparison to historical examples of insular traditional community.

However, heightened persistence and awareness may also have their costs. Social networks allow for the flow of information in the form of opinions, resources, and life events. While the flow of opinions could increase awareness of opinion diversity, an awareness of dissonant information about the opinions and beliefs of social ties could reduce perceived homophily, increase cognitive dissonance, and silence debate by heightening the perceived risk of discussing important matters (Hampton et al., 2017). While knowledge of resources embedded in social networks is generally viewed as valuable – increasing social capital – if people increasingly draw on informal support it can create new demands that exhaust resources and those who provide them (Hampton & Ling, 2013; Liebow, 1967). Similarly, higher levels of awareness of major life course events in others' lives, such as the illness or unemployment of a friend, can become a significant source of social stress (Hampton et al., 2016) or even spread depression and anxiety (Hampton, 2019). Such impacts are unlikely to be felt equally, but as with other types of affordances, changes to the structure of community will disproportionately affect some, based on their traits, skills, culture, and demographics. For example, women would seem to be both more aware of others' major life events and more likely to report higher levels of stress as a result (Hampton et al., 2016).

Might the reorganization of community structure into one in which relationships are again persistent and with more awareness of others' opinions and activities also bring about a return of the expedient and repressive sanctions that were common in a traditional community? Evidence of such a trend may already exist in the rise of mob morality and 'cancel culture', which has accompanied the online shaming of social transgressions and other behaviors captured by mobile phone cameras and shared through social media. Some examples are Californians 'drought-shaming' of excessive water users (Milbrandt, 2017), Singaporeans censuring those breaking civic norms (Skoric et al., 2010), the identification ('doxing') of white supremacists who attended 2017 rallies in Charlottesville (Ellis, 2017), the pejorative reference to the activities of 'Karens', and the public shaming of those who refuse to wear face coverings during the COVID-19 pandemic. Once again, the structure of community affords an informal watchfulness and a speed and severity of punishment that may supplant institutional, formal law. While some might find such informal social control beneficial (de Vries, 2015), it can also take clearly destructive forms such as online harassment (Podgornova, 2014). Yet others may withdraw from the uncertainties of participating in multiple partial networks and find refuge in more traditional bounded tribal solidarities that protect their identity and local autonomy (Wellman, et al., 2020).

Despite the continuing sound and fury from alarmed publics, politicians, and pundits, the evidence suggests that community has never been lost in the Western world. Communication, information, and transportation systems afford and constrain the shape and composition of the networks that make up communities. When researchers look for supportive relations within these networks, they find thriving communities, even as people suffer from continuing fears of untraditional unknowns. Recent technological changes are again reshaping the structure of community. Social media is making relations persistent and pervasive as well as finding and maintaining new ones. The fundamental nature of community is indeed changing as social media melds with in-person connectivity. Hence, there is a pressing need to understand what kinds of relations flourish and what communities do – and do not do – in this emerging restructuring. But, in facing such change, we must temper the persistent nostalgia for the supposed good times of the past and the unease that often comes with changing times. We need to recognize that although the structure of community may change, it has never been lost.

References

Bakshy, E., Messing, S., and Adamic, L. (2015). Exposure to Ideologically Diverse News And Opinion on Facebook. *Science*. doi:10.1126/science.aaa1160.

Bart, L., and Norman, F. (1959). *Fings Ain't Wot They Used to Be*. Stratford: Theatre Royal.

Bauman, Z. (2017). *Retrotopia*. Malden, MA: Polity Press.

Bellah, R., Madsen, R., Sullivan, W., Swidler, A., and Tipton, S. (1985). *Habits of the Heart: Individualism and Commitment in American Life*. Berkeley: University of California Press.

Berger, B. (1960). *Working Class Suburb*. Berkeley: University of California Press.

Brokaw, T. (1998). *The Greatest Generation*. New York: Random House.

Burgess, E. (1925). The Growth of the City. In R. Park & E. Burgess (Eds), *The City* (pp. 47–62). Chicago: University of Chicago Press.

Burt, R. (1992). *Structural Holes*. Chicago: University of Chicago Press.

Castells, M. (1996). *The Rise of the Network Society*. Oxford: Wiley-Blackwell.

Chaplin, C. (1936). *Modern Times*. Los Angeles: United Artists.

Chen, W. (2013). The Implications of Social Capital for the Digital Divides in America. *The Information Society*, 29(1), 13–25. doi:10.1080/01972243.2012.739265.

Chudacoff, H. P. (1972). *Mobile Americans: Residential and Social Mobility in the United States*. New York: Oxford University Press.

Clark, S. D. (1966). *The Suburban Society*. Toronto: University of Toronto Press.

Cooley, C. (1909). *Social Organization: A Study of the Large Mind*. New York: Scribner.

Cornish, D. (2006, October 13). Is Computer-glow the New Hearth-light? *Globe & Mail*. https://www.theglobeandmail.com/technology/is-computer-glow-the-new-hearth-light/article20415504/.

Del Vicario, M. et al. (2016). The Spreading of Misinformation Online. *Proceedings of the National Academy of Sciences*, 113(3), 554–559. doi:10.1073/pnas.1517441113.

de Vries, A. (2015). *The Use of Social Media for Shaming Strangers: Young People's Views*. Paper presented at the 2015 48th Hawaii International Conference on System Sciences, January 5–8.

Drouhot, L. G. (2017). Reconsidering 'Community Liberated': How Class and the National Context Shape Personal Support Networks. *Social Networks*, 48(supp C), 57–77. https://doi.org/10.1016/j.socnet.2016.07.005.

Durkheim, E. (1893[1993]). *The Division of Labor in Society* (1993 ed.). New York: Palgrave Macmillan.

Durkheim, É. (1897[1951]). *Suicide*. Glencoe, IL: Free Press.

Ellis, E. G. (2017). Whatever Your Side, Doxing Is a Perilous Form of Justice. *Wired Magazine*, August 17. www.wired.com/story/doxing-charlottesville/.

Engels, F. (1885[1970]). *The Housing Question* (2nd ed.). Moscow: Progress Publishers.

Engstrom, E. J., Hammond, J. R., and Scott, J. T. (2013). Capitol Mobility: Madisonian Representation and the Location and Relocation of Capitals in the United States. *American Political Science Review*, 107(2), 225–240.

Gans, H. (1962). *The Urban Villagers*. New York: Free Press.

Gibson, J. J. (1979). *The Ecological Approach to Visual Perception*. Boston, MA: Houghton Mifflin.

Goel, S., Mason, W., and Watts, D. (2010). Real and Perceived Attitude Agreement in Social Networks. *Journal of Personality and Social Psychology*, 99(4), 611–621.

Granovetter, M. (1973). The Strength of Weak Ties. *American Journal of Sociology*, 78(6), 1360–1380.

Grant, G. (1969). *Technology and Empire: Perspectives on North America*. Toronto: Anansi.

Grasshoff, A. (1972). *Future Shock* [film], Metromedia Producers Corporation.

Hampton, K. N. (2019). Social Media and Change in Psychological Distress Over Time: The Role of Social Causation. *Journal of Computer-Mediated Communication*. doi: 10.1093/jcmc/zmz010.

Hampton, K. N. (2016). Persistent and Pervasive Community: New Communication Technologies and the Future of Community. *American Behavioral Scientist*, 60(1), 101–124.

Hampton, K. N., Lee, C. J., and Her, E. J. (2011). How New Media Afford Network Diversity: Direct and Mediated Access to Social Capital Through Participation in Local Social Settings. *New Media & Society*, 13(7), 1031–1049. doi:10.1177/1461444810390342.

Hampton, K. N., and Ling, R. (2013). Explaining Communication Displacement and Large Scale Social Change in Core Networks: A Cross-National Comparison of Why Bigger Is Not Better and Less Can Mean More. *Information, Communication & Society*, 16(4), 561–589.

Hampton, K. N., Lu, W., and Shin, I. (2016). Digital Media and Stress: Cost of Caring 2.0. *Information, Communication & Society*, 19(9), 1267–1286.

Hampton, K. N., Sessions, L. F., Her, E. J., and Rainie, L. (2009). *Social Isolation and New Technology*. Washington, DC: Pew Internet & American Life Project.

Hampton, K. N., Shin, I., and Lu, W. (2017). Social Media and Political Discussion: When Online Presence Silences Offline Conversation. *Information, Communication & Society*, 20(7), 1090–1107.

Hampton, K. N., and Wellman, B. (2003). Neighboring in Netville: How the Internet Supports Community and Social Capital in a Wired Suburb. *City and Community*, 2(3), 277–311.

Harmon, A. (1998). Sad, Lonely World Discovered in Cyberspace, National Desk. *New York Times*, p. 1, August 30.

Jacobs, J. (1961). *The Death and Life of Great American Cities*. New York: Random House.

Jefferson, T. (1787). *Notes on the State of Virginia*. Self-published. Facsimilie retrieved September 14, 2018 from U.S. Library of Congress. www.loc.gov/resource/lhbcb.04902.

Katz, M. B., Doucet, M. B., and Stern, M. J. (1982). *The Social Organization of Early Industrial Capitalism*. Cambridge, MA: Harvard University Press.

Khaldun, I. (1377[2015]). *Muqaddimah: An Introduction to History*. Translated by F. Rosenthal. Princeton, NJ: Princeton University Press.

Kraut, R., and Burke, M. (2015). Internet Use and Psychological Well-Being: Effects of Activity and Audience. *Commun. ACM*, 58(12), 94–100. doi:10.1145/2739043.

Laslett, P. (1965). *The World We Have Lost*. London: Methuen.

Lee, F. E., and Oppenheimer, B. I. (1999). *Sizing Up the Senate: The Unequal Consequences of Equal Representation*. Chicago: University of Chicago Press.

Lennon, J., and McCartney, P. (1965). *Eleanor Rigby Revolver.* London: EMI.

Levitt, T. (2012). Chinese Cities 'Feel the Loss of Streetlife and Community'. *China Dialogue,* November 5.

Liebow, E. (1967). *Tally's Corner.* Boston, MA: Little Brown.

Lu, W., and Hampton, K. N. (2017). Beyond the Power of Networks: Differentiating Network Structure from Social Media Affordances for Perceived Social Support. *New Media & Society,* 19(6), 861–879. doi:10.1177/1461444815621514.

Marche, S. (2012). Is Facebook Making Us Lonely? *The Atlantic,* 2.

Marx, K. (1852). *The Eighteenth Brumaire of Louis Bonaparte, Karl Marx and Frederick Engels: Selected Works I.* Moscow: Foreign Language Publishing House, pp. 223–311.

Marx, L. (1964). *The Machine in the Garden.* New York: Oxford University Press.

Milbrandt, T. (2017). Caught on Camera, Posted Online: Mediated Moralities, Visual Politics and the Case of Urban 'Drought-Shaming'. *Visual Studies,* 32(1), 3–23. doi:10.1080/1472586X.2016.1246952.

Nisbet, R. (1962). *Community and Power.* New York: Oxford University Press.

Norman, D. A. (1988). *The Design of Everyday Things.* New York: Doubleday.

Pariser, E. (2012). *The Filter Bubble How the New Personalized Web Is Changing What We Read and How We Think.* New York: Penguin Books.

Parsons, T. (1943). The Kinship System of the Contemporary United States. *American Anthropologist,* 45, 22–38.

Podgornova, D. (2014). *Gay-Bashing and Slut-Shaming Online: Examining Digital Moral Activism of 'Occupy Pedophilia'and 'Check You'.* Budapest: Central European University.

Putnam, R. (2000). *Bowling Alone.* New York: Simon & Schuster.

Quan-Haase, A., Mo, G. Y., and Wellman, B. (2017). Connected Seniors: How Older Adults in East York Exchange Social Support Online and Offline. *Information, Communication & Society,* 20(7), 967–983. doi:10.1080/1369118X.2017.1305428.

Rainie, L., and Wellman, B. (2012). *Networked: The New Social Operating System.* Cambridge, MA: MIT Press.

Rainie, L., and Wellman, B. (2019). The Internet in Daily Life: The Turn to Networked Individualism. In W. Dutton and M. Graham (eds.), *Internet & Society* (2nd ed.). Oxford: Oxford University Press, pp. 27–42.

Simmel, G. (1903[1950]). The Metropolis and Mental Life. In K. Wolff (trans.), *The Sociology of Georg Simmel.* New York: Free Press, pp. 409–424.

Simmel, G. (1922[1955]). The Web of Group Affiliations. In K. Wolff (ed.), *Conflict and the Web of Group Affiliations.* Glencoe, IL: Free Press, pp. 125–195.

Skoric, M. M., Chua, J. P. E., Liew, M. A., Wong, K. H., and Yeo, P. J. (2010). Online Shaming in the Asian Context: Community Empowerment or Civic Vigilantism? *Surveillance & Society,* 8(2), 181–199.

Slater, P. (1970). *The Pursuit of Loneliness.* Boston, MA: Beacon Press.

Smith, M. P. (1979). *The City and Social Theory.* New York: St. Martins.

Starr, K. (1985). *Inventing the Dream: California Through the Progressive Era.* New York: Oxford University Press.

Starr, K. (1990). *Material Dreams: Southern California Through the 1920s.* New York: Oxford University Press.

Stein, M. (1960). *The Eclipse of Community.* Princeton, NJ: Princeton University Press.

Sunstein, C. R. (2009). *Republic.com 2.0.* Princeton, NJ: Princeton University Press.

Thernstrom, S. (1964). *Poverty and Progress: Social Mobility in a Nineteenth Century City.* Cambridge, MA: Harvard University Press.

Thernstrom, S. (1973). *The Other Bostonians: Poverty and Progress in the American Metropolis, 1880–1970.* Cambridge, MA: Harvard University Press.

Tilly, C. (1988). Misreading, then Rereading, Nineteenth-Century Social Change. In B. Wellman and S. Berkowitz (eds.), *Social Structures: A Network Approach.* Cambridge: Cambridge University Press, pp. 332–358.

Toffler, A. (1970). *Future Shock.* New York: Random House.

Tönnies, F. (1887[1957]). *Community and Society.* Translated by C. P. Loomis. East Lansing, MI: Michigan State University Press.

Turkle, S. (2011). *Alone Together*. New York: Basic Books.

Turkle, S. (2015). *Reclaiming Conversation: The Power of Talk in a Digital Age*. London: Penguin Press.

Turner, F. J. (1893). *The Significance of the Frontier in American History*. Paper presented at the American Historical Association, Chicago, IL.

Twenge, J. M. (2017). *IGen: Why Today's Super-Connected Kids Are Growing Up Less Rebellious, More Tolerant, Less Happy – and Completely Unprepared for Adulthood*. New York: Atria Books.

Wang, H., and Wellman, B. (2010). Social Connectivity in America. *American Behavioral Scientist*, 53(8), 1148–1169.

Webber, M. (1963). Order in Diversity: Community without Propinquity. In J. Lowdon Wingo (ed.), *Cities and Space: The Future Use of Urban Land*. Baltimore: Johns Hopkins Press, pp. 23–54.

Weber, M. (1946). *From Max Weber: Essays in Sociology*. Translated by H. Gerth and C. W. Mills. New York: Oxford University Press.

Weber, M. (1958). *The City*. Translated by D. Martindale and G. Neuwirth. Glencoe, IL: Free Press.

Wellman, B. (1979). The Community Question. *American Journal of Sociology*, 84(5), 1201–1231.

Wellman, B. (2001). Physical Place and Cyberspace. *International Urban and Regional Research*, 25(2), 227–252.

Wellman, B., and Wetherell, C. (1996). Social Network Analysis of Historical Communities: Some Questions from the Present for the Past. *History of the Family*, 1(1), 97–121.

Wellman, B., Wong, R., Tindall, D., and Nazer, N. (1997). A Decade of Network Change: Turnover, Mobility and Stability. *Social Networks*, 19(1), 27–51.

Wetherell, C., Plakans, A., and Wellman, B. (1994). Social Networks, Kinship and Community in Eastern Europe. *Journal of Interdisciplinary History*, 24(4), 639–663, Spring.

White, M., and White, L. (1962). *The Intellectual Versus the City*. Cambridge, MA: Harvard University Press.

Wilder, T. (Writer). (1938). *Our Town [Play]*. Princeton, NJ: James Naughton.

Williams, R. (1973). *The Country and the City*. London: Chatto & Windus.

Wills, G. (1978). *Inventing America: Jefferson's Declaration of Independence*. Garden City, NY: Doubleday.

Xu, Y., and Chan, E. H. W. (2011). Community Question in Transitional China, a Case Study of State-Led Urbanization in Shanghai. *Journal of Urban Planning and Development*, 137(4), 416–424. doi:10.1061/(ASCE)UP.1943-5444.0000077.

Yuan, S., Hussain, S. A., Hales, K. D., and Cotten, S. R. (2016). What Do They Like? Communication Preferences and Patterns of Older Adults in the United States: The Role of Technology. *Educational Gerontology*, 42(3), 163–174. doi:10.1080/03601277.2015.1083392.

22

Distracted by technologies and captured by the public sphere

Natalie Fenton

This chapter offers a critique of the ways in which we approach the study of civil society and digital technologies through the notion of public sphere theory. In it, I question whether public sphere theory is up to the job of dealing with a democratic deficit so large that it challenges the notion that liberal democracy should always be our 'go to' democratic frame. Classical public sphere theory begins and ends with liberal democracy as its overarching premise and ultimate political institutional arrangement. But what if we start from a different position where we acknowledge that liberal democracy has been so dismantled that it is now eviscerated and unrecognizable to many in civil society? Can a concept so undone really offer a critical perspective suggestive of democratic futures, or is it rather holding us back, capturing us in the comfort zones of liberalism that threaten ultimately to erode democracy yet further?

Captured by the public sphere

Any discussion of digital media and communication and their roles in enhancing democracy and political participation frequently falls back on Habermas' concept of the public sphere (1989). This is understandable as it is one of the few prominent theoretical frameworks that link the media and its practices directly to the exercise of democracy. This conceptual framing has increased in recent years (Lunt & Livingstone, 2013) with the Internet, in particular, lending itself to discussions around whether or not the space now available online for mass use constitutes a fully functioning public sphere – a space where all debates can be aired and issues discussed in a deliberative and rational manner. There are many problems with this approach, but perhaps the most obvious is that by foregrounding the media (in all its many forms) there is a tendency to reproduce the discourse of technological innovation as automatic democratic gain. This is a discourse that has many fault-lines, and in this chapter I focus on three of them: 'Liberal democracy undone' – the notion that liberal democracy is an adequate endpoint that should form our ethical horizon and be the focus of critical theory; 'Civil society empowered' – the myth that civil society is afforded more agency through digital communications; 'Public sphere expanded' – the assumption that the public sphere is expanded in the age of the Internet.

Liberal democracy undone

Public sphere theory is premised on the concept of liberal democracy: a system of governance that delegates power to elected representatives who will duly do the bidding of those who voted for them. It presupposes a crucial stage in the democratic process: that voters will be fully informed via the means of publicity available to them and through processes of deliberation will reach a rational understanding of all relevant issues. These processes of deliberation will then form a consensus view that is responded to by policy makers and, hey presto, liberal democracy is seen to be done.

Of course, actually existing democracy often falls far short of this ideal with societies characterized more by political disaffection (Streeck, 2014) than a citizenry satisfied that they understand all of the issues they are voting on, and when they do vote their views are taken heed of by their elected representatives. As Raymond Williams argued in "Democracy and Parliament," all too frequently we find ourselves confronted with "the coexistence of political representation and participation with an economic system which admits no such rights, procedures or claims" (1982, 19).

Crouch (2004, 2011) has famously termed our current democratic decay as a continuing process of dissolution toward 'post-democracy,' a state where "the forms of democracy remain fully in place," yet "politics and government are increasingly slipping back into the control of privileged elites in the manner characteristic of pre-democratic times" (2004, 6). If we accept this analysis, it raises the question whether interpretations of public sphere theory are captured by a liberal democratic frame to the extent that they cannot imagine a world beyond the forms and structures of a liberal democratic system? And if so, can public sphere theory any longer claim its status as critical theory where the purpose of critical theory is understood as seeking human emancipation (Fenton, 2016)?

What both Crouch and Williams remind us is that how we experience liberal democracy is bound up with political economic configurations and institutional/organizational formations and structures that have developed in articulation with media technologies. Specific configurations are likely to lead to different types of knowledge production. Furthermore, we cannot understand one without the others. So, for example, in the United Kingdom 2017 General Election the turnout was 68.8%, the highest since 1997. Moreover, many claimed a 'youthquake' with 55–62% of 18- to 24-year-olds voting compared to only 43% in 2015.[1] The apparent increase in young people voting was largely ascribed to social media and claimed as a sign of a fully functioning public sphere underpinning democracy in action. And it is true that many young people now get their news and information via social media (Newman, 2017). But what this response failed frequently to mention is that young people have also experienced an unprecedented attack on their socioeconomic conditions; state support has been withdrawn and left many young people in poverty; employment is precarious, homeownership is increasingly an unrealizable dream for many, and wages are low (Corlett, 2017). It is highly likely that these socioeconomic conditions played a large part in encouraging young people to vote alongside a Labour party manifesto that spoke explicitly to these concerns and, indeed, social media campaigns encouraging people to register and to vote.

In the economic realm, austerity, unemployment, high personal debt, extreme poverty and inequality feature heavily across many liberal democracies (Dorling, 2011, 2014). In the United Kingdom, the impact of these crises is particularly marked for working class and minority communities as well as for young people – whose experiences are also inflected by the 'war on terror,' student fees, housing inflation, urban riots, and youth unemployment. An important question for liberal democratic theory is whether social stability and consensus politics can prosper where poverty and inequality are apparent across so many intersecting fault-lines: young and old, black and white, religious and secular. Prominent reports in the United Kingdom have observed "[t]he need for change; the need to seek the voice of marginalized and disadvantaged people in decision-making processes is of undeniable and acute local, national and global relevance" (RSA, 2017).

The response in the United Kingdom to the 2008 global banking crisis was austerity politics designed to reduce national debt. In England, between June 2010 and March 2016 welfare reforms enacted reductions of £26 billion in UK social security and tax credits spending, with 'deficit reduction' being the primary goal of government (Tinson et al., 2016). Young adults (16–24) were particularly hard hit with "rapidly falling real wages, incomes and wealth" (Hills et al., 2015, 3). Poverty is also strongly linked with disability and ethnicity, with people from black and minority ethnic communities experiencing multiple forms of socioeconomic disadvantage (Hills et al., 2015).

Austerity politics has meant that local authorities in England have suffered a 49.1% cut in core funding from central government between 2010–11 and 2017–18 (National Audit Office). And so councils and other public agencies have sought further to outsource and share services as a means of reducing costs and improving performance (Whitfield, 2014). An emphasis on outsourcing has detached these services from democracy, depoliticizing decisions about public welfare and the public good. Citizens are recast as consumers as collective decisions are transformed into questions of individual need and choice (Cornwall & Gaventa, 2001; Lister, 2001). If, as media scholars, we insist on seeing liberal democracy primarily through a communicative lens, we miss noticing how crucial democratic processes have been eviscerated in the face of austerity and neoliberal practices.

A liberal democracy depends on citizen participation in systems of representation. Such aspirations and norms have been challenged (e.g., Mair, 2013) as political elites remodel themselves as a professional class, as nondemocratic agencies and practices proliferate and as inequality increases. In the United Kingdom almost all of the wealthiest people use the Internet, but this falls to 58% among the lowest income group (those earning less than £12,500) (Dutton et al., 2013). The picture is similar in the United States, with 93% of those in the income bracket of $100,000 plus using the Internet compared to only 48% of those earning less than $25,000 (File & Ryan, 2014). Just as patterns of inequality are replicated in access to health care and educational attainment (Wilkinson & Pickett, 2009), so they map onto access to technology (Pew Research Center, 2015). The digital divide is still a reality: Internet users are in general younger, more highly educated and richer than non-users, are more likely to be men than women, and are more likely to live in cities (Blank et al., 2017). Blank and Groselj (2014) point out that usage of the Internet is similar for all of us except when it comes to news and information when there are clear correlations to educational attainment and social class. Maybe it should come as no surprise then that in the UK 2017 general election the Labour Party saw the largest increase in vote share since 1945 with an increased turnout of 18- to 24–year-olds, many of whom access their news and information via social media; that most people with a degree voted Labour; and that these votes were also concentrated in urban areas. But we should not be duped into thinking that this then means democracy is well served.

Tilly (2007) developed an international comparative account of the macro-conditions associated, over the past centuries, with democratization. Defining democracy as "the extent to which the state behaves in conformity to the expressed demands of its citizens" – to be judged by the "breadth" and "equality" of the democratic process, its "protection" from arbitrary state interference, and its basis in "mutually binding consultation" (2007, 13), he isolated three macro-conditions:

1   The integration of trust networks into public politics;
2   The insulation of public politics from categorical inequality, and
3   The reduction of major non-state power centres' autonomy from public politics (2007, 23).

According to the Edelman Trust Barometer (2018), trust in government in the United Kingdom remains very low at 36%, with 47% believing that government is the institution that is most broken; only 32% of the UK population trust the media. In 2017, the same survey noted that Britain also has a significant 'trust gap' of 19% between 'informed publics' ('in the upper-income quartile, university educated, and with a declared interest in politics and the media') and those with an income of less than £15,000. Among the least affluent it hit a new low of just 20%, but it also fell significantly among the wealthiest, from 54% in 2016 to 38% in 2017.

Disenchantment with the political system is not new. The Hansard Society's 2016 Audit, undertaken before the Brexit referendum, found formal political participation had increased overall – with voter turnout in the 2015 general election at 65%, the highest since 2001, and more people claiming to be strong supporters of a political party (41%) than at any time since 2003 – but inequality had also increased: "there is now a 37 percentage point difference between the certainty to vote levels of those in social classes AB and DE, an increase of six points in 12 months" (Hansard Society, 2016, 6).

At the same time, overall confidence in the system, and especially in people's ability to influence decisions, is low:

> Only a third of the public think the system by which Britain is governed works well (33%) with those living furthest from Westminster most likely to be dissatisfied. Just 35% believe that when people like themselves get involved in politics they can change the way the country is run. Only 13% feel they have some influence over decision-making nationally although 41% would like to be involved in decision-making. More people (46%) would like to be involved in local decisions but just 25% currently feel they have some influence at the local level.
>
> *(Hansard Society, 2016, 6)*

This is the backdrop against which the United Kingdom's EU referendum turnout of over 72% took place, bringing to the surface deep divisions of class as well as generation that "cannot be divided from the economic dislocation that has taken place since the 1980s" (Dorling et al., 2016, 4). Studies by the Joseph Rowntree Foundation (Goodwin & Heath, 2016) and the Resolution Foundation (Clarke, 2016) both found that low-skilled and working-class voters in the most deprived regions were more likely to vote Brexit. The outcome of the referendum for the United Kingdom to leave the European Union came as a shock to many people – including those who voted for it, but it spoke to great swathes of society who felt abandoned by globalization and forgotten by a ruling elite all too willing to see their communities decimated and their social infrastructures weakened. At the same time, little attempt has been made to understand or address underlying structural inequalities. Instead globalization has tended "to be treated as an immutable economic fact rather than something that can be shaped politically" (Lister, 2001, 431). As Unwin argued, "people in the overlooked and too often ignored parts of the country . . . voted leave because they weren't satisfied with what they have. And they didn't feel able to change things" (2016, 4).

In the referendum campaign the mainstream media were accused of spreading anti-immigration discourses of hate and lies about the European Union – democracy was felt to be in dire disrepair. Fast forward a mere 12 months to the snap general election in 2017 and the likes of Michael Gove (a Conservative MP and key architect of the Leave Campaign) and Jeremy Corbyn (the leader of the Labour Party) both claimed that the power of the mainstream media had been evaporated by the veracity of social media and suddenly democracy was once more in the running. A convenient truth for both parties: for the Conservatives it is a response that removes the public gaze from their relations of intimacy with the mainstream media (MRC, 2017): if plurality is thriving online then we no longer need to be concerned about the concentration of ownership and lack of plurality in legacy media that can then be enabled and sustained by deregulation.[2] For Labour, it offers the prospect of hope without having to attend to the reproduction of inequalities online. Surely, a better response is to question what kinds of communities can act in what kinds of ways; and then to ask who (if any) are ascribed legitimacy by the mechanisms and practices of communication, and are listened to by those who govern?

I give this extended conjunctural analysis because if we then turn to technologies as the answer to our democratic futures we must do so with a deep understanding of what this means. Publics do not come into being simply through the public sphere – particularly when access to that public sphere is limited. Where should democratic theory go instead? It would do well to focus not on technologies but on people.

Civil society empowered through digital communications?

Many liberal democracies have witnessed a revival in collective social protest in recent years, reflecting an international resurgence in mobilization responding to the great political and economic crises of the early 21st century. Waves of collective action are not isolated, spontaneous events but rather speak to long histories of dissent and specific contextual changes in opportunities and resources – from the Anti-Globalization movement to the Indignados in Spain, to the Occupy movement scattered across the globe, Black Lives Matter and Climate Change Camps, among myriad others – as sociopolitical circumstances move and change so citizen responses to them adapt. One example is the emerging shift toward the unionizing of the precariat. In the United Kingdom this is manifest in traditional city bicycle couriers alongside Uber and Deliveroo food delivery couriers campaigns to gain the London Living Wage. In a largely decreasing trade union movement the Independent Workers Union of Great Britain (IWGB) has emerged, working creatively and on a small scale for workers' rights. Its members are predominantly low-paid migrant workers in London. In contrast to these emerging movements of protest and resistance, a turn has also been noticed toward new forms of 'survival tactics' and social organization based on solidarity and collective self-empowerment, such as neighborhood food banks, solidarity economy initiatives, cooperative community ventures, alternative currency networks, and new alternative media initiatives (Davis et al., 2020). Initiatives that have come out of a civil society response to a liberal democracy that they perceive as largely irrelevant to their lives.

Further afield we can see what David Harvey (2012) called the 'rebel cities' – Barcelona, Madrid, Valencia, A Coruna, Zaragoza, Naples, Grenoble, and many others – seeing a return to citizens' direct participation in decision-making processes, investing more resources in welfare, initiating housing that supports low-income residents, changing the rules of local tenders and procurements – trying to reinvent democratic practices from the grassroots in places that understand the multiple forms of exclusion that a representative liberal democracy has fallen foul of. Here too, the wider social, political, and economic context impacts not only on local areas but also on people's ability to participate and their power to influence the wider determinants of poverty and disadvantage that affect their lives and the life of their community. More people in more affluent communities have the time, skills, resources, and connections to engage in this way.

Digital technology can help, ostensibly facilitating opportunities for individuals to participate. But research also tells us that this online presence is most effective when linked to offline activities and opportunities to build solidarity: connective ties supporting collective action (Cammaerts, 2015). Civil society power is not increased through digital communications if the opportunities to be a democratic citizen are not open to you. Furthermore, when a growth in popular mobilizations appears to loom large, pleas for the legitimacy of established systems of governance have been the bidding of bourgeois democracy throughout history: look how democratic we are with the multiplicity of groups in the public sphere online contesting established political ideologies! Not only does this infer that democracy can be done better through an online system that is organized by and run for massive corporate monopolies in the form of Google and Facebook whose online architecture is designed to maximize profit; but it also conveniently forgets to mention that we still exist in a world with huge issues of digital exclusion.

In the week after the 2017 general election in the United Kingdom, Grenfell Tower (a large local authority–owned residential tower block in London) caught fire and killed 72 people. Grenfell Tower is a charred scar that reminds us of the damage that 40 years of neoliberalism has wrought – occupied by the poor, ignored by the rich, discarded by democracy. The tenants association had campaigned about fire safety to the local council but had not been listened to. Local papers had long since disappeared and the Internet simply wasn't up to the job of holding power to account because the people who lived in the tower were not those in networks where influence can be claimed.

Rather than focus on digital communications as the means to democratic gain, we would do well to turn to developing people's capacity to be and do (Sen, 2009; Nussbaum, 2003). For Sen, "the capability approach focuses on human life," shifting attention from "the means of living to the actual opportunities of living" (2009, 233). This is useful because it focuses on people's needs and aspirations to be engaged citizens and how these are shaped and constrained by "often unjust background conditions" (Nussbaum, 2003, 34), enabling us to ask different questions about how to promote human flourishing and the kind of society we want to live in. This might mean challenging the idea that economic growth is the ultimate goal for societies, that market mechanisms are the most effective way of determining human affairs, that an adequate public sphere is the route to better democracy, and turn our gaze instead toward increasing the space for, and autonomy of, civil society and citizen action.

The Internet as expanded public sphere

A key aspect of Habermas' understanding of democracy is the right of citizens to engage freely in debate and come to their own rational, critical interpretation. The extension of this act of deliberation in a democracy is that the views of citizens are taken into account in political governance. The principle is that participation in public debate leads to deliberation by a citizenry that can impact upon political decision-making. In public sphere theory, the means of public communication enables this practice and is seen as the route to democracy.

Loader and Mercea (2012) give an overview of this debate in relation to digital communication and argue that social media offers increasing opportunities for political communication and enables democratic capacities for political discussion within the virtual public sphere. In other words, citizens can challenge governments and corporations' political and economic power. Additionally, new forms of political participation and information sources for the users emerge with the Internet that can be utilized in online campaigns. They also point out that social media's dominant uses are entertainment, consumerism, and content sharing among friends.

Scholars such as Castells (2009) and Benkler (2006) advance rather different versions of an ultimately similar proposition wherein the promise of plurality that the Internet presents is foregrounded as the means to communicative and democratic freedom. In Benkler's (2006) analysis, the Internet has the potential to change the practice of democracy radically because of its participatory and interactive attributes that engender a more pluralistic public sphere and better civic engagement. Increased capacities to access the Internet and to produce and disseminate media content within expanding and thickening networks are argued to transform the relations of producer and audience, and enable all citizens to alter their relationship to the public sphere, to become creators and primary subjects engaged in social production. In Benkler's words,

> the high capital costs that were a prerequisite to gathering, working, and communicating information, knowledge, and culture have now been widely distributed in the society. . . [such that] . . . we have an opportunity to change the way we create and exchange information, knowledge and culture.
>
> *(2006, 473)*

In other words, citizens gain communicative freedom, and the more they gain, the more the public sphere expands.

Similarly, Castells (2009) argues that social movements that engage in oppositional politics – "the process aiming at political change (institutional change) in discontinuity with the logic embedded in political institutions" (2009, 300) – are now able to enter public space from multiple sources and positions raising the possibility for major social and political change: by using both horizontal communication networks and mainstream media to convey their images and messages, social movements increase their chances of enacting social and political change – "even if they start from a subordinate position in institutional power, financial resources, or symbolic legitimacy" (Castells, 2009, 302). Once again, information pluralism and communicative freedom work in tandem and in ever expanding circles: the more freedom one has, the more plurality is produced; the more plurality there is, the more freedom one has. While it is undoubtedly true that social media can mobilize and spread messages at speed, it is also true that the context of such activity is paramount and that simply spreading messages does not necessarily lead to power gained or to social change. There is a substantive chasm between feeding the democratic impulse and establishing shifts in political culture.

Social media platforms are also argued to work on the basis of 'people like you.' They function in an affective viral culture that is largely enclosed within ideological comfort zones, or what Pariser (2011) has called the 'filter bubble' effect, where people connect mostly with people who think like them. Latest research by Ofcom (2017) also notes that most news consumers in 2016 relied on 2 or fewer wholesale sources, less than they did in 2011. Although the extent of closure is contested (Newman, 2017), it is still hard to argue that the notion of a public sphere whose chief force is fostering critical rationality and better argument is well served on social media organized on the basis of a personal ecosystem.

Furthermore, Facebook curates content engineered to maximize consumer spend and serve corporate interest. The algorithms at work operate within a business model devised on the basis of extracting value from individuals through selling commodities and data – hardly the best premise for ensuring full and free debate. McChesney (2014) points out how the global power of new digital distributors has created the greatest monopolies in economic history with new digital industries moving from competitive to oligopolistic to monopolistic at a furious pace until the Internet has rested in the hands of a very few giant global corporations. McChesney argues that the hyper commercialism, advertising, and monopoly markets we now find online enhance rather than disrupt the contours of capitalism and lead to rampant depoliticization and undemocratic, commercial media policy as the point of government regulation pivots on helping corporate media maximize their profits rather than advancing the public interest

A closer consideration of who is communicating what to whom on social media also reveals that the majority of content is posted by a minority of users dominated by celebrities and mainstream media corporations which is then shared by the rest of us (Bruner, 2013). The notion of social media as an expanded public sphere is further sullied by the increase of bots (fake accounts operated by automated software), with some estimates putting them at 1 in 20 active accounts. Social bots are hard to spot. They are programmed to tweet and retweet; they have social quirks and create their own online histories; they can infiltrate popular discussions and generate content; they operate on sleep-wake patterns to make them more convincing (Ferrara et al., 2015). These robots inflate followers, influence the stock market, and sway political discourse as well as massively enhance marketing campaigns.

Astroturfing is also common practice on social networks. Just like artificial grass made to appear real, astroturfing online uses software to disguise the sponsors of messages to make it seem as if they have come from the general public and so give the impression of widespread support for a particular idea or product. It would seem, then, that identifying *who* is communicating on social media is not as simple as it first seems with social media traffic weighted heavily in favor of the corporate players and commercial agendas.

Of course, it is always possible to point to a flowering of alternative news websites that have emerged online. The problem is that counter publicity is less likely to be heard and taken account of by political elites and still comes way down the Google hierarchy. So while we may have more counter publicity than we ever thought possible on the Internet, so we have more inequality (Piketty, 2013) in society, more surveillance (Morozov, 2011), and more centralization of power than ever before (Jones, 2014). The explosion of counter publicity in a digital age does not necessarily translate into better democracy if the point at which "[t]he balance of power between civil society and the political systems [then] shifts" (Habermas, 1996, 379) is never reached. If we focus on the enhancement of the process and quality of deliberation, but the deliberation under question has little or no impact on the political administrative complex, then the public sphere is once more simply hollowed out (Fenton & Titley, 2015).

New claims of a greatly enhanced public sphere in the Internet age can only be evaluated when integrated into an assessment of intersecting forms of social, political and economic inequalities, the development of capitalism and the dramatic consequences of all of these dimensions for representative democratic systems. When such contexts are elaborated upon, it is clear that any *critical* examination of the democratic potential of new distributions of communicative power must address the material consequences of increasing inequalities in societies and their insidious relationship to vastly impoverished democracies.

Conclusion: distracted by technology

The premise of public sphere theory rests on the notion of liberal democracy. The basic tenet of liberal democracy is adequate political representation for all citizens within the sovereignty of the nation-state. Any focus on the citizenry and civil society must ask questions relating to social capacity that brings with it an emphasis on equality and inclusivity, and will require a systemic critique of power and not just be distracted by technology. Any democratic theory that is unable to do this is lacking and will not be able to provide the tools by which we can understand our current democratic deficit and a series of public issue crises: an economic crisis, an environmental crisis, a refugee crisis, and health and housing crises that actually existing liberal democracies have been unfit to deal with. Critical theory has a responsibility to reinvent our democratic futures, not recreate political arrangements and institutional formations and structures that have served the very few so very well.

Notes

1 Precise data on the ages of voters is still contested at the time of writing. The range of 55–62% offered here is based on a variety of estimates from different polling agencies.
2 The Conservative Manifesto pledged to repeal Section 40 of the Crime and Courts Act, a crucial element of the Royal Charter framework brought in after the Leveson Inquiry into phone hacking and not to go ahead with the second part of Leveson into the media and police corruption.

References

Benkler, Y. (2006). *The Wealth of Networks*. New Haven: Yale University Press.

Blank, G., Graham, M., and Calvino, C. (2017). Local Geographies of Digital Inequality. *Social Science Computer Review*. doi:10.1177/089443931769333.

Blank, G., and Groselj, D. (2014). Dimensions of Internet Use: Amount, Variety, and Types. *Information Communication and Society*, 17(4), 417–435.

Bruner, J. (2013). *Tweets Loud and Quiet* [online]. http://radar.oreilly.com/2013/12/tweets-loud-and-quiet.html.

Cammaerts, B. (2015). Technologies of Self-Mediation: Affordances and Constraints of Social Media for Protest Movements. In J. Uldam and A. Vestergaard (eds.), *Civic Engagement and Social Media: Political Participation Beyond Protest*. London: Palgrave Macmillan, pp. 97–110.

Castells, M. (2009). *Communication Power*. Oxford: Oxford University Press.

Clarke, S., Corlett, A., and Judge, L. (2016). *The Housing Headwind: The Impact of Housing Costs on Living Standards*. Resolution Foundation. www.resolutionfoundation.org/publications/the-housing-headwind-the-impact-of-rising-housing-costs-on-uk-living-standards/.

Corlett, A. (2017). *As Time Goes By: Shifting Income and Inequality Within and Between Generations*. Resolution Foundation. www.resolutionfoundation.org/publications/as-time-goes-by-shifting-incomes-and-inequality-between-and-within-generations/.

Cornwall, A., and Gaventa, J. (2001). *From Users and Choosers to Makers and Shapers: Public Participation in the Policy Process* Brighton: Institute of Development Studies.

Crouch, C. (2004). *Post-Democracy*. Cambridge: Polity Press.

Crouch, C. (2011). *The Strange Non-Death of Neoliberalism*. Cambridge: Polity Press.

Davis, A., Fenton, N., Freedman, D., and Khiabany, G. (2020). *Media, Democracy and Social Change: Reimagining Political Communications*. London: Sage.

Dorling, D. (2011). *Injustice: Why Social Inequality Persists*. Bristol: Policy Press.

Dorling, D. (2014). *Inequality and the 1%*. London: Verso.

Dorling, D., Stuart, B., and Stubbs, J. (2016). *Don't Mention This Around the Christmas Table: Brexit, Inequality and the Demographic Divide*. http://eprints.lse.ac.uk/70004/1/blogs.lse.ac.uk-Dont%20mention%20this%20around%20the%20Christmas%20table%20Brexit%20inequality%20and%20the%20demographic%20divide.pdf.

Dutton, W., Blank, G., and Groselj, D. (2013). *Cultures of the Internet: The Internet in Britain*. Oxford Internet Survey 2013. Oxford: Oxford Internet Institute, University of Oxford.

Edelman. (2018). *Edelman Trust Barometer 2017 – UK Findings*. www.edelman.co.uk/magazine/posts/edelman-trust-barometer-2017-uk-findings/.

Fenton, N. (2016). *Digital, Political, Radical*. London: Polity Press.

Fenton, N., and Titley, G. (2015). Mourning and Longing: Media Studies Learning to Let Go of Liberal Democracy. *European Journal of Communication*, 30(5), 1–17.

Ferrara, E., Varol, O., Davis, C., Menczer, F., and Flammini, A. (2015). The Rise of Social Bots. *Communications of ACM*, 59(7), arXiv:1407.5225v2 [cs.SI].

File, T., and Ryan, C. (2014). *Computer and Internet Use in the United States: 2013*. U.S. Department of Commerce, U.S. Census Bureau. www.census.gov/content/dam/Census/library/publications/2014/acs/acs-28.pdf.

Goodwin, M., and Heath, O. (2016). *Brexit Vote Explained: Poverty, Low Skills and Lack of Opportunities*. www.jrf.org.uk/brexit-vote-explained-poverty-low-skills-and-lack-opportunities.

Harvey, D. (2012). *Rebel Cities: From the Right to the City to the Urban Revolution.* London: Verso.

Hansard Society. (2016). *Audit of Political Engagement 13: The 2016 Report.* www.hansardsociety.org.uk/ publications/audit-of-political-engagement-13-the-2016-report.

Habermas, J. (1989[1962]). *The Structural Transformation of the Public Sphere.* Cambridge: Polity Press.

Habermas, J. (1996). *Between Facts and Norms: Contributions to a Discourse Theory of Law and Democracy.* Cambridge: Polity Press.

Hills, J., Cunliffe, J., Obolenskaya, P., and Karagiannaki, E. (2015). *Falling Behind, Getting Ahead: The Changing Structure of Inequality in the UK.* London: Centre for Analysis of Social Exclusion, LSE.

Jones, O. (2014). *The Establishment: And How They Get Away with It.* London: Allen Lane.

Lister, R. (2001). New Labour: A Study in Ambiguity from a Position of Ambivalence. *Critical Social Policy,* 21(4), 425–447.

Loader, B., and Mercea, D. (eds.). (2012). *Social Media and Democracy: Innovations in Participatory Politics.* New York: Routledge.

Lunt, P., and Livingstone, S. (2013). 'Media Studies' Fascination with the Concept of the Public Sphere: Critical Reflections and Emerging Debates. *Media Culture & Society,* 35(1), 87–96.

Mair, P. (2013). *Ruling the Void: The Hollowing Out of Western Democracy.* London: Verso.

McChesney, R. (2014). *Digital Disconnect: How Capitalism Is Turning the Internet Against Democracy.* New York: The New Press.

Morozov, E. (2011). *The Net Delusion: How Not to Liberate the World.* London: Allen Lane.

Newman, N. (2017). *Reuters Institute Digital News Report 2017.* Oxford: Reuters Institute.

Nussbaum, M. (2003). Capabilities as Fundamental Entitlements: Sen and Social Justice. *Feminist Economics,* 9(2–3), 33–59.

Ofcom. (2017). *News Consumption in the UK 2016.* www.ofcom.org.uk/__data/assets/pdf_file/0016/ 103570/news-consumption-uk-2016.pdf.

Pariser, E. (2011). *The Filter Bubble: What the Internet Is Hiding from You.* London: Penguin.

Pew Research Center. (2015). *Internet Seen as Positive Influence on Education but Negative Influence on Morality in Emerging and Developing Nations.* www.pewglobal.org/files/2015/03/Pew-Research-Center-Technology-Report-FINAL-March-19-20151.pdf.

Piketty, T. (2013). Should We Make the Richest Pay to Meet Fiscal Adjustment Needs? In *The Role of Tax Policy in Times of Fiscal Consolidation.* Brussels: European Commission, pp. 99–103.

RSA. (2017). *Citizenship 4.0: An Invitation to Power Change.* https://medium.com/citizens-and-inclusive-growth/citizenship-4-0-an-invitation-to-power-change-910bf07d319c.

Sen, A. (2009). *The Idea of Justice.* London: Penguin Books.

Streeck, W. (2014). How Will Capitalism End? *New Left Review,* 87, 35–64, May–June.

Tilly, C. (2007). *Democracy.* Cambridge: Cambridge University Press.

Tinson, A., Ayrton, C., Barker, K., Born, T., Aldridge, H., and Kenway, P. (2016). *Monitoring Poverty and Social Exclusion 2016.* York: Joseph Rowntree Foundation. www.jrf.org.uk/report/ monitoring-poverty-and-social-exclusion-2016.

Unwin, J. (2016). *Where Next for Civil Society? Inaugural Lecture for Wales Council for Voluntary Action.* www.jrf.org.uk/where-next-civil-society.

Whitfield, D. (2014). *UK Outsourcing Expands Despite High Failure Rate.* European Services Strategy Unit. www.european-services-strategy.org.uk/ppp-database/ppp-partnership-database/ppp-strategic-partnerships-database-2012-2013.pdf.

Wilkinson, R. G., and Pickett, K. (2009). *The Spirit Level: Why More Equal Societies Almost Always Do Better.* London: Allen Lane.

Williams, R. (1982). Democracy and Parliament. *Marxism Today,* 14–21, June.

23

Social movements, communication, and media

Elena Pavan and Donatella della Porta

The debate on the relationship between social movements and communication has been in general influenced by the specific types of media that were available for specific challengers in specific historical periods. If historians have pointed out the importance of the inventions of the printing press for the social movements of those times (Tarrow, 1994; Kielbowicz & Scherer, 1986), so the role of television has been looked at in the 1970s (Gitlin, 1980), and those of Fax in the 1990s (della Porta, 1996) and so on. At the beginning of the 21st century, with information and communications technologies going rapidly from "radical to routine" (Lievrouw & Livingstone, 2006, 1), the lines between "information, communication, and action" (Rainie & Wellman, 2012, 14) have blurred very rapidly. In this context, social movement studies addressed especially the use of digital media and their potential for multiplying public spaces for deliberation (della Porta & Mosca, 2005), even if their capacity to go beyond those who are already sympathetic to their cause, and reaching the general public is uneven (Bennett, 2004; Peretti & Micheletti, 2004). The digital divide, the uncertain effects of 'virtual' protest, the limited use of the participatory and deliberative potentials, have all been mentioned as shortcoming of computer-mediated communication (e.g., Curran, 2003; Rucht, 2004; Mosca & della Porta, 2009; Fuster Morell, 2009).

In spite of these limitations, the consolidation and the growth of a global system of digital media and communications did not simply entail the definitive overcoming of "one-way distribution configurations typically associated with mass society, mass production and consumption, and mass media" (Lievrouw & Livingstone, 2006, 5). More importantly, it led to some crucial transformations in the media field and, more particularly, to "1. New ways of consuming media, which explicitly contest the social legitimacy of media power; 2. New infrastructures of production, which have an effect on who can produce news and in which circumstances; 3. New infrastructures of distribution, which change the scale and terms in which symbolic production in one place can reach other places" (Couldry, 2003, 44). In turn, these transform how "the production of the message is self-generated, the definition of the potential receiver(s) is self-directed, and the retrieval of specific messages or content from the World Wide Web and electronic communication networks is self-selected" (Castells, 2009, 55). While "the media audience is transformed into a communicative subject increasingly able to redefine the process by which societal communication frames the culture of society" (ibid.:116), an increased capacity of citizens and activists to produce information has been noted as "people who have long been on the receiving end of one-way mass-communication are now increasingly likely to become producers and transmitters" (Bennett, 2003, 34).

Such a complex and multilayered media environment hosted the development and the spread of a new wave of protest movements aimed at denouncing the failures of neoliberalism, the corruption of democracy, and the crisis of political responsibility not only in advanced democracies in Europe or in the United States but also in South America and in the Middle East and the North African regions (della Porta, 2015, 13). On top of an increasingly pervasive Internet infrastructure, individuals, organizations, and their political agendas "aggregated" (Juris, 2012) within "personal, multiuser, multitask and multithreaded communication networks" (Rainie & Wellman, 2012, 7) that expand and enrich the relational milieu grounding collective efforts. While we are still far from having understood the variety of changes generated by the diffusion of digital media within protest dynamics (Earl et al., 2016, 355), an increasing number of studies is pushing extant reflections on the nexus between media and movements to a next stage looking not only at the old and new constraining effects that media logics and configurations can have on the unfolding on mobilizations (della Porta, 2013) but, more in continuity with reflections on alternative and radical media practices (Downing et al., 2001; Mattoni, 2009), at the empowering and transformative effects that networked and participative communication systems entail for collective endeavors.

Social movements emerging: mobilization context and predictors

In response to the pervasive diffusion of digital communications, observers begun to engage more thoroughly with the "environmental role of media in contentious politics" (Cammaerts et al., 2013, 3). In this respect, for example, Ward and Gibson speak about the emergence of a "technological opportunity structure" that comprises the communicational technological equipment with which movements are endowed and the extent to which it is strategically employed to compensate more or less narrow political opportunities (2009, 35). Broadly speaking, indeed, the networked nature and the low-cost of digital media endow movements with the possibility to organize horizontally within flexible coalitions, facilitate the sensitization of public opinion and the diffusion of alternative frames, allowing movements to "act like watchdogs" that safeguard the weakest interests, and provide possibilities to enrich tactical repertoires to address their targets (Mosca, 2014, 231).

However, digital media *on their own* are not necessarily conductive of any of these effects. To stress the necessary link between enhanced technological possibilities and activists' purposive orientation to seize them, scholars speak of an overall "mediation opportunity structure" (e.g., Cammaerts, 2012, 119). Under this conceptual framework, attention is given simultaneously to multiple elements: the complexity of the overall *media environment* from mainstream to alternative media and from analogue to digital outlets (Cammaerts et al., 2013); the multiplicity of *media practices*, i.e., the bulk of practices through which activists interact with media to generate and/or appropriate content but also interact with media actors like journalists and practitioners (Mattoni & Treré, 2014); and the "various ways in which media and communication are relevant to protest and activism" (Cammaerts, 2012, 118) – from the portrayals elaborated and transmitted by mainstream media and political elites, to movements' self-representations to mediated practices of resistance.

Common to these approaches is a conceptualization of communication as a complex process that can be fully understood only by adopting a "dialectical, mutual-shaping, or co-production perspective, where artefacts and social action are seen as mutually constitutive and determining"

(Lievrouw, 2014, 23). Hence, differently from previous accounts according to which media and movements are "ontologically separated entities" at best interacting reciprocally (Pavan, 2014, 444), contemporary reflections focus more poignantly on "sociotechnical systems" that result from the inextricable imbrication of material and social infrastructures (ibid.). In this sense, observers of contemporary movements tend to converge on the idea that the real asset to collective endeavors is not so much the widespread availability of easily accessible tools for communicating online but, more importantly, what these technologies "afford" individuals to do and the "structures" that result from these media practices (Bennett & Segerberg, 2013, 9). What is more, because different users perceive the same set of technological features and functions as "affording distinct possibilities for action" depending on their motivations, goals, expectations and levels of competence (Leonardi, 2012, 37), there can be different modes of appropriating and exploiting social media within contentious endeavors. For this reason, actual realizations of digital media material agency within contentious dynamics can neither be postulated *a priori* nor assumed to be invariable. Rather, they can be grasped only through a systematic empirical analysis which addresses the mutable role that digital media can play across different groups and over time "according to the state of the mobilization, the activities sustaining protest as well as the social actors who [are] using them" (della Porta & Mattoni, 2015, 41).

Moreover, scholars looking at the relevance of digital media for mobilization processes also suggest the existence of a non-linear relationship between the circulation of digital information and the actual participation of individuals in political activities. For example, Earl (2010) proposes that different uses of digital media affect in different ways the modes in which citizens engage in protest. More particularly, she argues that the simple diffusion of information generates a "supersize effect" (see also Earl & Kimport, 2011) for which movements manage to reduce the cost and, at the same time, are able to amplify the reach of their messages yet without significantly changing the way in which mobilization occurs or develops. A different case is, instead, when online social ties support the diffusion of "innovation" introducing new action repertoires (see the following section) or stimulating to action citizens who were not previously engaged in protest (Earl, 2010, 216). Finally, digital media affect more intensely collective action when protest spreads as a "heuristic for problem solving" thus becoming a "script" to address common concerns also outside the political terrain (Earl, 2010, 217–218). In this sense, political engagement is stimulated also by taking part in discussions hosted outside online spaces where to "talk politics" – as Graham et al. (2016) show by analyzing three UK forums devoted to discussing financial, parenting, and infotainment issues wherein almost half of the threads analyzed contained explicit calls to engage in conventional or unconventional forms of political action.

In summary, current reflections converge on a rather complex and multifaceted vision of both the contexts and the processes of mobilization. On the one hand, digital media offer movements the concrete possibility to overcome the limitations that were part of the previous mediascape but, on the other, they do not necessarily cause mobilization. Rather, their potentials enter in a direct relationship with political and social elements and, altogether, redefine in a sociotechnical way the overall field of action in which movements rise and dynamically unfold.

Social movements organizing: online networks and hybrid action repertoires

Over the last few years, fears of having offline activisms substituted by more "ephemeral" online activities (Earl et al., 2016) have been proved wrong by an increasing number of empirical studies which showed that, if the increased availability of digital information does not necessarily result in an increase in political participation, there is no evidence of a "negative effect" either (Christensen,

2011). Thus, reinforcing the idea that collective action can be organized within networks shaped by interactions between different political actors (see e.g., Diani, 2003), social movement studies have begun to engage more thoroughly in the attempt to understand how online and offline actions and networks jointly concur to determine contemporary forms of activism.

One first step in this direction consisted in conceptualizing online protest not as an *alternative to* offline activism but, rather, as a *form of protest in its own right*. In this respect, Earl and colleagues argue that online activism builds on a "new, alternative model of protest power, which research reveals can be effective in affecting agendas, policy decisions, corporate policies, etc." (2016, 356). Differently from traditionally studied forms of collective action that grow out of the work of a small core of "persistent activists," contemporary collective endeavors mediated by digital media "use a 'flash flood' model of power in which short, massive bursts of activity loosely (and even temporarily) engaged participants create pressure on targets" (*ibid.*) so as to maximize the effects of the "logic of numbers" but also to provide wider margins of manoeuvre to political actors within narrower political opportunity structures.

Crucial to this new form of protest power is the progressive retrenchment of the role of traditional social movement organizations (SMOs) as the primary hub to channel individual inputs into organized collectivities. Indeed, upon social media platforms personal expressions become actual contributions to a multiplicity of public discourses – what Papacharissi calls "civic narcissism" (2009, 236). Thus, while contributing and witnessing a myriad of inputs in the online public space, individuals find evidence that their claims are shared and, hence, legitimate. Motivated by their commonalities with strangers, citizens build connections regardless of their organizational attachments (Castells, 2012) and form networks that are sources of "social power" that challenge the status quo thanks to the continuous flow and exchange of texts, symbols, and audio-visual material (Castells, 2011). Therefore, digital media platforms become the new "organizational hub" to link individuals through a "connective logic" for which engagement becomes "relaxed and highly personalized" (Bennett & Segerberg, 2013, 11–13). Indeed, the very possibility to produce and circulate user-generated content of multiple types (i.e., text, videos, photos, mashups) facilitates the sharing of personal experiences as well as reciprocal recognition "at a fine-grained level" (Bennett & Segerberg, 2016, 375) – so that the mediation of SMOs is no longer strictly necessary to pursue social change.

What is more, the exercise of power, instead of being a matter of actors' status and formal properties, becomes strictly connected with their capability to control the construction of ties and meanings in the online space (Castells, 2011). For example, looking at Twitter networks González-Bailón and colleagues (2013) distinguish between *common users*, traditional "influentials" (i.e., celebrities), *broadcasters* that are more active in sending than receiving ties, and *hidden influentials* – that is, actors that are particularly central as they are often targeted by protest messages. Analogously, Padovani and Pavan (2016) propose to distinguish between *programmers*, actors that are often called upon by other activists through their online messages; *mobilizers*, actors that are particularly committed in sending messages and thus building online relations with other activists and bystanders; and *switchers*, actors bridging and coordinating different communities and groups.

Nonetheless, "crowd-enabled connective actions" (Bennett & Segerberg, 2013, 13) have not determined the complete disappearance of SMOs, which rather often adapt to this fluid context by switching role from promoters to connectors of mobilization efforts (Bimber et al., 2012) or by hybridizing their action strategies at the crossroads between different organizational repertoires (Chadwick, 2007). Moreover, as mentioned previously, the appropriation of digital media within collective endeavors does not always result in identical networks of actions. In this sense, Bennett and Segerberg (2014) speak about the possibility to find different "power signatures" in online networks depending on whether these networks represent "naturally emerging" efforts or result from a planned and intentional design by some key actors (Bennett & Segerberg, 2014, 425). Similarly, Pavan (2017) argues that, over time and depending on the type of political conditions in which actors operate, the same collective effort can occur within online networks that are shaped in different ways and, therefore, exert different levels of "integrative power."

Besides making the organizational infrastructure of movements more flexible and fluid, digital media also facilitate the overall enrichment of protest repertoires. In this respect, Van Laer and Van Aelst (2010) distinguish movement repertoires involving the use of the Internet along two dimensions. On the one hand, they envisage a dimension that opposes *Internet-based tactics*, such as email bombing or hacktivism, to *Internet-supported tactics*, that are more akin to traditional and conventional modes of protesting, such as demonstrations and boycotts, which can be organized more easily and on a larger scale thanks to the employment of digital media. On the other hand, the authors distinguish between *low* and *higher threshold* tactics depending on the levels of risk activists commit to when engaging in action. Thus, contrary to claims according to which online activities are easy to perform and "undertaken only by those that are too lazy to participate in more meaningful ways" (Earl et al., 2016, 356), Van Laer and Van Aelst argue that some online activities, such as launching a protest website or engaging in DoS attacks (i.e., Denial of Service), require a lot of resources and also entail a greater risk for activists – for example, of being accused and prosecuted for cyberterrorism or of suffering from personal attacks not only in the online space but also offline, in their everyday life.

Similarly, Lievrouw pushes past reflections on alternative media one step further and discusses how digital "artefacts, practices, and social arrangements [can be used] to challenge or alter dominant, expected, or accepted ways of doing society, culture, and politics" (2011, 19). In this respect, she reviews five "basic genres of contemporary alternative and activist new media projects" (ibid.). First, *culture jamming*, through which mainstream images and ideas are "monkeywrenched" with the aim of "making a critical point" about the very culture that generated them in the first place (Lievrouw, 2011, 73); second, *alternative computing* through which activists design or reconfigure digital systems to resist economic and cultural power but also to foster open access to alternative information (ibid.:98); third, *participatory journalism* to provide personal and alternative accounts of events (ibid.:121); fourth, *mediated mobilization*, though which digital media are "reprogrammed to become sites of action and change" (ibid.:149): and, fifth, *commons knowledge* that employ tools like folksonomies and crowdsourcing to create alternative systems of knowledge that "challenge the experts" (ibid.: 178).

Finally, also with respect to the consequences of digital media for movements' organization, current reflections consistently underline how their increased diffusion within protest and participation activities has not revolutionized already existent dynamics but, rather, has inevitably changed their nature by blurring the boundaries between the private and the public as well as between micro, meso and macro levels of action. Organization and action strategies can be certainly enriched by the affordances of digital media. However, there is no established formula to determine *a priori* the added value they will generate, or to establish how online action will intersect with offline protest, if at all. In fact, the diversified appropriation of digital media generates multiple effects depending on how their material features intersect social skills and desire for change.

Social movements ideating: the personalization of the collective

Digital media also play a part in determining how contemporary mobilizations become a consistent "action system" held together by a collective identity, that is, by "an interactive and shared definition produced by a number of individuals (or groups at a more complex level) concerning the *orientations* of their action and the *field* of opportunities and constraints in which such actions is to take place" (Melucci, 1996, 70, emphasis in the original). Indeed, the lack of a unique "control centre" within mediated protests does not make them anomic or irrational. Rather, it invites us to rethink how movements' identities are formed at the crossroads between the individual and the collective levels and at the intersection between material and social factors.

In this sense, Gerbaudo and Treré argue that contemporary processes of collective identity construction are played out in between the "interactivity" of social media (for example, the possibility to choose profile pictures or to update status messages) and the social appropriation of tools for "collective identification" such as likes, comments or retweets (2015, 868). The concurrence of technical features and cultural elements in the process of designing a "we" shape collective protest identities as inevitably fluid and evanescent (*ibid.*) but does not diminish their centrality for turning technology-enabled collectivities into actual collective actors (Pavan, 2014). In a similar fashion, Milan contends that social media platforms redefine the space of collective identity formation at the intersection between two processes: on the one hand, the active intervention of material features that condition the way in which the self is expressed in the online space, and, on the other, the emergence of an overall "politics of visibility" for which individuals select, appropriate, juxtapose, and publicly display digital cultural elements (e.g., photos, links, videos) that are consistent with their inclinations (2015, 895). Ultimately, this process of appropriation and re-composition is a continuous negotiation: an interactive tuning between the individual and the collective levels that elicits an inextricable and strong link between the private dimension of individuals' everyday life and their public performance of political engagement (*ibid.*). Beside amplifying the interactive and dynamic nature of collective identity formation, digital media also expand the inherent conflictuality of this process by establishing a tension not only between competing definitions and frames (Benford, 1993) but also between social and technological agencies. Indeed, as shown by Kavada (2015) in her reconstruction of how *Occupy!* was constituted as a collective actor, activists struggled to balance the principles of inclusivity and direct participation that defined the movement with the necessity to adapt to the material constraints of platforms such as Facebook and Twitter, which required them to reach out to other actors and to the wider public only with one collective voice.

Precisely because of the tight link that exists between the individual and the collective experience as well as because of the openness and the inclusivity that characterizes current mobilizations, contemporary movements' identities are also characterized by a strong emotional component. The expression of this emotional load can be highly disruptive and, as argued by Earl and colleagues (2016), can influence policy maker, the public opinion, and media coverage by "showcasing massive mobilization and attracting widespread attention" (2016, 356). For example, in reviewing how Egyptian and Spanish activists and supporters made use of Facebook pages, Gerbaudo describes the complex bundle of exchanges and expressions of support in terms of "digital enthusiasm – a necessarily transient phases of intense, positive emotional mood emerging in political online conversations in proximity to major protest events" (2016, 255). This overall intense atmosphere is jointly constructed through the interaction of two poles: on the one hand, social media pages' administrators who reach out to the public "constructing a hopeful emotional narrative"; and, on the other, supporters who testify their engagement by making use of Facebook functions to endorse and further specify this narrative (Gerbaudo, 2016, 255–256).

In a similar vein, Papacharissi speaks of "affective publics" as those "networked publics [that are] activated and sustained by feelings of belonging and solidarity, however evanescent those feelings may be" (2016, 310). In comparison to the original concept of "networked publics," for which social media create (non-neutral) public spaces that are also "the imagined collective that emerges as a result of the intersection of people, technology, and practice" (boyd, 2011, 39), Papacharissi's "affective publics" underline more explicitly the emotional investment that characterizes individuals' engagement within public discourses when technological affordances, like hashtags, are used to become part of a collective. Although affective publics can form for different reasons, it is always a "public display of affect that unites, identifies, or disconnect them" (Papacharissi, 2016, 308). Even in the absence of a formal commitment to an SMO or a political party and acting purposively but often discontinuously, individuals *choose to come together* under a "shared symbolic universe," as Melucci (1996, 58) called it, even if the building blocks of such a symbolic universe are volatile digital devices of thematic identification (like hashtags) or markers of addressivity (like retweets). In doing so, they participate actively in rendering "crowds into publics" (Papacharissi, 2016, 308), that is, into collective concerned actors that, not different from what traditional views of collective identities purported, are able of "making sense" of their being together (see Melucci, 1996, 20).

Although it is addressed less often than the environmental or organizational implications of digital media (Gerbaudo & Treré, 2015), the construction of movements' collective identity in the digital mediascape is a promising area of inquiry. While digital media affordances and communication possibilities have mobilization potentials which are somewhat distinct from those channeled by consistent and centrally defined "collective action frames" (Bennett & Segerberg, 2013), they have not eliminated at all the need for a common cognitive orientation under which dispersed actors can recognize and build an "action system" (Melucci, 1996). Echoing the claim made by Earl and colleagues (2016), the point is not whether contemporary "protest identities" or "affective publics" are as effective as movements' ideologies in achieving social and cultural change. Rather, the core issue remains understanding the circumstances and the modes in which digital media are appropriated and exploited beyond simple interpersonal interactions and to maximize the possibility to form "a crowd that permits *the feeling of being part of something* without *taking part* (. . .) [that] offers individuals the chance to take part in a 'collective' that remains undefined, that *leaves the options open*" (Melucci, 1996, 371–372, emphasis in the original). Even if mediated crowds are less structured than movements and can degenerate in individual panic and violent reaction, they can also be by all means "a potential collective in which individuals already interact in the production of meanings and orientation" (Melucci, 1996, 372).

The nexus between movements and digital media: looking ahead

As we argued at the beginning this chapter, in spite of the progress made in just a few years, much remains to be done to gain a fuller understanding of digital media implications for our societies and democracies. Very much open to further investigations are the processes through which less structured and sustained forms of political engagement can directly or indirectly contribute to achieve long-term consequences at all levels – stimulating offline protest, obtaining policy and cultural changes, generating media coverage and reshaping public opinion, but also impacting personal biographies (Earl, 2016). However, taking up this challenge implies a (necessary but not so easy to take) step beyond current event-based and protest-centered approaches looking at the nexus between digital media and mobilizations in the long run and in the context of non-conflictual action repertoires (Pavan, 2017).

Moreover, so far research efforts have addressed the nexus between digital media and movements according to the same "instrumental-structuralist" perspective (Johnston, 2009, 3) that has characterized movement studies in the past – that is, by considering movements and their structuring processes as the real object of interest. Hence, while we may have mastered our knowledge on movements and on how they exploit digital media to overcome political and cultural obstacles, we have admittedly paid less attention to investigate the contents of the "alternative political imaginaries and theories about how to actualise these imagined possibilities" (Chesters, 2012, 147) that movements elaborate at the crossroads between enlarged participation, inclusivity, and material constraints imposed by the technologies they decide to appropriate. Thus, accounting more systematically for the knowledge that movements produce in the current digital mediascape appears to be a necessary step to comprehend how fluid and ever evolving communication networks can become *agents of democratization*.

Of paramount importance is also accompanying current research efforts centered in digital media as tools for protest and activism together with a more systematic inquiry of engagement with media as *contested objects*. Research about alternative media already purported that media can become a terrain of social and political confrontation. However, even in its most recent realizations, this strand of research has focused more on the practices through which movements exploit digital media for realizing their alternative projects, than on how they may engage critically with their logics and politics. Moreover, in conjunction with the opening of new windows of political opportunities especially at the supranational level, media and communication governance issues have in fact become global contested issues (Hintz & Milan, 2007) around which civil society organizations, informal platforms, and even interested citizens have mobilized (Padovani & Pavan, 2009; Pavan, 2012). Yet, reflections on media as the substance of the protest have hitherto developed in a rather scattered way and have somewhat remained a niche within both communication and movement studies.

With 'big data' spreading as the mantra of our contemporaneity, a new phase of engagement with media and its less visible aspects seems to be on the rise. As noted by Milan and van der Velden, increased datafication (i.e., the ubiquitous quantification of social life, see Mayer-Schönberger & Cukier, 2013) and its analytic management through big data approaches are making citizens "increasingly aware of the critical role of information in contemporary societies" (2016, 57). The leak of documents by whistleblower Edward Snowden in 2013 functioned in this respect as a critical juncture, dismantling the mainstream narrative that "something new and special is taking place" (Mayer-Schönberger & Cukier, 2013, 6) thanks to the increased volume, variety and velocity of digital data produced by the so called "everyweare" (Kitchin, 2014). While it became evident that, beside allowing unprecedented analytical possibilities, massive data production and collection can be used to monitor people's lives, new forms of "*algorithmic resistance* that use the same advanced technological tools that the powerful deploy to [exert their] control" (Treré, 2016, 135) develop "to improve institutional output and democratic governance by means of software and data" (Milan & van der Velden, 2016, 58).

Because it addresses the networked infrastructure to provoke social and political change, data activism understood as the "composite series of sociotechnical practices that, emerging at the fringes of the contemporary activism ecology [to] interrogate datafication and its sociopolitical consequences" (Milan & van der Velden, 2016, 59) stands in continuity with already existing practices of cyber activism and hacktivism and, to be sure, with more radical orientations in the alternative media field (Downing et al., 2001). At the same time, it expands these practices by addressing how knowledge is produced within increasingly datafied contexts (Milan & van der Velden, 2016, 59) – struggling not only to subvert surveillance practice and re-establish privacy rights (Kubitschko, 2015) but also elaborating innovative "practices and imaginaries of open data" that prelude to the public sharing of raw data and to the elaboration of alternative knowledges that break the "interpretative monopoly of governments" (Baack, 2015, 3). Shifting dynamically from an interpretation of datafication as a threat to individual rights and an unprecedented set of opportunities for advocacy and social change, data activism adopts varied action repertoires that range from "obfuscating and resistance to making the most of datafication" (Milan & van der Velden, 2016, 68). While this fluidity is necessary to cope with the ever-evolving sociotechnical context in which data activism is rising, it also hampers the spread of these practices of resistance outside expert communities. As Dencik et al. (2016) show in their analysis, reactions to increased datafication have effectively implemented technical and legal solutions such as the use of encryption and the engagement in policy advocacy around issues of privacy and data protection. However, what seems to be missing is an overall frame of "data-justice" able not only to further clarify the urgency of the issues addressed by activists for all citizens but also to bridge data activism with the broader "social justice agenda" (Dencik et al., 2016) – a necessary step to pull out communication and data from the niche in which they lay too often and address more systematically their democratic implications.

References

Baack, S. (2015). Datafication and Empowerment: How the Open Data Movement Re-Articulates Notions of Democracy, Participation, and Journalism. *Big Data and Society*, 2(2), 1–11.

Benford, R. D. (1993). Frame Disputes Within the Nuclear Disarmament Movement. *Social Forces*, 71(3), 677–701.

Bennett, L. W. (2003). New Media Power, the Internet and Global Activism. In N. Couldry and J. Curran (eds.), *Contesting Media Power: Alternative Media in a Networked World*. Lanham: Rowman & Littlefield, pp. 17–37.

Bennett, L. W. (2004). Social Movements beyond Borders: Understanding Two Eras of Transnational Activism. In D. della Porta and S. Tarrow (eds.), *Transnational Protest and Global Activism*. Lanham: Rowman & Littlefield, pp. 203–226.

Bennett, L. W., and Segerberg, A. (2013). *The Logic of Connective Action*. New York: Cambridge University Press.

Bennett, L. W., and Segerberg, A. (2014). Three Patterns of Power in Technology-Enabled Contention. *Mobilization: An International Quarterly*, 19(4), 421–439.

Bennett, L. W., and Segerberg, A. (2016). Communication in Movements. In D. della Porta and M. Diani (eds.), *The Oxford Handbook of Social Movements*. Oxford: Oxford University Press, pp. 367–382.

Bimber, B., Flanagin, A., and Stohl, C. (2012). *Collective Action in Organizations: Interaction and Engagement in an Era of Technological Change*. New York: Cambridge University Press.

boyd, D. (2011). Social Network Sites as Networked Publics: Affordances, Dynamics and Implications. In Z. Papacharissi (ed.), *A Networked Self*. New York and London: Routledge, pp. 39–58.

Cammaerts, B. (2012). Protest Logics and the Mediation Opportunity Structure. *European Journal of Communication*, 27(2), 117–134.

Cammaerts, B., Mattoni, A. and McCurdy, P. (eds.). (2013). Introduction. In B. Cammaerts, A. Mattoni, and P. McCurdy (eds.), *Mediation and Protest Movements*. Chicago: Intellect, pp. 1–19.

Castells, M. (2009). *Communication Power*. Oxford: Oxford University Press.

Castells, M. (2011). A Network Theory of Power. *International Journal of Communication*, 5, 773–787.

Castells, M. (2012). *Networks of Outrage and Hope*. Cambridge: Polity Press.

Chadwick, A. (2007). Digital Network Repertoires and Organizational Hybridity. *Political Communication*, 24, 283–301.

Chesters, G. (2012). Social Movements and the Ethics of Knowledge Production. *Social Movement Studies*, 11(2), 145–160.

Christensen, H. S. (2011). Political Activities on the Internet: Slacktivism or Political Participation by Other Means? *First Monday*, 16(2–7). http://firstmonday.org/htbin/cgiwrap/bin/ojs/index.php/fm/article/view/3336/2767.

Couldry, N. (2003). Beyond the Hall of Mirrors? Some Theoretical Reflections on the Global Contestation of Media Power. In N. Couldry and J. Curran (eds.), *Contesting Media Power: Alternative Media in a Networked World*. Lanham: Rowman & Littlefield, pp. 39–55.

Curran, J. (2003). Global Journalism: A Case Study of the Internet. In N. Couldry and J. Curran (eds.), *Contesting Media Power. Alternative Media in a Networked World*. Lanham: Rowman & Littlefield, pp. 227–241.

della Porta, D. (1996). *Movimenti collettivi e sistema politico*. Bari: Laterza.

della Porta, D. (2013). Bridging Research on Democracy, Social Movements and Communication. In B. Cammaerts, A. Mattoni, and P. McCurdy (eds.), *Mediation and Protest Movements*. Chicago: Intellect, pp. 21–37.

della Porta, D. (2015). *Social Movements in Times of Austerity: Bringing Capitalism Back into Protest Analysis*. Malden, MA: Polity Press.

della Porta, D., and Mattoni, A. (2015). Social Networking Sites in Pro-Democracy and Anti-Austerity Protests: Some Thoughts from a Social Movement Perspective. In D. Trottier and C. Fuchs (eds.), *Social Media, Politics and the State: Protests, Revolutions, Riots, Crime and Policing in the Age of Facebook, Twitter and YouTube*. London: Routledge, pp. 39–65.

della Porta, D., and Mosca, L. (2005). Global-Net for Global Movements? A Network of Networks for a Movement of Movements. *Journal of Public Policy*, 25, 165–190.

Dencik, L., Hintz, A., and Cable, J. (2016). Towards Data Justice? The Ambiguity of Anti-Surveillance Resistance in Political Activism. *Big Data and Society*, 1–12, July–December.

Diani, M. (2003). Networks and Social Movements: A Research Programme. In M. Diani and D. McAdam (eds.), *Social Movements and Networks: Relational Approaches to Collective Action*. Oxford: Oxford University Press, pp. 218–299.

Downing, J. D. H., Villareal Ford, T., Gil, G,. and Stein, L. (2001). *Radical Media: Rebellious Communication and Social Movements*. London: Sage.

Earl, J. (2010). The Dynamics of Protest-Related Diffusion on the Web. *Information, Communication & Society*, 13(2), 209–225.

Earl, J. (2016). Protest Online. Theorizing the Consequences of Online Engagement. In L. Bosi, M. Giugni, and K. Uba (eds.), *The Consequences of Social Movements*. Cambridge: Cambridge University Press, pp. 363–400.

Earl, J., Hunt, J., Garrett, R. K., and Dal, A. (2016). New Technologies and Social Movements. In D. della Porta and M. Diani (eds.), *The Oxford Handbook of Social Movements*. Oxford: Oxford University Press, pp. 355–366.

Earl, J., and Kimport, K. (2011). *Digitally Enabled Social Change: Activism in the Internet Age*. Boston, MA: MIT Press.

Fuster Morell, M. (2009). Action research: mapping the nexus of research and political action. *Interface*, 1(1), 21–45.

Gerbaudo, P. (2016). Rousing the Facebook Crowd: Digital Enthusiasm and Emotional Contagion in the 2011 Protests in Egypt and Spain. *International Journal of Communication*, 10(2016), 254–273.

Gerbaudo, P., and Treré, E. (2015). In Search of the 'We' of Social Media Activism: Introduction to the Special Issue on Social Media and Protest Identities. *Information, Communication & Society*, 18(8), 865–871.

Gitlin, T. (1980). *The Whole World Is Watching: Mass Media in the Making and Unmaking of the New Left*. Berkeley and Los Angeles, CA: University of California Press.

González-Bailón, S., Borge-Holthoefer, J., and Moreno, Y. (2013). Broadcasters and Hidden Influentials in Online Protest Diffusion. *American Behavioral Scientist*, 57, 943–965.

Graham, T., Jackson, D., and Wright, S. (2016). 'We Need to Get Together and Make Ourselves Heard': Everyday Online Spaces as Incubators of Political Action. *Information, Communication & Society*, 19(10), 1373–1389.

Hintz, A., and Milan, S. (2007). Towards a New Vision for Communication Governance? Civil Society Media at the World Social Forum and the World Summit on the Information Society. *Communication for Development and Social Change*, 1(1), 1–23.

Johnston, H. (2009). Protest Cultures: Performance, Artifacts, and Ideations. In H. Johnston (ed.), *Culture, Social Movement and Protest*. Farnham: Ashgate, pp. 3–32.

Juris, J. S. (2012). Reflections on #Occupy Everywhere: Social Media, Public Space, and Emerging Logics of Aggregation. *American Ethnologist*, 39(2), 259–279.

Kavada, A. (2015). Creating the Collective: Social Media, the Occupy Movement and Its Constitution as a Collective Actor. *Information, Communication & Society*, 18(8), 872–886.

Kielbowicz, R. B., and Scherer, C. (1986). The Role of the Press in the Dynamics of Social Movements. *Research in Social Movements, Conflict and Change*, 9, 71–96.

Kitchin, R. (2014). The Real-Time City? Big Data and Smart Urbanism. *GeoJournal*, 79, 1–14.

Kubitschko, S. (2015). The Role of Hackers in Countering Surveillance and Promoting Democracy. *Media and Communication*, 3(2), 77–87.

Leonardi, P. M. (2012). Materiality, Sociomateriality, and Socio-Technical Systems: What Do These Terms Mean? How Are They Different? Do We Need Them? In P. M. Leonardi, B. A. Nardi, and J. Kallinikos (eds.), *Materiality and Organizing: Social Interaction in a Technological World*. Oxford: Oxford University Press, pp. 25–48.

Lievrouw, L. (2011). *Alternative and Activist New Media*. Cambridge: Polity Press.

Lievrouw, L. (2014). Materiality and Media in Communication and Technology Studies: An Unfinished Project. In T. Gillespie, P. J. Boczkowski, and K. A. Foot (eds.), *Media Technologies. Essays on Communication, Materiality, and Society*. Cambridge, MA: MIT Press, pp. 21–51.

Lievrouw, L., and Livingstone, S. (2006). Introduction. In L. Lievrouw and S. Livingstone (eds.), *Handbook of New Media: Social Shaping and Social Consequences*. London: Sage, pp. 1–14.

Mattoni, A. (2009). *Multiple Media Practices in Italian Mobilizations Against Precarity of Work* (PhD thesis), Florence, European University Institute.

Mattoni, A., and Treré, E. (2014). Media Practices, Mediation Processes, and Mediatization in the Study of Social Movements. *Communication Theory*, 24, 252–271.

Mayer-Schönberger, V., and Cukier, K. (2013). *Big Data: A Revolution That Will Transform How We Live, Work and Think*. London: John Murray Publishers.

Melucci, A. (1996). *Challenging Codes: Collective Action in the Information Age*. Cambridge: Cambridge University Press.

Milan, S. (2015). From Social Movements to Cloud Protesting: The Evolution of Collective Identity. *Information, Communication & Society*, 18(8), 887–900.

Milan, S., and van der Velden, L. (2016). The Alternative Epistemologies of Data Activism. *Digital Culture and Society*, 2(2), 57–74.

Mosca, L. (2014). Bringing Communication Back in: Social Movements and Media. In C. Padovani and A. Calabrese (eds.), *Communication Rights and Social Justice: Historical Accounts of Transnational Mobilizations*. New York: Palgrave Macmillan, pp. 219–233.

Mosca, L., and della Porta, D. (2009). Unconventional Politics Online. In D. della Porta (ed.), *Democracy in Social Movements*. London: Palgrave Macmillan, pp. 194–216.

Padovani, C., and Pavan, E. (2009). The Emerging Global Movement on Communication Rights: a New Stakeholder in Global Governance? Converging at WSIS but Looking Beyond. In L. Stein, D. Kidd, and C. Rodriguez (eds.), *Making Our Media: Mapping Global Initiatives Toward a Democratic Public Sphere* (vol. II). Cresskill: Hampton Press, pp. 223–242.

Padovani, C., and Pavan, E. (2016). Global Governance and ICTs. Exploring Online Governance Networks Around Gender and Media. *Global Networks*, 16(3), 350–371.

Papacharissi, Z. (2009). The Virtual Sphere 2.0: The Internet, the Public Sphere and Beyond. In A. Chadwick and P. Howard (eds.), *Handbook of Internet Politics*. Abingdon, Oxon: Routledge, pp. 230–245.

Papacharissi, Z. (2016). Affective Publics and Structures of Storytelling: Sentiment, Events and Mediality. *Information, Communication and Society*, 19(3), 307–324.

Pavan, E. (2012). *Frames and Connections in the Governance of Global Communications: A Network Study of the Internet Governance Forum*. Lanham, MD: Lexington Books.

Pavan, E. (2014). Embedding Digital Communications Within Collective Action Networks: A Multidimensional Network Perspective. *Mobilization: An International Quarterly*, 19, 441–455.

Pavan, E. (2017). The Integrative Power of Online Collective Action Networks Beyond Protest: Exploring Social Media Use in the Process of Institutionalization. *Social Movement Studies*, 16(4), 433–446.

Peretti, J., and Micheletti, M. (2004). The Nike Sweatshop Email: Political Consumerism, Internet, and Culture Jamming. In M. Micheletti, A. Follesdal, and D. Stolle (eds.), *Politics, Products and Markets. Exploring Political Consumerism Past and Present*. New Brunswick: Transaction Publishers, pp. 127–142.

Rainie, L., and Wellman, B. (2012). *Networked: The New Social Operating System*. Cambridge, MA: MIT Press.

Rucht, D. (2004). *The Quadruple "A": Media Strategies of Protest Movements since the 1960s*. In W. van de Donk, B. Loader, P. Nixon and D. Rucht (eds) Cyberprotest: New Media, Citizens and Social Movements. London: Routledge, pp. 29–56.

Tarrow, S. (1994). *Power in Movement*. New York: Cambridge University Press.

Treré, E. (2016). The Dark Side of Digital Politics: Understanding the Algorithmic Manufacturing of Consent and the Hindering of Online Dissidence. *IDS Bulletin*, 47(1), 127–138.

Van Laer, J., and Van Aelst, P. (2010). Internet and Social Movements Action Repertoires. *Information, Communication & Society*, 13(8), 1146–1171.

Ward, S., and Gibson, R. (2009). European Political Organizations and the Internet: Mobilization, Participation, and Change. In A. Chadwick and P. Howard (eds.), *Handbook of Internet Politics*. Abingdon, Oxon: Routledge, pp. 25–39.

24

Governance and regulation

Peng Hwa Ang

In digital communication governance and regulation, the most extensive and intensive discussions in this space have been around Internet governance. Two summits were organized by the United Nations (UN) in 2003 and 2005 to address it. Hitherto, there had never been two UN-level summits on any issue. Although intended to discuss the development of the information society for the world, the burning issue that emerged was that the Internet was run by the United States. Can the US Government cut the Internet's connection to a country so that its Internet infrastructure is unusable? As will be shown in this chapter, that major obstacle has been overcome. But the discussion around Internet governance has extended to other aspects of regulation around digital communication.

This paper addresses the origins of Internet governance, its significance and implications, and its limits. The governance of the Internet in practice reflects the divergent views of how the digital space, should be governed. It is old money vs new, International Telecommunications Union (ITU) vs the Internet Corporation for Assigned Names and Numbers (ICANN), traditional government-only vs the emergent multistakeholder model. The paper will also discuss the contentious issue of the role of civil society in the multistakeholder model as well as the regulation of content and disruptive technologies such as ride-sharing.

Evolution of Internet governance

The way the Internet operates requires a centralized directory of unique addresses and the management of that addressing system is undertaken by a US-company, ICANN, under the US Department of Commerce. What if, say, a country were to go to war with the United States? Can the Internet be pulled away from it?

Just such a scenario did play out. The national domain name for the country of Iraq, dot-IQ (.IQ) was in the hands, not of then ruler Saddam Hussein, his Baathist party or his cronies. It was in the hands of Bayan Elashi, a Palestinian-American who had developed the first Arabic-language personal computer (Whitaker, 2004). (In the early days of the Internet, Jon Postel gave out the right to register domain names to those who had the know-how and capacity to function as a register. In some countries, notably Japan, the national domain name register is in the hands of a private entity, not the government.) Because of sanctions imposed on Iraq, the US state department imposed "ridiculous" restrictions that made the. IQ domain name "useless," Elashi said. Then the company he owned that managed the. IQ domain name was raided in 2001. He was arrested in December 2002, just before the invasion of Iraq in March 2003, on charges of unauthorized sale of computer parts to Syria and other countries under US sanctions. This meant that when the war began, Iraq did not exist in the Internet space (Whitaker, 2004).

What do we mean by governance?

The Elashi case illustrated the criticality of the top-level domain (TLD), which in this case was supposed to belong to a sovereign country, Iraq. Although ICANN did not turn off access to the. IQ domain, it was ICANN that in theory could physically turn it off. The top-level domains such as. COM and. ORG as well as national country-code TLDs (ccTLDs) were under the control of ICANN. It was against this backdrop that the first World Summit on the Information Society (WSIS I) was held in Geneva in 2003. The original focus on the use of information for development shifted to governance of the Internet space. Unlike other summits, WSIS I nearly collapsed, without the customary declaration or statement. As a compromise, the Summit agreed that the UN Secretary-General would convene a 40-person Working Group on Internet Governance to report on the matter in a second Summit that was to be held two years later.

Governance can best be described as concerning, first, rules and second, rules about rules. That is, to talk about governance is to talk about rules, regulations and guidelines; these may be written or unwritten, such as rules of etiquette. But governance is also about how the rules are made. To paraphrase a more recent framing the issue of authority by Zuboff (2019, 107), it would be: What rules? Who decided the rules? And who decided who would decide the rules. What was the process in making the rules? Who decided on the process? If it was decided by a committee, who appointed the members of the committee?

The definition of Internet governance given in the Final Report of the Working Group on Internet governance (WGIG) sums it up well:

> The development and application by governments, the private sector and civil society, in their respective roles, of shared principles, norms, rules, decision-making procedures, and programmes that shape the evolution and use of the Internet.
>
> *(2005, 4)*

Three points in this definition should be noted. First, three stakeholders are mentioned. It is not just governments that make rules; the private sector and civil society have a role to play too. This is a major shift for a meeting held in the premises of the United Nations by a committee appointed by the Secretary-General. During meetings in 2004 and 2005 to discuss Internet governance, government officials would order out of the room non-government attendees, as happened to the author notwithstanding an invitation from another government official. The situation has since changed. Today, at international meetings on Internet governance, members of one stakeholder group often sit in on discussions organized by another stakeholder group. Rare is the occasion when discussions are strictly closed to the other two stakeholder groups.

Second, the definition prescribes each stakeholder having 'respective roles.' This qualification is a double-edged sword. On the one hand, it means that each stakeholder has a role to play. On the other hand, it seems to limit stakeholders to their specific roles. This qualification has led to controversy and will be discussed in more detail later in the chapter.

Third, principles, norms, rules, procedures, and programs were included to capture the breadth of rule-formation. Most obvious as rules would be principles, norms and rules. Less obvious would be procedures, which are the processes that might affect the outcome in rule-making. Still more often overlooked are software programmers themselves. As pointed out by Lessig (2008), the architecture of a software programmer has the effect of directing behavior. It is therefore a form of law. This third part means that governance of the digital space is not merely governance of technical matters. In fact, at the very opening session of the WGIG, when the Group was discussing the scope of its work, then Secretary-General of the International Telecommunication Union (ITU) Yoshio Utsumi had wanted the Group to focus only on ICANN and ICANN-related matters. To Utsumi, the ITU's handling of telephone codes and numbers was analogous to ICANN's handling of Internet Protocol (IP) addresses with the advantage of far more extensive experience. The ITU could handle telephone numbers; IP addresses were a series of numbers; therefore the ITU could also handle IP addresses. But it was clear that there were many issues regarding the Internet that were outside the experience of the ITU. The WGIG Final Report rejected that definition. In fact, the ITU appears once in the Final Report, and as a footnote.

Despite some limitations, considered later, no definition of Internet governance has been as widely accepted. It may be that it is because the definition emerged from the firepower of 17 of the 40-member WGIG. The major criticism of the definition is that alluded to earlier, that each stakeholder has a 'restricted' role. Some in the civil society sector feel that they should be able to 'negotiate' with governments at the same level. That is, civil society should not be restricted to merely giving feedback to proposed laws, the role typically understood to be that of civil society. Instead, civil society should have the same power to formulate rules. Such a position, however, is contentious even among civil society groups.

Some governments reject such a role for civil society by questioning the legitimacy of civil society as a stakeholder group. Governments can be said to represent their citizens; businesses can be represented by business associations. But it is not clear who civil society speaks for. Furthermore, civil society activists sometimes say that they do not speak for anyone but only for their own civil society group. But if so, the position raises the question of what such activists are doing giving policy input. In short, the definition, while arguably conceptually coherent, raises challenging questions in practice.

Origins of Internet governance

The governance of the Internet was a matter that few governments paid attention to in the early days of its public adoption in the early 1990s – that is, when the Internet left the universities and research institutions and was made available for wider public and commercial use. It was the explosive growth of the Internet, and the nature of the growth, that made governments pay more attention to the Internet and its governance. The number of domain names rose from about 627,000 at the end of 1996 to 1.5 million before the end of 1997; Internet traffic doubled every 100 days; Cisco Systems grew its sales on the Internet from $100 at the end of 1996 to $3.2 billion by the end of 1997; in that same one-year period, Amazon saw its sales soard from less than $16 million to US3.2 billion (Margherio, undated).

The rapid growth was probably best highlighted by the Initial Public Offering of a new loss-making company called Netscape. On its first day of trading on August 9 1995, its stock price, which had been offered at $28, shot up to $75 before closing at $58. This valued the company, which had no profits then, at US$7 billion (Lashinsky, 2015). The Internet was seen as the 'new oil,' a rich resource with the United States in charge and controlling it. This concern of the United States controlling a rich resource remains one of the drivers behind global Internet governance discussions.

In 1997, with the dotcom boom well under way, President Bill Clinton directed the Department of Commerce, to privatize the management of the Internet, of which it had oversight, and in particular the Domain Name System (DNS) (Clinton, 1997). The US government's aim of privatization was to encourage international participation as part of its Framework for Global Electronic Commerce. The Department of Commerce issued a Request for Comments the following day (1997). Over a period of seven weeks, it received more than 430 comments in 1,500 pages (Department of Commerce, 1998). Probably the most significant comment was that from the European Union (EU), which expressed its fears that the proposal was too US-centric. The proposal, presciently, was titled *International Policy Issues Related to Internet Governance* (EU, 1998). It was the first time the term Internet governance had been used.

Several themes in the EU comments and the responses to the US proposals are interesting to note. First, the comment was intended to represent all the EU member states. The number of people who knew about Internet governance issues then were limited; the EU proposal even had a glossary of Internet terms and relevant organizations. Second, because the United States controlled the Internet at the top-level of IP addresses, the EU therefore viewed US policy with some hesitancy, if not suspicion. Third, the EU comment called for global participation – code for avoiding US dominance – in discussing the US proposal (EU, 1998).

The US Government responded to the issues raised in a further consultation document, a Green Paper, entitled *A Proposal to Improve the Technical Management of Internet Names and Addresses* that was released by the US National Telecommunications Information Administration in early 1998. It called for discussion on the creation of a nonprofit corporation to manage the Domain Name System (DNS) by a globally and functionally representative Board of Directors. Over seven weeks, more than 650 comments were received (National Telecommunications and Information Administration, 1998). The Green Paper led in turn to the White Paper, which in many parts of the world is the color of the paper that sets out government policy for legislative change. Released in mid-1998, the *Statement of Policy Management of Internet Names and Addresses* (National Telecommunications and Information Administration, 1998) roused the industry associations to form the *International Forum on the White Paper* (IFWP). The Forum was intended to get feedback from stakeholders around the world to comment on the US proposal to move management of the DNS from the US government to a private nonprofit company.

Meetings were held in Reston, Virginia, for the Internet community in North and South America, in Geneva, Switzerland, for Europe (and that also included Africa and the Middle East), Buenos Aires, Argentina, for Latin America and the Caribbean, and in Singapore for Asia and the Pacific. Governments outside of North America and the EU were, however, not so ready to discuss governance of the Internet: at the August 1998 meeting in Singapore, many Asian participants from both the public and private sector said that they were learning of the issues for the first time (Greene, 1998).

Civil society for its part was, well, much less than civil. The author remembers the event in Singapore that had the most amount of vulgarities hurled by speakers at each other at a public global meeting that he had ever witnessed. Although some say a consensus of sorts was arrived at (Fenello, 1998), the IFWP "did not result in a specific proposal in response to the NTIA Paper (Boston Working Group, 1998, 1)." The IFWP as a bottom-up effort had failed. It was not surprising then that the final outcome was determined by the US government: the running of the Internet came under ICANN.

Meanwhile, the ITU considered ways to be involved in some aspect of the running of the Internet. The 1998 ITU Plenipotentiary Conference called for the holding of the World

Summit on the Information Society at the level of the United Nations. To be sure, it was not just the ITU that wanted a look into the issues of the rise of the information society. The oil-rich countries in the Middle East were concerned that information might be the 'new oil' and that they were being left behind. The result was the World Summit on the Information Society (WSIS), which was held in 2003 in Geneva. Such summits – hitherto always only on one topic – typically end with some declaration. The WSIS almost failed in issuing such a declaration. Countries wanted to discuss Internet governance, which was code for the dominance of the United States of the Internet space.

Puzzlingly, most of the reports of the saga around. IQ were in the UK press but not in the US; whenever the author has presented this, American audiences are astounded as they were hearing it for the first time. The. IQ domain was handed to the government of Iraq in mid-2005, when the WGIG Final Report was translated and just days before it was published. The reason given was that the Iraqi government was now stable. At WSIS, the US position was that countries did not know enough about issue and so were in no position to discuss the matter. There was some truth in that assertion but such a position also raised suspicion – especially after the. IQ saga – that the United States wanted to control and run the Internet on its own terms.

WGIG

This part of the discussion borrows from Ang (2005). Facing the prospect of a failed Summit, the Internet governance issue was sent to a committee called the Working Group on Internet Governance. This was a committee of 40 persons appointed by then-UN Secretary General Kofi Annan. The 40 were to be globally representative and to also to represent government, business and civil society.

The major accomplishment of the WGIG was a report that defined Internet governance and delineated its issues. On hindsight, it was this report that gave impetus to the discussion on Internet governance. Strictly speaking, there were two reports from the Group: the shorter and more frequently cited 24-page Final Report and the 76-page Background Report (www.wgig. org/WGIG-Report.html). The Final Report had the full consensus of the WGIG as it was heavily edited by the Group, down to the last comma; the Background Report included contributions from within and without of the Group, was much more lightly edited and conveys a better sense of the various issues discussed as they were discussed with more depth.

Public discussions, however, have tended to focus on the Final Report, of which the substantive part is 15 pages assessing the existent system of and mapping the most important public policy issues around Internet governance. The issues were:

- administration of the root zone files and system,
- allocation of domain names,
- IP (Internet protocol) addressing,
- multilingualism,
- spam
- interconnection costs Internet stability, security and cybercrime,
- intermediary liability,
- intellectual property rights,
- data protection and privacy rights,
- consumer rights,
- freedom of expression,

- capacity-building, and
- meaningful participation in global policy development.

The list reflects the breadth of issues under Internet governance, with an eclectic mix of technical matters, legal concerns, and "soft" policy issues such as capacity building and participation in global policy discussions. These were issues that went beyond merely technical concerns that the ITU confined Internet governance to. In fact, the substantive part of the Final Report mentions ITU just once, literally as a footnote. Instead, Internet governance was placed in the hands of a diverse group of stakeholders comprising the public and private sectors and civil society.

The discussion around Internet governance in the WGIG was a discussion around the vision of how the Internet should be governed. The WGIG Report recommended that the rule-making process concerning the Internet, that is, Internet governance, be transparent, democratic, multistakeholder and multilateral. It recommended who should be involved and how: governments, the private sector and civil society (multistakeholders) from many countries (multilateral) should be open (transparent) in their meetings and be consultative in acknowledging the majority's interests in their (democratic) decisions. The recommendation in effect repudiated the traditional government-only approach to governance (Ang, 2005, 11). An updated vision of Internet governance had prevailed.

Tunis commitment

The WGIG Final Report and its recommendations were sent to governments around the world. To discuss and debate before accepting the WGIG Report, the second part of the WSIS was held in November 2005 in Tunis. Developing countries wanted the WSIS meeting to be held in a developing country. And Tunis was the reward for Tunisia's role in launching the WSIS; and planned or otherwise, it would remind many of the role of Tunisia's information minister then, Mustapha Masmoudi, in the New World Information Communication Order of the 1980s. WSIS II was then unique. Hitherto, by definition, there had been only one summit for one topic. Having two summits was out of the norm. But since WSIS, there have been two-summit meetings, the most immediate following of which was on global climate change.

WSIS II adopted many of the recommendations of the WGIG Report, but only after extended discussions by governments. First, it was agreed that countries would have national sovereignty over their domain names. This defused the tension around the. IQ saga; in future, the United States would not be able the dictate the terms of use for a country-code domain, even if the country were to go to war with the United States. This means that while it may be physically possible to pull the plug on a country's top-level domain name, the United States has pledged that it will not do so. Second, it was agreed that Internet governance would be multilateral, multistakeholder and democratic. This meant that the United States would not hold sole oversight or authority over the Internet, particularly at the root zone of the addressing system. Third the recommendation to set up a "light weight" (meaning low cost) forums to discuss Internet governance issues was accepted. This was to be the Internet Governance Forum (IGF).

These recommendations were not easy for the US government to accept. It meant that its actions regarding the Internet could be scrutinized. The Internet Society, which was to represent all users adopted a position that aligned with that of the US government; US companies too adopted the position of the US government.

Debate around the IGF was also instructive. China and other countries such as Russia, India and Brazil were ready to go with a model where the IGF would be under the UN and governments had a more dominant role. The US position was that the IGF was not necessary at all as there were other fora that could undertake the role. In the end, it was the more moderate compromise position of the EU that was adopted: the IGF would be a forum for discussion and even though it was putatively under the UN, it would not have any decision-making power.

The trilemma of the Internet governance forum

More recently, however, the positions of these countries have seemingly flipped. The United States is now all for the Internet Governance Forum, seeing that it is a 'talk shop' and not a decision-making body. On the other hand, China and Russia in particular are disappointed that the IGF is only a talk shop and not a decision-making body. The Chinese and Russians would prefer a more centralized governance regime, as opposed to the more open and ground-up approach favored by the Internet community. The difference has been characterized as a contrast between Internet freedom and Internet sovereignty (Shackelford & Alexander, 2018).

The reality is of course more nuanced as there are other factors that explain the difference in receptivity. The very format of the open microphone format for giving input at the IGF shows the contrasting approach. While a minister from North America or Europe may be comfortable waiting his or her turn in formal attire behind a jeans-and-T-shirt-clad graduate student, those from other cultures are less so. Also, Asians and those from developing countries are generally more reticent about speaking up in public.

A frustration common to many governments is that while the mandate of the IGF allows it to make recommendations the Forum has been extremely reluctant to do so. Government officials are often frustrated at having to justify attending a meeting where the only output were notes and video recordings of the event posted on the IGF website.

For all its shortcomings, however, the IGF is the only global forum where all the stakeholders around IT can gather to discuss issues. It is probably the best forum to uncover emerging issues on law and policy around the Internet. The first five-year mandate of the IGF was renewed in 2011 for five years and then the renewed in 2015 for 10 years. The future of the IGF is not assured. The 2017 meeting was held Geneva a few days before Christmas when no country stepped forward to host the event. The same scenario repeated in 2018 when France stepped forward to be host; the date is similarly a week or two before Christmas.

The reluctance of governments to support the IGF raises the intriguing question: if the benefits for global agreement are so obvious (reduction of waste, common understanding) should it not be easy to arrive at them? Here is where a framework adapted from Dani Rodrik (2012) has proven useful. Rodrik's notion is that in any attempt to globalize, there are three competing forces at play: national sovereignty, democracy and globalization. National sovereignty refers to the desire of countries to assert their sovereignty in any international setting. It is an understandable but reflexive political response. Democracy refers to mechanism of rule-making, that the majority decision should prevail. At the international level, it means that agreements have to be arrived at through a democratic process. The global agreement then leads to globalization. In any trilemma, however, one can only pick two out of the three. Here, globalization tends to lose out because countries are extremely reluctant to surrender their sovereignty. (Ang & Pang, 2016).

Probably the most realistic way out of the trilemma is to have "thin globalization" where there is 'spotty' agreement at the international level. That is, international agreements are accepted and enforced unevenly (Ang & Pang, 2016). A solution, less acceptable to many, is to have "thin democracy." India, Brazil and South Africa have proposed a UN body to govern the Internet (Prodhan, 2011). Having Internet governance under the UN would mean the exclusion of business and civil society in decisions regarding the Internet. China, currently the world's second largest economy, has been most assertive in attempting to sway global consensus to its view of Internet governance. China, jointly with Russia, drafted the *International Code of Conduct for Information Security* (UN, 2011). The 13 pledges in the document that was drafted to be passed as a resolution of the UN General Assembly came across as neutral in tone. For example, Principle (g) said that countries that voluntarily subscribed to the Code of Conduct would pledge "to promote the establishment of a multilateral, transparent and democratic international Internet management system to ensure an equitable distribution of resources, facilitate access for all and ensure a stable and secure functioning of the Internet." This was language that could come from the WGIG Report. Nevertheless, only four other countries – Tajikistan and Uzbekistan in 2011 and Kazakhstan and Kyrgyzstan in 2015 – said they would subscribe to the Code. Most others viewed it with suspicion that this was an attempt to wrest governance of the Internet from the multistakeholder model to one that was dominated by national governments (Shackelford & Alexander, 2018). That these countries all rank low on the democracy proxy indicator of freedom of expression lends credence to the Internet freedom vs sovereignty contest.

The Snowden revelations

There is, however, no clear winner in the contest. While then Secretary of State Hillary Clinton may have delivered a well-received speech on Internet Freedom at the Newseum in 2010 (2010), it was overshadowed three years later when Edward Snowden revealed that the US National Security Agency had been conducting surveillance of phone data that went through the United States, including those of heads of states (MacAskill & Hern, 2018). Discussions around surveillance and privacy dominated the 2013 IGF in Bali, Indonesia. A cynical meme that circulated went that Internet freedom meant the freedom of the US government to spy on the rest of the world.

In response, China organized in Wuzhen the first World Internet Conference in 2014. In a ham-fisted attempt to demonstrate consensus, the organizers on the eve of the final day slipped a draft declaration under the hotel room doors of attendees that, among other things, called the international community to "respect Internet sovereignty of all countries" (Shu, 2014). The following year, China's President Xi Jinping in his keynote address reiterated the call to respect Internet sovereignty. The 2017 Conference saw the CEOs of Apple and Microsoft attend for the first time. At that 2017 Conference, President Xi repeated his call to "respect cyberspace sovereignty" (Deutsche-Welle, 2017).

The Snowden revelations angered Brazilian president Dilma Rousseff, who canceled a scheduled official visit to the United States (BBC, 2013). In September 2013, Rousseff condemned the NSA practices at the UN General Assembly and said that Brazil would "present proposals for the establishment of a civilian multilateral framework for the governance and use of the Internet and to ensure the effective protection of data that travels through the web" (UN General Assembly, 2013). At the IGF in Bali in October 2013, then-CEO of ICANN Fadi Chehadé in a meeting with civil society groups said that he had the support Roussseff to organize a meeting to discuss "Internet governance principles." This was understood to mean formulating principles and rules on surveillance.

Brazil had developed its own Regulatory Framework for the Internet, which had been called the Internet Bill of Rights, established principles concerning the use of the Internet in the country. Among these principles were freedom of expression, net neutrality, privacy and the protection of personal data. The NETmundial Global Multistakeholder Meeting on the Future of Internet Governance was intended to develop a similar set of principles for the global Internet community. More than 1,200 participants turned up in São Paulo on 23 and 24 April 2014

(Fraundorfer, 2017). Representatives from the multistakeholders – government, business and civil society – worked late into the night to deliver the NetMundial Multistakeholder Statement that was presented at the end of the meeting. This is no mean achievement considering especially that civil society groups are particularly fragmented because of their diverse interests (Haristya & Ang, 2015).

The NetMundial Statement emerged through an open process of the kind that the IGF had exemplified but had never executed. The initial draft was said to be a reasonable compilation from the more than 180 proposals received (Purkayastha & Bailey, 2014). The NetMundial Initiative (NMI) appeared to be an attempt to replace the IGF although that was denied by then-ICANN CEO Chehadé. The structure of the NMI Coordination Council further heightened fears. The Council was to have 25 members of which five of them – including ICANN and the World Economic Forum – were to be permanent members. The structure was reminiscent of the UN Security Council (McCarthy, 2014). Not surprisingly, the Initiative itself failed to take off and was boycotted by the Internet community (McCarthy, 2016).

Meanwhile, the Snowden revelations had created a trust deficit with the United States. Market research firm Forrester Research estimated that the United States would lose US$180 billion in business over three years from the Snowden revelations as companies insert "anywhere but the USA" clauses into contracts that concerned their data. To reduce the trust deficit, the US government privatized the IANA function of ICANN. As discussed earlier in this paper, privatization had been talked about since the presidency of Bill Clinton. The goal was to encourage greater use of the Internet and thereby encourage commerce online. But that did not happened. Instead after an exhaustive and comprehensive two-year study by volunteers around the globe, four states sued to block the privatization. US Senator Ted Cruz introduced a motion into the US Senate to stop it (Ang, 2016a). 'Ignorant patriots' – a term of art in political science – were under the impression that the United States was 'giving' the Internet away to authoritarian governments. As if illustrating how complicated and complex the whole Internet governance debate had become, the contrary course was actually the case. To continue to 'hang on' to the Internet would lead to the perception that the United States was continuing to control the Internet in order to spy on the world. To try to hang on would actually mean losing it as users move to alternative systems. The reality is that managing the master directory was a very small part that gave no power to the wielder to spy on content. Whatever the US government was giving up, it was giving away little.

The foregoing discussion indicates that the Snowden revelations have had a major repercussion on Internet governance. As Snowden himself said, "The people are still powerless, but now they're aware" (MacAskill & Hern, 2018). Privacy laws are being tightened globally. The EU's stricter privacy law in the form of the General Data Protection Regulation is a direct result of the Snowden revelations.

Other governance issues

There are other issues that impinge on governance in the digital space. As it is now more than 20 years since the Internet was made available to the general public, many have worked on with varying degrees of success in understanding and acceptance. The following are more salient issues.

Disruptions: leveling up or leveling down

As Internet technologies become more developed, new services are being developed that disrupt existing business models and regulatory frameworks. Two outstanding examples are Uber and Airbnb. Strictly speaking, both are illegal from their very start. In the case of Uber, it is the use of a private car as a taxi, a service that is ordinarily heavily regulated in cities around the world. In the case of Airbnb, it is the letting out of a room in a home for short stays on terms practically identical to that of a hotel, another service that is regulated around the world.

Technologies have become more disruptive because they incorporate components that disrupt current practices. For example, Airbnb is viable in part because technology enables remote locking and unlocking. Uber is viable because GPS (global positioning satellite) makes it possible to track both the car and the passenger. Computing power now enables computers to make judgment calls in areas that was once thought the exclusive domain of human beings. Disruptive technologies are therefore likely to be continued to be developed in future.

How should the rules apply to such disruptions? Before being allowed to operate within new rules, both Uber and Airbnb were disallowed or investigated on grounds of being illegal in countries as diverse as France (Schechner & Divac, 2015), Abu Dhabi (Parasie, 2016) and Singapore (Purnell, 2014). Disruptive technologies show the underlying resilience of the multistakeholder model. In most instances, the solution to the services was not straightforward, to be resolved only by government and business. Instead, the input from civil society was essential.

Content regulation

Censorship and content regulation had been a significant issue since the Internet was made publicly available. The euphoria of being able to deliver and receive all kinds of content has given way to the realism that some content can be harmful. The vexing question with content regulation of the Internet is the question of standards. Large companies such as *Facebook* and *Google* have tended to take a stronger stance in favor of freedom of expression. With evidence of how online content from extremists has been able to radicalize users, *Facebook* has had to hire tens of thousands of moderators to remove violent content (Lev-Ram, 2018). These moderators, however, have encountered psychological problems as a result of viewing the content (Hern, 2019). This raises the question of sustainability of such content moderation.

More recently, ever since the US presidential election of 2016, there has been heightened concern over fake news. *Facebook* and *Google* are also facing the accusation of spreading fake news. But they need to fix this in order to ensure that their respective platforms are sufficiently trustworthy for advertising. If the platforms are seen to be untrustworthy, users will not trust the advertisements and the advertisers will dry up (Ang, 2017). Regulation to minimize fake news would appear to require a multi-prong approach and the multistakeholder model. Governments alone cannot do the work, for example, of fact-checking. Civil society would have a role to play.

Role of government

The issue of content regulation leads to the question of the role of government in Internet governance. Quite clearly the government has a major role. The question is: how major should it be? The ideological divide would appear to be between the framework of Internet freedom vs sovereignty framework or government vs free market. Such frameworks, however, are a false binary. Matters such as human rights require intervention of the government. Similarly, government intervention to legislate for free and fair competition is necessary for markets to work. Wu (2013) argues persuasively that in fact, the US telecommunication industry, which is the foundation on which the Internet infrastructure is built, was supported by the US government.

The experience of the United States is that the Internet should be left to the private sector. But the private sector is not equipped to handle such matters as content that could lead to religious or communal violence and fake news. The tendency is for governments to step in, with the inherent danger that some of these actions may be for political ends. George (2016) shows for example that 'political entrepreneurs' use hate speech to further their own ends, instead of calming communal tensions. Again, the multistakeholder model would be the most sensible approach to take.

Trade agreement for the digital economy

One area where the multistakeholder model could be productively deployed globally is in crafting an international agreement for the digital economy. The Trans Pacific Partnership (TPP) was to have been the model for just such an agreement. It was to be a trade agreement among 12 countries in the Pacific Rim, with the notable exclusion of China. It was a trailblazing agreement because it was the first trade agreement for the digital economy. It prohibited spam, customs duties on digital products, the forced disclosure of software source code and data localization (the requirement that data be stored locally). It required privacy protection for consumers, cooperation in cybersecurity and legal immunity of Internet Service Providers (ISPs). Practically all of these terms are deemed best practices by the industry but a number are not practiced by China, which rules out China as a party to the TPP (Ang, 2016b). Indeed, the TPP was intended to be a counterweight to the growing economic influence of China (Peterson, 2018).

The Trump Administration, however, pulled out of the agreement notwithstanding that the biggest beneficiary of the provisions on digital trade would be US companies. The other 11 countries proceeded to sign the agreement, renaming it the Comprehensive and Progressive Agreement for Trans-Pacific Partnership (CPTPP), after removing some provisions, particularly those on intellectual property (Yamazaki & Yasoshima, 2018). The provisions on intellectual property primarily benefit US companies and were among the most contentious provisions in the TPP. As with previous trade negotiations, the TPP was negotiated by government and business. Civil society as a stakeholder group was left out. Understandably, civil society activists viewed the agreement as one that was conducted in secrecy (Palit, 2013). The result was major protests when TPP negotiations were held in New Zealand. The 11 countries still hope for the United States to join the agreement and the removal of the intellectual property provisions was meant as an incentive to join. With the experience of the TPP, future discussions on trade agreements are likely to use the multistakeholder approach.

Future

The aforementioned shows the waxing and waning of the multistakeholder approach to Internet governance. Deploying such an approach will not necessarily guarantee a positive result. But not deploying it is much more likely to lead to a negative outcome. The multistakeholder approach confers legitimacy on the decision-making process and also gives some comfort that with a fuller discussion, one is less likely to make mistakes in policy.

But as the aforementioned historical account has shown, while many of the issues around Internet governance have been resolved, there are also many that have yet to be. Many of these concern geo-politics. A clash of visions of Internet governance, between the United States and China in particular, continues. China in effect is conducting a natural experiment: how long can one country govern its Internet using the traditional mode of governance? The Chinese economy is big but its population is even bigger. The theory here would strongly indicate that the future for the Chinese Internet will not be as bright because of the weaker governance model. The multistakeholder is the best model for regulating the Internet. Notwithstanding its weaknesses, the alternatives are worse.

At the national level, Internet governance will be subject to domestic politics. The regulation of Uber and Airbnb is instructive as countries respond depending on the strength of resistance. At the global level, the main forum to discuss Internet governance issues appeared to be under threat of closure. For two years in a row from 2017, no government has stepped forward to offer to host the conference. In the end, it was the UN who came forward, hosting the 2017 at the UN Office in Geneva, four days before Christmas and the 2018 IGF at the UNESCO building in Paris. The 2019 IGF was held in Berlin and the 2020 planned for Poland. A digital trade agreement may be one constructive way to demonstrate the utility of the multistakeholder model. It would be an interesting outcome to see how the governance process for the online world spills over to the offline world.

References

Ang, P. H. (2005). The Legacy of the Working Group on Internet Governance. In D. Butt (ed.), *Internet Governance: Asia-Pacific Perspectives*. Elsevier, pp. 9–17. https://www.academia.edu/443274/Internet_Governance_Asia_Pacific_Perspectives.

Ang, P. H., and Pang, N. (2016). Going Beyond Talk: Can International Internet Governance Work? *SSRN Electronic Journal*. https://doi.org/10.2139/ssrn.2809214.

Ang, P. H. (2016a). Transfer of Control a Boon to the Internet. *Straits Times*, October 4. www.straitstimes.com/opinion/transfer-of-control-a-boon-to-the-Internat.

Ang, P. H. (2016b). Starting a Digital Economy Trade Agreement. *Straits Times*, November 30. www.straitstimes.com/opinion/starting-a-digital-economy-trade-agreement.

Ang, P. H. (2017). Fake News: Regulate Only Elections? *Straits Times*, May 4. www.straitstimes.com/singapore/fake-news-regulate-only-during-elections.

BBC. (2013). Brazilian President Dilma Rousseff Calls Off US Trip. *BBC News*, September17. www.bbc.com/news/world-latin-america-24133161.

Boston Working Group. (1998). *Letter to Ira Magaziner and Becky Burr*, September 28. www.ntia.doc.gov/legacy/ntiahome/domainname/proposals/bosgrp/submission-letter.html.

Clinton, H. R., Secretary of State. (2010). *Remarks on Internet Freedom*. Washington, DC: The Newseum, January 21.

Clinton, William. 1997. Presidential Directive—Electronic Commerce. July 1. https://clintonwhitehouse4.archives.gov/textonly/WH/New/Commerce/directive.html.

Department of Commerce. 1997. Request for Comments on the Registration and Administration of Internet Domain Names. July 1. https://www.ntia.doc.gov/legacy/ntiahome/domainname/DN5NOTIC.htm.

Department of Commerce. 1998. Statement of Policy on the Management of Internet Names and Addresses. June 5. https://www.ntia.doc.gov/federal-register-notice/1998/statement-policy-management-internet-names-and-addresses.

Deutsche-Welle. (2017). China's Xi Jinping Urges Respect for 'Cyberspace Sovereignty' at Internet Summit. *Deutsche-Welle*, December 3. Permanent link https://p.dw.com/p/2oh08.

EU, Commission of the European Communities. (1998). *International Policy Issues Related to Internet Governance*. Communication from the Commission to the Council. Brussels, COM(1998) 111 final, February 20. Permanent link https://eur-lex.europa.eu/legal-content/EN/ALL/?uri=CELEX:51998DC0111.

Fenello, J. (1998). *Personal Observations: Singapore, on Balance*, August 14. www.domainhandbook.com/singapore.html.

Fraundorfer, M. (2017). Brazil's Organization of the NETmundial Meeting: Moving Forward in Global Internet Governance. *Global Governance*, 23, 503–552.

George, C. (2016). *Hate Spin: The Manufacture of Religious Offense and Its Threat to Democracy*. Cambridge, MA: MIT Press.

Greene, L. (1998). *Singapore Notes – August 14, 1998*, August 14. www.domainhandbook.com/singapore.html.

Haristya, S., and Ang, P. H. (2015). *Multistakeholderism and the Problem of Democratic Deficit.* Internet Governance Forum (IGF) 2015 Best Practice Forum (BPF) on Strengthening Multistakeholder Participation Mechanisms, December 5.

Hern, A. (2019). Revealed: Catastrophic Effects of Working as a Facebook Moderator. *The Guardian.* September 17. www.theguardian.com/technology/2019/sep/17/revealed-catastrophic-effects-working-facebook-moderator.

Lashinsky, A. (2015). Netscape IPO 20-Year Anniversary. *Fortune,* August 9. http://fortune.com/2015/08/09/remembering-netscape/.

Lessig, L. (2008). *Code.* New York: Basic Books.

Lev-Ram, M. (2018). Why Thousands of Human Moderators Won't Fix Toxic Content on Social Media. *Fortune,* March 22. http://fortune.com/2018/03/22/human-moderators-facebook-youtube-twitter/.

MacAskill, E., and Hern, A. (2018). Edward Snowden: 'The People Are Still Powerless, But Now They're Aware'. *The Guardian,* June 4. www.theguardian.com/us-news/2018/jun/04/edward-snowden-people-still-powerless-but-aware.

Margherio, Lynn. (undated). The Emerging Digital Economy. *Secretariat on Electronic Commerce.* U.S. Department of Commerce. https://www.commerce.gov/sites/default/files/migrated/reports/emergingdig_0.pdf.

McCarthy, K. (2014). ICANN Creates 'UN Security Council for the Internet', Installs Itself as a Permanent Member. *The Register,* November 7. www.theregister.co.uk/2014/11/07/Internat_un_security_council_net_mundial_initiative/.

McCarthy, K. (2016). NetMundial Finally Dies. *The Register,* August 29. www.theregister.co.uk/2016/08/29/netmundial_finally_dies/.

National Telecommunications and Information Administration. (1998). *Statement of Policy on the Management of Internet Names and Addresses* [Docket Number:980212036-8146-02]. Washington, DC: U.S. G.P.O., June 5. www.ntia.doc.gov/federal-register-notice/1998/statement-policy-management-Internat-names-and-addresses.

Palit, A. (2013). TPP and Intellectual Property: Growing Concerns. *Foreign Trade Review,* 48(1), 153–159. doi:10.1177/001573251204800109.

Parasie, N. (2016). Uber Halts Abu Dhabi Operations as Drivers Detained; The Ride-Hailing Company and Middle Eastern Competitor Careem Are Seeking Information About the Fate of Drivers Held by the Authorities. *Wall Street Journal,* August 29 [online]. https://search-proquest-com.ezlibproxy1.ntu.edu.sg/docview/1814720390?accountid=12665.

Peterson, M. (2018). A Glimpse of a Canadian-Led International Order. *The Atlantic,* January 24. www.theatlantic.com/international/archive/2018/01/new-tpp/551405/.

Purkayastha, P., and Bailey, R. (2014). U.S. Control of the Internet: Problems Facing the Movement to International Governance. *Monthly Review,* 66(3), 103–127, July–August.

Purnell, N. (2014). Uber Faces Scrutiny from Southeast Asia Regulators; Thailand, Vietnam and Singapore Examining Ride-Sharing App's Legality. *Wall Street Journal,* December 3 (online). https://search-proquest-com.ezlibproxy1.ntu.edu.sg/docview/1629546842?accountid=12665.

Prodhan, G. (2011). BRICs Push for Bigger Say in Running of Internet. *Reuters,* October 3. www.reuters.com/article/us-Internat-governance/brics-push-for-bigger-say-in-running-of-Internat-idUSTRE7923DH20111003.

Rodrik, D. (2012). *The Globalization Paradox.* Oxford: Oxford University Press.

Schechner, S., and Divac, N. (2015). German Court Bans Uberpop Ride-Sharing Service; French Raid Is Part of a Preliminary Inquiry into the Legality of the Cheaper Uberpop Service. *Wall Street Journal,* March 18 [online]. https://search-proquest-com.ezlibproxy1.ntu.edu.sg/docview/1664229255?accountid=12665.

Shackelford, S., and Alexander, F. (2018). China's Cyber Sovereignty: Paper Tiger or Rising Dragon? China Wants to Reshape the World's Internet in Its Own Image. *Asia & The Pacific Policy Society,* January 12. www.policyforum.net/chinas-cyber-sovereignty/.

Shu, C. (2014). China Tried to Get World Internet Conference Attendees to Ratify This Ridiculous Draft Declaration. *TechCrunch,* November 21. https://techcrunch.com/2014/11/20/worldinternetconference-declaration/.

United Nations. (2011). *Letter Dated 12 September 2011 from the Permanent Representatives of China, the Russian Federation, Tajikistan and Uzbekistan to the United Nations Addressed to the Secretary-General*, September 12. A/66/359. http://repository.un.org/bitstream/handle/11176/290564/A_66_359-EN.pdf?sequence=3&isAllowed=y.

United Nations General Assembly. (2013). *Statement by H.E. Dilma Rousseff, President of the Federative Republic of Brazil, at the Opening of the General Debate of the 68th Session of the United Nations General Assembly*, p. 2, September 24. http://gadebate. un.org/sites/default/files/gastatements/68/BR_en.pdf.

Whitaker, B. (2004). IQ Test. *The Guardian*, Monday, July 5. www.theguardian.com/world/2004/jul/05/iraq.technology.

Working Group on Internet Governance. (2005). *Report of the Working Group on Internet Governance*. Geneva: Working Group on Internet Governance.

Wu, T. (2013). *The Master Switch: The Rise and Fall of Information Empires*. New York: Vintage Books.

Yamazaki, J., and Yasoshima, R. (2018). Eleven Countries Sign Revamped TPP in Chile: Pacific Trade Deal Brought Back from the Brink After US Departure. *Nikkei Asian Review*, March 9. https://asia.nikkei.com/Politics/International-Relations/Eleven-countries-sign-revamped-TPP-in-Chile.

Zuboff, S. (2019). *The Age of Surveillance Capitalism: The Fight for a Human Future at the New Frontier of Power*. New York: Profile Books.

25

Property and the construction of the information economy

A neo-Polanyian ontology

Julie E. Cohen

This chapter considers the changing roles and forms of information property within the political economy of informational capitalism. I begin with an overview of the principal methods used in law and in media and communications studies, respectively, to study information property, considering both what each disciplinary cluster traditionally has emphasized and newer hybrid directions. Next, I develop a three-part framework for analyzing information property as a set of emergent institutional formations that both work to produce and are themselves produced by other evolving political-economic arrangements. The framework considers patterns of interest-driven reoptimization of existing legal institutions for intellectual property, but it also encompasses patterns of ownership and control over information resources that traditional intellectual property institutions had excluded. In particular, it considers the ongoing datafication of inputs to economic production and the platform-based logics of economic organization within which datafied resources (and rights asserted over those resources) are mobilized. Finally, I consider the implications of the framework for two very different contemporary information property projects, one relating to data flows within platform-based business models and the other to information commons.

Property's disciplinarities

Legal scholarship on information property traditionally has been concerned with internal justifications and has relied for the most part on methods broadly associated with liberal political theory.[1] Models of intellectual property rights derived from neoclassical economics and analytic philosophy have favored ideal, abstract forms organized around considerations such as the presumptive connection between appropriation and productive development (e.g., Landes & Posner, 2003) or that between exclusive control and minimization of information and transaction costs (e.g., Smith, 2007). Models derived from liberal political philosophy link exclusive control with protection of the creator's natural rights (e.g., Epstein, 2011). (Although the above-cited works all favor maximalist approaches to intellectual property protection, important work favoring more restrained approaches also emanates from each of these methodological traditions. Some economic theorists of intellectual property emphasize the positive spillovers that flow from limiting rightholder control (e.g., Frischmann & Lemley, 2007) and some political philosophers of intellectual property emphasize the liberty and speech interests of audiences and users (e.g., Gordon, 1993; Benkler, 1999).) Meanwhile, like critical legal theorists more generally, critical legal theorists of intellectual property have focused on deconstructing legal categories to expose their arbitrariness and illuminate the relationships between property and power (e.g., Boyle, 1998; Jaszi, 1994).

Investigations of information property by scholars who study media and communications, meanwhile, traditionally have tended to focus on the social and cultural effects of intellectual property regimes. Preferred methodologies span the social science toolkit but tend to be infused with framing insights from critical social theory. For example, media and communications scholars have explored the linkages between copyright ownership of media content and hegemonic control of meaning (e.g., Bettig, 1996). Other work on a diverse collection of intellectual property–related topics including piracy, appropriation art, and other user-generated content draws on scholarly traditions that emphasize reader recoding and resistance (e.g., Coombe, 1998).

Each cluster of disciplinarities has contributed usefully to the study of information property, but (as many of the above-cited authors themselves have ultimately concluded) that project demands a hybrid methodological approach that includes institutionalist, materialist, sociological, and political economic lenses. Property arrangements are socially embedded institutions that systematically structure the conditions of resource access and use (Fennell, 2013). Such institutions may assume a variety of configurations (Cohen, 2015), so although the property label packs an important rhetorical punch, it is also important to pay attention to scope-defining rules and operational details.

This point leads directly into consideration of materiality. Although the very existence of intellectual property protection makes plain that property does not simply reduce to materiality and can exist without it (or, alternatively, that under the right conditions, the label 'property' can be deployed to reify intangibles), differences in materiality do correlate to systematic differences in the design of property institutions for different resources (ibid.). The material properties of digital objects and communications networks, however, are highly configurable. Digital protocols have afforded new points of leverage for coding in control of informational goods, thereby elevating physical control as a key determinant of de facto propertization (Lessig, 1998; Gillespie, 2007). Both for this reason and because the material configurations of media artifacts and infrastructures have a range of other (anticipated and unanticipated) affordances (Boczkowski & Siles, 2014; Lievrouw, 2014), materiality must be reckoned with as an important factor shaping both user experiences and societal implications more generally.

Other considerations affecting the design of intellectual property institutions are sociological; institutions need to 'work' within the communities that rely on them, and institutions that work to the detriment of disempowered communities can create pressing social justice problems. A diverse collection of scholars has begun to study these issues from a variety of perspectives, exploring the ways that intellectual property law shapes the experiences and behaviors of creators, firms, and others in an increasingly networked and globalizing economy (e.g., Burk, 2016; Chon, 2006; Cohen, 2012; Gray et al., 2007; Schur, 2009; Silbey, 2015); and investigating movements for information commons and the communities that support them (e.g., Benkler, 2006; Coleman, 2013; Frischmann et al., 2014; Kelty, 2008).

Lastly, property institutions are situated within evolving systems of political economy, and both parts of that compound term are important to understanding how and why particular institutions work as they do. To begin with, property institutions and the constructs on which they rely reflect (perceived) imperatives flowing from prevailing modes of economic development, production, and organization. In practice, property constructs, therefore, often both reflect and elide considerations of power, simultaneously entrenching various forms of privilege and masking them with just-so stories about property, productivity, and virtue. Property institutions also may express a wider range of political values, however. So, for example, Joseph Singer (2011) observes that property is a dominant modality of governance in democratic societies and that institutions facilitating widely distributed home ownership, in particular, have been understood as furthering democratic self-government. Bill Herman (2013) has charted the process by which public interest coalitions became a permanent fixture within the copyright legislative landscape.

Building on these observations about method and perspective, the next section explores the evolving relationships between legal institutions for intellectual property and the political economy of informational capitalism.

Institutionalizing transformation: intellectual property and evolving political economy

One way to think about the relationship between information as property and the emergence of the information economy might be in simple, syllogistic terms: Just as the transition from agrarianism to industrialism appeared to demand the appropriation of natural resources and the unbridled commodification of labor, land, and money (Polanyi, 1957), so the transition from industrialism to informationalism (Castells, 1996; Schiller, 2007) now appears to require the appropriation and commodification of other important resources. The relationships between intellectual property institutions and larger dynamics of economic and sociotechnical (re)organization are more complex than that formulation suggests, however.

Among economic historians, a useful frame for understanding the emergence of industrial capitalism has been Karl Polanyi's (1957) analysis of a 'great transformation' in the system of political economy that not only involved large-scale appropriation of resources but also moved on conceptual and organizational levels. The basic factors of industrial production – labor, land, and money – were reconceptualized as commodities, while at the same time patterns of barter and exchange became detached from local communities and re-embedded in the constructed mechanism of 'the market.' It was these developments that lent both momentum and legitimacy to the large-scale enclosures of land, the displacement of populations, the development and deployment of machinery for industrial production, and the accompanying large-scale extraction of natural resources. Together, these appropriative, conceptual and organizational shifts produced a decisive movement toward a capitalist political economy. Then, when the resulting dislocations become too extreme, they prompted a 'protective countermovement' aimed at ameliorating their effects.

Extending Polanyi's analytical frame into the present era, it is useful to frame the emergence of informational capitalism in terms of three large-scale shifts that together constitute a decisive movement toward informational capitalism: the propertization (or enclosure) of intangible resources, the datafication of the basic factors of industrial production, and the embedding of patterns of barter and exchange within information platforms. Whether the effects of those changes will elicit a meaningful protective countermovement is yet to be seen. In a book from which this chapter is adapted (Cohen, 2019), I explore the legal-institutional dimensions of the movement to informational capitalism. Here, I focus on the ways that forms of information property both work to produce and are themselves produced by emerging economic arrangements.

Metamorphoses of 'intellectual property'

This section traces the evolution of the major systems of intellectual property protection over the course of the modern era, identifying three large trends. First, and predictably, legal protection for patents, copyrights, and trademarks has grown stronger, longer, and broader, while at the same time the justifications for granting protection have come to refer more directly to the motivations and presumed needs of production intermediaries and corporate brand owners. Second, the movement to an informational economy has produced large structural and conceptual shifts in the ways that rightholders understand, exploit, and value patents, copyrights, and trademarks; in brief, intellectual property rights have begun to behave in more uniform, predictable, and monetizable ways – that is, more like other components of corporate asset portfolios. Finally, the increasing diversity and value of information flows has prompted corresponding diversification in the landscape of recognized intellectual property entitlements.

From the beginning of the modern era, debates about patent and copyright policy have concerned the relationships between individual creators and production intermediaries – industrial firms on the patent side and publishers, motion picture producers, and record labels on the copyright side. That focus reflected practical realities: Although governments funded some large-scale scientific and technical research, industrial firms with access to capital assembled the research teams and the material resources needed to solve other kinds of large-scale technical problems and amassed the capital needed to manufacture and distribute the resulting industrial and consumer products. Similarly, before the advent of powerful desktop computing platforms put professional-quality editing capabilities within easy reach, access to specialized equipment was necessary to produce cultural goods in forms suitable for the mass market. Some cultural production was publicly funded, but much was not. Additionally, dissemination of creative outputs required access to printing presses, newsstands and bookstores, movie theaters, or broadcast airwaves.

It is unsurprising, then, that the patent and copyright regimes that evolved over the course of the 20th century were optimized to facilitate industrial production and dissemination of intangible goods. New treaties and statutes altered the scope of patents and copyrights in ways that favored powerful new industries, giving patentable subject matter broad and openended scope, redefining copyright to cover the by-products of new recording, broadcast, and computer technologies, and granting copyrights uniform and lengthy terms (Litman, 1989, 2001; Merges, 2000). Today, the patent and copyright regimes in force in developed countries (and extended via the world trade system to developing and least developed countries) contain broad, general rights and narrow, specific limitations that eliminate latitude for many nonprofit and downstream uses of copyrighted works and patented inventions. Assignment of economic interests in intellectual property from employees to employers is routine. (In the US copyright system, corporate employers own their employees' creations from the outset.)

Twentieth-century debates about intellectual property policy also reveal a gradual shift in the tenor of the prevailing justifications for granting patents and copyrights. Although policy debates continued to refer to the motivations of individual creators, new strands of justification began to emerge that emphasized the claims of intermediaries more directly. In Continental European copyright debates, the rhetoric of individual creatorship increasingly was deployed to justify control by intermediaries such as performing rights organizations. In the United States, whereas 19th-century instrumentalist rhetoric had emphasized the public benefits to be gained from underwriting progress in science and learning, the distinctive flavor of instrumentalism that developed over the course of the 20th century focused more narrowly on incentives to production. The turn to incentives provided a point of entry for express consideration of the incentives of the production intermediaries without which, as the argument went, many intangible intellectual goods would not be produced and distributed at all (e.g., Landes & Posner, 2003). Most recently, in disputes raising questions about harmonization with international intellectual property developments, some courts and commentators have evinced a willingness to abandon creator-centric rhetoric altogether, focusing instead on concerns about the balance of power in international trade.[2]

The changes to trademark law have been equally dramatic. Within the traditional hierarchy of intellectual property rights that emerged over the 19th and early 20th centuries, trademarks were inferior rights that served principally to protect against unfair diversion of trade, not to confer broad property entitlements operative regardless of context (McKenna, 2007). More recently, economic justifications for trademark protection have emphasized signaling to consumers about consistent product quality. By the early 20th century, however, brands and branding had begun to assume very different persuasive and performative functions. A prime mover in that shift was the nascent marketing industry, which envisioned its role as that of identifying desirable types of customers and devising more effective ways to reach them (Turow, 1997). The shift to persuasion gathered velocity as mass media markets and technologies evolved in ways that facilitated market segmentation (ibid.; Ang, 1991). Consumers on the receiving end of contemporary marketing strategies also came to understand brands and branding differently, as both tools for self-articulation and heuristics for social sorting. Today, brands and branding underwrite complex systems of performative and fundamentally social consumption, enabling consumers to signify class allegiance and to draw conclusions about others' allegiances and social status. Those systems reflect the deliberate efforts of marketers who seem to have internalized the core tenets of poststructuralist thought about the cultural construction of identity and meaning (Holt, 2004; McDonagh, 2015).

As the expressive power of corporate brands assumed ever-increasing importance, both the legal framework governing brand-related activities and the justifications for affording protection adapted in response, conferring on brand proprietors increasingly broad protection over brand atmospherics (Beebe, 2010; Tushnet, 2015). So, for example, although courts and commentators initially thought that trademarks reproduced on logo merchandise served purely aesthetic purposes, mark owners eventually convinced courts that most such reproductions signified sponsorship and therefore required authorization. That result effectively sheltered an increasingly broad web of licensing designed to encourage performative consumption and bolster brand-based reputational entitlements. Although courts and commentators initially characterized infringement lawsuits against down-market counterfeits as doctrinally and economically baseless, mark owners eventually convinced courts to find infringement based on a theory of 'post-sale confusion,' or cognitive dissonance resulting from the mismatch between luxury signifier and down-market context.

As intellectual property doctrine, theory, and rhetoric have evolved to emphasize the primacy of corporate claims, deeper conceptual and structural changes in those doctrines also have been underway. Although individual patents, copyrights, and trademarks remain the theoretical basic units of protection, the industrial organization of cultural and technical production increasingly emphasizes amassing intangible capital at scale (Benkler, 2002; Desai, 2012; Parchomovsky & Wagner, 2005). Portfolio-based intellectual property strategies in turn have begun to reshape legal doctrines. So, for example, as character copyrights have become cornerstones of merchandising campaigns, the test for character copyrightability has become correspondingly more lenient. As patent portfolios have become more central to competitive strategy in a variety of industries, courts have allowed claimants in certain industries to draft key enabling disclosures broadly and vaguely, and firms also have learned to practice selective disclosure in ways that both strengthen their own portfolio positions and disadvantage their competitors. Legal protection for trade dress – originally understood to mean specific packaging elements associated with a product or service – now provides broad protection for the 'look and feel' of products, services, and even business establishments (Lee & Sunder, 2017).

As important corporate assets increasingly have become informational in character, perceived needs for methods of defining and valuing legal entitlements in intangible intellectual goods also have begun to reshape other areas of law relating to such matters as secured finance, securities regulation, and taxation. Each of those fields values certainty and predictability in asset definition, which in turn shapes the claiming, licensing, and litigation strategies of firms that develop, use, and transact in intangibles. So, for example, many disputes about consumer-oriented exceptions and limitations to copyright have become disputes about the weight to be given to norms and practices favoring licensing of particular kinds of uses. Courts in patent validity disputes have developed ancillary tests that emphasize commercial success as an indicator of nonobviousness. Strict rules barring the licensing of trademarks without quality control and prohibiting transfers of marks without the accompanying business goodwill have been relaxed, allowing complex webs of franchising, merchandising, and co-branding to flourish.

A final important set of changes involves reconfiguration of intellectual property regimes' traditional boundaries. As intangible intellectual goods have become more varied, more important, and potentially more profitable, carefully delineated taxonomies of rights that originated in an earlier era have come to seem increasingly inadequate. New types of informational entitlements have mushroomed around the edges of existing regimes: prohibitions against trademark dilution and 'cybersquatting' that bolster the economic power of brand owners; regulatory entitlements that expand the window of exclusivity for patented pharmaceutical and biomedical products facing competition from generics; expanded rights in industrial design; and protections against 'circumvention' of copy-protection technologies that effectively shield proprietary media platforms from unauthorized access. Some intellectual property scholars have decried the loss of conceptual purity, but from a different perspective these developments are entirely predictable; confronted with claims of economic urgency, seemingly arbitrary doctrinal obstacles to diversification of legal entitlements in information goods have begun to melt away.

Reimagining inputs to production as (appropriable) data

Two subjects conspicuously absent from the preceding section's narrative of expansion, reconceptualization, and augmentation of existing systems of intellectual property protection are data and algorithms, both of which have proved powerfully resistant to formal propertization. According to centuries-old intellectual property formulations, facts and formulas are public property. As the movement to informational capitalism has gathered momentum, however, the three inputs that Polanyi identified as the basic factors of production in a capitalist political economy are undergoing a new process of transformation. The movement to an industrial economy reconstructed labor, land, and money as commodities; the movement to an informational economy is reconstructing labor, land, and money as dematerialized inputs to new and highly informationalized modes of profit extraction – that is, as data. Data flows representing labor, land, and money have been joined by a new and highly lucrative fourth factor of production: flows of personal information gathered from and about individuals and groups. Property formalism notwithstanding, these datafied resources are the subjects of active appropriation strategies that represent both economic and legal entrepreneurship.

As the movement to informational capitalism has gained velocity, finance has become both increasingly detached from the real-world activities that it originally served to enable and increasingly informationalized (Arrighi, 1994; Van der Zwan, 2014). Aided by rapid increases in processing power, investment bankers began using sophisticated computational models to devise more complex trades and trading algorithms and to develop new, ever more exotic financial instruments for 'securitizing' a wide variety of activities. Meanwhile, new forms of intermediation have disrupted and restructured financial markets. The rise of hedge funds and proprietary exchanges for exotic derivative instruments, as well as the emergence of opportunities for 'flash trading' in brief, technologically mediated windows of market advantage, has partially disintermediated conventional trading exchanges (Brummer, 2015). At the same time, large financial conglomerates have developed their own trading platforms and devised a variety of other information-based strategies for (re)positioning themselves as the intermediaries of choice (Chiu, 2016). Volumes of fee-generating, cashless transactions have skyrocketed, profiting both traditional banks and new payment intermediaries (Levitin, 2017; Servon, 2017). In all of these developments, a common denominator driving new profit strategies is privileged access to flows of information about trades and transactions.

Similar processes of dematerialization and financialization have produced dramatic changes in the conditions of labor. As digital communications networks have enabled just-in-time extraction of raw materials and automated, on-demand manufacturing and delivery, those changes have engendered new just-in-time labor contracting and scheduling practices. In similar fashion, service economy employers rely on forecasting algorithms and mobile communications technologies to retain, schedule, and release workers according to varying patterns of demand (Kalleberg, 2009). In the terminology used by scholars of information-era labor practices, the proletariat has given way to the precariat, an intermittently employed workforce that is retained and compensated on an as-needed basis (Standing, 2011). Most recently, high-profile, platform-based 'disruptors' of existing labor arrangements have emerged in a number of service-related industries. These entities call themselves 'information businesses,' rather than, for example, temporary employment agencies or transportation businesses, and insist that, except for the people they hire to write their code and conduct their government relations operations, they do not actually employ anyone. Their true business, they argue, is disintermediation; they are simply facilitating the emergence of a new, freelancer-driven economy that is nimbler, more cost-effective, and less impersonal. Yet they also are reintermediators, converting the labor of user-workers (and user-customers) into flows of monetizable data (Scholz, 2017).

Of the three Polanyian factors of industrial production, land might seem the most difficult to dematerialize. Yet land too has come to play an important role in the ongoing dematerialization and reconstruction of industrial-era resources as modular, highly informationalized assets. Consistent with the pattern of informationalized 'innovation' in financial markets generally, new digital information and communication technologies have enabled the creation of new and increasingly complex derivative instruments based on the payment streams from mortgage lending (Levitin & Wachter, 2012). Although the securitization process has slowed in the wake of the 2008 financial crisis, the volume of data-driven lending and securitization that preceded (and helped precipitate) the crisis means that, as a practical matter, significant interests in both residential and commercial real property remain highly datafied.

Law's role in these processes typically is characterized as passive or obstructive. Well-known narratives link each set of developments described previously to the disintermediation of traditional regulatory institutions. The datafication of finance gained momentum as financial regulators removed regulatory barriers to the movement of capital, including both laws that prevented banks from engaging in certain kinds of speculation with the funds entrusted to them and those that prevented cross-border speculation in nascent global financial markets (Arrighi, 1994; Krippner, 2012). Similarly, both platform-based work arrangements and older workforce management techniques relying on freelance and temporary labor route around many of the protections traditionally provided under labor and employment regimes to fulltime employees (De Stefano, 2016). The underwriters who concocted mortgage-backed securities viewed the fees imposed by local real property recording offices in the United States as a drag on financial innovation, so they created the Mortgage Electronic Recordation System (MERS), a privatized registry. When a MERS member bank purchased a mortgage loan, it would enter MERS in the local property register as the 'nominee of record' and pay the required fee just once, while MERS member banks continued to exchange the note among themselves in the course of successive rounds of securitization and trading (Levitin, 2013). The MERS system and its participants did not maintain good internal records, a situation that has made it nearly impossible to reconstruct chains of title for many securitized loans and the underlying real properties.

Narratives about legal obsolescence are inaccurate, however, because law and legal institutions also have played active roles in the construction of new datafied realities. Participants in the datafication of labor, land, and money have mobilized legal resources, most notably contracts law, to help create both new derivative investment instruments and new intermediation structures. Over time, some new trading strategies have become reified as financial instruments with distinct names, contours, and parameters; although contractual in origin, the new entities also have features that are property-like (Cohen, 2015). Similarly, ad hoc contracting practices requiring temporary workers to disclaim many of the obligations conventionally understood as indicia of traditional employment relationships have coalesced into regularized boilerplate agreements (De Stefano, 2016). MERS, a creature of contract and corporations law, has pursued a litigation strategy that amounts to demanding that courts bless its unusual approach to title transfer on efficiency grounds. Practices of mortgage resale and securitization also rely on prior acceptance of the idea of negotiability – that is, owning debt obligations as tradable assets (Cohen, 2019).

The emergence of a new, fourth dematerialized factor of production – data extracted from people – has followed a similar path. Strategies directed toward cultivation, harvesting, and appropriation of personal data have catalyzed sweeping reorganizations of sociotechnical activity and underlie the emergence of vast and lucrative new markets organized around data collection and predictive profiling (Zuboff, 2019). Participants in the personal data economy have constructed technical architectures and business strategies that route around the obstacles posed by privacy and data protection frameworks devised for an earlier era. Their activities both rely on and work to constitute a different type of enabling legal framework organized around the legal construct of a public domain: a repository of raw materials that are there for the taking and that are framed as inputs to particular types of productive activity (Cohen, 2017). As in the cases of labor, land, and money, participants in the personal data economy also mobilize a variety of contractual tools to order their dealings with data subjects and with each other.

Platforms and the organization of appropriation

The processes of datafication and appropriation described in the preceding section point toward a third dimension of the ongoing movement to informational capitalism, which is structural and organizational. In the industrial-era economy, the locus for activities of barter and exchange was the market, an idealized site of encounter between buyers and sellers within which the characteristics, quantities, and prices of goods and services were regulated autonomically by the laws of supply and demand. In the emerging informational economy, the locus for those activities is the platform, a site of encounter where interactions are materially and algorithmically intermediated. Vibrant and fast-growing literatures explore the power that platforms exert over economic exchange, social interaction, and public discourse. My goal in this section is the more modest one of teasing out the connections between platform logics and the emergent design of legal institutions for information property. As the perceived imperatives of access to data and to data processing capacity have sharpened, the platform has emerged as a key site of appropriation, and platform-driven cycles of dis- and re-intermediation have emerged as a recurring motif in information-economy narratives about competition, innovation, and access.

Over the past several decades, scholars in a wide variety of fields have identified networks and infrastructures as important organizing concepts for studying the information economy. A network is a mode of organization in which hubs and nodes structure the flows of transactions and interactions. Network organization is not a unique property of digital information and communications networks; rather, as network scientists have shown, such networks simply make visible a latent characteristic of the many human activities that rely on communication and interconnection (Barabasi, 2002). Digital information and communications networks do, however, reduce many of the costs and lag times formerly associated with such activities. In addition, participants in networks reap generalized benefits, or network externalities (Katz & Shapiro, 1994), as those networks grow in size and scale, and the relatively low costs of digital interconnection have enabled digital networks to become very large. Infrastructures are shared resources that facilitate downstream production of other goods (Frischmann, 2012). Roads and electric power grids, for example, play essential roles as inputs into a variety of downstream goods, as do less tangible resources like linguistic and scientific conventions. Notably, infrastructures may be managed as commons but need not be: some infrastructures, such as the interbank wire transfer system, are club goods financed and controlled by their members; others, such as local electric power suppliers, are managed as utilities and financed based on metered consumption charges; and still others, including facilities for Internet access in most countries, are privately provided but subject to various regulatory obligations. Digital information and communications technologies function both as infrastructures and as networks.

Platforms are not the same as networks, however, nor are they simply infrastructures (cf. Plantin et al., 2018). The intertwined functions that platforms provide – intermediation between would-be counterparties and legibility of users – have important antecedents in 20th-century direct marketing and advertising practices. In the late 1980s, as proprietary infrastructures for radio and television broadcast began to give way to a far more complex media ecosystem, the proliferation of cable channels and home video recording technologies lent momentum to emerging practices of targeted marketing (Ang, 1991). The opening of digital communications networks for commercial exploitation engendered the development of new, highly granular techniques for measuring audiences and predicting audience appeal (Bouk, 2017; Turow, 1997). Ultimately, the melding of digital architectures and commercial pressures for legibility produced a striking inversion. Twentieth-century mass-media intermediaries had purchased market research as a standalone service from third-party providers, but as legibility assumed increasing normative force as an overarching frame for commercial endeavor, the legibility function began to burrow into the core of the infrastructure itself. A world with a vast diversity of information sources required intermediation, and legibility became the essential function for an intermediary to provide.

Platforms represent infrastructure-based strategies for introducing friction into networks in the interest of maintaining and preserving their own legibility function. They are information-era formations in two distinct senses: they pursue profit strategies that revolve around information and information processing, and those strategies both rely on and reinforce the centrality of a particular set of sociotechnical predicate conditions involving networked, mediated, digital communication (Helmond, 2015; Srnicek, 2017). Platforms operate with the goal of making clusters of transactions and relationships stickier – sticky enough to adhere to the platform despite participants' theoretical ability to exit and look elsewhere for other intermediation options. To accomplish that goal, platforms must provide services that participants view as desirable and empowering, thereby generating and enabling participants to leverage network externalities. But they also must thwart certain other kinds of networking by developing and policing their own protocols for access. The latter power is one that the fictionalized construct of the market lacked, and it comprehensively reshapes the conditions of economic exchange.

The exchanges constituted by platforms are two- or multi-sided: they serve buyers, the sellers seeking to reach them, and often advertisers seeking the buyers' attention. Because the platform forms relationships with members of each group separately, it can define the terms of each relationship differently (Rochet & Tirole, 2006). So, for example, it can charge little or nothing to participants on one side of a target market and make its profit on another side. A dominant platform can reduce prices to one group – for example, book buyers or consumers of professional networking services – below marginal cost and still maintain its dominance by charging fees to some other group, and a provider of free services to consumers can attain and maintain dominance by controlling access to the 'market for eyeballs.'

From the perspective of users, a group that for purposes of this analysis includes individuals but also advertisers and niche platforms, dominant platforms in particular function in a manner analogous to utilities, supplying basic information services now deemed essential to a wide variety of economic and social activities. Users therefore may experience platform services as both empowering and generative (Gillespie, 2010). At the same time, users typically know very little about the way the intermediation provided by the platform actually works.

From the perspective of the platform, its business model instantiates both horizontal and vertical strategies for extracting the surplus value of user data. Because that goal requires large numbers of users generating large amounts of data, the platform provider's goal is to become and remain the indispensable point of intermediation for parties in its target markets (Srnicek, 2017). Platforms use a variety of strategies to attain commercial success and pursue commercial dominance, including co-branding, preferential placement, and interplatform affiliation. Because the principal worry for any platform is disintermediation by a would-be competitor, however, the root strategies for competitive positioning involve preserving privileged access to data and algorithms.

Emergent formations of information property: two stories

In this final section of the chapter, I examine two emergent formations of information property that exist in growing tension with one another: the movement toward appropriation and enclosure of data as an economic resource and the countermovement toward construction of information commons within which appropriation and enclosure are prohibited. This exercise suggests some additional insights into the processes by which new institutions for information property first begin to take shape and the conditions that they require to flourish. In each case, new institutions for information property emerge via routine, strategic interactions between interested parties – that is, via processes that are fundamentally performative. Parties to these interactions rely heavily on a different legal institution – contract – to define and formalize terms and conditions through which tropes of appropriation, enclosure, and secrecy are iterated and reiterated. Put differently, they are intellectual property entrepreneurs, seeking to define, propagate, and destabilize particular types of arrangements. The success or failure of these strategies depends to some extent on the content of the terms but far more on other, contextual factors.

Platform-based property strategies for data

Platform-based competitive strategies revolve fundamentally around control of access in two different and complementary senses. Platform users seek access to the essential social, commercial, and cultural connectivity that platforms provide, while platform providers seek access to the data necessary to create and sustain competitive advantage in their chosen field(s) of intermediation. The result is a bargain that appears relatively straightforward – access for data – but that in reality is complex and importantly generative. One important by-product of these access-for-data arrangements is a quiet revolution in the legal status of data as (de facto if not de jure) proprietary informational property.

Platforms use contracts systematically to facilitate and protect their own legibility function, extracting data from users but shielding basic operational knowledge from third-party vendors, users, and advertisers alike. The particular form of the access-for-data contract – a boiler-plate terms-of-use agreement not open to negotiation – asserts a correspondingly nonnegotiable authority over the conditions of access that operates in the background of even the most generative information-economy service. Boilerplate agreements are contractual in form but mandatory in operation, and so they are powerful tools for both private ordering of behavior and private reordering of even the most bedrock legal rights and obligations (Radin, 2013). Through the terms-of-use agreement, the platform asserts "exclusive control over the surface on which the exchange takes place" (Andersson Schwarz, 2017, 381).

Platform contracts themselves, of course, are 'only words' – and, for that matter, words that most users do not read – but they gain powerful normative force from both their continual assertion and reassertion and their propagation within environments that use technical protocols to define the parameters of permitted behavior. The combination of asserted contractual control and technical control becomes the vehicle through which the platform imposes its own logics on the encounters that it mediates. Commenting on the legal arrangements used to effectuate the dematerialization of labor in the informational economy, Martin Kenney and John Zysman (2016) analogize the platform model to the 'putting out' of prefabricated pieces for assembly that occurred early in the industrial era. As anyone who has ever assembled a piece of prefabricated furniture or a modular closet system knows, piecework makes certain types of goods more widely accessible, but it is also tyrannical as to form; its component parts are intended to be assembled only in particular, predetermined ways. Boilerplate access-for-labor instruments, consumer finance contracts, and others work in tandem with platform protocols to configure data flows derived from land, labor, money, and people as modular inputs to production and profit extraction.

From an intellectual property perspective, the hybrid contractual-technical arrangements crafted by platforms and other information intermediaries function as points of entry for institutional entrepreneurship targeting the form and substance of legal entitlements in information. In a process that is fundamentally performative, such arrangements step in where the map of formal legal entitlements ends, providing a vehicle for leveraging trade secrecy entitlements into de facto property arrangements operative against large numbers of people with no direct relationship with the platform owner. Dominant platforms, in particular, jealously guard access to both data collected from users and the algorithms used to process the data. They offer advertisers placement but never direct access to the data or algorithms themselves; they offer developers access to carefully curated data sets, data structures, and programming interfaces (Helmond, 2015); and they vigilantly police automated crawling and data extraction by would-be competitors.

Notably, traditional intellectual property rights play helpful but secondary roles in processes of de facto propertization, functioning as sources of leverage that can be invoked to channel would-be users toward entering the access-for-data bargain on the platform's terms and/or to prevent would-be competitors from gaining access to information stored on the platform by other means. For example, access to a branded exchange may enable third-party vendors to position their products and services as more desirable to consumers. When access to a platform requires technical interoperability – as is the case, for example, with apps for desktop and mobile operating systems – patents and copyrights can supply important points of leverage against unauthorized access by third-party vendors and would-be platform competitors. As the example of Google shows, however, not all platform businesses consider copyrights a necessary tool for limiting access.

In sum, the access-for-data arrangement is both a concrete bargain and a complex act of institutional entrepreneurship, with a number of interrelated implications for the intellectual property system that are still playing out. In addition to their other roles, platforms are in an important sense intellectual property entrepreneurs, working to refine, propagate, and normalize appropriation strategies that serve their economic interests.

Commons versus/and/as property institutions

The shift to an informational economy also has catalyzed a vibrant movement for informational commons. Formally, the label 'commons' denotes an institution for resource management that is structured around nondiscriminatory sharing within the community of members (Frischmann, 2012). Many different types of resources may be managed as commons, but the low costs of producing many types of information goods and distributing them via digital communications networks make possible new types of commons-based production arrangements as well (Benkler, 2006). For many, the emergence of networked information and communication technologies has seemed to promise a wholly new era in which cultural production by decentralized communities of peers would largely displace cultural production by the copyright industries. So far, however, although some commons movements have become well established (Creative Commons, 2017; Thakker et al., 2017), the full extent of that promise has yet to be realized.

The relationship between commons and property-based notions of exclusivity is complex and underexplored. According to one well-known definition, commons are the opposite of property in the sense that 'no single person has exclusive control over the use and disposition of any particular resource in the commons' (Benkler, 2006, 61). That formulation is compelling but also somewhat misleading. Commons is the opposite of exclusivity in the sole-ownership sense, but both arrangements are types of property institutions. Notably, institutions organized as commons may exclude nonmembers from resource access and use, and may invoke notions of property to sanction and even exclude entirely those who attempt to benefit from access without accepting the accompanying obligations.

Institutions for commons-based resource management persist over time only if their rules effectively govern members' behavior and prevent defection. For this reason, most successful examples outside the informational context involve localized resources managed by small, well-defined groups (Ostrom, 1990). Within the networked digital environment, however, the same conditions that enable distributed production of information goods also have enabled construction of distributed institutions for commons-based management using legal instruments designed to help the terms and conditions spread virally. The two most prominent examples are the free/libre open-source licensing system (F/LOSS) and Creative Commons, both self-consciously framed as efforts to develop sustainable, 'copyleft' alternatives to existing copyright-based institutions. As in the case of platform-based propertization strategies, legal instruments for distributed commons-based management take the form of boilerplate restrictions that are contractual in form but mandatory in operation. As developed and pioneered by the open-source software movement, this strategy was self-consciously mimetic, relying on constructs of authorial control and take-it-or-leave-it licensing. For exactly those reasons, it has occasioned soul-searching among advocates for information commons (e.g., Dusollier, 2006; Elkin-Koren, 2005).

Thoughtful design and continual reiteration of narratives about boilerplate enforceability, however, are not the only determinants of success; materiality and economic organization also matter. Within both technical and cultural communities, powerful constituencies have resisted the viral spread of information commons (e.g., Pfaffenberger, 2000; Sporkin, 2011). In the open-source licensing context, persistent, thorny issues surround the interfaces between open-source and proprietary systems and modules. Open-source communities have wrestled publicly with questions about how far proprietary incorporation of open modules should be allowed to proceed before triggering viral licensing provisions; as a result, different versions of the major license agreements take different approaches to important issues (for a summary, see Ilardi, 2014). In the cultural context, dominant producers of popular culture for the most part do not wish to relinquish control over their products to the full extent demanded even by the most protective versions of the Creative Commons license. Because cultural network effects are weaker than coded interoperability protocols, the Creative Commons model has been incapable of compelling viral spread in the same manner and to the same extent as the open-source licensing model has done.

Both the open-source licensing movement and the Creative Commons movement also confront other ongoing challenges rooted in the material logics of the platform-based economy. As discussed previously, although networked digital communications infrastructures do enable distributed peer production, they also are highly configurable. Therefore, they have proved well-suited to strategies of reorganization, appropriation, and enclosure via platform-based business models (Cohen, 2019). The shift toward platformization has rippled through both technical and cultural production. Most obviously, platform logics facilitate efforts to control flows of proprietary cultural content; for example, dedicated platforms like Netflix or Hulu need not carry Creative Commons content, and zero-rating initiatives by access providers that privilege sources of proprietary content can effectively deprioritize other content. Open-source software has attained a more durable foothold, but access-control strategies based on patenting, on copyright control of application programming interfaces, and on digital rights management tend to be implemented in ways that are incompatible with the open-source ethos. Platform logics also have implications for new initiatives based on open content and/or data; such efforts sometimes have found themselves confronting appropriation and enclosure after taking root in user communities (Pessach, 2016).

A final set of complications confronting movements for information commons is political, and flows from the fact that commons and users' rights are not equivalent. As noted earlier, institutions designed as commons do not inevitably afford their members open-ended grants of users' rights. This is easiest to see in the case of commons that are constituted for the benefit of particular, well-defined groups, such as the grazing and water rights collectives studied by Ostrom (1990). In such institutions, the parameters of permitted access and use are strictly defined. Even in more widely dispersed commons regimes, however, users may not ignore the rules established by the governing institutions for those regimes. For example, someone who wants to violate the rules of an open-source license will not be able to rely on his or her license for permission, but will need to mount a challenge based on the background copyright law. Users' rights, meanwhile, generally are conceptualized as limited exceptions for personal private use that must be claimed on a case-by-case basis, rather than as common privileges automatically available to all (Litman, 2001).

These differences between commons and users' rights have created both political fragmentation and moral hazard (Elkin-Koren, 2005). Movements organized around users' rights, and particularly around peer-to-peer file-sharing and open entertainment platforms, have struggled to earn the approval of courts and policymakers. Many such movements now are explicitly framed as counter-movements in a way that many of the most high-profile and successful commons movements are not. Meanwhile, the copyleft movements' deliberate reliance on the antiradical rhetorics of authorial choice (in the case of Creative Commons) and business-friendly utility (in the case of some, though not all, open-source communities) have been important factors enabling them to take root and flourish. The result is that users' rights groups and commons movements do not always speak with a unified voice in copyright reform debates, a situation that has made the most lasting reforms advocated by both groups more difficult to achieve.

Conclusion

Information property institutions are not neutral tools for welfare maximization, as many economists and economically inclined legal scholars would have it, nor are they simply instrumentalities of hegemonic control, to paraphrase an oft-repeated refrain in media studies and critical legal studies. They play central roles in the evolving articulation of informational capitalism as a system of political economy, and in so doing they shape the evolution of both media content and media infrastructures. At the same time, the evolution of informational capitalism calls forth new propertization strategies and channels those strategies in particular ways. The examples of appropriated data flows and information commons illustrate two very different paths that process has taken.

Notes

1 Here I am acutely conscious of having left many important works and scholars out. A full list would go on for much longer; unfortunately, however, word limits prevent this chapter from doing so.
2 See, for example, Golan v. Holder, 132 S. Ct. 873, 889 (2012) ("Full compliance with Berne, Congress had reason to believe, would expand the foreign markets available to U.S. authors and invigorate protection against piracy of U.S. works abroad, thereby benefitting copyright-intensive industries stateside and inducing greater investment in the creative process.").

References

Andersson Schwarz, J. (2017). Platform Logic: The Need for an Interdisciplinary Approach to the Platform Economy. *Policy and Internet*, 9(4), 374–394.

Ang, I. (1991). *Desperately Seeking the Audience*. New York: Routledge.

Arrighi, G. (1994). *The Long Twentieth Century: Money, Power, and the Origins of Our Times*. New York: Verso.

Barabasi, A.-L. (2002). *Linked: The New Science of Networks*. Cambridge, MA: Perseus Publishing.

Beebe, B. (2010). Intellectual Property Law and the Sumptuary Code. *Harvard Law Review*, 123(4), 809–889.

Benkler, Y. (1999). Free as the Air to Common Use: First Amendment Constraints on the Enclosure of the Public Domain. *New York University Law Review*, 74(2), 354–446.

Benkler, Y. (2002). Intellectual Property and the Organization of Information Production. *International Review of Law and Economics*, 22(1), 81–107.

Benkler, Y. (2006). *The Wealth of Networks*. New Haven: Yale University Press.

Bettig, R. V. (1996). *Copyrighting Culture: The Political Economy of Intellectual Property*. Boulder, CO: Westview Press.

Boczkowski, P. J., and Siles, I. (2014). Steps Toward Cosmopolitanism in the Study of Media Technologies: Integrating Scholarship on Production, Consumption, Materiality, and Content. In T. Gillespie, P. J. Boczkowski, and K. A. Foot (eds.), *Media Technologies, Essays on Communication, Materiality, and Society*. Cambridge, MA: MIT Press, pp. 53–76.

Bouk, D. (2017). The History and Political Economy of Personal Data Over the Last Two Centuries in Three Acts. *Osiris*, 32(1), 1–22.

Boyle, J. A. (1998). *Shamans, Software, and Spleens: Law and the Construction of the Information Society.* Cambridge, MA: Harvard University Press.

Brummer, C. (2015). Disruptive Technology and Securities Regulation. *Fordham Law Review*, 84(3), 977–1052.

Burk, D. L. (2016). On the Sociology of Patenting. *Minnesota Law Review*, 101(2), 421–452.

Castells, M. (1996). *The Rise of the Network Society.* New York: Wiley-Blackwell.

Chiu, I. H.-Y. (2016). Fintech and Disruptive Business Models in Financial Products, Intermediation and Markets: Policy Implications for Financial Regulators. *Journal of Technology Law and Policy*, 21(1), 55–112.

Chon, M. (2006). Intellectual Property and the Development Divide. *Cardozo Law Review*, 95(2), 2821–2912.

Cohen, J. E. (2012). *Configuring the Networked Self: Law, Code, and the Play of Everyday Practice.* New Haven: Yale University Press.

Cohen, J. E. (2015). Property as Institutions for Resources: Lessons from and for IP. *Texas Law Review*, 94(1), 1–57.

Cohen, J. E. (2017). The Biopolitical Public Domain: The Legal Construction of Informational Capitalism. *Philosophy and Technology.* http://dx.doi.org/10.1007/s13347-017-0258-2.

Cohen, J. E. (2019). *Between Truth and Power: The Legal Constructions of Informational Capitalism.* New York: Oxford University Press.

Coleman, E. G. (2013). *Coding Freedom: The Ethics and Aesthetics of Hacking.* Princeton, NJ: Princeton University Press.

Coombe, R. (1998). *The Cultural Life of Intellectual Properties: Authorship, Appropriation, and Law.* Durham, NC: Duke University Press.

Creative Commons. (2017). *State of the Commons 2016.* https://stateof.creativecommons.org/.

De Stefano, V. (2016). The Rise of the 'Just-in-Time' Workforce: On-Demand Work, Crowdwork, and Labor Protection in the 'Gig-Economy'. *Comparative Labor Law and Policy Journal*, 37(3), 471–504.

Desai, D. R. (2012). From Trademarks to Brands. *Florida Law Review*, 64(4), 981–1044.

Dusollier, S. (2006). The Master's Tools v. the Master's House: Creative Commons v. Copyright. *Columbia Journal of Law and the Arts*, 29(3), 101–123.

Elkin-Koren, N. (2005). What Contracts Can't Do: The Limits of Private Ordering in Facilitating a Creative Commons. *Fordham Law Review*, 74(2), 375–422.

Epstein, R. (2011). What Is so Special About Intellectual Property? The Case for Intelligent Carryovers. In G. D. Manne and J. D. Wright (eds.), *Competition Policy and Patent Law Under Uncertainty: Regulating Innovation.* New York: Cambridge University Press, pp. 42–74.

Fennell, L. A. (2013). The Problem of Resource Access. *Harvard Law Review*, 126, 1471–1531.

Frischmann, B. M. (2012). *Infrastructure: The Social Value of Shared Resources.* New York: Oxford University Press.

Frischmann, B. M., and Lemley, M. A. (2007). Spillovers. *Columbia Law Review*, 107(1), 257–302.

Frischmann, B. M., Madison, M. J., and Strandburg, K. J. (2014). *Governing Knowledge Commons.* New York: Oxford University Press.

Gillespie, T. (2007). *Wired Shut: Copyright and the Shape of Digital Culture.* Cambridge, MA: MIT Press.

Gillespie, T. (2010). The Politics of 'Platforms'. *New Media & Society*, 12(3), 347–364.

Gordon, W. J. (1993). A Property Right in Self-Expression: Equality and Individualism in the Natural Law of Intellectual Property. *Yale Law Journal*, 102(7), 1533–1609.

Gray, J., Sandvoss, C., and Harrington, C. Lee. (2007). *Fandom: Identities and Communities in a Mediated World.* New York: New York University Press.

Helmond, A. (2015). The Platformization of the Web: Making Web Data Platform Ready. *Social Media and Society.* doi:10.1177/2056305115603080.

Herman, B. D. (2013). *The Fight Over Digital Rights: The Politics of Copyright and Technology.* New York: Cambridge University Press.

Holt, D. B. (2004). *How Brands Become Icons: The Principles of Cultural Branding.* Cambridge, MA: Harvard Business School Press.

Ilardi, T. J. (2014). Client Counseling for Common OSS Licensing Problems. *The Computer and Internet Lawyer*, 31(12), 1–18.

Jaszi, P. (1994). On the Author Effect: Contemporary Copyright and Collective Creativity. In M. Woodmansee and P. Jaszi (eds.), *The Construction of Authorship: Textual Approaches in Law and Literature.* Durham, NC: Duke University Press, pp. 29–56.

Kalleberg, A. L. (2009). Precarious Work, Insecure Workers: Employment Relations in Transition. *American Sociological Review*, 74, 1–22, February.

Katz, M. L., and Shapiro, C. (1994). Systems Competition and Network Effects. *Journal of Economic Perspectives*, 8(2), 93–115.

Kelty, C. M. (2008). *Two Bits: The Cultural Significance of Free Software.* Durham, NC: Duke University Press.

Kenney, M., and Zysman, J. (2016). The Rise of the Platform Economy. *Issues in Science and Technology*, 32(3), 61.

Krippner, G. (2012). *Capitalizing on Crisis: The Political Origins of the Rise of Finance.* Cambridge, MA: Harvard University Press.

Landes, W. M. and Posner, R. A. (2003). *The Economic Structure of Intellectual Property Law.* Cambridge, MA: Harvard University Press.

Lee, P., and Sunder, M. (2017). The Law of Look and Feel. *Southern California Law Review*, 90(3), 529–92.

Lessig, L. (1998). *Code and Other Laws of Cyberspace.* New York: Basic Books.

Levitin, A. J. (2013). The Paper Chase: Securitization, Foreclosure, and the Uncertainty of Mortgage Title. *Duke Law Journal*, 63(3), 637–734.

Levitin, A. J. (2017). Pandora's Digital Box: The Promise and Perils of Digital Wallets. *University of Pennsylvania Law Review*, 166(2), 305–376.

Levitin, A. J., and Wachter, S. M. (2012). Explaining the Housing Bubble. *Georgetown Law Journal*, 100(4), 1177–1258.

Lievrouw, L. A. (2014). Materiality and Media in Communication and Technology Studies: An Unfinished Project. In T. Gillespie et al. (eds.), *Media Technologies, Essays on Communication, Materiality, and Society.* Cambridge, MA: MIT Press, pp. 21–52.

Litman, J. (1989). Copyright, Compromise, and Legislative History. *Oregon Law Review*, 68(2), 275–362.

Litman, J. (2001). *Digital Copyright.* Amherst, NY: Prometheus Books.

McDonagh, L. (2015). From Brand Performance to Consumer Performativity: Assessing European Trademark Law After the Rise of Anthropological Marketing. *Journal of Law and Society*, 42(4), 611–638.

McKenna, M. P. (2007). The Normative Foundations of Trademark Law. *Notre Dame Law Review*, 82(5), 225–294.

Merges, R. P. (2000). One Hundred Years of Solicitude, Intellectual Property Law, 1900–2000. *California Law Review*, 88(6), 2187–2240.

Ostrom, E. (1990). *Governing the Commons: The Evolution of Institutions for Collective Action.* New York: Cambridge University Press.

Parchomovsky, G., and Wagner, R. P. (2005). Patent Portfolios. *University of Pennsylvania Law Review*, 154(1), 1–78.

Pessach, G. (2016). Beyond IP – The Cost of Free: Informational Capitalism in a Post IP Era. *Osgoode Hall Law Review*, 54(1), 225–251.

Pfaffenberger, B. (2000). The Rhetoric of Dread: Fear, Uncertainty, and Doubt (FUD) in Information Technology Marketing. *Knowledge, Technology and Policy*, 13(3), 78–92.

Plantin, J.-C., Lagoze, C., Edwards, P. N., and Sandvig, C. (2018). Infrastructure Studies Meet Platform Studies in the Age of Google and Facebook. *New Media and Society*, 20(1), 293–301.

Polanyi, K. (1957). *The Great Transformation: The Political and Economic Origins of Our Time.* Boston, MA: Beacon Press.

Radin, M. J. (2013). *Boilerplate: The Fine Print, Vanishing Rights, and the Rule of Law.* Princeton, NJ: Princeton University Press.

Rochet, J.-C., and Tirole, J. (2006). Two-Sided Markets: A Progress Report. *RAND, Journal of Economics*, 37(3), 645–667.

Schiller, D. (2007). *How to Think About Information*. Urbana: University of Illinois Press.

Scholz, T. (2017). *Uberworked and Underpaid: How Workers Are Disrupting the Digital Economy*. New York: Polity Press.

Schur, R. D. (2009). *Parodies of Ownership: Hip-Hop Aesthetics and Intellectual Property Law*. Ann Arbor: University of Michigan Press.

Servon, L. (2017). *The Unbanking of America: How the Middle Class Survives*. New York: Houghton Mifflin Harcourt.

Silbey, J. (2015). *The Eureka Myth: Authors, Innovators, and Everyday Intellectual Property*. Stanford: Stanford University Press.

Singer, J. (2011). Property Law as the Infrastructure of Democracy. In M. Allen Wolf (ed.), *Powell on Real Property*. New Providence, NJ: Lexis-Nexis Publishing, pp. 11–17.

Smith, H. E. (2007). Intellectual Property as Property: Delineating Entitlements in Information. *Yale Law Journal*, 116(8), 1742–1822.

Sporkin, A. (2011). *Publishers Applaud 'Research Works Act,' Bipartisan Legislation to End Government Mandates on Private-Sector Scholarly Publishing*. Association of American Publishers, December 23. www.webcitation.org/64VQfm6rv?url=www.publishers.org/press/56/.

Srnicek, N. (2017). *Platform Capitalism*. Malden, MA: Polity Press.

Standing, G. (2011). *The Precariat: The New Dangerous Class*. London: Bloomsbury.

Thakker, D., Schireson, M., and Nguyen-Ha, D. (2017). Tracking the Explosive Growth of Open-Source Software. *TechCrunch*, April 17. https://techcrunch.com/2017/04/07/tracking-the-explosive-growth-of-open-source-software/.

Turow, J. (1997). *Breaking Up America: Advertisers and the New Media World*. Chicago: University of Chicago Press.

Tushnet, R. (2015). Stolen Valor and Stolen Luxury: Free Speech and Exclusivity. In H. Sun, Barton Beebe and M. Sunder (eds.), *The Luxury Economy and Intellectual Property: Critical Reflections*. New York: Oxford University Press, pp. 121–143.

Van der Zwan, N. (2014). Making Sense of Financialization. *Socio-Economic Review*, 12, 99–129.

Zuboff, S. (2019). *The Age of Surveillance Capitalism: The Fight for a Human Future at the New Frontier of Power*. New York: Polity Press.

26

Globalization and post-globalization

Terry Flew

Globalization is a concept with deep roots in communication and media scholarship. Definitions of globalization generally refer to its relationship to changes in consciousness and experience that arise from access to global communication technologies. This is seen in the highly influential definitions of authors such as Anthony Giddens, Roland Robertson, and David Held and Anthony McGrew:

> Globalization can . . . be defined as the intensification of worldwide social relations which link distant localities in such a way that local happenings are shaped by events occurring many miles away and vice versa.
>
> *(Giddens, 1990, 64)*

> Globalization as a concept refers both to the compression of the world and the intensification of consciousness of the world as a whole . . . both concrete global interdependence and consciousness of the global whole.
>
> *(Robertson, 1992, 8)*

> Globalization . . . denotes the expanding scale, growing magnitude, speeding up and deepening impact of transcontinental flows and patterns of social interaction. It refers to a shift or transformation in the scale of human organization that links distant communities and expands the reach of power relations across the world's regions and continents.
>
> *(Held & McGrew, 2002, 1)*

Many of the most famous metaphors of globalization have their roots in communication. Marshall McLuhan's famous concept of the 'global village' foresaw the relationship of broadcasting to globalization as one where "electric circuitry has overthrown the regime of 'time' and 'space' and pours over us instantly and continuously the concerns of all others" (McLuhan & Fiore, 1967, 16). More recently, the Catalan sociologist Manuel Castells defined the global network society as arising in the first instance out of digitally networked media and communication technologies. For Castells, the economic base of the network society as the informational mode of development is one where "the source of productivity lies in the technology of knowledge generation, information processing, and symbol communication" (1996, 17). This "new information technology paradigm provides the material basis for its pervasive expansion throughout the entire social structure" (1996, 469). Castells also proposed that cultures are defined primarily through their dominant communication technologies, "because culture is mediated and enacted through communication, cultures themselves . . . become fundamentally transformed . . . by the new technological system" (1996, 328).

In considering the significance of globalization in the field of digital media and communication studies, three issues present themselves as being of fundamental importance. The first is whether globalization marks an unprecedented era of human history – the strong globalization thesis – or whether it is symptomatic of the evolution of other historical forces, such as the development of capitalism. Examples of strong globalization claims include Ulrich Beck's argument that "globality is an unavoidable condition of human intercourse at the close of the twentieth century" (2000, 15), or Anthony Giddens' argument that globalization marks "a shift in our very life circumstances" (2002, 19). Strong globalization arguments typically see a fully integrated global political-economic system as having developed through global networks of technology and communication, with a series of associated changes, including markets now operating on a global, real-time scale, the declining power of nation-states, and a shift in cultural identities away from nationalism toward hybridized and non-territorial forms of belonging and solidarity (e.g., Piertese, 2015). By contrast, critics of such strong globalization theories would argue that global interconnectedness has been a feature of global capitalism going back at least as far as the 15th century, and much of what is deemed as novel and unprecedented has clear antecedents. Arif Dirlik has argued that "if globalization means anything, it is the incorporation of societies globally into a capitalist modernity" (2003, 275), while Hirst et al. (2009) argued that the current phase of global economic interconnectedness and the mass migration of people have a clear historical parallel in the period from 1870 to 1914.

The second question concerns the explanatory power that we attribute to the media as a driver of globalization. Media is clearly important to globalization. The technical infrastructures through which information is circulated globally have generally been provided by media companies, and the content through which we develop cultural identities and make sense of other peoples and societies around the globe is provided to us by media. If we follow Winseck (2011) and define media companies broadly to include telecommunications, Internet, and ICT companies, then these corporations are clearly at the forefront of global expansion. The 2019 Interbrand survey of the world's top 100 global brands placed ten such companies among the top 20: Apple (number 1), Google (2), Amazon (3), Microsoft (4), Samsung (6), Disney (10), Intel (13), Facebook (14), Cisco (15), Oracle (18), and SAP (20).

But this raises a methodological question around media-centric modes of explanation. The influence of critical theory on mass communication studies was to demand that empirical research be better grounded in social theory, but this in turn raised the question of what theory. For one of the most important early approaches to global communication studies, which was the political economy approach pioneered by Herbert Schiller, the accompanying social theories were dependency theories of global political economy and theories of cultural imperialism pioneered by Latin American cultural scholars (Miller & Kraidy, 2016, 26–32). More recently, communications researchers such as Grabe and Myrick (2016) have posited the need for a media-centric approach to analyzing citizen participation in political life, as conventional political theory routinely underestimates the significance of entertainment media, 'soft news,' and visual culture in the formation of affective publics engaging in political action. By contrast, David Morley (2009) has explicitly called for a non-media-centric approach to media studies, which questions sharp divides between 'old' and 'new' media, and material and 'virtual' culture, and asks sociologically sharper questions about whose lived experiences are being transformed by global communications and media flows.

A final question concerns what we now mean by the media. Historical accounts of mass media often equate the rise of print media with the formation of nation-states as they required common national languages and broadcasting with the formation of national cultures arising from the capacity of such media to generate unifying populations through media events that have a 'space binding' influence (Gorman & McLean, 2009). From this perspective, the Internet marks a systemic break between 20th-century mass communication media and what Castells (2009) was termed the 'mass-self-communication' of the 21st century, that is global, bottom-up, distributed, and facilitated by digital platforms such as Facebook and YouTube, in contrast to the top-down, highly concentrated and territorially bound broadcast model.

At the same time, it is apparent that this dichotomy greatly oversimplifies what is occurring in media systems around the world. Traditional media providers have a very significant presence online, and as they have adopted convergent multi-platform distribution models, audiences have been drawn to their professionally produced content and away from more amateur, DIY media and so-called fake news, as long as they can access that content at any time and on any platform or device. While it is early days in researching online user preferences for local content, significant studies (e.g., Taneja & Wu, 2014) suggest that in key global markets such as India and China, users are showing a strong preference for locally produced online material, which has parallels with the long-observed tendency for local audiences to prefer local broadcast content (Xu et al., 2013). Finally, nation-states continue to play a significant role in regulating online media spaces. This has long been apparent in countries where media content restrictions have parallels in other forms of restriction on cultural expression on religious, political, or other grounds, such as China, Iran, and Saudi Arabia. But a preparedness to set territorially based laws on Internet content providers has become apparent in many parts of the world (Flew & Waisbord, 2015), with the European Union's rules around data privacy, the 'right to be forgotten,' and other laws and regulations marking a significant intervention in the operating environment of global Internet companies such as Google and Facebook (Holt & Malčić, 2015). This points to a more general question about the continuing significance of nation-states and national media systems in the context of globalization.

Paradigms for understanding global media and communication

The historical roots of global communications studies reside in two sources. First, there is the tradition of communication technology studies associated with authors such as Canadian communication scholars Harold Innis (1991) and Marshall McLuhan (1964; cf. McLuhan & Fiore, 1967). This tradition has placed a particular importance on both the historical and the geographical dimensions of different media technologies. It is notable because, with a relatively small number of exceptions (e.g., Robins & Morley, 1995; Adams, 2009), an interest in the relationship of media to geography has been relatively weak, particularly when compared to the extensive scholarship on the role played by media in historical change, such as its relationship to modernity, the development of capitalism, and the rise of nation-states (Thompson, 1995).

The second major source of influence has been development communication. Hamid Mowlana has made the point that the first US-sponsored communications programs established in developing countries were different to those on US campuses at the time, in that they were not focused upon mass communication studies or particularly interested in establishing communication as a stand-alone social science discipline. Rather, they were a part of highly interdisciplinary programs "relating to and drawing from fields as diverse as economics, international studies, politics, sociology, psychology, literature and history" (Mowlana, 2012, 272). Their focus was primarily on developing leadership communication skills for elites and on the process of public opinion formation, in the context of the geopolitical struggle for global influence between the United States and the Soviet Union.

Early work in development communication was strongly influenced by the modernization paradigm of development, which attributed underdevelopment to adverse cultural factors such as the influence of traditions that discouraged social mobility and entrepreneurial achievement. The sources of underdevelopment were typically seen as internal to the countries and regions themselves, and modernization was explicitly understood as "the process of change towards those types of social, economic, and political systems that have developed in Western Europe and North America" (Eisenstadt, 1966, 1). The modernization paradigm drew upon the sociology of Max Weber, particularly his notion of a modern 'mental type,' and the idea that the "spirit of capitalism has had to struggle [with] . . . that type of attitude . . . which we may designate as traditionalism" (1978, 59). With regard to the media, broadcasting in particular was seen as a modernizing force in developing countries, which could communicate the values and attitudes associated with modernity, as well as building a sense of a shared national identity aligned with development goals.

Critical political economists such as Herbert Schiller (1969, 1976), Oliver Boyd-Barrett (1977), and others critiqued the modernization paradigm as simply reinforcing the power of domestic political and economic elites in the service of dominant Western interests. In contrast to the focus on internal factors found in modernization theories, these authors drew attention to the structural inequalities of the global capitalist system. They drew upon the work of dependency theorists such as Immanuel Wallerstein (1974), who argued that the capitalist world-system as it had evolved since the 15th century was founded upon relations of dependency and exploitation between the 'core' nations of Europe – and, later, the United States – and the colonized periphery of the Third World. While the post–WWII period had seen decolonization and the rise of independence movements throughout Asia, Africa, Latin America, the Middle East, and the Caribbean, what had been subsequently developing was neo-colonialism based upon economic power more than political force. It was argued that the ruling elites in developing nations, who for the most part had control over the media, were more closely aligned to global elites than to their own people. In this regard, the media were seen as forces promoting cultural imperialism (Schiller, 1976) in developing nations, as well as promoting and facilitating the dominance of Western political and economic interests and the desire of corporations to expand their global market reach.

The rise of the critical political economy paradigm as an alternative to modernization theory greatly sharpened the methodological questions associated with global media and communication. Of the many questions opened up in the field of global media and communication studies, three are worth exploring. First, there was the question of whether the world's media was in fact dominated by Western content. The UNESCO study by Nordenstreng and Varis (1974) found that over half of the world's television content was imported from a very small number of Western countries, with the United States accounting for about 90% of imported entertainment content. But a subsequent study by Varis (1984) found that about one-third of television content was imported, and that the highest levels of importation were from the poorest countries, but that there were also significant regional sub-markets for television content, complicating the picture of global media flows being a 'one-way street' from the West to the rest of the world. More generally, Straubhaar (1991, 2007) drew upon extensive surveys of Latin

American television to argue that the domination of television schedules by imported media content was a feature of less developed national media systems, but as these systems evolved over time, there was a strong 'localization' dynamic, where imported content was displaced by locally produced material, as the national media industries respond to the challenge of competition with imported media programs.

The second issue concerned the reception of Western media content. The cultural imperialism thesis implicitly drew upon a version of media effects theory, and the operating assumption that exposure to certain types of media content influenced attitudes and behavior in relatively predictable ways. This was challenged by new approaches to audience studies influences by cultural studies models of active audiences, reception studies, and cross-cultural ethnography. The implication of this work was that there was a need for closer analysis of how global media content is "actively and differentially responded to and negotiated in concrete local contexts and conditions" (Ang, 1996, 153). Such critiques of the cultural imperialism thesis have been associated with wider debates around the globalization of culture, and in particular the questioning of claims that expanded global connectivity leads to the homogenization of cultures and the destruction of local cultures and identities (Tomlinson, 1999). It should be noted that this debate is far from concluded. Some critical political economists (e.g., Herman & McChesney, 1997) argue that the issue is not one of how individuals respond to particular media texts but rather the overall systemic influences of commercially dominated media and exposure to large-scale advertising. Sparks (2012) has also observed that recent debates about the relationship of global media to soft power share attributes of the cultural imperialism thesis, but invert the consequences: while authors such as Schiller saw the influence of US media as pervasive and having negative effects around the world, authors such as Joseph Nye (2004) also see its influence as pervasive but having benign or positive global effects.

The final issue relates to the continued competitiveness of national media companies in the face of global competition, and the distinctiveness of national media systems. Critical political economists have generally posited that one consequence of globalization has been policy convergence toward a global free market model, as political ideologies such as neoliberalism have "become a dominant force in supranational and national communications policy [as] corporations have also increased their influence to unprecedented levels" (Hardy, 2014, 192). From this perspective, the globalization of media production and the development of global production networks in fields such as film, television, and games have been seen as consolidating a New International Division of Cultural Labor (NICL), where global outsourcing and runaway productions are driven by lowering wages and offering tax incentives and reduced regulation, leading to a 'race to the bottom' for workers in these industries, while 'Global Hollywood' retains control over copyright, finance, and decision-making (Miller et al., 2005; cf. Mirrlees, 2013).

While this is certainly one trajectory of media globalization, there is also the important counter-tendency toward the rise of competing media capitals (Curtin, 2009). National governments have invested strongly in developing globally focused media clusters in many cities around the world, often under the rubric of a creative industries strategy (Karlsson & Picard, 2011; Lee & Lim, 2014). Cities such as Seoul, Shanghai, Sydney, Beijing, Dubai, Manchester, and Wellington have been officially designated 'media cities,' competing alongside those cities that have seen the audiovisual industries grow more organically out of commercial entrepreneurship, such as Mumbai, Beirut, and Miami. Whether such ventures succeed in economic terms is contingent upon multiple factors – particularly their ability to attract creative talent from overseas – but the fact that there is such strong nation-state intervention to promote 'national champions' and media spaces that are attractive to global investment capital is a reminder that the role of the nation-state toward media globalization is not inevitably a passive one. Surveying more general trends, the economic geographer Allen Scott has made the observation:

> Although Hollywood's supremacy is unlikely to be broken at any time in the foreseeable future, at least some of these other centers will conceivably carve out stable niches for themselves in world markets, and all the more so as they develop more effective marketing and distribution capacities. . . . This argument, if correct, points toward a much more polycentric and polyphonic global audiovisual production system than has been the case in the recent past.
>
> *(2004, 475)*

The Internet as a force for global transformation

Many of the debates around the political economy of global media have been framed in the context of film and television. The question thus arises about the extent to which the questions surrounding media globalization are fundamentally transformed by the Internet environment. This is at the core of Manuel Castells' 'network society' thesis: developments in the Internet and digital technologies and processes of globalization are mutually reinforcing (i.e., as a society becomes more digital it becomes more global, and vice versa). A variety of other consequences are seen to follow from this, including the declining power of nation-states, the emergence of global elites, the reshaping of urban centers, networked oppositional politics, post-national cultural identities, and so on. Anthony Giddens observed that "globalization is political, technological and cultural, as well as economic. . . [and] influenced above all by developments in systems of communication" (2002, 37). The very shape of the Internet, as a global network linked by technical protocols rather than agreements among nation-states, and where content of all forms moves almost instantaneously across space, served as a metaphor for the shift toward a global media culture. Moreover, while other technologies for global distribution of media content, such as satellite dishes, could have access regulated or banned, the cost-benefit ratio of regulating the Internet was considered too high for national governments, partly for reasons related to the technical aspects of the Internet, but also because access to a high-speed Internet is central to global business activity. It was the latter set of considerations that were critical to the decision of a country like China to embrace what it termed 'informatization' in the mid-1990s, whatever the reservations about opening up to foreign media content.

Political economists have tended to be digital media skeptics, seeing the Internet as marking a technological change in media, but not a more significant social change. They point to the continued dominant place of corporations as the key players on the Internet, the centrality of commercial activity on digital platforms, and the need for revenues derived from advertising, direct sales, and subscriptions as evidence that the Internet marks the latest phase in the development of capitalist media, rather than a platform that transcends the constrains of 20th-century mass communication media. Wider claims about the transformational capacity of digital media have often been viewed as 'cybertarian rhetoric' (Miller, 2009) that ignores the material dimensions of digital media production, distribution, and content. Dan Schiller summarized the critical perspective on the Internet when he argued that

> far from delivering us into a high-tech Eden, in fact, cyberspace itself is being rapidly colonized by the familiar workings of the market system . . . the Internet comprises nothing less than the central production and control apparatus of an increasingly supranational market system.
>
> *(2000, xiv)*

It is argued that while the Internet notionally provides the opportunities for the emergence of a new digital public sphere and emergent forms of deliberative democracy (Dryzek & Dunleavy, 2009) or monitory democracy (Keane, 2011), such normative claims are tempered in practice by the economic relations that underpin the Internet and social media. The question of affordances of digital media, for instance, needs to take account of questions of access and the digital divide between information 'haves' and 'have-nots' or 'have-less' (Qiu, 2009). While the proliferation of content across digital platforms has clearly challenged incumbent media giants, they have been able to maintain a strong presence online and make use of copyright restrictions and forms of content 'bundling' to continue to generate monopoly rents. Moreover, the strong 'winner-take-most' economics of digital platforms has seen a new set of global social media giants emerge, such as Google, Amazon, Facebook, and so on. Finally, as digital media platforms remain primarily reliant upon the ability to generate revenues from business, it leads them to privilege content that drives traffic to websites that can maximize their commercial returns. Political economist Christian Fuchs (2015) has argued that social media have the potential to promote new forms of political movements and revivify the public sphere, but that such strategies challenge the commercial demands of social media platform providers to commodify big data and sell user information to advertisers, as well as the growing role being played by state agencies in accessing personal data for political surveillance.

In addition to discussions about the changing economics of global digital media, we can also note their impact on both domestic and international politics. The key questions here are whether globalization and the Internet are working in tandem to weaken the power and capacities of nation-states, and whether they are transforming the global political economy away from a historic system of states. Concerns about the 'hollowing out of state authority' (Strange, 1995) preceded the popularization of the Internet, but the growing convergence of 'traditional' and digital media has raised questions about the capacity of nation-states to continue to pursue long-standing media policy goals, such as the regulation of media ownership and content (Flew, 2016, 2018). Indeed, in some more libertarian accounts, the entire rationale for media regulation has collapsed, as online consumers are free to access content of their choosing from around the globe, subject only to increasingly ineffectual domestic institutions seeking to control and classify such material (Berg, 2014).

In the field of international relations, some have argued that globalization and the Internet point in the direction of a 'new medievalism' in world affairs, fundamentally challenging nation-state sovereignty (Freidrichs, 2001). As Robert Gilpin observed, "in the era of the Internet, governments have lost their monopoly over information and can therefore be successfully challenged by non-government actors" (Gilpin, 2011, 243). Wikileaks provided an exemplary case in this regard (Flew & Wilson, 2011). Radical political theorists such as Hardt and Negri have seen this as presaging the rise of a digitally networked global multitude, with information and cultural workers at its core (Negri & Hardt, 2011), while David Held (2016) argued the case for a 'new cosmopolitanism' and global governance, with an attendant need for state actors to agree to share power, not only with one another but also with a plethora of non-state actors that constitute global civil society. In the media sphere, Mansell and Raboy have argued that new forms of multi-stakeholder engagement in global policy fora are indicative of the ways in which, in media and communications policy, "the arena has shifted from the nation-state to the global" (2011, 4), while Padovani and Raboy observed "a shift from vertical, top-down and state-based modes of regulation to horizontal arrangements. . . [where] governing processes have become more permeable to interventions form a plurality of players' (2010, 153).

Claims about the decline of the nation-state in the face of globalization and digital technologies appear to be misplaced. The experience of multilateral forums and organizations is that their capacity for action remains contingent upon the support of powerful nation-state governments. Whether it be the opposition of countries such as China and Russia to proposals to link communication rights to human rights or the decision of the Trump administration in the United States to withdraw from the Trans-Pacific Partnership – in spite of the United States having been instrumental in establishing the TPP – it is apparent that there is no smooth ceding of powers and responsibilities form the national to the supranational realm. Moreover, the legitimacy of multilateral institutions remains integrally tied to the preparedness of nation-states to acknowledge their right to make decisions to which they are legally or morally bound, and their preparedness to implement policies that arise out of such decision-making processes. As the recent history of the European Union has confirmed, such processes are far from smooth once there are multiple nations involved, even when there is shared commitment to overarching goals.

It has also become more apparent that the Internet is a governable communications platform. There have always been controls over online content in some countries, such as China, Iran, and Saudi Arabia, and the number of countries that have chosen to restrict access to some forms of content on either a temporary or permanent basis has been growing over time (Gillespie, 2017). Freedom House (2019) has estimated that at least 56% of the world's online user population are in countries where there has been some form of content filtering or blocks placed on social media platforms by governments. It is also notable that laws governing the Internet are not necessarily synonymous with state censorship. For example, the Marco Civil da Internet, passed by the Brazilian government in 2014, sought to safeguard net neutrality and provide privacy protections for Brazilian citizens using US-based social media platforms. Internet governance is typically a complex mix of supranational rules and norms, nation-state regulations, and rules of use applied by the platform providers themselves, and exist around a diverse array of goals, which can range from policing copyright infringement to blocking access to extreme pornography to restricting access to material that may incite violence or terrorist activity (Flew, 2018). What is apparent is that any form of international norms or agreements needs to be connected to local laws and regulations in order to have any impact and, as with other fields of law and regulation, there has not been a wholesale transfer of sovereign powers from nation-states to supranational institutions.

Post-globalization

Whatever the debates about the pros and cons of globalization, there has until recently been an agreed set of observations about what it involved. At the core of the process was the leading Western economies, led by the United States, advocating an opening up of the global economy to greater freedom of movement of goods, services and capital, overseen by multilateral institutions such as the World Trade Organization, the World Bank, the International Monetary Fund, and others. Arguments for globalization were typically driven by political leaders from the English-speaking world, be they conservatives such as Margaret Thatcher, Ronald Reagan, or G. W. Bush, or 'Third Way' leaders such as Bill Clinton, Tony Blair, or Barack Obama, and the underpinning ideologies have been variously referred to as neoliberalism (Springer et al., 2016) or globalism (Sklair, 2002; Steger, 2005). Critics of this global neoliberalism were most prominent outside of the Western world, in countries such as China, Russia and Venezuela, while in the West it was assumed that anti-globalization protests would, over time, come to take the shape of global anti-capitalism, with a particular focus on the need for shared global stewardship of resources in response to the challenge of climate change.

By the mid-2010s, the picture was starting to change dramatically. In the United States, the election of Donald Trump as Republican President in 2016 was on an explicitly protectionist, anti-immigration and 'America First' platform, making Trump the first US president since World War II to explicitly question the merits of expanding US trade and influence globally. In the same year, voters in the United Kingdom narrowly chose to leave the European Union, with the 'Brexit' vote promising Britons the opportunity to 'take back control': this result overturned over four decades of largely bipartisan political support for EU membership in the United Kingdom, and occurred in spite of strong support from industry and most academic experts for the status quo. The 2010s had seen a surge in support for populist parties with a nationalist message across Europe, such as the Front National in France, the Party for Freedom in the Netherlands, the Freedom Party in Austria, the UK Independence Party, and the Alternative für Deutschland in Germany. Populist opposition to globalization had taken a strongly nationalist turn – contrary to the predictions of many on the left – and events that catered for the transnational political and economic elites, such as the annual World Economic Forum (WEF) in Davos, Switzerland, began to look bleak, with even relatively mainstream politicians such as former UK prime minster Theresa May proposing that "If you believe you're a citizen of the world, you're a citizen of nowhere. You don't understand what the very word 'citizenship' means" (May, 2016).

If so-called Davos Man as the exemplar of post-national global citizenship was now looking increasingly beleaguered (Tett, 2017), the political savior of the globalization project also took an unlikely shape: China's President Xi Jinping. In his January 2017 speech to the WEF, Xi strongly endorsed economic globalization and multilateral institutions that support free trade, arguing that "whether you like it or not, the global economy is the big ocean that you cannot escape from" (Xi, 2017). This message was reinforced at the Boao Forum for Asia (the 'Asian Davos') held in Hainan, China, in March 2017, which positioned Asia as the global leader in committing to globalization and free trade. It was also reinforced by China in its renewed commitment to the Paris Climate Change Accord targets, in the face of the United States moving away from the targets signed off by the Obama administration under Donald Trump.

The significance of these global geopolitical shifts for understanding the relationship between digital media and globalization is not clear as yet. They do point in the direction of an uncoupling of globalization as a political-economic project from the development of the Internet and digital media. The rhetoric of China about its support for free trade and economic globalization has not typically been extended to supporting the free flow of media content: the entry of foreign broadcasters into China is highly restricted; platforms such as Facebook, YouTube, and Twitter are not allowed into China; and there remains strong state censorship of media content within China as well as policing of the online environment. China is developing technology giants that rival the big Western players, such as the so-called BAT group (Baidu, Alibaba and Tencent), and there are growing partnerships in the media and technology space, which range from US–China film co-productions (Keane, 2016) to strategic alliances, such as Tencent buying an equity stake in Tesla. But the big Chinese corporate players retain strong links to government, and the general consensus is that China under Xi has been moving more in the direction of stronger state controls over media than media liberalization.

At a conceptual level, three implications for future research around digital media and globalization can be noted. First, there is the issue of what Curran and Park referred to as "a certain fuzziness in the way in which three different categories – American, Western, and capitalist – can be used almost interchangeably" (Curran & Park, 2000, 6). At certain points in time, there is an alignment across these three categories: the 1990s was a notable example, where the global Internet could develop in the context of an unquestioned hegemony of the United States in global affairs and in setting the rules for global laws and multilateral institutions. But there is little doubt that the global environment of the 21st century has returned to multi-polarity and competing claims to ascendancy among major regional powers. It is a global environment, moreover, where the competing claims of various state actors exist alongside the challenges to such power presented by non-state actors. With the global rise of China as an economic power, the extent to which capitalism in the 21st century can be presumed to be Western, let alone American, is clearly up for grabs.

The implications of this multi-polar global environment for the future development of the Internet and digital media are particularly important. Whereas previous eras of superpower conflict, such as the Cold War between the United States and the former Soviet Union, occurred in a context where their media systems were largely independent from one another, economic globalization has created complex interdependencies between governments and businesses in different countries. The Chinese government is by no means hostile to Western digital technology companies: Apple had an almost iconic status in China during the Steve Jobs era. But the engagement is selective, and on China's terms, as seen with Google's ongoing challenges in dealing with the Chinese authorities and the sensitivities around allowing Facebook in China. At the same time, China's national champions have been able to fill the vacuum left by the absence of these Western giants, with WeChat being a preferred alternative to Facebook and Baidu occupying the web search space that Google claims elsewhere. As the Chinese tech giants look to go global, they will bring new functionalities to the digital media environment – the integration of search and payment is more advanced in China than anywhere else in the world – but there will also be questions asked about their relationship to government in an environment where national security concerns are becoming heightened.

This means that we can no longer speak of a single global Internet. Governments around the world shape the content available to their citizens online, from proscriptions on the promotion of Nazism on German websites to the blocking of the swimsuit issue of *Sports Illustrated* in Saudi Arabia. The Chinese case, however, points to the possibility of distinctive national digital media ecologies emerging, similar to the ways in which broadcasting systems remain largely national despite over three decades of routine access to imported media content. Work on national preferences online suggests that such tendencies are already identifiable, and this will present a research challenge for digital media scholars, as it points to the need to bring back consideration of national laws, policies, and regulations into analyses of the Internet and digital media. It also suggests that the meta-frameworks that have been considered here, such as globalization theories and critical political economy, will need to engage with more applied, empirical work on particular national and regional cases.

References

Adams, P. (2009). *Geographies of Media and Communication*. Malden, MA: Wiley-Blackwell.

Ang, I. (1996). *Living Room Wars: Rethinking Media Audiences for a Postmodern World*. New York: Routledge.

Beck, U. (2000). *What Is Globalization?*. Cambridge: Polity Press.

Berg, C. (2014). *In Defence of Freedom of Speech*. Melbourne: Institute of Public Affairs.

Boyd-Barrett, O. (1977). Media Imperialism: Towards an International Framework for the Analysis of Media Systems. In J. Curran, M. Gurevitch, and J. Woolacott (eds.), *Mass Communication and Society*. London: Edward Arnold, pp. 116–135.

Castells, M. (1996). *The Rise of the Network Society: The Information Age: Economy, Society and Culture*. Malden, MA: Wiley Blackwell.

Castells, M. (2009). *Communication Power*. New York: Oxford University Press.

Curran, J. and Park, M.-J. (2000). Beyond globalization theory. In J. Curran and M.-J. Park (eds.), *Dewesternizing Media Studies*. London: Routledge, pp. 3–18.

Curtin, M. (2009). Thinking Globally: From Media Imperialism to Media Capital. In J. Holt and A. Perren (eds.), *Media Industries: History, Theory, and Method*. Malden, MA: Wiley- Blackwell, pp. 108–119.

Dirlik, A. (2003). Global Modernity? Modernity in an Age of Global Capitalism. *European Journal of Social Theory*, 6(3), 275–292.

Dryzek, J. and Dunleavy, P. (2009). *Theories of the Democratic State*. Basingstoke: Palgrave Macmillan.

Eisenstadt, S. (1966). *Modernization, Protest and Change*. Englewood Cliffs, NJ: Prentice-Hall.

Flew, T. (2018). *Understanding Global Media* (2nd ed.). Basingstoke: Palgrave Macmillan.

Flew, T. (2016). Global Media and National Policies: The Return of the State. In T. Flew, P. Iosifidis, and J. Steemers (eds.), *Global Media and National Policies: The Return of the State*. Basingstoke: Palgrave Macmillan, pp. 1–15.

Flew, T., and Waisbord, S. (2015). The Ongoing Significance of National Media Systems in the Context of Media Globalization. *Media, Culture & Society*, 37(4), 620–636.

Flew, T., and Wilson, J. (2011). WikiLeaks and the Challenge of the 'Fifth Estate'. In M. Ricketson (ed.), *Australian Journalism Today*. Melbourne: Palgrave Macmillan, pp. 168–181.

Freedom House. (2019). *Freedom on the Net 2019: The Crisis of Social Media*. https://freedomhouse.org/report/freedom-net/2019/crisis-social-media (Accessed March 16, 2020).

Freidrichs, J. (2001). The Meaning of New Medievalism. *European Journal of International Relations*, 7(4), 475–501.

Fuchs, C. (2015). *Culture and Economy in the Age of Social Media*. London: Routledge.

Giddens, A. (1990). *The Consequences of Modernity*. Cambridge: Polity Press.

Giddens, A. (2002). *Runaway World: How Globalization Is Reshaping Our Lives*. London: Profile.

Gilpin, R. (2011). *Global Political Economy: Understanding the International Economic Order*. Princeton, NJ: Princeton University Press.

Gillespie, T. (2017). Governance of and by Platforms. In J. Burgess, T. Poell, and A. Marwick (eds.), *Sage Handbook of Social Media*. London: Sage.

Gorman, L., and McLean, D. (2009). *Media and Society into the 21st Century: A Historical Introduction* (2nd ed.). Malden, MA: Wiley-Blackwell.

Grabe, M., and Myrick, J. (2016). Informed Citizenship in a Media-Centric Way of Life. *Journal of Communication*, 66(2), 215–235.

Hardy, J. (2014). *Critical Political Economy of the Media: An Introduction*. London: Routledge.

Held, D., and McGrew, A. (2002). *Globalization/Anti-Globalization*. Cambridge: Polity Press.

Held, D. (2016). Elements of a Theory of Global Governance. *Philosophy & Social Criticism*, 42(4), 827–836.

Herman, E.S., and McChesney, R. W. (1997). *The Global Media: The New Missionaries of Global Capitalism*. London: Cassell.

Hirst, P., Thompson, G., and Bromley, S. (2009). *Globalization in Question* (3rd ed.). Cambridge: Polity Press.

Holt, J., and Malčić, S. (2015). The Privacy Ecosystem: Regulating Digital Identity in the United States and European Union. *Journal of Information Policy*, 5(2), 155–178.

Innis, H. (1991). *The Bias of Communication*. Toronto: University of Toronto Press.

Karlsson, C., and Picard, R. (2011). *Media Clusters and Media Cluster Policies* [online]. Stockholm: Centre of Excellence for Science and Innovation Studies. https://ideas.repec.org/p/hhs/cesisp/0246.html (Accessed October 2, 2016].

Keane, J. (2011). *The Life and Death of Democracy*. New York: W.W. Norton & Company.

Keane, M. (2016). Going Global or Going Nowhere? Chinese Media in a Time of Flux. *Media International Australia*, 159, 13–21.

Lee, H.-K., and Lim, L. (2014). Cultural Policies in East Asia: An Introduction. In L. Lim and H-K. Lee (eds.), *Cultural Policies in East Asia: Dynamics Between the State, Arts and Creative Industries*. Basingstoke: Palgrave Macmillan, pp. 1–14.

Mansell, R., and Raboy, M. (2011). Foundations of the Theory and Practice of Global Media and Communication Policy. In M. Raboy and R. Mansell (eds.), *Handbook of Global Media and Communication Policy*. Malden, MA: Wiley-Blackwell, pp. 1–20.

May, T. (2016). *Speech to the Conservative Party Conference*, October 5. www.telegraph.co.uk/news/2016/10/05/theresa-mays-conferencespeech-in-full/(Accessed December 13, 2017).

McLuhan, M. (1964). *Understanding Media*. New York: Mentor.

McLuhan, M., and Fiore, Q. (1967). *The Medium Is the Message*. New York: Bantam.

Miller, T., Maxwell, R., McMurria, J., Govil, N., and Wang, T. (2005). *Global Hollywood 2* (2nd ed.). London: British Film Institute.

Miller, T. (2009). Can Natural Luddites Make Things Explode or Travel Faster? The New Humanities, Cultural Policy Studies, and Creative Industries. In J. Holt and A. Perren (eds.), *Media Industries: History, Theory, and Method*. Malden, MA: Wiley- Blackwell, pp. 184–198.

Miller, T., and Kraidy, M. (2016). *Global Media Studies*. Cambridge: Polity Press.

Mirrlees, T. (2013). *Global Entertainment Media: Between Cultural Imperialism and Cultural Globalization*. New York: Routledge.

Morley, D. (2009). For a Materialist, Non – Media-Centric Media Studies. *Television & New Media*, 10(1), 114–116.

Mowlana, H. (2012). International Communication: The Journey of a Caravan. *Journal of International Communication*, 18(2), 267–290.

Negri, A., and Hardt, M. (2011). The Fight for 'Real Democracy' at the Heart of Occupy Wall Street. *Foreign Affairs* [online]. www.foreignaffairs.com/articles/north-america/2011-10-11/fight-real-democracy-heart-occupy-wall-street [Accessed March 5, 2017].

Nordenstreng, K., and Varis, T. (1974). *Television Traffic – a One-Way Street? A Survey and Analysis of the International Flow of Television Programme Material*. Paris: UNESCO.

Nye, J. S. (2004). *Soft Power: The Means to Success in World Politics*. New York: Public Affairs.

Padovani, C., and Raboy, M. (2010). Mapping Global Media Policy: Concepts, Frameworks, Methods. *Communication, Culture & Critique*, 3(2), 150–169.

Piertese, J. (2015). *Globalization and Culture: Cultural Mélange* (3rd ed.). Lanham, MD: Rowman & Littlefield.

Qiu, J. L. (2009). *Working-Class Network Society: Communications Technology and the Information Have-Less in Urban China*. Cambridge, MA: MIT Press.

Robertson, R. (1992). *Globalization: Social Theory and Global Culture*. London: Sage.

Robins, K., and Morley, D. (1995). *Spaces of Identity: Global Media, Electronic Landscapes and Cultural Boundaries*. New York: Routledge.

Schiller, D. (2000). *Digital Capitalism: Networking the Global Market System*. Cambridge, MA: MIT Press.

Schiller, H. I. (1969). *Mass Communications and American Empire*. Boston, MA: Beacon Press.

Schiller, H. I. (1976). *Communication and Cultural Domination*. New York: International Arts & Science Press.

Scott, A. J. (2004). Cultural-Products Industries and Urban Economic Development: Prospects for Growth and Market Contestation in Global Context. *Urban Affairs Review*, 39(4), 461–490.

Sklair, L. (2002). *Globalization: Capitalism and its Alternatives* (3rd ed.). New York: Oxford University Press.

Sparks, C. (2012). Media and Cultural Imperialism Reconsidered. *Chinese Journal of Communication*, 5(3), 281–299.

Springer, S., Birch, K., and MacLeavy, J. (2016). An Introduction to Neoliberalism. In S. Springer, K. Birch, and J. MacLeavy (eds.), *The Handbook of Neoliberalism*. London: Routledge, pp. 1–14.

Steger, M. (2005). *Globalism* (2nd ed.). Lanham, MD: Rowman & Littlefield.

Strange, S. (1995). The Defective State. *Daedalus*, 124, 55–74.

Straubhaar, J. (1991). Beyond Media Imperialism: Assymetrical Interdependence and Cultural Proximity. *Critical Studies in Mass Communication*, 8(1), 39–59.

Straubhaar, J. (2007). *World Television: From Global to Local*. Los Angeles: Sage.

Taneja, H., and Wu, A. (2014). Does the Great Firewall Really Isolate the Chinese? Integrating Access Blockage with Cultural Factors to Explain Web User Behavior. *The Information Society*, 30(5), 297–309.

Tett, G. (2017). Davos Man Has No Clothes. *Foreign Policy* [online]. http://foreignpolicy.com/2017/01/16/davos-man-has-no-clothes-globalization/(Accessed March 5, 2017).

Thompson, J. (1995). *The Media and Modernity*. Cambridge: Polity Press.

Tomlinson, J. (1999). *Globalization and Culture*. Cambridge: Polity Press.

Xu, X., Fu, W., and Straubhaar, J. (2013). National Self-Sufficiency in Broadcast Television Programming: Examining the Airtime Shares of Homemade Versus U.S.-Made Programs. *Journal of Broadcasting & Electronic Media*, 57(4), 543–561.

Varis, T. (1984). The International Flow of Television Programs. *Journal of Communication*, 34(1), 143–152.

Wallerstein, I. (1974). The Rise and Future Demise of the World Capitalist System: Concepts for Comparative Analysis. *Comparative Studies in Society and History*, 16(4), 387–415.

Weber, M. (1978). *Economy and Society* (2 vols.). Berkeley, CA: University of California Press.

Winseck, D. (2011). The Political Economies of Media and the Transformation of the Global Media Industries. In D. Winseck and D. Y. Jin (eds.), *The Political Economies of Media and the Transformation of the Global Media Industries*. London: Bloomsbury, pp. 3–47.

Xi, J. (2017). *Opening Plenary Address to the World Economic Forum 2017*, January 17. https://america.cgtn. com/2017/01/17/full-text-of-xi-jinping-keynote-at-the-world-economic-forum.

27

Toward a sustainable information society

A global political economy perspective

Jack Linchuan Qiu

Does the arrival of digital media contribute to sustainable development of Planet Earth? When personal computers started to spread in the 1970s and 1980s, they carried the promise of a 'paperless office' that would save trees (Sellen & Harper, 2003). When the Internet began to diffuse in the 1990s, it was believed it would reduce gasoline consumption because people no longer needed to commute (Cairncross, 1997). A digital world, as Bill Gates famously put it, is supposed to be "friction-free" (1995). But how come a generation later, we see more signs of global warming, environmental distress, and planetary apocalypse, to the extent that the turn of the Anthropocene (Ellis, 2018) has become a focal point of interdisciplinary investigation, including media studies? Could the opposite be true – that is, as John Peters (2016) argues, human communication, including its latest forms through digital media, in fact encourages more consumption and produces a more unsustainable lifestyle?

One way to answer these hard questions is to take a critical political economy approach, which, according to Wasko, Murdock, and Sousa, has four defining features (2011, 2, emphases added):

> Firstly, it is *holistic*. Rather than treating 'the economy' as a specialist and bounded domain, it focuses on the *relations between economic practices and social and political organization*. Secondly, it is *historical*. Rather than concentrating solely or primarily on immediate events, it insists that a full understanding of contemporary shifts must be grounded in an analysis of transformations, shifts, and contradictions that *unfold over long loops of time*. Third, in contrast to economics that severed its historic links with moral philosophy in an effort to present itself as an objective science, critical political economy continues to be centrally concerned with the relations between the organization of culture and communications and the constitution of *the good society grounded in social justice and democratic practice*. Fourthly, critical analysis places its practitioners under an obligation to follow the logic of their analysis through into *practical action for change*.

This chapter takes such a holistic, historical, normative, and action-oriented approach to critically examine the global political economy of digital media and their relationship with sustainable development. In so doing, I shall emphasize issues of ownership, class, worker's voice, and what Dyer-Witheford calls "the rate of struggle" in the "vortex" (2015, 19, 28) of global capitalism, now powered by digital media. My global perspective pays particular attention to the Global South, especially Chinese workers and the factory zones of South China, where I have been conducting research since 2002.

The gravity of Sustainable Development Goals

But first of all, what is sustainability? The Sustainable Development Goals (SDGs) of the United Nations, adopted by the UN General Assembly on September 25, 2015 (https://bit. ly/2wNGf3t), is the obvious starting point to discuss sustainability in the 21st century. With broad support from global civil society and UN member states, the SDGs include 17 goals that cover a wide range of issues such as poverty alleviation, gender equality, peace, justice, and environmental protection, to be reached by 2030 or earlier. This is, of no doubt, a historic document that contains critical discursive resources at the transnational level for politico-economic analysis toward a better world. It is also key to a new politics of visibility in that it throws light on issues formerly rendered invisible by capitalism and authoritarianism.

More than a discursive resource for high-level diplomacy, the SDGs have special importance for media and communication scholars because, finally, there is a closure to the old debate on "the right to communicate" (d'Arcy, 1979, 117). Is media access, especially Internet access, a basic human right? Scholars, myself included, have been saying yes for a long time, which means we had to debate with the naysayers. But now, SDG 9.c sets out the goal to "[s]ignificantly increase access to information and communications technology and strive to provide universal and affordable access to the Internet in least developed countries by 2020." This is more than mere discourse. It's a clear message: Let's stop debating. Let's get things done!

We, however, should not worship SDGs as if they are sacred commandments that can, by themselves, guarantee a better Planet Earth. Rather, they should be taken as the beginning of a dialogue and the start of a social movement, as an invitation to a new sociological imagination – to reimagine sustainability.

Multiple contentions lie beneath the seemingly smooth surface of the SDGs. But political economists would ask: Who owns the sustainability discourse? What are the policy outcomes? With what consequences for the people of the lower classes the world over? A fundamental contradiction lies between a proprietary Internet owned by a few tech giants and commons-based peer production whose ownership is truly decentralized (Benkler, 2006; Fuchs, 2014). Another opposition is between a corporate sharing economy as exemplified by Uber, on the one hand, and the global movement of platform cooperativism, on the other (Scholz, 2017). Before the future landscape of the Internet fully emerges, too often sustainability is imagined as little more than regulatory protections from Silicon Valley, an imagination that is inadequate and problematic especially at the global level (Larkin, 2008; Qiu, 2009; Chan, 2013; Ekstein & Schwarz, 2014).

One such problematic imagination is post-industrialism: the notion that our economy has evolved from atoms to bits and our world from an industrial era defined by production to a post-industrial era defined by consumption. While this may apply to regions of the OECD countries, we have to remember that these countries of the Global North represent less than 20% of the world's population and that more than 80% of humanity are still living in industrializing or preindustrial economies. The continued industrialization of the world economy, for instance in the BRICS countries – Brazil, Russia, India, China, and South Africa – is very much behind the shift that Fareed Zakaria calls "the rise of the rest" (2009).

It may be helpful to take a reality check by looking at the real numbers: since the 1970s, total global industrial output has in fact more than tripled from $2.56 trillion in 1970 to $8.92 trillion in 2011, measured in constant 2005 US dollars. Although the digital economy is often seen as post-industrial and celebrated for its immateriality, look at our handsets, laptops, iPads, or any other electronic gadgets – none of them is windfall from the sky. All of them are industrially produced with tangible materiality. Let us do not forget: before the data mine, there has to be the assembly line.

From assembly line to the data mine

Since 2002, I have studied digital media being made and used, tinkered and domesticated in the 'workshop of the world' of the early 21st century, the Chinese factory zones, especially those in the Pearl River Delta of South China (Qiu, 2009). I have conducted interviews, focus groups, questionnaire survey, mapping, and participatory action research. More recently, my work has turned comparative in *Goodbye iSlave* (Qiu, 2016), where I attempt to theorize my observations in China through comparisons with transatlantic slavery from the 1600s to the 1800s, learning especially from African struggles, following a political economy approach that is holistic, historical, and social justice oriented.

A substantive question raised in *Goodbye iSlave* is: 'Does slavery exist not only along the assembly line but also in the data mine?' In asking this question, I side with Christian Fuchs (2015, Loc 4883), who maintains that we need a broader definition of digital labor beyond Western conceptions focusing on either the knowledge/creative labor or gig workers and the "precariat" (Standing, 2011). Instead, we need to confront the full gamut of the International Division of Digital Labor (IDDL), spanning the Democratic Republic of the Congo (where key minerals for electronic devices are extracted from mines controlled by warlords), the factory zones of China (where manufacture happens), and every world region of the Global South from Latin America (Chan, 2013) to Africa (Larkin, 2008) to Asia (Ekstein & Schwarz, 2014).

The techno-social reality of this great digital diffusion in the Global South is however often marginalized, if not neglected, in Western and Asian studies of digital media, in favor of almost exclusive attention being paid to hackers, artists, and, above all, consumers. This Western-centric, postindustrial imagination hampers realistic investigations of digital media research in China, ignoring not only the epic story of industrialization but also the heroic acts of collective struggle by the working people.

My analysis of "social media on the picket line" (Qiu, 2016, 140) has documented the ways in which smartphone and Chinese social media (especially QQ group, Weibo, and WeChat) have been deployed in worker struggles in the manufacturing sector. Meanwhile, there are notable instances of labor solidarity extending beyond manufacture, such as workers in the 361 Degree Shoe Factory forming an alliance with hackers to ambush management following their strike in 2009, in an online guerrilla war. The picket line, online and offline, has extended to other industrial sectors. On May Day, 2018, crane operators in construction sites of nearly 20 Chinese provinces went on strike to demand higher pay. They have succeeded (Hoie, 2018). In June 2018, truck drivers using Yunmanman (an Uber-like digital platform) in a dozen Chinese provinces protested corporate monopoly and official corruption, a struggle still ongoing at the time of writing. Increasingly common in such industrial actions is (a) workers are now digitally connected, (b) they have developed media literacy against surveillance and censorship, and (c) they increasingly target Uber-style digital platforms in addition to conventional employers and the Chinese state.

A focal point of my analysis is Foxconn, the world's largest electronic manufacturer that at one point employed 1.4 million Chinese migrant workers assembling iPhones and iPads, a massive army that was more numerous than all the armed forces of the US military combined (Mozur & Luk, 2013). In my historical comparative project, I found an appalling parallel between Foxconn and the slave ship during the notorious "Middle Passage" smuggling of Africans from West Africa to the Americas: the suicide-prevention nets.

According to Olaudah Equiano (1995), a slave boy who survived the Middle Passage in mid-1700s, he witnessed the jumping of his fellow Africans through the anti-jumping nets, because they wished to die and free themselves from the miseries of enslavement. At the time, anti-jumping nets were standard equipment for slave ships before they became obsolete after the abolition of slave trade in the 19th century. However, in 2010 they reappeared on top of Foxconn buildings, where our digital gadgets are made. There are three levels of netting in the modern 'slave ships' so to speak: on top of the buildings, 'Sky Net'; at the bottom, 'Ground Net'; all windows and corridors are sealed with the 'Middle Net' (Qiu, 2016, 76–77).

Foxconn claimed to have taken down the anti-jumping nets, and China's media censorship means we do not have full account of suicides in Foxconn. But the suicides have continued. In Foxconn Zhengzhou, Henan Province, where most of the latest iPhones are made, my research team still found anti-jumping nets in the dormitory buildings in 2017. From time to time, we still had reliable sources about yet another worker who committed suicide.

What can we learn from these tragedies in the factories that make our laptops and smart devices? What lessons can be drawn about labor struggles toward sustainability?

We can zoom into one worker, Xu Lizhi, who also happens to be poetically gifted. After jumping from the seventeenth floor of a Foxconn building, he is now posthumously recognized as the most renowned worker-poet in Chinese literary circles. This is the last poem by this young worker, who leaped to death at age 23.

> I want to take another look at the ocean,
> behold the vastness of tears from half a lifetime
> I want to climb another mountain,
> try to call back the soul that I've lost
> I want to touch the sky, feel that blueness so light
> But I can't do any of this, so I'm leaving this world
> Everyone who's heard of me
> Shouldn't be surprised at my leaving
> Even less should you sigh or grieve
> I was fine when I came, and fine when I left
>   (translated by Li Fei and Zhang Xiaoqi https://bit.ly/1txlq7H)

Xu Lizhi named this poem 'A New Day,' with a subtitle 'On My Deathbed.' He published it online in his blog webpage on October 1, 2014, which was also the National Day for the People's Republic of China. Xu already died in the late hours of September 30, 2014. But he programmed the blog site so that his last poem would be automatically published online on October 1, the day that celebrates 'A New China.' Was this an act of defiance against the Communist Party? Was it an ironic comment on Foxconn and the IT industry? Or perhaps both?

Literary critiques Jomo and Mamos interpret Xu Lizhi's act as "revolutionary death" (2014, 8). In doing so, they quote Huey Newton, cofounder of the Black Panther Party, as saying:

> Revolutionary suicide does not mean that I and my comrades have a death wish; it means just the opposite. We have such a strong desire to live with hope and human dignity that existence without them is impossible. When reactionary forces crush us, we must move against these forces, even at the risk of death.

From the deathbed of Foxconn to the transatlantic trade of slavery to the historical birth of a New Day, a New China which represents one of the most uplifting moments of communist revolution in world history achieved by the Chinese people – we can see that the struggles of the working class are not just triggered by unsustainable practices of industrial-capitalist alienation; they also produce new imaginations of sustainability by themselves – in this case, through the words of immortal poetry.

Reflections

Back to the SDGs, we have to ask: Whose sustainability are we discussing? Is it the sustainability of capitalism, of authoritarianism, of those structures that allow the 1% to dominate the 99%? Is it about what can be called the new 'sustainability industry' that instrumentalizes UN discourse for the sales of corporations?

One may ask, how to draw the line between instrumentalized and non-instrumentalized sustainability? At the risk of oversimplification, I submit that genuine sustainability – for digital media industries, for the human species now and in the future, and for Planet Earth – has to be postcapitalist. The road ahead can be socialist, anarchist, feminist, postcolonial, Indigenous, open source, and environmental. The paths are diverse. But they need to lead us out of the swamp that Dan Schiller calls 'digital capitalism' (2000), which revives slave-like conditions in the 21st century. Digital abolition will not succeed in the shadow of historical capitalism. That was a conclusion of *Goodbye iSlave*.

Another line to draw is that we cannot simply rely on career bureaucrats for the realization of SDGs. A case in point is to remember the Millennium Development Goals (MDGs), adopted by 191 UN member states in September 2000, declaring to "eradicate extreme poverty and hunger," "achieve universal primary education," "promote gender equality and empower women," among eight goals by 2015 (https://bit.ly/1N1BCFa). But what happened to the MDGs? As I write in 2020, have we eradicated extreme poverty and hunger? No. It has probably gotten worse in recent years regarding MDG #1. Have we achieved universal primary education and empowered women? No. Consider Malala. Consider #MeToo. Have we ensured "environmental justice" and succeeded in meeting MDG #7? No. Otherwise, we would not need those five SDGs from #11 to #15.

Career bureaucrats are good at translating lofty ideals into diplomatic language. But they are less effective at translating language into impactful action. This is not to portray a negative stereotype for those who labor behind the MDGs and SDGs, many of whom I know from the UN headquarters and across Asia. Most of them are well-intended, hard-working people. Some read the same poetry I read, and they complain to me about their frustrations. "The SDGs are just another way to justify territoriality with the UN system," a senior official told me. His cynicism is understandable. After all, if these goals are all met, how could the UN ask for money to solve the world's problems?

Money, indeed, is a root reason why we cannot rely on career bureaucrats. My observations are that many UN agencies have been disciplined and infiltrated by powerful corporations and resourceful nation-states, using carrot and stick made of US-dollar incentives. For example, today at the United Nations Educational, Scientific, and Cultural Organization (UNESCO) many young bureaucrats have never heard about the NWICO, the New World Information and Communication Order, struggle from the 1970s to 1980s (MacBride & Roach, 1989). This is not only because their supervisors thought the historic movement has become outdated but also because they dare not to talk about it for fear of offending US representatives. Yet shamefully, the United States withdrew anyway, this time using the excuse that UNESCO is too friendly to Palestine (Rosenberg & Morello, 2017).

This is how bureaucracy works, in reality, in vain. If UNESCO has so little power to make the United States pay its due of more than half a billion – (yes, the United States now owes UNESCO $550 million membership fees (Rosenberg & Morello, 2017), which is probably the real reason for the US withdrawal, not Palestine) – how can we expect them to change the behaviors of Wall Street that so often obstruct the realization of the SDGs? How can we rely on them to fight the digital media and tech giants, which Vikki Meyer at the ICA Prague conference called 'MAFIA,' that is, Microsoft, Apple, Facebook, IBM, and Amazon – plus Google, of course, as well as Alibaba, Tencent, and Baidu?

This analysis does not stop at the UN level. The same structural limitations exist in other intergovernmental organizations and most national and local governments. Reflecting on this reality, we have to be mindful that 'sustainability' is already a loaded word that cannot be taken at face value. Otherwise, its problematic usage can lead to the very opposite of democratic media, inclusive communication, and global justice. To achieve genuine, long-term sustainability, we have to transcend the SDGs. We have to take things into our own hands.

What is to be done?

So what is to be done? Every reader of this chapter has multiple identities. We are students as well as consumers of digital media. We are citizens. Many of us are also media producers and activists, committed to causes of sustainable change that is truly democratic, egalitarian, and emancipatory. Regardless of the struggle, let us practice what we preach. "Be the change we want to see in the world," as Mahatma Gandhi famously put it.

Be mindful, next time we buy a smartphone, we shall try to seek a brand that is less tainted with workers' blood, for instance, the Fairphone (www.fairphone.com/en/). Be mindful, next time we write a paper, we shall try to cite colleagues from the South whose scholarship is as good as those from the North (Chakravartty et al., 2018). Changing systemic bias in processes of knowledge production is urgently needed, and it is not that hard.

We shall not end with blind optimism as I am keenly aware that things have deteriorated, in China for workers as well as digital media researchers, in the United States, the United Kingdom, and so many Western as well as Asian, African, and Latin American countries where populism, isolationism, and xenophobia have disrupted the political, economic, and media systems, particularly for critical scholars holding unconventional views. As Oliver Boyd-Barrett (2015) contends, imperialism is back, carried forward this time by corporate algorithms and military drones. To resist and to prevail, I would emphasize the need to invest our intellectual resources in three types of praxis, that is, the praxis of hearing, of outreach, and of stealing. Let me elaborate.

First, we have to hear the voices of the working people – in the Congolese mines, along Chinese assembly lines and the picket lines, as well as inside the data mine. Workers are never voiceless. As we have learned from cases of worker struggles in Foxconn and the Chinese factory zones, the real problem is: can we can hear workers' voices effectively using old-school qualitative and quantitative methods as well as new digital methods?

In one of my ongoing projects, I am lucky to collaborate with GlobalWorks (http://globalworks.se/), a group of social scientists and data scientists in Sweden, who have developed a new methodological toolkit that uses machine learning to analyze Chinese workers' online discussions. In this study, we have scrapped a corpus of nearly nine million posts in the online public forum Baidu Tieba, which will allow us to not only produce new scholarly knowledge but also help upgrade the global labor auditing system under new conditions of social media.

Big data, artificial intelligence (AI), machine learning – these tools of digital media research can be reappropriated for democratic communication research, including critical political economy analysis of digital media. We shall use these new methods, instead of leaving them to neoliberal imperialists or racist algorithms (Noble, 2018).

Second, we need to seriously broaden the scope of media and communication research by engaging in interdisciplinary discussion with colleagues in other social science and humanities disciplines, engineering, health, biology, and computer science. The list goes on. But the direction is clear. Following Yuezhi Zhao (2011), Toby Miller and Marwan Kraidy (2016), I'd like to stress: we ignore things outside the media-centric framework at our peril. In the Chinese contexts, for instance, we have to consider industrial systems, industrial relations, the role of the state, labor struggles online and offline, environmental justice and social justice for all suppressed people, before gaining a holistic understanding of sustainability.

Third, we need to 'steal' as Fred Moten and Stefano Harney argue beautifully in their book *The Undercommons* (2013, Loc 195). Structures of power have always stolen from the powerless. The University is one such structure. Progressive intellectuals shall therefore steal at least three types of things from the University: (a) informational resources – ideas and data, historical knowledge, findings from cutting-edge research that are relevant to grassroots activism; (b) social network resources – the prestige of professors, the brand name of higher education, connections with media, politicians, investors; and (c) personnel resources – putting activists on college payroll, getting them travel entry visas, and most importantly, training our students into new participants and leaders of social movements.

We steal not for individual benefits but for existing moral economies to sustain and expand, for the creation of a new digital commons, for instance, in the global movement of 'platform cooperativism.'

Let me conclude with an invitation to this new movement that is particularly important to students and researchers of digital media. Spearheaded by Trebor Scholz and his students and colleagues in the New School, platform cooperativism is connecting time-honored traditions of cooperatives with the latest inventions of digital platforms (https://platform.coop/). The goals are, first, to empower workers so that they become co-owners of the platform economy, against exploitative corporate platforms like Uber, and, second, to grow coops into new socioeconomic bases for post-capitalist society (Scholz, 2017). The success of this movement will mean that, based on our critical political economy praxis of digital media, we can offer the working people things much better than right-wing populism and neoliberal deceit.

We can win back the working class – starting from the White working class in Western countries, Latinos, Blacks, and all minority groups to the working people in Asia and the world over. We can win back their hearts and minds and souls through economic empowerment, autonomy, integrity, and democratically managed digital platforms. Collaborating with them and their organizations large or small, be they unions or coops or social enterprises, we can build a sustainable planetary communication system that hears workers' voices and respects workers' rights, along the assembly line and in the data mine.

You are welcome to join us. Welcome to the platform cooperativism movement, for a better, sustainable world.

References

Benkler, Y. (2006). *The Wealth of Networks: How Social Production Transforms Markets and Freedom*. New Haven, CT: Yale University Press.

Boyd-Barrett, O. (2015). *Media Imperialism*. London: Sage.

Cairncross, F. (1997). *The Death of Distance: How the Communications Revolution Will Change Our Lives.* London: Harvard Business Review Press.

Chan, A. S. (2013). *Networking Peripheries: Technological Futures and the Myth of Digital Universalism.* Cambridge, MA: MIT Press.

Chakravartty, P., Kuo, R., Grubbs, V., and McIlwain, C. (2018). #CommunicationSoWhite. *Journal of Communication,* 68(2), 254–266.

d'Arcy, J. (1979). The Right to Communicate. In J. Richstad and M. Anderson (eds.), *Crisis in International News: Policies and Prospects.* New York: Columbia University Press, pp. 117–136.

Dyer-Witheford, N. (2015). *Cyber-Proletariat: Global Labor in the Digital Vortex.* London: Pluto Press.

Ekstein, L., and Schwarz, A. (2014). *Postcolonial Piracy: Media Distribution and Cultural Production in the Global South.* London: Bloomsbury.

Ellis, E. (2018). *Anthropocene: A Very Short Introduction.* Oxford: Oxford University Press.

Equiano, O. (1995). The Interesting Narrative of the Life of Olaudah Equiano; or, Gustavus Vassa, the African, Written by Himself (London, 1789). Reprinted in Carretta, V. (ed.), *The Interesting Narrative and Other Writings.* New York: Penguin.

Fuchs, C. (2014). *Digital Labor and Karl Marx.* New York: Routledge.

Fuchs, C. (2015). *Reading Marx in the Information Age: A Media and Communication Studies Perspective on Capital (Vol. 1).* London: Routledge.

Gates, B. (1995). *The Road Ahead.* New York: Viking.

Hoie, B. (2018). Crane Operator Strikes Take Place Across China on International Workers' Day. *New Bloom Magazine,* May 6. https://newbloommag.net/2018/05/06/china-may-day-crane-operator/.

Jomo and Mamos (2014). Ghost in the Machine: The Poetry and Brief Life of Foxconn Worker Xu Lizhi. *Pacific Rim Solidarity Network,* December 2. https://parisolnet.files.wordpress.com/2014/12/foxconn-formatted-2.pdf.

Larkin, B. (2008). *Signal and Noise: Media, Infrastructure and Urban Culture in Nigeria.* Durham, NC: Duke University Press.

MacBride, S., and Roach, C. (1989). The New International Information Order. In E. Barnouw (ed.), *International Encyclopedia of Communications.* Oxford: Oxford University Press, pp. 3–10.

Miller, T., and Kraidy, M. (2016). *Global Media Studies.* London: Polity Press.

Moten, F., and Harney, S. (2013). *The Undercommons: Fugitive Planning and Black Study.* New York: Autonomedia.

Mozur, P., and Luk, L. (2013). Gadget Maker Foxconn. *Wall Street Journal,* February 20.

Noble, S. (2018). *Algorithms of Oppression.* New York: New York University Press.

Peters, J. (2016). *The Marvelous Clouds: Toward a Philosophy of Elemental Media.* Chicago, IL: The University of Chicago Press.

Qiu, J. L. (2009). *Working-Class Network Society: Communication Technology and the Information Have-Less in Urban China.* Cambridge, MA: MIT Press.

Qiu, J. L. (2016). *Goodbye iSlave: A Manifesto for Digital Abolition.* Urbana, IL: University of Illinois Press.

Rosenberg, E., and Morello, C. (2017). U.S. Withdraws from UNESCO, the U.N. Cultural Organization, Citing Anti-Israel Bias. *Washington Post,* October 12. www.washingtonpost.com/news/post-nation/wp/2017/10/12/u-s-withdraws-from-unesco-the-u-n-s-cultural-organization-citing-anti-israel-bias/?noredirect=on&utm_term=.02cbe845b72f.

Schiller, D. (2000). *Digital Capitalism: Networking the Global Market System.* Cambridge, MA: MIT Press.

Scholz, T. (2017). *Uberworked and Underpaid: How Workers Are Disrupting the Digital Economy.* Malden, MA: Polity Press.

Sellen, A., and Harper, R. (2003). *The Myth of the Paperless Office.* Cambridge, MA: MIT Press.

Standing, G. (2011). *The Precariat: The New Dangerous Class.* London: Bloomsbury.

Wasko, J., Murdock, G., and Sousa, H. (2011). *The Handbook of Political Economy of Communications.* Malden, MA: Wiley Blackwell.

Zakaria, F. (2009). *Post-American World and the Rise of the Rest.* New York: Penguin.

Zhao, Y. (2011). *Communication and Society: Political Economy and Cultural Analysis.* Beijing: The Communication University of China Press (in Chinese).

Index

Note: Page numbers in *italics* indicate a figure on the corresponding page.

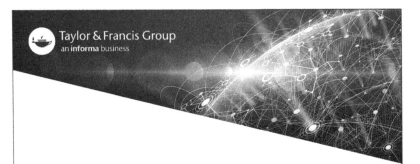

Printed in the United States
By Bookmasters